THE OXFORD HISTORY
OF ENGLAND

Edited by SIR GEORGE CLARK

THE OXFORD HISTORY OF ENGLAND

Edited by SIR GEORGE CLARK

THE
FIFTEENTH
CENTURY
1399–1485

BY

E. F. JACOB

Sometime Chichele Professor of Modern History
in the University of Oxford

OXFORD
AT THE CLARENDON PRESS
1961

Oxford University Press, Amen House, London E.C.4

GLASGOW NEW YORK TORONTO MELBOURNE WELLINGTON
BOMBAY CALCUTTA MADRAS KARACHI LAHORE DACCA
CAPE TOWN SALISBURY NAIROBI IBADAN ACCRA
KUALA LUMPUR HONG KONG

PRINTED IN GREAT BRITAIN

PREFACE

WHOEVER starts to write the history of the fifteenth century in England is likely to be impressed more by its deterrents than by its opportunities. The sheer bulk of the material available in the Public Records, the small progress made with private archives, now, however, becoming more accessible, and the need for a revaluation of the literary and chronicle sources are formidable things, to say nothing of the historian's continual problem of understanding the minds of men in a period of contradictions. Yet great advances both in record scholarship and interpretation have come about during the last forty years. People are ceasing to regard the age as the gloomy culmination of those disorders which it was the business of Tudor sovereigns to prevent. 'Morally, intellectually and materially it was an age not of stagnation but of ferment.'[1] The truth of Kingsford's remark is becoming evident.

Naturally since his day, as the exploration of public and private records developed, there has been, on the part of scholars, a concentration on aspects of the period not fully covered by the older monographs or general histories. In the first place the study of the greater families, of the means by which they preserved their inheritances, of their competitive acquisitions of land and property, their connexions with their neighbours and their influence on local administration, is likely to have no small effect upon the central theme of fifteenth-century history. The organized noble household with its council, its domestic organization, and its retained supporters stands as a social element making for order as much as, on occasion, for its opposite. Along these lines the civil wars may begin to appear less as a unique dynastic contest than as a series of episodes characteristic of the rivalries and conflicts between magnate houses of the later middle ages. The greatest of magnates is the duke of Lancaster become king.

In the second place, research in the personnel of parliament has focused attention upon the social composition of the commons' house, their affinities with the lords and with their

---

[1] C. L. Kingsford, *Prejudice and Promise in Fifteenth Century England* (1925), p. 66.

burgess colleagues in the legislature, and upon methods of election. This has served to emphasize the importance of the knights as a class in parliament and in the county and to show that the advance in their claims to be an essential element in legislation as well as in granting taxation is continuous, though they suffered a setback when the minority council was formed in 1422. Through the Speaker, they guaranteed their own freedom of speech, though, because of the predominant position of the council, their power of action was limited. Their interest in the financial affairs of the kingdom was continuous and on the whole relevantly applied. In this respect they were constantly eager to assure an adequate income to the household and to augment revenue both by the resumption of crown property alienated or leased on too favourable terms and by rigid control of annuities.

A third line of investigation has been the credit system of the government, particularly during the later stages of the Hundred Years War. The loans made to the crown have been investigated and classified, and the relation of the king, as borrower, to the different social and occupational groups has been made plain. This displays the poverty of the crown at various epochs, although it had great territorial resources many of which its own administrators undervalued. English finance was, however, deeply complicated by the war abroad after Henry V's death: the maintenance of Normandy and its garrisons might be paid for from the conquered areas, but not the cost of extensive military operations: these at intervals had to be met from 1429 onwards. The expedients resorted to for meeting the increasing indebtedness of the Lancastrian government and the new fiscal methods of Edward IV form one of the more interesting aspects of recent research.

Fourthly, diplomatic study has set the Congress of Arras (1435) in the forefront of political events: it marked the virtual end of the treaty of Troyes and the Anglo-French dual monarchy. The motives of Henry V and his optimism in fighting for the Troyes settlement have been recently brought under review: the risk he took was enormous, but there are indications that the war policy had behind it not only the claims of *justitia* (reassertion of 'right' against broken treaties) but also of the soldier-capitalist, determined to make what he could out of the rewards and the ransoms of war. Henry V appears as a man who thought that he could make both the war and the peace settlement pay.

Work on social and legal records has pointed to the serious threat to order and discipline offered by the fellowships grouped round the magnates and by intimidation on the part of powerful persons, a problem not surmounted even by Edward IV. The work of the chancery, the crown side of the King's Bench and the council reinforcing that of the local commissions of the peace, may have kept the worst outrages under, but the position, from the side of the judicature, was serious enough. Individuals and groups alike used the technicalities of procedure and delay to evade appearance: or used pardons to extinguish what many could not forgive. The same licence was in practice accorded to piracy, which might be regarded by some as the school of mariners, but caused a great deterioration of relations with the Hansa and with other powers and was a nuisance rather than an advantage. Inland there was considerable mobility of population owing to the migrations of the textile workers, some of it due to the flight of the discontented unfree from the old conditions of customary tenure. The economic background is, at any rate before 1460, of a mixed kind as far as agrarian life is concerned: a scarcity of labourers, agricultural depression, depopulation either through migration to towns or the extension of sheep farming: but in some counties, in the new cloth-producing districts and in certain special areas of the north and south-west, income steadily overtaking expenditure. In London some expansion and, as in Bristol and Newcastle upon Tyne, hopeful trading conditions, new houses being built, an atmosphere of stir and prosperity.

With the ferment there was everywhere energy and vitality: no intellectual impoverishment, but a certain isolation from the main stream of humanism and the currents of philosophical life abroad. A revival of piety that came very near to the Netherlands movement, one that opened men's hearts but did not necessarily improve their minds. Noble towers, superb wood carving, gracious alabaster plaques and retables: over the tombs, canopies that nearly rivalled Beverley: a new realism in manuscript illumination; a great demand for books of all kinds especially from the Lollards who persisted, particularly in East Anglia, throughout the century and were never suppressed; learned foundations and an active collegiate life.

People have been very generous in helping me with this book: for the use to which their advice has been put I alone must be responsible. I must thank Professor J. S. Roskell for reading the text and sending many useful notes; Dr. R. L. Storey for his assistance with the first section of the bibliography and for information about Bishop Langley's administration; and Dr. A. R. Myers for comments on the central chapters. Among those who have patiently answered my questions or provided information are Principal A. B. Steel; Mr. K. B. McFarlane, from whose guidance in research so many workers on the fifteenth century have profited; Dr. R. H. Hilton; Mr. J. L. Kirby, Dr. Frank Taylor, Dr. Ethel Seaton, Mr. R. H. Bartle, Miss A. M. Taylor, and Miss Margaret Avery. I am especially indebted to Dr. C. D. Ross for letting me use his thesis on the Yorkshire baronage, and to Dr. G. L. Harriss, whose doctoral dissertation upon the finances of the Court in the middle of the century was of great assistance, for valuable criticism. I have gained much from the studies of Dr. B. P. Wolffe upon the Acts of Resumption and the reforms of Edward IV; and from the theses of Dr. A. L. Brown upon the Privy Seal, and of Dr. R. M. Jeffs upon the fifteenth-century shrievalty. I am grateful to all these. Lastly I thank the staff of the Clarendon Press for their services.

E. F. J.

CONTENTS

VII. THE CHURCH

VIII. (a) THE KING AND THE GENTLE FOLK

VIII (b) THE TRADER AND THE COUNTRYMAN

VIII (c) THE TOWNS

XI. EDWARD IV (1)

ABBREVIATIONS USED IN
REFERENCES AND BIBLIOGRAPHY

Arch. Nat.	Archives Nationales (Paris)
Bull. Inst. Hist. Res.	*Bulletin of the Institute of Historical Research*
B.M.	British Museum
Cal. Close R.	*Calendar of Close Rolls*
Cal. Ch. R.	*Calendar of Charter Rolls*
Cal. Fine R.	*Calendar of Fine Rolls*
Cal. inq. p. m.	*Calendar of Inquests post mortem*
Cal. Pat. R.	*Calendar of Patent Rolls*
C. & Y. S.	Canterbury and York Society
C.S.	Camden Society
D.K.R.	*Reports of the Deputy Keeper of the Public Records*
D.N.B.	*Dictionary of National Biography*
E.E.T.S.	*Early English Text Society*
Econ. Hist. Rev.	*Economic History Review*
Eng. Hist. Rev.	*English Historical Review*
Hist. MSS. Comm.	Historical Manuscripts Commission
K.R.	King's Remembrancer
L.T.R.	Lord Treasurer's Remembrancer
N.S.	New Series
O.S.	Old Series
P.P.C.	*Proceedings and Ordinances of the Privy Council*
P.R.O.	Public Record Office
R.S.	Rolls Series
Rot. Parl.	*Rotuli Parliamentorum*
S.R.	Statutes of the Realm
T.R.	Treasury of Receipt
Test. Ebor.	*Testamenta Eboracensia*
Trans. Roy. Hist. Soc.	*Transactions of the Royal Historical Society*
Vict. County Hist.	*Victoria County History*

The Paston Letters are cited by volume and page in the Library Edition of Dr. James Gairdner (1904).

ERRATA

Page 26, lines 22, 23. *For* abbot of Colchester *read* abbot Colchester
  ,,   38, last line. *For* Penynydd *read* Penmynydd
  ,,   64, footnote. *Read* E. W. M. Balfour-Melville
  ,, 113, line 24. *For* Saint-Foy *read* Ste-Foy or Sainte-Foy
  ,, 113, ,, 31. *For* Chateauneuf *read* Châteauneuf
  ,, 113, ,, 30. *For* Poitievs *read* Poitiers
  ,, 114, ,,   9. *For* Chateauneuf *read* Châteauneuf
  ,, 116, ,,   7 from bottom. *For* Merton *read* Melton
  ,, 127, last line. *Add footnote 1 after* granted in 1412: This episode
           (from line 30) is quoted from R. L. Storey's *Thomas
           Langley and the Bishopric of Durham, 1406–1437* (1961),
           p. 111, to whom my sincere apologies are due for
           the lack of reference.
  ,, 129, ,,   6. *For* Montague *read* Montagu, *and throughout*
  ,, 132, note 1. *For* MacFarlane *read* McFarlane
  ,, 133, line   8 from bottom. *For* Clayton *read* Claydon
  ,, 180, ,,   7. *For* Nantes *read* Mantes
  ,, 181, ,, 13.   Ditto.
  ,, 182, ,, 16.   Ditto.
  ,, 183, ,, 20.   Ditto.
  ,, 186, ,, 12 from bottom. *For* Clement *read* Clément
  ,, 189, ,,   2. *For* Nantes *read* Mantes
  ,, 205, ,,   2 from bottom. St. Valéry has accent
  ,, 214, ,,   9. *For* Henrci *read* Henrici
  ,, 218, ,,   8 from bottom. *For* Aluwide *read* Alnwick
  ,, 223, note 3. *For* Combeworth *read* Comberworth
  ,, 236, line 12 from bottom. *For* Guiliemo *read* Giuliano
  ,, 239, ,, 13. *For* la Hirè *read* la Hire
  ,, 239, ,, 14. *For* Poton de Xantrailles *read* Poton de Xaintrailles
  ,, 239, ,, 24. *For* Maconnois *read* Mâconnais
  ,, 240, ,, 15. *For* Saintongè *read* Saintonge
  ,, 241, ,, 11 from bottom. *For* Tanguy *read* Tanneguy
  ,, 247, ,, 16. *For* Meuny *read* Meung
  ,, 257, footnote 1. *For* Joyce *read* J.G.
  ,, 282, line 30. *For* Gardner *read* Gairdner
  ,, 299, ,, 27. *For* Jessop *read* Jessopp
  ,, 320, ,,   5. *For* Montaque *read* Montagu
  ,, 332, ,, 29. *Omit* William
  ,, 336, ,, 20. *For* FitzWalter, Burnell *read* Beaumont, Lovel
  ,, 344, note 1. *For* Lit. *read* Library
Pages 421, 543, 614, 621, footnotes. *For* du Boulay *read* Du Boulay
Page 513, line 23. *After* authority *add footnote*: The following par-
           ticulars of the restoration of the Crown's authority
           I owe to Dr. G. L. Harriss.
  ,, 536, ,, 16. *Insert after* Somerset *footnote 1*: Scofield, *op. cit.* i. 352
  ,, 586, note 1. *For* Foedera, XI. 814, 825 *read* Foedera, V. iii. 44, 48
  ,, 679, ,,   1. *For* 1935 *read* 1955
  ,, 686, line 14. *For* Alvastia *read* Alvastra

PART I · LANCASTER

I

THE USURPATION

THE revocation (18 Mar. 1399), on a pure technicality, of the letters patent permitting the attorneys of Henry earl of Derby to receive the inheritance of the duchy of Lancaster after John of Gaunt's death, gave the signal for the momentous events leading to the capture and deposition of his cousin, Richard II, and the establishment of a usurping dynasty on the English throne. Henry was an exile living in Paris when the news came: he gave no sign of emotion, though the sentence implied perpetual banishment and confiscation. Very soon he must have heard from the constable of Kenilworth, Roger Smart,[1] about the grants made out of the duchy to Richard's supporters: to the duke of Exeter who had the south Wales group of estates, the duke of Albemarle who was given the Midland honours, and the duke of Surrey, Richard's nephew, on whom the honours of Lancaster, Clitheroe, and Tutbury were conferred. As if to penalize only more pointedly the true successor to the duchy, Richard had confirmed the annuities that had been granted out of the estates by John of Gaunt.

With Henry in France were the dispossessed archbishop of Canterbury, Thomas Arundel, and his nephew, the young earl Thomas FitzAlan of Arundel, whose father had been murdered in the reaction against the Appellants; and three old companions of his expeditions to the Baltic and the eastern Mediterranean, John Norbury, Sir Thomas Erpingham, and Sir Thomas Rempston, all intimate *familiares*, along with the constable of Pevensey castle, Sir John Pelham, who may have been Henry's main link with the duchy officials in England. In their company Henry sailed from Boulogne on or about 24 June 1399, to recover his ducal inheritance. The story that he made a landing

[1] Sent by Sir William Bagot to Henry in France: *Chronicles of London*, ed. C. L. Kingsford (1905), p. 53.

at Pevensey may arise from the fact that Pelham was put ashore there and captured his own castle which at the time was being held for Richard. The duchy was on the alert: its officers may well have been planning the return ever since Richard improvidently crossed to Ireland. It was safer now for Henry to disembark in the north, in Holderness, where he would get immediate help and support from his own castles and followers in Yorkshire, than on the Kent coast, where the earl of Wiltshire would assuredly have attacked him. When, therefore, he landed at Ravenspur on the Humber on a day early in July, there were his old household officials ready to greet him: the Waterton brothers, Robert his master of horse, now steward of the manor of Pontefract, with some 200 foresters from Knaresborough, and John, later steward of the Lincolnshire honour of Bolingbroke; along with the notable John Leventhorpe, probably the ablest administrator in Lancastrian circles, Henry's own receiver-general, and soon to pass into the wider service alike of the duchy and of the kingdom. The reunion had been well arranged. Henry passed by Pickering which at once surrendered, to Knaresborough, which fell after a short resistance. Thence to Pontefract, the most formidable of his strongholds, where he was joined, as the Kirkstall chronicler puts it, by 'a great force of well-born knights and esquires with their retainers from the counties of York and Lancaster'. The northern contingents of the duchy were coming in.

When he left England the devoted Londoners who believed in him had sped him on his way to Dartford. Since the spring of 1399 the tide had been swelling strongly against Richard, at any rate in the boroughs and counties which he had forced to submit and take out pardons; and there was a general expectation, of which Henry could not yet be fully aware, that the disinherited would return and that something more than the correction of Richard's misrule would follow. The duke, through his wrongs, was the man to gather sympathy and harness much of this vague emotion. The able son of an able and resplendent father, Henry shared John of Gaunt's love of magnificence and desire for military glory abroad. Impressive not only in his lineage, but by his bearing and his personality, he was more than a great English noble: he was a prince of high rank, who expected and received at the foreign courts he visited in the expedition of 1392–3, a proper amount of deference and consideration. A relative of Queen Anne of Bohemia was well received in parts of Europe governed by the children of the Emperor Charles IV, and in Italy it would be remembered that through his uncle, Lionel duke of Clarence, he was a kinsman of the Visconti. On his journeys abroad he moved with a great retinue, sending his heralds before him to announce his arrival and to paint the escutcheons that were put up over his lodgings. The alms he gave were princely: he seldom missed a shrine. His appearance is recorded by no death-mask as it is with Edward III; neither the recumbent laten figure, nor the stone effigy in the choir-screen at Canterbury, that portray him with regular, if somewhat heavy features and a short beard, present more than a conventional portrait of a king approaching middle age, nor call to mind that even in his twenties he had challenged attention by his strength and skill in jousting, when all eyes followed the figure in the inlaid armour of Italy.

The young Derby had ardour, a high spirit, and an independence of character which in 1389 took him out of the circle of the Appellants—he had been their commander at Radcot bridge—and led him to see the sinister points in the duke of Gloucester, led him to serve Richard with loyalty until the clash with Norfolk unmasked the real designs of the king and showed him that his cousin could never be trusted. These experiences had not disillusioned him, but had made him reticent, determined, and cautious. For all his activity he was a man of a studious nature, and liked reading works of moral philosophy. Of music he was a passionate devotee. On his expeditions his household band—trumpeters, percussion, pipers—followed him everywhere. His treasurer's accounts are filled with gifts to minstrels and musicians of all sorts. Wherever he went he was played to. Yet sources of weakness are apparent. On occasions, an impulsiveness, or rather a headstrong obstinacy, when he would follow no warning nor advice; and uncertain health. Great mental strain would prostrate him physically, and in the later stages of his reign he was certainly a neurotic, to say nothing of his other and more positive ailments.

He was strong enough now, when close to Doncaster he was met by the earl of Northumberland, and by Henry Percy, 'Hotspur', his son of the same name; by Ralph Neville, earl of Westmorland, who had married Henry's half-sister, Joan Beaufort: by William Lord Willoughby and the experienced marcher warden, Ralph Lord Greystoke. In 1403 Henry Percy was to charge the king with perjury because at the Doncaster meeting he had sworn that he would not claim the kingdom, but only his own inheritance and lands, and—a wild exaggeration—that Richard should reign with the control of affairs vested in a council of magnates, ecclesiastical and lay. This is Hardyng's first (Lancastrian) version of events; the Dieulacres version is more cautious, making Henry promise to give way should a more suitable candidate to the throne be forthcoming. There are grounds for thinking that the story of a promise or undertaking is suspicious.[1] But even if he did say something which was construed as a promise, how could he feel himself bound by undertakings made at a time of high excitement when the situation was developing from hour to hour? When he landed he knew only that his presence in the country was a mortal challenge to the man who had vowed 'that the Duke of Lancaster, that now ys, whulde never kome into England while he was on lyve'; he did not know how many people outside the duchy would support him in that challenge. It was a great hazard and he was prepared to see what would happen. He can only have begun to realize his popularity when the Border began to move, and in less than a week his little force had reached 30,000. By the time he reached Gloucester at the head of a substantial army (which Adam of Usk put at 100,000) he must have understood in whose direction people were looking for fair government again. Yet if he had sensed the general feeling aright, he was still very cautious: at Bristol, whither the confederates marched when they turned west to seize Richard's ministers, it was the earl of Northumberland who offered the garrison their freedom, if they submitted, and had Scrope, Green, and Bussy arrested.

The wording of Richard II's more important documents issued during his stay at Chester and on his way south (Aug.) suggests that at Doncaster or soon afterwards Henry had at any rate agreed to take the leading part in a baronial council for the restoration of order and confidence, for he was named after Archbishop Arundel and before the earls of Northumberland and Westmorland and 'other lords and magnates of the Council'. By September Percy and Neville are no longer specifically mentioned, the form of Richard's letters being 'by the advice of the

---

[1] Ably adduced by J. E. W. Bean, 'Henry IV and the Percies', *History*, xliv (1959), pp. 218–19.

duke of Lancaster' with (or without) the assent of the council.[1]
The northern leaders may have had as their model the council
established by the Appellants, though there was sufficient precedent stretching back to the Council of Fifteen in 1258 or to
the body specified in the Montfortian *Forma regiminis*, for an
aristocratic group, headed by an important magnate, undertaking the government of the country with the king being more
or less in tutelage. Such experiments had never lasted long; and,
whatever northern minds might think, 1399 was different from
1258–65 or from the crisis resulting in the Ordinances or even
1386–8. In the last two years Richard had resorted to acts of
intimidation and revenge incompatible with government by the
law and custom of England, and people did not feel secure. It
was doubtful, as Henry must have seen, whether Richard's continued participation in any form of government would have
been tolerated, particularly in view of the unpopularity of his
highly placed friends and relatives. The governing council of
the northern leaders, if it included a king of this kind, had little
to recommend it, and if it did not, might become a battle-
ground for antagonistic magnates. It was towards the solution of
a king governing with the advice of those qualified by birth and
position to give it, the old 'natural counsellors' with an infusion
of legal or sub-noble elements for part of the professional work,
that Henry found himself impelled by the logic of the situation.
The warm greeting of the Londoners; the need for a powerful
individual of unchallenged status among the nobility to take
responsibility; the need, in fact, for a man rather than the young
earl of March, eight years old, to restore confidence and
solidify a government that was rapidly going to pieces in the
country: these and the ambition of the high Lancastrian were
the factors that must have turned Henry's mind towards claiming the kingdom itself rather than to any conciliar expedient.

Yet the domination to which he was irresistibly led was
dependent upon the co-operation of a nobility more calculating
and less moved by fear or dislike of Richard than the county
gentry or the burgess class. To them, provided that he could be
kept reliant on their counsel, Henry was a good risk. It was important to get the king out of the hands of a courtier or palace

---

[1] *Cal. Close R., 1396–1399*, pp. 522–4; *Cal. Pat. R., 1396–1399*, pp. 589, 590, 594, 596.

entourage, to emphasize his dependence on a ministerial nobility ready to act as representatives of royal justice and royal power. Service of the crown, both military and governmental, was the aim of many of the younger elements in the magnate class: in return, they must be restored to their rights and territories, where these had been usurped or abandoned, and be adequately rewarded for the duties undertaken; and if it were necessary for them to shoulder public burdens without full remuneration, they must be given full recognition for their patriotism and allowed to recoup themselves when opportunity occurred.

These are but rough generalizations. The magnates were not a homogeneous class, and in their attitude towards Henry several strands can be detected. First there were the highest-ranking courtiers who had supported Richard and reaped their reward in dukedoms or other honours, but under pressure were prepared to desert him. Several of this class were holding confiscated lands of the Appellants. The duke of Albemarle (Edward, son of Edmund of Langley) and the earl of Gloucester (Thomas Despenser) were in possession of the late earl of Arundel's properties, and, like Thomas Percy, earl of Worcester, Gloucester had also certain possessions of the banished earl of Warwick (Thomas Beauchamp). The duke of Exeter (John Holand), who had been Arundel's jailer, the duke of Surrey (Richard's nephew, Thomas Holand the younger), and the earl of Wiltshire (William Scrope) had also benefited from the confiscations; they were the Ricardian courtiers, more so than the slow-moving regent, Edmund Langley, duke of York, who could not bring himself to act and to join Henry in the early stages. Thomas Percy, retained by Richard and an executor of John of Gaunt, Henry was prepared to treat as a friend and to make adviser to Thomas, his second son. To all these, save only to the earl of Salisbury (a personal enemy), Henry displayed a leniency in sharp contrast to the resentful suspicions of the commons, and indeed of some of the younger lords to whom a man like Albemarle was particularly obnoxious. His forbearance was intended to attract their loyalty, but was not justified by later events; and though he was favourable and considerate to the young Earl Marshal, Thomas Mowbray, son of his old rival Norfolk (who died in Sept. 1399 at Venice on his way back from Jerusalem), the reward he got was nothing but disloyalty and rebellion. The commons were perhaps correct in their diagnosis of the reliability of Richard's friends. Yet they cannot be called representative of the nobility as a whole.

The northern earls took the greatest part in the revolution. Genuine supporters were not lacking in the baronage south of the Trent. The immediate adhesion of two of Richard's ablest captains, the friendly attitude of the East Anglian magnates, and the powerful help among the greater landed families in the south and west showed him that it was not going to be an all-northern revolution. On Richard's expedition to Ireland were Lords Mowbray (Norfolk) and Lovel (Oxfordshire). John Lovel was perhaps Richard's best fighting commander; a confirmed supporter of the king, Lovel had been expelled from the court in 1387 for his opposition to the duke of Gloucester and in 1388 had been forced to swear that he would not enter the king's house save by permission given in parliament. In 1394 he was retained by Richard for life and various grants were made to him. Lovel was one of the first of his opponents to join Henry, and did so while the king was at Chester, followed soon after by Mowbray. The East Anglians were Walter Lord Fitzwalter, a young man of twenty-one, whose estates lay in Norfolk, Suffolk, and Essex; Robert Lord Scales of Newcells in Berkway, Hertfordshire, who had lands near Lynn, and Ralph Lord Cromwell of Castle Rising and Tattershall, whose son was to play an even greater part in Lancastrian fortunes. Before he reached the midlands, Henry had been joined by the Lincolnshire magnate Henry Lord Beaumont, a youth of nineteen, whom he was to make a knight of the Bath on the eve of his coronation, and before 19 August, when Richard's writs for parliament were out, he had received the allegiance of one of the largest midland landowners, Edmund earl of Stafford, son-in-law of the murdered duke of Gloucester, whom he was similarly to decorate on 12 October and in time to invest as a knight of the Garter. Stafford, still a young man, was later killed when in command of the royal forces at Shrewsbury, and two others of his family were to shed their blood for the house of Lancaster. Outside London, Henry's main strength in the south and west proved, apart from the commoner Sir John Pelham, to be Lord Camoys in Sussex, and, when he returned from Guernsey, Lord Cobham in Kent; in the Gloucester–Shropshire area and the Welsh borderlands, Lords Berkeley and Burnell. Hugh Lord Burnell, captain of Bridgnorth, was a son-in-law of Michael de la Pole;

and like Fitzwalter and Cromwell he was one of those who counselled the secret imprisonment of Richard in the October parliament. Thomas Berkeley is more important, and it is likely that his services to Henry were essential. Tradition repeated by Holinshed and by the seventeenth-century biographer Smyth assigns Berkeley Castle as the place where on 27 July Henry with the northern earls met the duke of York, and the decision was taken to act against Richard's officials in Bristol. The place taken by Lord Berkeley in the events of the autumn, when he acted as representative of the lords in abjuring homage to Richard, and his other activities in parliament show him to have been one of the two principal co-operators in the revolution.

But it was on the northern marchers and their tenants that Henry relied the most. Ralph Neville, earl of Westmorland, lord of Raby and Brancepeth, Middleham, and Sheriff Hutton, retained by Richard at the same time as John Lovel for a yearly sum of £130, and strengthened by politic marriages in the royal house, took the decisive step of his life and of his dynasty when he came to greet Henry at Doncaster. By his first marriage with Katherine, daughter of Hugh earl of Stafford, Ralph was brother-in-law to the present earl, and to Thomas Holand, duke of Surrey. His eldest son by this marriage, John Neville, seems to have had no landed estate, but in right of his wife, Elizabeth Holand, he was lord of a considerable inheritance extending over eleven counties: of her share of the lands of the earls of Kent, the bulk lay in Yorkshire and included the important manor of Cottingham near Hull and the North Riding manor of Kirkby Moorside. The story of Neville's house illustrates the tendency discernible in the English baronage as a whole towards the absorption and concentration of territories in the hands of a few families or family groups. Neville's second marriage with its fourteen children to whom the territorial rights of the first brood were steadily and unscrupulously transferred, implanted, as will be seen, his sons and daughters throughout the great families of England. In the north the lordships of Furnivall, Fauconberg, and Latimer were brought into the Neville inheritance: Furnivall in 1383, when Joan the only daughter and heiress of the fifth lord of that name, married Ralph's brother, Thomas Neville, second son of John Lord Neville of Raby, and so conveyed the title to her husband. Thomas Neville, Lord Furnivall, became one of the conspicuous figures of Henry's earlier years, proving his value to the dynasty in the rebellions of 1402–5. Having fought against Hotspur at Shrewsbury, he played a leading part in the summer of 1403 in obtaining the surrender of the northern castles held by the Percy interest, and after the rising Berwick, Alnwick, and Warkworth were committed to his charge. In November 1404 he was made a war treasurer in the Coventry parliament and in December treasurer of England in succession to William Lord Roos. The Furnivall country was the Sheffield area, and the Furnivalls were the most reliable supporters of the cause in south Yorkshire.

The earl of Northumberland and his son Henry Percy were marcher powers of the first order, a barrier to the Scots and in their Yorkshire lands second only to the dukes of Lancaster. By his first marriage to Margaret, daughter of Lord Neville of Raby, the elder Percy became uncle to Ralph Neville whose advancement in the royal favour he regarded with a jealous eye. Both were fighting captains from their youth, the earl with John of Gaunt in the expedition to Castile in 1366–7, Henry Percy in the border warfare of 1378, when he was only sixteen, then on and off for the next six years till he was captured by the Scots at Otterburn and was helped to pay his ransom by a grant of £1,000 from the king's council; but his father was also a diplomat and an administrator, for besides being successively keeper of the West and the East March and sheriff of Northumberland for life (1372) he was made governor of Calais in 1389, in 1394 was prominent in the negotiations between England and King Robert of Scotland, and in 1396 took part in the mission sent to get Isabella of France for Richard. Lord of a notable string of castles in the north-east, Bamborough, Alnwick, Warkworth, Newcastle, Prudhoe, and Langley, after his second marriage with the sister and heiress of Lord Lucy and widow of his cousin Gilbert de Umfraville earl of Angus, he secured in 1392 the castle and honour of Cockermouth with nine important manors, including Wigton and Aspatria, and after the death of his second wife the lordship of Egremont. In Yorkshire the Percies had been established since early post-conquest days. If their earliest fee was in Craven, they had estates in all the Ridings from Cletoft and Giggleswick in the west to Seamer and Ayton near the coast. Their castles were at Spofforth and Topcliffe on the Swale as well as at Healaugh, where Henry Percy was staying

when he wrote the famous Mattathias letter to Henry IV in
June 1403. Their favourite east Yorkshire haunts were Leconfield near Beverley, and Wressell, the manor and castle acquired
by Sir Thomas Percy, and in the glorious Beverley Minster the
decorative sculpture of the fourteenth century seems to reach its
climax in the Percy tomb. In the south the Percy lands extended
to Sussex (Petworth and Ashdown Forest). So far from living
'apart from English life' or acting as 'a border robber holding
his lands by the sword', as Dr. Wylie put it,[1] Earl Henry Percy
had been deeply involved in English public life ever since he
supported Wyclif in 1377, and his relations with the duke of
Lancaster and with Richard show that he was, if a difficult, at
any rate an indispensable magnate, without whom it was impossible to handle northern affairs; one sensitive to any attempt
on the part of the crown to advance his Neville cousins and
always ready to believe that his services in the north had not
been properly recognized. No longer a palatine earl, the creation of 1377 constituting a purely comital honour, Percy frequently behaved with all the freedom of a sixteenth-century
elector of Saxony. His son was less subtle, more constant. The
magic of Shakespeare still clings so closely to Hotspur that it is
hard to realize that the best soldier and probably the ablest
mind of the family was Northumberland's brother Thomas,
whom Richard made earl of Worcester. From a military point
of view the younger Percies were typified by Thomas. Hotspur's
fighting experience was not as extensive; but among his contemporaries he had the greater reputation: personal valour, the
halting and, when it came, explosive speech, the peculiar courtesy
that could impress (1394) even a Lusignan king of Cyprus,[2]
made Percy exactly the man to send as governor of Bordeaux
(1393): these are some of the ingredients in a character more
reminiscent of the twelfth than of the fifteenth century: such
qualities may have had a powerful influence on the future
Henry V when their owner had charge of the prince in Chester.

In any exposition of the events of September and October
1399, the historian is faced with two serious difficulties. The
first is the now familiar doubt cast by an important group of
sources upon the official version of Richard's deposition in the

---

[1] *History of England under Henry IV* (1884–98), i. 24.
[2] 'Ipse dixit sua curialitate et nobilitate quid sibi placuit': James I of Cyprus to
Richard II in E. B. de Fonblanque, *Annals of the House of Percy* (1887), i. Appendix.

parliament roll, which appears to be an account drafted in the Lancastrian interest. This version is described as the 'Record and Process of the Renunciation of King Richard the Second after the Conquest, and the acceptance of the same renunciation together with the deposition of the same king'.[1] It is incorporated in the roll of the first parliament of Henry IV which met on Monday, 6 October, in accordance with writs issued in the new king's name on Tuesday, 30 September. How far is the official account to be trusted? The second difficulty may also be put in the form of a question: was it Henry's intention to seek the approval of parliament for his title or did he take steps to avoid such parliamentary recognition? In answering these questions it will be remembered that we are trying to fathom the mind of a man in an extremely critical situation, seeking justification from the most representative jury of his fellow-countrymen for a series of unprecedented decisions which were to end in his eleva-tion to the throne: and seeking it—this is the important point—within a short time limit, one forced upon him partly by the rapid development of events and the movement of opinion in the country, partly by a pre-existing schedule of parliamentary dates. Delay might have frustrated everything, even the recovery of the heritage of Lancaster. If he hesitated too long, there were others ready to step in. There was little time for lengthy academic discussion: genealogists, historians, even common lawyers had to be kept in their places. Using the device of representative delegations and committees, the jurists advising Henry had to devise the procedure of deposition and appointment without sacrificing speed to that care for justice and for consistency of statement which so crucial a change might have been supposed to require.

The official account represents everything going smoothly. On the morning of 29 September a committee of lords spiritual and temporal, of representatives of the landed gentry and of the law, deputed as the result of consultations between the lords and their legal advisers, called upon Richard at the Tower to claim the fulfilment of his promise to abdicate made at Conway before he had been taken prisoner, and presented him with a previously drafted form of abdication. Richard asked for time to consider this and desired to see Henry and Archbishop Arundel. These arrived with certain of the lords in the afternoon, and Richard

[1] *Rot. Parl.* iii. 416 f.

then read the document aloud and signed it, adding that if he had any say, he would wish Lancaster to succeed him. He thereupon appointed the archbishop of York (Richard Scrope) and the bishop of Hereford (John Trefonant) as his proctors to declare his cession and renunciation of the crown to all the estates of the kingdom, so that they might announce his intention to all the 'people'; and he handed Lancaster his signet, doing this, as he said, that all the estates might see the token of his intent. On the next day, 30 September, the scene shifts to Westminster Hall, where the lords spiritual and temporal and the people were assembled in great numbers, *propter factum parliamenti*, and the throne stood vacant, covered with a cloth of gold. To this assembly Archbishop Scrope read the king's abdication, and the 'estates and people' (*status et populus*) expressed their unanimous acceptance of the act: but, the roll adds, in order to remove all scruple and suspicion, it was thought advisable that the grounds of the abdication should be stated. Consequently the Coronation Oath and a 'list of grievances' against Richard were read in full to the 'estates and people'. Thereupon 'the estates and the communities' accepted the suggestion made to them that the king, having broken his coronation oath and being thereby guilty of perjury, deserved to be deposed, and established a commission described as having been deputed 'per pares et Regni Angliae . . . et ejusdem regni communitates omnes ejusdem regni representantes' to report, in accordance with historical precedent, on the advisability of this step. This body, sitting as a tribunal in front of the vacant throne, read out a statement to the effect that in view of the perjury, crimes, and other offences of Richard, and of his own confession, published by his own choice and mandate to the estates, that he was unfit to govern, they, after careful deliberation with the estates, pronounced him useless, unfit, and insufficient for the government of the kingdom, deserving to be deposed from all royal dignity and honour, if any such remained in him, and by their definitive sentence then and there deposed him. After this the estates appointed the commissaries as their proctors to resign and refuse their homage and fealty to Richard and to inform him of the proceedings.

The throne was now legally vacant. Rising up in his place and crossing himself, Henry claimed it in his mother tongue as descended by right line of the blood from Henry III, in virtue of which 'God of his grace hath sent me wyth helpe of my kyn and of my friends to recover it'. Richard no longer king, he was the next heir by hereditary right. His claim through Edmund of Lancaster, now implicitly alleged to stand above Edward I in seniority, had been vindicated by the divine aid given him in his mission of recovery. The lords spiritual and temporal were asked severally and collectively what they thought of the claim, and 'the said estates, with the whole people' agreed that the duke should reign over them. The new king then showed the estates the signet Richard had given him as a token that he should succeed and the archbishops enthroned him. This was followed by Arundel's sermon (*vir dominabitur populo*) justifying the rejection of Richard the childlike (as well as of Edmund Mortimer) and the selection of the manful Henry. It remained for the newly chosen king to assure the estates that the conquest of his rightful inheritance did not imply any lack of respect on his part for law and custom, and to start the administration going under new authority. To keep the personnel of the estates still in London, Henry explained that writs had been made out to the persons present summoning a parliament for the following Monday (6 Oct.); and he assured the estates that this 'shortening of the day fixed for parliament' was not intended to prejudice them. On the following day, 1 October, proctors of the lords and commons visited Richard in the Tower, and through Chief Justice Thirning made known to him the acceptance of his abdication and the cause and procedure of his deposition.

It is now generally admitted that the account of the proceedings given in the parliament roll is tendentious and in certain details completely erroneous. Largely on the strength of it, and of the St. Albans chroniclers (the author of the anonymous *Annales Ricardi Secundi et Henrici Quarti* and Walsingham) and of Adam of Usk, Stubbs accepted the promise to abdicate made at Conway, concluding that Richard 'made no attempt to stem the tide of desertion and ingratitude'. After a conference held at Conway he 'offered to resign the Crown'. The evidence of the Dieulacres chronicle supporting Creton's[1] story of the terms offered to Richard at Conway, and confirmed by the Whalley

---

[1] *Chronique de la traison et mort de Richard II* (Eng. Hist. Soc. 1846), pp. 106 f. 'Apart from Creton's omission of Archbishop Arundel, the Dieulacres story of what happened at Conway is the French version, shorn of its rhetoric and propaganda': M. V. Clarke and V. H. Galbraith, 'The Deposition of Richard II', *Bull. John Rylands Lib.* xiv (1930), 144.

continuator of the *Polichronicon*, shows that on Henry's behalf
Northumberland and Arundel offered Richard to leave his
kingly dignity intact provided that certain conditions—the trial
of five of his councillors and the reference to parliament of his
claim to be hereditary ruler—Creton says—were fulfilled. The
'full' resignation at Conway is a Lancastrian fable: under cover
of promises made to him then, Richard was lured to Flint, when
he was made prisoner, thence he was taken to Chester. The
chronicle does not bear out the statement of the official account
that Richard displayed a cheerful countenance (*gratanter, ut
apparuit, et hillari vultu*) when he read the document of abdication
presented to him by the commissioners who visited him in the
Tower: instead Richard asked that he 'should not enter parliament in horrible fashion, as it was said, and placing the crown
of the kingdom upon the ground he resigned his right to God'.
'Resignation to God instead of to Bolingbroke is a last gesture
characteristic of Richard' the editors of the Dieulacres chronicle
comment.[1] Next, in the parliament roll's account of the proceedings at Westminster on 30 September, no mention is made of the
protest evidently voiced by the bishop of Carlisle on Richard's
behalf, that the king should at least be heard before being
deposed. The anonymous Chronicle[2] known as Giles's Chronicle
shows that the question was raised whether, as the king was in
prison, his resignation was genuine or made under duress, and
so whether it was not advisable to ascertain from him his real
intentions. It was to counteract this line of defence that the
gravamina against Richard, printed in the roll, were put forward.
He was never allowed any defence.

A brilliant and elaborate thesis has been advanced contending that the terms in which Henry stated his claim to the throne
are incompatible with any theory that derives his title from
parliamentary action:[3] a parliamentary deposition, and equally
a parliamentary title to the throne was what Henry IV most
wanted to avoid: and he was therefore careful that the revolutionary proceedings of 29–30 September should take place in an
assembly that was authoritative but at the same time did not
possess the true character of a parliament.

---

[1] M. V. Clarke and V. H. Galbraith, 'The Deposition of Richard II', *Bull. John
Rylands Lib.* xiv (1930), p. 146.   [2] In Royal MS. 13 C.1.
[3] By Dr. G. Lapsley, 'The Parliamentary title of Henry IV', *Eng. Hist. Rev.* xlix
(1934), 423–49, 577–606.

Early in September, according to Adam of Usk, a committee of learned men was set up to discover a way by which under the forms of law Richard could be deposed and Henry made king. The commission considered the charges against Richard—it has been suggested that this body may actually have drafted the articles preferred against him and enrolled on the parliament roll—and decided that he must be deposed 'by authority of the clergy and people'.[1] In other words, that the precedent of 1327 should be followed. The problem of how to make Henry king must also have been discussed, and it would be remembered that in the previous reign the question of the succession in the event of Richard's remaining childless had been settled by parliament's declaring Mortimer the heir. Parliament might now be recommended to alter its decision and elect Henry to the throne. It has been argued that the plan of summoning a parliament and submitting to it a scheme for the removal of Richard and the substitution of Henry had been settled as soon as the king was a prisoner;[2] and it was the work of the more moderate and constitutionally minded of his supporters. The objector to this course was, however, Henry himself. In his idea, it was necessary that the abdication should be accepted in as public and formal manner as possible: on the other hand, it was just as necessary that his title should not depend upon an act which later on the estates might regard themselves as competent to revoke. The case of Edward II had given the crown lawyers an exact precedent for associating the estates with the act; for in that instance it was held that the abdication could not be carried out by unilateral action, it required the advice, if not the assent, of the estates of the kingdom.

But Henry, with the 'might and wilfulness' that Northumberland was later to attribute to him, did not want the parliamentary title: he preferred 'to substitute a title of legitimate descent, vindicated by conquest and admitted by some form of popular acclamation'.[3] The new course, formed after a somewhat astonished commission had rejected his plea (25 Sept.) for succession by conquest, was in one sense a compromise: it gave parliament the opportunity to proclaim the heir as king. This concession was, however, rendered nugatory by Arundel's declaration that the cession of the crown had invalidated the

---

[1] *Chronicon Ade de Usk*, ed. E. Maunde Thompson, pp. 29, 30.
[2] By Lapsley, op. cit., p. 588.   [3] Lapsley, op. cit., p. 596.

parliamentary writs which had been issued by its authority. The body, therefore, that did the acclaiming may have looked like parliament, but obviously could not be so. It was sufficiently like parliament to give the revolution a good claim to be following in the line of 1327; legally it was not a parliament, and Henry's title was not limited by its actions or resolutions. Henry had, in fact, the best of both worlds; maintaining a constitutional appearance, in fact, he enjoyed an unhampered reality in his title to the throne.

The danger in interpreting these events is that we may read into them a subtler constitutional significance than they can bear. The truth may be simpler and vaguer. Without doubt there was much searching for precedent, as much searching of chronicles and scrutiny of constitutional events from Edward II's deposition down to the warnings given to Richard II by the magnates in the parliament of 1386; but the commission on precedents was given less than a month to discuss and deliberate; and from Michaelmas 1399 Henry was applying the guillotine and allotting—the decision is almost incredible—no more than fifteen days for Richard's deposition, his own election, and his own coronation. He must get it all over somehow, and confront doubters and opponents with the accomplished fact. Parliament or no parliament, there were the magnates to hand, the hereditary advisors to the crown; there were the knights and the burgesses; and there was the *populus*—the citizens of London, in accordance with ancient precedent, to 'collaud' or acclaim him. These elements, in whatever confusing language they are described by contemporary chronicles, were at hand: they must not be allowed to depart before they had dismissed Richard and approved his own claim to succeed. But parliamentary title? It has been rightly pointed out that the idea of a parliamentary deposition involves a conception of crown and parliament as two distinct entities which is 'contrary to all that we know of their constitutional relations in the fourteenth century or long after'.[1] If 'parliamentary title' means that the kingship is held in virtue of the claim to succeed having been warranted or approved by parliament, the answer is that in point of fact Henry had no such title, because the body that met on 30 September was not a parliament at all: it was a meeting of the

---

[1] B. Wilkinson, 'The Deposition of Richard II and the Accession of Henry IV', *Eng. Hist. Rev.* liv (1939), 220.

elements which normally, with the king, would have constituted parliament, and were to constitute it in a week's time, but now at the moment were an assembly convened to record the fact that Richard II by his conduct had divested himself of the 'character' of king and that the throne was vacant. It was this assembly that set up the committee of deposition, accepted its report, and approved Henry's challenge of the crown, the decision being followed by an *electio in regem* in which the *populus*, the Londoners, took their traditional part by acclamation. A convention, perhaps, but not a parliament.

But to imagine Henry as alarmed at the thought of a parliamentary title smacks of the first half of the seventeenth century. Such a hypothesis isolates crown from parliament, whereas the old maxim that the medieval king holds his court in his council in his parliaments represents the true line of English constitutional doctrine. In parliament the king is integrated with his natural counsellors, the lords spiritual and temporal, in a governing organism, that possesses the fullness of judicial and executive power. By their advice he takes his decisions in important matters of state; at their counsel he replies to the less routine petitions submitted to him. If Henry deliberately avoided the approval of parliament why did he let it be enacted and enrolled that he was the lawful sovereign, and that the succession should be fixed in his sons? Why all the elaborate provision made by parliament for the young Prince Henry of Monmouth?[1] We are left, it seems, with the conclusion that Henry presented his case to a body that had no claim to be called a parliament but was summoned as one and was sufficiently like one to mislead the contemporary chroniclers and to make public opinion think that it was; that he had no objection in principle to using parliament to ratify the changes upon which he was set. Speed was his aim: rapid action must forestall second thoughts in the north and a possible move by the French king.

Before the authentic parliament met, provisions for the continuity of government had to be made. The judges, and the lieutenants of counties, along with the escheators, collectors of customs, and other agents holding appointments from the king whose offices automatically terminated with the abdication, had their commissions renewed: the sheriffs were prolonged until the normal November change-over. Archbishop Arundel

---

[1] *Rot. Parl.* iii. 426, 428, 441, 525.

resumed the chancellorship, but resigned it on 5 November to John Scarle, a former *custos rotulorum* and a familiar figure in the chancery; John Norbury, Henry's companion in exile and for years a member of his household when earl of Derby, was made treasurer and lost no time in handling the finance of the revolution,[1] and the stalwart Sir Thomas Erpingham became chamberlain, on 30 September being made constable of Dover Castle and on 9 November warden of the Cinque Ports for life. The privy seal remained in the hands of Richard Clifford, a supporter of Richard, who on submitting to Henry was pardoned and allowed to retain office. Henry made his second son, Thomas, steward of England and assigned him as his assistant Thomas Percy, who for the fourth time was now made admiral (15 Nov.). The king's resolve to retain the personnel of the judicature and to attach some of them to his interests by more than mere renewal of their commissions was a counsel of prudence; less so, in the long run, was the long list of annuities and pensions granted after 30 September. These grants were normally payable out of the customs, the revenues of the counties, the farms of towns, royal manors or manors in royal occupation, and escheats of various types; those granted for the months of October–November alone amounted to an annual charge of £2,125,115. The grants were continued at a substantial rate for the rest of the first royal year, a point that may be remembered when the commons protest against the 'outrageous' sums granted to petitioners; for large numbers of those who claimed to have assisted Henry petitioned for grants from the crown.

It was natural that a king whose elevation had been so hasty and so dubious in legal precedent should call ceremony to his aid. The coronation was fixed for 13 October. On St. Edward's Day, therefore, Henry was crowned. Adam of Usk who was in the sanctuary and attending the archbishop throughout the service noted that among the lords bearing the regalia, the earl of Northumberland bore the Lancaster sword, the one worn by the duke at his landing, the young prince of Wales the unsheathed Curtana representing justice without vindictiveness,

[1] In M. D. Legge, *Anglo-Norman Letters and Petitions* (1941), no. 389, 1399–1401, Norbury shows that he had letters written by privy seal clerks to persons capable of making loans to the crown. No. 361 (same date), a privy seal warrant for letters to the customers of Hull and Boston asking them to pay the earl of Northumberland 'before all others' the sums due to him from the customs and subsidies.

and the earl of Westmorland the rod. He heard Henry swear, just before the actual crowning, to take heed 'to rule his people altogether in mercy and truth'. At the banquet in Westminster Hall he saw Sir Thomas Dymock (whose claim to act as king's champion he had himself drafted) ride in to challenge any who denied the king's right and caught Henry's confidential words: 'if need be, Sir Thomas, I will in my own person ease thee of this office'.

The king's first parliament had met on 6 October. Seventy-four belted knights were present, representing thirty-seven English counties; and 173 citizens and burgesses were returned on the existing writs for eighty-five cities and boroughs. Arundel's pronouncement emphasized the king's resolve to be 'counselled and governed by the honorable, wise and discreet persons of his kingdom' and *not* 'by his own will, voluntary purpose or singular opinion'; and his determination to protect the liberty of Holy Church, to maintain the statutes and ordinances of his predecessors and to ensure that all liberties and franchises should be respected. The archbishop then asked the lords individually to consent to the continuation (adjournment) of parliament until the morrow of the coronation (Tuesday, 14 Oct.). The receivers and triers of petitions were appointed, and the serious business began on that Tuesday, with the presentation of the Speaker, Sir John Cheyne, his enforced withdrawal under pretext of health, and the appointment of John Doreward in his place. The author of the *Annales Henrici Quarti* makes it clear that Cheyne was suspected by Arundel for his Lollard opinions and that the convocation of Canterbury were alarmed at his possible influence in parliament.

Though parliament and the convocation of Canterbury normally, for obvious financial reasons, had their meetings synchronized, it is not often that the same day was fixed, as now (6 Oct.), for both assemblies. On it Henry sent the earls of Northumberland and Westmorland and Sir Thomas Erpingham to the provincial assembly of Canterbury, waiting for them in the Chapter House of St. Paul's, to bear a message perhaps more optimistic than practical: abjuring any immediate collection of the tenth, the commissioners promised on the king's behalf not to tax the clergy 'nisi magna necessitate guerrarum et inevitabili necessitate ingruente', but asked for prayers for the king, especially in event of war (from several sources it is clear that

after the deposition Henry expected hostile action from France):
they also guaranteed on their master's behalf the liberty of the
Church; Henry would destroy, in her interest, heresies, errors,
and heretics. The support of the clergy was at the moment
valuable to Henry, and his promise of vigilance against Lollardy
was not merely a diplomatic move, however much his contemporaries might suspect him of favouring unorthodoxy. This
reassurance was the more important in view of a *gravamen*
brought forward by the clergy in the convocation of Canterbury,
warning the archbishop of a move by Lollard sympathizers in
parliament to produce new legislation 'against the liberty of the
Church' and asking him and his suffragans to resist.[1] Parliament, however, did not come off as lightly as the convocations:
it voted the king the subsidy on wool and woolfells (50s. on
denizen and 60s. on alien merchants) for three years, and a
grant of the tenth and fifteenth promised to Richard II, though
the half-tenth and half-fifteenth to be paid at Michaelmas 1399
were to be cancelled and the collection restored. It was stipulated
that the grant was not to be taken as a precedent. Behind any
such concession lay the assumption, dear to parliament, that
under normal circumstances the king should live of his own,
that is on the revenues of his own estates and the proceeds of his
jurisdictions and franchises.

The chief business of the parliament, expressed in the main
through the common petitions presented, was to undo the legislation, and the penal measures against his opponents passed
during Richard II's last three years. This involved the repeal of
the acts of the 1397–8 parliament, the restoration of those wrongfully deprived and exiled, the remnant of the Appellants,
measures to prevent private forces being recruited and maintained for the advantage of the crown just as much as of the
magnates, and the permanent and effective custody of the late
king, round whom any rebellion was bound to centre.

The repeal of 1397–8 and its sequel was the first petition of
the commons (15 Oct.), granted with the reservation that any
profitable clause contained within that legislation might be
brought up again for re-enactment in the common petitions of
the current parliament. The corollary of this was the reaffirma-
tion of the acts of the Merciless Parliament, 11 Richard II
(1388), with a parallel reservation about the rights of the

---

[1] No. 29 of the list: Wilkins, *Concilia*, iii. 242.

commons to petition against any undesirable or unprofitable point these contained. The commons then asked for the restoration of Thomas Arundel, displaced as archbishop by Richard's clerk and secretary, Roger Walden. They petitioned that he should have the administration of Walden's goods and the issues and profits of the temporalities he had seized. With equal success they sought the restoration of the Arundel heir, Thomas FitzAlan, to his father's estates and dignities and the restoration to the treasury (from which they had been abstracted) of his title deeds, and the rehabilitation of Thomas Beauchamp, earl of Warwick, condemned to exile and the forfeiture of his estates in the parliament of 1397–8. The measures against Richard II's highly placed friends and agents were the Liveries Act and the trial in parliament of the dukes and other magnates who had appealed Arundel and Warwick of treason. The Act prohibited any subject from using or giving any livery or token of company inside the realm. The king alone was excepted, but any persons to whom he granted it were not to wear it save in his presence, unless they were abroad or on the frontier or on the march in time of war. It was not to apply to domestic retainers in the service of magnates, but was a measure aimed at the recruitment of auxiliaries like Richard's Chester archers as well as at the bands of extra-domestic supporters brought by powerful lords to parliament, with consequent danger to the peace. All this was plain sailing compared with the consequences of the demand (16 Oct.) made by the knights of the shire for the arrest of the evil counsellors of Richard II. These included Sir William Bagot, the dukes of Albemarle (Edward, son of Edmund duke of York and formerly earl of Rutland), Surrey (Thomas Holand, earl of Kent), and Exeter (John Holand, earl of Huntingdon), the marquis of Dorset (John Beaufort, earl of Somerset) and the earl of Gloucester (Thomas Lord Despenser). By bringing Sir William Bagot to book (Bussy and Greene had already been executed at Bristol) the commons were made aware that the question of who was responsible for Gloucester's murder had been raised. Bagot's implication of Albemarle, in whose favour Richard had professed himself ready to abdicate when he had secured obedience to the crown throughout England, led to denials by the duke and angry rebuttals and challenges by other lords and finally to the examination of the late duke of Norfolk's servant, Hall, who was doorkeeper to the duke of Gloucester's chamber at Calais and knew the yeomen alleged to have been sent by Albemarle to do the work. When examined privately Albemarle and the other dukes and lords inculpated in the murder pleaded *force majeure*. On 29 October they, along with Bishop Thomas Merke of Carlisle, were brought to answer the charge in parliament. Merke made no attempt to claim his clergy, and asserted his innocence of complicity before the assembled lords: the others who had pleaded coercion were leniently dealt with. The dukes were to revert to their original titles as earls of Rutland, Kent, Huntingdon; Dorset and Gloucester were to return to their old styles as earl of Somerset and Lord Despenser, and after a token imprisonment in the custody of the abbot of Westminster, William of Colchester, were set at liberty. Only the earl of Salisbury, who had been challenged to single combat by Lord Morley, was not immediately liberated. How little resentment Henry IV felt can be seen by his appointment of Somerset as chamberlain of England (9 Nov.) and of the earl of Rutland as justiciar and keeper of the New Forest and of all the forests south of the Trent, while in December both Rutland and Huntingdon were present as regular members of the council.

Before the ending of the process against the lords the fate of Richard himself, at the moment in the charge of Sir Thomas Rempston, was decided. On 21 October the commons petitioned that he might be brought to answer for the misdeeds alleged against him. Henry gave no answer until the lords spiritual as well as temporal were present. On 23 October, at a full meeting of the lords, charged by Archbishop Arundel to secrecy, the earl of Northumberland asked each one present what was to be done with the former king. Fifty-eight, whose names are given in the parliament roll,[1] advised that he should be removed to safe custody, where no mob could rescue him and that no former member of his household should have access to him. On 27 October the king told the parliament that by the assent of the lords spiritual and temporal Richard had been condemned to perpetual imprisonment, the place of his custody to be secret. And just as he had not been permitted on 30 September to appear and state his case or to have his case stated for him, so now there was no semblance of trial. Richard had to be put away as secretly as possible. On 28 October he was moved in

---

[1] *Rot. Parl.* iii. 426–7.

disguise from the Tower to Gravesend, and thence to Leeds Castle in Kent. Soon afterwards he was transferred to Ponte-fract, when he was in the custody of Robert Waterton and Sir Thomas Swynford, later governor of Calais.

If this was the winding-up of the past account, Henry was equally concerned with the dynastic future. On 15 October Arundel on his behalf informed parliament that the king was proposing to create his eldest son Henry prince of Wales, duke of Cornwall, and earl of Chester, and asked that he should be declared heir apparent to the throne. The revival of the Black Prince's titles for Henry envisaged not only the future of Henry's house, but had a more immediate purpose: the establishment of the king's son with a military and administrative staff in a commanding position within a county formerly pledged to the support of Richard, and economically the chief market for a large part of north Wales. The prince was invested with ring and rod, and was led by the duke of York to a special seat assigned to him in parliament. On 23 October the prince was made duke of Aquitaine. Very soon afterwards (10 Nov.) he was given the liberties and franchises of the dukedom of Lancaster, and bore the name of duke, although by the Great Charter of the duchy (1399) the Lancaster inheritance remained the personal property of the sovereign as a separate system of estates, not merged into the other properties of the crown, and the Lancas-trian kings held it because they were dukes of Lancaster of hereditary right.[1] The advancement of the prince by assented proposals made to the lords and commons in parliament, which are recorded on the parliament roll, was the first of a series of such measures: as was suggested above, it does not square with the view that Henry wished to avoid parliamentary recognition of his successful claim.

The common petitions of Henry's first parliament are natur-ally coloured by the revolutionary emergency. One in particular reflects the anxiety of the commons at the king's liberal grants to individuals claiming reward for their support of his invasion, by asking that the 'outrageous gifts' should be 'resolved by good deliberation'. The reply proferred the king's willingness to be

---

[1] R. Somerville, *The Duchy of Lancaster* (1946), i. 150; cf. p. 151: 'The dispositions of the Duchy made by the Lancastrian kings in connexion with their wills show how the Lancastrian kings considered it to be their personal property in a sense that the crown lands were not. They put large parts of the Duchy in the hands of feoffees' (examples given).

advised by the wise men of his council: and conceded that any soliciting for lands, rents, offices, or annuities should make express mention in their petitions of the value of what was requested, and should state whether they already had received any gift from the king or his predecessors. If they failed to do this, the grants made to them were to be null and void. Another petition asked that any persons who had suffered trespass or spoliation when the king arrived in the summer should, save in the county of Chester,[1] have remedy at common law. The king, in reply, could make no promise of compensation for those living in the path of his army, but elsewhere aggrieved parties might sue at common law. Not dissimilar was the case of persons who, upon information sent to the king, had been ousted from their lands, and had seen them granted to others. The reply came that if the lands had been granted by letters patent where the king had no legal claim to dispose of them, the owners might be granted a special assize by the chancellor against the deforciants, and if the claim was successful, threefold damages might be awarded. Such petitions almost point to an interlude of *tempus turbationis* upon Henry's arrival in the country. The annalist from the northern midlands, who wrote what is popularly known as Giles's Chronicle and was well informed about proceedings in parliament, adds that the king granted the prayer of the commons (*vulgus*) who petitioned him not to take measures of revenge for treason or for bad government or to pursue his rivals (*aemulos*) for their misdeeds, and for the time to separate, in the best way he could, the penitent from the obstinate.[2] This shows a less vindictive temper than was displayed in the City of London at Henry's lenience towards Richard's dukes and counsellors; but the king was unaffected by this, and parliament was dissolved on 19 November with a declaration of political amnesty for all save those present at the murder of the duke of Gloucester.

The obstinate were not long in raising their heads. It was perhaps fortunate that they did so now instead of waiting till external dangers and internal rebellion had combined against the first Lancastrian. The degraded dukes, reduced to their

---

[1] Where Henry, on arrival with his army, had allowed his men to run amok: 'Havock' super eam (Cestriam) et eius comitatum proclamato', Dieulacres Chron. in *Bull. John Rylands Lib.* xix (1930), 171.

[2] [*Incerti scriptoris*] *Chronicon Angliae*, ed. Giles, p. 5.

former earldoms, were soon in positions of royal confidence. Kent, Rutland, and Huntingdon were now members of the council, Salisbury was at liberty through the latter's intercession with the king, and Thomas Merke, the ex-bishop of Carlisle, was conspiring in London with two of Richard's partisans, Sir Thomas Blount and Sir Benedict Cely. On 17 December 1399 Huntingdon, Kent, Rutland, and Salisbury along with the bishop met at the house of William Colchester, abbot of Westminster, to concoct plans for the destruction of the king and his sons at Windsor, just before the tournament arranged for the Epiphany, and for the restoration of Richard, impersonated till the real character arrived by a priest named Richard Maudelyn. Even as late as 1414, when Oldcastle made his attempt, the abbey was under suspicion as a centre of Ricardian sympathy, with (as approvers stated) the archdeacon of Westminster taking the place of the abbot and smuggling away prominent Lollards who had taken sanctuary there.

Details of the present plan, which seems to have filtered through in a vague way to the court, were revealed by Rutland to his father the duke of York, and Henry was quickly informed (4 Jan. 1400). Immediately the king took the risk of leaving Windsor with his sons and making straight for London. Less than twelve hours after they had departed from Windsor, the rebels arrived, and though they found no king, were able to seize the castle and to circulate the story that Henry was on the run, that Richard had escaped and was gathering a force in the valley of the upper Thames. At this crucial moment the City of London stood by the king. Recruiting started at high rates of pay, and by 6 January Henry had an army of about 20,000 men, from which a strong reconnaissance force was detached and sent up the Thames to locate and engage the rebels. At Maidenhead Kent fought a successful delaying action, and got away to join Salisbury at Cirencester, while the slippery Rutland deserted his friends and joined the king. But at Cirencester the rebels were caught. The terms of their surrender were that their lives should be spared until they had seen the king, but their guardians were set upon and overpowered by the local mob, and on 8 January Kent and Salisbury were beheaded in the streets of the town. Lord Despenser, the former earl of Gloucester, escaped from Cirencester, but fell to a similar act of lynching at Bristol; and Huntingdon, captured near Shoeburyness in Essex, was taken to the countess of Hereford's castle of Pleshy and by her order delivered over (15 Jan.) to the revengeful men of Essex. The countess was sister to the late earl of Arundel; her daughter had been the wife of the late duke of Gloucester, and it was hardly to be expected that she would feel merciful towards Richard's supporters. Sir Thomas Blount was put to death with appropriate barbarity after trial before the king at Oxford. Preceded by a grisly collection of the heads of his opponents, in sacks or on poles for exposure in the City of London, Henry returned to Westminster on 15 January. Then, as was again to happen in 1414, courts of inquiry were held into treason within the city, and measures were taken against churchmen supporting the rebellion, who were not allowed benefit of clergy. All the clerks arraigned were found guilty; Merke himself was condemned to death, but the sentence was not carried out, for the Pope never gave permission for his formal deposition. Translated by Boniface IX to the see of Samothrace, he received a conditional pardon (28 Nov. 1400), and after being appointed (June 1401) to the prebend of Masham in Yorkshire, was presented by the now more merciful crown to a living in the diocese of Salisbury (14 Nov. 1403) where he made himself useful as an assistant bishop until his death. Roger Walden and the abbot of Colchester were both set at liberty, Walden to become bishop of London from December 1404 to January 1406. Henry did not dislike Richard's former secretary.

After the rebellion the old bishop of Norwich, Henry Despenser, who according to the St. Albans chronicler had had the courage to move an armed force against Henry IV on his arrival, wrote to his niece the countess of Gloucester a stoical letter of condolence upon the Lord Despenser's death. Not unnaturally the bishop had come under suspicion during the rising, but he was ready with a convincing alibi to prove that he had no part in the treason. 'Like myself', he writes, 'who make reason sovereign over the foolishness of my flesh, you should so make your reason also: reason tells us that to watch, think, work and imagine how to recover a thing that is recoverable is well: but to grieve, sigh, languish, weep and groan over an irrecoverable thing is often the greatest folly that can be. For first, it is great displeasure to God and a sin to murmur against his will; secondly it is a most horrible sin against nature, since by such grief a man consumes himself to death and causes himself to die'; and having sketched the disastrous results of such grief, he continues: 'And therefore for God, dear and sweetly loved niece, banish such folly and silliness from your heart and make reason the head of your council and your chief governor.' He promises to do all he can for her honour and comfort, 'for if you so please, I will henceforth be to you father, uncle, husband and brother to the best of my power, and if God will, you will find this not only a fair promise, but a perfect gift.'[1] In such terms of compassionate realism, beyond all hope, but not beyond simple affection, wrote the scourge of the rebellious peasants (1381), the leader of the Flemish crusade.

It only remains to deal with the pathetic figure around whom the plot was woven. Richard at Pontefract was dead by the end—in all probability by the middle—of January 1400. He may have been put to death; he may have starved himself to death. One story relates that on hearing that his friends had failed to secure his rescue, he fell into a morbid melancholy, refused food until it was too late, and died of starvation. The normal tradition is that he died by violence. On 29 January the French king and his council referred to him as dead. But in view of current rumours that he was alive the council had Richard's body conveyed to London and shown at various places where the column stopped. The body lay for two days in St. Paul's, where Henry attended a solemn service himself bearing the pall. It was then removed to King's Langley in Hertfordshire, where it remained in the charge of the Black Friars and was buried in the presence of the bishop of Lichfield and the abbots of Waltham and St. Albans.

Sentiment in favour of Richard kept on cropping up, particularly in the north and in the midlands, till well into the reign of Henry V. Henry IV was confronted with the opposition of many Franciscan convents, where in 1401–2 sympathy for Richard's cause was widespread and vocal. Apart from the Minorites of Llanfaes who in 1401 were to join the Welsh insurrection and to be severely punished for it, a friar from one of the Norfolk convents was imprisoned for preaching in favour of Richard, and a priest of Ware who had circulated a list of the names of men whom he declared ready to rise in favour of Richard was also put under arrest. Early in 1402 the first execution of a Franciscan for treason occurred when a lay brother of

[1] *Anglo-Norman Letters and Petitions*, ed. M. D. Legge, pp. 111–12.

the Aylesbury convent laid information against a priest of the house, alleging that he had declared himself exceedingly glad that King Richard was alive. Examination revealed that the friar favoured Richard as a benefactor of the Order and opposed Henry in as far as he ought by right to be duke of Lancaster and not king. The author of the *Eulogium Historiarum* who must have had access, or drew information from a friend who had access, to the *Coram Rege* rolls, gives a series of detailed accounts of the proceedings against the Minorites. Chief among them was the trial of two brothers, Roger and Richard Frisby, of the Leicester convent.[1] One of the conspirators in the Leicester convent, Walter Walton, who turned approver, denounced Richard Frisby as 'an old Master in Theology who speaks evil of you and says that Richard shall wage war on you'. It had been arranged, he said, by the conspirators that the informer himself and ten other friars of the Leicester convent were to join an assembly of 500 men, clerical and lay, who would be mobilized at Oxford on 23 June 1402 with the intention of finding and joining the forces which Richard II was collecting, and this charge was put in the indictment. The Franciscan plot to overthrow Henry was suppressed and at the Provincial Chapter held significantly at Leicester on 15 August 1402, all the friars were prohibited on pain of life imprisonment to utter a word against the king. The clearest statement of their position was given by Richard Frisby who according to the *Eulogium* was questioned by Henry IV himself at the trial. The dialogue may be quoted in detail:

The King. . . . Did you say that King Richard is alive?
Frisby. I do not say that he is alive, but I do say that if he is alive he is the true King of England.
King. He abdicated.
Frisby. He did abdicate; but under compulsion while in prison, and that is not a valid abdication.
King. He abdicated right willingly.
Frisby. He would never have resigned had he been at liberty. And a resignation made in prison is not a free resignation.
King. Even so, he was deposed.
Frisby. While he was king, he was captured by force of arms, thrown into prison, and despoiled of his realm, while you usurped his crown.
King. I did not usurp the crown, but was duly elected.

[1] Printed from the *Coram Rege* Roll in *Eng. Hist. Rev.* xxxii (1917), 560–1.

Frisby. An election is null and void while the legitimate possessor is alive. And if he is dead, you killed him. And if you are the cause of his death, you forfeit all title and any right which you may have to the kingdom.

King. By this head of mine, thou shalt lose thine!

After the trial of those implicated by Friar Walton the *Eulogium* makes one of the condemned, as he was about to die, say 'It was not, as our enemies say, our intention to kill the king and his sons, but to make him the duke of Lancaster, which is what he ought to be'. The friars were prepared to recognize and honour him as duke, but not to supersede the legitimate Richard. It is evident also that the Franciscans revealed their knowledge that Richard had not abdicated 'of his own will'.[1] The English convents implicated were those of Aylesbury, Leicester, Stamford, Nottingham, and Northampton. According to the *Eulogium* an interesting point is that Richard was not known to have extended any special favours to the Friars Minor:[2] it was from among the Dominicans that he chose his confessors.

---

[1] Attention is drawn to this and other references to the Franciscan attitude by D. W. Whitfield, 'Conflicts of Personality and Principle', *Franciscan Studies*, xvii (1957), 326–35. His translation of the passage from the *Eulogium* is given above.

[2] Noted by Whitfield, op. cit., p. 334, n. 49.

II

HENRY IV: REBELLION

Not before the capture of the Glyn Dŵr strongholds in Wales during 1408 can it be said that the new dynasty was safe from its enemies. The coincidence of attacks from without, the problem of defence and the growing tide of criticism from within were to give Henry IV no respite. There were years when Scotland, Wales, France (including both Calais and Gascony), as well as Ireland, called for a burden of military expenditure with which no English monarch had been faced since the end of Edward I's reign. If, after the battle of Shrewsbury in 1403, Henry had looked forward to a breathing space in the north, there was to be no such thing. He was confronted by the disloyalty of potential rivals and a different type of pressure, the vigorous criticisms of many loyal persons at Westminster, who thought his organization of war and finance inadequate, the grants and rewards he made to his followers excessive, and his tendency to regard the kingdom as an enlarged private estate unduly exclusive. In the country at large, a government continually asking for money is bound to become disliked and when the first enthusiasm for Henry had faded under the strain of taxation and the demand for loans to the crown, he was even less popular than his predecessor. All these anxieties Henry met with courage and resilience. The prolonged effort cost him his nervous health and the house of Lancaster much political good will. That he survived the ordeal and was able to hand over to a son was due partly to his own unremitting energy and almost unbelievable power of driving himself virtually beyond the limit; partly to the loyalty of his administrators and the support of certain leading churchmen. In the present chapter the hostile and treasonable reactions will mainly be described: the constitutional effects will be analysed in the following.

Until at least 1404 Henry mainly relied upon his duchy servants, the officers and relatives of John of Gaunt and upon the members of his own household. The magnates who had helped him to the throne, his 'natural' counsellors, looked to him to govern by their advice and consent; his first council therefore, was unusually large and aristocratic, an average of fifteen members attended for normal business. In 1400 the average fell to seven and the atmosphere changed. Tolerant and polite, Henry made what concessions he could, but was determined to uphold his own prerogative and to govern through the administrators closest to himself: the same knight, Sir John Pelham, who had been with him as early as 1389; Sir Thomas Erpingham, influential in Norfolk; John Woodhouse, constable of Rising Castle; John Leventhorpe, receiver-general of the duchy; Hugh and Robert Waterton, both Lincolnshire men, the former now ageing, chamberlain of Henry since 1386 and with him on the expeditions of 1390–1, 1392–3; the latter chief steward of the duchy in the north; Thomas Chaucer of Ewelme, retainer of John of Gaunt and constable of the duchy castle of Knaresborough, speaker-to-be of the commons in 1407, 1410, 1414, and 1421; not least Walter Hungerford, of a family long in the duchy service, later to be treasurer of England after taking a distinguished part in diplomacy. Locally the king-duke could rely, in the county of Lancaster, for support, and, as will be seen, notable service in the field, upon men like Sir Nicholas Haryngton of Farleton, connected with the Nevilles of Hornby; or Ralph Staveley, steward to Henry on the expedition to the East (1393) and connected with the Asshetons, a prominent family in the parliamentary history of Lancashire. But the duchy and the county palatine did not exhaust Henry's supporters: his appeal was to many of those shire knights who were to be most restive in parliament under his personal conduct of affairs. For personal it certainly was. If there was any revolution in 1399, it was not in the central organs of administration. The king kept very close to him the man and the instrument whereby the royal will was transmitted to those responsible for its execution. By 1400 the privy seal had formally gone out of court and become a public department like chancery or exchequer. It is true that the keeper had his own staff of clerks and his own hostel or establishment, and drew 20s. a day in wages: but he was treated as a member of the royal household, as it travelled about the country, and was often in close and immediate personal contact with the king. Even more than the chancellor, Thomas Langley, the keeper, was the king's man and occupied the central position in the royal administration.[1] From his

[1] See R. L. Storey's forthcoming *Thomas Langley and the Bishopric of Durham, 1406–7.*

office warrants went out to every department, and the privy seal was bound by no strict traditions such as those governing the chancery or the exchequer. It was a flexible instrument: the letters were not enrolled, but its activities can be measured by the surviving warrants of chancery and from chancery letters that cite their authority. These are very numerous: it has been estimated that from 3 November 1401 until 2 March 1405, a period of three years and four months, 1,340 warrants survive in the chancery files: instructions to royal ministers of all ranks and in all parts of the country, mandates to officers in Chester and in Wales, to collectors of customs in the ports, to castellans, military officers, and so forth.

The range of operations conducted by, and the informal character of, the privy seal, made its control a matter of great importance. While under it certain letters could be issued as a matter of course, it was normally set in motion by a higher authority and that authority was the king. It was Henry IV who, in the early years of his reign, directed the keeper and governed the country with a small body of specialist councillors who were the three main officials, the chancellor, the treasurer, and the keeper, together with a few retainers of knightly status whom he had personally chosen. It was an administrative rather than an advisory body, and the fact is characteristic of Henry's mentality: as such it was attacked in parliament in January 1404 and again in the Long Parliament of 1406.[1] This reaction brought an increase in the magnate element besides eliciting regular salaries for councillors. In 1407 there was a reaction to the older type of larger and more representative council, the sort of council in which, as Stubbs remarked of 1422, 'every honoured name appears'; it was not entirely of the king's choosing and did not last, for in 1410 there appeared a small aristocratic body, the pattern of the councils of Henry of Monmouth, whether as prince of Wales or (later) as king. Now despite the amount of business transacted by the council, that body had no seal of its own, but used the privy seal to give effect to its decisions and the keeper's association with the council was very close. Not only was he one of its most prominent members, but his officials carried out the council's secretarial work: one of his clerks usually acted as clerk to the council. The connexion of the privy seal with the council was to

---

[1] Cf. Chap. IX, below.

reach its fullest development during the minority of Henry VI.

For a monarch holding personal views of government and presiding in his council much as he might have sat with his duchy officers, a sensible administrator who would respect the royal prerogative and at the same time profit from the lessons of Richard II's reign, was necessary. It was characteristic of Henry IV's discrimination to appoint first as keeper of the privy seal and later as chancellor (1405–7) the Lancastrian clerk, Thomas Langley. Langley, a native of Middleton, six miles to the north of Manchester, owed his rise to John of Gaunt, whose executor he became. Within a fortnight of Henry IV's accession he is described as 'king's clerk' and on 29 October 1399 became archdeacon of Norfolk. On 1 July 1401 he was given the deanery of York and, on 3 November of that year, made keeper of the privy seal. Later he was promoted by Innocent VII to the see of Durham (14 May 1406), after an ineffective attempt by the king and Archbishop Arundel to promote him to the see of London. While in Durham, this versatile man established himself as a solicitous and acceptable diocesan; to the government he was an indispensable administrator. His resignation from the chancellorship in 1407 may indeed have sprung from a desire to do his duty in his diocese, rather than being, as Stubbs thought, the result of parliamentary criticism. That he was not under any disfavour in 1407 can be seen from the fact that on the same day as he resigned the Great Seal, he was appointed a member of the king's council with an annual salary of 200 marks. Henry, like his son later, felt respect and even affection for this robust, discreet, and moderate man. But neither Langley nor the ten treasurers who were appointed and removed in as many years were more than very partially responsible for the inefficient administration of the king's resources which the knights of the shire were so vigorously to challenge.

After the displacement of Richard and his queen, Henry could hardly have expected amity with France. If as duke he had been treated well while in exile there, the fate of Richard and the humiliation of Queen Isabel must have forewarned him of the hostile preparations made by Charles VI: the closing of the Somme at Abbeville and the assembly of a fleet under the count of St. Pol at Harfleur in preparation for a descent upon the coasts of Wales, while the duke of Bourbon was sent to Agen from which to stir up disaffection against the English. The appearance, however, at Bordeaux of the English admiral Thomas Percy with a force of men-at-arms and archers prevented revolt. But there were other ways of threatening England: one at least through an understanding with the Scots. The Scots historian Bower makes Henry apprehensive of the friendly relations between the two countries and refers to the capture by the king's men at sea of letters addressed by Scottish magnates to France in which Henry was described as a traitor. The king's attack on Scotland in 1400 has been represented as nothing more than a raid to gain prestige, and much has been made of his words to the canons of Leith that he had appeared in Scotland, not to do the country harm, but to discover whether Robert III, after calling him a traitor, would dare to fight with him. Such simplicities may be dismissed. A king who had newly and at great hazard acquired a kingdom, did not leave it and march to Edinburgh for reasons of this sort.

The invasion discussed in the meeting of the great council at Westminster on 9 February 1400, which arranged for the necessary loans, had undoubtedly as one of its aims the discouragement of the French alliance. Henry was determined to force Robert III and his subjects to observe the Anglo-French agreement of 1396 which named Robert as ally of the French king and therefore bound to maintain peace with England. He was anxious to retaliate for the Scottish raid of the previous autumn, and, more important still, to make a reconnaissance in force so as to test the allegiance of the Scottish magnates to their own king and to see how far the Lowlands were prepared to admit the overlordship of the English monarch. There is substantial evidence that in the summer of 1400 Henry was collecting all the evidence he could to support a fresh claim to the Scottish homage. On 15 July John Norbury the treasurer brought him evidence taken from various charters and muniments on the subject of homage. A transcript of Edward I's transactions with Scotland from 1291–6 was delivered to the king,[1] and from the *Rotuli Scotiae* and other sources the case against Scotland was presented in a convenient form. When he went north Henry took with him a dossier put together from royal archives.

[1] E. L. G. Stones, 'The Records of the "Great Cause" ', *Scottish Historical Review*, xxxv (1956), 98, suggests that Glasgow Univ. Lib. MS. BE 10-y. 3 together with Cotton Vitellius E. XI, foll. 178–255, were compiled for this purpose early in Henry IV's reign, and that these may be the evidence submitted by Norbury.

It is doubtful whether he would have gone at all had he not received an important new ally from beyond the Border. George Dunbar, earl of the Scottish March, had procured the marriage of the heir of the Scottish throne, the duke of Rothsay, to his daughter Elizabeth, but, after its consummation, had been outbidden by the earl of Douglas, in favour of his daughter Margaret, on the pretext that the Dunbar engagement had not been approved by the estates. March had protested to Robert III in vain: thereupon he wrote on 18 February 1400 to Henry asking that either Lord Neville of Furnival or the earl of Westmorland might be sent to confer with him on the Marches and praying for a safe conduct to enter England and reside there with a retinue of one hundred. Henry granted the safe conduct on 8 March and the earl crossed the Border, leaving Dunbar Castle in charge of his nephew, Sir Robert Maitland, who promptly handed it over to the eldest son of the earl of Douglas. In reply March joined Henry Percy in a raid through the Lothians as far as Hailes where they were turned back and defeated by Douglas at Cockburnspath. Armed with a fresh safe conduct, March set out to meet the English king. Henry, who had left Pontefract to talk with March at York, rejected a Scottish proposal of peace based on the lines of the treaty of Northampton of 1328, which would have given the Scots Berwick, Jedburgh, and Roxburgh beside opening the way for a claim upon Northumberland. From York he made for Newcastle upon Tyne, whence on 7 August he issued a proclamation to all the nobles of Scotland asking them to induce Robert III to do homage at Edinburgh on 23 August, or, failing that, to perform it themselves. Henry took a considerable force into Scotland, with a fleet co-operating at sea. The Border was crossed on 17 August; the army marched first to Haddington, then to Leith. Edinburgh was firmly held, and on 23 August, the day for the homage to be performed, Henry received no reply. The Scots maintained a continuous guerilla warfare and Henry was anxious about his commissariat. All he could achieve at an interview with a representative of the Scottish court was a promise to give consideration to the claim of overlordship. He recrossed the Border on 29 August, marching by Newcastle upon Tyne.

The expedition evoked a retaliation which might have been serious had it not been for the resistance of the Border castles and the defeat at Redesmuir (in Redesdale) of a large Scots force by Sir Richard Umfraville. Apart from this, the total result of Henry's Scottish expedition was a truce of six weeks made on 9 November, but no permanent peace. A settlement might have been possible while the duke of Rothsay was in power (i.e. to the end of April 1401), and indeed Northumberland and Rothsay arranged to meet at Melrose on 25 March. But with the rise of the earl of Douglas a more militant policy prevailed and the chances of reconciliation diminished.

Henry took his claims to the overlordship of Scotland very seriously. Before negotiations were resumed, in the summer of 1401, he had searches made in monastic chronicles to prove his claim, and the extracts were shown to the Scots in the autumn: he made a note of the homage done by Edward Balliol, and his representative at the negotiations brought forward a dossier constructed from the letters of Edward I and other contemporary documents from the *gesta publica* in the royal archives (*in archivis regiis*).[1] Henry commissioned his envoys on 1 September and Robert III his on 1 October 1401. Douglas and Northumberland were the heads of the two delegacies, and the meetings were held on 17 October at Yetham in Roxburgh and later at Carham and Alnwick. The proceedings appear to fit the instructions given to the English envoys. They were to take up 'the matters touching Scotland at the time when the king and his army were at the Cross between Edinburgh and Leith': if the Scots could produce no valid evidence against the king's claim, the envoys were to agree upon a final peace 'to their best judgement': but if they produced evidence and doubts arose about the supremacy, there was to be a reference back to Henry, who would try to persuade the Scots to refer the question to an expert committee of persons mutually agreed upon, and if their report favoured the Scots, the English were none the less to press for homage, but to offer 1,000 marks or £1,000 worth of land in England and a force of 500 men-at-arms to fight for the king when required by way of return. If the Scots proved obdurate, then a general or particular truce must be asked for but England must keep the 'castles and towns of Berwick-on-Tweed, Roxburgh and Jedworth' (Jedburgh). If the Scots came to any reasonable terms, the envoys might go farther and treat for

---

[1] Note 1, p. 34, above. Henry's chronicle extracts, which are not those made by Edward I, included a chronicle *iuxta tumbam sancti Cuthberti*, evidently a Durham book.

marriages of 'lads and ladies of both courts as the king might find expedient'.[1] The tone of the instructions is not optimistic. Evidently it was not expected that the Scots would agree to more than a truce, but in any such the earl of March was to be included 'as the king's ally'. The earl had indeed burned his boats; he had been rewarded with lands in England, the manor of Clippstone in Sherwood Forest, and the castle of Somerton in Lincolnshire, for life, and £100 a year during pleasure. Gawain his son also received an annuity of £40 on his own account. Dunbar was taking an active part in the attacks of Henry IV upon Scotland, devoting his attentions particularly to the lands on the east Border. The English had not yet accustomed themselves to raiding as far as East Lothian; but March showed the way and many persons living around Haddington, both peasantry and men of estate along with much booty were hailed off with impunity to England. On 3 February 1401 March, with Henry Percy and a large following, made a surprise visit to Papple, where they burned and spoiled as far as East Linton, made two attacks upon Hailes Castle, and fired the townships of Hailes, Traprain, and East Markle. The earl's accession to England worsened the prospects of negotiation with the Scots: incidentally there were, as will be suggested later, those who found the forceful Scot an embarrassing ally.

We left Henry at Newcastle early in September 1400 on his way south. He was at Northampton on 19 September, where he heard of the quarrel that had broken out between Owain Glyn Dŵr, lord of Glyndyfrdwy and Cynllaith, and Reginald Grey of Ruthin, lord of Dyffryn Clwyd, a large landowner in eastern England and a member of Henry IV's council. Whether the dispute arose from a maliciously intended delay on the part of Grey to serve the summonses upon Glyn Dŵr for the expedition to Scotland, with the Welshman's consequent misrepresentation as a traitor; or whether it was the result of a boundary dispute, a contest that had been some time in progress over lands claimed by Glyn Dŵr as part of his inheritance and forcibly denied him by Grey, is uncertain: what is clear is that on 16 September 1400 Owain took up arms along with his eldest son, his brother Gryffyn, and his brother-in-law, Philip Hanmer, was proclaimed prince of Wales and on the 18th burned Ruthin and for the next three days ravaged the English settlements at

[1] *P.P.C.* i. 168–73. For the Scots commissioners', *Rotuli Scotiae*, ii. 159.

Denbigh, Rhuddlan, Flint, Hawarden, and Holt. The insurgents had it their own way until 24 September, when Hugh Burnell with the levies of Shropshire, Staffordshire, and Warwickshire met Owain's forces near Welshpool and inflicted on them an incisive defeat. This proved a temporary breathing-space only: a larger movement was to follow.

The Wales of 1400 was not the tribal Wales of popular imagination. Both before and after the Edwardian conquest there had been growing up a new class of gentry and, in certain districts, a régime of large integrated individual estates had to a large extent displaced the *gwely*, the semi-communal holding of land by a group of relatives. The change from tribalism had been in part brought about by a closer association with England and with the feudalism of the Marches; most of all, however, by the growth of the state and the existence of centralized administrative institutions. This growth necessitated an administrative bureaucracy, and an official aristocracy of *ministeriales* began to develop, members of which were often rewarded with grants of land little related to the tribal pattern. After the Edwardian conquest new factors reinforced this trend: lands forfeited to the crown by rebellion were often leased to individuals on non-tribal terms: in the neighbourhood of the English boroughs in north Wales, the gains of industry were increasingly spent on land; while even with the *gwely*, individual tribesmen could often buy up the portions of less fortunate or less effective kinsmen.[1] The restraints imposed by Welsh custom on free trade in land were gradually being broken down. It was in such a developing society that the rise of certain ministerial families can be observed: to the support given by a group of these the rebellion of Owain Glyn Dŵr owed much of its initial success.

Prominent among these families were the descendants of Ednyfed Fychan, senechal to Llewelyn the Great and to his son Dafydd from about 1215–46. By 1334, when the survey of Denbigh was completed, the descendants of Ednyfed are found distributed over a wide area in Rhos and Rhwfoniog. The most important of these, in the middle of the fourteenth century, were the sons of Goronwy ap Tudor, Howel, and Tudor ap Goronwy who in Anglesey held jointly the vill of Trecastle and half of the vill of Penynydd. Howel was archdeacon of Anglesey and therefore

---

[1] Glyn Roberts, 'Wyrion Eden', *Trans. Anglesey Antiq. Soc. and Field Club* (1951), pp. 35–36.

had no progeny; but Tudor, famous in Welsh legend for his defence, before Edward III, of his own assumption of knighthood, had five sons, Goronwy, Ednyfed, Gwilym, Rhys, and Mareddud. Of these Gwilym ap Tudor of Clorach and Rhys ap Tudor of Erddreiniog were, in 1398, in Richard II's pay, and the evidence points to the supposition that they stood in some sort of personal relationship to him. Of the part played by the brothers in the Glyn Dŵr rising there can be no doubt. Their mother Margaret was the sister of Helen, daughter of Owain ap Tudor ap Llewelyn, who by Gruffyd Fychan was the mother of Owain Glyn Dŵr. They were therefore first cousins and were of his party from the outset. Along with Glyn Dŵr, they were excepted by name from the pardon granted in March 1401 to the original rebels, and it was their capture of Conway Castle on 1 April that year that signalized the renewal of the revolt. But, as it has been observed,[1] the Tudor contribution to the Glyn Dŵr rebellion cannot be rightly assessed if attention is concentrated on the brothers alone. The Tudors had wide connexions. In the list of Anglesey men who in November 1406 abandoned the cause of Owain Glyn Dŵr and were allowed to make fine at Beaumaris before the commissioners appointed by Prince Henry to receive surrenders,[2] some of their affiliations are made clear: the names of Rhys, Gwilym, and Mareddud appear along with their connexions, men like Tudor ap Goronwy the son of Goronwy ap Tudor of Penmynydd or Gruffydd ap Gwilym ap Gruffyd and others, which suggest vividly the background of clan and kinship that forms the setting of the rebellion and shows the close relationship between the families of Glyn Dŵr, Pengwern, Mostyn, and Tudor. The evidence points to 'the central position of the Tudors in the network of families involved'.[3] The list enumerates the friars who were to prove rebellious at Llanfaes and shows why Henry burned their house. Less local are the outlaws enumerated at the close of the list, among them many non-Anglesey names, besides the three Percies, Lord Bardolf, William Langby, friar of Guisborough, John Scalby, Lewis Byford, bishop of Bangor, the prior of Beddgelerth, and other important clerks including Gruffyd Young, archdeacon of

[1] By Prof. Glyn Roberts, op. cit., p. 51.
[2] Printed from Peniarth MS. 405D by Glyn Roberts, 'The Anglesey Submissions of 1406', *Bulletin of the Board of Celtic Studies*, xv, part i (1952), pp. 39–61.
[3] Glyn Roberts, 'Wyrion Eden', p. 58.

Merioneth and the abbot of Conway (supporting Glyn Dŵr as early as October 1400).

The immediate crisis was over, owing to Burnell's action, when Henry reached Shrewsbury on 26 September 1400, but it was evident that the revolt had spread northwards to the Conway valley and, as we have seen, to Anglesey. Henry accordingly made a punitive circuit of north Wales crossing to Beaumaris where he was attacked by Rhys the Black of Erddreiniog, and returning by Bangor to Shrewsbury. He received the submission of numerous Welsh and prevented the revolt spreading south. On his return the estates of Gruffyd and Philip Hanmer were declared forfeit: all the manors and lands of 'Owinus de Glendordy' were granted to John Beaufort, earl of Somerset, but the northern lands remained in Owain's hands until the prince of Wales's raid in May 1403.

Owain, as Sir John Lloyd observed, was in 1400 one of the few Welsh landowners who held directly from the crown lands which their ancestors had ruled as princes. 'He was the representative of the northern line and heir of the princes of Powys Fadog.'[1] From his ancestors, in particular from Gruffyd Fychan, son of Gruffyd ap Madog (d. 1289), he had inherited lordships on either side of the Berwyn Hills; 'the fourth part of a commote in the county of Merioneth attributed to him lay in the Dee valley between Corwen and Llangollen, just by Carrog',[2] the other estate centred at Sycarth which is the same as Cynllaith Owain; and his mother had brought into the family a part of the Cardiganshire inheritance of Rhys ap Eddwr, lands in Iscoed and Gwynionydd. Married to the daughter of Sir David Hanmer, from 1383 judge in the King's Bench, Glyn Dŵr was a landowner of position. He had been 'an apprentice-of-law' probably under his future father-in-law in the Inns of Court; he had been on the Scottish expedition of 1385, during the course of which Iolo Goch describes him while at Berwick 'wearing in his helmet the scarlet feather of a flamingo', and he was of sufficient status to give evidence at the Scrope and Grosvenor trial, having seen Grosvenor bear the arms that Scrope of Bolton denied him. He is found there, as Sir John Lloyd says, 'in

---

[1] In J. E. Lloyd, *Owen Glendower* (1931), p. 22.
[2] The house a mile west of the village of Glyndyfrdwy, between the present Holyhead road and the railway, on the site of the fir-topped tumulus, a prehistoric earthwork named on the Ordnance map 'Owain Glyndwr's Mound'.

a crowd of well-born young squires, learned in heraldic distinction and the customs of chivalry'; and later, as a man of substance, was celebrated (as any rich person might be) by his bard.

Glyn Dŵr's revolt was to spread to the whole of Wales and to reach its climax in 1405. By the end of 1401, in the absence of Henry Percy who, after being demoted from his command in Anglesey, had returned to Northumberland, he had received the counties of Caernarvon (not Caernarvon Castle) and Merioneth and was master of the majority of north Wales. He had not yet claimed to rule as an independent prince: all he wanted was recognition of his claim as a Welsh landowner. Still in possession of Cynllaith and Glyndyfrdwy, he might have been content with the return of his south Welsh properties and have refrained from extremities. There is reason to think that he had the confidence of Northumberland and his son. There were elements in the king's council which might advise negotiations and the end of 1401 was not unfavourable to peace, for just before November 1401 he asked the earl for a pardon and was told that if he submitted without reservation, Northumberland would make a plea for his life: he replied that having seen what the commons did to certain of the earls in the rising of 1400 he did not dare to submit.

The author of the anonymous chronicle printed by Giles which, as we have seen,[1] reveals a north midland–Yorkshire trend of opinion, not unfavourable to Henry Percy, represents Hotspur as interviewing the Welsh leader in the hope of bringing him back to the king's allegiance. The condition Glyn Dŵr made was a royal pardon and some evident testimony of the king's good will, along with a three months' armistice; 'but certain of the council said that it neither was nor could be honorable and befitting the king's majesty to remit to such a malefactor his offence', and others went so far as to advocate murdering him when negotiations were in progress: to which Percy replied 'that it was not in keeping with his rank to use the oath of fealty as a means of deception'.[2]

Branded as a traitor Glyn Dŵr prepared for stronger measures, for enlarging the struggle by appealing to Irish chiefs and approaching Robert III of Scotland in a letter which claimed

---

[1] Above, p. 24.
[2] *Incerti Scriptoris Chronicon Angliae*, ed. Giles (1848), p. 31.

kinship on the ground that both were descended from Brutus. Aiming first at Reginald de Grey, whom he suspected of frustrating all attempts at an accommodation with Henry, Glyn Dŵr attacked Ruthin and carried off much plunder. In April 1402 he had the skill and fortune to capture Grey himself very near to his own castle, and on 22 June no less a person than Edmund Mortimer, younger brother of the late earl Roger (d. 1398), in an action in Radnorshire, when the Welsh archers in the English forces turned against their commanders. The royal counter-measures envisaged a general muster at Lichfield on 7 July, but in the event the campaign was postponed: there were other dangers to meet.

In August 1402 Glyn Dŵr appeared for the first time in South Wales, while the Welsh of Glamorgan rose in sympathy. The royal forces, in three separate armies based on Shrewsbury, Chester, and Hereford, undertook a general advance upon the insurgents, but Glyn Dŵr avoided capture and the royal army was discomfited by unusual weather conditions which caused the greatest hardship to the English expedition in early September. A different sort of pressure was Glyn Dŵr's alliance with Edmund Mortimer: the Welsh leader was able to make play with the slowness of the English government to ransom Mortimer in contrast with the speed they showed in ransoming Grey. At the end of November Mortimer became Glyn Dŵr's son-in-law and on 13 December he wrote to Sir John Grendor of Herefordshire, Hywel Fychan of Rhayader and Radnor, and others of that area signifying his adherence to the Glyn Dŵr programme: which was to place the Mortimer earl of March upon the throne and to secure Glyn Dŵr 'his right in Wales'. The capture and defection of Mortimer meant that Maelienydd and the Mortimer lordships of the middle and upper Wye as well as that of Blaenllyfni on the upper Usk were lost to the English cause and a great hole had been made in the loyal marcher centre. Even though the prince of Wales might in the course of the next spring capture and fire Glyn Dŵr's family house of Sycharth and make havoc of his properties along the river Dee, the homeless chieftain was far from being suppressed.

He was shortly to become the centre of a conspiracy wider than ever before. To this we shall pass very shortly. For the moment it is worth observing how the Welsh revolt ranked among the items of business considered by Henry's small council of administrators, for beside the official view of the administrators about Wales, there was the view of the commons and there was also the view held at the prince's headquarters at Chester. The commons at any rate did not underestimate the danger. On 21 February 1401 they showed the king evidence of disaffection among the Welsh at the universities and pointed to the departure of Welsh labourers from England to their homes in preparation for resistance: at the same time they successfully petitioned for the withdrawal of certain privileges enjoyed by native Welshmen residing in England and in the Welsh Marches and for the protection of native Englishmen from malicious sentences on the part of Welsh juries. Barons resident in the marches were to garrison and equip their castles adequately—a requirement frequently met with hereafter. Among the assented petitions were arrangements for the attachment of Welshmen's goods in retaliation for the seizure of English goods and chattels in Wales; and the enactment that all Englishmen taking on Welsh tenants should take from them securities of good behaviour. Furthermore, it was successfully petitioned that no Welshman should be permitted to purchase lands or tenements in England.

In the parliament of October 1402 there was a crop of common petitions, of an extremely drastic kind, on the subject of justice and order in Wales. Some of them could be assented directly; others involving complete anglicization of officials, taking hostages among a Welshman's family for his good behaviour, or making leading Welshmen responsible to the king for the peace in their own lordship, were referred to the council for decision and action.[1] In 1404 the commons suspected that the Marcher lords were not garrisoning their castles adequately, and that more energetic steps might be taken to raise men-at-arms and archers in the border counties. Most of all did they show anxiety that the prince of Wales should have, for the defence of Wales, the full sum of 1,000 marks granted to him for his conduct in the Percy rebellion. Not all the measures suggested by the commons could be carried out. The proclamation of 1402 which made it

---

[1] *Rot. Parl.* iii. 508–9. One of these (no. 90) shows that Welsh minstrels and bards were circulating through the country, reciting to popular gatherings. For the bards, cf. J. E. Lloyd, op. cit., pp. 154–7. Mr. E. D. Jones makes the interesting suggestion, based on a revision of the commonly accepted dating, that Davydd Llwyd, at a tender age, took part in Owain Glyn Dŵr's rising: 'Some Fifteenth Century Poetry relating to Montgomeryshire', *The Montgomeryshire Collections*, liii, part i (1953), pp. 3–17.

illegal for English people to trade with Welsh was disregarded
and large quantities of goods were smuggled across the border.
The people of Chester, Shropshire, Hereford, and Gloucester
thought less of patriotism than of their pockets. The attitude of
many persons living in the border was unwarlike, and an
economic blockade of a country in which large districts consisted of English and Welsh living side by side was out of the
question. The English hold upon Wales depended on the safe
custody of the castles: and never was the Edwardian policy of
castle-building more clearly vindicated. The custody of central
Wales turned upon Conway and Caernarvon in the north;
Harlech and Llanbadarn (Aberystwyth) in the centre. After the
royal expedition of 1400 large forces were not employed in north
Wales. In June 1401, before he left north Wales, Henry Percy
marching from Denbigh routed the Welsh in an engagement at
Cader Idris,[1] and in June also John Charlton, lord of Powys,
narrowly missed catching Owain Glyn Dŵr in the mountains,
but capturing part of his armour and a cloth 'painted with
maidens with red hands'.[2] This may have been a prearranged
movement, Percy doing the attack and Powys, moving north-
east, surprising the Welsh as they retreated. In November 1401
Northumberland had advised a concerted movement against Glyn
Dŵr's lands. He suggested that if Welshpool was well defended
the garrison, Edmund Mortimer, and the other marchers could
move in from the south-east and the garrisons of Carmarthen
and Harlech from the west and north, while he himself would
advance into north Wales 'par M' (probably Mould).[3] This
never materialized and during the first years of the Welsh revolt
Prince Henry had to rely upon the castellans without any large-
scale movements.

The local defence was primarily the concern of the prince's
council at Chester, headed by Henry Percy as justice of Chester
and north Wales, who held Anglesey and was keeper of the lordship of Denbigh; and secondarily of the Marcher lords themselves.
Percy held his position effectively—save for his failure to prevent
the capture of Conway, 1 April 1401, by William and Rhys ap
Tudor—until June 1401, when he resigned on the ostensible
grounds of inability to pay his men, and Hugh le Despenser,

[1] *P.P.C.* i. 153: letter of Henry Percy dated 4 June 1401.
[2] *Anglo-Norman letters and Petitions*, ed. M. D. Legge (1941), no. 226.
[3] Ibid., no. 244.

with an extended commission covering all Wales, took his place. Though at an early age the prince showed that he had a will of his own, he had to take orders from Henry IV, and the solicitous father did not give him and his council much elbow room. If the prince was allowed to make representations about his own governor, when Hugh le Despenser died, it was Henry IV and the council which put forward names from whom one, Thomas Percy, earl of Worcester, was selected. The prince's receiver, John Spencer, and his chancellor, the chancery clerk William Ferriby, were also central appointments. It was the king in council who appointed the custodians of the castles and sent any extra military assistance that was needed.[1] Henry looked to the prince to hold the key castle of Aberystwyth firmly: 'considering, dearly beloved son, that it costs less and is simpler to keep the said castle (Llanbadarn) than to gain and recover it from the hands of the rebels, if they have taken it'.[2] The prince's letters show lively feelings for his own staff. Hugh le Despenser's death was 'a great weight of sorrow to my heart', and Ferriby's health (he suffered from sciatica) was the prince's special concern.[3] But the main topic of the letters to his father is scarcity of ready money and anxiety at its results.

Henry Percy was happier in the north. He was keeper of Berwick Castle and warden of the East March, and northern campaigning among his own people was more to his taste. In 1401, in order to avenge the losses of 1399 and 1400, certain of the Scotch magnates had been arranging, with the encouragement of the earl of Douglas, raids upon England, one of which came to grief at Nesbit on 22 June with considerable loss. At the same time a large Scottish army set out for Carlisle, but hearing of the defeat at Nesbit, transferred itself to the eastern side. Accompanied by Murdoch, Albany's eldest son, and by the earls of Angus, Orkney, and Moray, the army got as far as Newcastle, but on its return was met in the valley of the Till by the English under Northumberland, Henry Percy, and the earl of March, and suffered disaster at Homildon Hill, where seven prominent nobles were killed, twenty-eight taken prisoner (including four earls among whom was Murdoch, earl of Fife), as well as some thirty French knights. In all there were taken no less than eighty Scottish barons and knights of rank and a large

---

[1] e.g. in 1402, the earls of Arundel and Stafford.
[2] *Anglo-Norman Letters*, no. 236. [3] Ibid., no. 223.

host of fighting men. In the autumn parliament of 1402 the earl of Northumberland brought on 20 October, Murdoch Stewart, son of the earl of Albany, and six of the chief prisoners taken at Homildon. The earl of Douglas was not produced. Henry Percy had refused to hand him over: the ransom would help to recoup him for the heavy losses he had incurred on behalf of the king. Hardyng reports an angry scene with Henry when Henry Percy, pressed to give up his prisoner, asked that his brother-in-law Edmund Mortimer should be allowed to ransom himself as Lord Grey of Ruthin had done.[1] Percy had no possible case, for the crown's right to the main enemy prisoners was generally admitted.

To the author of Giles's Chronicle, perhaps too unreservedly a Hotspur partisan, the convulsions that were to follow in 1403 derived from internal rivalries. If it was clear to him that the Percies were dissatisfied with their treatment since 1399, there were also those he says, whose policy was to foment rather than heal the antagonisms. Some were anxious to procure the death of the king, others were jealous of Henry Percy:

and especially the two principal lords who encouraged that evil work, men who could have extinguished all these bitter thoughts at the beginning and even almost at the end of the business, to wit, the earls of Dunbar and Worcester: since one of them, Dunbar, desired the death of Henry Percy that he might dominate more easily in parts of Northumbria, and the earl of Worcester desired the death of the king, that with him out of the way he might be more easily the principal power under his cousin.[2]

Sub consanguineo suo meant the earl of Northumberland. While no view of the situation that is so much dependent upon personalities is likely to be complete, the stress laid by the chronicler upon the opposition between Dunbar and Henry Percy should not go unnoticed. Homildon Hill made an English advance into southern Scotland a distinct possibility and March successfully petitioned Henry IV that the castles and lordships formerly belonging to him, that had been conquered by the English, should be restored to him to hold for the English crown. He had been granted in 1401 an annuity of 500 marks, part secured on lands, part made up from customs at Boston.

Once on the English side, he was a new and disturbing element inserted into the Percy sphere of influence. When he faced Percy

---

[1] *The Chronicle of John Hardyng*, ed. H. Ellis (1812), pp. 360–1.   [2] Giles, p. 33.

as his Scottish counterpart, Marcher–Warden in the eastern lowlands, he was a formidable opponent, known and proved: as the
ally and tenant of Henry IV he was, for the Percies, a more
difficult and questionable factor; nor, by 1403, had Hotspur
any scruple in giving him the slip. Early in that year Dunbar
advanced, with Percy's assistance, to besiege Cocklaws Castle in
Teviotdale, which the governor had agreed to surrender if not
relieved by 1 August. When he got there he found the siege
already raised. Henry Percy had withdrawn his troops to the
west of England to co-operate with Worcester and Mortimer
against the crown. Furthermore, the chronicler's mention of
Northumberland ruling, or at least nominally ruling, has some
significance, even if the passage was written after 1405. For it
foreshadows the tripartite agreement for the division of England
between the earl, Edmund Mortimer, and Glyn Dŵr made that
year, and suggests that Northumberland may have thought of
himself as more than a northern viceroy. At the moment (May
1403) he was the alarmed and frustrated feudatory. The letters
which he wrote to the council in May 1403 witness to his
apprehension at an expected Scottish riposte to the campaigns
that ended in Homildon Hill. The duty of the overlord was to
support his loyal lieges when in danger: an extreme emergency
was at hand, for there was reason to believe that the Welsh and
the French were co-operating with the Scots. Money, whether in
immediately available cash or got by loan (*paiez ou chevez*),
should reach him by 24 June; if payment was not made speedily
disaster would follow. Henry replied that he had ordered a
certain sum to be sent without delay, though he gave no indication of its amount or precisely when it was to be paid. From the
manor of Healaugh near Tadcaster, the earl replied that time
was short: if he and his son had really received the £60,000
which certain people had wrongly informed the king that they
had received, it would have been well, but as much as £120,000
were due now. Alive to the danger from the Scots, Henry, with
characteristic energy, decided to go in person to reinforce the
Percies, after which it was his intention to pass over into Wales,
there to remain until the rebellion was ended. He therefore made
northwards, through Higham Ferrers to Lichfield. On 13 July,
while at Nottingham on his way north, he received news that
Henry Percy and his father were in revolt, and that the younger
Percy had issued a proclamation in Chester, alluding to the

king as Henry of Lancaster and spreading the well-worn story that Richard II was alive. It then appeared that Hotspur was collecting an army in Shropshire preparatory to uniting with Owain Glyn Dŵr, Edmund Mortimer, 'the Cheshire and the Welsh archers and men-at-arms',[1] and that he was accompanied by the earl of Douglas and by the prince's own governor, Thomas Percy, who had removed his treasure from London as well as from Chester—wherewith to pay his rebel troops.

To Henry the movement was plainly treasonable. It was to place the young earl of March upon the throne.[2] It was, at the time, camouflaged by constitutional propaganda which deceived not a few. Under their seals, wrote one annalist, the leaders canvassed the magnates and people throughout the country (*regni proceribus necnon et incolis*) asserting that the proposal they were making was not contrary to their allegiance or the fealty they had undertaken to the king, nor had they resorted to arms for any other end, save that they might enjoy the indemnity of their own estates and correct the present system of government by establishing wise councillors for the profit of the king and kingdom. They pointed out that the taxes and tallages granted to the king for the safekeeping of England had not been employed to their rightful use, but devoured and consumed to no profit. Moved by their consciences, they proclaimed that they had been compelled in the public interest to assemble their forces so as the more easily to provide remedies. The implication was that the rightful use of the grants received was to subsidize the Percies as wardens of the two Marches of Scotland, and that they had not received the sums for which they asked for the purpose of defence. Henry did his best to counteract the complaints that the money had gone elsewhere: the earl of Northumberland and his son had received by far the larger part of the sums granted for the safeguarding of the March: and as for the story, put about by the Percies, that it was unsafe for them to approach him, so far was this from being the truth that he would grant them a personal interview immediately.

How far was Henry right in his contention not to have failed the Percies financially, since this was a major point in question? The Issue Rolls show that between October 1399 and July 1403

---

[1] *Annales Ricardi Secundi et Henrici Quarti*, p. 361.

[2] The various authorities for this are cited by J. M. W. Bean, 'Henry IV and the Percies', *History*, xliv (1959), p. 221.

the Percies, father and son, received, in cash or in assignment, sums not far short of £50,000: but assignments are different from cash: normally made over in tallies cashable by other officers or accountants of the crown with money in hand, very frequently they could not be realized at all. On 7 December 1402 Henry Percy sent into the Exchequer of Receipt eight tallies amounting to £4,115 which he had been unable to cash with the accountants to whom they were presented, and was given tallies cashable by the collectors of the customs and subsidy 'in divers ports of England'. In the euphemistic words of the issue roll, he delivered the tallies representing a loan (*mutuo liberavit*) but he had been trying to realize them since the previous 13 March.[1] It was no voluntary loan. A commentator on Henry IV's financial policy has pointed out that over £10,778 of the £50,000 mentioned above was made up of 'bad' tallies,[2] and it is difficult to see how Henry Percy could have paid his troops regularly under these conditions. It was in keeping with such delays that on 19 April 1402 he received £200 in assignments for charges incurred when he was beseiging Conway Castle for a period of four weeks at his own expense (April 1401).[3]

Delay in payment is always vexatious, but it was of such common occurrence, and long-term borrowing so general, that it seems questionable whether the grievances of the Percies were financial[4] rather than personal and political.

They may have recognized that in supporting Henry they had made a mistake. Even if both Scottish Marches, eastern and western, were in their hands, and Ralph Neville had been relegated to the command of Roxburgh Castle, they were, in reality, no better off than under Richard: probably with less opportunities for aggrandizement, since their neighbour on their Yorkshire estates was now their king. It was idle for them to

[1] P.R.O., E. 403/574, m. 6.

[2] Between 1399 and 1402: 'which may perhaps be fairly regarded as an additional source of aggravation, leading up to their (the Percies) revolt against the king they had helped to the throne', Steel, *The Receipt of the Exchequer* (1954), p. 139: cf. pp. 86–87. 'Bad' is, however, too decisive an epithet: they were tallies that could not be met immediately. Cf. below, chap. iii.

[3] *ad custos suos proprios sine adiutorio alicuius persone preterquam gencium patrie illius*: E. 403/573, m. 3. In May 1401, from Denbigh, Hotspur had written to the council a strong appeal for money. *P.P.C.* i. 151.

[4] 'Careful consideration of all the figures in the Issue and Receipt Rolls suggests that the Percies were not unfairly treated in their financial dealings with the crown': Bean, op. cit., p. 223, where a table of the Percies' revenues as wardens of the Marches, 1399–1403, is given.

plead, as they did in a manifesto sent at the beginning of July 1403, that Henry was violating the oath made to them at Doncaster in 1399, not to claim the kingdom but merely his own inheritance of Lancaster, while Richard should continue to reign under the control of a council of prelates and barons. On 2 August 1399 Henry appointed Northumberland warden of Carlisle and the west March by his commission under the seal of the duchy of Lancaster.[1] The office was accepted, granted though it was in an irregular form, and this fact, together with Northumberland's presence in London to support the new régime at the end of September 1399, and Henry Percy's acceptance of the justiciarship of Chester and the guardianship of Henry of Monmouth, suggest that the Percies had agreed to the change of government and dynasty.

The three other points in the manifesto were equally doubtful justifications for revolt. Henry, they said, had departed from his promise not to exact taxation from clergy and people, save with the advice of the three estates in parliament, and then only for great emergency: a reference to his alleged undertaking, made at Bristol or elsewhere on his journey through southern England, either to remit or at least to abate lay and clerical subsidies. A second was that after swearing to maintain the law, he had advised his sheriffs in every county to return to parliament only such knights as would favour his wishes. A third charge was that he had refused to ransom Edmund Mortimer from captivity and had kept the young earl of March from succeeding to the throne. The first of these, even if the undertaking had been given, was pedantry: as he moved southwards after his landing, Henry may well have promised not to burden the estates, but as king he could not dispense with some reinforcement of his ordinary revenue: many of the pensions and annuities awarded by Richard II had to be confirmed, and from sheer expediency he was bound to make a number of his own. Then with the emergency in Wales, French hostility, and the king's determination to clarify the position in Scotland, to say nothing of the expenses of the royal marriage, obligations began to mount. Without the parliamentary subsidy, the real (as opposed to the book-keeping) revenue for each exchequer term might fall below £40,000, a grotesquely small yield from which to finance the necessary operations. Even

---

[1] P.R.O. Exch. Warrants, E. 404/15/46, in R. L. Storey, 'The Wardens of the Marches of England towards Scotland', *Eng. Hist. Rev.* lxxii (1957), 603.

the grants of the January parliament of 1401 and of the Michaelmas parliament of 1402 could not prevent the revenue being
overburdened with large assignments. For the second charge
which interestingly anticipates Henry's tactics before the 'un-
learned' parliament, from which lawyers were excluded on the
king's instructions, there is no clear evidence. The third charge
was only too true: to Henry's realistic mind, Reginald Grey,
now admiral for service in the north, was of much greater importance for his contribution to the defence of the country than
Mortimer. These recriminations, some of which will be found
to recur in the manifestos of 1405, reflect the grievances of the
country latent since the early part of 1402. In May that year
two significant commissions had been issued: one, directed to
William Barrow, bishop of Carlisle, Earl Henry Percy, and the
sheriff of Cumberland and Westmorland, ordered the arrest
and imprisonment in the two counties of all persons resident
there who asserted that Richard II was still alive; the other,
sent to a group of seven to ten leading men in each county, was
for the arrest and imprisonment of those guilty of spreading
false rumours against the king. These rumours include 'preaching . . . that the king had not kept the promises that he made at
his advent into the realm and at his coronation and in parliaments and councils, that the laws and customs of the realm shall
be observed'.[1]

The news of the Percies' treason which Henry heard at
Leicester made him turn westwards: from Burton-on-Trent he
asked the sheriffs of the Midland counties to meet him with all
available forces (16 July), and in the meantime to act against
any suspected of supporting the rebellion. On 12 July he moved
on to Lichfield, whence he sent the council a request for immediate personal service, and a demand for loans to be raised
and forwarded to him by the treasurer, who was instructed to
stay in London for that purpose. There was only one other
thing to do. Henry Percy was moving upon Shrewsbury with
all speed to capture the prince of Wales at his headquaters,
and the king must get there first. On 20 July Henry IV entered
the town, and Hotspur, with a force estimated at 14,000, on
learning of the king's advance, withdrew with his uncle Thomas
Percy along the Whitchurch road, a couple of miles to the
north-west. Owain Glyn Dŵr was not at hand to help. The

[1] *Cal. Pat. R., 1401–1405*, p. 126.

Dunbar earl of March advised the king not to give him any chance to arrive, but to strike before the earl of Northumberland and the Welsh leader had time to reinforce the rebels. It was wise counsel: if battle was joined quickly, the Percies could expect no assistance, while help could still soon be had by the king from the south and south-west. Instead, therefore, of waiting for the insurgents' attack which had been timed for Monday, 23 July, Henry, on the 21st (Saturday), moved towards his opponents and prepared to fight near the village of Berwick about two miles to the north-west of the town: yet even when, after a formal defiance issued by the rebels, the royal army was in battle formation, its three divisions commanded by Humphrey earl of Stafford, Henry himself, and the prince of Wales, the king was still ready to support negotiations, and sent Thomas Westbury, abbot of Shrewsbury, together with the clerk of the privy seal, offering, if the rebels should disperse, to consider any statement of grievances that they might send; or, if Henry Percy preferred to communicate privately with the king, to receive a confidential envoy.

To this attempt at peace at the last moment Thomas Percy was sent with a negative reply. The story of the earl's treachery in representing to his nephew, not indisposed to believe the king's word, that Henry was in reality bellicose and uncompromising, derives from the author of the *Annales* who is bitterly hostile to Thomas Percy throughout (he is *incentor, ut dicitur, totius mali*): it may well represent a genuine difference of opinion between uncle and nephew about the value of the king's promises. Whatever may be the truth, some two or three hours were at least spent in parleying before Henry gave the word to attack. The Percies had stationed themselves on rising ground, with a thick tangle of crops in front of them, and the English right had to force its way uphill on a narrow front against a barrage of arrows from the Cheshire archers who were deadly shots. The fight lasted all day until nightfall and the carnage was considerable. Recognition of coat armour seems to have been a weak spot on both sides and there was much confused battering and belaying, in the course of which the king, the object of ferocious quest by Hotspur and Douglas, was astutely removed from his battle station by George Dunbar, to prevent his death becoming a reality instead of the noisy rumour that was already current. Henry Percy himself was surrounded and killed: the earl of Stafford and Sir Walter Blount cut down, and the earls of Douglas and Worcester taken alive. By nightfall Hotspur's death and the capture of the rebel leaders had made the issue clear, though fighting went on over a wide area until both sides were exhausted: the one which maintained its standard and a semblance of headquarters held the field. Henry IV and the prince, the latter wounded in the face, had survived, but the royal casualties appear to have been heavy. Apart from the dead, estimated at 1,600 on both sides, at least 3,000 were wounded of whom the greater part died of their injuries or were dispatched by pillagers working amongst the booty during the night. Percy's corpse was first buried by Lord Furnival at Whit-church, but soon after exhumed and exposed at Shrewsbury, and after being carved up, portions were sent to different cities, while the head, appropriately, went to York, to be fixed on Micklegate Bar. Thomas Percy was tried and beheaded on the Monday, and Sir Richard Venables, lord of Kinderton, and Richard de Vernon died similar deaths. Worcester's head was set up on London Bridge with those of Venables and Vernon until it was given burial, with the body, in St. Peter's abbey at Shrewsbury. The fate of the traitors thus received the utmost publicity.

It was necessary for the king to make an immediate assault on the head and source of the trouble, the earl of Northumberland. Orders were issued to Ralph Neville to raise the forces of North-umberland and Yorkshire, and attack and capture the earl, who was to be brought alive into the king's presence. Meanwhile Henry hurried north via Nottingham and Doncaster to Ponte-fract (4–6 Aug.). Northumberland was close to Tadcaster, preparing to reinforce his son. On hearing that the earl of Westmorland and Sir Robert Waterton were collecting troops in his rear, he retired northwards and gained admittance to Newcastle upon Tyne, but only on condition that he was accom-panied by his private retinue and that his troops were left out-side. By this time he had heard of Henry Percy's death and, with Westmorland and the king pursuing him, concluded that resist-ance was hopeless. He was making for Warkworth when he received a letter from Henry offering to take him back into favour, if he would meet the king at York. To York, therefore, Northumberland came for his formal submission. His life was to be spared, but he was kept under close guard, while the castles of Berwick, Cockermouth, Alnwick, Warkworth, Prudhoe-on-Tyne, and Langley (on the south Tyne) were to be governed by royal officers. (Orders might be issued to this effect, but, as will be seen, Alnwick and Warkworth continued to be held for the earl.) He was deprived of his office of constable, which was given to Prince John. The east March was entrusted to the prince of Wales, the west to Ralph Neville (4 Mar. 1404). The sequestration of Northumberland's estates was supervised by the steward of the household, and the duchy treasurer, John Leventhorpe, collected the rents. Elsewhere the plundering of Henry and Thomas Percy's estates began immediately, and had to be suppressed, for it was the king's intention to grant their forfeitable possessions away. George Dunbar, earl of March, did well out of the confiscations: he was granted the wardship of Gilbert de Umfraville, lord of Kyme,[1] which had been in Hotspur's hands, as well as Hotspur's London house in Bishopgate Street. His manors, castles, and lands in Cumberland were granted to Prince John.

It was now time to deal with south and west Wales. Early in July 1403 Glyn Dŵr had appeared in the upper valley of the Towy, and with general support from the Welsh made his way via Llandilo and Dryslwyn to Carmarthen, surrendered to him on 6 July, and then on to Pembrokeshire, well described by Sir John Lloyd as 'the chief obstacle to the conquest of West Wales'.[2] John Fairfield, receiver of Brecon, depicted the revolt thus: 'the whole of the Welsh nation in these parts are concerned in this rebellion'.[3] Writing to Henry he asked the king 'to ordain a final destruction of all the false nation aforesaid', and an instant plea for the king to come in person was made by 'the sheriffs, knights, esquires and commoners of your county of Hereford',[4] as well as by other royal officers such as the constable of Kidwelly. In the Carmarthen area, however, Glyn Dŵr's forces received a sharp reverse from Thomas Lord Carew: it may have been this that deterred him from marching to Shrewsbury, though it is more likely that the sheer pace of the king's movements forestalled him and that he was not at Shrewsbury because he could not get there in time. Yet the

---

[1] The Umfravilles, lords of Redesdale, were closely related to the Percies. The wife of Gilbert de Umfraville, Matilda de Lucy, had married the earl of Northumberland on Gilbert's death (1381).   [2] *Owain Glyndwr*, p. 67.
[3] *Royal and Historical Letters of Henry IV*, i. 142.   [4] Ibid. i. 148.

royal victory did not materially alter the situation, and there was the greatest alarm in the March until Henry appeared at Hereford on 11 September and marched through the valley of the Usk and later through the Vale of Towy with Carmarthen as the objective. But, as not seldom happened on Welsh expeditions, lack of the means to maintain a large army forced Henry to retire, so that in October he was back again in Hereford with Somerset left at Carmarthen to complete the work of pacification.

But Glyn Dŵr was by no means defeated. He had begun to contract an alliance with Charles VI, and French ships were already aiding the Welsh in their attacks upon the maritime castles. To avoid pitched battles and to strike unremittingly at the castles in English hands was Glyn Dŵr's policy: hill fighting or raids without a very large concentration of troops along with French assistance were his methods. In November 1403 the town and castle of Caernarvon were assailed by French ships commanded by Jean d'Espagne. From Caernarvonshire French forces advanced to attack Beaumaris. Writing from Chester on 6 January 1404 William Venables of Kinderton and Roger Bracey, constable of Chester, described the castle and town as in great peril; the keeper Maredudd ap Cynwrig had been captured. Small wonder, for on the 12th one of the keepers of Conway had written that the whole of Caernarvonshire purposed to raid Anglesey and sweep the place bare, 'leste Englishmen shulde be refreshitte therwith', and that the French were bringing up all available ordnance against the town.[1] During the first half of 1404 Harlech and Aberystwyth were lost. They were places of great value to Glyn Dŵr as arsenals and victualling depots, but more, they formed two defensive posts guarding the extremities of a solid block of territory which owed him allegiance. So unchallenged was his power now that Adam of Usk can attribute to him the summons of a parliament: it was, Adam says, a fiction of a parliament,[2] and clearly justice and finance were less the aim than a formal declaration of Owain as prince. Tradition has assigned the meeting to Machynlleth or, with more probability, to Pennal, on the Machynlleth–Aberdovey road; but it would be more accurate to reserve the assembly at Pennal till later and to place the first of such

---

[1] Ellis, *Original Letters illustrative of English History*, 2nd series, ii. 34, 35.

[2] 'celebrat, ymmo symulat seu confyngit parliamenta', *Chronicon Adae de Usk*, p. 86.

representative gatherings at Dolgelly from which place Glyn
Dŵr wrote (10 May 1404) to the king of France announcing the
dispatch of two envoys, Griffith Young and John Hanmer, his
own brother-in-law, to discuss an alliance. At Dolgelly it was
arranged for four representatives to be chosen from each commote to meet there, and it seems a likely conjecture that Glyn
Dŵr's later ecclesiastical proposals for a Welsh church independent of Canterbury and a metropolitanate at St. David's were
first made public at Pennal.

Glyn Dŵr's ambassadors arrived at the French court before
the end of June, bearing his request for an immediate supply of
weapons and, later, for an expedition to be led by the count of
La Marche. They were well received and within a month had
concluded their negotiations. The treaty (14 July 1404) made at
the house of the French chancellor, Arnaud de Corbie, bound
the French king and the *Princeps Wallie* in an alliance against
Henry of Lancaster, and stipulated that neither side should
make a separate peace, while each power should give a welcome
to the shipping and merchants of the other. There was no mention of a French expedition to north Wales, though one was
obviously expected, but the chronicler of St. Denys asserts that
Glyn Dŵr had fully informed the French about the Welsh ports
and Welsh topography. The expedition did not come immediately: a force under the command of La Marche put to sea
in August, cruised about the channel, but did not touch Wales.
The naval war was on, and the French preferred to raid the
Devon coast and assail Dartmouth, a costly operation, rather
than to sail round Land's End into the Irish Sea. They could
probably have reached the south Welsh coast without difficulty,
for, by the end of 1404, Glyn Dŵr had firmly established his
authority in Glamorgan: so much so that it seemed a desirable
retreat to the countess of Gloucester, widow of Earl Thomas
Despenser, who had been put to death for treason in the conspiracy of the earls. Lady Despenser had conceived the idea of
taking to Wales the two young sons of the earl of March, one of
them in the true line of succession to the throne, and of there
establishing contact with Glyn Dŵr and with the uncle of the
boys, Edmund Mortimer. The scheme failed, the party having
been overtaken and arrested at Cheltenham; but the episode
showed that there was a harbour for the enemies of the house of
Lancaster, if they could only reach it.

By 1405 so strong did Glyn Dŵr's position appear that it is possible to attribute to the early months of this year the famous tripartite indenture. The initiative for this singular document appears to have been the earl of Northumberland's, who entered into a relationship with Glyn Dŵr and Edmund Mortimer called a *ligia et confederatio*. On 28 February 1405[1] a compact was sworn to and sealed by their deputies 'in the name of the archbishop of Bangor'. Bishops Trevor of St. Asaph and Byford of Bangor were probably among the intermediaries, both later joining Northumberland and Bardolf. The three principals contracted, in a pact of mutual loyalty, to defend the realm of England against all men, 'saving the oath of alliance sworn by Glyn Dŵr to the king of France'. The remarkable clause is the one that fixed the boundaries of their respective dominions: 'Item, if by God's disposing it appears to the said lords in the course of time that they are the same persons of whom the prophet speaks, among whom the rule of Great Britain should be divided and partitioned, then will they labour, and each will labour, to have this brought to effect.' It was unanimously agreed that Glyn Dŵr should have the whole of Wales, with a boundary running 'along the Severn to the North Gate of the city of Worcester, thence to the ash trees on the main road from Bridgnorth to Kinver: thence by the high way, called the ancient way, to the source of the Trent, then to the source of the Mersey, and so along that river to the sea'. The earl of Northumberland was to have the northern counties running down into the midlands, to include Leicester, Northampton, Warwick, in East Anglia Norfolk; Mortimer was to have 'the whole of the rest of England, to him and his successors', and it may be noted that this remainder did not include the great Marcher properties of the family.[2] Clearly it was an arrangement between Northumberland and Glyn Dŵr.

The French expedition landed at Milford Haven between 1 and 7 August 1405. Thence an attack was made upon Haverfordwest, the town being captured, but not the castle: then Tenby was assaulted, although at the sight of the English relieving ships the attackers withdrew; shortly afterwards the town and castle of Carmarthen fell, and Glyn Dŵr himself got control of Cardigan and the Teifi valley; the next stage was a move

[1] Lloyd, op. cit., p. 93, n. 1, corrects Wylie's dating of the document.
[2] Printed by Ellis, *Original Letters*, II. i. 27–28, from Sloane MS. 1776.

eastwards through Glamorgan and south Wales to the vicinity of Worcester. Woodbury Hill, eight miles from the city, was the farthest point reached, but if Glyn Dŵr and the French had had a better organized commissariat, they might have marched on into the midlands. Henry was at Leicester on 19 August and reached Worcester on 22 August: his army was growing daily in answer to the summonses he had sent out and Hereford was indicated as the place of muster on 29 August; but by that time the rebels had found that they could go no farther: none the less such of the French reinforcements as remained with Glyn Dŵr through the winter of 1405 were of great assistance to the Welsh cause, and even Pembrokeshire was found ready to buy off the invaders by £200 in silver till May 1406. During Lent the French forces left. They had been disappointed in not being able to force a way into England. Accordingly 1406 saw the beginning of the Welsh decline. The help which Glyn Dŵr expected from English dissidents, especially from the northern counties, had been frustrated the previous year by the failure of the conspiracy led by Archbishop Scrope.

There is no conclusive proof that the tripartite convention was connected with the Scrope conspiracy, yet there is general support for Sir John Lloyd's assignment of its date to 1405, the year of greatest danger to the crown. We should probably be correct in denying to Scrope himself the manifesto which Wharton printed and attributed to him under 1399.[1] Drawn up in the form of articles of protest by a number of proctors who are unnamed, it may well be, as Wylie suggested (though he was inclined to attribute it to a single author), an exercise of a formal character by Oxford clerks of the northern nation, for the text speaks of the authors having taken oaths 'tam in Romana Curia quam in Oxonia', and the interests said to have been offended or violated by Henry are always in the first instance those of church and churchmen. The document is a good example of the sort of anti-governmental propaganda which is to be associated with the years 1403–7; its exact date is extremely difficult to establish, but it breathes the spirit of reaction against the Coventry parliament of 1404 and the fear of the clergy that the Church was not being adequately protected from the anti-clerical knights of the shire. The duke of York's suspected plot against Henry at the end of 1404; the admission of the earl

---

[1] *Anglia Sacra*, ii. 362 f.

marshal that he knew what was afoot; and the fact that even Archbishop Arundel[1] had to clear himself from suspicion will show the atmosphere of tension at court, and there is little wonder that the discontented in the north were now ready to do what they had not time to attempt in 1403.

Archbishop Scrope had not protested against the usurpation. He had assisted in displacing Richard and had helped in Henry's coronation. But two years before he had, at Shrewsbury, been claimed as an ally by Northumberland and Hotspur, and for the intervening time, certainly till April 1405 (when he was present at a great council), he was probably backing both sides. Now, however, he had made his decision. His confederates were the earl marshal, Lord Bardolf, and his own nephew Sir William Plumpton. The author of the *Annales* implicates Lord Clifford who had married Hotspur's daughter, and Clifford, at Brougham Bridge and Appleby, involved a great part of Westmorland. Nearer York, Cleveland, Northallerton, and the Percy manor of Topcliffe sent contingents, and the presence of Sir John Fauconberg, one of the family holding property in Cleveland and Holderness, who was heir to Skelton Castle, displays the range of Northumberland's influence.[2] Their manifesto or list of grievances (to be distinguished from the one just described) which was fixed to the doors of monasteries and posted 'in the ways and streets of York', was in a rude English which the author of the *Annales* himself saw and turned into a literal Latin. There were three main articles giving the points needing reform: the bad government and impossible burdens which all estates of the clergy suffered; the rigours suffered by, and the indignities done to, the estates, and the subjection and annihilation that threatens the secular lords contrary to their rights of birth and their position in the country; and the excessive intervention of the government (*excessivis gubernationibus*), the unbearable taxes and subsidies which burden the gentle class, the merchants and the commons, 'and the destruction of those who ought to be true supporters to all the estates spiritual and temporal'.[3] The

---

[1] 'non ignorans quam amaro animo eum perstringebant familiares regii', *Annales Henrici Quarti*, p. 399.

[2] There were other north Yorkshire knights and religious prelates too: Sir Ralph Hastings of Slingsby and Allerston; Sir John FitzRandolph of Spennithorne, near Middleham; Sir John Colvil of Daletown in Ryedale and Arncliffe near Stokesley; Robert Takell, prior of Warter near Pocklington; and Geoffrey Wyveswold, prior of the Gilbertines at Old Malton.   [3] *Annales Henrici Quarti*, pp. 403–5.

manifesto asked for the punishment of those who recklessly spent the money received from the *generosi*, the merchants, and the commons. Such sums must be restored for the safety of the kingdom and 'the amendment of the estate of the faithful commons'. If the articles complained of could be remedied, Englishmen might then labour to resist foreign foes and to foster[1] their merchants 'who ought to be one of the substantial riches of our land'. This being done, 'we' have the full promise of satisfaction and contentment from those now in rebellion in Wales, peaceful now as they were in Edward III's and Richard II's time. The document with its alarming anticipation of a lean time for the nobility, its appeal to the parliamentary 'estates' (*status*), and its obvious attempt to draw in the York merchants, was aimed, as will be seen, at the groups most susceptible to propaganda. It was the anxious endeavour of the *generosus* to maintain his estate intact against all depredation, not least against the attempt of the crown to tax income from land; for, as will be seen, at the Coventry parliament, a 20*s*. tax on every £20 of income from land over 500 marks value per annum was ordered.[2] A 5% land-tax had been sanctioned in the previous parliament, but the record of the grant and collection had been destroyed to avoid creating a precedent. Furthermore, if the *generosus* held any annuity, sinecure, or grant of profit, he had been asked to surrender the current year's income to the king, and proclamation had been made that all who held patents of grant since 40 Edward III should bring them to be scrutinized by the council. The York merchant community had less cause for grumbling, but it was policy to represent the *mercenarii* (as the annalist has it: one might, in the York context, mistranslate 'the mercers') as adversely affected by the present régime.

If the manifesto was shrewdly aimed, its authors lacked the drive of true revolutionaries. The earl of Westmorland had been moving south with all speed to divide the Cleveland rebels from the forces marching down the York Road from Clifton and Masham. The Cleveland forces were attacked at Topcliffe, where they were waiting for the earl of Northumberland, but even so Westmorland was outnumbered when he took up his

---

[1] This word, or one like it, is omitted in the manuscript.

[2] According to the *Eulogium* (iii (Rolls ser.), 406) the manifesto included a demand 'quod iurisperiti ad parliamentam veniant', a protest against the 'Illiterate Parliament', at Coventry, where, as Wylie remarks, 'the knife of retrenchment had been set in deep and firm'.

position at Shipton Moor, about six miles north-west of York. The archbishop's forces faced him for three days, at the end of which (29 May) the earl got possession of the rebel leaders by a stratagem, under cover of a promise of unfettered discussion of their articles by the leaders of the two sides. Meanwhile the citizens of York and the Dalesmen had melted away, and the archbishop and his colleagues were left as prisoners to face the wrath of the king when he arrived to find them at Pontefract. On 4 June a judicial commission, including the Chief Justice of the King's Bench, Sir William Gascoigne, was appointed to try the captives, and on 6 June the king moved to Bishopthorpe, whence he could make an example of the leaders of the revolt that might be seen by the disloyal citizens. Despite the warning of Archbishop Arundel who, foreseeing a judicial disaster, had arrived early on the 5th, Henry sent for the Chief Justice and directed him to pass sentence of death on the archbishop and his associates. At the crucial moment Gascoigne, who knew his precedents[1] as well as the canon law, drew a distinction between the laymen and the archbishop, who he alleged could not be legally sentenced by the secular court. He had the courage to maintain his position, and, on failing to secure its acceptance, to resign from the tribunal. A new president of the court was appointed, and Scrope, the earl marshal, and Sir William Plumpton were sentenced to death and executed at Clementhorpe just outside the city. Bootham Bar received the marshal's head, Sir William Plumpton's was fixed on Micklegate, but the archbishop's head and body were carried to the Minster by the vicars-choral and buried there.

To permit the traitor to lie forthwith in his own cathedral was, to say the least, unwise, for the archbishop had many supporters among the clergy. Aiding his rebellion were five vicars-choral and one chaplain of the Minster, as well as several York parish priests and chaplains. At Shipton Moor there were members of the four mendicant orders: some may have come from Beverley or Malton, but the York convents evidently contributed, though the exact provenence of the Franciscans whom the royalists stripped of their clothes and left to run away is uncertain. The royal pardon of the city granted on 24 August 1405 mentions more than a score of persons described

---

[1] Alexander Neville, archbishop of York (1388), and Archbishop Arundel himself (1397) found guilty of high treason. Neither received a capital sentence.

as 'of York' and many were townsmen—mercers, fishmongers, tailors, and the like—who must have come from the city. Naturally the 'holy bishop, the blessed confessor', soon began to work miracles from his tomb in St. Stephen's chapel, and, as with Simon de Montfort after Evesham, the government issued agitated orders against any veneration of the rebel. In the York Memorandum Book is entered a petition of four of the York sergeants to Henry IV, complaining that they had been dismissed from their posts for carrying out a command of the king's son, John of Bedford, to track down any people who offered at the tomb of the archbishop and seeking restoration of their offices. The king immediately demanded the reinstatement of the sergeants,

And upon that [the record continues], the said reverent letter [of the king] being read and heard, the said mayor, aldermen and sheriffs and all the commonalty made resistance to the said evil suggestion, to the great cost of the commonalty, as is well known to all people. And the following year when the sergeants were elected, they were made to swear, under heavy money penalties, that if at any time they were removed from office, they would make no suit for restoration to anyone, save to the mayor and council.[1]

In this act of defiance the influence of the powerful William Frost, six times mayor of York, can unquestionably be traced. Officers of the Alma Curia, the Consistory of York, also come into the picture. In 1459 William Langton, clerk to master Robert Esingwold, proctor of the court, was left by his godson, the York ecclesiastical lawyer, John Dawtry, a book that had belonged to Dawtry's father, a lawyer like his son, 'which book the blessed Richard Scrope had and bore it in his breast at the time of his beheading', the testator directing that it should be chained in the Scrope chapel after Langton's death. Dawtry was brother-in-law of Guy Fairfax of Steeton, made a justice of King's Bench in 1478, and to Guy Dawtry left 'a great register which once belonged to William Gascoigne, justice of England'.[2] Gascoigne, famous in later days for his critical attitude towards the procedure dictated for Scrope's trial, recalled a tradition of legal independence and there were men in York to keep it alive.

There was little doubt where the incentive for northern rebellion was to be found. This time Northumberland made no

---

[1] Ed. M. Sellers (Surtees Soc. 120), i. 236–8.
[2] *Testamenta Eboracensia*, ii. 231, 233.

submission when called upon to do so. He freed Robert Waterton, whom he had imprisoned at Warkworth, Alnwick, and
Berwick, on condition that his brother John would act as a
hostage, then moved northwards to Berwick where he secured
admission. He was there when Henry entered York. This time
there had to be real confiscation, and the king advanced into
the country of the Percy castles. Warkworth fell on 1 July: and in
it, according to Hardyng, Henry found documentary evidence
of the sympathies of the English barons in the earlier movement of 1403. On 20 July Langley Castle on the south Tyne was
taken over by Robert Umfraville, Prudhoe had already been
surrendered like Cockermouth, and only Alnwick held out.
Percy himself had no desire to risk capture in Berwick. Having
previously sent on his grandson, Hotspur's child, he crossed the
border into Scotland, Lady Bardolf with him. The fall, before
12 July, of Berwick and, by 14th, of Alnwick completed the
seizure of the Percy strongholds and confiscation could also
begin of Bardolf's estates in Norfolk and of the earl marshal's
properties. A number went to the earl of March; the Essex
lands at Bradwell at the mouth of the Blackwater went to Prince
John, who also received custody of the castles of Langley, Prudhoe, and Alnwick, and of all the Northumberland property in
York, Carlisle, and Newcastle, besides Calais. The marshal's
castle of Framlingham in Suffolk was given to the prince of
Wales, and, to make up the arrears in her dower of 10,000
marks a year, Queen Joan was to receive Wressell Castle, the
Percy manors of Healaugh (Yorkshire) and Petworth (Sussex),
with other properties of the earl of Northumberland. The
earl of Westmorland had originally been granted Wressell,
Healaugh, and Petworth, but as has been pointed out,[1] the
queen's grant was later (10 Aug.), but if he did not get the
profitable Sussex manor, he did at least secure Cockermouth
Castle as well as the Isle of Man. The queen's grant was very
considerable, including all the Bardolf and Mowbray possessions
which had not been granted away to the king's sons and his half
brothers, Henry and Thomas Beaufort, to the countess of Hereford (his mother-in-law), and to his niece Constance. It was
shortly afterwards cancelled as illegal, and provision was made
for her from other sources. Another variation upon Westmorland's original grant was that the Isle of Man was granted

[1] By Wylie, op. cit. ii. 281, n. 11.

(4 Oct. 1405) for life to Sir John Stanley of Knowsley (the estate acquired through his wife Isabel Lathom) on its forfeiture by the earl of Northumberland. The annual income was about £400 per annum, and helped to establish the fortunes of the remarkable man who had had long experience of Ireland, partly as deputy of Robert de Vere, during Richard II's reign, and later as king's lieutenant, and was to succeed Sir Hugh Waterton as constable of Windsor Castle.

After the collapse of the Scrope rebellion the young Henry Percy and James the heir of Scotland were sent to the household of Bishop Wardlaw of St. Andrews. The old king of the Scots did not, however, think that James was safe with the ambitious Albany about and resolved after his death to send him to the court of France, where David II had formerly gone. A merchant ship of Danzig picked him up at the Bass Rock, but as it made southward it was captured off Edinburgh Head by Norfolk pirates, and James was taken to Henry IV at Westminster. This was the beginning of an eighteen-year captivity, which only ended in March 1424. The news killed the Scottish king who realized that it meant the governorship of Albany: this, when a council-general at Perth had met to settle the government, became a fact, for while James, whose title was clear under an act of 1373, became king, Albany was made 'Governor' of the kingdom, and Albany's foreign policy, if he had one, was to secure the release of his son, captive in England, and to leave James in captivity. As it has been acutely observed: 'his success is to be measured by the fact that when he died in September 1420, Murdach became governor in his place, and James was still the prisoner of the English king'.[1]

Early in 1406 Northumberland and Bardolf found Scotland unsafe: they got news of a plot to seize and exchange them for certain Scottish prisoners captured at Homildon Hill. Accordingly they left the country and settled in Wales, where their aid to Glyn Dŵr was mentioned in parliament when the declaration of treason was made against Northumberland on 30 November 1406.[2] Early in June that year they had been defeated by Edward Charlton, Lord Powys, and finding that they were making little progress in Wales, betook themselves to France to seek the assistance of Louis of Orléans. This was not forthcoming

[1] E. W. B. Balfour-Melville, *James I, King of Scots* (1936), p. 35.
[2] *Rot. Parl.* iii. 606–7.

and they returned in 1407 to Scotland to raise rebellion in the course of the winter 1407–8. On 19 February 1408 at Bramham Moor near Tadcaster the small force of Northumberland and Bardolf was defeated by the sheriff of Yorkshire. Northumberland was killed in the encounter and Bardolf died of his wounds. One of the prisoners taken was Bishop Byford of Bangor. Northumberland's death meant the end of serious rebellion. Ralph Neville was fairly established in the north, and Percy tenants and supporters were to be among the strongest adherents of Henry IV.

The failure of Northumberland was a blow to the cause of Glyn Dŵr. In the year that followed Bramham Moor the two castles of Aberystwyth and Harlech, the basis of his authority in central Wales, were lost to him. In the summer of 1408 Prince Henry, renewed in his commission as king's lieutenant in central Wales, returned to the attack on Aberystwyth which he had already begun, and it appears that the castle fell before the end of September 1408. Harlech took longer to reduce. Gilbert Talbot of Goodrich and his brother John Talbot, Lord Furnival, maintained a close siege and by March 1409 the castle had surrendered. The fall of Harlech involved the capture of Glyn Dŵr's family, including three daughters of Edmund Mortimer, himself dying in the siege, as well as the family possessions. Owain with his son Maredudd vanished into the moors and forests. What happened to him before 1410 is not known; but attention has been drawn to letters sent on 23 November 1409 to the earl of Arundel, Richard Lestrange, Edward Charlton of Powys, and Reginald Grey directing them to repudiate the action of their officers who were apparently making truces with Owain and his followers to the detriment of the king's faithful lieges.[1] It appears as if Owain had gone back to the region where his family seats of Sycharth and Carrog were located. The last attempt he made was in 1410, when he lost three notable captains, especially Rhys ap Gruffydd of Cardigan, known as Rhys the Black, while his cousin Rhys ap Tudor, who had been active at Conway in 1401, was put to death at Chester. After this he is heard of spasmodically till 1413, when he disappeared from view, then, as earlier in his life, to be the subject of legend. At the beginning of his reign Henry V was prepared to treat with him and restore him, if he so wished, and another attempt

---

[1] *Foedera*, iv. i. 163.

was made to win him over in 1416. It was unavailing. His son
Maredudd was pardoned on 30 April 1417, by which time Owain
was dead.

The Welsh annals of Owain Glyn Dŵr leave him at 1415.
Owain, they say, went into hiding on St. Matthew's Day in
harvest (21 Sept.): thereafter his hiding-place was unknown.
'Very many say that he died: the seers maintain he did not!'
But to those who know the course of Dee from Corwen to
Llangollen, the name Glyndyfrdwy, where the splendid river
sweeps into its gorge under the Berwyn Hills, may recall the
'cywydd' or ode (1400) of Gruffydd Llwyd to Owain in his prime:

> Eryr digrif afrifed
> Owain, helm gain, hael am gêd,
> Gore wir fab (gair or orfod),
> Gruffudd Vychan glân ei glôd;
> Mur Glyn meistir rhaddlyn rhwydd
> Dyfrdwy fawr, dwfr diferydd.[1]

---

[1] 'Thou delightful eagle Owain, with thy bright shining helmet, generous in
bestowing riches, thou art the brave and ever conquering son of Gruffydd Vychan
of noble renown; thou art the bulwark, the graceful and liberal possessor of the
vale of Dyfrdwy, a great and rapid stream.' Translation in *Memoirs of Owen
Glendower*, Supplement to *A History of the Island of Anglesey* (London, Dodsley,
1775), p. 84. The ode is printed in Lewis, Roberts, and Williams, edd., *Iolo
Goch ac Eraill* (1925), pp. 130–3.

III

HENRY IV: POVERTY AND CONSOLIDATION

FROM the outset numerous indications made Henry realize how vulnerable his position was. He had to secure himself from internal revolt and the pressure of invasion, as well as to establish his position with the powers of Europe. The latter effort is written very large in the diplomatic activity of the period. It involved both marriages and conventions and the passage of a constant stream of envoys to the Continent.

The diplomatic missions began in 1401, with the proposals for the return of Isabel to France. Charles VI was raising the claim for repayment of 200,000 francs dower and English representatives who on 1 April 1401 met the French at Leulinghen, mid-way between Boulogne and Calais, put forward demands for the outstanding ransom for King John and for redress for infringement of Henry's rights in the duchy of Guienne. The discussions ended in the promise being made by the English that Isabel should be sent home without delay and that further discussion should settle Charles's claim and the English objection to the action of the French king in Guienne. Isabel was taken over by Thomas Percy, earl of Worcester, on 28 July and delivered to the French on 31 July. Her escort from England numbered 500 persons and the total estimated expense came to £8,242. 0s. 10d.: more serious than the expense was the fact that at a time of great difficulty at home, Henry had given up a valuable bargaining counter: French hostility now grew and threats of invasion multiplied as soon as Isabel had been returned, and Henry's hope of a marriage alliance with the Valois, which Bishop Walter Skirlaw, Thomas Percy, and others had been commissioned, late in 1399, to discuss,[1] came to nothing. But Germany looked more promising. Rupert III of Bavaria had recently been elected king of the Romans in place of Wenzel of Bohemia, brother-in-law of the deposed Richard, and propaganda done on his behalf might help Henry with a greater project which he had begun to set in motion, the

[1] *Foedera*, III. iv. 178.

marriage of Rupert's eldest son, Lewis count palatine of the Rhine and duke of Bavaria, to his elder daughter Blanche. From 12 May to 9 August 1401 an embassy consisting of Sir Walter Sturmy, master John Kington, canon of Lincoln, and Robert Waterton, who had been with Henry in Prussia, was sent to obtain homage of the duke of Guelders (who had already recognized the duke of Lancaster) and secure his recognition of Rupert III as emperor. Sturmy, a north Hampshire landowner, who had sat as knight of the shire for Hampshire (Apr. 1384–Nov. 1390), Devon (Nov. 1391), and Wiltshire (Jan. 1390, Jan. 1393, Oct. 1399, and Jan. 1401), and had married the widow of Sir John Beaumont of Sherwell in Devon, been closely connected with the court and had already been employed abroad in negotiations with the rival Popes Boniface IX and Benedict XIII.[1] This successfully over, Sturmy and Kington were sent again, after their return from Guelders, to Germany to arrange the marriage alliance and once more, on 16 February, sailed from London bearing the indenture under which Henry undertook to pay a dowry of 40,000 nobles, 16,000 of which were to be paid over at the wedding: the remainder to be forthcoming in instalments over the next two years. Further, Henry had had resort to the feudal aid *pur fille marier* and to loans, and the princess with her party would have crossed the sea before, but for the slowness with which the money came in: it was not fully paid when Henry IV died, and it has been shown that thirty-one years after the death of the Princess Blanche, 5,000 nobles were still outstanding. She was escorted to Germany on 27 April 1401 by three envoys, Bishop Clifford of Worcester (soon to be keeper of the privy seal and bishop of London), John Beaufort, earl of Somerset, and Lord FitzWalter, who, with Sturmy (the steward of her household) and Kington, were commissioned to treat for alliances, both with the duke of Guelders and with the emperor. It was typical of missions abroad that Sturmy had to write for his expenses, having been granted money for fifty days only, which he had exceeded by nearly the same amount. The entente did not last long, for Blanche, to the general sorrow, died in May 1406.

A second marriage project was for union with the ruler of

[1] See J. S. Roskell, 'Sir William Sturmy, Speaker in the Parliament at Coventry, 1404', *Transactions of the Devonshire Association for the Advancement of Science, Literature and Art*, lxxxix (1957), 78–92.

Denmark and Norway, through the energy of Queen Margaret, now combined with Sweden, under the federal Union of Kalmar (1397). It was an elective monarchy and the first king was Eric duke of Pomerania, then fifteen, a grandson of Queen Margaret's elder sister. The suggestion was for Eric to marry Philippa, Henry's second daughter, while Henry prince of Wales was to marry Katherine, Eric's sister. In 1402 formal undertakings were made both by the princess and by Henry, but the latter project was dropped and Philippa's marriage did not materialize until 1406. Distance, the problems of finance, and the preoccupation of the council with the Welsh revolt and with internal troubles may have contributed to the delay: but the question of communications and of safe transit within the Baltic area was of no small importance, and it happened to be the time when a breach had occurred between England and the Prussian and Baltic towns of the Hanseatic league. The purpose of the alliance was not solely a good match with a young ruler of promise; it also aimed at the expansion of trade with countries of northern Europe, and any such attempt on the part of English merchants was bound to bring them into conflict with the Hansa. This was the great empire of trading ports centred originally upon the cities of Lübeck and Hamburg which controlled the points at which goods brought by sea were unloaded for passage across the Jutland peninsula, natural centres also of traffic going northward to the ports of Scandinavia and south to the grain-bearing districts of eastern Saxony, Brandenburg, and Mecklenburg. To the east of these were the towns of Prussia grouped about the important city of Danzig, marking a stage towards Livonia and Russia. The principle of Hanseatic growth had been the regulation of internal competition and the defeat of all competition from without: it has been well said that the four great German factories, the Steelyard in London, the Hanseatic community in Bruges, the court of St. Peter in Novgorod, and the German bridge in Bergen were outlying termini of a commercial system spreading, in centipede fashion, all along the great trading route and all over northern Europe. In Scandinavia the Hanseatic power in the course of the late thirteenth and early fourteenth century had acquired a hold over the mineral wealth of Sweden, the fisheries of Skania, the fish and fur trade of Norway. This had not been effected without war, undertaken against Denmark by the league in 1367, and the Hansa made it its object 'to organise military and political action against possible economic change and commercial competition'.[1]

Margaret's successor Eric had reacted against this control: his attitude was encouraged by new entrants to the northern trade, English and Dutch. The Prussian towns were ready at first to avail themselves of the new carriers, and the policy of Cologne or Prussia itself was becoming progressively more separatist. This was the time when English penetration into the Baltic reached its height, with the desire of English merchants, themselves in a number of cases the manufacturers, to sell in the markets of Scandinavia and eastern Europe, as they were doing alike in Flanders and in Aquitaine (particularly Toulouse) and Spain. With Prussia the trade was increasingly important, for Prussia was the chief distributor of English cloth in Poland and western Russia. The attempt of the English traders to establish themselves in Danzig occurred at a time when, with the new separatism within the league, municipal privilege and monopoly were being desperately defended, but at the same time in England the concessions and special position accorded to the London Steelyard were under attack.[2] Although Henry IV on his accession confirmed the Hanseatic privileges, in 1402 the Prussian towns, which had in 1396 decided to restrict English rights of residence, put into force the rules against English settling in the country 'with wife and childer' and trading with foreigners or in the interior of Prussia. The dispute would have remained confined to Prussia, had it not been for blatant acts of English piracy against the Hansa as a whole. In March 1405 the Diet at Lübeck prohibited the trade in English cloth and the export of Baltic goods to England. This followed the action of Danzig on 31 May 1404 in prohibiting the annual voyage from the Baltic to this country.

The action of the Danzigers alone would not have stirred the parliament of Coventry (1404) to action: but a prohibition of English cloth imports generally could not be neglected, and at the end of the parliamentary session that experienced traveller in Germany, now the Speaker, Sir William Sturmy, together with Dr. Kington and William Brampton, alderman and

---

[1] M. Postan, 'Anglo-Hanseatic Economic Relations', *English Trade in the Fifteenth Century*, ed. Power and Postan (1933), pp. 93–94.
[2] Cf. below, Chap. VIII.

parliamentary burgess for London, were ordered to go upon a diplomatic mission to Conrad of Jungingen, master of the Teutonic Order, and the mission left England on 31 May. Its members were received at Marienburg on 8 August 1405, when the embargo on trade was lifted and the period of a year fixed for the settlement of claim and counter claim. Brampton's ship foundered on the way back, but his two colleagues Sturmy and Kington made a progress through the Hanseatic ports and addressed a united gathering of the Hanseatics at Dordrecht on 15 December, when they arranged a truce for nineteen months. They were back in London on 18 February 1406. A comparatively trifling episode occurred to show how easy it was to break the truce. The master mariner of Dordrecht whom they had engaged to take them across was arrested, brought before the mayor and sheriff of London in the Guildhall and detained. In a petition for his release the two envoys explained that this not only broke the truce, but infringed their own letters of protection which applied to their servants as well as to themselves.

To assume, as Wylie did, that Henry's marriage (Feb. 1403) to the duchess regent of Brittany, Joan, widow of John IV, was a provocative act which had to be carried out in conditions of semi-secrecy[1] is a criticism of the king that neglects contemporary economic facts and past relationships between the two countries. Duke John IV's friendship for England, which has led him to be called by the historian Borderie *le valet du roi Anglais* (Edward III had installed him as duke in 1362), provoked French antagonism at different times during the later fourteenth century, but his reign saw the beginnings of a peaceful reorganization of the duchy and a great advance in its economic life. The restoration of its fortunes coincided with the beginning of the north European quest for fresh supplies of salt. The salines of Brittany, particularly of Bourgneuf Bay, the English monopoly of which Edward III had granted to Henry of Lancaster, were already famous, and the dukes showed particular concern for the industry: John V (1399–1442) granted numerous leases on favourable terms to tenants prepared to rent desolate lands and build salines thereon.[2] The dukes were earls of Richmond

---

[1] 'Threatened to let loose a desperate struggle, and open another century of bloodshed and civil war', *History of England under Henry IV*, i. 259.

[2] A. R. Bridbury, *England and the Salt Trade in the Later Middle Ages* (1955), pp. 67–69.

(though Henry IV in October 1399 granted the castle and honour to Ralph Neville, earl of Westmorland),[1] the connexion going back to the twelfth century, to Alan III of Richmond, lord of the honour 1137–46, who married Bertha, daughter and heiress of Conan III of Brittany, though his son Conan had been the first to style himself earl of Richmond.[2] To marry into Brittany was to marry into a duchy which had already showed at different times a provoking independence in French eyes, but which to Henry might constitute a valuable economic asset, and, perhaps of even more immediate value, might now prove itself an exception in the hostile coastline on the French side of the Channel. For the moment things did not work out that way. Joan's arrival in England coincided with the attacks of the Bretons on the wine convoys coming from Bordeaux to the ports of Bristol, Dartmouth, Plymouth, and Southampton. The running sea-warfare going on between English pirateers and Breton shipmasters led to various incidents and provoked an English concentration, mainly of London vessels commanded by William de Wilford, against Brittany. The capture of a convoy of thirty ships from Belle Isle and the landing of a large force by Wilford in Breton country to burn and ravage it, coupled with the privateering activities of John Hawley of Dartmouth, enraged the Breton nobility who sent a force under Guillaume du Chastel and the Sire de la Jaille to land near Dartmouth; and though it was defeated, it (like similar descents by the Flemish) created considerable alarm.

The plan of Channel defence through the establishment of a linked and friendly Brittany proved a disappointment; and Henry had to make every effort farther north to stop the depredations of Flemish corsairs, and preserve the integrity of Calais and its March. The embassy of Sir Hugh Lutterell, Sir John Croft, Dr. Nicholas Risshton, and John Urban which took up its quarters at Calais tried to bring the Four Members of Flanders (Bruges, Ghent, Ypres, and the 'French territory') to an engagement to observe the truce with France which it was commissioned to renew and if possible convert to a more lasting peace, and made every effort to bring about a settlement: but a little war was going on round Calais, conducted by Walerand

[1] *Cal. Pat. R., 1399–1401*, p. 241.
[2] R. Gale, *Reg. Honoris de Richmond*, App. 101 : *Vict. County Hist.* Yorks., N. Riding, i. 3.

count of St. Pol, who having married Richard II's sister had been prevented by the revolution of 1399 from securing the English domains she brought him; and the support of Louis duke of Orléans for these hostilities against the English made negotiations difficult and enormously protracted. The embassy was costing a great deal and the government found it extremely difficult to pay its members. The French council eventually agreed to a prolongation of the truce (27 June 1403),[1] but the Four Members of Flanders proved a greater obstacle, and Croft and Risshton had to ask Henry for further instructions and implore him for naval protection and for the proper defence of the king's French subjects in Gravelines and the castles in Picardy. This was essential if a separate treaty applying to Flanders was to be made. The overlord of the Flemings was the duke of Burgundy, Philip the Bold. Upon his death early in 1404, his duchess Margaret did what she could to advance the settlement, but while Flemings, Bretons, and French were conducting hostile raids on the English coast, making the Channel difficult for English merchandise, and while English reprisals (as up the Zwin in May 1405)[2] were in progress, little could be done, and it was not until 15 June 1407 that a commercial agreement could be made, lasting in the first instance for a single year, but successively renewed, and reinforced in July 1416 by a treaty of 'abstinence from war'. This agreement was of the highest importance for England if only for the safeguarding of the route to Calais against Flemish depredations.[3]

When the duke of Lancaster seized the crown he can have had little notion of the financial burden which was to weigh upon him for the rest of his life. As duke he was excellently served by his receiver-general and the local fiscal agents. His earlier expeditions, when he was earl of Derby, were more than adequately subsidized by his father: wherever he went he could entertain as well as fight, and there was enough over for

---

[1] *Foedera*, iv. i. 46. The work of the embassy at Calais and Leulinghen is admirably illustrated in Gilliodts van Severen, *Le Cotton MS. Galba B. 1: Documents pour servir à l'histoire des relations entre l'Angleterre et la Flandre, de 1341–1473*, who prints Bruges documents from 2 Sept. 1402 to 2 Sept. 1403, and Henry IV's instructions to his ambassadors, p. 191 (12 Nov. 1404) and no. lxxxvi (p. 193) which shows that Henry suspected the French of not repairing the *attemptata* or acting in the spirit of the truce.   [2] Gilliodts van Severen, op. cit., no. xxvi.
[3] Paul Bonenfant, *Du meurtre de Montereau au traité de Troyes* (1955), pp. 11–12.

almsgiving. From the larger organization of the duchy his household drew as much as it needed: the revenues were more than sufficient. Through his wife he also had a life interest in half the possessions of his father-in-law, Humphrey de Bohun, earl of Essex, Hereford, and Northampton, which were to pass to his son when he died.

This affluence was hardly a preparation for his new responsibilities. The duchy, the largest of all private franchises, was not the kingdom and could never have been confronted with the extraordinary demands made upon the crown. Two instances may be taken. In the Hilary parliament of 1404 the chancellor, in enumerating the emergencies to be met, included Calais, the Isle of Wight, Guienne, Ireland and Scotland, the expenses of the Percy rebellion, and the Welsh revolt. In the October parliament of the same year, when a grant of two fifteenths and two tenths was made (12 Nov.), the wording ran: 'considering the East March and the West March of Scotland, the rebellion in Wales, the alliance of the Welsh, Scotland, France and Brittany, the safe-guarding of the sea, the March of Calais, Ireland, the recovery of Guienne, and the defence of the country'. In the worst years (1401–7) there were seldom less than four or five extraordinary demands upon the revenue, mostly concurrent.

To meet these demands it was necessary to borrow: current revenue was insufficient. From the early fourteenth century loans had been, in the words of a financial historian, 'an indispensable and normal part of the financial system of the Crown', in peace as much as in war.[1] This involved giving creditors adequate security, often from the royal treasure and *jocalia*, and repaying them from funds not already too heavily mortgaged. Only a portion of the royal revenue was at any time physically in the Treasury of Receipt: much of it was in the hands of collectors, keepers, and other officials, who, like local banks, could be drawn upon, if authorization was given, to meet the demands of the king's creditors. Of these the customs, the largest single source of royal income (varying £35,000–48,000 a year), were the most utilized, and next in order came the collectors of the subsidy, lay or clerical, if and when granted. It frequently happened that these proved to be already assigned to other creditors of the king before the money came to hand, and the disappointed creditors had to get their tallies reassigned

[1] E. B. Fryde, 'Loans to the English Crown', *Eng. Hist. Rev.* lxx (1955), 198.

and presented to collectors or officials in charge of some other more likely source of revenue. In most cases there would be considerable delay, even though the creditor had done his best to secure preferential treatment: he might get only part of the sum he wanted, along with a promise to pay the balance later, or he might be asked to defer his demand until more ready cash was available; sometimes he only got repaid at a discount. Often creditors would go so far as to name the source from which they thought that repayment was likely to be had, and in certain instances the party who was being asked to lend would not do so unless the king was prepared to meet other debts which he had incurred. It can be imagined how vexatious to the crown heavy demands for repayment could be when they coincided with the need to raise and train in the field even a moderate-sized force. Merely the payment of a long list of annuities might be a difficulty when all available cash was required for an expedition; and in any case the household departments were persistently drawing upon the more promising sources of royal revenue.

The concern of every medieval treasurer was not only with the existing sources and collection of revenue, but with the problem of how to create funds devoted to specific purposes and, most of all, how to maintain them, when new emergencies were constantly suggesting that they should be raided. Accumulate a fund, and almost immediately an imminent mutiny in the Calais garrison or urgent demands for increased expenditure on Welsh castles or a request from the king's lieutenant in Gascony might threaten its integrity. A letter from the treasurer, Lawrence Allerthorpe, at the end of 1401 may illustrate the position in which Henry IV found himself that year: he hopes that the king will remember the great programme of expenditure which he has been commanded with all speed to undertake, both for Ireland and for Guienne. He has done his best to carry it out according to his discretion and ability,

Considering the divers payments which I have made of late, 1,000 marks for the expenses of your household, 1000 marks for the wages of the Queen's servants, £300 paid to the Prince [of Wales] and divers other payments which I have had to make by force of your letters and mandates continually sent to me by various persons, i.e. to my lord your son £1,000, my lord your cousin £2,038. 6. 8d., my said lords being still for the greater part in arrears of what they should have had for the first half-year. Wherefore, revered and gracious lord, because the revenues of your kingdom are burdened so outrageously[1] that there can be no relief, and also because the major part of the fifteenth and tenth was assigned before I took over office, as I have often told you before this, will your gracious highness abstain now from charging me beyond my power to pay or else hold me excused for not accomplishing your said letters and command-ment? For truly, revered lord, there is not in your Treasury at the moment enough to pay the messengers who are to bear the letters which you have ordained to be sent to the lords, knights and esquires to be of your council, so that the said sum of £3933. 6. 8d. being in arrears to my said lords, as written above, cannot be paid to them on the day assigned unless loans (chevance) are resorted to by the aid of your gracious power and of my lords of your council.[2]

The *chevance* probably did not take place until the following May. In February 1402 two citizens of London, William Parker and Thomas Oyster, lent £700 between them, and on 28 February the bishop of Bath and Wells lent 1,000 marks; but the majority of the loans were raised on or about 11 May 1402, when sixty-one loans brought in £14,020: the chief lenders being the London draper, John Hende (£2,000), the bishop of Bath and Wells more than £1,000, Richard Whittington £1,000 and the City of London £1,353. 6s. 8d.[3] Mr. Steel has shown, *inter alia*, that the peak years of borrowing were between 1400 and 1402, and 1407–8, and that the greater part of the sums received from London came from a group of mercers, one of whom, Whitting-ton, had already begun to be active before 1400 and contributed two-thirds of the whole effort.[4]

After the costly Scots expedition (July–Sept. 1400) the year 1401 was in many respects a bad one for the treasurer. In December 1400 the Emperor Manuel, who had undertaken a journey to western Europe to collect money for the defence of Constantinople, now hard pressed by the Turks, after a visit to

[1] The word echoes that used by the commons in the first parliament of Henry IV. Cf. above, p. 23.

[2] *Anglo-Norman Letters*, ed. M. D. Legge, no. 331. Assigned to 1410, obviously a slip. Allerthorpe was treasurer 31 May 1401–27 Feb. 1402.

[3] A. B. Steel, *The Receipt of the Exchequer, 1377–1485* (1954), pp. 86–87: 'This desperate activity should all be connected with the progress of the dangerous Welsh rising, which had started, in the previous year, the rumour that Richard II was still alive in Scotland which reached London in May; and the imminent threat, shortly to be realised, of a full-scale Scottish invasion.'

[4] Ibid., pp. 142–3.

Calais which cost the Exchequer £133,[1] arrived in England attended by the prior of the Hospitallers, spent two months at Eltham, and in February 1401 was granted 3,000 marks out of the Exchequer. He took away with him £2,000, rather more than the grant, part of it money payable from a previous collection, part the liberality of the king. The summer brought a letter (20 Aug.) from the archbishop of Dublin, writing to complain of the straits to which the government of Thomas of Lancaster, Henry's second son, had been reduced through inability to pay wages. The lieutenant was so destitute of money that 'he had not a penny in the world', and in February 1402 Thomas followed it up by drawing his father's attention to the threat of his captains to leave him, if wages were not paid.[2] At Chester the prince of Wales professed himself kept equally short. This was a serious matter, since the payment of the garrisons in the castles of north Wales came through the prince's treasurer at Chester and any weakening in the garrisons at this time might have sinister results. From a subsequent period when the position had somewhat improved (1405-7) we know that the constables of Caernarvon paid, for three years, forty-seven days, £561. 1s. 2½d. in wages to their captains and archers, and got back £478. 18s. 3½d. from Chester, leaving £82. 12s. 11d. still to be found.[3] This was consequent upon a reform in payments, so the position at the earlier date is likely to have been critical.

Medieval financial practice regarded contingencies like rebellions as in a class beyond the normal categories of supply. The sources of revenue upon which the crown could in the normal course draw were roughly eight: the ulnage (fees paid for the inspection or measurement of cloth); the proffers of the sheriffs which included money from the escheators as well as the mulcts imposed upon officials for failure of duty; the farm of lands comprising crown rights of various kinds, mostly royal demesne; the fee-farms of towns; the issues of the Hanaper and the Marshalsea; and the crown estates which fell into six groups. There were the duchy of Cornwall, with lands in a number of counties beside Cornwall and Devon; the two groups of royal lands in north and south Wales: the county and lordship of Pembroke and the three lordships of Tenby, Cilgerran, and Ystlwyf; the counties

---

[1] Not £300, as Wylie states.
[2] *Royal and Historical Letters of Henry IV*, i. 74, 87.
[3] P.R.O., E.101/43/39.

and lordships of Chester and Flint; and the lordship of Rich-mond (Yorkshire) which included manors in Lincolnshire, Nor-folk, Suffolk, and Cambridgeshire in addition to the Yorkshire lands. These six groups, it should be said, by no means exhausted the tale of crown lands scattered throughout England, some granted out for life or for a term of years free of rent. The above sources constituted the 'ordinary' revenue; but there was in addition the casual revenue from forfeitures, compositions of all kinds made with the crown, amercements imposed in the course of judicial proceedings, windfalls such as money payable under treaty arrangements, temporalities; and there was the extra-ordinary revenue from lay and clerical taxes and from the customs. To Sir John Fortescue the notion that the expenses of government should be met from 'grete lordshippes, maners, feeffermys and other such demaynes' was fundamental. Customs and taxes should be granted as a supplement to meet occasional expenses. This is a theory underlying the acts of resumption and is clearly stated in Fortescue's *Governance of England* (cc. 6, 10, 11, and 14). Despite the fact that since the reign of Edward III parliamentary grants of taxation had come to be made with regularity and the king was granted the customs as a matter of course, these subsidies, however firmly the council might count upon them, still remained grants of special grace, dependent upon the good will of the commons.

Throughout the fifteenth century the commons took the greatest interest in public finance. This was not only because they saw in the king's fiscal difficulties the opportunity to increase their own authority by trying to insist upon the granting of their petitions before they made their vote of supply (as in 1401), or by having the council nominated in parliament so that it might be answerable there for money spent; they were also concerned to ensure that the king should have the fullest possible revenue from, and make the best possible use of, his own resources. In this policy the knights of the shire, who took the leading part, were determined to preserve the classic distinction between the ordinary and the extraordinary revenues of the crown. They were determined to treat all extraordinary revenue, including the proceeds of clerical tenths, just as much as of the secular subsidy, as coming within their purview and they were anxious to ensure that it was properly spent; from time to time they were deeply suspicious of the king's advisers, the members of his council, and particularly of his household as well as of the temporal and spiritual lords who had got into their hands by grants or leases or other methods the endowed revenues of the crown. These men, in the words of a contemporary poem, had 'pulled the pears off the royal tree' and 'were licking even the leaves'. A 'librarie of lords' were engaged, they thought, in 'licking of the lordship that to the coroune longeth'.[1]

The first duty, they thought, was to restore the king's livelihood both by resumption of the alienated lands and by careful control of the grants and of the instruments under which they were made. And as their eyes were also turned longingly to the larger accumulations of clerical property, particularly to the possessions of the exempt religious orders, they were not infrequently charged with Lollardy (which was certainly true of some of them); one reason perhaps why the Benedictine chronicler Walsingham was so bitter against them was their hostility to those religious orders who were under no obligation to contribute to taxation.

At the time of greatest financial pressure (1404–6) the knights were prepared to co-operate with the king in ensuring him an adequate revenue on condition that a real financial reconstruction of the crown's resources was undertaken. Their agitation probably began in Henry IV's first parliament. Walsingham, writing of the Coventry parliament of 6 October 1404, makes Archbishop Arundel successfully oppose the plan of the parliamentary knights to confiscate for a period the temporalities of the clergy. In this, says the chronicler, he was assisted by Mercury, the bishop of Rochester. The Speaker is made out to be the Lollard knight, Sir John Cheyne, but by the time of the Coventry parliament the bishop of Rochester, Bottlesham, of whom he speaks, was dead and the see was vacant: Cheyne was in fact chosen as speaker in the 1399 parliament, though he excused himself on the ground of illness to make room for John Doreward, elected by the commons because they realized Cheyne to be unsuitable; and from this it appears likely that the 'excusation' of the Speaker took place as soon as the danger of the anticlerical tendencies was realized by the archbishop. If this is so, the movement must have started early; plans for a resumption of royal grants and leases were in fact put forward as early as

[1] From *Mum and the Sothesegger* (E.E.T.S. 1936), cited by B. P. Wolffe, 'Acts of Resumption in the Lancastrian Parliaments', *Eng. Hist. Rev.* lxxiii (1958), 587.

Henry's first parliament, to apply to all grants made since 1327.

Bringing in the council to control grants, they petitioned that all requests for annual grants should, when assented, expressly state that they were made *per l'advis de vostre Conseil*. A petitioner asking for an annuity and not complying should forfeit a year's grant and his letters patent were to be cancelled. The king replied that he wished to be advised and counselled by the wise men of his council when such gifts or grants were to be accorded and made. In September 1402, under the speakership of Sir Henry de Retford, they were evidently thinking of further measures to control the grant-making power of the crown, and asked for the collaboration of certain lords in advising them how to proceed: Henry agreed, but sent William Heron, steward of the household, and John Prophet, the clerk of the council, to point out that it was neither a duty nor a custom on the part of the king to grant such communication, but a matter purely of grace. In their petitions they returned to the vexed questions of grants by asking that upon the death of any annuitant or grantee of crown rights from Henry or his predecessors, the revenues granted were to revert immediately to the Exchequer *saunz les doner a nully* and were not to be petitioned for or anticipated. The king's answer was that he intended to abstain from making any such grants save to those who deserved them,[1] as it seemed best to king and council: it was a compromise, for Henry would not bind himself not to make such grants.

So far had the pressure gone by the January (Westminster) parliament of 1404 when the commons again asked for the advice and counsel of the lords. In this assembly they were concerned that the prince of Wales should be more effectively financed, to the point of asking that the duchy of Cornwall should be restored to its old territorial extent and that the prince should recover what had been alienated, for the duchy, as they said, had been *demembrez*. More serious a step, though not without its precedents, 1215 and 1258, was their onslaught upon aliens in the household of the king and queen and upon supporters of the anti-pope: French, Bretons, Lombards, Italians, and Milanese might stay in the country, but must quit the household. Meanwhile, in an ordinance of the household, they attempted to fix its income from the various sources of crown

[1] *Rot. Parl.* iii. 495.

revenue as £12,000 by stating the proportions payable from each source. In return for the grant made, the king accepted the institution of war treasurers (Lord Furnival and Sir John Pelham) 'certains tresorers de meme le grant' to ensure that the collected money was actually 'mys sur les guerres'. These men were both treasurers and paymasters. The commons returned to their pressure on aliens after 29 April 1406, when expulsion was brusquely demanded of those whose names were on a list given to the steward of the household, though Hanseatic and other merchants were to be exempt.[1]

In 1404 at the Coventry parliament, despite strong criticism from the temporal lords and a marked reaction of the bishops against the confiscation measure proposed for the temporalities, a parliamentary act of resumption was passed, to apply to all grants and leases made since 1366. At Coventry the gravity of the financial crisis was emphasized because the king, after rescinding his decision once, had been forced to declare a financial *moratorium*. He gave his consent to a petition for resumption, but managed to secure a respite by promising a commission of inquiry, composed of lords spiritual and temporal, justices and the sergeants-at-law, to determine what were the crown lands and what had been alienated since 40 Edward III. For the moment, he told the commons, it would not be honest or expedient for him to revoke outright patents under the Great Seal, because of repercussions abroad and the inevitable murmurings at home. As an immediate measure, however, all who held annuities, sinecures, or grants of profit under patent would be ordered to surrender the current year's income to the king, and proclamation would be made that all holding patents of grant since 40 Edward III should bring them in for scrutiny by the council before the Feast of the Purification of 1405.[2]

By these far-reaching promises Henry got his grants of two tenths and two fifteenths. Further, in anticipation of reform, parliament voted a novel tax of 1s. in the pound on rents of land, and 20s. on every £20 of income from land over 500 marks value per annum. This had first been discussed in the previous parliament, but all records of the grants and collections were destroyed to avoid creating a precedent. From the *Annales Henrici Quarti* for 1404[3] it is clear that the impost, a 'new and

---

[1] Ibid. iii. 571.   [2] Ibid. iii. 459.
[3] p. 379: 'novam concessit et exquisitam taxam.'

ingenious tax', applied to chattels as well as land. Holders of chattels to the value of £40 paid 2s.; of each £20, 1s. All who held lands and annuities from the crown without obligation of service were to contribute; as well as those profiting from marriage settlements or wardships, and the tax was to cover the possessions of the Hospitallers. Half was to be paid at the coming Whitsuntide, and half at All Saints' Day. The Coventry parliament directed that the mixture of income and land tax should be entered upon the parliament roll; but of the committee of inquiry nothing further was heard.

The 1406 parliament was the longest of Henry's reign. It started in March 1406, was adjourned on 3 April, resumed on 25 April, and continued till 19 June. Then came an adjournment till 15 October when the session was continued till late in December. The commons had already showed considerable boldness in the parliament of 26 February 1401. They had asked that they might have a reply to their petitions before they made their grants. The answer was given that such a step was without precedent. They should have, as before, 'no reply to their petition before they had shown and carried out all their other business of parliament, whether there was any grant to make or otherwise'.[1] By now they had overcome the royal resistance to a committee of liaison with the lords, and on 19 June 1406, in spite of Henry's angry retort that kings were not wont to render account, they obtained the royal promise and got it enrolled, of a parliamentary audit of the novel land tax voted at Coventry in 1404. On 22 December they over-reached themselves by demanding a personal guarantee from council members still present in parliament that they would be responsible for refunding any grant that had been misspent. Very naturally this provoked an explosion from the king, for the commons having attempted to curtail his own prerogative were trying the same tactics on the council.

In 1406 a new flexibility of procedure is witnessed. At the outset the young Speaker, John Tiptoft, who tried to escape duty because of his youth 'et par defaute de seens et discrecion' (evidently not admitted), made on behalf of the commons various petitions 'par bouche'.[2] One was that Richard Clitheroe, one of the admirals, should give place to Robert Clifford, who was to be authorized 'to appear in parliament in their two names,

---

[1] *Rot. Parl.* iii. 458.   [2] Ibid. iii. 568, 572.

as if both were present'. The Speaker had a formidable task, which only a man in full vigour could undertake, of carrying through for Henry the parliamentary declaration of the succession cancelling the earlier declaration, of negotiating with the king and the lords the formation of the new council and of securing the adherence, made by solemn oath in the presence of the estates, of those nominated to serve on it to obey new articles devised for the council's conduct of business. At each step the diplomatic form in which the conciliar act was to be made had to be discussed, which required a negotiator who had the confidence of the king and of the commons alike. Thus after the council had been nominated in parliament (22 May) and it had been conceded that bills passed by the chamberlains and others under the royal signet, as well as other mandates issuable to the chancellor, treasurer, and keeper of the privy seal, should be endorsed and made by the 'advice of the Council', it was agreed that the new arrangement should be made by the king himself, and the 'bill' nominating the council was recorded as being *de sa mocion propre* and entered, with the request of the lords that this change should be effected, upon the parliament roll. The close co-operation of the Speaker and the clerk of the parliament (John Rome) was required in these complicated matters of record.

The main constitutional battle was, in a sense, over, for the *avis du conseil* in the matter of grants and the nomination of the council by the estates had been secured. But would the lords nominated join the council and subscribe to the articles? Archbishop Arundel answered that 'if sufficiency of goods be found, for which proper provision could be made, they would undertake the work: otherwise not';[1] in other words, they would agree to serve if the arrangements for providing an adequate revenue were satisfactory. It was this provisional nature of their assent which was reflected in the final article limiting the force and effect of the projected rules from the end of the present to the beginning of the next parliament: this might be anticipated as about a year. How optimistic of the commons to consent to so short a period—or was it the lords who limited the time out of dislike for the new arrangement? Before the regulations were laid down the commons cheerfully asked for an inquiry into the value of all types of lordships, manors, lands, tenements, alien

[1] Ibid. iii. 573.

priories, wardships, marriages, or other possessions let at farm
or granted by the king and his predecessors for life or a period
of years for annual rent or for nothing; and if they proved to be
of higher value than the figure at which they were let, powers
should be given to the council to increase the amount of those
annual farms or rents. To hold such an inquiry would have consumed an immense amount of time, a longer period than the
life of the regulations, though the subject, as will be seen
presently,[1] was entirely relevant and of high importance.

The chief purpose of the articles for the conduct of the council
was to regulate and control access to the king for the purpose of
obtaining grants or favours, and at the same time to secure a
settled revenue for the household by preventing certain classes
of revenue being assigned elsewhere. Nothing was to pass under
the Great Seal or privy seal that should not of right or law pass.
No one was to invoke the king's prerogative in suits that should
be terminated by ordinary process of law, and if the council
discovered that this was being done for purpose of private gain,
the official, if he was a member of the household, was to lose his
position there, his fees and annuities, and pay £20 to the
Exchequer to be paid as wages for Calais or the Marches or for
the king's use. The suspicion that members of the household
were using their privileged position to get grants is patent. Only
on Wednesdays and Fridays, the days to be assigned for the
reception of petitions, should the *familiares* of the king make
any requests for grants. The council only is to hear matters not
determinable at Common Law; and as the council is a judicial
body, councillors must not act as pursuants or litigants. All
councillors are to swear not to take anything outside their
official salaries. No judicial officer or official of the household or
one serving in any of the courts was to be given a life appointment, but only an appointment at pleasure.

In the Gloucester parliament of 1407, Thomas Chaucer the
Speaker reminded the lords and commons that the lords appointed to the council, who had been sworn to keep the articles,
had not been thanked for their services and for the substantial
credits which they had granted the crown (*grandes creances par
lour obligations propres*). Through him they asked for their discharge and for release from their oaths. *Creances* is interesting,
for the expression can be borne out by the figures in the Receipt

[1] See below, Ch. XII.

rolls. Was that year's service on the part of the lords a method by which Tiptoft and his friends thought that additional finance might be provided for the king? In any event it is important not to take the parliamentary nominations of the council more seriously than they deserve. In 1401 the proposals were not intended to limit the royal prerogative in favour of the council: this was specifically stated.[1] The charge is to be given to the members 'apart', 'hors du parliament en la presence du Roy en aucune lieu come pleura au Roy'; just as his household officers are charged. In 1404 the parliament rolls merely stated that on account of repeated requests by the commons, the king had ordained certain lords and others to be of his great and continual council. The twenty-two councillors nominated on the parliament roll had all served on the council previously: the number attending council meetings did not change because of the nomination; and attendance was not confined to those who had been nominated. The same applies to the council nominated in parliament in 1406. What then was all the pother about? The commons regarded the act of publicly reading out the names of the councillors in parliament as of importance. It cannot be believed that the commons thought that they had secured a council responsible to them. It is more likely that they thought that by having the council now (1406) formally charged *in* parliament, they might be able to bind its members to restrain the king's liberality and ensure some measure of economy. It was on avoiding the 'outrageous' grants that their minds were set. Yet when Henry promised to be advised by the 'sages de son Conseil', he added 'sauvant toute foitz sa libertee'. On the other hand, the noxious grants by letters patent, particularly to members of the household, were in fact restricted; and privy seal warrants to the Exchequer were also made with the assent of the council more often than in the past. The Exchequer warrants for issue show the most obvious change. Only 20·6 per cent. of those dated before 22 May 7 Henry IV were made with the assent of the council, while 60 per cent. of those dated after 22 May record its assent.[2]

Yet neither the threefold nomination of the king's council in the 1406 parliament nor the list of articles which its members

---

[1] Cf. K. B. McFarlane's observations in *Camb. Med. Hist.* viii (1936), 369.
[2] A. L. Brown, 'The Privy Seal in the Early Fifteenth Century' (Oxf. Univ. unpubl. thesis, 1955), pp. 75–76.

were obliged by oath to observe, nor the subsidy granted in December, could produce, within the time that circumstances now demanded, the necessary cash. By the beginning of March 1407, £25,000 had been paid into the exchequer, but even so it was necessary to borrow, and the earl of Westmorland came forward with £900 and Sir Thomas Knolles with £200. This was not nearly enough, for the problem of Calais demanded immediate attention. Arundel (chancellor succeeding Langley) and the council were informed that the wages of the garrison had been in arrears for a considerable time and that the soldiers had seized the wool stored in the merchants' warehouses before being sold to the Flemings. Edward III had fixed the staple at Calais; wool export was then the country's largest type of trade and the ready money it brought in was the most readily accessible form of wealth. It had been the practice to earmark part of the subsidy in wool for the Calais garrison, which was itself guarding the market where the wool was sold, so that by a simple operation of credit it had been possible to pay the troops at Calais with the cash received from the merchants. This system worked well enough if the exchequer had ample cash and credit for the king's current expenses in England: but this was not so now, and to maintain, in addition to the current expenses, an establishment in Calais fixed at 800 men in time of peace (400 being stationed in the town itself, the rest in the parts around) and at 1,000 in war meant a considerable effort. The average cost of the garrison was £17,000 a year, a large slice out of an annual income substantially below £100,000. On 29 and 30 April it was announced that Richard Whittington and other merchants of the Staple had lent the king £4,000, and had been promised that they should have full repayments from the first moneys collected on the wool subsidies in certain ports. Whittington was both mayor of London (his second term of office) and also mayor of the Staple at Calais. With the possible exception of John Hende (who had already lent the crown money) he was the wealthiest citizen in London. Hende lent £2,500, in return for which he was promised the keeping of the cocket seal in the port of London. The English and the alien merchants lent on this and the earlier occasions the sum of £8,000 which was still short of the arrears due to the garrison at Calais, amounting, as one scholar thinks, to probably £20,000.[1] By a special effort, to

---

[1] J. L. Kirby, 'The Council of 1407 and the Problem of Calais', *History Today*,

which John Norbury, formerly treasurer, contributed in the sum of £2,000 and the earl of Westmorland in a further £500, the figure was raised to £12,000. This sum was paid to the treasurer of Calais on 12 June 1407. On 30 June the collectors of the customs were told about the loans and the arrangements made for collecting and repaying the money lent. It was decided that half the wool subsidy was to be earmarked for the payment of the current wages at Calais, and the other half to the repayments, and bonds guaranteeing the repayment of loans were sealed by every member of the council who had been named in parliament the previous December.[1] The Calais crisis of 1407 certainly shows that the new council was utilized financially in an extreme emergency, and proved effective for the time being. Yet, despite the salaries they received, the desire of the councillors to have their tenure of office strictly limited is fully understandable.

It would be an exaggeration to say of this 1406 parliament that the demands of the commons and the concessions of the king almost amounted to a supersession of the royal authority.[2] The articles were not permanent: still less was the scheme of reform drawn up by the council which prescribed a grant of £1,000 to the household from the subsidy to be collected, and recommended that a permanent headquarters for the household be established, to avoid the expense of constant movement; for Henry IV, when he was well, was unusually mobile, even when not pressed by revolt.

It was worth making concessions to extract from parliament and the two convocations the grants tabulated in the Appendix to the present chapter.[3] They represent extraordinary revenue only: to gain a full and accurate picture of Henry's annual income from these and all other sources, still more to find out what seems to be actually disposed of in a given period is more difficult. It would be necessary to study his credit operations. Richard's average annual revenue seems to have been about £116,500, certainly below £120,000. Henry's 'real' average was below £90,000. Now in 1401 the council had before it figures from the treasurer showing that more than £130,000 was

---

v (1955), p. 49. For a general picture, cf. id. 'Calais sous les Anglais', *Revue du Nord*, xxxvii (1955), pp. 19 f.

[1] Archbishop Arundel, the bishops of London, Winchester, and Durham, the duke of York, the earl of Somerset, Lords Grey, Burnell, and Roos, Sir John Stanley and John Prophet (keeper of the privy seal).

[2] Stubbs, iii. 37.   [3] See below, p. 118.

required for administration and defence. It was not stated whether the household expenses were included in this figure, but probably they were not. If so, Henry, *before* he became heavily involved in financial demands from Wales, Ireland, Gascony, Calais, and naval defence, had to find at least £140,000 a year; and by 1404–6 considerably more. It was therefore necessary to call upon all available extraordinary revenue and to maintain a proper flow of the customs.

Taxation comes in slowly: troops and supplies will not wait. The data extracted by Mr. Steel from the Receipt rolls of the Exchequer show that the king was borrowing actively and that his creditors were not being repaid as fully or as punctually as Richard II's in the last ten years of his reign. But before this is considered, there is one technicality which is worth notice. With one exception, very much larger sums were received by the Exchequer of Receipt in cash from and after Michaelmas 1406 until 1409 than either before or after those dates. This may perhaps be the result of the abundant taxation granted by the commons from 1404 onwards, the collection of which was now making itself felt: the cash payments appear large because in previous years, years of mounting strain, most of the grants had been assigned and the Receipt itself simply acted as the accountant. (The exception is Michaelmas 1407–8 when there is a comparatively high cash payment into the Receipt (£33,166. 12s. 7½d.), while as much as £47,272. 11s. 9½d. or 52 per cent. of the total on the Receipt roll was assigned.)[1] The reason may be that the revenue was being more efficiently collected, and that the council's articles were having some effect.[2] But the main interest of Mr. Steel's data lies in the wider and more important conclusion that Henry, in the loans he contracted, had resort more than his predecessor to a small group of wealthy independent Englishmen. He raised appreciably more from members of the household, somewhat more from magnates and from bishops than Richard had done, considerably less from monasteries, county gentry and the smaller boroughs, and substantially less from aliens. From the royal household Henry Somer, from London great capitalists such as

---

[1] Steel, op. cit., pp. 96–97.

[2] It is possible, of course, that in this period (1407–9) assignment was being deliberately restricted for fear of the king's death: the Exchequer would not want to issue large numbers of doubtful tallies, if there was this possibility.

John Hende, Richard Whittington, or Thomas Knolles, from the bishops Henry Beaufort (after 1410) helped him, men who could wait some time for repayment. He relied on a few big lenders of money and providers of military service (e.g. the earls of Westmorland and Northumberland). But Richard II repaid his creditors much more conscientiously than Henry IV; and here we reach a celebrated interpretation of political history from Exchequer statistics. The figures completed, Mr. Steel maintains, show that 'the face value of worthless tallies cut by Henry's Exchequer was over three times as much as under Richard, viz. (in round figures) £135,000 against £15,000 and £37,000 for the two periods of Richard's reign respectively (1377–89, 1389–99).' There was therefore an 'enormous increase in untrustworthiness and insecurity of payment under Henry'.[1] This generalization rests upon the clear distinction drawn between the 'genuine' and the 'fictitious' loan, the latter represented by the tally which cannot be cashed and has to be returned to the Exchequer for reissue to the creditor, thence to be drawn upon some other collector or official who was now asked to meet it. To contemporaries this uncertainty in reimbursement must have reflected badly upon the government and produced ill will towards the dynasty.

What happened when a loan was made? The creditor who made it received from the Exchequer of receipt a tally which enabled him later to recover the sum from an official in charge of public funds, whether he was a collector or a customs official or a sheriff. The official might accept the tally and pay the creditor: he might be unable to meet it, or might meet only part of it, and later pay the whole in full. Or he might say that his funds were already over-assigned, and that it was impossible for him to pay. On the other hand, the tally might be defective, through some error in form, or it might be uncashable because the sovereign had died or the collectors had been changed. In 1404 the commons petitioned that those who held assignments for goods supplied to the royal household or for money lent should have them renewed if they became void by the changing of the king's officers. Such changes led important civilian or military creditors to ask, when receiving tallies from the Exchequer, that they should be changed if they proved ineffective. In cases where the tally could not be met and was taken or sent

[1] Steel. op. cit., pp. 114–15.

back by the creditor to the Exchequer, it was the practice of clerks to cancel the original entry in the Receipt roll and credit the holder with a fictitious loan, recorded close to the cancelled entry. This both preserved the totals on the roll and recorded the Exchequer's obligation to the creditor for the undercharged sum. The loan might take a long time to pay: but, as a commentator on these loans has acutely observed:

> as a general index to financial stability the simple equation of fictitious loans with bad tallies and uncancelled assignments clearly will not do. An uncancelled entry can indicate a promptly discharged assignment: but it might well mean that a creditor had been content or compelled to wait for payment, had perhaps sold the tally at a discount or even, in some circumstances, had failed to secure payment at all. ... A tally returned to the Exchequer might indicate that the revenue it assigned, through over-assignment or inefficient collection, had failed to bear the strain imposed upon it, but equally it may have been rendered invalid by an administrative hitch or by the removal of the collector.[1]

Readers of the *Calendar of Fine Rolls* for the period will notice the number of times in which the collectors of the customs, that source of revenue so heavily assigned, were changed. Some caution is therefore required before passing, on these technical grounds, an adverse judgement on the financial difficulties of the first Lancastrian.

In his St. Albans Chronicle (Bodleian MS. Version)[2] Thomas Walsingham gives paramount attention to two critical phases in the latter part of Henry IV's reign: negotiations to end the Great Schism and the advantage taken by Henry's government of the offer of the French princes to draw the king into their struggle against the duke of Burgundy. A tendency to discount English participation in Conciliar events has led historians to pass over the genuine efforts made by the king to restore unity in the Church and to achieve some measure of reform by a general council; the second of these phases, the expedition to Acquitaine, raises the problem of Anglo-Burgundian relations and calls for some estimate of the personalities and politics of Henry's later years.

The government's preoccupation with rebellion and with the

---

[1] G. L. Harriss, 'Fictitious Loans', *Econ. Hist. Rev.*, 2nd ser., viii (1955–6), 198–9.
[2] MS. Bodl. 462, ed. V. H. Galbraith as *The St. Albans Chronicle, 1406–1420*.

problems of finance had diverted most people's attention from the major contemporary European problem, until the death of Innocent VII raised the question whether a fresh papal election would not merely prolong the impasse of the Schism. But that eventuality had been anticipated earlier, for Henry showed himself anxious, in harmony with the trend of French diplomacy, to bring about the cession of the contending parties. In the second recess of the 1406 parliament Sir John Cheyne and the chancellor of Salisbury, Dr. Henry Chichele, were sent on an embassy to the Pope and cardinals in Rome, probably to achieve a basis for the eventual resignation of Innocent VII and Benedict XIII. Before they left they were joined (6 Oct. 1406) by Hugh Mortimer, chamberlain to Prince Henry of Monmouth, with the object of presenting to the French court a proposal for the marriage of Henry with one of Charles VI's daughters or at least of emending the existing truces. They reached Venice late in January 1407; but already on 6 November 1406 Innocent VII had died, and letters from England now instructed them to ascertain whether the cardinals intended to elect or suspend the election of a successor. Henry IV expressed himself in favour of suspension and for concerting measures to end the Schism. He did not, as yet, put forward the views already tentatively expressed by Oxford and, more positively, by Cambridge University (1399) in favour of a council. The intervention came too late. On 30 November 1406 Gregory XII (Angelo Corrario) had been elected, but Cheyne and Chichele had other business to carry out at the Curia, and their commission was renewed on 26 April 1407. For a year they were at Gregory's court and in the spring of 1408 moved to Lucca. On 9 May Gregory took the fateful step, when most of his own cardinals left him, of creating a new batch, which led to the decision of the dissident cardinals of both obediences, now a majority of the Sacred College, at Pisa on 13 May to summon a general council. The letters went out on 24 June for its assembly at Pisa on 25 March 1409, and shortly afterwards Richard Dereham, chancellor of Cambridge University, returned to England with messages from the Pisan cardinals which he communicated to Henry on 11 July. The king made no decisive proclamation of his attitude till the visit, in November 1408, of the archbishop of Bordeaux, Cardinal Francis Uguccione: already the abbot of Westminster and the bishop of Carlisle had been advocating the *Via Concilii*, but it was the speech of Uguccione, reported fully in Arundel's register,[1] that turned the scale and convinced the lawyers—for the legitimacy of the summons was in question—that the cardinals were in the right.

England therefore sent representatives to the council: the king's were the abbot of Westminster, Sir John Colville, a king's knight with considerable experience in diplomacy, and the papal auditor, Nicholas Risshton, a Lancashire clerk who had represented his country in the difficult negotiations with the Flemings at Calais in 1401–3. The royal envoys were told to persuade Gregory XII to come to the council of Pisa and there make his formal resignation. They visited him at Rimini on 28 February 1409. Colville made an eloquent speech to him in Italian; the abbot delivered a little sermon on the text *coadunate senes et congregate parvulos*, in which 'proceeding very deliberately and elegantly in the matter of union, he exhorted the Lord Gregory to come to Pisa'; then the auditor, appropriately on the text *audi nos domine*, 'used many varieties of persuasive arguments in asking the Lord Gregory to come to the general council at Pisa and there renounce his right, as the letters of Henry IV had urged him to do'. Gregory declined and gave his reasons for preferring a general council to be summoned by himself. The ambassadors, not content, pressed him to answer Henry's inquiry. Would he go to Pisa and resign? He replied that when he had read the king's letter he would readily reply.[2] He wrote, in fact, a letter to the two bishops, Hallum and Chichele (the latter of whom by now he himself had provided to the see of St. David's), representing the province of Canterbury, along with Thomas Chillenden, prior of Christ Church, Canterbury, at the council of Pisa, which was to catch them on the way. He asked the two bishops to inform themselves of the attitude already adopted by the king of Hungary, the doge of Venice, and the orator of King Rupert, and by Charles Malatesta of Rimini—in other words, his own supporters.

The ambassadors got no satisfaction. The feeling of the English Church about Pisa is best expressed in the appointment of Robert Hallum, bishop of Salisbury, to lead the delegation.

---

[1] Printed from Prof. Hamilton Thompson's transcript in Galbraith, *The St. Albans Chronicle, 1406–1420*, pp. 136–52.

[2] Johannes Vincke, *Briefe zum Pisanerkonzil* (*Beiträge zur Kirchen- und Rechtsgeschichte*, i.) (Bonn, 1940), pp. 175–6.

Arundel's former auditor was a keen reformer himself, and it was for him that a friend at Queen's College, Oxford, Richard Ullerston (himself, like Hallum, recently chancellor of the university), wrote in 1408–9 the treatise *Petitiones quoad reformationem ecclesie militantis*, the most important English treatise written on the reform of the Church by the general council. Hallum had the friendship of the prince of Wales and persuaded Ullerston to dedicate to him, when king, his treatise on knighthood (the possibility of Henry's residence for a while at any rate as a *commensalis* of Queen's must not be ruled out). Nor should Hallum's colleague, Henry Chichele, be regarded as a purely ambassadorial type. It is known that at Pisa he discussed reform within the religious orders and he was later to protest to Hallum, at Constance, his dislike of monastic exemptions. But in any event, a jurist was wanted to help Risshton and Richard Dereham, the Cambridge chancellor, in the process against Gregory and Benedict. Risshton was one of the clerks appointed for receiving the testimony and examining the witnesses against the two popes, and it is on record that Dereham testified to the charge of collusion between the two popes in refusing to repair to a common meeting-place. Dereham was also present, he said, in the cathedral of Lucca when Gregory created his cardinals; and the abbot of Westminster and Sir John Colville both gave evidence about Gregory's refusal to obey the summons.[1] English participation in the council was both active and effective. The clerical representatives of Canterbury and York, as they passed through Paris on the way to the council, heard an address of congratulation from Jean Gerson, the *Proposicio facta coram Anglicis*, in which he rejoiced that the two countries were at one in their support of the council.

Dr. Haller's opinion that the English king cared more for unity in the head than for reform should be treated with caution. Henry's letter to Alexander V, exhorting him 'to persist with the Council', was copied by John Prophet, formerly clerk of the council now keeper of privy seal, into his letter-book, to record the king's hope that 'certain detestable abuses cease through the proper reformation of many errors'.[2] At the same time he was on his guard against any attempt by the newly unified papacy to try any novelties which would be 'derogatory

---

[1] See the recent new material on the council of Pisa summarized in *Bulletin of the John Rylands Library*, xli (1958), 33–38.   [2] Harleian MS. 431, f. 42.

to our crown or *regalia*', nor attempt anything against the statutes and ordinances published by the consent of the estates. Several 'moderations' or relaxations of the second Statute of Provisors (1390) had been asked for and sanctioned in parliament: but those were exceptional *ad hoc* measures, made for the benefit of the university clerks, and not of general application. There were, as will be seen later on, other administrative reforms in the Church which, without raising controversial issues, Henry thought might be undertaken.

Above all it was essential that in the universal Church and in any gathering of it, England should stand for orthodoxy in the faith. This was to be emphasized most fully in the personnel and the tactics of the English delegation at the council of Constance: but the problem of Lollardy and its political influence was especially prominent in the mind of Archbishop Arundel, chancellor (1407) in succession to the invaluable Langley. It was an all-round heresy by now, almost with a literature of its own, in academic Latin, but only on one side, the side of the aggressors, in English: orthodoxy had no such translators as Wyclif's helper John Purvey. The second translation of the Bible, probably not Purvey's, can be dated to *c.* 1396: it was not a Lollard version, but would help the bible-readings that went on in different parts and further the simple-minded testing of current doctrine and institutions by reference to Word of God. Though Archbishop Courtenay and his bishops had been concerned and active about Lollardy since 1382 and the council had come to share their anxiety, it was not till the Twelve Conclusions of the Lollards affixed to the doors of St. Paul's in 1395 and the subsequent resolution of the convocation of Canterbury that an approach was made to Rome and Boniface IX asked to press the king for action. The council had indeed been asking the ecclesiastical authorities for the suspension and punishment of preachers, and various mandates had been sent;[1] but heavier penalties seemed necessary and in the Hilary parliament of 1397 the bishops of both provinces asked the king and the lords for a statute, providing for the execution and forfeiture of heretics who refused to repent. To get it they had to wait until Arundel's restoration, when in 1401, at the petition of the clergy

---

[1] H. G. Richardson, 'Heresy and the Lay Power under Richard II', *Eng. Hist. Rev.* li (1936), 16–20, enumerates letters sent to the University of Oxford and to municipal authorities.

of Canterbury, it was enacted that if the diocesans should find anybody contravening the rules of the Church against unlicenced preaching, such persons should be arrested and kept in prison until they adjured. Within three months the diocesan had to proceed against them, and if they proved obdurate, they were to be handed over to the king's officers in the area, who were to receive the heretics and have them publicly burned. This procedure put the *onus* of proving the heresy upon the diocesan authorities: they did not have to hand over the suspects, but they could keep them in prison for a time proportionate to the offence, for not all culpability in this respect merited death.

The Statute, called the *De heretico comburendo*, and the supplementary measure of 1406 by which the State and the Church authorities were commissioned forcibly to inquire into and arrest Lollards in their districts, were deficient in a number of ways. There was no regular method of inquiry save for what the ordinaries could themselves devise; few people were aware of the canonical rules on preaching; and heresy being often a highly technical matter, the bishop's court was not always the most expert place where the degree of suspicion could be established and the amount of the accused person's obduracy determined, or the right penance prescribed. There was also the problem of the relapsed and contumacious heretic who had gone back upon his earlier adjuration. The last of these categories Arundel dealt with by using the provincial council of convocation as the tribunal. In the case of William Sawtry from the diocese of Norwich, brought to trial actually before the Statute of 1401 was promulgated, the condemnation took place in convocation on 23 February, Sawtry was degraded and, the king anticipating the Statute, was handed over the same day to the London civic authorities for burning, which took place shortly afterwards at Smithfield. This sentence, as it was meant to do, alarmed Wyclif's secretary, John Purvey, when brought from Arundel's prison in Saltwood before the same provincial council, into submission and later he regained the archbishop's confidence to the extent of being instituted to West Hythe in the Canterbury diocese, though he resigned in 1403 and vanished into neutral obscurity. With John Badby, the tailor of Evesham who denied transubstantiation, the provincial procedure was not applied, for the accused was brought before a tribunal of bishops and secular lords over which Arundel presided at the Blackfriars on 1 March 1410, when the sentence of the diocesan, Thomas Peverell, was confirmed and Badby, despite the efforts of the prince of Wales and Arundel to save him, assigned to the civic authorities for a peculiarly horrible death. In this case the temporal lords present, though appealed to by Arundel, had declined to show mercy. Arundel's successor, Chichele, always employed a strictly ecclesiastical form of procedure and had severe cases reported on to convocation by theological experts and sometimes by canon lawyers.

The problem of unlicensed preaching was treated in the convocation which Arundel summoned to Oxford in 1407, and the resulting constitution was issued at St. Paul's in the assembly of 1409. William Lyndwood later regarded this as the main enactment on heresy in a province where the inquisitor was the metropolitan in his judicial capacity. It was the violation of this constitution that was to constitute the ground of action against suspected persons. If this could be proved against a man, Lyndwood said, 'immediately that the crime has been committed the accused person loses not only the administration of goods but also their ownership'. To the Church proof of heresy involved automatically the loss of all possessions.[1] Mainly on the strength of the preaching enactment Arundel felt free to deal with one of the most difficult problems in his own eyes: the attitude of the University of Oxford towards heresy.

Oxford was the home as well as the platform of two able but suspected academics, Peter Payne and William Taylor. Payne, who lived to become the official responsible for foreign affairs in the revolutionary Czech state under Prokop and Zizka, came early under the influence of John Purvey and made himself a champion of Wycliffite influence in the schools, and early in his career became notorious for an escapade whereby, as Thomas Gascoigne wrote, 'he stole the common seal of the University under which he wrote to the heretics of Prague that Oxford and all England, save the false mendicant friars, held the same beliefs as they did in Prague'. The letter in question was taken to Prague by two Czech scholars, returning home during 1407 after a visit to Oxford made for the purpose of copying, among Wyclif's works, the *De Ecclesia* and the *De Dominio Divino*. It has been pointed out that before a statute of 1426/7 there was no

---

[1] *Liber Provincialis*, v. 5, s.v. *auctorizatus est*: ed. 1679, p. 289.

serious obstacle to prevent the issue of letters under the university
seal being obtained as the result of a snatch vote in the poorly
attended congregation of regents, and that a small and militant
party of regents might very well profit by the fact.[1] By 1411
Payne was principal of St. Edmund Hall, living in the annexed
White Hall. The other *degener filius*, Taylor, 'Master of Arts of
singular opinions and of the new sect', is reported, in Arundel's
register, to have advocated the seizure of the possessions of the
Church 'quasi per violentam cedicionem (sedicionem) populi';
and it is thought that he may have been the Oxford clerk whose
sermon at St. Paul's Cross was vigorously defended by the
Oxford Wycliffite, William Thorpe, in an altercation with Archbishop Arundel when he arraigned Thorpe for heresy.[2] Taylor,
also master of the Hall, was eventually brought before Chichele
at Lambeth in February 1420 as one 'who had been for a long
time and still was vehemently suspected of divers errors, heresy
and Lollardy', abjured his errors and relapsed. Two Oxford
principals do not make a heretical movement, but Arundel was
also aware that his direction in the Preaching Constitution of
1407–9, that no book or treatise of Wyclif was to be used in the
schools unless it had been first approved by a committee of
twelve to be appointed in each university, had been disregarded,
and he was aware that the university had been slow to execute
his order that the heads of colleges or principals of halls should
inquire, once a month at least, into the orthodoxy of their
scholars. He had listened to various ill-founded accusations
against Richard Fleming:[3] but it was not till the committee of
twelve had submitted to the southern convocation a complete
list of 267 heretical and erroneous conclusions in March 1411
that Arundel felt able to carry out a visitation of the university.
Oxford claimed to be exempt by a bull of Boniface IX and
Arundel's attempt to procure an oath from two resident members
of the university that they would not maintain any of the 267
errors stung the university into strong opposition. When on

---

[1] Actually, 'in October 1411 a letter bearing the seal of the University was sent
to the king announcing that the University, in spite of his express command to the
contrary, had reelected the Chancellor and Proctors who had impeded the Archbishop in his visitation. The University hastened to appease the royal indignation
by explaining that this letter . . . was a *fabrica epistola* for which certain *degeneres
fratres nostri* were to blame': A. B. Emden, *An Oxford Hall in Medieval Times* (1927),
pp. 141–2.   [2] Ibid., p. 127.
[3] On his foundation at Oxford, see below, p. 673.

7 July he came to St. Mary's for the visitation he found the church locked and barred, but in the end succeeded in gaining entry. At the end of his sermon a mandate arrived from Henry IV summoning the chancellor and proctors to appear before him on 9 September. Thereupon Arundel broke off the visitation and placed St. Mary's under interdict. At Henry IV's request John XXIII revoked Boniface IX's bull of exemption, and the publication of this revocation, in congregation during 1412, marked the victory of the king and Arundel. That they became reconciled to the university is stated in the *Statuta Antiqua* under 1412 to have been due to the *instancias, supplicationes et media* of Prince Henry, the university undertaking to sing Mass of the Holy Ghost for the king on 31 October every year so long as he lived, and other exequies and mass for him that day and the morrow yearly 'after he shall have resigned the breath of his life of the Most High'.[1] Undoubtedly it was the visitation rather than the suspicion of Lollardy which the university resented.

If Arundel exaggerated Oxford's feeling for its leading philosopher of the later fourteenth century, he was more justified in his suspicion of the attitude of the commons towards the Church. Walsingham copied into his history the petition of the parliamentary knights ('or, as we may more rightly say, satellites of Pilate'), not to be found on the parliament roll, but evidently circulated in the city and elsewhere. Calling themselves 'all the faithful Commons', they asked for the confiscation of the 'temporal goods' of the bishops, abbots, and priors, out of which the king could be endowed with £20,000 a year, fifteen new earls each with 3,000 marks annually, 1,500 knights each with 300 marks, and 6,200 esquires each with 40 marks, and a hundred hospices or almshouses each with an income of 100 marks annually under good secular management; and the authors of the badly calculated plan then coolly enumerated the sees and religious houses that might yield the required figure. It is a very odd document. 'All the faithful Commons', as one knows from other petitions,[2] cannot be taken too literally. But that there were powerful critics of those religious houses which made no contribution to the grants made by the convocations there is no doubt; and some of the best diplomatic servants of the crown, men like Sir John Cheyne of Beckford, who was to be Speaker

---

[1] S. Gibson, *Statuta Antiqua Universitatis Oxoniensis* (1931) p. 210.
[2] See below, p. 410.

of the commons, in their wills lamented their Lollard past, while county families like those to which Sir William Latimer and Sir Lewis Clifford belonged were implicated in unorthodoxy. Against both types, anti-clerical or genuinely Lollard, Henry IV stood firmly beside Archbishop Arundel.

It has been customary to regard Henry IV in his later years as very much of an invalid, increasingly disinclined towards the burdens of state and unequal to its cares. This has gone as far as to suggest that he 'retired' from his duties, and that the alleged attempt of Prince Henry to seize power was in no small measure due to his father's reluctance to conduct business and deferment to the unpopular Arundel.

That Henry had so many bouts of illness that they seriously incapacitated him is well attested. In his later years he became a neurotic, much alarmed about his condition and therefore all the more liable to physical collapse: but like many neurotics he was capable of remarkable recovery, and only when he was very ill was he prepared to delegate his duties. About Easter 1405 he expressed himself as improving in health through God's help and spoke of the benefits of his 'convalescence'. After the Scrope rebellion the *Eulogium* reports that the king 'began to appear like a leper' and Giles's Chronicle says that the king was struck with incurable leprosy at the very hour of the archbishop's death. It was probably a nervous breakdown which temporarily affected his appearance, but by July he was thanking his Maker for his excellent health. At the end of April 1406 he was suffering from pain in the legs, and by the third week in May he gave over most of his work to a council of seventeen, consisting of the permanent officers and most of the prominent lords. In August–September 1407, when he was moving about in Yorkshire, we are told that his 'failing health' brought on a nervous dread of infection 'and constant change of place was deemed the only safeguard when the air was charged with pestilence'.[1] Constant change of place was not unusual when Henry was in the north, and on this occasion he was anxious to recruit all available men between the ages of sixteen and sixty to fight the Scots. After the great Northumberland rebellion (Feb. 1405), and his return from Pontefract, he became very ill, when staying at Archbishop Arundel's manor at Mortlake

[1] Wylie, op. cit., iii. 110.

(19 June–12 July),[1] lost consciousness, and was reported by Walsingham to be dying. It was a mild stroke. He recovered, however, to be urged by the archbishop to give thanks to God for his restoration and to amend his misdeeds, a story perhaps rather too closely resembling that of his illness after the Scrope trial. But in December 1408 he certainly was convinced that he was soon to die and his son Thomas was sent for from Ireland: on 21 January 1409, at Greenwich, whither he had been moved to get better air, he made his will with Arundel and the great officers and other members of the council standing by, the prince of Wales being made executor. Of this more will be said later: here it may only be noted that on 6 April, in a letter written to Archbishop Arundel in his own hand, he spoke of the 'good hele that I am ynne', and by the first week in May he was preparing to hunt at Windsor. Until July 1411 there is no hint of illness, but during that summer his health would not allow him to cross the Channel in person in the expedition that was being fitted out to help John the Fearless, but when it was proposed that he should abdicate and the prince take over the government, he had the will to refuse. Henry IV retained a large measure of personal control till his final illness in 1413.

On the other hand, the authority of the council over financial affairs was greater after the autumn of 1407. This phase lasted till November 1411, when the prince of Wales's friends no longer attended and the two archbishops and the professional administrators did the work. It is characterized by the greater share of Prince Henry in the government, his frequent attendance in the council, and a determined effort to remedy the financial situation by careful planning. From the council itself the knights and esquires dropped out. Their number had already begun to decline in 1406. In the council nominated in the parliament on 22 May 1406 there were three, John Cheyne, Robert Waterton, and Arnold Savage. These figure in the council assigned on 27 November, but they did not appear on that occasion, nor were they with the other counsellors on the last day of parliament. The last meeting of the council at which they are recorded as having been present was 26 November, when Savage alone appeared. After this date there is no record of any knight

---

[1] The traditional date for Henry's supposed attack of leprosy is 8 June 1405, but as Wylie, op. cit., ii. 249, has shown, there is no likelihood of this disease.

or esquire having attended a council meeting during the remainder of the reign, and payments to them ceased.

From the beginning of December 1406 the prince of Wales
began to attend meetings and to judge by the existing but very
limited evidence he attended pretty regularly until 30 November 1411, when he and his friends were dismissed. For his
services he was given 1,000 marks. Unquestionably he was paid
off; but it would be erroneous to think that this meant a deep-
set quarrel with his father. There were diplomatic as well as
financial issues on which the earlier combination of Arundel
and the king was reasserting itself, and the prince's inability to
back the foreign policy now adopted should not be construed in
any way as disloyalty. If he was critical of the new trend, that
was because he could not approve the anti-Burgundian leanings
of Arundel and his brother Thomas, and after all he was the
declared and approved heir and successor to a king whose tenure
of life was very uncertain. Prince Henry had been plunged into
great events at a very early age, and had commended himself
to Richard II who, when Henry of Bolingbroke was banished
(1398), took young Henry to Ireland and during the visit
knighted him. The prince was only thirteen when put in charge
of north Wales and the Marches. The initiative, naturally
enough, came from a council of which the justiciar of north
Wales, Henry Percy, was the chief member. At that stage Henry
had a tutor or governor, Sir Hugh Despenser, to whom he was
much attached. A certain amount of the prince's correspondence
has survived,[1] to show that, even at an early stage, he was more
than a figure-head; and from the beginning his father, though
he kept his son short of money, constantly sent information
about the movements of Owain and about any decisions which
the king's council was proposing to take or had taken in cases
where the prince was concerned. Though resident at Chester
he had, as prince, general charge over Wales as a whole, and
one letter written before November 1401 shows him appointing
his own 'master' or governor, Sir Hugh Despenser, to deal
with a fresh rebellion in south Wales. The prince looked well
to the care and advancement of his own staff when they were ill
or required promotion. A number of letters refer to the prince's
requests for benefices on behalf of his household. One, as we
saw, addressed to an abbot asked that his clerk, Master William

[1] Printed in M. D. Legge, *Anglo-Norman Letters and Petitions*, pp. 280 f.

de Ferriby, might have the attentions of an inmate of the abbey who was expert in curing rheumatism. He was in close touch with his father, sending him letters on which he sought advice, or dispatching councillors to bear news from north Wales.[1] Early in his time he experienced the difficulty felt by all responsible officials of the crown in obtaining ready money for defence purposes, for although in 1402 the king had assigned him the sum of £1,000 *en eide de noz custages*, by the late summer he had only received £200 of it, and he asks the official to whom he is writing (possibly the chamberlain of the Receipt) to let the bearer have any ready money that is about. He may have found a more ready ear in Archbishop Arundel to whom he wrote a series of letters from 1403–5. He was sustaining with wages of war 'all the men of our household' (*tous noz gens meignalx*)[2] employed in safeguarding Herefordshire and the March, and lack of means to pay them was causing desertions among them. Would Arundel approach Henry and his council and put the case to them? In June 1404 he wrote to Arundel asking him to make representations with the king on his behalf. The king had ordered him to Worcester, but there was no indenture or other document binding him to undertake the governance of Wales; nevertheless he had gone, but so far received nothing for this, and even had been obliged to pawn his plate to get there. He approached Arundel as one of those 'nearest to our blood', one who had, as he thankfully recognized, 'such great tenderness to our estate as no other man has'.[3]

By the time that the prince returned to Westminster, Aberystwyth being securely in English hands again, he had learned something about garrisons left in semi-hostile territory and about victualling and maintaining outposts such as these. He had been able to judge of the inadequacy in Wales of short campaigns in force, fought with troops who, although salaried, were anxious to get home; he had learned the value of speed, and the importance of good supplies and had acquired some knowledge of siege-craft. By 1408 he had taken part in practically every important engagement; in 1406 he had been given command over the whole Welsh front, north and south Wales and the Marches, with power to receive and pardon all rebels, and

---

[1] M. D. Legge, *Anglo-Norman Letters and Petitions*, pp. 305, 311.
[2] From *mesnée*.
[3] *Anglo-Norman Letters*, pp. 356–6, 359–60.

his new command had brought him into touch with the best soldiers of his day, leaders like the earl of Warwick and Edward duke of York, military families like the Talbots and the Stanleys, and with the knights on whom he had to rely for the administration and defence of the Marcher counties: men like the Oldcastles of Almeley, Sir Richard, his brother Thomas, sheriff of Hereford in 1407 (as his father had been), who had been present with the prince at the siege of Aberystwyth, and his son, the notable Sir John, captain of Builth and administrator of other castles, now, through his marriage with Joan, the Cobham heiress, Lord Cobham and owner of Cooling Castle in Kent: Roger and John of Beckford; Sir Roger Acton, in 1403 squire of the household, an annuitant of Richard II: Sir Thomas Clanvowe, Sir John Greindor, and others who had come under the influence of Herefordshire Lollardy. The prince, as his action at the Badby trial was to show, was entirely orthodox; but defence against the rebels was the paramount need, so that even when John Oldcastle had convicted himself before convocation and should have been handed over to the secular arm for burning, the king (as he was then) 'had compassion on the knighthood of the said apostate': he remembered what Oldcastle had done and the place of the *miles* in the State.

Closer to the prince, because in high position, were the three sons of Catherine Swinford and John of Gaunt, born while their mother was in the castle of Beaufort near Angers, John, Henry, and Thomas Beaufort. John, who declined the offer made in parliament to restore him to the marquisate of Dorset which he had lost on Henry's accession, was earl of Somerset, and became chamberlain of England as well as captain of Calais, but died on 16 March 1410. Henry, the future cardinal who became bishop of Winchester in 1404, is reported by John Rous to have been chancellor of Oxford at the time when the prince was at Queen's College, and acted as his guardian. He was elected chancellor of Oxford in 1397,[1] the year when the Beauforts were legitimized. As a rich young *commensalis* (he was liberally endowed with prebends), Beaufort had rented rooms at Queen's in 1393–4[2] and appears to have resided after that date, when he had taken his Master's degree and was reading theology. He had resigned the chancellorship by July 1398

---

[1] A. B. Emden, *A Biographical Register of the University of Oxford* (1957–9), i. 140.
[2] *Vict. County Hist.* Oxon., iii. 133, n. 19.

when he was consecrated bishop of Lincoln. It is possible that both uncle and nephew were members of the same college, so that, if Rous is right, Henry must have been ten to eleven years old in 1397–8, probably studying grammar as a preliminary to the arts course. The tutelage did not last long, but the impression Beaufort made must have been lasting; he was with the prince on Richard II's expedition to Ireland in June 1399, but on his return gave his allegiance to Henry Bolingbroke, and in 1402 was made a member of the council. As bishop of Winchester (in 1404) he moved quickly to the centre of English diplomacy, and was to become the chief financial prop of the Lancastrian dynasty, with his wool exports and the manors of the bishopric as the basis of a vast, income. In character and judgement the third Beaufort, Thomas, was perhaps the best of the three: less brilliant and far-scheming than the bishop, he could carry great responsibility without self-seeking as (in this reign) admiral of the north and west, of Ireland, Aquitaine, and Picardy, commander of Calais, and for a period chancellor of England. He was one of those who understood the problems of naval defence and had a general appreciation of the importance of overseas possessions and of the need to retain Gascony.

On 28 February 1409 the prince was appointed constable of Dover and warden of the Cinque Ports. When John Beaufort died (1410) he took over the captaincy of Calais, with Sir Thomas Pickworth as his lieutenant and effective governor, though this fact did not absolve him from final responsibility as can be seen in the charge of misappropriation of the wages of the garrison brought against him in 1412. The captain was responsible for large sums. For two years up to 29 March 1412 the detailed accounts of Robert Thorley, the treasurer of Calais, are extant, to show that in the first year he received £1,000 from the Exchequer, £11,000 from the collectors of the customs in England, and £1,100 of local receipts from Calais (£13,100). One of his predecessors, Nicholas Usk, from 1399 to 1403 disbursed £46,000 on the wages of the garrison; from the Exchequer he received £18,000, from collectors of customs £29,000, and from local receipts in Calais £4,400, a total of about £52,000 for four years. But he had many other expenses than wages, and when the account was closed he still owed £12,000 to various captains (e.g. the captain of Marck) and part of the debt was still owing when Roger Salvayn took over in July 1413. The maintenance of the great fortress, the wages and victualling of the garrison, the harbour works that continually needed keeping in order, and the soldiery in the defensive posts and castles in the March, was an expensive business. To assume control must have cost the prince some resolution, but his acceptance was evidently part of a general reconstruction of defence and responsibility for which he and Beaufort were mainly responsible.

At the end of December 1409 Archbishop Arundel resigned the chancellorship, and for a month nobody was appointed to take his place. Tension had been growing in the council for some time previously between Arundel and his critics. When the legitimation of the Beauforts was confirmed by Henry IV on 10 February 1407, a clause (*excepta dignitate regali*) was inserted excluding them from all claim to the crown, and this, in the view of Stubbs,[1] was a victory for Arundel over Beaufort, indicating at least one cause of friction. It seems doubtful whether the Beauforts could have ever expected to be in the succession: there are indications of another sort, independent action by the prince supported by other lords in the council both in 1408 and 1409, and of an understanding with the Beauforts against Arundel and Henry's brother Thomas. The prince's petition had support in the commons. The parliament which met in January 1410, in which there was much anti-clericalism, framed a series of articles presented in the interests of 'good and substantial government', the first of which requested the king 'to ordain and assign in the present parliament the most valiant, wise and discreet lords of the realm to be of his Council', who were to be publicly sworn along with the judges. When the king answered this, he stated that certain lords whom he had selected had excused themselves for adequate reasons. These may have been the archbishop and his friends.[2] At any rate the new council, when nominated, was small and aristocratic, and omitted the knights and esquires of previous selections. It was composed of Bishop Beaufort of Winchester, Langley of Durham, and Bubwith of Bath and Wells: the earls of Arundel and Westmorland and Lord Burnell. The professional element was the new chancellor, Sir Thomas Beaufort when appointed, Lord Scrope of Masham, treasurer, and John Prophet, keeper of the privy seal. Langley and Ralph Neville were soon found to be

[1] *Const. Hist.*, iii. 59.
[2] J. F. Baldwin, *The King's Council* (1913), p. 162.

needed in the north, and in their place came Henry Chichele, bishop of St. David's, and Richard Beauchamp, earl of Warwick. The new council accepted office and gave their oath to govern in accordance with the articles on condition that sufficient supplies were made available to the government: but in the end all, the prince excepted 'because of the highness and excellence of his honourable person', gave way and swore unconditionally.

The question of adequate supply was vital because the prince and his friends were determined upon a more active policy towards English possessions abroad. The essential point in English commerce with Europe north of the hinterland of Bordeaux and the Mediterranean region was the town of Calais. Calais, conquered in 1347, peopled with English, defended by an English commander, was a small portion of England overseas. Ecclesiastically it was part of the diocese of Canterbury. It had the staple of wool, leather, skins, lead, and tin. By the treaty of Brétigny, Calais, along with its March, consisted of the seignories of Marck, Oye, Sangatte, Wissant, Hervelinghem, Hammes, and the country of Guînes, and was incorporated into the English crown with absolute sovereignty. The garrison of Calais under its lieutenant was, as the figures given above show, a major charge upon English revenue and the remarkable thing in its history is the extraordinary length of time during which the garrisons seemed able to subsist without mutiny upon little or no wages at all. Calais was to be the centre of the merchants of the staple exporting wool to the Low Countries. To hold it and control the narrows was a cardinal point of English policy. It is, therefore, understandable that the dukes of Burgundy regarded it enviously and, as will be seen, John the Fearless made a determined attempt to secure possession. Alongside of English Calais must be placed in importance English Bordeaux, the indispensable port and capital of Gascony. It need only be remembered that it was in the main over the possession of Gascony that the Hundred Years War began. Bordeaux was the heart of the wine trade which in the thirteenth and first half of the fourteenth century had absorbed a very large proportion of English shipping, though wine was also part of native and Italian cargoes. As the result of the Hundred Years War English imports of wine had fallen substantially and much was going elsewhere, but Bordeaux was still the place most loyal to

England and the maintenance of English rule there was a necessity in the municipality. It was better to be governed by the representatives of a far-distant suzerain than by the bailiffs and agents of the nearer French king. Gascony was not only Bordeaux, it was the lordships of the Dordogne, the Garonne, the Landes, and the Pyrenees, and it was the policy of Charles V and his successors to buy, or otherwise detach, the great families to their side and to employ fighting companies to recover these regions. The families of d'Albret, Armagnac, Foix, military leaders like Captal de Buch, La Hire, Poton de Xaintrailles provided a sort of *condottiere* element wooed by both sides. Round Bordeaux and among the Bastides originally built by Edward I, the line of possession fluctuated from year to year. The English possessions had originally included Poitiers, Saintes and the country of the Charente. But in the course of the fourteenth century, even after the treaty of Bretigny, but especially during the reign of Charles V, territories were won by the French king, and the local families, particularly the family of d'Albret, from supporting the English side, came over to the French. Not a little was done by compacts concluded between Bordeaux and its neighbouring towns to resist French penetration. The support of Gaston Phoebus of Foix secured by the duke of Burgundy in 1389 was an important attachment of a great ally. And even when the French king was nominally at truce with the English, the process of attrition and infiltration through financial assistance given to towns that had suffered from the war went on. Among the archives of the Dordogne there is a letter of remission and exemption granted by Charles VI to the town of Sarlat, describing its situation, standing on the frontier, close to eight enemy fortresses. Though faithful to the defender of the French crown, Sarlat had been, in spite of truces, constantly ravaged by troops, and the inhabitants against their will had been obliged to traffic with the English.[1]

It is impossible at any one time to make a clear map of English and French spheres of influence. But in 1393, before Richard II had concluded his long truce with the French, the French were prepared, in return for a clear promise of homage by the English king to the French crown, to offer besides Bordeaux and the Bordelais, Bazas, Dax, Bayonne, and farther

[1] Republique Française, Archives Departmentales, dép. Dordogne, IV. E., Sarlat.

north, the Agenais, Périgord, Bigorre, Saintonge with the Charente, Quercy without Montauban, along with considerable money payments. This shows the classic areas of English domination at the end of the fourteenth century: the Agenais, Périgord, and Saintonge were not then in English hands. Roughly speaking English Gascony ran from the Gironde past Blaye and Bourg, through Libourne, Saint Emilion, as far as Bergerac, and included the area called *entre deux mers* in the north, and in the south extended as far as Bayonne, with its main centres at Dax and Tartas. It was a country, as M. Boutruche has pointed out, of lords, burgesses, and peasants. The burgesses on the whole were faithful to England, the lords swung between the two powers, and the peasants, with extraordinary tenacity and resilience, had to adjust themselves to their changing masters, but did so with a steady power of acquiring lands and territories, acting as a cushion, so to speak, between war-battered Gascony and the demands, when they came, of Charles V.

The government of France was in the hands of an administration which did not know when the king would be in his senses and when not. Control of policy was in the hands of the royal dukes, Burgundy, Berri, Bourbon, or Orléans, with the latter increasingly in the ascendant until he was murdered in 1407. It was not a businesslike government and there were rifts within its policy. Orléans, allied with the Visconti, was essentially an adventurer, who looked to the south. He was detested by the people of Paris, who put their faith in the duke of Burgundy. When the king was sick the duke of Burgundy usually had the upper hand. Burgundy at first possessed far greater resources of his own and he managed to draw repeatedly and extensively upon the treasury. But in these operations he was excelled by Orléans, who in the opening years of the fifteenth century derived large sums from the *aides*, while he also received from his royal brother enfeoffments giving him territory in France which in extent approached that of Philip of Burgundy. In 1404 Philip the Bold of Burgundy died. Orléans had himself made lieutenant and captain-general of Normandy and Picardy and secured the betrothal of the Princess Isabel, widow of Richard II, to his son Charles. The new duke of Burgundy proved an even more determined opponent of Orléans. It was in an atmosphere of growing tension within the French council that most of the negotiations with England were conducted.

They fall roughly into two divisions, separated by the deliberate murder of the duke of Orléans in 1407. The first period is governed by the truce made between Richard II and Charles VI in 1396. In that year Isabel of France was both betrothed and married to Richard II, and a truce of thirty years agreed between the two countries. But the death of Richard II, and Henry IV's determination to retain Isabel and marry her to the young prince, led to embittered relations, and even when Isabel had been restored, a state of hostility existed between the two countries. Henry IV was anxious to secure a marriage treaty with the French king. But he was determined to negotiate from a vantage-ground of strength, which could not for the moment be secured. His own Gascon subjects realized this. The French seneschal of Guienne, Archambaud de Grailly, Captal de Buch, under the blandishments of the constable d'Albret, deserted the English side, but the town of Bordeaux itself, with the help of the Archbishop Uguccione and the mayor, held firm, and in August 1401 the earl of Rutland was nominated as the king's lieutenant, and with Gaillard de Durfort as seneschal the position began to be restored.

Between 1403 and 1405 the French policy was to encircle Gascony, Charles d'Albret operating against the border fortresses in the north of the Bordelais, Périgord, and Saintonge, Armagnac trying to secure the English enclaves in the Agenais and the Bordelais itself (e.g. Langon)[1] and the count of Clermont fighting between the Dordogne and the Dropt. The main attack was against Blaye and Bourg, by sea and land, but the home government scarcely appreciated the danger, and Archbishop Uguccione of Bordeaux had to tell Henry (30 June 1406) that 'nous sumes en perilh de perdition'; and in October he complained to Henry of being abandoned, while only three days afterwards a herald of the duke of Orléans presented an ultimatum to Libourne and St. Emilion. With Henry deaf to all appeals, Bordeaux had to act on its own, and raise forces and requisition ships. The improvised fleet prevailed over the French vessels and Orléans had to raise the siege of Bourg. But if Bordeaux took the initiative, she had to bear the expense and make the Gascons share it. Defence in the interest of herself and of England meant an economic struggle: the remarkable thing is

[1] On which cf. the note (2) of R. Boutruche, *La Crise d'une société* (1947), p. 220.

that the *jurade*, for all the rebuffs suffered from an English council beset with demands from many quarters, was prepared for the effort of taxation necessary to maintain the English régime. Nor was Bordeaux alone in its English sympathies: Bergerac, though in French hands, petitioned Henry IV to be taken back into protection for a year, and four years' protection was granted to both it and to Maureux. Libourne, though a quarter of it was occupied by enemy forces, went to the assistance of Fronsac in March 1408, very nearly captured from its small garrison, and brought in supplies provided by a London merchant, John Arnold. Not till 1409 did assistance from the English council reach that important castle, when Thomas Swinburn, mayor of Bordeaux, was sent from England to Fronsac with £1,000 in cash for the pay of the garrison.

Yet in spite of this reluctance to take active measures in Aquitaine, there was much pro-Gascon sentiment in England, not least in the ports, and in the city of London connexions between the two countries were far-reaching. There were numerous business contacts, particularly between Bordeaux and Bristol. The English king as duke had a well-organized administration in Gascony, in which nationals of both countries took part; English soldiers and English officials took their share in the defence of Bordeaux and of the Bastides; and there were English feudatories holding land and performing military service. In Richard II's reign the English esquire, John de Stratton, who married Isabel of St. Symphorien, lady of Landivas, received lands and rents in the Bordelais to which the king added; the Speaker, John Tiptoft became through his wife a great seigneur in the Landes before Henry IV gave him possessions on the Garonne; and there were a number of Gascons and Englishmen holding lands in both countries.[1] Not only rich English merchants but English tradesmen and artisans had settled in Gascony, and the total is considerable.[2]

The question that faced the council when the prince came back to Westminster was not exactly new. It was how to make an agreement with France that would guarantee to the English as much as possible of the lands and rights assured them in the treaty of Brétigny which in its first form awarded Calais and Ponthieu and the duchy of Aquitaine (not merely Gascony) to the English king, on condition of his renouncing the claim to the

---

[1] R. Boutruche, *La Crise d'une société*, pp. 129–35.   [2] Ibid., p. 135 and nn.

French throne. The French had fully revealed their hand in 1405, when they took part in the rebellion of Glyn Dŵr. None the less overtures began in 1406 for the marriage of Prince Henry with a daughter of the French king and for a settlement, more stable than the truce, which should vindicate the English king's absolute right to the territories which he claimed to hold in Aquitaine. From 1407 onwards marriage was in the forefront of the English requests and the dowry demanded of the lady is adjusted to the facts of the political situation. So far the English had acted as petitioners; but after 1407, when strife between the duke of Burgundy and what had now become the Armagnac party reached its height, England was approached by both sides and her help solicited in the new civil war. In July 1411 Duke John the Fearless opened negotiations to secure English aid in resisting the dukes of Orléans and Berry. He professed himself ready to hand over four Flemish towns—Gravelines, Dunkirk, Dixmuiden, and Sluys—and to help the English reconquer Normandy. He also proposed the marriage of his daughter Anne to the prince of Wales. He made no mention of English claims to Aquitaine under the treaty of Brétigny; nor was there a clear statement (this point was to come up again in 1416) whether the duke was prepared to go to war against his own sovereign, should Charles VI become associated with the combination of Orléans–Bourbon–Berry–Armagnac. The English embassy that met John the Fearless at Arras[1] asked him this and whether he would help the English in the reconquest of Aquitaine. John was too cautious to answer. But the English council thought it had enough to go upon. It was decided to send 800 lances and 2,000 archers under the command of Arundel to join the duke of Burgundy at Arras on 2 October 1411, and the allied force, marching by Peronne, Roye, Beauvais, and Pontoise crossed the Seine at Meulan, where it was met by 3,000 Parisians with Burgundian devices, to enter Paris on 22 October: the object of the march was to disperse the Armagnac forces which at St. Denis and St. Cloud were cutting the supply lines of the city. The English forces then helped the Burgundians to recover Étampes and Daudan, before retiring to Calais. John the Fearless followed this up by an embassy to discuss with the council the dispatch of a larger force next year. But before any conclusion

---

[1] *Foedera*, iv. i. 196. The embassy consisted of Bishop Henry Chichele, Thomas earl of Arundel, Francis Court, Hugh Mortimer, and John Catterick.

was reached on this point, Berry, Orléans, and Bourbon had made an offer, supported in the south by Armagnac and Charles d'Albret. The embassy was in England from 1 February till 4 March 1412.

By the latter date the prince had ceased to preside over the council. On 11 November the king had replaced him by his brother Thomas, and Arundel had succeeded to the chancellorship. The change was the result of Henry's sharp reaction to the manœuvres of the prince and the Beauforts. When the Burgundian alliance was accepted, Henry had decided to lead the expedition in person. In August 1411 it was proclaimed that he was going over to Calais to prevent the invasion of the March by the French and the council made preparations for the strengthening of the fortress, calling upon the Cinque Ports for their service of fifty-seven ships which had to be at London by 23 September. Everything was ready when Henry decided not to go. He was not well enough, but he may also have seen that he would be required to move farther than the Calais March, and to undertake the campaign that was to bring the English contingent to Paris and its neighbourhood. It was at this point that Bishop Beaufort suggested that he should abdicate in favour of his son and Henry indignantly refused. He was not at the opening of the November parliament, but he was determined to have no pressure put upon him to resign the crown and declared to Thomas Chaucer that he would have no 'novelleries' in this parliament. The prince must go, and the councillors of his group with him. On 30 November the prince, Bishop Beaufort, Langley and Bubwith and Chichele, the earls of Arundel, Warwick, and Westmorland were thanked for their services before the termination of parliament. On 19 December 1411 Thomas Beaufort gave place to Archbishop Arundel as chancellor: three days before Henry Lord Scrope ceded to Sir John Pelham as treasurer. It had all been done quietly and, in public at least, without recrimination. But the change in the council must have reflected divided views on the attitude to be adopted to the contending parties in France, even if no Armagnac embassy had arrived when the matter was discussed in the council. Was the attack to be made north of Paris or south of Loire?

The autumn parliament had added to the second half of the convocation tenth (one to be collected from midsummer to Michaelmas 1411) the subsidy on wool, three-quarters of which was due for the protection of Calais, and a tax of 6s. 8d. on every £20 of annual income from lands or rents which was to be at the royal disposal. The second part of the lay fifteenth and tenth, due on 11 November, raised the total which could now be used, if it was required for the postponed expedition. Arundel and the traditionalists were for re-establishing the English position in Aquitaine and seizing any opportunity to make effective the settlement projected, but never carried into effect, by the treaty of Bretigny. The Armagnac offer, when it came, gave them the chance, for John the Fearless had made any resumption of the Anglo-Burgundian co-operation impossible by announcing the fact that Charles VI had entrusted him with the task of expelling the English from Aquitaine. The offer, conveyed by the embassy, was agreed to at Bourges. The French magnates, Walsingham says, undertook to assist Henry, to co-operate in the recovery of Aquitaine which belonged to him by hereditary right, and to put at his disposal their sons, daughters, nephews, and nieces for Englishmen to marry, as well as their castles, manors, furniture, and treasure and those belonging to their friends and helpers among the clergy, merchants, and the bourgeoisie generally;[1] to restore all Aquitaine that had been lost to him since 1300; to do homage to him for the properties, strong towns, and *seigneuries* they held; to hand over to him twenty fortresses in the south, including Bazas, Saint-Foy, Saint-Macaire, La Réole, occupied by French troops. For Poitou the duke of Berry was to do homage to the king of England, who was to invest him, but on the duke's death the county was to revert to England: and similarly with Périgueux in the care of Charles of Orléans, while the count of Armagnac was to do homage for four castelries. As security, Henry IV was to occupy Poitievs, Niort, and Lusignan and Chateauneuf on the Charente in Angoulême. In exchange for this Henry IV was to defend the princes against the duke of Burgundy and was not to treat with him without their consent. He was to indemnify them for all damage caused by the Burgundians, and to send to France a force of 1,000 lances and 3,000 archers. The agreement of Bourges was guaranteed at Westminster by representatives of the princes and by the king's four sons Henry, Thomas, John, and Humphrey in the presence of their father. The attendance of the prince of Wales is to be noted, for in 1415 he was to make

---

[1] *The St. Albans Chronicle*, pp. 63–64.

good propaganda out of the undertakings of the Armagnac leaders.

This singular document, which Walsingham cheerfully reproduces at length, became known through a piece of carelessness on the part of Berry's proctor, to Charles VI. Either the original itself or a copy was read to the king on 6 April 1412, and provided John the Fearless with an excellent opportunity for an outburst of moral indignation and a good excuse for marching against the French lords. Having taken the *oriflamme*[1] at St. Denis he moved with Charles VI to La Charité-sur-Loire, to besiege Bourges. This could not in fact be taken, but from Sancergues on the Loire Charles sent his orders to Berry, revealing that the conspiracy had been discovered and calling upon him and his colleagues to revoke the alliance. On 22 July Berry, Orléans, Bourbon, the constable d'Albret, and to crown all the duke of Burgundy renounced their accord with England. There followed a series of touching but insincere reconciliations. These moves were not known in London, where the English expedition was preparing under the command of Thomas, now promoted earl of Albemarle[2] and duke of Clarence. A notable force was being equipped, to include besides Clarence the duke of York with 260 men and 800 archers, Thomas Beaufort (240 and 700), the earls of Ormonde (James Butler), Oxford (Richard de Vere) and Salisbury (Thomas Montague), and Sir John Cornwall with 90 lances and 270 archers: all bound to five months' service, the knights paid at 2s. a day, the esquires 1s. 6d., and the archers 9d. for the first two months, and afterwards 'according to what the lords of France should pay'.[3] The force landed, captured Chateauneuf, St. Rémy, and Bellême, passed through Anjou to the neighbourhood of Blois, where the duke of Clarence wrote to the French dukes declining to accept their volte-face. Then, as no pay was forthcoming from the French side, Clarence entered the duchy of Orléans, captured Meung, and having crossed the Loire, marched through Sologne to the valley of the Indre. By this time the French dukes were anxious to buy the English out, and arranged to pay them 150,000 crowns, 100,000 to be forthcoming on 30 November 1412, and the rest at Christmas.

---

[1] The sacred banner of St. Denis.

[2] Owing, as Wylie points out (iv. 75), to his possessions in Holderness, the lordship of which was always associated with the Honour of Albemarle.

[3] Wylie, op. cit.

Ready money was, however, not forthcoming and an agreement was made by which the total payable by the French was raised to 210,000 crowns but that 75,000 were to be found immediately, and seven hostages, including the young count of Angoulême, were given for the balance. The English captains made their claims: Sir John Cornwall, 21,375 crowns, shortly paid entire; the duke of York demanded 36,170 crowns and received 5,430 with a large gold cross of Damascus work, valued at 40,000, as pledge for the remainder.[1] The duke of Clarence asked for 120,000 crowns, of which he received about 40,000 together with a gold crucifix (15,000 crowns) with three large diamonds in the hands and feet and a ruby in the wounded side. This and other treasures came from the duke of Berry's private chapel at Bourges; its great glory was its large gold cross, both a valuable object and a reliquary (it had one of the nails with which Christ was fixed to the Cross), which was handed to Clarence, who passed on into Gascony to winter at Bordeaux: he was prepared to fight for the recovery of English territory, but met with resistance from Armagnac, and on his father's death returned to England.

The prince of Wales was not with the expedition, otherwise he would have commanded it. Walsingham says that he was unpopular with the king's *familiares* 'who as it is said sowed trouble between the father and son'; so, in order to refute the schemes of his detractors, he sent an open letter to all parts of the kingdom, stating that he had been bidden to go with the king's army 'for the recovery of his duchy of Aquitaine', but had only been allowed to take a force so small that it could not provide for the safety either of his parent or himself. He had therefore asked permission to hold a conference with his kinsmen and friends in order to find means of increasing the number and had gone to Coventry to do so; but that this had made the sowers of discord even more active, to the extent of spreading a rumour that he was trying to seize the throne; and further that he was doing his best to impede the expedition to Aquitaine. He protested his love and respect and filial obedience to his father and repudiated any such suggestion. The letter was written 'under our signet in our city of Coventry, 17 June (1412)'.[2] Walsingham goes on to relate that the prince sought an interview with his father in

---

[1] Wylie, iv. 83, who gives details of the jewels.
[2] *The St. Albans Chronicle*, pp. 65–67.

which he again protested his loyalty and asked 'this one thing' that his detractors should be properly punished after their false-hood had been discovered. The king 'appeared to agree', but told the prince to wait for the summoning of parliament when *hi tales* could be punished by the judgement of their peers. The chronicler would probably have heard this from his abbot.

There seems no reason to doubt Walsingham's story of a slanderous campaign against the prince. He had fallen out with his brother Thomas, and the *judicium parium* referred to suggests that members of the lords were hostile. The story of the crown-wearing which occurs in Shakespeare's *Henry IV Part II*, where in the presence of his dying father the prince tries on the crown, is an invention of Monstrelet from whom it passed to Holinshed and so to Hall. But the anonymous translator of the *Latin Life of Henry V* by Titus Livius, a man responsible for inserting a number of stories which he heard from his patron, the seventh earl of Ormonde (they may have been inherited from James Butler, the fourth earl), has noted of the prince 'the greate recourse of the people unto him, of whom his courte was at all times more abundant than the Kinge his father's', and speaks of the sinister suspicions roused in Henry IV's mind by those who drew attention to the comparison. The suggestion made to the king by Beaufort and the princes in 1411 had not been lost on the royal household. The translator does not fail to colour Walsingham's tale of Henry's visit to his father by making the prince disguise himself, secure entry to his father's room, and presenting him with a dagger request the king to kill him if he was suspected of treachery.[1] Which is the more likely version of the facts it does not take much imagination to discover. The prince was loyal, but evidently he had stolen his father's thunder.

After 19 September 1412 when he was at Canterbury—Arundel was a good friend and the king was there for a number of days in his last year—Henry did not go far from the London area. A certain amount of time was spent at Merton Priory, and he kept Christmas at Eltham. In the New Year he was twice at Lambeth, then went down the river to Greenwich, where the air was better. Thence he paid his visits to the February parlia-ment, but he collapsed and finally died (20 Mar.) before the assembly was over. He was buried at Canterbury behind the high altar of the north side of St. Thomas's shrine. The effigy

[1] *The First English Life of Henry the Fifth*, ed. C. L. Kingsford (1911), pp. 11–13.

with its forked beard is fine, but conventional. Henry was not an old man, but his constitution was played out. Walsingham is one of the few chroniclers to give him a word of praise, and that a true one. He had reigned 'gloriously': supported, one may add, through the worst times by the officers of his duchy, now the confirmed upholders of his dynasty. But for that great administrative training-ground and his own magnificent endurance, Henry might have been buried as duke, not as king.

APPENDIX TO CHAPTER III

Lay and Clerical Taxation, Henry IV (Cal. Fine Rolls, 1399–1405, 1405–1413)

Regnal year of collection (Fine Roll)	Lay grant, with date (P = parliament)	Clerical grant, with date	Subsidy on wool, woolfells, &c., tunnage and poundage	Special features L = Lay C = Clerical
2 Henry IV	P. 1401, Jan. 1/10, 1/15	1401, Jan. 1/10. Cant. Conv. 1/10. York Conv.		L. ½ Trinity, ½ All Saints 1401. 8–9 collectors in each county interviewing 2 men and reeve from each township, 4 men from every city and borough
3 Henry IV	20s. Aid *pur fille marier* (Princess Blanche)			
4 Henry IV	P. 1402, Sept. 1/10, 1/15	1402, Oct. 1½/10. Cant. Conv. 2s. on every 20s. on every benefice or office ecclesiastical unassessed over 100s. a year	Subsidy on wool, woolfells, cloths, &c., for 3 years. Customs on wine, 2s. on every tun, 8d. in pound on other wares. Tunnage and poundage granted for 2½ years	
5 Henry IV	P. 1404, Mar. 20s. on every knight's fee; 12d. on every 20s. annual value of land not held by military tenure; or 12d. for every £20 of personal property. King to have £12,000			L. That the commissioners are to levy the subsidy in each shire with 2 controllers associated with them. To be appointed by king and council from persons who did not come

Lay and Clerical Taxation, Henry IV (contd.)

Regnal year of collection (Fine Roll)	Lay grant, with date (P = parliament)	Clerical grant, with date	Subsidy on wool, woolfells, &c., tunnage and poundage	Special features L = Lay C = Clerical
	to recompense him for Shrewsbury campaign and other labours; rest to go to treasurers who are not knights nor burgesses at this parliament			by writ and election to that parliament
6 Henry IV	P. 1404, Oct., Coventry. 2/10, 2/15. A lay subsidy of 20s. on every £20 of land of 500 marks a year and over. One year's proceeds of any royal grant by Richard II or Henry IV to be surrendered to Exchequer	1404, 24–28 Nov. 1½/10. Conv. Cant. *N.B.* Abbot of St. Albans is collector for the exempt jurisdiction of St. Albans: grant from stipendiary clergy demanded by Henry but refused	Custom on wine increased: 3s. on every tun, and 12d. in £1 for all wares for import and export	L. 1/10 at Christmas next (1404); ½/10 at Midsummer, 1405; ½/10 at Martinmas 1405. Great difficulty found in securing the second half tenth. K. has to get advances from 'certain of the richest and most sufficient lay persons', the money to be at Exchequer by 26 Sept.
7 Henry IV	P. (Long Parlt.) 1406, Mar.–Dec. with adjournments. (i) 20s. on each knight's fee; 20s. on every £20 of land, held immediately in socage in Cumberland; *pur fille marier*	1/10 Cant. Conv. 6s. 8d. from beneficed persons, (i.e. chaplains, stipendiaries serving cures) unaccustomed to pay 10th	Custom and subsidy granted. 1 year	C. The 1/10 and the 6s. 8d. to be allotted entirely to defence. This grant not to be a precedent
8 Henry IV	(ii) 1406, Dec. 1/10, 1/15			

Lay and Clerical Taxation, Henry IV (contd.)

Regnal year of collection (Fine Roll)	Lay grant, with date (P = parliament)	Clerical grant, with date	Subsidy on wool, woolfells, &c., tunnage and poundage	Special features L = Lay C = Clerical
9 Henry IV	P. 1407. Oct. Gloucester. 1½/10, 1½/15.	28 Nov. 1407. St. Frideswide's Oxon. 1½/10 Conv. Cant.	Subsidy on wool and customs for 2 years	
10 Henry IV		1/10 from Conv. York. Collected, Dec. 1408		C. Exceptions: all dignities, prebends, offices in St. Peter's Minster, York, because of work on the fabric: monasteries of Selby, Watton, Ellerton, Cockersand, Holmcultram, Ferriby, Madersay, Rufford, Felby, Eglinton
11 Henry IV	P. 1410. Jan. 1½/10. 1½/15	1410, 17 Feb. St. Paul's. 1½/10, Conv. Cant.		
12 Henry IV		1411, 23 May. 1/10 Conv. York		C. No royal writ for collection
13 Henry IV	P. 1411, Nov. 6s. 8d. on every £20 worth of land or rent in lay hands	1411, 21 Dec. ½/10, Conv. Cant.; 1412, 20 Jan. ½/10 Conv. York	Subsidy, tunnage, and poundage	L. No record of collector. Grant in Rot. Parl. iii. 671; cf. Stubbs, iii. 69

The subsidy (col. 4) consisted of (i) the *nova custuma* granted to Edward I; (ii) the customs and subsidy on wools, hide, and woolfells: 50s. on each sack of wool from denizens, 60s. from aliens; woolfells, figures on every 240 woolfells. On each last of hides, 100s. from denizens, £6 from aliens or 8 marks. On cloths, wool, or worsted: on every cloth of assize, 14d. from denizens, 21d. from aliens; on every cloth of scarlet or other cloth of whole grain, 2s. 4d. from denizens, 3s. 6d. from aliens. For cloth of half grain, half these figures.

CHAPTER IV

HENRY V: 1413–1417

THE reign of Henry V has sometimes been depicted as an interlude, a sort of Indian summer between two troubled periods, 1399–1413 and the minority of Henry VI. This view needs much qualification: it is true that after 1415 the crown had no immediate peril or fear from within and that instead of warding off danger as it did in Henry IV's time, both in the Welsh Marches and in the north, it was now able to take the initiative and lead the nobility and the country gentry on foreign expeditions of its own choice. It is also true that there was a greater co-ordination of effort which made itself felt both in parliament and in the administration: taxes were collected with reasonable promptitude and large sums of money were extracted both in subsidies and in loans that were repaid. But Henry V's policy in France was based on anticipations that could scarcely be realized; difficulties both fiscal and political deepened the moment that the treaty of Troyes had come into being, while the maintenance of the dual kingdom at which Henry V aimed was to strain the country and in the end to bring about a deterioration of English finances as well as the loss of the Burgundian alliance. The efforts of the crown to secure unity on the basis of aristocratic leadership with the compliance of leading churchmen were only temporarily successful, depending as they did upon the personality and continued life of a single man. None the less it can be said that for several years England played a leading part in European politics, and that this lead was not due simply to military victories or to a successful role in the general council of Constance, but to the coherence of the upper and middle ranks of society under the determined direction of the monarchy.

Henry himself made so powerful an impression that for modern minds he is one of the most difficult historical figures to evaluate. He cannot be accepted as the biographers after his death accepted him; nor should he be made the target of cynical attacks on medieval English nationalism. His position, in the verdict of historians, has been powerfully influenced by Tudor historiography. Even during his lifetime he was the subject of numerous stories, for a royal commander who showed himself so frequently to his troops and interested himself so much in routine and the work of his chapel in the field, was an obvious subject for legend and, indeed, for poetry. Ballad literature and poems like that of John Page on the siege of Rouen grew around him, and after his death the saga multiplied. The posthumous Henry, the medieval hero-king, must obviously be distinguished from the Henry of strictly contemporary record. If it is the biographies which were mainly responsible for the legend in its usual forms, one at least gives a convincing contemporary picture. The *Gesta Henrici Quinti*, from 1413 to the autumn of 1416, was written by a clerk, clearly a priest in the king's chapel, who has been identified, but not on very convincing grounds, with Thomas Elmham, the Cluniac prior of Lenton; largely because of the similarity between the *Gesta* and the authentic Thomas Elmham's *Liber Metricus*, the Latin poem written by the prior with the double intention of showing how Henry triumphed over the duplicity of the French and over the rising of the Lollard, Sir John Oldcastle. It has been said that the *Liber Metricus* would rank high as a source for Henry V's reign did it not duplicate much of the material in the *Gesta*: but medieval literary propriety being what it was, there is no reason why the *Liber Metricus* should not have been written from the *Gesta* by a totally different person; and all who maintain the Elmham authorship have to face the question whether it is likely that the prior appointed (1414) to the Cluniac house of Lenton in Nottinghamshire, the man who in early autumn of that year drew up a scheme for the reformation of the English Cluniac houses and in 1415 at Henry V's request was made vicar-general and chamberlain of the Cluniac province of England and Scotland, should, at Agincourt, be sitting on his horse 'at the back of the battle' in and among the transport. The *Gesta* must be the work of a less prominent eye-witness, a clerk who appears to have been also a royal *scriptor*, with access to the records which the king carried about with him in the field, and possibly lending a hand to that section of the privy seal office which Henry took with him to France. The events this biographer witnessed cover only six months of the three and a half years of which he treats, but almost two-thirds of the narrative is devoted to them. Throughout the *Gesta* there runs the theme which is given fully in the opening words about Henry: he set himself with all devotion to achieve

those things which make for the honour of God, the extension of the Church, the freeing of his country and the tranquillity of kingdoms, and especially of the two kingdoms of England and France that they might be more coherent and united, which from long and unhappy times past had damaged each other and caused deplorable effusion of human blood.

This exactly echoes the king's aims set forth in official documents to which the writer evidently had access.[1] Henry is represented as desiring above everything else peace, but a peace with justice, implying the restitution to the crown of its inheritance and rights in France. It is emphasized that when the way of peace was denied him, the king was compelled to take up the sword. The author of the *Gesta* lays stress on the efforts of the king to secure peace by negotiation: when this fails, the *athleta Christi* makes war. Again, this is in harmony with the opening *pronuntiatio* in several parliaments of the reign.[2] It is the conception of the *Justus Rex* on which the *Gesta* lays stress, and combined with this is found the assertion that Divine Providence aided the king in his efforts to recover his inheritance. Sluys and Poitiers as well as more recent successes in France are instanced as judgements of God, the just judge, in favour of the English, and the biographer prays that the proud and stiff-necked French who prefer to submit to vengeance rather than to justice, may be turned from their obstinacy and understand this: *utinam resipiscat gens Francorum*. Thus, to take one instance out of many, Henry is represented as refusing to be dissuaded from marching his small force to Calais after the fall of Harfleur, because of his belief that victory depends not on numbers but on God. This is not merely a pious remark put into Henry's mouth by an orthodox cleric: Henry himself when prince of Wales, writing to his father to report the defeat of a superior Welsh force, stated the same thing: 'Mais il est bien voir que la victoire n'est pas en la multitude de poeple . . . mais en la puissance de Dieu.' The sentiment is by no means original. The picture given in the *Gesta* is of a profoundly orthodox king and there is little doubt that Henry was one of his own most voluble propagandists,

[1] *Foedera*, IV. ii. 107. The English ambassadors to France (March 1415) represent their master acting with these aims.
[2] *Rot. Parl.* iv. 62, 92, 106, 116.

unwearying in his belief in the justice of his claims and in God's favour. The French 'against God and against all justice' are keeping from the king what belongs to him. The conviction was almost an obsession, particularly where Normandy was concerned. Rouen, he told the starving inhabitants who met him during the siege to seek terms, was his own city: they could not bargain with the proprietor. In similar accents the author of the *Gesta* when describing the evacuation of Harfleur, 'a noble portion of his inheritance', depicts the women and children in tears at losing their 'awonted but wrongfully detained dwelling-place'. 'And so', he writes, 'by the true judgement of God they were proved to be guests (*hospites*) where they thought themselves denizens.' Henry's consciousness of superior right can be seen in the challenge he sent by Guienne Herald to the Dauphin immediately after Harfleur fell: 'de mettre toute nostre querelle en la grace de Dieu par entre nostre personne et vostre',[1] as well as in the over-riding of the advice given him not to attempt the march from Harfleur to Calais, although it is arguable that, from a military point of view, the risk was worth taking.

So far, and along such lines, Henry was shrewdly and accurately observed by his ingenuous chaplain-biographer. The legends which principally concern his disputes with his father and his wildness as prince are mainly due to two sources: the official biography by Tito Livio of Forlí and the English translation of Livio's work which Mr. C. L. Kingsford edited as 'The English Life of Henry V'. The first of these, which Hearne printed in 1716, was completed between March 1437 and the middle of 1438. Livio was a Ferrarese humanist and a servant of Humphrey, duke of Gloucester, who made him his poet and orator. He was also a playwright of some distinction.[2] The *Vita* is a commissioned biography in classical Latin based on the events given in the English or *Brut* chronicle and on material supplied by Humphrey himself. It deals mainly with the French war, giving particulars of the second expedition, from August 1417 to May 1419, and of the later campaign, which may be explained by the fact that Humphrey was the leader of the war party in England after the breach with Burgundy caused by the treaty of Arras, and was naturally anxious to magnify English war exploits. Therefore it is the official biography of Henry V,

---

[1] *Foedera*, IV. ii. 147.
[2] Cf. *T. Livii Forojuliensis opera*, ed. C. W. Previté-Orton (1932).

and, as Kingsford said, 'contributed the principal historical basis of the popular conception of the Hero'. While the events of the later stages of the war are narrated with care, Henry had become stylized in the humanist's Latin as the hero-king, and it was the *Vita* which Tudor historians knew well, though Holinshed depended on the sixteenth-century translator. Henry is now the hero, who from a wild youth, is suddenly converted into a serious king. Whereas the author of the *Gesta* simply says of Henry that he was *aetate juvenis maturitate senex* in the present account, the king now emerges 'washed in the laver of repentance and decently adorned in the garment of virtue'. The fact of a change in his manner of life was noted by Walsingham, but this may not imply past misdemeanours but simply point to a gravity induced by his new responsibilities. We have already seen that the causes of the prince's dispute with his father may have been partly due to substantial differences of view on the attitude to be adopted towards the Burgundians and the Armagnac leaders.

The English translator of Livius made his version in 1513, but into his translation he inserted material from various sources, mostly from Monstrelet and from stories which were current in the family of the earls of Ormonde. James Butler, fourth earl, accompanied Henry V to France in 1415; he was in Normandy in 1418 and served with Thomas duke of Clarence in the siege of Rouen. He died in 1453. This fourth earl of Ormonde made a collection of reminiscences illustrating matters such as the duties of a prince and the law of arms. The translator, Mr. Kingsford thought, got his Ormonde information from the seventh earl in whose household he appears to have held a place, and in inserting the stories, some of which may represent no more than the gossip of the court, he has conserved at any rate the substance of extracts from a work written in the middle of the fifteenth century: e.g. the account of Prince Henry's dissension with his father in 1411–12, makes him put on a disguise when he came to seek the reconciliation reported in the St. Albans Chronicle; and the stories of the prince's wildness, when he robbed his father's receivers, struck the Chief Justice, and so forth, are here. Some of these tales, for instance that of Duke Humphrey riding into the sea with drawn sword to extract from the Emperor Sigismund, when landing, the promise not to attempt to exercise any jurisdiction in England, are not lightly to be dismissed. But later dramatic figments, such as the Boar's Head tavern with all its engaging scallywags, will have to go. By 1413 the prince was already a hard-bitten leader with experience of campaigning under conditions where the personal influence of the commander rather than the cash at his disposal was responsible for holding the troops together; a leader with a shrewd knowledge of men and an important following among the nobility. In person Henry did not resemble a warrior. A Frenchman, Jean Fusoris, who visited the king at Winchester in 1415, observed that while the duke of Clarence really looked like a soldier, Henry had the fine manner of a lord and a noble stature, but seemed more suited to the Church than to war. From other sources he appears, in his times of relaxation, as an athletic figure: a runner and a jumper, but not a hunter. He is certainly not the traditional Englishman: there is something of an Este or a Gonzaga about Henry. Much of his diplomacy may be judged Italianate, but the comparison must not be too closely drawn; with 'reason of state' he combined a more than conventional piety. He supervised in closest detail the services of his chapel and took special pains over the choice of his confessors and, most of all, of his bishops. His liturgical interests can be seen in his request to convocation for the increased devotion to be paid to St. George of Cappadocia and in the choice of psalms and responses after the procession and litany which, after his return to England in November 1415, preceded his daily Mass. The Latin *Brut* notes that because the victory of Agincourt was obtained on the day of the martyrs SS. Crispin and Crispinian, Henry ordered that every day as long as he lived commemoration of them should be made at Mass.[1] His bishops were not always chosen for their administrative qualities. As archbishop, when Canterbury fell vacant, he chose, not an aristocrat of the type of Arundel, nor a royal administrator like Langley or Nicholas Bubwith, but an ecclesiastical lawyer who had served him well in diplomacy, had valuable connexions in the City of London, and was above all else a man of the university, with high standards for his clergy. Henry Chichele was a characteristic choice. Richard Ullerston, fellow of Queen's College, Oxford, who between 1404 and 1408 dedicated to Henry a treatise on the moral and spiritual requirements of a

[1] Ed. Kingsford (the Longer Version) in *English Historical Literature in the Fifteenth Century* (1913), p. 326.

knight, spoke of his 'desire for spiritual study'. This was when Henry was quite young. But interest in moral and theological questions never left him. His consultation of recluses, his visits to shrines, his refusal to be interrupted even by his magnates during the course of divine service, his zeal for the purity of the Benedictine Order, his final hope to recover Jerusalem, are facets of a predominantly clerical nature, signs that he took the sacring at his coronation more seriously than his predecessors, and that for him the prestige and success of his country were connected with the moral and religious qualities of the monarchy.

However carefully Henry IV had provided for the succession of his other sons, were Henry of Monmouth to die, it was plain that the continued life of the dynasty depended on one man alone. John of Lancaster, employed on the Scottish March, had still to develop the qualities that won him recognition as a sound diplomat and wise leader; Clarence was an ardent soldier and a keen herald[1] but little else, and Humphrey was as yet too young. The Lancastrian usurpation had done little to satisfy the nobility who encouraged it. Financial inability to meet any serious demand adequately, religious rigidity, a sense of frustration at the poor results of intervention abroad, lack of a guiding personality in the council, all these things had translated themselves into discontent, and, at the beginning of Henry's reign, there was almost as much lawlessness as in the later days of Edward II. The justices of the peace were barely able to maintain order in the counties. There was rioting in the Midlands and East Anglia. The northern franchises observed no law and in a great palatinate like Durham the landed class was no less violent than the country workers. In May 1411 Sir Robert Hilton rode into Sunderland with a considerable following 'in warlike manner' and insulted a certain John Duckett. At his master's orders one of Hilton's servants fired an arrow into Duckett's throat and when he lay dying a second servant struck him with the pommel of a sword. A few days later Sir William Hilton and others executed bonds to the bishop in a thousand marks that neither he nor his retainers would do any harm to certain men of Sunderland. A similar bond was made for Sir Robert Hilton. These pledges were presumably honoured, and the reward was a pardon for Duckett's murder, granted in 1412. In 1422 Sir

[1] Cf. A. R. Wagner, *Heralds and Heraldry in the Middle Ages* (1956), pp. 59–64.

William Hilton and Ralph Eure undertook under pain of a thousand marks each to keep the peace towards Sir William Claxton. But making of bonds was often too late and followed, rather than prevented, riotous behaviour. Excommunication was the method resorted to by Bishop Langley of Durham in his palatine franchise. Much disorder arose from the fantastic system of outlawry following non-appearance in court, and the patent rolls record many instances of restoration of men outlawed for purely technical offences. Violence was only just below the surface. The scenes in St. Dunstan's church in the City of London on Easter Sunday 1417 when Lord Lestrange and his household made a murderous attack on Sir John Trussell and a parishioner who went to his assistance were not isolated examples. Violence to the persons of the clergy as well as the sacred buildings were a constant subject of complaint. If churchmen were sometimes responsible for breaches of the peace, it could be retorted that they were frequently the victims of malicious prosecutions for felony by the laity, while the practice of castrating clerks for sexual delinquency was becoming more prevalent. The first problem of Henry's reign was not how to treat France, but how to repress a disorder closely linked with the anti-clerical movement which had grown in explosive force and vehemence the more Archbishop Arundel proscribed it.

None the less the king's policy was, within limits, one that began by conciliation and peace. On 9 April 1413 he gave notice of a pardon that might be obtained before 1 August by all malefactors save those guilty of murder and rape, with certain categories of reprobates and persons awaiting trial in prison excluded. Richard of York, Duke Edmund Langley's son, he made earl of Cambridge. With the advice and consent of parliament he showed himself ready to believe that the duke of York was a good and loyal liege, both to his father and to himself, and restored him to the 'estate, name, fame and honours' which he had possessed before the judgement given by Henry IV in the rebellion of the earls. The enmities of the last reign were to be forgotten. In December 1413 he had the body of his old patron Richard II, who had predicted great things for him as a boy, brought from Kings Langley to Westminster, to lie beside Queen Anne of Bohemia in the sarcophagus which Richard had erected during his lifetime, in the choir. It was appropriate that the banners made for the funeral of Henry IV at Canterbury should have been used for this service, which followed exactly the details laid down in the late king's will. On the other hand, neither the king nor parliament were prepared to take too heavy risks. During the autumn of 1413 security was taken from leading persons including the earl of Arundel to be of good behaviour towards king and people. Earl Thomas Montague of Salisbury whose father had been in the 1400 rebellion and adjudged a traitor to Henry IV with the loss of his lands and tenements, appealed for restoration 'in blood, estate and dignity', alleging errors in the record of the trial. This was because the earl had been put to death by the people without being accused or having a chance to reply, and Thomas pleaded that he could not legally forfeit his lands without judgement of parliament. The declaration of treason was, he urged, made to the king by temporal lords alone. In parliament the case was referred to the sergeants-at-law, who opined that the attainder was a common law attainder, with the implication that Thomas had to be satisfied with the recovery of all his father had in fee tail. The reversal of the judgement did not take place till 1461.[1] On the other hand, Henry was determined to restore Henry Percy, Hotspur's son, to the earldom of Northumberland, and the trust which he imposed in his father's opponents in the north of England was rewarded by the loyalty of the Cheshire knights and squires against whom measures had been taken in previous reigns.

But conciliation was not enough to allay deeper discontents. Elsewhere an attempt has been made to explore the tenets of Lollardy,[2] but here it is only necessary to say that the policy of Archbishop Arundel since the convocation of 1409 had provoked a large and growing volume of discontent. Soon after the proposal for the disendowment of the *possessionati* in 1410 came Arundel's visitation of the University of Oxford (July 1411), and the measures taken in the dioceses to repress unorthodoxy must have acted as a stimulant to stronger action culminating in rebellion. In the convocation of March 1413 damning evidence was produced against the Herefordshire knight Sir John Oldcastle, who, as we saw,[3] had married Joan, daughter of Sir John de la Pole (d. 1380), inheritor of the lands of her grandfather, John Lord Cobham (d. 1408). One of Oldcastle's chaplains had been preaching heresy in Kentish churches, and he

---

[1] *Rot. Parl.* v. 484.   [2] Ch. VII.   [3] See above, p. 103.

himself had been caught through the discovery, in an illumina-
tor's bookshop in Paternoster Row, of certain heretical tracts.
At first Arundel had told the king, and at a meeting at Kennington a number of passages in the books were read aloud, in Oldcastle's presence. The knight excused himself by saying that he
had not fully understood their character. In convocation much
more information against him was produced. The lower clergy
pressed for his trial on the ground that he harboured and protected heretics in the dioceses of London, Rochester, and Hereford. As he was one of the king's intimate friends it was agreed
that Henry should again be consulted and Henry did his best
to secure submission. This was not forthcoming, and in August
1413 Arundel was authorized to proceed in accordance with the
law. Whereupon Arundel issued citations affixed to the doors
of both Cooling Castle, where Oldcastle had barred himself in,
and of Rochester Cathedral. At first the citation was ignored
but eventually Oldcastle paid another visit to Windsor and
was arrested and put in the Tower (23 Sept.). He declined to
submit and obtain full forgiveness, but put in an imprecise
statement of his views, particularly in the matter of transubstantiation and auricular confession. Arundel persisted with him
but had little hope of securing his conversion. When the trial
continued (25 Sept.) Oldcastle maintained that he would
not be absolved by any save God. He then asserted that bread
remained bread after consecration and that confession was not
necessary to salvation, and ended by declaiming against the
hierarchy and warning his hearers that his judges were deceivers
and were leading them to hell. There was no need for further
proof and the archbishop had only to record the judgement of
the court, which asked that Oldcastle should be excommunicated
and left to the secular arm.

The king still hoped to save him and, 'under hope of leading
back the sheep into the fold, put off sentence of fire and death'.
Oldcastle was given a respite of forty days to think the matter
over in the Tower. During this stay of execution his friends, later
described as a Warrington Franciscan, a Shropshire scrivener and
a London parchment-maker, contrived his escape on the night
of 19 October 1413. For two months he was in the neighbourhood of London, planning a rising which had as its intention
the destruction of the king and his brothers during or immediately after the Christmas festivities which were to be spent at

Eltham. Henry's spies got to know of the plan afoot. From
Eltham the king quietly moved to Westminster on the night of
8 January 1414, and on the evening of Tuesday the 9th, under
cover of darkness, took up a position in St. Giles' Fields outside
the city. The Lollards expected that the Londoners would rise
and pour out of the gates to meet them, but the city gates were
shut, and as they moved in towards the town in scattered parties
they were caught by the king's guard and marched off to prison.
The leading victims seized in London were hanged on 13
January; probably there were not more than sixty. Many were
artisans or countrymen, but the leaders were more important.
Oldcastle's chief lieutenant, Sir Roger Acton of Sutton in Worcestershire, Sir Thomas Talbot of Davington near Faversham
in Kent, who like Acton had fought in the Welsh March,
Thomas Maureward, ex-sheriff of Warwickshire and Leicestershire, and two esquires of London, Robert Horley and Richard
Colfox, were involved, as well as Thomas Noveray a Leicestershire gentleman who had had an interesting career as an active
Lollard propagandist. On 11 January commissions of inquiry
were issued in twenty-one counties and London. The returns
had to be made to the chancery and a considerable number
have survived. From them it is clear that while the plan for the
armed revolt was defective, the preparations for assembling
forces in each county were made, as in 1381, with thoroughness.
In each one or two persons, whether priests or laymen, were
responsible for organization, for letting Oldcastle's supporters
know at what time they were expected in London, doling out
money to them, arranging for the billeting of those who came
from a distance, and bribing those who could not be persuaded
to rise. In the midlands most of the insurrection took place on
3 and 4 January. Leicestershire, where there was a considerable
amount of heresy, was largely organized by Walter Gilbert, a
chaplain who in Derbyshire was known under the name of
Walter Kibworth. Another chaplain named William Ederick,
who had been very active in Derbyshire, was presented as
bribing villagers to join the insurgents. While in Derbyshire and
Leicestershire the rising was fairly widespread in the villages, in
Warwickshire, Coventry alone seems to have been affected. The
St. Albans annalist showed considerable alarm about the activities
of Robert Morley of Dunstable. But here and in Hertfordshire,
only a small group of volunteers were effective. Attention has

been drawn[1] to the influence of the family of Cheyne of Drayton
Beauchamp, which had put heretics into livings in its possession.
Three Cheynes were implicated, while Amersham and Little
Missenden sent their contingents. Farther west, Bristol sent a
considerable party composed of forty craftsmen, mainly weavers,
headed by six chaplains. In Essex the organizers were John and
Thomas Cook, supported by their father. The Cooks were
offering sixpence a day to all who would support Oldcastle and
actually paid some of the money in London. The names presented
show in the towns a preponderance of artisans, weavers, turners,
webbers, smiths, and in the country, graziers, corndealers,
husbandmen, and so forth, led by local chaplains. In Bristol,
Northamptonshire, and Leicestershire scriveners also are found.
Although the various city commissions did not sit simultaneously,
a good many of the returns, made in the first instance by the
commissioners, give an identical account of the struggle. A long
preamble relates that Sir John Oldcastle, a convicted heretic
and traitor, having gathered together a band of 20,000 supporters from various parts of England, maliciously plotted to
subvert the catholic faith, to destroy churches and monasteries,
and afterwards was contriving the death of the king and all his
nobility. One return charges him with designing to destroy the
Holy Church. A considerable number of men are presented
as being 'a common Lollard', but there are some theological
charges, e.g. men are presented for saying 'it is not meritorious
to go on pilgrimages to St. Thomas (of Canterbury) nor to
other centres of devotion': that it is 'not healthful for the souls
of Christians to honour images or to visit on pilgrimage the
bodies of the saints'.

Yet it is not from these returns, suggestive as they are, but
from the trials in the King's Bench that the most significant
facts emerge; much relevant detail did not come out until six
or seven years after the main rebellion, but the immediate
trials, 1414-15, which deal with cases of treason as well as of
Lollardy, reveal that Oldcastle was at large in the capital from
19 October 1413 till nearly five weeks after the rebellion:
he had lived in various retreats, e.g. with a Robert Arnold
(not Robert Arnold the grocer, as was first suspected) in Aldrich-
gate Street, in the house of William the parchment-maker in

[1] By Mr. K. B. MacFarlane, *John Wyclif and the Beginnings of English Noncon-
formity* (1952), p. 175.

Smithfield; and that he was suspected of being in hiding at West-minster when early in February 1414 the duke of Clarence came to search for him. An approver deposed that the monk arch-deacon of Westminster was involved in getting him away from London. It is curious that such a hammer of the religious orders should have been protected by people of no less standing than the abbot of Shrewsbury and the Cluniac prior of Wenlock. Returns of a number of inquisitions show how he got food and maintained himself for the next three years in the midlands[1] and in the west of England,[2] and that in 1417 he was actually living in his own Herefordshire manor.[3]

In Henry V's first parliament (15 May 1413), which made full provision for the expenses of defence as well as of govern-ment—besides the wool subsidy a fifteenth and tenth was granted for the keeping of the sea—the commons spoke emphatically about the weakness of the last reign, of disobedience to the laws, and the lack of public order. The judicial findings and the alarm of the Lollard revolt led to stronger measures in the Leicester parliament of April 1414. Another statute was now passed against heretics, by which the secular power took co-operation of the Church with the laity a stage further than in 1401. In cases of heresy, lands held in fee simple were now forfeit to the overlord, and any lands held of the bishop who convicted the offender were to remain with the king. All justices and local officials were to strive their utmost for the suppression of the Lollards: the justices of the King's Bench, and the justices of the peace and of assize were authorized to make search for Lollards, and any persons they arrested were to be delivered over to the ordinary within fifteen days. In 1415 the London skinner John Clayton was brought before the ordinary after first being ar-rested (*primitus arrestatus*) under this process. The Lollard statute was, however, only a part of the business at Leicester. The commons first asked for an assurance about petitions, which they received (Henry's prerogative right to grant as much as he liked of them reserved) to the effect that no enactment should be engrossed as a statute which would change the meaning and in-tention expressed in the petition. They then set about tightening

---

[1] In Northamptonshire: P.R.O., K.B. 9/209, mm. 6, 27 (Byfield). In Notting-hamshire: Gaol Delivery Roll J 13/195, no 37; Warwickshire, K.B. 9/209, m. 50.
[2] In the Wenlock area: K.B. 9/212, m. 88: evidence of William Carswell of Witney, approver.   [3] K.B. 27/634, Rex, xj.

up measures for law and order particularly by making lords of franchises liable for misconduct occurring in areas such as Tynedale, Redesdale, and Hexhamshire where the king's writ did not run. Measures were taken to strengthen the existing law against rioting, and in one special case, the disputed election at Fountains Abbey, the king, to end disorder in Yorkshire, put one of the contending parties in possession. In Shropshire and Staffordshire defiance of the law had reached an extreme pitch, for in the former county the collectors of the tenth and fifteenth granted in the last parliament had been attacked by the servants of Robert Corbet and Richard Leighton, the two knights representing the shire in that particular assembly, and had only escaped with difficulty, while Corbet himself appears to have barred their way and maltreated one of them at Dunstable, when they were travelling to London to render their November account. Disorder, as has been noted, had long been extended to the sea, and the Leicester parliament took special measures to repress piracy. In the previous summer John Hawley junior of Dartmouth had been arrested, the government having at last brought itself to take measures against one of its abler captains. The new enactment was for the establishment, in every port, of an officer of standing, a man of at least forty librates of land, to act as president of a local court entrusted with the admiral's powers except for questions involving capital punishment. This official had to keep particulars of every vessel clearing from the port, with the name of the owner and particulars of crew and cargo, and all prizes captured at sea had to be notified to him as 'Conservator of truces and safe-conducts'.[1] The statute, like many other attempts to harness piracy, had no lasting success, and return was allowed to the older system of reprisals by letters of marque.

In other respects the Leicester parliament was notable for the petition that the king should take over confiscated property of French religious houses in England, not properly conventual in character. These confiscations had in the main taken place under Edward III and Henry IV. Quite a fair number had not been seized, the houses having secured charters of denization and so being permitted to retain most of their property and escaping from the duty of sending contributions to their mother houses overseas. The king gave the assurance, especially

[1] *Rot. Parl.* iv. 22–24.

welcomed by the farmers of the confiscated houses, that the confiscations should not be annulled, if peace were made with France; after the treaty of Troyes holders of the lands or possessions of such alien priories had to appear in the chancery and prove their titles. It was intended by Martin V that the lands and possessions should later be converted into endowments for churches and religious houses, after compensation had been paid to the parent houses in Normandy:[1] but the king's death seems to have frustrated this pious, if only equitable, provision.

But peace with France was at a distance and Henry, after the disillusionments of 1411 and 1412, was thinking of the *voie de fait*. None the less, the way of fact had to have its diplomatic preparation. He could go the whole length and demand the French crown; or he could fall back upon the unfulfilled treaty of Brétigny, by the famous twelfth article of which it was provided that the king of France was to give up sovereignty and *ressort* (the right to give judicial decisions which could not be challenged in a higher court) in all the lands to be acquired by Edward III under the treaty, in return for which the English king was to renounce all claim to the crown of France and to the sovereignty of Normandy, Touraine, Anjou, Maine, Brittany, and Flanders. When the treaty was ratified at Calais on 24 October 1361 the article was deliberately omitted and the word sovereignty dropped throughout the text. The omissions were compensated by a separate agreement known as the clausula *Cest assavoir* which postponed the renunciations until specified lands and fortresses[2] were surrendered to the English king by John II. The lands in question were to be surrendered before 1 November 1361, but by that date the places had not been handed over, and Edward for his part was not going to make renunciations until he was sure that the territorial advantages accorded to him in the treaty would actually materialize. The non-execution of the renunciation clauses was the factor governing Anglo-French diplomatic negotiations until the conferences held between

[1] Wylie, *The Reign of Henry V* (1914–29), i. 342, on the strength of a statement made at the council of Basel in 1434: he points out that there is 'no statement to this effect in the Papal Letters'.

[2] Poitou and the town and castle of Poitiers, Thouars, Belleville, Agenais with the town and castle of Agen, Périgord with the town and castle of Périgueux, Quercy with the town and castle of Cahors, and the Limousin with the town and castle of Limoges. On these negotiations, see Pierre Chaplais, 'Some documents regarding the fulfilment and interpretation of the Treaty of Brétigny', *Camden Miscellany*, xix (1952), 6–7.

1373-6, by which time the French had declared Aquitaine forfeit to Charles V (in the *parlement*, 2 May 1369) and had reopened the war. To the English this violation of the peace of Calais by Charles was a justification for resuming their claim to the French crown. The two papal nuncios who tried to bring the parties to an agreement at Bruges in June 1377 found that failing this the English would be content with nothing less than the re-enactment of the Calais treaty and its complete acceptance and observance by the French, including the unfulfilled exchange of renunciations. Various proposals made for the partition of Aquitaine, though seriously considered, came to nothing. The *détente* and the truce of Richard II's reign did not alter the fundamental difference of opinion between the two countries. Frenchmen, like Charles V, were still convinced that the Hundred Years War was, as M. Perroy has aptly said 'essentially a feudal quarrel between a Gascon vassal and his French overlord'.[1] Henry was determined to show them that it was more than that.

The first preparations for a French expedition were made shortly after the Lollard revolt. Large quantities of arms, siege materials, bridging, and other equipment were being accumulated in the early summer of 1414. The operation was prepared for by a series of loans starting in June–July 1413. In July 1413 Richard Whittington lent £2,000, and a year later £1,000 was forthcoming from John Hende and £2,000 from the citizens of London corporately. Bishops, including Beaufort with £1,333 6s. 8d., and abbots put up substantial sums. This was the first instalment of Beaufort's loans which amounted to £35,630 in Henry V's reign. After the breakdown of the promises made by the Orleanist lords to restore the ancient boundaries of Aquitaine and to guarantee the return of Normandy to the English allegiance, there could be only one direction for Henry V's policy. The problem was not whom to fight, but *with* whom. It was important to sound Burgundian intentions. In June 1413 a Burgundian embassy landed at Dover and stayed a week in Canterbury, probably to study preliminaries to the formal discussions which were to take place in the later summer and autumn. The English party, consisting of Henry Chichele, bishop of St. David's, Richard Beauchamp, earl of Warwick,

---

[1] 'The Anglo-French negotiations at Bruges, 1374–1377', *Camden Miscellany*, xix (1952), p. xix.

William Lord Zouche, lieutenant of Calais, and Henry Lord Scrope of Masham, crossed to Calais at the end of July 1413. Their commission included the redress of the infringements of the truce with Flanders, but they were also to approach the French king and offer to meet any envoys whom he might appoint with a view to obtaining a more friendly understanding. The four ambassadors to Burgundy met the French representatives at Leulinghen (Pas-de-Calais) but there is no record of the result. With Burgundy, on the other hand, they negotiated 'on certain secret articles and matters'. The duke himself they met at Bruges on 15 September after he had been forced to leave Paris, and in a further interview at Lille on 19 October the proposal was made that Henry should marry one of the duke's daughters, and receive with her the fortresses of Cherbourg, Le Crotoy, and Caen. But the arrival in November of French envoys from Paris cut short the proposals; yet intercourse with Burgundy did not cease with the return to England of the ambassadors. There were claims constantly arising out of breaches of the truce between England and Flanders, which acted as the formal occasion for diplomatic meetings with France.

The truce was due to expire on 31 December 1413 and commissioners were appointed to meet the English envoys at Leulinghen on 1 September. All that was effected at this meeting was a prolongation of the truces, a local truce for the area between Nieuport and the Somme to last for eight months from 1 October 1413 and a general truce (16 October) to last until the following Easter. But the meeting also witnessed the production, on either side, of evidences for and against the English claim to the French crown made by Edward III in right of his mother Isabel. The French brought forward the treatise of Jean de Montreuil challenging the right of the English kings to be dukes of Aquitaine, and therefore impugning the whole basis of the treaty of Calais; and the English for their part brought forward the evidence which they had extracted from trustworthy historical sources supporting Edward III's claim and refuting the French case based on the Salic Law which allegedly established a bar against the succession to females. Naturally the Leulinghen discussions were preliminaries. On 8 October 1413 the archbishop of Bourges, Guillaume Boisratier, and Charles d'Albret, constable of France, received commissions to treat with Henry V, and the discussions led to a truce, dated 24 January 1414, to operate for twelve months from 2 February. The document embodying it was drawn in French and Latin, the latter being the language advocated by the English. The French left during the middle of February and appear to have reached Paris at the same time as an English group of negotiators including Henry Lord Scrope, Hugh Mortimer, Henry V's chamberlain when prince of Wales, and Master Henry Ware, a civil lawyer already experienced in diplomacy, who became dean of the Arches in 1415. The English group were commissioned to arrange a match between King Henry and Charles VI's youngest daughter Catherine, of whom Henry had heard an enthusiastic report from the duke of York, recently (Feb.) back from Paris. On the basis of marriage a permanent peace might be made out of the truce; but Henry had no intention of surrendering his major demand that the king should restore all rights and heritages belonging to him. The examination and discussion of these claimed rights was the object of the largest and most imposing embassy as yet sent to France. This left after the Leicester parliament (April–May 1414) and contained Bishops Langley and Courtenay, Thomas Montague, earl of Salisbury and, again, Master Henry Ware. A great council summoned at the time held that the king's claims to France should be made known, and that if Henry was prepared to modify them and the French then refused to accept the concession, this should be regarded as all the more strengthening his case. The suggestion that Henry should moderate his claims or make an 'offre that were moderyng of youre hoole title or of eny of youre claymes beynde the see' is an evident indication that some concession by the king in the interests of peace was considered desirable.

The embassy crossed on 11 July 1414. The king gave them an exemplification of the French king John's declaration of his liability to pay 1,600,000 crowns for his ransom (the original sum was 3,000,000 gold crowns—£500,000, the crown being the English half noble), a claim revived when the French pressed Henry IV for Queen Isabel's dower. The embassy was allowed to promise on the king's behalf that he was prepared to engage himself in the future or to be immediately betrothed to the Princess Catherine, provided that a satisfactory solution was reached about her dower. While to the French Henry professed himself thus prepared to treat, the king was simultaneously listening to the overtures of Duke John the Fearless whose envoys were in London with the express purpose of arranging an alliance with England through the marriage of Henry with the Duke's fifth daughter Catherine (still under age). Catherine had once been promised to Louis count of Guise, the eldest son of Louis II of Anjou, titular king of Naples, Jerusalem and Sicily, when he was only six. In May 1414 she was seen by an English embassy which probably described her in favourable terms, but she did not live long enough to matter. At Leicester Henry received envoys from Duke John proposing a perpetual alliance and a marriage between him and one of the duke's daughters. The agreement, a secret document, arranged that the English king was to send 500 men at arms and 200 archers to help the duke conquer the possessions of the dukes of Orléans and Bourbon and of his enemies. The duke and Henry V were then to divide the takings in proportion to the forces employed. The English embassy which followed upon these overtures included beside Scrope and Mortimer, Thomas Chaucer and Philip Morgan (future bishop of Worcester), and was empowered to accept on Henry's behalf one of the duke's daughters and to arrange about a dower. They were to conclude an alliance with the duke and were in addition authorized to prolong the truce with Flanders indefinitely. In July the ambassadors saw John the Fearless and reached a detailed agreement by which the Burgundian not only undertook not to oppose Henry's attempt to gain the French crown, but declared himself ready to attack his own sovereign. How much practical assistance Henry hoped to gain from the duke it is impossible to say. He was notoriously difficult to pin down, and probably Henry hoped for little more than the absence of opposition to his *viage*, though he was to return to the charge in the autumn of 1416 in an attempt, on a grander scale, to secure positive help from Duke John. It seems, as Dr. Wylie suggested, likely that Henry's negotiations with each contending party, the Burgundians and the Armagnacs,[1] were intended each to enhance the price of his support to the other.

To the Armagnacs the price was certainly formidable. The embassy, led by Courtenay and Langley, reached Paris on 8 April 1414; fêted and entertained by the duke of Berry, it got to business on 10 August when Courtenay, in asking for the hand of the Princess Catherine for Henry, made it a condition

---

[1] The party, successor to the Orleanist faction, led by Bertrand VII, count of Armagnac. Wylie's view is in *The Reign of Henry V*, i, 416.

that the crown and kingdom of France should be yielded up to
England. After this *demande incivile* as it was called, he indicated
that Henry was prepared to abate his claim a little and be
content with suzerainty and with *dominium* in perpetuity over
Normandy, Touraine, Anjou, Maine, Brittany, Flanders, and
the old duchy of Aquitaine: the territories specified in the treaty
of Brétigny. The French wanted to give priority to the marriage
question. But the English insisted upon putting territorial claims
first, including a demand for a moiety of the county of Provence,
the title to which had belonged to Thomas and Henry, sons of
Edmund Crouchback, who derived his right from his aunt
Eleanor of Provence, Henry III's wife. Eleanor was the second
daughter of Raymond Berenger, count of Provence. The fantastic
claim had been maintained by the English throughout the
fourteenth century. These territorial demands and the claim for
the balance of King's John's ransom the English put first, but
indicated that when the matter of Catherine's dower was reached
it should be at least 2,000,000 crowns. In reply to these requirements (made in writing) the French professed themselves ready
to make considerable territorial concessions including Agen,
Périgueux, Tarbes, Saintes, and the Saintonge, south of the
Charente: they were willing, in fact, to restore the old limits of
Aquitaine from the Charente to the Pyrenees, as the Orleanist
lords had promised to do in 1414. The question of Provence they
said must be arranged with the duke of Anjou. Consideration of
King John's ransom they wished to defer until the king had
finished extending his dominions, but they suggested that they
might reach as much as 600,000 crowns for the dower. In other
words, the English territorial demands were treated seriously,
even if the claim to the French crown was not admitted. The
English ambassadors themselves received every mark of attention. There is probably no justification for the story, very shortly
circulating in England, that Henry's overtures had been laughed
at or treated contemptuously. But opinion hardened: the double
tenth and fifteenth granted by the November parliament of
1414 and the pronouncement made therein by the chancellor,
Bishop Beaufort, to the effect that the king had set his mind on
recovering his inheritance and the rights belonging to his crown,
and that his subjects must fight for justice, even if it led to their
death, clearly indicate the way the wind was blowing. None the
less the Speaker, Thomas Chaucer, advised Henry on behalf of

he commons, that before he undertook hostilities, he should
irst send ambassadors to France and gain his rights by peaceful
nethods if possible.

Henry took the advice and sent Bishops Langley and Courtenay,
vith whom he associated the earl of Dorset, Lord Grey of
Codnor, Sir William Bourchier (constable of the Tower in 1416),
nd Sir John Phelip: the clerks were Philip Morgan and the
York lawyer Richard Holme. The French negotiators whom
hey were to meet were again Berry's chancellor Boisratier,
Pierre Fresnel, bishop of Noyon (Oise), Charles, count of Eu,
nd Guillaume Martel, lord of Bacqueville. The conversations
indertaken by this second English embassy opened on 12 March
1415, and Bishop Courtenay again led the delegation. He
eiterated the demand for justice, but on the subject of the
marriage made use of the revelations of St. Bridget, who had
dvocated a match between the royal houses of France and
England, so as to stop the existing strife. As to Catherine's dower,
he English were prepared to 'descend' to one million crowns,
provided that the king of France was ready to furnish the
rousseau. On their side the French, while refusing to concede
ny of Henry's pretensions, were willing to restore those portions
of Aquitaine which had been recovered from the English in the
previous reign, and to go as far as 800,000 crowns for a dower
ogether with the princess's clothes and jewels. The English
ambassadors professed to have no power to agree to such
proposals, although, as they said, their master had 'offered to
eave his said adversary a great part of what in law belonged to
him' (Henry).[1] At the end of March 1415 the English returned
sans aucun exploit reporter de lour ambassade'. In spite of this
he truce, due to expire on 1 May 1415, was prolonged until
8 June with a further extension to cover the visit of the French
embassy to England during the summer.

The final effort of the French king was made when Henry had
already started on his journey to France to join the fleet at
Southampton. At Winchester he heard that the French ambassadors had arrived, and sent for them to Wolvesey Castle.
They had landed at Dover on 17 June and ridden through
Canterbury to London. The chief members were the archbishop
of Bourges, the bishop of Lisieux (now Pierre Fresnel), the
count of Vendôme, and Charles lord of Ivry, with a large

[1] *P.P.C.*, ii. 150.

retinue. The meeting held while the royal forces were assembling round Southampton, lasted from 2–6 July, and this time
ended in a complete rupture. The question of the dower might
have been settled peaceably since the archbishop was prepared
to raise the figure to 850,000 gold crowns, but the French would
settle no date for bringing over the Princess Catherine; and as
far as territorial demands by Henry were concerned, they professed themselves uncertain as to how they were held, i.e. whether
Henry's claim was equally valid for each. The English king
quickly retorted that he was the rightful king of France and
that he intended to have the crown, to which the archbishop is
reported to have replied that Henry had no right to the crown
of England, and that the French should be dealing with the
heirs of Richard II. The situation was now beyond argument
and Bishop Beaufort read another ultimatum demanding the
surrender of all Aquitaine, Normandy, Anjou, Touraine, Poitou
Maine, and Ponthieu, in default of which Henry would cross to
recover them and would seize the crown of France. Henry called
God to witness that he was compelled to do this by the refusal
of his cousin to do him justice. To hold on to his claim had now
become a matter of conscience. Even in a last letter written on
28 July 1415 Henry might declare that he was prepared to give
effect to the precept in Deuteronomy to a leader proposing to
besiege a town, that is, to offer peace first, and to accept a figure
suggested by the French for a dower; but he could not conscientiously give up his claim to his rights in France and by
doing so disinherit his successors. Henry's chaplain, who wrote
the *Gesta*, complained of the 'almost adamantine hardness' of
the French in the matter of the claims.[1] They were of two kinds
there were both the throne and the territories never in fact
acquired after the Brétigny settlement, with Normandy in a
special position because it was an ancient English possession
forced from King John by a legal decision followed by an act of
disseisin, which successive English governments had never tolerated. It will be seen that the claim to the French crown hardened
and became more axiomatic for Henry as his campaigns proceeded. But until Rouen fell and he saw the way clear to Paris
he was prepared at a pinch to be forced back on to the demand
for Normandy along with the other territories. The problem
that confronts the modern reader is to know how genuine were

[1] *Gesta Henrici Quinti*, ed. Williams, p. 107.

the negotiations on either side, whether there was any serious expectation of peace and, in matters of form, whether offer and counter-offer, modification and counter-modification were not merely set-pieces, unaccompanied by discussion and dialectic. The formality of ambassadorial procedure in the first half of the fifteenth century was extreme, as was to be seen at the council of Arras.[1] There was no 'round table' atmosphere of any kind, the only serious debate often being over the language in which the proceedings were to be conducted: the English asking for Latin, the French for French.

The army that had been brought together in the Portsmouth–New Forest–Southampton area and the transport that was to convey it were the result of many months of preparation and hard work. On the army side it was the product of the indenture system, by which each captain contracted with the king to provide an agreed number of men-at-arms, 'well mounted, armed and arrayed as belonged to their estate', and of archers, for a definite period. He agreed to provide and to make periodical musters of his retainers before persons appointed by the king. In return for these soldiers the king agreed to pay wages. The documents recording these transactions, the indentures themselves, muster rolls, commissions of array, and so forth, mostly represent Exchequer determination to pay effectives only for services rendered, and to guard against remuneration twice over for the payment of absentees. The indenture laid down the size and composition of the force, the rates of pay, the place of assembly, the length of service, and such privileges as 'rewards' or *regarda* to which all men were entitled. It was, generally speaking, a force of all arms, including the mounted men-at-arms with their esquires, pages, and horses, called in the indentures for the Agincourt campaign and in other documents lances (and a 'lance' generally meant three or four persons, only the principal one, a *generosus*, being named); mounted and foot archers, hobelars who were light horsemen, with horse unprotected by armour; spearmen or pikemen on foot, as well as miners, artificers, surgeons, and so forth. The men-at-arms were fully armoured knights and esquires. Their weapons were the lance, sword, and the dagger. For protection they had small shields. The horse was covered with a housing of mail, over which

[1] pp. 261 f.

there was a *caparison*, charged with the arms of the rider. In an action the normal practice was for the men-at-arms to dismount while their horses were led to the rear by their pages. A considerable headquarters staff or company, as we might put it, went with an army. The best example of which is perhaps the king's own retinue in the Agincourt campaign. There were tradesmen of all kinds, beginning with the German master-gunners and the stuffer of bassinets, i.e. the man who padded and adjusted the helmets; their armourers, surgeons, clerks of the stable, and household servants (clerks of the spicery, poultry, scullery), along with the carpenters and the very important fletchers and bowyers. Finally, if it was a royal force, as on the present occasion, there were the clerks of the king's chapel, the dean and chaplains among whom, on Henry V's first campaign, was the author of the *Gesta Henrici Quinti*. Finally came the band, consisting of trumpeters, pipers, and fiddlers under the leadership of the master minstrel. Each member of the household staff brought with him a number of archers: thus the sergeant of the king's tents and pavilions provided 28; the king's smith, Mr. William Smith, 41; and the yeomen of the king's household jointly 86. On the present campaign the master carpenter had 124 archers and the chief minstrel John Stiff also had his contingent. The archer was lightly armed and was probably the most mobile element of the force.

The term of service varied from a traditional forty days to a full year or longer. In 1353 the Black Prince's engagement had been 'during the king's pleasure'. Arrangements for pay were vital. In 1359 the prince of Wales's retinue consisted of seven bannerets at four shillings a day each, 136 knights at two shillings, 143 esquires at one shilling, and 900 mounted archers at sixpence. The duke of Lancaster's retinue had more men at arms, 486, and 423 mounted archers. The cost of maintaining forces of this kind was considerable. In the first English expedition to the Low Countries, July 1338–February 1340, the accounts of the keeper of the wardrobe[1] show that the expedition cost no less than £386,546 apart from the normal household expenses of £23,748. On that occasion Edward III and his council authorized an abnormally high rate of wages, double the usual amounts, from 22 July 1338–16 November 1339.

---

[1] On the keepers of this period and the expenses they had to meet, cf. T. F. Tout, *Chapters in Medieval Administrative History*, iv. 113 f.

The Crécy–Calais campaign was proportionately expensive. The wages of war for the three and a half years amounted to just over £150,000 to which £1,027 was added for the garrisoning of Calais. In the invasion of France in 1359–60 the prince of Wales was owed no less than £24,400 for the wages of war for three-quarters of the war. None the less warfare might be, and often was, an extremely profitable business.[1] For no one had the profits of war been more valuable than for Edward III who had the good fortune to take prisoner a king of Scotland and a king of France, besides many other magnates only slightly less illustrious. It has been reckoned by Professor Perroy that between 1360 and 1370 Edward III received the large sum of about £268,000 from three major ransoms. Much royal income from war was, directly or indirectly, devoted to war, and it soon became a criticism of the crown if the war did not pay for itself, as it seemed that this should be easily possible. The crown obtained the ransoms and spoils not only from princes and from barons, but from a continuous series of smaller men through the custom of demanding one-third of the winnings of its captains and one-third of their thirds when they or their men took prisoners or spoils. All the advantages of war, as they were called, were usually granted by the king to the other indenting party. To this rule there were two main exceptions: the king reserved for himself the most important castles and lands, and he also reserved the most influential prisoners of war, promising, however, to pay the actual captors a reasonable reward. The system is outlined in the first of the General Ordinances of War issued in 1385 which regulated the discipline in the royal army and formed the basis for the subsequent code issued by Henry V. They were issued for the forces advancing against Scotland and are printed in the Black Book of the Admiralty.[2] Clause 16 runs: 'that each man pays a third to his lord or master of all manner of gains of arms'. This applies to non-retained men just as much as to soldiers in the indentured retinues. It is unlikely that Richard II could have invented a claim so large as one-third, and a third of a third, without raising criticism, and it is probable therefore that the ordinance represents the custom prevailing throughout the fourteenth century. The same applied to naval warfare. The king had a right to all prisoners taken at

---

[1] Cf. H. J. Hewitt, *The Black Prince's Expedition, 1355–1357* (1958), chap. vii, 'Ransoms, Rewards, Pardons'.   [2] Rolls ser., i. 282–94.

sea, if he chose to exercise it, but habitually he conceded a portion of the spoils, usually one-half, to the crew of the victorious ship. Where the ship was not a royal vessel the king got only one-quarter, the other quarters going to the owner. The admiral's share in the prizes crystallized at one-tenth, but the whole matter of proportions at sea was a very lively question for a long while to come.

The king left Winchester on 6 July 1415 for Southampton. On the way he stayed with the Premonstratensians at Titchfield, where John Stevens, one of the archbishop's clerks, made copies of the agreements entered into by the Armagnac lords in 1412, offering parts of Aquitaine in return for English help. These were to be circulated, for propaganda purposes, in the council of Constance. From Titchfield Henry moved on to Porchester Castle to supervise operations.

It was here that he was given confidential information by the earl of March of a plot which necessitated immediate action. Richard, earl of Cambridge, brother of the duke of York, Thomas Gray of Heton, and Henry Lord Scrope of Masham, were immediately seized on a charge of conspiring to kill the king and his three brothers. Edmund, earl of March,[1] was in it, but less heavily engaged than the others. It was Earl Richard's plot and nobody suspected him of it, since he had accepted the earldom given him in May 1414 and had indented with the king to bring a force of 2 knights, 57 esquires, and 160 mounted archers. Richard had married, as his second wife, Maud Clifford, whose brother John Lord Clifford, had married Elizabeth Percy, Hotspur's daughter. The projected restoration of Hotspur's son, Henry Percy, had not pacified the north: it had been proposed that he should be exchanged for Murdach, son of the duke of Albany, at a ransom of £10,000, to be paid by the Scots by midsummer, but at the persuading of French envoys, the transaction never took place. Murdach was seized out of the hands of his English guards in Yorkshire when he was being taken north and it was now planned to use Henry Percy to raise the north, to take the earl of March into Wales and proclaim him king, while the Scots should lend assistance, and the old conspirators, Oldcastle and Glyn Dŵr, would be brought in to co-operate in the west. This proposal was revealed to Thomas

---

[1] Knighted at Henry V's coronation, summoned to the Leicester parliament, and a trier of petitions there (*Rot. Parl.* iv. 16).

Gray by the earl of Cambridge at Conisburgh. The ringleaders thought that Robert Umfraville, keeper of Roxburgh Castle, and John Widdrington would join in, but in the event Umfraville let the Scots in through the border only to destroy them. On his way south Gray was told that the earl of Arundel and Henry Lord Scrope were bound to help March, though Scrope had advised him either to cross to France and Flanders and work up the Percy cause from there, or else to join the disaffected in Wales. Scrope's adhesion was the more surprising since Henry IV had made him treasurer of England and a member of the Order of the Garter. It is unnecessary to suspect that he had been bought by France: there were other treasonable contacts; the dead archbishop, Scrope's own second wife Joan, who had been second wife to Edmund duke of York, and family influences and friendships may have broken down his sense of duty, for Gray seems to have approached him as soon as he reached Southampton. The earl of March, whose innocency, as the *Gesta* has it, both Gray and Scrope did their best to assail,[1] gave away the whole story on the very day on which the assassinations were to have taken place (1 Aug.). A meeting of nobles hastily summoned at Porchester advised the arrests and trial, and Cambridge, Scrope, and Gray confessed their guilt. A commission of lords and two judges was appointed and a jury of Hampshire men collected for the trial, which took place on 2 August. Gray was condemned to death for treason, but the others claimed trial by their peers. This presented no difficulties: the twenty selected contain, interestingly enough, the names of the earl of March, Lord Clifford, and the duke of York who had never been informed of the plot by his brother. The three prisoners were sentenced to be drawn, hanged, and beheaded, but the hanging was remitted, and Gray and Cambridge were spared drawing. In 1461 the sentences at Southampton were annulled and called 'an erroneous judgement' although they were evidently the only possible course in a crisis of emergency, one to be confirmed at the Westminster parliament which met in November 1415.

The first invasion of France, whatever was originally planned, turned out to be a raid on a large scale, and no more. It was begun with a total effective force of 2,000 men at arms and a little more than 6,000 archers, more than half of the latter

---

[1] 'cujus innocentiam in hoc exitiali proposito attentassent', *Gesta*, p. 11.

mounted. With the specialist troops and headquarters unit, the total was about 9,000. Fifteen hundred ships were required and it took three days to assemble them along the coastal harbours from Gosport to Southampton, with the king's own ship lying in the Solent. Henry embarked on 7 August, and on Sunday 11th the signal of departure was hoisted. It was late in the year for the sort of campaign that could result in permanent occupation of territory. In his message to the mayor and aldermen of London assembled at the Tower on 10 March 1415, Henry had spoken of his intentions 'with no small army to visit the parts beyond the sea, so that we may duly reconquer the lands pertaining to the heirship and crown of our realm, which have for long, in the times of our predecessors by enormous wrong withheld',[1] and for the great gold S.S. collar pledged in security the city had lent Henry 10,000 marks to be repaid on 1 January 1416. The formal resolution to attack Armagnac France was taken on 11 April. Why, then, was the expedition so long delayed? Can Henry have been hoping for a favourable outcome in the discussions with France? It seems likely that he had scanty expectations from them, but a comfortable show of legality was of value to him for propaganda and other purposes, and it is quite possible that all along he was only intending to establish a defended area on the lower Seine, one that commanded the river traffic and could be made in time into a second Calais: after which he would undertake a reconnaissance in force up the Seine, ending in a withdrawal southwards, perhaps even as far as Bordeaux. If during the reconnaissance he met with opposition, he was confident of defeating it, and, given the division of opinion existing among the Armagnac captains, he did not anticipate that he would be confronted with an army of any size. Had not Clarence in 1412 made a long and unopposed march through the south of France? Henry's journey from Harfleur to Calais has sometimes been condemned as an imprudent and hazardous adventure. But if his knowledge of the relations existing between Burgundy and the Armagnac leaders, which the peace patched up in February 1415 had not seriously improved, is taken into account, and if it is remembered that he had confidence in being able to repeat the tactics of Crécy were he to be encountered by heavy armed troops in the

---

[1] In H. T. Riley, *Memorials of London Life in the 13th, 14th and 15th Centuries* (1867), p. 604.

open field, it was a justifiable movement, and one which would serve to reveal the state of preparations in France. The events of September, the siege of Harfleur and the loss of part of his force by dysentery, shortened his reconnaissance, but did not alter the general plan. Should such a view of the Agincourt campaign be accepted (and it is assumed that the supplies of siege equipment taken by Henry, the gunners and the engineers, were for the purpose of reducing Harfleur only), a more lenient verdict upon his strategy than the one normally held is likely to result. He may originally have been set upon a full-scale invasion, but the casualties which he suffered at Harfleur, the departure of many of his transport vessels, and the length of time he had been detained at the mouth of the Seine was the reason why he shortened his reconnaissance march, while at any rate making some warlike display in France to satisfy his creditors in England.

The expedition made for the Chef de Caux on the Seine estuary and landed on 14 August. On the 17th Henry marched to Graville about four kilometres west of Harfleur, and by the 19th the latter was surrounded. Harfleur was called by Monstrelet the principal key to France. It was difficult to take since it was defended by a curtain wall with three strongly defended gates, each with drawbridge, portcullis and 'angle towers according to the doctrine of Master Giles' (Giles Colonna), as the author of the *Gesta* observed. Outside the wall was a deep ditch. The river Lézarde which ran through the town was flooded in the north of the place, and ran through the defended harbour that could be closed at high tide. Nobody was holding the northern bank of the Seine and the whole force could get ashore and occupy a place at the foot of the high ground to the west of Harfleur. This was not in sight of the town, but when the English came nearer they found the western side strongly defended with a circular bastion called a bulwark which projected into the moat and was built from tree trunks and constructed so as to leave emplacements and loopholes for the fire of guns and cross-bows. The king's first move was to send a party by a circuitous route round the north of the town, avoiding the flooding of the Lézarde. This gave total investment of the place by land. At sea the English fleet was in the Seine estuary, preventing any relief force reaching the town. The besiegers settled down to trench-digging and mining. Henry hoped to reduce the place by about 12 September. But the heat and the damp from the marshes were not long in producing dysentery among troops only too ready, in the heat, to drink the polluted water, and the casualties were considerable. The numbers who died have been put as high as 2,000, but it seems more likely that the figure includes men sent home by royal licence. Of the 40 men-at-arms in the party of, and including, the earl of Suffolk, the earl himself died (17 Sept.) and 8 others returned ill by royal licence, but out of his 120 archers only 2 are recorded as having returned to England through illness. One or two others may have died, but the accounts record 90 archers present at Agincourt, a creditable total, and 21 left behind to garrison the town.[1] The sickness appears to have hit the *generosi* more freely than the rank and file. Bishop Courtenay, Henry V's young and gifted friend, the eldest son of Sir Philip Courtenay of Powderham and a Devonshire landowner; John Phelip, a Suffolk man who came from Denington near Framlingham and had fought in the expedition to aid Burgundy (1412); William Butler, lord of the manor of Warrington; and the earls of Suffolk and Arundel were among those who died. The dwindling of the army induced Henry V to make a final effort to capture the town and on 18 September after a nightlong cannonade, the assault was delivered. The besieged had received no help from Rouen and food was running out. Early in the morning Clarence on the east side of the town received an offer of surrender if no help reached the place by 22 September. At first the king was for unconditional capitulation. But eventually he decided to listen to the French proposal that the siege should be suspended and the town handed over if no help arrived by the specified date. By that day none of the French commanders had stirred to help Harfleur. The constable Charles d'Albret was at Honfleur on the southern bank of the Seine, and Marshal Boucicaut, appointed lieutenant and captain-general for the French king on 28 July 1415, was waiting for the English at Caudebec, but did not approach the town. The Dauphin remained inactive at Rouen. Henry, therefore, had Harfleur at his mercy, but there was to be no pillaging. His purpose was to make it into a second Calais. The captains of the garrison, the commander, the Sieur de Gaucourt, and others were 'divided up among the English commanders', and on 23 September Henry left his headquarters

[1] P.R.O., E. 101/46/24.

and entered the town barefoot to offer thanksgiving at the parish church of St. Martin. He then had the town surveyed, and all who were willing to take the oath of allegiance were allowed to retain their goods and possessions. The better sort of burgesses who refused to accept the king's conditions were transported to England until they could ransom themselves. Two thousand of the poorer residents along with the women and children were escorted out of the town as far as Lillebonne whence they were sent by Marshal Boucicaut in boatloads to Rouen. On the eve of the surrender Henry wrote a letter to the mayor of London announcing the capture of the town and on 8 October a proclamation was issued to the merchants, victuallers, and craftsmen of London and other large towns in England, offering free houses and other advantages to all who were prepared to settle in Harfleur. Henry permitted the leading defenders of the town (60 knights and 200 gentlemen of the best-known families) to depart on parole: the condition being that they delivered themselves up 'as faithful captives' at Calais by 11 November, if a general submission had not already been arranged. The date is worth observing as it shows that Henry was not proposing to fight throughout the winter. The prisoners would, of course, be safe in Calais, but they were too important to be left there. They were going back with the king's army when it crossed early in November.

From these assignments and other contemporary testimony it is clear that Henry had taken the decision to march through Normandy to Calais. His total force including the headquarters unit did not reach 6,000. There were scarcely 5,000 archers and 900 men at arms, as Elmham's *Liber Metricus* has it. At the beginning of September he had been proposing to go by Monti-villiers, Dieppe, and Rouen to Paris, but the weakening of his force had precluded the larger plan. The dangers of a demonstration march through maritime Normandy were pointed out to him by his captains, but he was perfectly confident of his ability to engage a much larger force than his own within his own duchy. The assurance of Divine aid to which his chaplain biographer alludes was also based on intelligible military calculations. He did not think that his opponents had the morale or the unity to interfere with him. The exhibition of their supinity given during the siege of Harfleur strengthened the opinion. He must have expected to be watched and pursued, none the less the march ending in Agincourt was not a foolhardy expedition, it was a limited operation, enabling him to gauge the strength of the French command, and the careful dispositions made for that march, the severe discipline exercised in the army, the screening scouts ahead, show that he was taking precautions.

Starting on 8 October[1] Henry brought his force, marching as lightly as possible, without the baggage-wagons, past Fécamp and the castle of Arques to Eu (12 Oct.), where a large French force awaited him, but offered no fight, and into Ponthieu, making towards the mouth of the Somme. Already there were rumours of a large army waiting to dispute his crossing of the river and the chaplain biographer reports that there was much speculation whether the French would have the spirit to oppose him now or later. Two bodies of the French forces come into consideration: the advance guard under the constable Charles d'Albret and the main body under the dukes of Orléans and Bourbon. Waurin records that d'Albret, Arthur of Richmont, the duke of Alençon, and others were present on the Somme near Abbeville when the English army approached the river. The advance guard was evidently the force which is known to have been deputed to shadow Henry from the north bank of the Somme. It seems to have rejoined the main body at Bapaume after that force had moved up from Péronne. From Eu Henry, deciding to follow the track of Edward III before Crécy, was approaching the ford of Blanche Taque when a Gascon prisoner asserted that the ford had been staked and was being watched from the north bank by Marshal Boucicaut with a force of 6,000 fighting men. In fact it was not Boucicaut, but d'Albret who was awaiting Henry, but the king believed the report and concluded that the party which had been sent by the Calais garrison to establish contact with him after he had crossed the river had not reached its destination. Hostile elements in Boulogne and Étaples had been alerted. French sources relate that this English connecting force had been dissipated before reaching the area at all. It was therefore necessary for Henry to find a crossing farther up the river, and so began the long search for the right place, given the hard fact that the bridges were down and the causeways through the marshy river valley broken.

[1] Following A. H. Burne, *The Agincourt War* (1956), who does not accept the date given in the contemporary Chronicle of London (Cleopatra, C. IV, *Chronicles of London*, ed. Kingsford, p. 119) as the 'firste day of Octobre', nor Wylie's 6 Oct.

Henry's movements were shadowed by a force marching parallel on the north bank. The French tactics were to compel him to march up into the area of Péronne where a large army was waiting to deal with his starved and dispirited troops. It was not thought necessary to engage him before he got there.

Between 13 October and 19 October when it was marching up the river by Boves (16 Oct.), Corbie (17 Oct.), and Nesle, the army was living on meagre rations; but at the latter place Henry received information that the fords at the villages of Béthancourt and of Voyennes were unguarded, even if the causeways leading to them were destroyed. It was found possible to fill the gaps in the *pavé* with timber and brushwood, but it took a whole day (19 Oct.) to pass the force over the two crossings, and the French army, at Bapaume, should have attacked it at its most vulnerable moment. As it was, every man was across by the evening and the French leaders at their head-quarters at Péronne had to make up their minds whether to follow and engage Henry or to let him march on to Calais. If wisdom had prevailed, the advice of the constable d'Albret and of Marshal Boucicaut to let the English get away and to con-centrate on the recovery of Harfleur would have been followed and Henry would have trailed home with only the capture of a single coast town to narrate to the mayor and citizens of London who had helped him so liberally. To Henry's satisfaction the French leaders were determined upon a set battle and from Péronne sent heralds to tell him that they would fight him before he got to Calais. Henry told the heralds that they must come and find him in the field. His men were wet and tired with marching in the rain and food had not been plentiful, but he was determined to keep going and not to let himself be manœuvred into a position favourable to the French heavy armour. To make the best use of the archers, the ground and the weather was all-important. This accounts for the substantial distance covered in the next three days (20–23 Oct.). The Ancre was crossed at Miraumont, the Canche at Frévent, while all the time the French were marching parallel with his right flank and somewhat ahead of him. For three days the two forces moved close to one another without being aware of the fact: when eventually the armies came within sight, after the English had crossed the Ternoise, and had reached the high ground on the right bank of the river (24 Oct.), Henry saw that he could not select his position as he had hoped, for the French were now effectively barring the road to Calais and he would have to fight his way through.

The position they eventually chose lay between the woods surrounding the villages of Agincourt and Tramecourt. There was no circumventing the greatly superior French army, stated by the author of the *Gesta* to be 'thirty times more than our own', but probably, according to the latest computations, to be reckoned as at least 40,000 to 50,000. The attempt of the distinguished French historian, M. Ferdinand Lot, to argue, on the basis of three single lines of men-at-arms filling the battle front, that the French force only just exceeded 5,000 has not been found convincing. To the French it was a matter of numbers. They could not fail to overwhelm a small tired force which, according to the account later given by Jean Jouvenel des Ursins, had asked to be engaged before the date originally fixed (26 Oct.) owing to its exhaustion. The French chroniclers state that Henry offered to restore all he had taken and give security to pay for damage done, if only he might be allowed to pass: Walsingham avers that he was prepared to give up 'omnia oppida et castra potenter requisita in Normannia et Francia'. But the chaplain, whose account of Agincourt is the most circumstantial, relates nothing of this. On the night of 24 October the English lay at Maisoncelles, the southernmost of a triangle of villages of which the others were Agincourt and Tramecourt. Each little commune lay within a wood. The French had their left on Tramecourt: their right behind the cluster of houses and farms that was Agincourt, while their communications extended back to Ruisseauville. The outposts of the two forces lay close to one another, between the woods of Agincourt and Tramecourt, so close that one side could hear the talking and hammering of the other. Each army filled the open space between the woods, a newly sown wheat field, saturated by the rain that fell all through the night. Next morning the French formed up on three battles with a vanguard estimated at 5,000 to 10,000 men-at-arms with spears and lances; the second mass behind had a depth of some twenty to thirty ranks and there was a rearguard for reinforcement if necessity arose. There were very few archers on the French side, but on either wing of the vanguard detachments of horse were stationed, whose duty it was to ride down and break up the English archers. The small numbers of the

English allowed of no reserve. Their only advantage was the narrowness of the front into which the large French force had to fit itself. There was plenty of room behind towards Ruisseauville, but the road to Calais lay between the two woods and the French counted on crushing the English by sheer numbers in the narrow gap. Henry, commanding the centre, threw out two wings in echelon under the duke of York and Lord Camoys, while all along in front in a half circle were the archers, grouped in cones or herces, each consisting of 200 men in open order, with the apex of the wedge inwards. Each archer had planted in the soft ground before him the sharpened stake prepared at the Somme crossing, so as to break the force of the French mounted attack. For three hours in the morning of 25 October there was no move, but at 9 o'clock Henry ordered the baggage with the royal chapel to move up and the English army advanced. The French horse tried to ride down the archers, but with little success, owing to accurate English shooting. The vanguard then met the full force of the English barrage, but their better numbers made the English recoil at first, until the lances recovered and held firm while the archers poured their arrows into the sides and rear of the French battle, and when arrows were done came in with swords and hatchets. Very soon these flank attacks told and the French centre gave ground, while all the time the dense ranks behind them were pressing forward until there was no room to manœuvre, and a great body of men in heavy armour and close order presented a vulnerable target to the lightly clad troops and mobile English, who butchered their opponents 'like sheep'. In half an hour the issue was clear, but it took between two to three hours for the English to pound and destroy their opponents whose last line never attempted to enter the mêlée at all. It also took considerable time to extract the French leaders who were found to be alive, and to assign them to their captors. While they were being pulled out, the cry was raised that reinforcements had reached the French. It was, in fact, a hopeless attempt on the part of Anthony of Brabant, the brother of John the Fearless, to rally the second line. At the same time news was received that the baggage had been plundered, including the coffer containing jewels along with the seals of the chancery, the sword of state, and the crown. The apparent danger caused Henry to give the fateful order to kill the prisoners who were awaiting distribution, and under adverse demonstrations this was carried out in the case of all save captains of the highest rank. The order is probably responsible for the high number of French killed rather than taken prisoner, and there were cries of protest in the army at the loss of so many valuable ransoms. Relieved from all danger in the rear, the English went on to deal with the second French contingent, but the enemy gave little resistance, while those who were mounted got away as quickly as they could.

On the French side the slaughter was immense. The greater part of the chivalry of France had been lost. Among the dead were the dukes of Alençon, Bar, Brabant, the constable d'Albret, the admiral Jacques de Châtillon, Philip count of Nevers, another brother (like Brabant) of John the Fearless, the counts of Vaudémont, Marle, Blamont, Roucy, Dammartin, Vaucourt, and Fauquembergue, more than 1,500 knights and 4,000 to 5,000 men-at-arms. On the English side casualties were unbelievably low. The chaplain gives 13–15, other accounts anything from 20–40. It seems most likely that it was below 300.[1] The two principal captains dead were the duke of York and the earl of Suffolk, the young Michael de la Pole, and six or seven knights including two Welshmen, one of whom, David ap Llewelyn also called Davy Gam, was knighted on the field.

Henry was correct in attributing the French disaster to lack of control and insubordination. The troops were not collected and brought to their jumping-off grounds till too late. There was no unity of direction. Units were unpunctual in moving to their stations and there was a general lack of co-ordination because commanders were too independent to submit to the discipline of a staff. After the failure of the French initial cavalry charge to destroy the archers, discipline in the movements of the heavy armed forces was essential, and the bunching of the French men-at-arms can only be explained by disorder from the outset. These material factors received less consideration from the English chroniclers than immaterial reasons: Divine aid, the verdict of God against France for her iniquities, invoked by Bishop Beaufort when he enumerated in parliament a 'trinity of divine judgements' upon the justice of the English cause. Observed more coolly, the campaign just fought brought only two advantages to the English: the possession of Harfleur, which

---

[1] See the discussion in J. H. Wylie, *The Reign of Henry the Fifth*, ii. 183. The figures given by English chroniclers are certainly underestimated.

was in effect to prove a doubtful blessing, and the ransoms, when they could be paid, of a number of high-born captives. Many of the minor sort of prisoners were released on parole or redeemed at less than their true value and in Calais batches were bought and sold locally. Calais citizens and English returning troops entered into bonds with the king to pay various sums into the Exchequer before the following summer, on the chance of making what they could out of their captives. A certain number were taken into the service of the English, but on the whole only the higher type of prisoner was brought back, such as the dukes of Orléans and Bourbon, Lord Gaucourt, and the senior defenders of Harfleur. On 5 October 1415 the place was named as the rendezvous for all knights and esquires and valets desirous of crossing over to Normandy; and all merchants, victuallers, and artificers willing to reside there were exhorted to go there 'with all speed with their goods and harness and the captain of the town (the earl of Dorset) would provide them with homes, and when settled there the king would grant them a charter of liberties'. Another entry in Letter Book I of the City of London invited merchants and others to speed to the king 'beynge at Harfleure' with all manner of victual, shetys, breches, doublettys, hosene, schone, clothing, armour and artillery' and to be ready 'between this and to-day sevennight' and in the meanwhile to go to the mayor 'who would assign them y redy shippyng and passage.'[1]

The importance attached to Harfleur is strikingly illustrated in 1416. The victuals and supplies coming from England were inadequate and the garrison left behind by Henry when he started his march to Calais had to make raids into the surrounding country. It is in these expeditions that the name of John Fastolf, who in November 1415 led a raid to within six miles of Rouen, is mentioned. In January 1416 the garrison was relieved by an enlarged body of men, 900 men-at-arms and 1,500 archers. When Dorset, who had gone on leave, returned in March 1416, a specially large foray was mounted to make a three-day raid to the north-east. On its return it ran into French patrols at Valmont. The army had been observed by the French, and now found itself opposed by a force of 3,000–4,000 men. This was under the command of Bernard d'Albret count of Armagnac who had brought 6,000 Gascons from the south. The French

[1] Riley, *Memorials*, p. 628, from Letter-Book I, f. clxviii (ed. R. R. Sharpe, p. 161).

cavalry cut their way through the thin English line, but instead
of turning back and rounding on the English men-at-arms and
archers, set about attacking the grooms and the baggage. This
gave time to Dorset to re-form his troops and take them off to a
flank where there was a large garden surrounded by a tall hedge
and a ditch. This garden he lined with troops and the position
was not one which Armagnac liked attacking. Negotiations, as
before Agincourt, accordingly took place, but the terms exacted
by the constable were too high: it was by now late for them to
attack, and under cover of darkness the English force was able
to escape westwards, going probably through Fécamp and
turning south-west till they reached at dawn the wood of Les
Loges four miles east of Étretat. They were still there throughout the second day but on the third they marched along the
coast for twenty miles, rounding the Cap de la Hève to the
Seine estuary, until they were stopped by a mounted column, a
patrol of the Marshal de Loigny, who dismounted upon the
high ground and ran down upon the tired English troops: but
the effort threw the assailants into disorder and they were never
able to bring a sufficiency of men into conflict with the English;
the French were, in fact, cut up and the English had to scrounge
what they wanted and strip the bodies.

Armagnac did arrive, with the main body, and when the
English, engaged in stripping corpses, perceived the new enemy,
they picked up their arms again and charged straight up the
cliff against the French. Armagnac's column fled back to
Caudebec, making for Rouen. The route here led the fugitive
force past Harfleur, and the remainder of the Harfleur troops
took to their horses and pursued them. This gave Harfleur a
respite: but it was only a respite, for the count of Armagnac
had determined, however much the French council were ready
for peace, to reconquer the place. Harfleur was much more
vulnerable than Calais; at Calais the English Channel is at its
narrowest: at the Seine estuary four times as wide. The French
aimed at securing a local command of the sea and maintaining
a blockade which would starve Harfleur into submission. France
had insufficient naval reserves for this, but she had recourse to
Navarre and above all to Genoa.

To return to 1415. Henry himself crossed with the chief
prisoners from Calais on 16 November. He was met and
carried ashore by the barons of the Cinque Ports, passed through

Canterbury, Dover, and Rochester (19–20 Nov.) to Eltham and entered a much decorated London on 23 November 1415. The great crowds, the symbolical figures, the choirs dressed as angels and priests to meet him were described by the chaplain as a rapturous background to the grave and reserved figure of the king, who may well have been reflecting on the narrowness of his escape. The expedition had brought him great prestige in every quarter, but its positive results were small. The chronicler of St. Denys notes that before he returned from France, a deputation from the English parliament had crossed to urge Henry to follow up his victory as soon as the winter was done. After Agincourt and on the way to Calais the captured French dukes had been encouraged by him to suggest to Charles VI that negotiations should be opened immediately. Which was Henry to do? In the November parliament Bishop Beaufort urged that the king's journey had only just begun and that parliament must do for the king as he had done for them. It was therefore resolved to grant him the customs from Michaelmas 1416 for the whole of his life (43s. on every sack of wool, 100s. on every last of hides; foreigners to pay 60s. and 106s. 8d.) along with a tunnage of 3s. on wine and a poundage of 1s. on all other goods entering the country. The commons stipulated that this grant should not be made a precedent for future reigns. They also granted a further tenth and fifteenth payable by 11 November 1416. This grant of the customs has been the subject of adverse comment as being a surrender, made in the flush of enthusiasm, of the right to control supply. But it will be remembered that the customs were the most productive source of assignment with which to finance any expedition and the commons were clearly anticipating that Henry would continue his campaign.

Henry made no secret of his determination to continue. At the beginning of 1416 he began strong anti-French propaganda among kings he knew to be favourable to his cause and by 23 January 1416 started consultation with his own lords, knights, and esquires about the future conquest of France. With Flanders the truce was extended (25 April 1416 until 15 June 1417) and a further series of negotiations was undertaken to hold open the trade routes between England and the Burgundian dominions. John the Fearless, while maintaining a semblance of devotion to the interests of France, had no desire to close the Flemish ports.

But there were constant infractions of the truce on which commissions periodically had to adjudicate. Continual diplomatic contact was preserved between England and Burgundy, which, while ostensibly concerned with trade, could take on a political aspect if occasion arose. In the case of France Henry characteristically prepared for war and negotiated for a peaceful settlement.

CHAPTER V

HENRY V: 1417–1422

A LEADING factor in Anglo-French relations was the Emperor Sigismund. That the visit he paid to England, intended by him initially as a measure of pacification, should have terminated in an offensive and defensive alliance with the empire was not a result that could have been foreseen; but it was one that had considerable effect upon English policy in the council of Constance, while it completed the encirclement of France aimed at by Henry V. From England there had been of late two approaches to the empire. In February 1411 Hartank van Clux and Dr. Stokes had gone over to discuss 'certain leagues, alliances and friendships', and 'the method, form and assessment of aid, subvention or subsidy to be given to each other in time of necessity, as well as trading and other relationships between the subjects of either'.[1] It is probable, as Caro originally suggested, that Clux and Stokes were sent primarily to encourage Sigismund to arbitrate in the dispute between Poland and the Teutonic order, a matter in which Henry IV was much interested: but the terms of the commission suggest a much wider reference. When Henry V succeeded to the throne, Sigismund wrote to him to remind him of the negotiations which had been in progress with a view to co-ordinating policy on conciliar matters, and mentioned that these points had been raised with Clux and Stokes.[2]

After December 1413, when John XXIII's bull of summons was issued, the council was a live political issue, and in the early summer of 1414 Clux was sent to Sigismund once more. The commission given to him and the outcome of the embassy are alike unknown: but on 23 July 1414 a further embassy led by Sir Walter Hungerford was dispatched; and the preamble to Hungerford's commission states that Clux had discussed with Sigismund *foedera amicitiarum et ligarum*.[3] The new embassy was

---

[1] *Foedera*, iv. i. 187.

[2] 'et enim alia tractare pertinentia ad concilium generale', H. Finke, *Acta concilii Constanciensis*, i. 226, n. 1.

[3] *Foedera*, iv. ii. 86. F. Schoenstedt, 'König Sigismund und die Westmächter 1414–1415', *Die Welt als Geschichte*, Jahrg. 1954, Heft 314, pp. 154–5, argues that

M

to follow up and bring to a definite conclusion the proposals discussed by Clux; the main question canvassed had been the coming council, and Sigismund had emphasized his desire for a tripartite undertaking between France, England and himself to ensure the council's success, whatever line of action the three popes decided to follow.

But Sigismund was also anxious over Burgundian intervention. A memorandum that can be dated about the end of August 1414 envisaged a joint move against Duke John by Charles VI (whose adhesion to the council Sigismund had obtained in the treaty of Trino), Henry and Sigismund. Henry was to be promised enfeoffment with the imperial lands in Flanders in return for his co-operation. There is no clear evidence that Hungerford concluded anything definite with Sigismund under this latter head, but a letter sent round by Sigismund to notabilities of the time advertised the emperor's aim of reconciling England and France and of doing so, if he could, in the council. In the council Sigismund said that he had had frequent conversations with Henry V's ambassadors, in which they emphasized Henry's hereditary rights in France and his attempts by negotiations to have those rights honoured. He can have been left in no uncertainty about the English attitude towards that country, and Henry's ambassadors were given every encouragement to attach the emperor by pointing out to him the advantage of an English alliance against France. Henry was sincere in his attitude towards the problems of faith and reform with which the council was dealing: he sent the strongest delegation he could, but he had above all a political purpose, seeing in the council a convenient platform for stating his case against the old adversary.

The journey of Sigismund which took him away from the council after the flight and formal deposition of John until the early days of 1417 was undertaken, partly to secure the allegiance of the Spanish legation in the council (effected by the treaty of Narbonne), but most of all in order to reconcile England and France by periodical visits to both kingdoms. It is unlikely that, at first, Sigismund had any expectation of seeing England, for France needed him badly as a mediator after the failure of her last embassy (July 1415). He was then planning

a formal treaty with England was made some time between the end of Aug. and the beginning of Oct. 1414.

his journey to Nice to negotiate the withdrawal of Spanish obedience to Benedict XIII which took place in the capitulation of Narbonne, and it was suggested to him that he should go to Paris, if Lewis of Bavaria was prepared to pay the expenses of the journey. The project did not materialize: but while the discussions were in progress with the Aragonese at Perpignan in September, the news of the capture of Harfleur arrived, and Sigismund decided to send envoys to England to propose an armistice. Two arrived, but Henry did not postpone his march. After Agincourt, Sigismund tried to meet Henry at Calais, but the movements of Burgundy negatived his plans for the moment. In February 1416 he saw his opportunity, and raised sufficient funds for the journey by conferring a dukedom upon Count Amadeus of Savoy.

In Paris, where he arrived with a liveried company of 800, he found the French council divided. The dukes of Berry and Bourbon were for peace: but Count Bernard of Armagnac, heartened by his success against Dorset at Valmont, was for starving out the English garrison by an efficient sea blockade and by strong forces guarding the roads; for the English were now hopelessly on the defensive, and Bernard was determined that Harfleur should not become another Calais. The French were looking to Sigismund to induce Henry to moderate his demands, but with this deeper cleavage of opinion on Harfleur, what clear lead could Sigismund obtain in Paris? He resolved to transfer the negotiations to England, where Henry was entirely ready to receive him and impress him with the justice of his case. The visit was typical of the emperor. He liked personal meetings with heads of governments, but was far too optimistic about the effect of his own interventions in the Anglo-French quarrel. He had a sense of occasion but no sense of time. Already for more than ten months he had been absent from the council of Constance, which he had instructed to take no fundamental resolutions on policy during his absence. He did not see that the longer he stayed in England, the more would his financial dependence on his hosts accumulate, and that if Harfleur was not relieved he would be swept into the maelstrom of national indignation against the duplicity of the French who talked peace, but in fact were blockading an English possession. He arrived at Dover on 1 May and was given a reception increasingly impressive the nearer he approached

London. Arrived in the capital, he was installed in the palace of Westminster, Henry himself going to the archbishop's manor of Lambeth. He was given the gold S.S. collar which he wore at public ceremonies thereafter, and installed (24 May) as a knight of St. George at Windsor, while parliament was kept in being so that he might see how it worked. Everything was done for his comfort and entertainment and Sigismund expressed himself duly delighted and grateful: on his departure his entourage scattered leaflets containing encomiums of England (*felix Anglia et benedicta*) and from the money which Henry had supplied to him he gave, on this occasion at any rate, liberal quantities to members of the royal household. Sigismund was not the only foreign notability now concerned with the question of Anglo-French peace. On 28 May another knight of the Garter, Count William of Holland, Zealand, and Hainault, arrived at the suggestion of the French king. He was the husband of Margaret, daughter of Duke Philip the Bold of Burgundy, and the Dauphin, Jean, had married his only daughter and heiress, Jacqueline. It was through the joint efforts of Sigismund and Count William that the king's projected expedition, indentures for which were being drafted in May 1416, was postponed for a time, while a French embassy headed by the archbishop of Rheims visited London, and the leading French prisoners were brought into the discussions.

On 20 June Henry had announced his imminent arrival at Southampton where the military and naval forces which had foregathered were instructed to wait for him. On the 28th he was sending commissioners to France to negotiate a truce, so that a change must have come over the situation towards midsummer. The chronology is difficult to disentangle but it is clear that Harfleur was the nodal point of discussion and that Henry must have been satisfied between these dates that the blockade would not be pressed by the Armagnacs. The town had been besieged by a Franco-Genoese naval force with the strong encouragement of the count of Armagnac ever since the end of May, and Henry's attitude towards the government in Paris depended upon whether it was prepared to leave off the blockade and negotiate in all good faith. In the peace negotiations, at which the emperor, Count William, and the French negotiators were present, Henry began by including in the terms on which he was willing to treat with France the proviso that he should be given possession of Harfleur and enough of the surrounding country to support a garrison. At this stage he was prepared to waive his claim to the French throne provided that he was given all the lands assigned to him in the treaty of Brétigny—the whole of western France except Brittany. A proposal was then made that while negotiations were in progress Harfleur should be handed over to the emperor and the count of Holland. To this there was so much objection on the part of the commons that it had to be dropped. It was even suggested that the chief prisoners should be released upon giving hostages for their return in the event of the conversations breaking down. The failure of both these projects seems to have been due to external pressure, in the main to opinion in the City of London. But it was eventually agreed that, subject to the French king approving, commissioners should arrange for a three years' truce and that within five weeks from its conclusion the kings of England and France, the emperor and Count William of Holland should meet on the frontier of English Calais to prepare for the new discussions. The French ambassadors, accompanied by Lord Gaucourt, returned.

This was at any rate some advance towards peace. The fact that the negotiations broke down was due neither to the demands of the English embassy nor to the wariness of Charles VI, who was quite prepared to call a meeting at Beauvais to settle the terms of the truce: but to the intransigeance of the count of Armagnac, who in the council held at Paris on 5 July to consider arrangements for the personal interview between the two kings,[1] represented that the proposed three years' truce was nothing but a device for saving Harfleur, and urged that no English embassy should be received. The outcome of this opposition was the worst possible solution for France: it was decided that negotiations over the treaty should be drawn out, while a stranglehold was to be kept upon Harfleur in the hope of its speedy surrender. The English embassy, when it arrived, quickly perceived, and was not slow in complaining, that negotiations were being protracted merely to gain time for Harfleur to surrender: by the end of July the position of Harfleur was critical and there could be no delaying the English countermove.

[1] St. Denys, vi. 24.

No opportunity was lost in England of convincing Sigismund of the reality of *Gallicana duplicitas*. Until late in July he had done his best to bring the parties together: he had sent (21 June) the count palatine of Hungary and others of his own entourage to Paris, an embassy followed almost immediately by the archbishop of Rheims and his colleagues, who having accompanied Sigismund to England, were granted a safe conduct on 20 June, allowing them twenty-three days in which to visit France and return; and secondly by Lord Gaucourt and five companions. He had received from Gaucourt a favourable reply to the points specified by the English council, and communicated news of it to Henry. Then, two days later, had come the news of the French occupation of the Isle of Wight and blockading of Portsmouth[1] and shortly after that of the bad treatment given to the English embassy of 28 June. Although it was decided, on 29 July, that representatives of both sides should be at Calais and Boulogne on 16 August for a further discussion, the danger of prolonging the agony of Harfleur was manifest. It was under this disillusionment that Sigismund made, at Canterbury, on 15 August, a treaty[2] of mutual help and alliance with Henry: it was a document which in its reversal of imperial policy towards France and her allies had a profound effect upon the English and German nations at the council of Constance and, for the time being only, upon the balance of power in contemporary Europe.

It was, in a sense, a naïve document, setting forth Sigismund's disappointment at the failure of his plan to reconcile France and England in the interest of restoring unity to the Church. He had done all he could to get certain articles, agreed by himself and the count of Holland, accepted by the royal house and by the French council, but the French king, loving deceit, had rejected them in order to destroy the unity of the Church, just as he had been the source of opposition to Sigismund at Perpignan: and when he came over to England to help his brother get his due, the French had treated him with derision. Determined to bring such provocations to an end, he had now resolved to make a treaty of perpetual friendship with Henry and his sons or, failing sons, his brothers, to resist attack from any quarter, saving only the Pope and the Church. Natives and merchants of either side were to have free access

---

[1] St. Denys, vi. 64.   [2] Termed *Alligantia*. *Foedera*, IV. ii. 171–2.

to the territories of the other, so long as they paid the necessary
dues and obeyed existing laws: neither side was to harbour the
traitors, rebels, or banished exiles of the other; each power was
free to move against the French king, Sigismund to recover lost
lands, rights, and possessions, Henry to reconquer his kingdom
of France and other inheritances and rights that were his, and
each would assist the other in 'such recovery'. If peace 'which
we have laboured so much to secure' could be established,
Sigismund would recognize the territorial settlement and assist
Henry to maintain his possessions and his rights; if it could not
be made, or was broken, the alliance should stand firm: the same
applied on the English side towards imperial acquisitions. If
through any agreement with France the king of the Romans
received back lost rights or possessions, Henry was to recognize
this settlement. In all alliances to be made outside the treaty
by the parties, there was to be a clause saving the rights of
either king. For greater security, Henry was to have the treaty
ratified and confirmed in parliament, Sigismund by the
electors of the empire: and the document was to be affirmed
on either side by corporal oath taken on the gospels.

'Pro bono pacis in Angliam descendimus.' Sigismund was
convinced that the schism in the Church and, in particular, the
obstinate survival in the Holy See of Benedict XIII was due to
the quarrel between France and England, and writing to the
Germans at Constance he justified (22 Aug. 1416) his long
absence by the necessity of securing peace between the two
countries with the resulting union in the Church, and by the
fact that already Henry V had instructed the English nation
at Constance to vote as the German did.[1] It is remarkable that
he should have still gone on regarding himself as a mediator,
but all his hopes were on the forthcoming triangular council
at Calais, at which the duke of Burgundy was expected as well
as the ambassadors of the French king. Evidently he still
thought that by means of individual alliances between the
empire and France, England and Burgundy, the conditions of
a general pacification in the west could be achieved. He was
allied to Charles VI at Trino: with England by the 'league' of
1414 and now by the treaty of Canterbury: Burgundy, with
which he had to settle certain scores, remained; but his new
partner Henry was also hoping for an understanding with John

[1] H. Finke, *Acta concilii Constanciensis*, iv. 468–9.

the Fearless, and in the eyes of Henry's chaplain biographer it was the duke who held the key to the situation. The position in the Channel had gradually improved. By the battle of the Seine (15 Aug.) Bedford had broken the siege of Harfleur and relieved the town, and an English convoy had no difficulty in getting across the narrows where earlier it might easily have met with Genoese opposition. On 5 September Henry crossed from Sandwich to Calais to find the emperor waiting to greet him; and for six weeks negotiations, about which tantalizingly little information survives, were in progress. The importance of the Calais meeting is attested not only by the number of lords in the town, but by the presence of the chancellor, the keeper of the privy seal, and Archbishop Chichele, who, in his diocese, had appointed a vicar-general and expected to be away from his province for some little time. The archbishop, an expert in the negotiations for the French marriage, was joined by Sir Ralph Rochford, Robert Waterton, and Philip Morgan, the three envoys sent to negotiate at Beauvais. By 9 September the archbishop of Rheims, Gontier Col, and the other French envoys had arrived, and the talks, initiated by a schedule addressed to Sigismund as mediator, had begun. The French proposals offered to reopen the marriage question, which Henry had refused to consider while the French were besieging Harfleur, and to pay down a large sum of money. It was suggested somewhat optimistically that if the English declined to agree, the emperor might give them 'aid' from his own imperial lands in addition to the money already put down. If the English would not be content with this, then Sigismund was asked to inform the French, so that a clear reply might be given by Charles VI. The allies (*confoederati*) of each side must be comprised in any treaty made and a special truce for carrying out the terms established in the area between the Somme and Gravelines. It soon appeared that no terms of this sort could be conceded, and that a truce was the immediate solution. With difficulty Sigismund obtained one to last from 9 October to 2 February 1417, which has been considered simply as a means to 'cover up' Henry's warlike preparations. It may have been a device to get rid of the French envoys, for the duke of Burgundy was approaching and upon the conversations between him and Henry V much was to depend.

The interviews with Burgundy, for whose security while at

Calais Duke Humphrey of Gloucester had stood as a hostage, lasted until 13 October. At the time their nature did not transpire, and the author of the *Gesta* opined that like all Frenchmen Duke John would be found 'double-dealing': 'one person in public and another in private'. But he was not playing with the king: he acknowledged the justice of Henry's claim to the French throne and recognized him as his sovereign, but decided to postpone doing homage until they had conquered some 'notable part' of the French kingdom. He would help him secretly; though he would not be seen to assist him against the actual French king, and indeed had to make the correct exception against taking arms against his suzerain: such an undertaking was a pure convention to which no importance need be attached. This singular agreement is not untrue to the character of John the Fearless, but raises a question of the recompense made him by Henry for such a settlement. No evidence of this is forthcoming, but it cannot have been very much; for in the summer of 1417 he sent no help when called upon by Henry to do so; and in the following year, when Henry was moving into the area of the Upper Seine, his conduct was quite at variance with his promises. Towards Sigismund he proved himself equally unreliable. It has been pointed out[1] that although he did homage to Sigismund for his possessions in the counties of Burgundy and Alost, no sooner had he left than he entered into negotiations with the estates of Brabant and undertook to protect them against any attempts made by Sigismund to bring them back into the empire.

The repercussions caused by the treaty of Canterbury at the council of Constance were considerable. The favours bestowed on his return by Sigismund upon the English delegation were not lost upon the French cardinals, especially Fillastre, who viewed with suspicion the influence of the bishop of Salisbury (Robert Hallum) in the council. After an abortive attempt in November 1416, in December Cardinal Pierre d'Ailly, acting as protector of the French kingdom at the council, raised an objection to the English being reckoned a nation for voting purposes in the council, the problems of priority having been posed by the advent of Spanish representatives who claimed to represent more territory than the English. When Sigismund returned on 27 January 1417 the whole council, 'even the

---

[1] By Wylie, op. cit., ii. 29.

Cardinals' (as Fillastre observes), went out to meet him, and
in the cathedral the sermon was preached by Bishop Hallum.
It was not long before the emperor took up the question raised
by d'Ailly and showed his displeasure at the trend of opinion
revealed in the council against the English.[1] Between the
autumn of 1416 and the spring of 1417, a marked change of
climate took place through the attempt of the Latin bloc to rob
the English of their position as fourth nation, and only the support from the Germans and the fear of dividing the council
restrained the Spanish, French, and Italian delegates from
embodying so extreme a measure in a decree. As it was, the
new grouping produced prolonged tension in the council when
it was a question whether to carry through Sigismund's plan of
enacting reforming measures before the selection of a new
pontiff, a question not solved until in September 1417 Henry V
decided to 'drop' (*dimittere*) the emperor and tell his delegation
to vote for an immediate conclave.

The naval victory won by Bedford on 15 August 1416 had
led to the strengthening of the fortifications and garrisons along
the Norman coast. The truce concluded with the English from
3 October 1416 to 2 February 1417 gave the Armagnacs a short
period of respite, but they were constantly harried by companies in the service of the duke of Burgundy, in Vermandois,
Eu, Aumale, and the Beauvoisis, while in the south-east, the
Upper Seine especially, the duke was aided by men-at-arms
sent by his sisters in Austria and Savoy. There was always the
raiding by the companies against which the French government
had to provide, the primary anxiety being the capital itself.
Meanwhile the problem was to raise sufficient money for the
defence. In February 1417 a second *aide* (the first had been
levied in the autumn of 1416) was imposed, to be collected in
March, while the Dauphin extracted what loans he could from
the cities, while £60,000 was extracted on loan from sixty-seven
leading men of the kingdom then in Paris. In May or early June
a third *aide* was imposed, and on 9 June 1417 a scheme for
quick raising of money was put forward: it was proposed to
increase the income from the gabelle, to impose a tax upon the
clergy, and to abolish both exemptions from *aides* and other
exemptions made since 1407. The general impression was that

---

[1] Quia notorie favebat Anglicis et odio habebat Gallicos', H. Finke, *Acta concilii
Constanciensis*, ii. 90.

every device had been resorted to with the aim of keeping the army in being. Rouen and Caen were put into a state of defence, and instructions were issued to municipal *prévôts* to look to their fortifications and repair them.

By the end of 1416 the English war preparations were well under way. The parliament that met at Westminster on 19 October 1416 voted two-tenths and two-fifteenths, and in November 1416 the convocation of Canterbury, at the urgent request of the king, conveyed through members of the council, voted two-tenths conditionally upon the postponement of one of the tenths granted in the convocation of November–December 1415. This heavy grant was to be repeated in the meeting of 20 December 1417 (again conditionally upon the postponement of an earlier grant). Between 5 and 12 January 1417 the convocation of York granted 'a whole tenth'. Some £136,000 was provided by these taxes upon the laity and clergy. Much attention was paid to the naval preparations. The French had a Genoese squadron of nine carracks stationed at Harfleur, against which the earl of Huntingdon was dispatched, as a preliminary to the invasion, to win a victory off the Chef de Caux. On 23 July 1417 the English force embarked. There were some 12,000 men in all, with about 10,000 fighting effectives. The transports, many hired from the Netherlands and some from opportunist Genoa, amounted to just under 1,500.

The destination was Touques rather than Harfleur, as the French had expected. There was little opposition to the landing and the castle itself capitulated on 3 August, consenting to surrender within six days if no relief came. The Dauphin was at Rouen with an army, but made no move to help. At the same time Deauville Castle, at the mouth of the Touques, surrendered to Salisbury—the English were thus some ten miles along the road from Harfleur to Caen, and, if they preferred, could go up the river Touques to Lisieux. Henry had decided to winter in France. It was his intention now to annex territory rather than to fight his adversaries in a demonstration foray, and he had to secure substantial bases before the winter approached. He was therefore unable to pillage the country, while at the same time his troops must be adequately fed. The problem led him into lower Normandy where the country was prosperous and there were good sea communications between the army and England and Harfleur. Caen was the obvious base but before he attacked it, he sent Clarence to occupy Lisieux. He did not advance to the siege until he was sure that he would not be attacked from the east. Meanwhile the transports were sent back for reinforcements and the earl of March had to 'skim the sea' and preserve communications. Caen was invested on 18 August and subjected to a continuous battering: by 4 September all save the castle had been taken, and the approach of Gloucester from the successful capture of Bayeux heralded its fall: on 8 September the garrison was given letters of safe conduct. The town was ruthlessly pillaged, unquestionably in order to strike terror into the Norman countryside, for the surrender of the smaller places soon followed. Rumours about the size of the English army, estimated at from 30–40,000 men, and the prodigious size of Henry's engines of war also had their effect.

The first phase of the English conquest ended with the fall of Falaise on 16 February 1418. After Caen had capitulated (Sept. 1417) Henry might have been expected to go into winter quarters, but he could not do so. The reason was the activity of John the Fearless on the Oise. The duke had set himself to capture Paris and the first move in his campaign was to isolate the capital from Picardy and Normandy, thus hindering the supplies from reaching Paris from these regions. At the beginning of September John the Fearless captured Beaumont-sur-Oise, largely on account of the treachery of the Seigneur de L'Isle Adam, who deserted the Armagnac cause. On 11 September the Burgundian troops took Pontoise. Senlis had fallen on 8 September. After Pontoise was lost the Seine towns were occupied; Meulan, Mantes, and Vernon submitted and in an enveloping movement on the western side of Paris, Chartres was besieged and surrendered in October. The Burgundian tactics largely determined Henry's actions. It would be unwise to strike at Paris immediately, for a union of France and Burgundy had to be avoided. To go into winter quarters with Burgundy active on the north of the Seine was inadvisable. Before moving to the river Henry chose to attack lower Normandy: for the time being he avoided Falaise. At the beginning of October he advanced, keeping the earl of Warwick as a screen between him and the enemy to guard against any movement from Falaise, and Sir John Talbot to the west of Bayeux as a precaution against enemy enterprises from the Cotentin.

On 10 October the English advance guard was at Alençon, and by the end of the month English forces were at Mortagne, while farther south Warwick had secured Bellême. Alençon became Henry's headquarters for the time, to the alarm of the Angevins, who suspected that Le Mans would soon be captured as a preliminary to the conquest of Maine and Anjou. They also disliked the Burgundians being in Vendôme and threatening Anjou from the east, but their appeals to Paris met with the reply that the government could only afford to protect Paris and that they were advised to make a truce. The outcome was a truce made by Henry with Brittany, Anjou, and Maine on 16 November (1417) to last till Michaelmas (29 Sept.) 1418. In the middle of November 1418 the Burgundians were in Chartres, but the English, while moving up to Verneuil, took no steps to attack the enemy but contented themselves with raiding in the direction of Dreux. Henry had already secured a good deal; with the reduction of Falaise the whole of western Normandy was consolidated beneath him. The place agreed to surrender on 1 February 1418 (if not relieved by 16 February), and its fall, as has been well observed, 'ended the first phase of the English Conquest'.[1]

The Burgundian movements on the Upper Seine were a source of anxiety to Henry as well as being ominous for the Armagnacs. By 23 February 1418 there were Burgundian garrisons at Rouen, Vernon, Mantes, and Caudebec.[2] In the spring of 1418 Louviers and Évreux surrendered to the Burgundians from despair of receiving any help, and a Burgundian official was appointed by John the Fearless to exercise 'un gouvernement sur les marches et fins du pais de Normandie', with headquarters at Vernon, co-operating with the (now) Burgundian captain de L'Isle Adam at Pontoise and with Guy Boutellier at Dieppe and Rouen. For the moment Henry let his captains complete the conquest. Gloucester was sent into the Cotentin along the road through Vire, St. Lô, Carentan, and Valognes, while Gilbert Umfraville, captain of Caen, kept open communications with the latter place by occupying Neuilly l'Evêque. Huntingdon was sent against Coutances, which capitulated on 16 March; and in the south the capture of Avranches and the establishment of a garrison at Pontorson and

[1] R. A. Newhall, *The English Conquest of Normandy* (1924), p. 80.
[2] Cited by Newhall, op. cit., p. 90.

St. James de Beuvron were effected. Warwick was directed against Domfront, the capture of which would give a secure frontier to the south, opening the way into Maine. He was not, however, to storm it, but to reduce it by starvation. On 10 July the French agreed to surrender if by the 22nd the duke of Alençon had not relieved the place. To draw the line of effective English occupation in Maine is, as will be seen, extremely difficult. Complaints were made by the Angevin authorities that the garrisons south of Alençon had been imposing contributions and subsidies on the parishes under the rule of the queen of Sicily, and that estates and manors to which Henry had no claim were being seized. There seems to have been little control exercised over the English captains in these districts. In fact, attention of headquarters was being directed to what was for the immediate present the chief problem: how to extend the Norman frontier eastward without risking a clash with the Burgundians; later it might be necessary to oppose them, but for the moment a position must be seized from which it would be possible to take the initiative, whatever might be happening in the internecine war of Burgundian and Armagnac. Accordingly to Clarence was assigned the task of clearing the valley of the Touques; whence he moved on to the Risle and thence to Harcourt. By 4 April Auge, Orbec, and Pontaudemer had put themselves under English protection, but the abbey of Bec held out. It was besieged throughout April and surrendered, unable to obtain relief, on 4 May 1418.

From this vantage-ground, with Lower Normandy for the most part in his power, Henry had no longer any need to consider Burgundian susceptibilities. Another thing had happened to change the course of French politics. The Burgundians had entered Paris and seized power; Armagnac himself had been taken prisoner and the Burgundians were trying for a peace with their opponents, so as to present a united front against the English. On 5 June the Burgundian leaders and the French lieutenant-general in the *baillages* of Gisors, Rouen, and Caux (now captured) concluded a truce and alliance of all the Norman garrisons against the English. The immediate purpose of this was the mutual strengthening of position held along the Seine. Pont de l'Arche, commanding the passage of the Seine along the road from Louviers to Rouen, was Armagnac: but unless the place received assistance from the Burgundian garrison at Rouen, it could easily be taken, and so, within the larger alliance, an understanding between Rouen and Pont de l'Arche came into effect, to last till Michaelmas. Not that there were particularly good relations between the two, for on the day after the truce was signed Braquemont was removed from the office of admiral and replaced by a Burgundian, and Armagnacs were held in suspicion at Rouen. Henry did not delay. On 27 June 1418 he seized Pont de l'Arche, and a small body got across the river. On 5 July the captain of the fort undertook to surrender by the 20th, unless relieved by King Charles or the Dauphin; with a footing on the north bank a larger force under Clarence passed over and constructed a bridge of boats. By 14 July the English army was across, a signal for the fort to capitulate. Meanwhile Burgundy with Picard forces was now marching for Paris, and on 14 July he made his formal entry. Next day, the chronicler of St. Denis relates, the captain of Pont de l'Arche sent word of his agreement with the English, and shortly afterwards there arrived in Paris a herald from Henry to ascertain whether the duke would observe the truce prorogued at Bayeux till Michaelmas: a defiant reply was received from duke John, who proclaimed that he would fight for Rouen: but the Burgundian did nothing to save Pont de l'Arche which surrendered as agreed on 20 July.

It was now Rouen's turn. The duke of Burgundy in Paris realized that at the moment he could not prevent the English moving downstream. He was very far from being master of the country round the capital. The Armagnacs had both Meaux and Melun, controlling respectively the Marne and the Seine, and in the south-west they were in Montlhéry, blocking in these positions the main channels of the city's provisioning system. On 21 July 1418 they seized Compiègne which they garrisoned strongly enough to control the trading routes into Picardy. Only with the Dauphin's co-operation would Duke John be able to free Normandy from the English. What he could do was to open up the communications between the Parisis and Maine, Perche and Beauce, so as to facilitate an attack on the English on their southern boundary, to procure aid from abroad through embassies to Scotland, Lorraine, Navarre, and Foix, and come to terms with the Dauphin. This last was effected in the short-lived peace of St. Maur-des-Fossées, which the Dauphin could not be brought to ratify. The new

combination must have put Henry on the alert and made him
see that he could not concentrate upon a really big siege until he
was certain of Lower Normandy through the capitulation of
the greater castles. Domfront fell at the end of July, but the
garrison of Cherbourg did not ask for terms until 22 August
1418. Its fall enabled Henry to bring all his effectives into the
siege of the Norman capital.

His forces were engaged in this operation from 30 July 1418
to 19 January 1419. Apart from the accounts in Henry's
biographies, it is described at length by John Page, an English
soldier in the contingent led by Gilbert de Umfraville, lord of
Redesdale, whose version of events became incorporated in
certain texts of the Brut Chronicle. Page was in a position to
record that when on 31 December hunger induced the inhabitants to sue for terms, it was, of all the English captains they
shouted at, only Gilbert de Umfraville on the south side who
took the message and passed on the report to the king.[1] When
at the end of December the Dauphin moved from Pontoise to
Beauvais the position of the defenders was judged hopeless. In
the course of the siege the captain, Guy le Boutellier, had been
obliged to eject many of the older and poorer people, the useless
mouths, into the city ditch to die of starvation, and the sight
merely angered the king, who refused to have his compassion
aroused by an act for which he was not responsible. After much
bargaining, the negotiations were broken off: but the fury of
the townsfolk at this overcame the negotiators, and on 13
January, partly through the intervention of Archbishop
Chichele, and with the help of the clergy of the city, a settlement was reached. If no help arrived by 19 January the city
was to submit entirely to the king's mercy, pay 300,000 crowns,
and give up all war material. The Normans in the garrison
were to be held as prisoners: but citizens prepared to take the
oath of homage to the king were to retain their own property.
When the terms were reported to the duke of Burgundy he
blamed the Dauphin for not having attacked the English and
advised the Roueners to make the best terms they could. The
Parisians were assured that he would guard the capital and
maintain the food supply, and relieve it if an attack was made
before May: he promised not to withdraw from Provins except
for grave necessity. Wisely he avoided Paris and having placed

[1] *Historical Collections of a London Citizen*, ed. J. Gairdner (1876), p. 26.

garrisons on the frontiers of Normandy and Picardy, and in other *baillages* where Burgundians were strong (Sens, Meaux, Melun, and Chartres), he retired to Provins. The treaty of St. Maur-des-Fossées had not remedied the fact that, outside Normandy, there were two governments in France, the Burgundian and the Dauphinist, each hostile to the other, both hostile, though not irretrievably, to the invader.

The fall of Rouen did not, to Henry's mind, involve an immediate further advance into territory now held by the Burgundians. Before advancing to the conquest of France he had first to consolidate Normandy: but France, during 1419, was being re-created not at Paris nor at Provins or Troyes, but on the Loire. Henry's move upon Rouen had freed lands in the power of the Armagnacs from being invaded from Normandy. No longer had the Armagnacs to defend Paris. For the moment, it has been well observed, they were too weak or too wise to attempt its recovery:[1] what they could do, or did, was to negotiate with Spain and Scotland for help, to make themselves firm in Touraine, where Tours was now in their hands, and to strengthen and garrison the castles north of the Loire. The southern frontier of the English conquest was the weak point. There was no natural barrier along which a strong system of defence could be constructed. To advance southwards in force meant dividing Normandy and exposing it to reconquest from the east by Burgundians. In the south, frontier garrisons had to maintain the position, while the main front was made against Burgundian Paris rather than against the Armagnac Loire. As far as foreign aid was concerned some Scots had been brought by the Genoese to La Rochelle to join the Dauphin's army, and it was arranged that a larger force estimated at between 8,000 and 10,000 men should follow, recruited in 1419 by the count of Vendôme and the chancellor, who went on an embassy to Scotland. By 28 June 1419 the Castilians promised to provide an armed fleet to convey them to Havre, but already, early in that month, the first contingent of Scots had begun fighting in Lower Normandy and their exploits nerved the French to take, on 18 June, Avranches and Pontorson by assault. These places were recovered by the earl of Salisbury, the royal lieutenant in Normandy, but the episodes show where the English defence was weak. They also encouraged the more intractable of the

---

[1] Newhall, op. cit., p. 135.

Armagnac garrisons to the north-east and in the south along the Maine frontier to hold firm against the invader.

Meanwhile there was no cessation in diplomacy. While the siege of Rouen was in progress both French factions were negotiating with Henry. After feelers had been put out by the Dauphin's party, in November 1418 a strong party of negotiators was sent to Alençon to treat for his marriage with the French king's daughter Catherine; Normandy was to be ruled out of consideration, and if the French offered lands it must be from those not yet in Henry's possession. Once more the demand for the terms of the treaty of Brétigny was pressed, along with Flanders and the coast between Gravelines and the Somme. But if a peace was not immediately practicable, and a truce proved more acceptable, Henry would suspend his claim to the French crown on condition that the French made a substantial gift in return. After some dispute as to who was to make the first offer and in what language the proceedings were to be conducted, the French read a written statement of their readiness to give up Saintonge, the Agenais, Périgord, the Limousin, Angoumois, Rouergue, and Poitou, without mentioning the territories already in Henry's possession. This the English negotiators did not consider sufficient. After some delay, the French on 14 November said that they were prepared to offer all Upper Normandy north of the Seine, except Rouen and its administrative district, and promised that if Henry and the Dauphin captured Artois and Flanders from Burgundy, the English should have a share in the territories gained. The Dauphin still thought in terms of the civil war, but for the English the new offer was territorially inadequate, and they kept on returning to the terms of Brétigny. Finally, after Henry V's claim to the French throne had been firmly and emphatically stated, the French were induced to offer what they alleged to be the concessions made in that treaty, but they were not prepared to agree to handing over to Henry the lands unconditionally in full sovereignty. This they had no power to do. There were further fruitless interchanges and the conference broke up. In reporting the indecisive ending Dr. Wylie, who took his account from the notarial report of Richard Cowdray, considered that the English envoys had full powers, thus rendering *rationabiliter et plenarie instructos*.[1] It seems more likely that

---

[1] *The Reign of Henry the Fifth* (with W. T. Waugh), iii. 156.

Henry regarded the meeting as a sounding-board and the conversations as an encounter which would tell him how far the
French were prepared to go, rather than as an authoritative
negotiation. He knew that Burgundy was making inquiries
about possible terms of peace with England, and had accredited
envoys to speak in the name of the king of France, a group with
which Cardinal Orsini, seeking to mediate, had associated
himself. On this occasion, when they met the Burgundians the
English party which included Warwick, Langley the chancellor, and Archbishop Chichele, was reinforced by Hungerford,
Philip Morgan, and Dr. John Stokes, who had been at
Alençon. Here again the Burgundians wanted to negotiate in
French, and Henry urged Cardinal Orsini to sanction Latin as
the language of the conference because neither he nor his
council nor his negotiators knew how to speak French and they
could not understand it—a remarkable admission for the
grandson of John of Gaunt. The language question was solved
by the modern method of letting each party speak in its own
language; but the Burgundian envoys were not ready to admit
Henry's territorial claims immediately: he asked for Normandy,
Aquitaine, Ponthieu, and other places named in the treaty of
Brétigny as well as 1 million gold crowns as the dowry of the
princess. The demand would have to be reported to the French
king and queen and the duke of Burgundy. John was still a
Valois prince.

The Dauphin was not deterred by the failure of the negotiations. Before Rouen had fallen he made attempts to arrange a
personal meeting with Henry, and after that event his ambassadors arrived in the Norman capital to treat with an English
delegation, mainly composed of high-ranking clerics, for 'a
final peace'. The two sides agreed that Henry should meet the
Dauphin on 26 March, the interview to be at some place
between Évreux and Dreux. Meanwhile there was to be an
armistice for the country lying between the Seine and the
Loire. Henry turned up at Évreux on 25 March; but the
Dauphin was not at Dreux; no rendezvous had been appointed
nor did any meeting take place. It did not matter very much,
because there was an alternative to hand, an embassy from the
duke, the king, and the queen at Provins, which proved more
forthcoming than the Dauphin's; and was prepared, when the
English asked for the duchy of Normandy and the lands ceded

by the treaty of Brétigny, to yield them (though without declaring whether they were to be held absolutely or not) and to
treat further for a marriage alliance and a permanent peace.
This promise was made on 30 March 1419 and it was arranged
(7 Apr.) by representatives of both sides that Henry should
meet the king, the queen, and the duke of Burgundy on 15 May
between Nantes and Pontoise. Meanwhile a truce was to be
observed in the lands between the Seine and the Somme as well
as in the Burgundian possessions between the Seine and the
Loire. Persons of the Armagnac party were excluded from the
truce. It was allotted to Warwick to make arrangements for
the formal meeting, ultimately fixed for Meulan on 30 May.
There, opposite the Isle Belle in the Seine, the meeting-place
was elaborately prepared, each nation, limited to 1,500 armed
men, parked within a fence, with the middle space reserved for
the principals and negotiators.

On the third day of the conversations Henry had his first
view of the Princess Catherine and was overcome by her beauty
and charm. The meetings of the great personages were the more
social and decorative aspect of the detailed negotiations undertaken, on the English side, by a group consisting of Archbishop
Chichele, Bishop Beaufort, and the dukes of Clarence, Exeter,
and Gloucester, with full powers to treat of a final peace and a
marriage between Henry and Catherine. When the French got
to grips with the English demands, it was clear that their pliancy
of two months before had been optimistic: Henry's claim that
he must be undisputed sovereign of Normandy and the Brétigny
lands aroused opposition: nor would the English king listen to
the French request that he should renounce all claims to Maine,
Anjou, Touraine, Brittany, and Flanders in return for an
equivalent amount of land in Aquitaine. The French also asked
that 600,000 crowns should be deducted from the dowry of
800,000 already promised to the Princess Catherine, because
this sum should have been returned with her sister Isabel,
Richard II's wife. Then there were other demands and claims,
and the fact that Henry already knew that Burgundy was
moving towards an alliance with the Dauphin did not increase
his readiness to treat with either party. The Meulan discussions
lasted till the beginning of July, when the duke of Burgundy
declined to negotiate any further. The fact was that during the
Meulan conferences, emissaries of the Dauphin were actively

at work in Pontoise, and, a week after the English had been warned off, a formal treaty of peace was signed between him and the duke (11 July). The duke undertook to be true and loyal to his kinsmen and the Dauphin did the same in an instrument drafted in the form of a feudal alliance, with past offences and grievances forgotten, while an end was to be put to the faction names Burgundian and Armagnac. The two leaders promised to live in harmony and make no alliances with the king's enemies, repudiating any so made.

Henry's truce with Burgundy expired on 29 July. It was time to bring home to the parties making the new alliance the consequences of their action. A strong party was sent out of Nantes to secure Pontoise. On the morning of the 30th a storming party under Gaston de Foix surprised the garrison which fled at the approach of the earl of Huntingdon whose force had made a wide détour to the east in order to prevent help arriving from Paris. On 6 August Henry transferred his headquarters thither from Nantes. It was a notable capture, of great strategic importance; Henry was now in possession of the whole Vexin. The threat came home when Clarence made a demonstration raid up to the gates of Paris; and there was more than threats: with Pontoise lost, many essential supplies were denied to the halles. The future of the city and indeed of France turned upon the treaty between the Dauphin and the duke. It had been stipulated that within a month they were to concert together with the aim of driving out the English. John the Fearless had as a precaution moved from St. Denys to Troyes (7 Aug.), leaving the Parisians indignant at the supposed desertion. From there he wrote to urge the Dauphin to meet him as soon as possible. The Dauphin's reply suggested Montereau, where the Seine and the Yonne join, on 28 August, a date found by Burgundy to be too early and the meeting was fixed for 10 September. On the appointed day Duke John, when he had entered the fenced enclosure upon the bridge, was felled by an Armagnac axe, while Armagnac troops attacked the Burgundians drawn up in front of the castle. The Dauphin's formal responsibility for the deed is undoubted, but the murder must have been carefully planned by his entourage and it is most unlikely that he himself devised any such thing. Burgundian sources indicate Tanneguy du Chastel as the author of the crime and the murderer in one; and if in 1425 he protested his innocence to Duke Philip, his conscience can hardly have been clear.

The deadly stroke led in the end to one of the most fateful treaties upon which England has been induced to enter. For the moment Henry, who quickly grasped the significance of the murder, could profit by the sentiments of revenge both at the French court and in Burgundian circles. On 20 September 1419 Queen Isabel wrote to urge him to avenge the duke's death and to continue the negotiations interrupted at Meulan, while in the north the duchess of Burgundy was appealing for justice to the Pope and cardinals as well as to the emperor, and young Duke Philip was mobilizing the sympathy of the Flemish towns. On 24 September Henry nominated representatives to meet those of the French king and arrange terms of peace, and on 1 October Duke Philip appointed a group of six to negotiate an alliance with England. When they reached Nantes (26 Oct.) Henry spoke to them in the firmest possible language. While commending Duke Philip's determination to avenge his father, the king warned their master that he could not be treated as the late duke had treated him: in that event he would go on with his conquests. Paris was ready to receive him. He would give the duke a fortnight to declare himself and come into line against the dauphin. On 27 October Henry outlined to them the dynastic plan which had been forming in his mind since the end of his first expedition or at least since 1416. If he married Princess Catherine, her parents should not be charged with any dowry, for a larger one was at hand: he was to be heir to the French kingdom, Charles was to keep his throne, and the queen her present state, but when that king died, Henry and his heirs were to have the crown; equally he was to be governor of the kingdom while Charles was ill. If Burgundy agreed, Henry said that he would have the murderers punished, and arrange for the marriage of one of his brothers to a sister of the duke. But if he wanted the crown of France for himself Henry said that he would make war upon him to the end, for he would rather see the duke of Orléans upon the throne than the duke of Burgundy.[1] In considering the later conduct of the duke, it will be well to keep this high and intimidating language to his envoys in mind. However much he may have desired action against the murderers, Philip had practically no choice; the

[1] Report of the Burgundian ambassadors quoted in Wylie, op. cit., iii. 190.

alliance with England had to be made on Henry's terms, not his own. Monstrelet reports that in the assembly of local estates which met at Arras on 17 October, while it was decided to support Philip's policy of alliance with Henry, fears were expressed lest an English personnel would replace the French court and French civil servants.

Then began the series of diplomatic moves which were to end in the treaty of Troyes. Two sets of preliminaries were necessary, an alliance of Duke Philip with Henry and a truce between Charles VI and the English king. The first of these was signed on Christmas Day 1419. It was a mutual defensive alliance made on the understanding that not only should Henry marry the Princess Catherine, but also that one of his brothers should marry a sister of the duke. Henry was to make every effort to track down the Montereau murderer and his accomplices, and to secure the grant to the duke by Charles VI of lands worth 20,000 *livres parisis* a year. While the details of this alliance were being settled, Henry was closing in upon Paris. Gisors surrendered on 17 September and the castle on 23 September. From Gisors Henry turned to Nantes, but sent out detachments to secure Meulan, Montjoie, and St. Germain. Meulan fell on 30 October and the other two towns made little resistance: and before the middle of December 1419 Henry had received news of the fall of Richard I's 'saucy castle', Château Gaillard, the English taking possession on 8 December.

By this time there was little resistance in Normandy: in the spring of 1420 large numbers of safe conducts were issued to Normans making their submission: by the end of the year some 1,500 had been registered. Meanwhile Anglo-Burgundian operations against Armagnac centres of resistance were taking place in mid-winter in the north-eastern and central northern districts of France: the English forces under the earl of Huntingdon and John Cornwall, the Burgundian under John of Luxemburg and Hector de Saveuse. It was during the operations at Roye that the English and Burgundian commanders nearly came to blows over the conduct of the English in killing and taking prisoner men whose lives and safe conduct had been guaranteed by the Burgundians. The French were prickly, the English overbearing and insolent: none the less the alliance held, and in February 1420 the duke of Burgundy announced officially his negotiations with the English, and moved southward, being joined at St. Quentin by the earl of Warwick, the earl marshal, Lord Roos, Gilbert de Umfraville, and Lewis Robesart, Henry's representatives. After spending a fortnight near Laon, when the Burgundians took the fortress of Crépy-en-Laonnais, the force marched through Laon, Rheims, and Chalons, to enter Troyes on 23 March, to be received with a ceremonial welcome by the king and queen. During the next week there were conferences: but the issue was already clear and was embodied in the document of 9 April 1420. Its terms were, as Henry had foreshadowed, that he should marry the Princess Catherine, the expenses of the dowry to fall not on the French, but on the English Exchequer, which was to provide the usual *aurum reginae* of 40,000 crowns a year: that upon Charles VI's death he should inherit the kingdom of France, but that Charles and his queen were to be maintained on the throne while they lived, the French king's writs to run in places subject to the French crown. On the death of Charles the crown was to pass to Henry and his heirs for ever, and, as Charles was in poor health, the regency should be exercised by Henry with the counsel of the nobles and wise men of France. Then followed certain articles of great importance for the future. Henry undertook to reduce to obedience all France then subject to the Dauphin. All conquests to be made in the kingdom of France outside the duchy of Normandy should be to the profit of the French crown (*utilitatem nostram*); the possessions of loyal subjects of Charles VI which were included in the conquests were to be restored to their owners; so also those who favoured the Burgundian side and would swear to obey the present force, were to have their lands in Normandy and elsewhere in the kingdom restored to them. Evicted clergy beneficed in the duchy of Normandy or elsewhere in the French kingdom who obeyed Charles or Philip were to be restored to their benefices. When Henry succeeded to the French crown the duchy of Normandy was to become an integral part of the French kingdom. These clauses were not of simple application. The restoration of Charles VI's subjects to their territorial possessions in the newly acquired territory involved the collection of much information, and the exercise of some administrative skill; most of all, how was 'our profit' to be interpreted while Charles VI was alive? Were *ministri* of Charles VI to be put in to collect the profits and the rents?

Charles VI further stipulated that letters of justice and crown appointments to offices or benefices should be in his own name, though provision was made, in unforeseen circumstances or in any emergency, for Henry's letters to run. The royal governmental machinery was to be preserved. Henry, when he assumed the regency, was to take the same oath as the kings of France at their coronation. The authority and prestige of the *parlement* was to be maintained; the offices of justice and of the royal demesne should be filled by zealous and able Frenchmen; the peers, nobles, the churches, universities, and colleges were to be upheld in their present states, with their liberties and *franchises* intact; and there were to be no 'impositions nor exactions' save for 'reasonable and necessary' reasons. Henry was not to nominate himself king, but *héritier*, heir of France, during Charles's lifetime. All these provisions were to be guaranteed by the oath of the nobles and estates, both spiritual and temporal, of the 'cities and notable communities and the citizens and burgesses of the towns' now obedient to Charles; they were to swear to obey Henry while exercising, as regent, the *de facto* government, to accept the settlement of the French throne, and after Charles VI's death, to regard Henry as their liege lord and to lend no aid to any plot against him.

It will be seen that the English king was taking on large obligations: both to conquer territories still holding out, to restore loyal subjects dispossessed by the Armagnacs, to maintain the government and legal systems of France, and, in due course, to cease treating Normandy as the special heritage of the English crown. The document in which all this was embodied ended by making provision for the personal meeting of Charles, Henry, and the duke of Burgundy at Troyes.

The treaty itself, sealed at Troyes on 21 May 1420,[1] contained practically all the draft, strengthened certain clauses and added others.[2] Henry was to marry Catherine, he was to be the heir to the French kingdom, which on the death of Charles was to pass to him and his heirs for ever. By a new clause (24) Henry undertook to labour to his utmost to secure by the advice

---

[1] E. Cosneau, *Les Grands Traités de la guerre de Cent Ans* (Paris 1889), gives the date as 28 May, the date accepted by Charles Samaran: *Thomas Basin, Histoire de Charles VII*, ed. C. Samaran (1933), i. 68 n.

[2] e.g. the clause providing for compensation, out of newly acquired territories, for lands belonging to supporters of Charles or Philip which had been granted away. Where no such grants had been made, they were to be restored forthwith.

and consent of the estates of both kingdoms that when he succeeded, both crowns 'shall for perpetual future time remain
and be in one and the same person' for his life and then 'in the
person of his heirs that shall successively be, one after another;
and that both kingdoms shall be governed, from the time that
Henry or one of his heirs reaches them, under one and the same
person'.[1] Clause 26 stipulated that allies and confederates of
Charles and of Henry V who within eight months from the
signature of the treaty declared in writing that they wished 'to
adhere to the concord' (be included in the treaty) might do so,
with a saving clause providing for the pursuance of claims or of
remedial actions on the part of either power against the people
so joining, 'if such were deemed necessary'. Henry was made
responsible, with the counsel of the duke of Burgundy and
other nobles of the kingdom, for looking after Charles and
ensuring him an honourable estate. In his entourage were to
be native-born French only. At the end of the treaty stood the
joint undertaking of all the parties to make no peace with the
Dauphin in consideration of his enormous crimes: the duke

avoit traictié et pourparlé avec le roy d'Angleterre sur ce que dit est,
et avoit promis de faire son loial povoir envers le Roy nostre souve-
rain segnur, de lui faire ratifier approuver et confermer ledict
traictié lequel il avoit rapporté et fait exposer au Roy, presens ceulz
qui dit est.[2]

The words of the *greffier*, Clement de Fauquembergue, state un-
equivocally the part played by Burgundy in the negotiations
that led up to Troyes. For the citizens of Paris there could only
have been one course. Henry had an economic stranglehold
upon the city, having demanded and having been accorded
(29 Feb. 1421) the castle of Beaumont-sur-Oise, which could
prevent the arrival of food from Normandy and Picardy.[3]
When the terms thus provisionally agreed were put to the gathering for agreement, they shouted yes. The peace was proclaimed
to the city on Whit Monday (27 May); 'and now', as an
English official writing to a friend at home said, 'English men
goon into Paris, as ofte as they wil, withowte any saaf conduct

[1] *Foedera*, iv. ii. 173. 'Non divisim sub diversis regibus pro eorum contextu
temporis, sed sub una et eadem persona quae pro tempore erit utriusque Rex et
Dominus supremus . . . non subiciendo quoquo modo unum dictorum regnorum
alteri eorundem.'

[2] *Journal de Clément de Fauquembergue*, ed. A. Tuetey (Soc. Hist. France), i. (1903),
360.   [3] Ibid. i. 349.

or any lettyngs'. In the University of Paris an oath to maintain the treaty was made obligatory upon all members of the faculties proceeding to degrees.[1]

Henry's marriage to Catherine took place in the cathedral of Troyes on 2 June. He did not stay long, for by the treaty just signed he was under obligation to reduce the Dauphinist–Armagnac fortresses. On 4 June, accompanied by Catherine and Queen Isabel, he left, to besiege the Armagnac stronghold of Montereau. On 24 June the tower was carried by assault, for the Anglo-Burgundian forces to secure the body of Duke John whence it was transported to Dijon: the castle capitulated on 1 July and Henry moved down the Seine to besiege Melun, a town divided into three quarters by the Seine with the island of St. Etienne, on which stood the castle, in the middle. It was strongly defended on both sides by a comparatively small garrison under a Gascon commander. The duke of Bedford brought 800 men-at-arms and 2,000 archers to reinforce the Anglo-Burgundian assailants, while from Germany, Henry's brother-in-law, Louis count palatine of the Rhine brought 700 men at Henry's cost; but in spite of large numbers and of their guns of unexpected calibre the allied force made little progress against a determined defence, and disloyalty affected a number of the Burgundian leaders. Nevertheless, by the middle of October hunger began to tell, and when the garrison saw that no help was forthcoming from the Dauphin surrender terms were arranged (17 Nov.). All in the town, whether combatants or civilians, were spared their lives, were to deposit their arms in the castle, and be held as prisoners until their ransoms were paid; before they were released they had to give security not to serve against the English king on any future occasion. From these terms English and Scots who had taken part in the defence were excepted. In Melun there were twenty Scots mercenaries under their captain. King James of Scotland had been specially brought from prison in England to appeal to them to surrender: they refused and were hanged by Henry's orders for disobedience to their king. After Melun had fallen Henry joined Charles VI at Corbeil, prior to a ceremonial entry into Paris.

---

[1] Thomas Basin, *Histoire de Charles VII*, ed. C. Samaran (1933), i, 69. This was done upon the recommendation of the English nation: Denifle and Chatelain, *Chartularium universitatis Parisiensis: auctarium*, ii. 303.

On 1 December 1420 the two sovereigns and the duke of
Burgundy were welcomed by the parliament, the university, and
the burgesses, and next day arrived the queens, accompanied
by noble ladies. The main purpose of the visit was to secure
ratification of the treaty from the Estates, to make obedience
to it a matter of statutory obligation on oath, and secure con
demnation of the murderers of the duke of Burgundy a
Montereau. The states general met on 6 December and passed
a series of ordinances giving effect to the requests they had
already made on the subject of the treaty: one of them stipu
lated that any oath to observe it should be taken by all entering
upon ecclesiastical benefices or public office and by all who did
homage for their lands. The trial of the unapprehended
murderers took place on 23 December, in which at the instance
of the duke, his mother, and his sisters, a number of leading
members of the Dauphin's supporters were arraigned, notably
the lord of Barbazan,[1] Tanneguy du Chastel, Guillaume le
Bouteiller, Arnaud-Guilhem, and Jean Louvet. While nothing
definite could be proved against these persons, those involved
were pronounced guilty (though they were not there to defend
themselves), and were declared to have committed treason and
to be incapable of holding any dignities, offices, or property
while their subjects and vassals were released from all obliga
tions against them. Some condemnation, if only in very general
terms, of the murderers of John the Fearless was obviously
required, and no means of satisfying Burgundian demand
could be neglected, even if the results were, for the moment
nil. It was some, though a very limited, satisfaction to issue a
formal summons to the Dauphin, and, when he defaulted, to
pronounce him contumacious, sentence him to banishment
and declare him incapable of succeeding to the crown or to his
own states. Judgement to this effect was passed upon him by
the king's council and by the parliament.

Before this took place, Henry and Catherine had left for
Normandy. The king was anxious to meet the three estates of
Normandy and of the other conquered territories. The 'con
quest', by which the newly acquired lands outside Normandy
were described, was a vague term embracing what had actually
been won by the sword before the treaty of Troyes: any land
conquered from the Dauphinists after the treaty were to go, a

[1] Called by Thomas Basin (op. cit., p. 73) 'notable et brave chevalier'.

has been pointed out, to the profit of the French crown. The pre-Troyes 'conquest' included the *bailliage* of Nantes (in English hands) extending to a dozen miles from Paris. North of the Seine, Pontoise, Beaumont-sur-Oise, and Chaumont were in the control of the *bailli* of Gisors. South of Alençon there were also parts of Maine in English hands, but by no means the whole: at the beginning of 1421 the English authority extended a short distance south of Beaumont-le-Vicomte. It is not recorded what contribution was made to Henry's direct taxation by these lands outside the duchy, but the presumption is that they were asked to contribute. The Norman estates meeting at Rouen granted a total of 400,000 *livres tournois*,[1] the clergy consenting to pay two-tenths and the towns a *taille*, while nobles, men bearing arms, and the entirely poor were exempt. The lay tax was to be on the basis of 20 *sous* a hearth to be collected in three instalments. 100,000 *l.t.* was to be received by 1 March. The yield would not be sufficient to provide for the reforms in government requested by the estates as well as for defence; but the estates pleaded poverty and Henry could only accept what they offered and arrange for its immediate collection. His other concern, besides finance, was to overhaul the machinery of the duchy which during the past three years had been largely provisional.

His design was to govern Normandy and 'the conquest' as a separate state which was to pay for itself and to continue upon the lines of administration already established. There was to be no essential change in the system of local administration. The eight *bailliages*—Cotentin, Caen, Alençon, Évreux, Rouen, Caux, Gisors, and Mantes—were to remain undisturbed, but from the beginning of 1420 until the end of Henry's reign the *baillis* with one possible exception were Englishmen. Below the *bailli* the civil officers were practically all French and, as Professor Waugh has noted, apart from small settlements at Harfleur, Honfleur, and Caen, there is no sign of any attempt to anglicize the population of Normandy.[2] The military administration, however, remained almost entirely in English hands. In 1421 the English garrisons have been estimated at

[1] The *livre tournois* was about 3*s*. 6*d*.– 3*s*. 8*d*. in English currency. The *écu* was the crown of five francs.

[2] 'The Administration of Normandy, 1420–22', *Essays in Medieval History presented to Thomas Frederick Tout* (1925), p. 352.

about 4,700 men, their captains and lieutenants almost all English. On the road connecting Cherbourg, Caen, and Évreux there were about 150; on the southern frontier between Avranches and Verneuil, approximately 1,600, in the Seine valley 1,100, and on the eastern boundary, Pontoise to Eu, roughly 950. There were in addition sixty enfeoffed castles with their garrisons; and those receiving Norman lands from Henry had to furnish mounted troops totalling some 1,400. 'It seems safe to estimate, therefore', wrote Professor Waugh, 'that besides those paid by the king, there were in Normandy 2000 soldiers, nearly all of whom must have been English.'[1] The military authorities were technically under the civil, the head of whom was the chancellor, Bishop John Kemp of Rochester, who before Henry died was translated first to Chichester, then to London. The ancient seneschalship, powerful in the days of Henry II, but suppressed when Philip Augustus seized the duchy, was revived and placed in the hands of Richard Woodville, who was given the supervision of all officers, civil or military, in the area subject to Henry V. His main duties were to hold musters when he saw occasion, reporting to the treasurer-general; to inquire into the feeding and administration of the garrisons and to investigate abuses of power by the captains, when they occurred. He was, however, excluded from finance and from any control over the Norman treasury which remained at Caen. Its main official was the treasurer-general and receiver-general, William Alington, paid on much the same scale (4 *l.t.* daily) as the seneschal who received one mark *per diem.* The treasurer was charged with the collection and receipt of most of the revenue from the conquered territories. Some of this was spent locally by the *vicomtes* and allowed them when they came to reckon at Caen. Over the treasury the *Chambre des Comtes*, also at Caen, had control: its barons, if one may borrow the English term, were not exclusively English; from 1420–2 there were at least three Frenchmen, and its president was a Norman knight who, taken prisoner at Caen, had made his peace with Henry.

The senior military commander in the lands of the conquest was Thomas Montague, earl of Salisbury, the king's lieutenant. He was both captain of the defence and the leader of offensive operations against the Dauphinists. Beginning as the royal

[1] *The Reign of Henry V*, iii. 241.

ieutenant in the south-west, with his forces based upon Alençon
and covering the conquest as far as Le Mans, he had to retrieve
the position after Clarence's imprudence had lost the English
the battle of Baugé and prevent a French advance into
Normandy from the Dauphin's headquarters at Le Mans.
When the French decided to advance north-east from Le Mans
towards Chartres and recovered a good deal of Beauce, Salisbury was able to strike at Anjou and make a foray south as far
as Angers. After Henry's death and under Bedford's regency
he was transferred (1424) to the south-east of Paris: commis-
sioner or governor of Champagne, Brie, and the *baillages* of
Melun, Sens, Auxerre, the Nivernais, Dunois, and the Maconnois and Soissonois, he was the most formidable soldier in this
area, and at one time he looked likely to threaten Lyon. In the
big French effort that led up to Verneuil he was with Suffolk
reconnoitring the movements of the enemy, and after the battle,
again with Suffolk, he was in the vigorous offensive that aimed
at bringing the English to the Loire. Salisbury, a fighting
commander, was thus far less an administrative official than
the seneschal who had to do with the permanent work of
the garrisons, but all alike were subject to Henry's council, the
great council at Rouen. This was the body responsible for the
defence and administration of the conquered territories; pre-
ided over by the chancellor, staffed by the senior officials
(though not, apparently, the treasurer-general), and by a small
number of councillors paid for their attendance. At Caen,
alongside the council, was the *camera compotorum* or *chambre
de comptes*, apparently separate from the Exchequer, the functions of which were largely judicial. It has been suggested that
this *scaccarium* was probably the original undifferentiated organ
of administration, over which John Tiptoft presided, and that
as the 'conquest' and the administrative machinery it entailed
grew larger, so the *camera compotorum* became necessary as the
bursarial office of the acquired territories.

The sum collected by the English officials at the first levy of
the *taille* by 20 August 1421 was 85,000 *l.t.* The first of the levy
of clerical tenths produced no more than 12,000 *l.t.*, and in
view of the reluctance to pay, fourteen bishops and their vicars-
general had recourse to the secular arm. When in December
1421 the bishops were ordered to collect the second instalment
of clerical taxation, considerable opposition was encountered.

By 1 May less than 1,000 *l.t.* had been collected; in the nex
four months not more than 5,000 *l.t.* were paid in, and th
total was disappointing. The diocese of Rouen furnished a
much as 3,400 *l.t.* of the total, and nothing was forthcoming
from the dioceses of Évreux, Sées, Bayeux, and Avranches
There had been no attempt to implant an English clergy in
Normandy, and though Henry kept a firm hand on the appoint
ment to sees, the appointments to ecclesiastical offices or
benefices recorded in the Norman rolls for 1421 and 1422 were
predominantly of Frenchmen. In spite of this, the clergy were
worse contributors than the laity who were allowed to pay in
four instalments. Of the 400,000 promised, in the end Henry
is thought to have received about 270,000 *l.t.* It must be re
membered that the collection was in progress during Henry's
reform of the currency. In April 1421 the silver coin commonly
in use, the *gros* or *royal*, which had carried an exchange value o
1*s.* 8*d. t.*, was officially proclaimed to be worth 5*d. t.*, and a
petit blanc of 5*d. t.* was issued to replace the *gros*. A month late
a silver *gros*, worth 1*s.* 8*d. t.*, was issued by the mints of Rouen
and St. Lô. This scaling down of the exchange value had a
serious effect upon individual fortunes. The reduction in th
value of the *gros* was made more unpalatable by the deman
of the council that all taxes should be paid in money that really
bore the value attributed to it, not in face-value coin. The
attempt at currency reform in Normandy was of little per
manent effect because there was not enough coin for the area
counterfeit money was constantly coming in and the govern
ment made no attempt to make the new coinage the sole lega
tender. 'The unique feature of Henry V's military achievement
is the continued effort which he maintained during a series o
years in a foreign and conquered country.' Dr. Newhall's
judgement[1] is made to depend on the fact that while Henry's
opponents were financially embarrassed most of the time, the
king 'had a sufficiency of money'. It will be worth while examin
ing this statement in due course.

Henry left Rouen half-way through January 1421. With
Catherine, the king of Scots, the duke of Bedford, the ear
marshal, and the earls of March and Warwick, he passed
through Amiens, Doullens, St. Pol, and Thérouanne to Calais

[1] *The Conquest of Normandy*, p. 142.

and on 1 February landed at Dover. After offering at Canterbury, he went on to London without the queen, who followed
on 21 February. On the 23rd Catherine drove through the
decorated streets to be crowned by Archbishop Chichele in the
Abbey, and afterwards was enthroned in the palace of Westminster; in Westminster Hall a formal banquet followed,
attended by the English nobility, the judges, a number of
ladies, Bedford as Constable of England, and the mayor and
senior citizens of London. At the palace there was free food and
drink for the generality.

The king had been away three and a half years. It was thought
that he would return before Christmas 1420, and in the opening
speech in the parliament which met on 2 December the Chancellor voiced the general desire to have him back. More significant were his allusion to the poverty and distress into which
the king's subjects had fallen, attributed by him mainly to the
scarcity of money throughout the country; and three petitions
of the commons relating to the treaty of Troyes. One invoked
the example of Edward III who, when it was feared that his
succession to the throne of France might involve the subjection
of England to the new kingdom, declared and ordained
(*vouloit, graunta e establyst*) that his realm and his people should
never be obedient to him as king of France, and successfully
asked that this statute of 1340 might be confirmed in the present
case; another, anticipating that the king, now governing two
kingdoms, might return while parliament was sitting, asked
that his arrival should neither on this nor any future occasion
cause the dissolution of parliament; and a third referred to the
statement made by several lords that petitions submitted to the
duke of Gloucester as *custos Anglie* were not allowed to be
engrossed (i.e. decided and recorded) before they had been
sent overseas to the king, and requested that petitions of the
commons made to the duke might be replied to and 'terminated'
within the kingdom and without being sent abroad. This latter
was firmly refused, for even while outside the kingdom Henry
was determined to keep the reins of government in his own
hands. The actual treaty he himself caused to be submitted to
parliament on the first day that it met, 12 May 1421, rehearsing
what had been done in the hall of the king's palace in Paris on
6 and 10 December the previous year, when upon Charles VI's
instructions the three estates of France along with the cities,

towns, and communes ratified the peace. The chancellor, Bishop Thomas Langley, at Henry's order made a full statement of its provisions, and further 'our lord King commanded his same Chancellor that the said three estates should inspect and see with their own eyes (*visitarent*) the provisions of the said peace': the estates did so, and approved and authorized the treaty and 'bound themselves, their heirs and successors to observe and fulfil its terms'. This solemn undertaking, in full parliament, has seldom received the emphasis it deserves. The next reign was to witness a protracted struggle to maintain its provisions.

Between the coronation of Queen Catherine and the May parliament Henry had made a tour of the country. The journey was not for recreation nor was its purpose mainly devotional or charitable, though he worshipped at the shrines of Bridlington, Beverley, and Walsingham. The visits he paid to Bristol and, via Herefordshire, to Shrewsbury, enabled him to see areas of disaffection, and after he had been joined by the queen (12 Mar.) at Plesantmaris (in Kenilworth) his presence recorded in Coventry and Leicester and later (2 Apr.) at York can be connected with a desire to give an account of his doings and a lively hope to gain money and reinforcements for France. Such hope must have been all the stronger when, very soon after leaving Beverley, he received through a messenger the news of Clarence's death at Baugé. The news of the catastrophe he characteristically hid from his entourage until the following day, when the magnates accompanying him were told the truth and could only agree with the requests of the commanders in France for his speedy return. The shock did not prevent him completing the tour by visiting Lincoln for the enthronement of Richard Fleming as bishop and making his way back through Lynn, Walsingham, and Norwich. He had in his mind a definite time-table, fixed before he heard of the disaster of Baugé, and was aiming at returning to France by midsummer, after he had raised the money necessary to pay the fresh troops he was due to bring over. The need for money was urgent. On 6 May 1421 a financial statement submitted to the king revealed the state of the treasury, giving the anticipated revenue for the exchequer year ending in Michaelmas 1421 and the charges upon it. The total revenue was put at £55,743. 10s. 10d. of which the customs were to furnish £40,676. 19s. 9d., and the casual revenue £15,066. 11s. 1d.; against which were to be set expenses of £52,235. 16s. From the small balance of £3,507. 13s. 11d. provision had to be made for the chamber, the household, and the privy wardrobe, the king's works, the new tower at Portsmouth, the clerk of the king's ships, the custody of the king's lions and the fee of the constable of the Tower, the artillery and other ordnance for the king's wars, the keeping and feeding of the king's prisoners, the 'king's embassy', messengers, parchment and office expenses, and the expenses of the duchess of Holland.[1] No provision had yet been made for the debts of Harfleur and Calais, or for the debts of the wardrobe and household and the sums owing, to say nothing of Henry IV's unpaid bills and 'the debts of the king while he was prince'. This ill-assorted but pitiless catalogue shows on how small a margin Henry was conducting the war.

To have appealed to parliament would have damaged his cause, especially when the treaty of Troyes needed all the support it could receive. Loans therefore were essential. The money began to come in on 10 May when thirty-seven lenders produced £1,701, but on the 13th, £34,131 was received in 535 loans on a single day: the king's journey and the commissioners appointed had been successful. The largest lenders were Beaufort with three loans totalling £17,666. 13s. 4d.; the City of London (£2,000), and Queen Catherine £1,333. 6s. 8d.; Richard Whittington and Nicholas Bubwith, bishop of Bath and Wells, each lent £666. 13s. 4d. It has been pointed out[2] that while twenty-four of the larger loans produced as much as £25,125, by way of contrast the remaining £9,000 was spread over 501 lenders: most of these smaller loans were collective, levied from whole towns and villages and districts as well as individuals. 'The whole episode', Mr. Steel writes, 'may be held to illustrate, if not Henry's popularity, the strength of his hold upon the country.' It was not until after the last parliament of the reign met at Westminster on 1 December that repayment could be seriously undertaken, though the first instalment of the 15th and 10th payable in February 1422 was allowed to be paid in nobles worth 5s. 8d. instead of 6s. 8d.[3]

While making his tour of England, Henry had been keenly observing conditions within the religious orders. He himself had

[1] Waugh, op. cit. iii. 274.   [2] By Steel, op. cit., p. 163.
[3] Ibid., p. 164; Rot. Parl. iv. 151.

been a pious founder. His father, in making his peace with Gregory XII in 1408, had been directed, in expiation for the deaths of Richard II and Archbishop Scrope, to build three religious houses. Five years passed before his son started building a Carthusian house on the river bank to the north of the royal residence at Sheen, 'the House of Jesus of Bethlehem of Sheen', the foundation charter of which was given on 1 April 1415; but besides this he had founded on the opposite bank of the Thames the Bridgettine house of Mount Syon of Sheen in the park of Twickenham (the charter is dated 3 March 1415). The connexion of his chamberlain, Lord Fitzhugh, with Vadstena and the presence of his sister Philippa in Sweden led to the transfer of four Swedish nuns and two brothers to the new house, for it was a double monastery, consisting in 1420 of 24 nuns, 5 priests, 2 deacons, and 4 lay brothers, and originally endowed with 1,000 marks annually at the Exchequer, but later with funds from the alien priories and from appropriations.

Henry's conception of his duty to the Church and to the religious orders is illustrated by the action he took in March 1421 after he had received complaints, according to Walsingham, from certain 'false brethren' about laxity within the Benedictines. On 16 March he wrote to the abbot of St. Edmund's asking him to summon a meeting of the Black Monks at Westminster on 5 May: the abbot replied that the next general chapter was not due till July 1423, and that authority to summon such a meeting lay with the presidents of the last chapter, who were the abbot of Winchcombe and the prior of Worcester. Henry accordingly wrote to these presidents who, seeing that the king was intent upon an immediate conference, sent round a messenger to all their prelates for an assembly on 7 May. At this gathering at which there were 60 prelates and over 300 monks, doctors, and proctors present, the king made a speech 'on the early rule of the monks, the devotion of his own ancestors and the ancestors of others in founding and endowing monasteries and the negligence and carelessness of the present-day monks'. In his capacity as 'founder' and 'patron', he urged them to reform; ending by telling them how greatly he had relied on and benefited from their prayers on the morning of the battle of Agincourt.[1]

---

[1] The sequence of documents here is given by W. A. Pantin, *Chapters of the English Black Monks, 1215–1540* (C.S. 1931–7), ii. 98 f., and particularly 106–8.

The king's points present little that is new to a student of
monastic visitations: insistence that abbots who had establishments entirely separate from their monasteries, should participate fully in the life and worship of their convents, not
dwelling for more than three months in their manors; that all
such religious superiors, exempt or not exempt, should render
account within a month from Michaelmas of goods belonging
both to their monasteries and to themselves; that from the
middle of September to the beginning of Lent restrictions upon
flesh eating should be more strictly observed, with the exception
of Sundays and greater feasts; that the growing habit of private
accumulations of money, plate, and other articles of *proprietas*
should be suppressed; that women should not be allowed to
visit monks in their cells, and that prelates should be forbidden
to allow their monks freedom to make visits in town and city.
Such precautions as these occur in the *capitula* or inquiries put
to religious houses at earlier dates: but the novelty of the king's
articles lay in the fact that they were directed at exempt and
non-exempt houses alike, not by the bishops nor chapters
general, but by the greatest of all *fundatores*, the king. They were
communicated to the religious by three royal representatives
and 'considered by six representatives of the monks' including
the abbot of St. Albans and the Cluniac prior of Lenton, to
whom twenty-four others were added, with power to discuss
and to draft proposed legislation. Henry's articles in their
original form were rejected, and in their place the abbot of
St. Albans put forward a new set of rules which the monks
promised to observe. The king's article demanding the restriction of flesh eating was one of those decisively negatived, on the
ground that in many houses distant from the sea it was difficult
to get fish and also that it contravened the discretionary power
of the abbots to relax the prohibitions where this was needed.
Another so declined was the ninth, *de recepcione pecuniarum*,
asking that the statute of Benedict XII against private hoarding
should be observed, partly because the Holy See had already
declared its readiness to allow monks to possess money *pro
minutis recreacionibus et solaciis* as well as for other necessary
lawful objects, partly because by Chapter 33 of the Rule of
St. Benedict a monk could rightly and lawfully possess whatever
his abbot allowed him to possess. In general the king's appeals
to the original rule were countered by stressing the dispensing

power of the abbot or by invoking much later canonistic authority. If a legate be excepted, nobody but the king could have moved the Black Monks to meet and anticipate some of the legislation which they were to pass twenty-three years later. But Henry's simple hope that by 1421 the *pristina religio mona-chorum* could be restored came to nothing.

His determination to be master in his own church can be seen in his whole treatment of the problem of papal provisions and papal intervention. He had, of course, no intention of inter-fering with the ordinary course of diocesan and provincial administration; but like his predecessors he was determined to limit, primarily in his own interests, the system under which appointments were sought in or made by the court of Rome over the heads of the ordinary collators or in contravention of his royal rights. He was similarly resolved to control the acti-vities of special emissaries from Rome who threatened to com-pete with his own demands for clerical taxation. He was entirely opposed to the existence of any cardinal legate in England. Martin V, whose primary object in dealing with England was to get rid of the obnoxious statutes of Provisors and Praemunire (in the versions of 1390 and 1393), attached great importance to the residence of a permanent legate in England, and intended to use Henry Beaufort in this capacity as the spearhead of the attack upon the offending statutes. He was to be, the Pope later said, the means of recovering 'the pristine liberty of the Church in that most Christian nation'. In March 1418 Archbishop Chichele wrote of two important matters to Henry while campaigning abroad. In the previous autumn (1417) the king had told him that no petition was to be made to the newly elected Pope until he (the king) and the Pope had exchanged letters and the royal permission had been given for the restoration of communications with Rome. So far permission had not been given and now Bedford and the council in England were seeking instructions on the matter. The other matter was more significant: Chichele reported that he had received word that Beaufort was to be made a Cardinal,[1] permitted to hold his see *in commendam* and given a legatine commission to run throughout the king's dominions. This, the archbishop pointed out, was contrary to precedent, detrimental

---

[1] The sequence of events in this case is analysed by K. B. McFarlane, 'Henry V, Bishop Beaufort and the Red Hat, 1417–1421', *Eng. Hist. Rev.* lx (1945), 316.

to Church discipline, and dangerously wide and vague in its scope. It was likely to interfere with the normal system of clerical taxation. Henry acted quickly by seizing and impounding the ominous commission; but Beaufort, undeterred, obtained a fresh bull from Martin. By this action he had exposed himself to prosecution under the statute of Provisors. The king, who was having his uncle watched and reported upon by Thomas Chaucer, made it clear to him that the penalties were the forfeiture of his goods and degradation from his see. Beaufort, who knew that he had infringed the statute, was given time to consider the alternatives, which seem to have been freely discussed in a hard-headed way between Chaucer and himself; whether to leave the country altogether, ostensibly on pilgrimage, and make room for a successor at Winchester, or to seek his nephew's leave to remain in his present status and expiate his offence. The latter alternative was eventually chosen, and by instalments Beaufort contributed to the war finances the prodigious loan of £22,306. 18s. 4d.

Against Martin's attack upon the statute of Provisors the king held firm. In Normandy he disposed freely of prebends and other benefices, and though later he promised not to apply the statute there, for the present (1418, 1419) he wanted a free hand. With the bishoprics he took no risks. In September 1419 Chichele wrote to his agent in the Curia about the promotion of John Langdon, doctor of theology and monk of Canterbury, to the see of Lisieux, expressing surprise that the Pope was delaying to make it 'since in truth he will suffer no Frenchman in the Gallican Church until the land is more quiet and peaceful'. In October 1419 Martin sent his protonotary, Henry Grünfeld, to the king at Mantes to raise the question of the statute of Provisors. The king answered the Pope that for the time being he was too busy in the field to deal with this request. The statute was older than himself or his father: it had been solemnly established in parliament during the course of the previous century and his coronation oath forbade him to tamper with it save with the consent of the three estates. Henry got as far as promising that the matter of the statute should be examined in parliament upon his return: but it was never done. From a memorandum sent by Chichele to Rome in 1421 we know that Henry refused to admit the provision of Cardinal Nicholas Albergati to the archdeaconry of Lincoln: 'the lord

Cardinal of Bologna should be told that touching this matter
of the archdeaconry of Lincoln our lord king in no way dis-
penses with the statutes of England over provision etc. that have
been issued in parliament.'[1] As long as the king lived the
offensive was kept at arm's length. His death precipitated the
onslaught which, as will be seen, reached its climax in the years
1427–8. With Henry, Martin who owed so much to the English
desertion of Sigismund at the council of Constance in September 1417 and to English support in the conclave that elected
him, could never proceed to extremities. With the council of
Regency it was different. Henry's death released Beaufort,
as it were, for service in the Papal interest, and the attack on
Provisors could be pressed home.

The sudden removal of this powerful regal will is the domi-
nating fact of the English history in the Lancastrian period.
Baugé had hastened Henry's return to France. The Dauphinist
revival had to be fought in Picardy as well as on the borders of
Maine; but having crossed to Calais Henry heard that the
Dauphin and troops had crossed Perche to besiege Chartres,
whereupon he changed his plans and hastened to Paris: he was
about to lead the English force along the Seine between Mantes
and Meulan to relieve Chartres when he heard that the
Dauphin had retreated into Touraine. Henry followed him to
the Loire, on the way taking Dreux (8 Aug. 1421) and bringing about the surrender of most of the forces between it and
Chartres. Thence Henry marched along the right bank of the
Loire to the suburbs of Orléans, and passed on to Nemours
(18 Sept.) and Villeneuve-le-Roy on the Yonne (22 Sept.).
Nowhere did the French oppose him in the field; and Henry
accordingly turned to the reduction of the Dauphinist strongholds in northern France. He had decided to spend the winter
in reducing the formidable Meaux, situated on a loop in the
Marne where the market, protected on three sides by the river,
practically constituted a fortified island. The town held out for
five months, but the market defended itself till 2 May 1422.
The Pseudo-Elmham terms this siege 'the most harmful of all
that Henry undertook'. Not only did dysentery carry off many
of the English troops, but it was here that Henry contracted the
same disease that ended his life. After Meaux had fallen, Henry
went to Paris to meet Catherine, whose son was born on

[1] Bod. Lib., MS. Arch. Seld. B. 23, ff. 145ᵛ, 146.

6 December 1421. Whitsuntide was spent at the Louvre but after a fortnight Henry, already ailing, moved to the country air of Senlis. Here he received from the duke of Burgundy an appeal to relieve the Burgundian garrison at Cosne-sur-Loire from the Dauphinist pressure. It was politic to do all that was possible in aid of a Burgundian force faced with surrender, and Henry started, but at Corbeil was too weak to command and had to hand over to Bedford. He tried once more, at Charenton, but was unable to ride and was carried to Bois-de-Vincennes, where he died on the last day of August 1422. Had he lived another two months he would have become king both of England and of France; for Charles VI was to die on 11 October.

What he said in his final hours has been the subject of differing reports and much controversy. He had with him, besides the duke of Bedford, his uncle Thomas Beaufort, duke of Exeter; Richard Beauchamp, earl of Warwick; Sir Lewis Robessart and several others. He exhorted his commanders to fight on 'until peace is gained'; protested that he had not entered upon his wars from any other motive than of prosecuting his just title and of obtaining 'both peace and my own rights'; and gave his entourage a long discourse upon 'the just and right ways they were to follow and the method of government they were to observe'. He showed them his will and the codicils in which he had directed how Henry IV's debts were to be paid and had arranged that the members of his personal staff were to be rewarded. All this is straightforward. It is the arrangements which Henry made for the government of France and England, and particularly the latter, which have been disputed. Most of the English chroniclers say that Henry had decided to make Bedford responsible, during the minority, for the government of Normandy, and the regency of France; the St. Albans Chronicler, Thomas Walsingham, observes, however, that the king provided for Bedford to be *custos Ducatus Normannie*, but that the duke of Burgundy, on whose loyalty depended the maintenance of the treaty of Troyes, was to be *Regens regis et regni Francie*.[1] Walsingham may have been right.

Henry had allowed himself so little time for the elegances and the humanities of kingship that it is hard to depict him away from the pursuit of his great ambition: to settle once for all the question of France. He made a deep impression on his

[1] *Historia Anglicana*, ii. 345.

contemporaries by his character, his sense of discipline, and his love of justice. He was unquestionably formidable, for he could diagnose the weak points of his opponents and had the gift of severity and the power to coerce with a passionate dialectic of his own. In the last analysis he was an adventurer, not a states-man: the risk he took in the creation of a dual monarchy was too great, depended on too many uncertainties, and funda-mentally misread the nature of France. In the adjoining note on the financial aspect of the English conquest one or two points about Henry's *damnosa haereditas* will be considered. But if judgement has to be passed upon the king, one proviso seems necessary. To the fifteenth century the inducement of immediate gain by successful warfare was always more com-pelling than remoter considerations of economic security or political achievement. In 1413 there seemed to be a genuine opportunity to succeed where Edward III had in the end failed: either to enforce the English claim to the French crown or to see that the treaty of Brétigny was carried out without any reservation, and to acquire the duchy of Aquitaine in full sovereignty with no obligations of any sort to the French king. Events brought Henry face to face with the first of these alter-natives. Holding the view of his relations to Normandy that he did, he would have found it hard to accept the Brétigny settle-ment without reserving the duchy, and that was not in the Calais agreement. He made the claim therefore to the French throne and through military ability and the disunity of his opponents was awarded the greater prize, but with obligations and reservations that could only have been carried out had he been there for the next twenty years to supervise, negotiate, and fight for the completion of the treaty of Troyes, and above all by his own great personal influence to hold the duke of Burgundy to his engagements. Even granted abundance of days, would he have been successful? As it was, he had only made a beginning; and he had bound his country to a settle-ment which quickly became out of date.

NOTE A

It may be useful to consider the statement, quoted above,[1] that 'while Henry's French opponents were financially embarrassed, he himself had a sufficiency of money'. Both parliament and the

[1] See above, p. 192.

convocations were, for three years at least, generous. The grants
from November 1415 to the end of the reign were:

Laity (1) 4 Nov. 1415: 1/15 and 1/10, by Martinmas (11 Nov.)
1416; subsidy, wool and woolfells 43s. 4d., leather 100s.;
alien merchants, wool 120s., leather 106s. 8d.

(2) 16 March 1416: the last 1/15 and 1/10 accelerated to
Whitsun (7 June).

(3) 19 Oct. 1416: two 1/15 and 1/10. 1½ 1/15 and 1/10 to be
levied on 2 Feb. 1417; the remaining half by Martinmas, 1417; this half to be reserved for the repayment of
loans made to the crown.

(4) 16 Nov. 1417: two 1/15 and 1/10: 1/15 and 1/10 on
2 Feb. 1418; the other 1/15 and 1/10 on 2 Feb. 1419.

(5) 16 Oct. 1419: One and a third 1/15 and 1/10; the entire
1/15 and 1/10 on 2 Feb. 1420; the third by 11 Nov.
1420. The third, devoted as before to repayment of
lenders, to be levied for their benefit before Martinmas.
(Ordinance for money to be kept within the realm. *Rot.
Parl.* iv. 118.)

(6) 1 Dec. 1421: 1/15 and 1/10: half on 2 Feb. 1422.

Seven and three-quarter tenths and fifteenths in little more than six
years. The effort of the clergy in the convocations has been described
in detail elsewhere;[1] the main facts for the convocation of Canterbury are:

(1) 18 Nov. 1415: two 1/10 on assessed tithe-paying benefices,
payable 11 Nov. 1416, 1417; and two 1/10 on un-
assessed benefices of £10 *verus valor*.

(2) 1 April 1416: one of the tenths granted above to be
advanced to 24 June 1416.

(3) 9 Nov. 1416: two 1/10, 1½ payable on 2 Feb. 1417, ½ on
18 April 1417: but the 1/10 due under grant on (1), i.e.
on 11 Nov. 1417, to be put off until June 1418.

(4) 26 Nov. 1417: two 1/10, payable on 2 Feb. 1418, 1419;
on condition that the tenth, originally granted in (1),
which in (3) was postponed until 24 June 1418, should
be put off until 2 Feb. 1420. York Convocation voted
1/10 only.

(5) 3 Oct. 1419: half 1/10, to be levied along with the tenth
due on 2 Feb. 1419: and a noble (6s. 8d.) from chaplains of parochial chantries of 7 marks annual value
upwards, and from all unbeneficed secular chaplains of
similar income.

[1] *Reg. Chichele*, iii. 522 f. where the exemptions are listed.

(6) 5 May 1421: one tenth, half payable on 11 Nov. 1421, half on 11 Nov. 1422.

In the concession of 1421 there were some significant conditions. No prelate, clerk, or agent of his should be forced to contribute to the secular fifteenth or to any advance on secular taxation; secondly, clergy who had either made or had promised that year to make loans to the king should receive preferential treatment in the clerical grant. When the new reign came the exhaustion of the clergy was so great that in the October 1425–February 1426 convocation they made no grant at all, and earlier in 1425 all that the council could extract from them was the promise of a half-tenth, payable at Martinmas 1425, while the same figure was offered for April 1426, and it was two years before the full tenth was resumed.

The immediate effort of laity and clergy was therefore notable. It has been computed[1] that under the grants of November 1415, March and October 1416, sums amounting to £216,868. 9s. 10d. were collected; on the other hand, the cost of maintaining Harfleur, of negotiations with Sigismund and Burgundy, of arranging the naval expedition of 1416, and preparing the flotilla that crossed to France in 1417, amounted to £256,885. 15s. 10d. There was thus a deficit of more than £40,000. The expedition of 1417 had therefore to be financed by 'chevance' (*chevisance*) or loan, and letters were sent to the leading men of the realm inviting them to meet the king at Reading, while similar requests went out to the clergy on a wide scale. The commissioners who had been authorized to accept loans told the people quite unreservedly and openly what they were expected to pay, and the remarkable thing is that so many complied. 286 loans produced the sum of £31,595, but, as on the occasion analysed just above, Beaufort is credited with £14,000 of this amount: apart from him, there were loans of 1,000 marks from Bristol, £1,860 from London, and from Richard Whittington and the prior of St. John of Jerusalem £1,333. 6s. 8d. each.[2] There was more besides and the total sum borrowed during the period 11 April–29 September 1417 was £34,146. 17s. 7d.: in addition there were considerable sums from the prisoners, instalments of their total ransom money or the complete ransom itself. Among them the count of Vendôme's ransom proved in 1418 a useful source of assignment for the household expenses. Between 1417 and the spring and summer of 1421 there is a gap in the borrowing, and the buoyancy in the revenue is kept up by the taxes collected in 1418, 1419, and the two collections of 1420; the great loans of 1421 were sought and obtained because of the failure of Henry's approach to parliament. It is interesting that it was the convocations rather than parliament

---

[1] By Newhall, op. cit., p. 144.   [2] Steel, *Receipt*, pp. 156–7.

which were prepared to concede taxation during the summer of that year. Henry, then, had a sufficiency, but not more.

Professor Newhall has argued that from 1418 onwards, the real burden of the war was gradually being transferred to Normandy.[1] None the less he has to concede that when Henry died, the English Exchequer had a deficit of some £30,000 contracted during 1416–22 and augmented by outstanding debts that amounted to £25,434. 2s. quite apart from expenses not yet met for the Agincourt campaign. It was, however, the policy to make Normandy pay for itself and later to contribute, at critical periods, to the general war effort. The first complete account of the treasurer-general, William Alington, shows that all save 5,121. 6s. 11d. l.t.[2] of Norman revenue was expended for Norman affairs, and a comparison of Alington's fourth account with that of the treasurer of war, Sir William Phelip, for the same period shows that Alington paid nothing towards the household expenses except for provender ordered by the king, while the treasurer, Phelip, accounted for receipts from the Norman chancery, the Rouen mint, the ransom of Rouen and from *vicomtés* and *baillis* and other officials in France and Normandy. Evidently the treasurer of war was getting sums direct from these sources, not mentioned in Alington's accounts. But by 1423–4 relations were clear: the account of the treasurer-general of Normandy, Pierre de Surreau, shows that more than 80,000 l.t. were paid to John Barton, treasurer of Bedford's household, of which 29,437 were to go as wages for the household troops and 52,000 l.t. was for 'household expense'. This 52,000 l.t. became part of the annual budget, not chargeable to the gabelle or to quarterages, i.e. the fluctuating taxation. It was a reasonably manageable sum as long as the Norman treasurer-general did not have to finance large military operations: but when this was the case and he had to call troops out of the garrisons where they were normally financed locally, and to pay them, the same sum could not be maintained. Good instances of this occurred in 1423 and 1424 when Bedford was pursuing a largely defensive policy. In February 1423 the duke asked for 50,000 l.t. from the Norman estates at Vernon (as well as a clerical tenth) to be used for paying the army engaged in counteracting aggression against Norman frontiers. He was also drawing upon the French receipts to pay the force besieging Meulan and defending St. Valery and Gamaches, as well as attempting to tax the French clergy. By the summer of 1423 he found that

---

[1] Op. cit., pp. 150–1: 'The financial burden . . . tended to become lighter as he extended his authority in France.' The financial burden should not be thought of in terms of direct taxation, but of loans extracted; and it would be truer to say that it became lighter only for certain classes of the community, not for all.

[2] The sums passing into and out of the Norman exchequer are given in pounds Tours (abbreviated *l.t.*).

the expenses of the operations (with little success) exceeded his resources. He could not pay, on 24 June, his troops engaged in the defence of Normandy, 'for there is nothing to give them because the funds intended for the soldiers have been spent on the siege of Le Crotoy, which still drags on, on the journey to Amiens and on the expeditions into Champagne and Brie'.[1] He therefore had to convene the estates once more at Vernon and persuade them to vote another *taille* of 60,000 *l.t.* for paying his army defending Normandy and operating southwards. This did not prove sufficient and for a third time the Norman estates were summoned, on this occasion at Caen, and assented to the government's request for a grant of 200,000 *l.t.* for the recovery of certain places and the suppression of brigandage—almost the worst danger Normandy had to face.[2] Although the border vicomtés could not produce anything, the collection elsewhere was pretty successful, but only sufficient to finance the war for about nine months. The military preparations culminating in the battle of Verneuil (1 Aug. 1424) were such a strain that the Norman estates were again convoked, on this occasion to Paris, where they voted another levy of 60,000 *l.t.* Of this 50,000 *l.t.* was for the wages of the troops up to Michaelmas 1424, 3,000 *l.t.* was for the fortifications at Harfleur and Honfleur, and the remainder (7,000 *l.t.*) to help with the expenses of the expedition to Mont St. Michel. On this occasion only 49,371. 16s. 4d. *l.t.* was collected by the specified date, and of this nearly half was diverted to help subsidize the expedition which was being ordered against Maine. Normandy and the conquest scarcely gave the English government a safe margin to provide for operations on any scale. Within sixteen years, from 1419, there were twenty-four meetings of the Norman estates and 3,150,000 *l.t.* of impositions were voted. From them, it may be noted, the nobles and clergy were exempt. There was no cessation in the demands. The English government asked for 140,000 *l.t.* in 1429; 200,000 *l.t.* in 1430; 410,000 *l.t.* in 1431; 80,000 *l.t.* in 1432; 160,000 *l.t.* in 1433; 344,000 *l.t.* in 1434 and 230,000 *l.t.* in 1435.

Apart from direct impositions the main revenues of Normandy came from the rents payable by tenants of the demesnes, and from the income of lands seized, after the confiscation order of 9 February 1419, from the rebels. The order extended to the lands and rents held by churchmen who had not sworn fealty to Henry. These sources have the satisfactory figure of 92,132. 2s. *l.t.* in 1419–20; but grants to prominent captains and restorations to Normans who had promised obedience reduced the figure proportionately: to 79,953 *l.t.*

---

[1] Newhall, op. cit., p. 181.

[2] The section on expenses incurred in the suppression of brigandage in Alington first account, P.R.O., E. 101/188/7, is worth careful note.

in 1421–2, and 48,842. 11s. 2d. l.t. in 1423–5. By 1429 it was down to 33,245 l.t. Other income was the gabelle on salt, in 1419–20 not less than 26,615. 10s. 4d. l.t.; the Quatrieme or tax on wine, cider, and other beverages, and a sales tax on all merchandise. The Norman receipts and expenses of the treasurer-general, William Alington and Peter de Surreau, have thus been calculated:[1]

1 May 1419–30 Apr. 1420	1 May 1421–31 Aug. 1422	16 Nov. 1423–15 Jan. 1425	1 Oct. 1425–30 Sept. 1429	1 Oct. 1433–30 Sept. 1434
RECEIPTS:	l.t. s. d.	l.t. s. d.	l.t. s. d.	l.t.
164,161 4 3	377,633 0 10	429,256 12 4	434,458 13 3½	320,000
PAYMENTS:				
150,896 12 5	396,899 6 6	431,491 14 0	459,568 19 6	377,622

The apparent buoyancy of the four years 1421–5 derives from the *tailles*, from which 170,036. 7s. 4d. l.t. were gathered in 1421–2, and 265,535 l.t. in 1423–5. The peak year is, none the less, 1428–9 when the collection was not in; even so, the expenses to be set against the 434,458 l.t. are no less than 459,568. 19s. 6d. l.t. The real drop comes after the year of the siege of Orléans, when English forces were deployed against France on every front. Then the receipts from Normandy were lower than in any year save 1419–20. This is partly due to the destructive influence of brigandage, eloquently described by Thomas Basin in his Chronicle[2] and the cumulative effect of the taxation; the resentment so caused appears from the decision of the government in September 1428 to collect and hand over to the local commanders of garrisons the *compositions des guets*, the sums by which the inhabitants of these military districts compounded for the duty of keeping watch and ward (lt. *excubiae*). The *guet*, which originally stood at 20s. a year, was a particularly irritating form of tax collected on the *feu* or hearth. The account of Martin Bezu, collector in Harcourt and Brionne for the period 1 January 1426 to 20 May 1427, survives[3] to show that the collector was badly down on the payments due from the *feux* in his two districts. Out of an expected 360. 10s. l.t. he had only gathered 199. 4s. 2d. l.t. because the parishes would only pay at a 10s. rate; and when the collector seized the goods of defaulters and exposed them for sale, the people of Harcourt and the neighbourhood assembled before Richard Anquetin, sheriff of Harcourt, pointing out that in the neighbouring *chatellenies* the inhabitants had been paying at the half rate for some

[1] By R. Doucet, 'Les Finances anglaises en France', *Moyen Age*, 2ᵉ série, xxxvi (1926), 294, 301.   [2] *Histoire de Charles VII*, ed. C. Samaran, i. 109–15.
[3] Archives Nationales, KK. 325 A. Harcourt, which became an English possession in 1418, came into the hands of Anne of Burgundy, Bedford's wife.

time. The note of this assembly which occurs after the account puts
the gathering on 5 May 1428. The change in the scale was decreed
in September and with it came a change in the collection. The controller of the receipts, the receiver-general of Normandy, Peter de
Surreau, prepared his account of the *guet*, from Michaelmas 1428
to Michaelmas 1430,[1] with the king's letter authorizing the receiver-
general to receive the compositions from the local collectors; by
the Rouen ordinances of September 1428 he was himself to send the
moneys to the commanders and castellans, whereas previously the
commanders were collecting and handling the money. The compositions were to be sent by the controller of the receipts when the commanders received their wages and pay, and the military officers were
not to collect them, 'par occasion d'aucunes plaintes qui en furent
faictes de plusieurs exactions qui se faisoient par les diz cappitaines
à l'occasion'.[2]

In the conquered territories apart from Normandy there were
very small receipts from the demesne; not more than 2,000 francs in
Picardy and Vermandois (each); the two most important sources
were the *aides* and the fourth on wine and liquors (10,000 francs)
and the gabelle which brought in 15,000 francs. A document of
1427–8 emanating from Bedford's treasury, which is described as 'a
declaration of estate and value by way of an approximate financial
estimate of outgoings and receipts, rents and emoluments of the
kingdom of France lying under the obedience and power and in the
seisin of John regent of France . . .' from 1 October 1427 to 30
September 1428,[3] puts the receipts at 129,240 francs out of which
all current administrative expenses, the salaries of the administrators, and the pay of the garrisons had to be found. The latter
amounted to 175,000 francs, which is in excess of any deficiency on
similar items in the accounts for Normandy, 1418–34. Such deficiencies outside the duchy are probably the reason for the continued
pressure upon the Norman estates.

But a satisfactory statement of the whole picture in any year after
the death of Henry V is very difficult to obtain. The problem of
estimating the financial position of the conquered territories outside
Normandy is due to lack of records: nor are all the items in the
surviving accounts quite clear. Did the 2,000 francs entered by
Bedford's receiver as receipts from (the profits of) 'Justice' include
the profits of the Great Seal? Almost certainly not. All sorts of
licences, pardons, safe-conducts were, under the English rules for the
conquered territories, being continually petitioned for and granted
under the Great Seal and the Signet, for which substantial sums

---

[1] Arch. Nat., KK. 325 B.   [2] Ibid., f. 5.
[3] Printed in J. Stevenson, *Letters and Papers Illustrative of the Wars of the English in
France during the Reign of Henry VI*, ii (1864), part 2, pp. 532–40.

were forthcoming. An account survives, for Maine alone, of the profits of Bedford's seals collected by the receiver Nicholas Molineux, for the period 1 October 1433 to 29 September 1434.[1] It records chiefly payments made by individuals and communities or groups of persons for safe-conducts, for protections, for permits of various kinds and letters testifying to the loyalty of the petitioners. Most of the safe-conducts are for people to go *hors cette obéissance* for the purpose of trade or of hawking and hunting (*voler, gibayer, chasser,* &c.), or to enable them to dwell for periods *en pays appatissé,*[2] that is, in land of Dauphinist sympathies but paying sums for the English protection. A good many parishes collectively had taken out *bullettes de ligeance*[3] to protect them from raiding parties, and the community just as much as the individual could obtain '*congés*'—'pour aller en payees appatissé fair leur labour et pourchassier la deliverance deulx et leurs biens pris par les adversaires . . .'.[4] Persons going on pilgrimage had to be similarly protected, just as much as French prisoners in English hands going, some with attendants, to borrow money for their ransom in Dauphinist France. In the brief period of a year, from 1 October 1433 to 29 September 1434, Molineux and his officer Giles de Ferrières at St. Suzanne accounted for 20,061 *l.t.* In the first quarter (Oct. 1433–Jan. 1434) the receiver took 4,086. 16s. *l.t.* at Le Mans, and his subordinate 2,607. 17s. 8d. *l.t.*[5] These 'profits' are for one district only. Such payments can scarcely have been popular, though they may have been the only hope for Frenchmen forced to live in occupied or 'protected' areas.

A letter from Henry VI, written on 7 September 1428 to the receiver-general of Normandy modifying the amount of the *guet* to be exacted alluded to the many complaints which Bedford, as regent, had received about the oppressions and abuses for which the English as well as the French captains were responsible in Normandy and the conquered lands:[6] remonstrances had been received from churchmen, nobles, and communities representative of the three estates of Normandy and the conquest about the violent attacks of bandits and malefactors upon peaceful subjects, the holding to ransom of persons and goods alike, and the robbery and raiding of villages and hamlets by these ruffians, 'to provision their fortresses'. Instances of undisciplined foraging and the 'ransoming' of possessions illegally seized by armed members of the English garrisons are to be found throughout the letters of pardon issued by Henry VI's chancery in France, demonstrating what opportunities for private gain offered themselves not only to the upper ranks in the English garrisons, but

---

[1] Arch. Nat., KK. 324.   [2] Ibid., f. 2, 10.   [3] Ibid., ff. 109–18.
[4] Ibid., f. 136ᵛ.   [5] Ibid., f. 108.
[6] Arch. Nat. KK. 325ᴮ, at the beginning of the account of the receiver-general, Peter de Surreau, Michaelmas 1428–Michaelmas 1430, for the *guet* (*excubiae*).

also to the ordinary rank and file. There is, for example, the pitiful story of the English archer from the garrison of Alençon who seized goods from the homes of labourers and insisted upon their providing him with transport to visit the villages of the countryside, where he entered the homes of the people, took their belongings, and 'ransomed' them by selling them back to their owners. Eventually the peasants who had been forced to convoy him could stand it no longer and belaboured him to death.[1] The impression one gains from the pardons issued by Henry VI's chancery 'is that of the misery of the ordinary (*menu*) people, held to ransom indifferently by the English soldiery and the French partisans, only escaping the regular troops to fall under the power of the brigands defying the common law; crushed by taxes voted by the estates and by forced contributions for protection (*appatis*) levied by the captains of the armed bands'.[2]

---

[1] *Actes de la Chancellerie d'Henri VI*, ed. Le Cacheux, i. 253 f. Cf. ibid. i. 267 for the ransoming of the members of a parish priest's household, and i. 357-9 for the account of the lamb stolen by a squire of Sir John Clifton.

[2] Ibid. i, p. xv: the editor's comment.

VI

THE MINORITY OF HENRY VI TO THE CONGRESS OF ARRAS (1435)

EALIZING how dangerous a long minority might be, Henry V tried to safeguard the dynasty by providing for the royal power to be principally exercised by his younger brother Gloucester. France was to be governed by the duke of Burgundy or, if he declined, by Bedford. The latter arrangement he could secure without the need of English assent: the former he could not. By his will Henry appointed Gloucester to some form of regency in England. The course of the duke's life and his whole attitude towards the council were largely to be determined by the rejection of Henry's plan by the magnates in the first parliament of the new reign, and by the establishment, under parliamentary authority, of the office of protector, in a much more restricted sense than the one it bore in 1216. The protectorship was to be subordinate to the council and to lack the prerogatival powers which the council had claimed to exercise on behalf of the king during the minority.

Very few leading magnates were in England when Henry V died. Of the lay peerage, no more than the three earls of Westmorland, Northumberland, and Devon, and twelve barons had been summoned to attend the parliament of the preceeding December, held under John, duke of Bedford. Only the duke of Exeter (Thomas Beaufort), the earls of Warwick and March, Henry Lord FitzHugh (Henry V's chamberlain), Ralph Lord Cromwell, and the bishop of London (John Kemp, ex-chancellor of the duchy of Normandy) came home with the body: Bedford had joined Henry in May 1422 and stayed on in France, as did the earls of Salisbury and Suffolk. Humphrey earl of Stafford, who returned to England and John de Vere, earl of Oxford (who did not), were still minors. Not until 5 November could a representative meeting of the great council be called. Before that, at a meeting of available magnates on 28 September, summoned for them to perform homage and swear fealty to the infant king, it was decided that parliamentary sanction for whatever constitutional form of government was adopted was necessary. The writs went out on Michaelmas Day for a meeting on 9 November, and were tested by the king, being warranted 'by king and council' and not by the *custos Anglie*. Gloucester himself received a summons although neither he nor Bedford had received one while acting as *custos*, the available lords spiritual and temporal seem to have assumed that the exercise of the royal authority had devolved upon them by reason of Henry V's death and the tender age of the heir. Being, as one of their minutes on 1 October alleges, the 'maior et sanior pars omnium dominorum et procerum regni', it was they who must act, pending the appointment of a royal council of the regular kind. This had happened at the very beginning of Richard II's minority.

This interim council saw fit to secure from the parliament of 1422 its ratification of their acts. On 5 November a large and more representative council met: the archbishop of Canterbury the bishops of Winchester, Durham, Norwich, Exeter, Worcester Lincoln, and Rochester; the dukes of Gloucester and Exeter; the earl of Warwick, the earl marshal and earl of Northumberland and the Lords Ferrers, Talbot, Botreaux, Clinton, Dudley, Fitz-Hugh, Poynings, Berkeley, and Cromwell. They were met to consider the terms of the duke of Gloucester's commission to begin, conduct, and terminate the forthcoming parliament. In this council there came to a head, for the first time, the problem of Gloucester's ambition to be regent. A form of commission had been drafted and its terms set forth that Gloucester, on his royal nephew's behalf, was to open, conduct, and dissolve parliament *de assensu concilii*. This phrase Gloucester disliked: it would be he maintained, *in prejudicium status sui*: the phrase never came in previous commissions when he was acting as *custos*; if it were included, the lords could keep parliament in being for a year on end, if they so wished. The lords held out for the phrase and in the end Gloucester agreed to their petition. In this the influence both of Beaufort and of others lords could be traced Of course the tactical weakness was that at the end of September when Gloucester might have protested, he had accepted his obligation to receive and obey a summons to parliament Nearly six years later, on 3 March 1428, when seeking from the lords in parliament a definition of his power and authority as protector, Gloucester was reminded by the lords that he had

[1] *P.P.C.* iii. 4.

been summoned to parliament as duke of Gloucester, upon his faith and allegiance 'as other lords be and non otherwise', and they humbly requested, but also in the king's name *required*, his attendance as legally obligatory. His failure to assert his position in September 1422 was to prejudice him very considerably: and now to talk about his *status* and his *libertas*, as he did in the council of 5 November, created suspicions of his political designs. His only hope could be that the lords would fall in with any wishes that Henry V may have expressed in his written testament or by word of mouth on his death-bed.

What had Henry decided during his fatal illness? Here there is discrepancy among the chroniclers. The latest will of Henry V along with its codicils is lost. The earl of Stafford, Lords Bourchier and Hungerford when asked in the council what words Henry V had in his final instructions used about the government of Normandy professed themselves to have been so upset at the time that they could scarcely remember: but in so far as they could, it was that Bedford should 'drawe hym doune into Normandie and kepe that contray as well as the remenant of his Conquest . . . with the revenuz and the profitts thereof, and do therewith as he wolde do with his oune'.[1] As for France, all the important English chroniclers extant say that Bedford was to become responsible for the government of Normandy and the regency of France: all, as we said, save Walsingham, who states that Henry had provided for Bedford to be *custos Ducatus Normannie*, but that the duke of Burgundy should be *Regens regis et regni Francie*. Monstrelet, in whose exact knowledge of affairs some confidence may be placed, confirms Walsingham, but makes it clear that Burgundy's regency was naturally to be conditional upon his accepting it. If Burgundy was to refuse the offer, Bedford was to undertake the government of France as well as of Normandy. This is what in fact happened. The *Vita Henrici V* of Titus Livius says that Exeter was entrusted with the keeping and instruction of Henry VI: other chronicles associate one of the magnates with him in this: the Pseudo-Elmham makes the two Beauforts charged with the duty. Henry certainly showed the magnates who were with him in his last hours the testament, drawn up on 10 June 1421, when he left England for the last time, as well as the codicils to it. There is reason to think that one of these dealt with the

[1] *P.P.C.* iii. 248.

arrangements in England during the heir's minority: in a memorandum which Gloucester was to submit to the lords in the 1422 parliament[1] the duke stated that he had been granted *tutelam et defensionem principales* of the king, in a codicil of Henry V's will. It is interesting to find some of the very same words of the codicil appearing in the *Vita* of Titus Livius when he describes Henry V's death and draws Henry VI's attention to the claims of Gloucester on his gratitude: 'testamento tamen ante tui [Henrci VI] tutelam primasque defensiones et curam Humfrido Gloucestrie duci . . . [Henricus Quintus] . . . legavit.' The chroniclers in referring to the oral instruction of Henry V only tell part of the story. When Gloucester submitted his memorandum to the lords in 1422, he referred in that statement to their already expressed objection to the word *tutela* as a term used in Roman law (a term of 'law civil') and their refusal to allow its use in whatsoever commission Gloucester was to be granted. The Roman *tutor* was in fact first and foremost the controller of the property of his ward in the time of the latter's incapacity to administer it himself. This was apparently what Henry V wanted Gloucester to be. Henry's desire to create a *tutela* explains the omission of Catherine of Valois from the nominated personal custodians of Henry of Windsor. 'Gloucester then must have based his claims to the regency of England during Henry VI's minority on the knowledge that what his royal brother had conferred upon him in his will was the principal administration and defence of the inheritance of his heir, which, if the kingdom could be regarded as the property of the king (and in Henry V's mind it still evidently could be), included the inherited attributes of regality.' In other words, the lords rejected Gloucester's 'Romanist interpretation of the Romanist formulae of Henry V's will'.[2]

Even when the will had been read he could not have got much assurance that the codicil would be respected. In the sermon delivered at the ceremonial opening of parliament on 9 November, 'Principes populorum congregati sunt cum Deo', Chichele found a biblical analogy for the present position in the Old Testament story of the Exodus, in the wise counsel given by

[1] Printed by Professor S. B. Chrimes, 'The Pretensions of the Duke of Gloucester in 1422', *Eng. Hist. Rev.* xlv (1945), 102.

[2] J. S. Roskell, 'The Office and Dignity of Protector of England, with special reference to its Origins', *Eng. Hist. Rev.* lxviii (1953), 230-3.

Jethro to Moses, 'Duc des gens de Israel'. Moses had been found by Jethro to be overworked in fulfilling the obligations of the government: Jethro had told him that this was not a good thing: 'stulto labore consumeris et tu et populus iste qui tecum est: ultra vires tuas est negotium . . .'. When Jethro advised the appointment of assistants from among the powerful and worthy, Moses accepted the advice given him: 'et electis viris strenuis de cuncto Israel, constituit eos principes populi'. Gloucester was Chichele's Moses, Chichele's own was the part of Jethro.[1]

Later on, in the answer given on 3 March 1428 to Gloucester's request to be furnished with a definition of his power as protector and defender, it appears that the duke in 1422 made a twofold claim in parliament to the governance of England. It was his right 'as wel by the mene of birth as be the last wylle of the Kyng that was' (Henry V). The lords had debated this and in the end, after consultation with the lawyers, rejected his claim in both its aspects as being 'not grounded in precident, nor in the law of the land'. The claim to governance by birth was incompatible with the law and 'against the right and freedom of the estates of the land', and as for the will, it was not a valid bequest if its result was to 'altre, change or abroge withoute the assent of the thre estates or to commit to any persone governaunce of this land longer than he lyved'. The statement of the lords in 1428 then described the commissions which Gloucester received: in the absence of Bedford, he was to be 'chief of the Kynges Council' and should have a name different from other councillors, that of protector and defender, with such powers as parliament had allowed and specified. That is the account, a very careful one given in 1428, of the fate of Gloucester's claim in 1422. One more precedent was carefully studied and produced as the necessary means towards co-operation. In 1377, when Richard II succeeded to the crown at the age of ten years, his uncle John of Gaunt had not then been granted the name or authority of governor, and after the coronation, but *before* Richard's first parliament met, a great council of prelates and lay magnates nominated twelve councillors who were virtually an interim council of regency, and when parliament did meet, the lords, being formally moved to do so by a petition of the commons, nominated in parliament a salaried council of nine, to hold office for one year in which the three estates were

[1] Roskell, ibid.

represented in some sort of proportion: three bishops, two earls, two baronets, and two knights bachelors. But Gloucester was not satisfied with this. He, too, had been looking at precedents. He had, he said, been granted *tutelam et defensionem principales* and had gone back to the time when in 1216 William Marshal, created earl of Pembroke in 1199, was appointed *rector regis et regni*. If the title of governor was not palatable, he was, however, prepared to compromise: he would drop the *rector regis*: but the real difficulty was the *tutela* and to that he clung. Under Roman law the *tutela* was designed to protect the interest of the tutor as well as that of the ward, and to protect those who would succeed to the estate if he died while still under age. The main objection of the lords to the word *tutela* was probably that it implied a right to administer the estate of the ward with a responsibility to account only to him, and not until he reached maturity: and in this connexion one should compare the report, made to the lords in 1427, that Gloucester would answer for what he had done touching the king's estate to none save Henry VI when he came of age.

Gloucester was, therefore, in this 1422 parliament granted the title of protector and defender of the realm and church in England and principal counsellor of the king. But he could assume these duties only when Bedford was not in the country, and it was the intention of the magnates to keep the two brothers in that order: they emphasized the dependency by making the appointment, not for the minority, but at pleasure. It could be revoked. This was what the lords remembered in 1428: but in Gloucester's Memorandum the lords are represented as having originally accepted Henry V's will. It certainly does not represent them as having questioned on principle and from the beginning the rightfulness of Henry V's action in leaving the 'regency' of England to Gloucester by his will alone, and therefore without the concurrence of the estates. It appears therefore that, unless Gloucester was guilty of misrepresentation, the lords changed their minds and after once accepting the codicil of the will they came to reject it outright as the legal basis of any part of Gloucester's authority. There is nothing of this rejection in the 1422 record of parliament: it was not to be made explicit until early in 1428 when Gloucester refused to attend parliament and the lords prepared a statement of what had happened in 1422. The settlement of 1422 resulted, therefore, in the establishment of a protectorship with safeguards for the ultimate superiority, under the king, of the lords spiritual and temporal, whether assembled in parliament, or great council, or the ordinary continual council. It became a precedent.

The reign of Henry VI was to see a protectorship set up on two other occasions, in 1454, when the king became temporarily insane, and again in 1455 when he was once more out of his mind. On the first occasion Richard, duke of York, was chosen by the lords to take Bedford and Gloucester's former title and powers by parliamentary authority, and with the same formal limitation that his office was terminable at the royal pleasure. Yet there was a difference. York was more distantly related: in 1454 the king's nearest male relative was his son Edward of Wales, but he was only an infant of less than two years: so it was provided that when he reached the age of discretion the office was to devolve on him if he wished to assume it. In 1455 the protector's title, powers, and warrant were as before, but this time it was to be for the lords to determine in parliament when the royal pleasure should apply the closure. York undertook not to proceed to the execution of his office without the approval of the council chosen by the lords, to which was reserved the 'politique rule and governance of the land'. No such safeguards seem to have been furnished in 1483 in the next establishment of a protectorship, when Richard duke of Gloucester, the only surviving brother of Edward IV, took upon himself the powers of regency on behalf of his twelve-year-old nephew. He was in fact determined to avoid them.

The minority of Henry VI (1422–37) may not in itself be considered a compact historical period: yet it offers the historian a chance to survey the government of the country by the king's council during a period of peculiar difficulty and tension: the aftermath of Henry V's conquests in France when the implications of the treaty of Troyes have begun to make themselves felt and a group pledged to the furtherance of peace and the promotion of trade was, as the result of financial stringency and of continuing reverses abroad, making itself felt. During the period, at any rate from 1424, there is a mounting conflict of interests in the council, partly on public and partly on personal grounds, between the militant, Renaissance-minded, and quasi-protectionist Duke Humphrey and those who saw in the

Anglo-Burgundian alliance a guarantee for English exports and an avenue for a wider system of treaties with other powers, not excluding the allies of France. The treatment of Scotland and the question of the French prisoners were two of many issues that saw friction aroused. The constitutional crisis in which the minority began, raising as it did the question of oligarchy against regal prerogative sustained by princes of the blood, unquestionably started the fission: but it would not have led, as it did, to a party division and a party structure, had not the self-interest of the leaders and the allurement of the protective lordship they offered to those prepared to join them made competition so intense that even a physically and mentally strong Henry VI would have had great difficulty in asserting the royal authority after it had been so long in commission.

Seldom had a royal council started so strenuously and with such devotion to work. It was a large body that was nominated 'at the request of the commons, by the advice and assent of all the lords aforesaid': two dukes, Gloucester and Exeter (Thomas Beaufort), five bishops, Chichele, Beaufort, Kemp (London), Wakering (Norwich), and Polton (Chichester); five earls, March (Edmund Mortimer, still the hope of the discontented), Warwick (Richard Beauchamp), the earl marshal (John Mowbray), Northumberland (Henry Percy), and Westmorland (Ralph Neville); the chamberlain Lord FitzHugh of the great Yorkshire landowning family, FitzHugh of Ravensworth, brother of the bishop of London; and four knights, Ralph Cromwell,[1] Walter Hungerford, John Tiptoft, and Walter Beauchamp. The three officials of state who attended most of the meetings, Bishop Thomas Langley, chancellor, John Stafford, treasurer, and William Aluwide, keeper of the privy seal, were not formally appointed, as their presence was a matter of duty. The contemporary minutes show that besides the three, the most regularly attending were Chichele, Beaufort, and the four knights: but it was a highly representative and distinguished committee all round. Of the bishops, Chichele (archbishop of Canterbury), Beaufort, Wakering, and Polton were royal administrators and had been in the royal employ-

---

[1] Treasurer in 1433. He was sixteen on the death of his grandmother in 1419. J. F. Baldwin, *The King's Council*, p. 171, says that he 'still ranked as a knight at the age of twenty-eight'; but he received summonses to parliament from 29 Sept. 1422 to his death in 1456. Lords are frequently described by the knightly title.

ment on special business; Beaufort as chancellor, Wakering as keeper of the privy seal; Polton was a curialist in close touch with Rome. The knights had only one newcomer to administration—Ralph Cromwell, the owner of Tattershall Castle in Lincolnshire, a young man of nineteen, later to be king's chamberlain, and treasurer of England; the others were practised hands: Hungerford was a soldier and a diplomat who had served Henry IV and Henry V, had been Speaker of the commons in 1414, and had represented the king both at Sigismund's court and in the council of Constance. John Tiptoft had been Speaker in the parliament of 1406, and had been (Dec. 1406 to July 1409) treasurer of the household; while Walter Beauchamp from Worcestershire, cousin of Richard Beauchamp, earl of Warwick, had been Speaker in 1416. Round Chichele, Hungerford, Cromwell, and the permanent officers much of the history of the minority council could be written. On 9 November it was ordained in parliament that it should not be necessary to sue, with payment, for the continuation or confirmation of charters or patents of annuities, daily wages or offices, such confirmation to be granted gratis under the great seal with the word *concedimus*. It was also agreed that Bedford or, in his absence, Gloucester should have the nomination of foresters, parkers, and warreners in England and Wales, of clerks to parish churches rated at between 20 and 30 marks, to all royal prebends in royal chapels, the deanery in each excluded; the lords of the council were to appoint the sheriffs, escheators, customers, the comptrollers, weighers and searchers, saving rights already bestowed upon Beaufort:[1] they were to dispose of the wardships, marriages, and other casual sources of revenue belonging to the crown.

The quorum was to be four, plus the officers; and if the matter was normally one for the king, the council were not to proceed without the advice of Bedford or Gloucester. Measures were taken to tighten the custody of the receipts, keys being given to the treasurer and both chamberlains; and appointments by the treasurer were to be ratified by letters patent emanating from the chancellor to the appointees. The attendance was, for the first half year at any rate, exemplary: much of the business was routine: the issue of protections, the disposal of prisoners and the remuneration of their keepers, licences to abbeys and

[1] Cf. below, p. 227.

priories to elect their superiors, leasing of temporalities of vacant religious houses and appointments, particularly of Thomas Beaufort to be justice of north Wales. On 12 February 1423 the salary of the chief councillor was regulated. Gloucester, while in office as protector and chief councillor was to have 8,000 marks, including 4,000 out of the Lancaster lands, 1,000 from the Roos minority, 800 from the Neville minority (from the lands of Ralph, son and heir of Ralph Neville, son and heir of John Neville), and 1,700 out of the Exchequer. An oath was taken by the councillors, probably not in parliament, for on 26 January Hungerford was entered in the council minutes as 'assumptus ad concilium regis et admissus' at the Blackfriars; and the commons in 1423 made special request to know who were the persons 'assigned and chosen' to be of the council, whereupon for their 'ease and consolation' a list was read.[1] The original councillors had accepted office under the conditions specified above: the present council, which contained two new names, those of Thomas Chaucer of Ewelme, a cousin of the Beauforts, and purveyor of wine and other commodities to the royal household, and William Alington, who had been treasurer-general of Normandy, asked for five articles which seem to have gone farther than the original ones, and were aimed largely at the protector. They asked that all offices and benefices not directly and specifically excepted might be filled by their advice alone; that all the favours, wards, and marriages should be theirs to distribute; that a quorum of six, apart from the professional administrators, should be required for acts to be valid, and that the officials of the Exchequer were not to divulge what the king had in his treasury, save only to the lords of the council. They asked that neither the duke nor any other member should grant any favour in bills of right, office, or benefice which belonged to the council. In relations with foreign countries, nobody on the council, they stipulated, was to write in its name: the requirement that six or four persons outside the professional administrators was still the needful quorum was repeated. As to councillors' salaries, the council took up the matter in 1424 and a yearly scale was arrived at: an archbishop, a duke, the chancellor, and the bishop of Winchester each received £200; other bishops, earls, and the treasurer got 200 marks; barons and knights £100 and esquires

---

[1] *Rot. Parl.* iv. 201. Cf. Baldwin, *The King's Council*, p. 172.

£40.[1] Deductions were made for absence, but the amounts
demanded from the Exchequer were pretty large. They were
paid in assignments which could not always be met and in some
instances accounts fell as much as twelve years or more in
arrears. In March 1423 Gloucester was by way of getting his
8,000 marks from the receivers of the duchy of Lancaster.[2]

At the beginning of December 1422 the interconnected
problems of Scotland, the Marcher garrisons, and Calais became
urgent. At Calais the king's lieutenant received warrants for
2,000 marks for the wages of the soldiers of Calais and the
Marches. On 15 January it was agreed to pay £2,000 in money
to the troops there, and that they should receive an assignment
of 13s. 4d. on every sack of wool coming from the Staple, and
from the revenues of the town and Marches.[3] By 21 February
1423 the council were discussing the question of distributing
the sum of £5,000 in Calais to be divided as £4,000 to the
garrison and £1,000 to the March, and on 2 March ordered the
payment from the customs of 13s. 4d. on every sack of wool and
on every 240 tanned skins exported from Calais for the wages
of the garrisons of the town and Marches.[4] The £4,000 was in
fact lent to the government by the mayor and merchants of the
Staple at Calais after the wool had been seized by order of the
council, and steps were taken to reimburse the staplers. This
sum was to be repaid out of the arrears of royal tenants in north
and south Wales. Such arrears could only be paid by instalments.[5]

The difficulty experienced by the defenders not only of Calais
but also of the Scottish border was to get their assignments
cashed: for the Border, new tallies had to be made out on the
customers of Kingston on Hull and Boston,[6] while the earl of
Northumberland, captain of Berwick and warden of the east
March, was given a bond for £3,000 for the payment 'as much
of the old debt as of the new' on condition that he sent his
uncashable tallies to the Exchequer.[7] The earl had nearly as
much cause as Henry Percy to grumble at the slowness of the
government in repaying its debts; it was perhaps a counsel of
prudence, in view of past history, to accept the disagreeable
position of creditor. Such persons could have seen that Ireland

[1] Baldwin, op. cit., p. 176.
[2] *P.P.C.* iii. 51–52.
[3] Ibid. iii. iv.
[4] Ibid. iii. 49–51.
[5] Ibid. iii. 89: pp. 77–78.
[6] Ibid. iii. 73.
[7] Ibid. iii. 69.

and Gascony were no less exacting in their demands. The earl of March, who had fallen foul of Gloucester, had to be given a yearly allowance of 5,000 marks as lieutenant of Ireland; and alarmed by the depressing account of Guienne given by Sir Thomas Swinburn, the constable of Fronsac, the council ordered payment to be made to the keeper, Sir John Radcliffe, of the 1,000 marks a year, the retaining fee promised him by Henry V. Nor had Sir John Tiptoft, whom Henry V had appointed seneschal of Gascony, been paid for the work which Henry had commanded him to do on the castle of Bayonne: this had now to be rectified. Commitments and arrears mounted up: the annuity granted by Henry V to Lewis duke of Bavaria had to be recognized as an obligation; and then there were the French prisoners, valuable, but for the time being comparatively expensive assets, to be paid for. To a number the council accorded three months' leave, to find their ransoms.[1] Certain of them taken at Harfleur, were prepared to take the oath 'to be our liege men and true subjects' and were released to go where they would. Most of the greater Agincourt and Meaux prisoners had been allotted to their respective keepers and were maintained as their rank demanded, either by the Exchequer, if they were the king's prisoners, or by their captors or those granted the ransom. Until Easter 1435 the dukes of Orléans and Bourbon were paid for by their custodians who accounted with the Exchequer; after which time they were compelled by the council to find their own expenses: but men like Arthur of Brittany, the count of Eu, and Marshal Boucicaut cost 23s. 4d. a week while stationed under guard and 33s. 4d. a week 'while travelling'. Their keeper, Sir Thomas Burton, who had had them since 15 June 1417 had claimed £300. 16s. 8d., but only £178. 10s. 10d. was allowed for this 'long labour and heavy and dreadful charge'.[2] In one notable case the council was prepared to buy a prisoner, no less than Louis de Bourbon, count of Vendôme, from his keeper, Sir John Cornwall, for 5,000 marks, 3,000 of this sum to be furnished in instalments of £500 from the lands of the heir of Sir John Arundel then under age, and the rest to be the subject of a special arrangement; for the larger sum the permission of the next parliament was required, otherwise security was to be given him for the whole sum and the money raised by different methods. In the meantime

---

[1] *P.P.C.* iii. 135, 137. [2] Ibid. iii. 132.

the count was to remain in the custody of Sir John. The facts were that the count had been taken prisoner at Agincourt by Sir John Cornwall, but that Henry V had claimed him and had paid no compensation:[1] the new arrangement recognized Sir John's right as captor, but left the ultimate ransom in the hands of the council. Meanwhile Sir John was to have 600 marks compensation for his expenses in the long suit for the recovery of his prisoner, to come out of the Arundel lands, immediate payment in three instalments to be made by Henry V's feoffees in the duchy of Lancaster. It may be added that in the October parliament of 1423 he was given the right to the ransoms of the lords 'Gaucourt and Toteville' (Estoutville) to enable him to negotiate the liberation of his stepson the earl of Huntingdon,[2] a prisoner in French hands, to whom the king was heavily in debt for war wages. Sir John Cornwall of Burford, a soldier and a hard-headed, shrewd financier, who had been present at the siege of Rouen, had married, as her second husband, Elizabeth Holland, daughter of John of Gaunt and sister of Henry IV. He was given in 1429 the custody of the duke of Orléans, who had been in the hands of Sir Thomas Comberworth.[3] He is an example of a highly placed speculator in ransoms.

The Speaker in the October parliament of 1423, John Russell, when welcoming the infant Henry, brought by his mother to parliament, gave thanks for the two noble and mighty princes '. . . your full worthy uncles of Bedforde and Gloucestre' by whom the land had been protected, and for the confusion of the enemies of the kingdom, 'a full, noble and commodious meen that God hath provyded for us all the which is the truth and wysdome and kyndernesse of all yure other lords spirituelx and temporelx beyng of yure high and sadde counseill'.[4] The full, noble, and commodious meen (company) was to be tested severely in the early days of the February following (1424), when, as the London Chronicle states, 'bills' against the Flemings began to circulate. 'And somme were sette upon the Byshoppes gate of Wynchester and on other Byshops'

---

[1] He had originally been bought in 1417, for £5,000, two-thirds of which was paid by the Florentine financiers John Vittore and Gerard Danys, Sir John Cornwall paying a third. Steel, op. cit., p. 156 n.   [2] *P.P.C.* iii. 122.

[3] *Rot. Parl.* iv. 339. Sir Thomas Combeworth had transferred to him the duke of Bourbon, previously in the care of the duke of Bedford.

[4] *The Great Chronicle of London*, ed. A. H. Thomas and I. D. Thornley, p. 129.

gates.' Beaufort judged it expedient to occupy the Tower in strength by sending in Richard Wydeville, 'with men of army as though it had been in Londe of werre'. The Chronicle then mentions arrests of, and appeals of treason against, London citizens that followed at the bishop's 'excitation'[1] (incitement). As a London patron he was alarmed at Beaufort's friendliness to the Burgundian element in the city: the episode leads him to devote considerable space to the famous dispute between the bishop and the duke which came to a head at the end of October 1425.

The antagonism was both personal and constitutional. Under the latter aspect it has been argued that the bishop spoke for an element that was to become increasingly important in the council: a group of the lords, some holding office, some powerful through their experience and assiduous attendance. In other words, Gloucester came up against the *domini de consilio*, who had special functions and responsibilities. To what extent these *domini* could be called a group with specified powers and attributes is a matter which will be discussed later. But it may here be said that *domini de consilio* in our view simply stands for baronial members of the council and it was some of these who watched the claims and tactics of the duke with suspicion. He had, as we have seen, given them some reason to do so. The lords were prepared to grant Gloucester that in the absence of his brother he should be 'chief of the Kynges Counsail', as their statement in 1428 put it; and should be styled protector and defender with such powers as parliament had specified, the position to last 'as long as it like the Kyng'. In effect an oligarchy had assumed the executive power and had done so through parliament.

Hardyng is explicit in attributing the restrictions placed upon the protectorship to Beaufort.[2] But in 1428 the lords represented the decision they made in 1422 as a corporate one, and much that bears upon it can be gleaned from the interviews which the council held with the dukes of Bedford and Gloucester on 28 and 29 January 1427. Here it was clearly stated on behalf of the council that the king, being as yet of tender age, the council 'representing his persone as toward execucion of

---

[1] 'And there he arrested many worthy man of the cite'; *The Great Chronicle of London*, ed. Thomas and Thornley, p. 136.

[2] 'The bishop aye withstood all his intent', when Gloucester claimed the regency. But it will be remembered that this was written some thirty years later.

the said pollitique rule and governaille of his land and observance and keping of said lawes without that any oo (one)
persone may or owe ascribe unto himself the said rule and
governaille, savyng alweyes unto my said lord of Bedford and
of Gloucester that that is in especiale reserved and applied unto
hem by act of parlement'.[1] It was natural that Beaufort should
find a plurality more to his taste than that one of his nephews
should exercise regal power during the minority. The second or
alternative account of Gloucester's reply, when at the interview
with the council he was asked for a declaration of loyalty towards that body, shows how unguarded had been his language
and how impetuous his reactions on a grave constitutional
issue: enough to deter a young man like Cromwell, anxious
to be on the right side, as much as it did the great-uncle of
Henry VI. There was considerable provocation, needless to
say. The duke was greatly restricted in the matter of petitions.
No councillor, Gloucester or anybody else, was allowed any
'favour, grant neither in bills of right ne of office ne of benefice
that longeth to the Council', but should refer all petitions to the
council as a whole. There was another crucial conflict: control
over foreign policy, in the present case relations with France
and Burgundy. Gloucester was not prepared to delegate this
to the council, and hence, the country was found speaking
with two voices. One of the 'provisions' made for the good of
the land in the autumn of 1423 declared it to be 'too great a
shame that into strange countries our sovereign lord shall write
his letters by the advice of his Council, and (despite this fact)
singular persons of the Council to write the contrary'.[2] The
duke's marriage to Jacqueline of Hainault, the wife of John of
Brabant, who had taken refuge in England, caused serious
difficulties with the duke of Burgundy and with Bedford himself, who was betrothed to Anne, Burgundy's sister (June 1423).
Gloucester was determined to recover Jacqueline's inheritance
and Bedford tried his utmost to mediate between the two.
There was something to be said for Gloucester's contention that
Jacqueline's marriage with Brabant was illegal: there was
nothing to be said for his proposed invasion of Hainault, which
Burgundy declared a *casus belli*. None the less, Gloucester left
for Hainault in October 1424, an expedition that proved a
hopeless failure. In April 1425 Gloucester returned to England,

---

[1] *P.P.C.* iii. 233–4.   [2] *Rot. Parl.* iv. 201.

leaving Jacqueline to fall into the hands of Burgundy. Her lady-in-waiting, Eleanor Cobham, was to take her place in his affections.

While he was away the government of the country was practically in Beaufort's hands. On 23 February 1425 the bishop was voted by the council a special salary of 2,000 marks in addition to his existing emoluments as chancellor and member of the council. He was given this because of his near relationship to the king, and on account of his labour and the expenditure sustained in discharging his office, charges likely to recur. The third reason given was interesting: he had ever been and was now generous in lending money and in other services on behalf of the king and the preservation of his realms of France and England. This suggests that the 2,000 m. represents the *damnum et interesse* of the big loans. Mr. Steel has calculated that Beaufort's own loans, including contributions from the see of Winchester, amounted to £35,630 under Henry V and £45,413 for the first ten years of Henry VI. His adversary, however, retained his influence. On 22 May 1425 a resolution of the council granted him the custody of the lands of the deceased earl of March, which were for the time in the possession of the crown, during the minority of the late earl's heir, the duke of York. In parliament Gloucester, for all his expedition to Hainault, received support. The earl marshal, who had commanded for him there, was awarded precedence over the earl of Warwick, which was to create a dispute between the two captains: the duel to which Gloucester had been challenged by Burgundy was forbidden and the quarrel committed to the duke of Bedford and the dowager queens of England and France for arbitration, and Gloucester was compensated for the disappointment he might feel at being so prohibited or for parliament's decision to negotiate with Burgundy for the release of Jacqueline, by parliament's recommending a loan of 20,000 marks in four yearly instalments to meet the necessities of the king's 'fair uncle of Gloucester', for which the lords of the council were asked to give the necessary security.

Placed where he was in the council, with the opportunities for observation which he possessed, Humphrey of Gloucester must have watched with interest the tactics of his uncle over a long period. Except for the two years (1427–8), when he was abroad in the service of the Pope, there was no time when the

Exchequer was not more or less heavily indebted to him. Though he normally received ample security for, and punctual settlement of, his loans, for more than twenty-five years he was prepared to forego the chance of making money elsewhere. It is most unlikely that he failed to extract interest from what he lent. The normal interest at which the Lancastrians borrowed was 25–33 per cent. Fortescue himself when discussing the borrowing of the crown made the point that the king's 'creauncers' would 'win upon him the fourth or the fifth penny of all that he dependeth'. Creditors would never be satisfied and continued to press and 'defame his highness of misgovernaunce and default of keeping days: which if he keep he must borrow also much at the (these) days as he did at first: for he shall be then poorer than he was by the value of his fourth or fifth part of his first expenses and so be always poorer and poorer unto the time he be the poorest lord of his land'.

In order to evade the usury prohibitions the Exchequer had its own ways of expressing this interest: 'to chevise' or borrow £1,000 meant in fact to borrow a good deal less; the sum recorded was understood to include both principal and consideration.[1] If a *mutuum* of £1,000 was entered on the receipt roll, it did not mean that this was the literal sum borrowed by the Exchequer. It was the statement of a sum to which the creditor was entitled, not proof of the amount which had actually been received. When Henry V died he owed Beaufort the balance of two loans contracted 12 June 1417 and 13 May 1421 which amounted on 31 August 1422 to £20,149. 0s. 5d.[2] By the settlement made when the second loan was arranged Beaufort held a 'long commission on the port of Southampton and its subsidiaries, the terms of which enabled him to appoint one of two customers and enjoy all the profits of the port from customs, subsidies, tonnage and poundage, excluding assignments made and annuities granted from them before 18 July 1417, until full repayment was made to him'. He was to hold the great crown of England as security unimpaired either by the king's death or by his own, and if war prevented Southampton remaining a mercantile port the bishop should have

[1] K. B. McFarlane, 'Loans of the Lancastrian Kings: the Problem of Inducement', *Camb. Hist. Journal*, ix (1947), 51.
[2] For this and much that follows see K. B. McFarlane, 'At the deathbed of Cardinal Beaufort', *Studies in Medieval History presented to F. M. Powicke* (1948), pp. 412–13.

the right to compensate himself by taking over the port o
London on the same terms as he had been granted South
ampton. This clause provided for an alternative in case wa
and its contingencies caused a cessation of the passage o
merchandise in and out of Southampton: it was not intended
to be interpreted as Beaufort interpreted it after Henry V'
death. For, as Mr. McFarlane has pointed out, when in
November 1422 the commons reduced the rate of taxation upor
native merchants, lowering the customs and subsidy on woo
from 50s. to 40s., Beaufort, realizing that the reduction woulc
retard the repayment of his loans, claimed his right to assume
control of the ports and on 17 November began to nominate
his own customers. On 15 February 1423 he was formally
permitted to appoint one customer in every English port, from
which time the whole of the government's most stable source
of revenue became diverted to his use.[1] From the end of 142
he had received as much as £11,000: it was not until 21 May
1425 that the whole of Henry V's debt was paid off. He hac
received what that writer has termed 'the beginnings of a
stranglehold over royal finances which might easily have
become permanent', one only broken by the settlement which
followed his armed conflict with Gloucester in October 1425,
involving his withdrawal from England for service with the
Roman Curia. Gloucester and other observers would have
noted how, starting merely with the temporalities of his see,
Beaufort had by 1424 made his name celebrated for great
wealth. In that year he lent £4,000 which is the only loan not
repaid. When money was being raised by the council for the
campaign of Verneuil Beaufort's contribution was fixed at
14,000 marks, and in return the council agreed to repay 8,000
by immediate assignment on the customs and to hand over the
crown jewels as security for the remainder; with the proviso
that if the latter (6,000) were not forthcoming by Easter 1425,
the pledges were to be forfeit. The value of the jewels which
were given as security had to be agreed with him 'not with-
standing that the said jewels have been priced at a greater price
than that at which our said cousin shall perhaps wish to receive
them': and this is what happened. The council must have been
in dire straits if these were the terms made, for Beaufort stood
greatly to gain if the Exchequer did default or fail to honour

[1] McFarlane, op. cit., p. 414.

the bond in good time. That may well have been the cause of the charge made by Gloucester in 1440 when he accused Beaufort of defrauding the king of his jewels 'keeping them still to his own use to your great loss and his singular profit and avail'. Detailed examination of the records has shown that there was substance in a charge which has often been dismissed as exaggeration. It was in fact a considerable time before he began to disgorge the jewels and even shortly before his death, when in codicils to his will he was bequeathing them in driblets (often actually specifying the use to which they were to be put), Beaufort was insisting that they were at his own disposal.

Matters came to a climax between the duke and the bishop over the custody of the royal infant. On 29 October 1425 Gloucester sent for the new mayor of London, John Coventry, and the aldermen and besought them to 'keep well the city that night and make good watch'. He had evidently heard of a coup planned to take place from the Southwark side on the 30th, when Beaufort's men were preparing to force their way into the city, probably to capture the Tower and perhaps later to take possession of the king at Eltham. Between 9 and 11 a.m. an armed force (knights and squires) of Beaufort's men removed the chains and obstacles on the southern end of the bridge and occupied positions for firing from the houses built upon it. The news spread in the city, the shops were shut, and within an hour the citizens came pouring out towards the bridge. At this point Archbishop Chichele and Prince Peter of Portugal, who was a cousin of Gloucester and, by being a son of Philippa, eldest daughter of John of Gaunt, a nephew of Beaufort, intervened. Acting as mediators, they had to ride constantly between the parties before the threat of fighting was removed: the presence of a large number of Londoners in force was a sufficient threat to the great majority of peaceable citizens. But Bedford had not come yet and Gloucester was in control. On 5 November he brought the young Henry to London and on that day the council agreed to lend him 5,000 marks repayable when Henry was fifteen. The loan he used in dispatching a force to Hainault to help Jacqueline. But within two months it had come to grief. On 20 December Bedford, who had received an agitated summons from Beaufort, landed with his wife in England, and for the present Gloucester was protector no more, neither chief counsellor.

It was Bedford's task, having called the council, to reconcile the parties. On 29 January a deputation from the council at St. Albans was sent to urge Gloucester to meet Bedford at Northampton on 13 February. So far Gloucester had refused to meet the chancellor, and the emissaries, obviously instructed by Bedford, had to reassure the duke about the bishop's intentions and urge him to be present at the Leicester parliament. Gloucester had now taken the offensive against his opponent (previously it had been the other way round) and declined to be pacified until at the parliament on 7 March he gave his consent to a commission of nine peers hearing his complaint and issuing an award. A strong group presided over by Chichele contained besides Bishops Stafford (Bath) and Polton (Worcester), the duke of Exeter and Lord Cromwell, friendly to Beaufort, and the duke of Norfolk and the earl of Stafford, if anything on the side of Duke Humphrey, along with William Alnwick, keeper of the privy seal. Before this body Gloucester laid a number of written complaints and Beaufort replied in defence of his action. Beaufort defended Wydeville's action in denying Gloucester the Tower; he scouted the idea that he was trying to capture Henry VI; and when Gloucester alleged that Beaufort had tried to thwart his purpose by going to Eltham in person, the chancellor was able to reply (the episode of London Bridge on 30 October) that, alarmed by stories of bodily harm purposed against him by Gloucester, he had acted in self-defence. Lastly Gloucester brought up the earlier legends of the disloyalty of Beaufort to his sovereign, in one case Henry IV, when he instigated Prince Henry of Monmouth to claim the governance of the country for himself. This was an old legend. To meet it the chancellor could utter a general protest that he had been loyal to all sovereigns, particularly to Henry V who would not have bestowed so great a trust on him in making him a chancellor if he had been suspicious. We have seen that on one occasion, at any rate, Henry had found him acting disingenuously: the occasion on which he defied the statute of Provisors in 1418.

This contest the council saw fit to interpret in terms of personality rather than of principle. They were concerned to secure from the parties a declaration that they had remitted all rancour ('alle hevynes or displesaunces') towards one another and that each of them should be 'good lord to all adherents, counsellors and favorers of the other'. It was decided that there must be a statement of mutual forgiveness and respect in parliament. The arbiters awarded Beaufort the opportunity to repudiate all disloyalty in Henry IV's reign and to state his complete fealty towards Henry V and his loyalty to his son. This done, Bedford declared him a 'trewe' man and directed him to assure Gloucester that he never 'imagined or purposed (any)thing that might be hindering or prejudice to youre person honour or establishment': after which they were to take each other by the hand in the presence of the king and all parliament. Beaufort had indeed cleared himself at Leicester, but the rancour was merely driven underground. On 14 March he resigned the chancellorship, now his third, making way for a man almost as ambitious as himself, John Kemp, bishop of London, and now to be translated to York. Reading the account of the dispute in the Great Chronicle makes it clear that Beaufort had had the worst of it. To have been forced to repudiate in full parliament the story that he was privy to an attempted murder of Prince Henry of Monmouth ('be myne excitation'), or of his incitement of the prince to replace his father, must have been a blow to Beaufort's dignity. His intervention at the Tower, even if the council raised no formal protest, could not be justified; but what emerges from the actual fracas is that while Gloucester's support among the Londoners was spontaneous and effective, Beaufort had at his disposal an organized and trained force. If Gloucester could count upon some of those who had been with him in the Hainault campaign, Beaufort could bring up the knights and squires of his own retinue.

But the incident and certain remarks made by the parties had left suspicion in the minds of the council. There was a need for conciliar action to preserve the authority which, at a moment of crisis, had nearly slipped from its grasp. That authority must now be exercised on behalf of the crown and the question which must have arisen was the duration of the protectorate: for when the king was crowned, even this carefully controlled régime would be terminated, and it was essential to secure that during the rest of the minority no powerful prince of the blood should seek to control the council to his own ends. This was the purpose of the remarkable interviews to which allusion has already been made between the council and the two princes in January 1427, when the council sounded Gloucester and Bedford upon their views as to where the ultimate authority during the minority lay. This was done cautiously, the councillors protesting that they had no intention of diminishing authority accorded to the dukes or arising naturally from their estate; but firmly establishing the point that the king had as great authority 'of governaille' . . . 'duryng his said tendre age as ever shal be here after whan he shal come with Goddes myght to yeers of discrecion'.[1] The executive function, 'standeth as now in his lords assembled either by authority of his parliament or in his consail and in especiale in the lords of his consail'. This authority did not rest in any one person but in all the lords together, saving the authority granted to Bedford as protector and in his absence to Humphrey of Gloucester. Bedford had been sent for, Archbishop Chichele explained, so that the council might discover whether his views were in harmony with those just stated. It was an uncomfortable task for the primate, but Bedford eased the tension by thanking them for giving him the opportunity to avow his complete loyalty and obedience to the council, a statement which he affirmed on oath, whereupon the council, as well as Bedford himself, were moved to tears of relief. Gloucester was ill, and the next day Kemp as chancellor went to interview him in his room and, after reporting Bedford's agreement with the council's terms, questioned him about certain matters previously put to him which his answers had shown to be not at all to his liking, and expressed the concern of the council if this was actually the case. Gloucester made a courteous reply, desiring the council's correction if he 'should happen to do or err hereafter against the lawes of the land' and professing his readiness to abide by their decisions. 'The law of the land' was not meant inadvisedly. In Sir John Fortescue's treatise *De Laudibus Legum Anglie* the common law and civil law are compared to the disadvantage of the latter, and Gloucester was well known to be one who preferred the Roman-law procedure. Does this refer to Gloucester's doctrine of the prerogative of the prince, or is it an allusion to the resentment he must have felt at the restrictions placed upon him in answering petitions and to his thwarted desire to deal with them in the name of the king? The council must have been aware of his discontent and may have done their best to pacify him, for on 21 October during the parliament of 1427 they were to give him

[1] *P.P.C.* iii. 238.

3,000 marks for his 'great labor and expense'. They had had to
work against a background of grievances dating from Henry V's
campaign. In the 1427 parliament both Gloucester and the
earl of Salisbury asked to be compensated for payments made
to their troops for the second quarter of the Agincourt campaign, and on later occasions, which the Exchequer had dis-
allowed, while it had claimed the thirds and the third of thirds
won by the two captains in the campaign of 1415 and later.
The duke's petition for redress was discussed by lords and
commons and Humphrey had been allowed to keep the valuable
objects (*jocalia*) which he had received as security for payment
by the crown, because of his expenses 'not only at the siege of
Harfleur but also for his capture of Cherbourg and the thirty-
two castles, defended towns and strongholds'. But the difficult
question of authority was not to be slurred over by the granting
of such requests. After an adjournment of the parliament for
Christmas, when on 3 March 1428 Humphrey declined to
come into the parliament chamber until he was told precisely
what his powers as protector were, the spiritual and temporal
lords had to give an opinion which they had deferred doing
in two previous sessions. The lords replied reminding the duke
of his first approach to the subject in 1422, when he 'desired to
have had the governance of this land, affirming that it belonged
to you of right as well as by the means of your birth, as by the
last will of the king that was your brother. . . '. Great search was
then made for precedents, the lords said, but the duke's desire
was not supported by any: furthermore, in the matter of
Henry V's will, King Henry could not by his will alter the
governance or rule of the land without the assent of the three
estates. The duke was not suspected of any such plan; and to
maintain peace and to appease him, it was advised that in the
absence of the duke's brother Bedford, he should be chief of the
privy council, and the name of protector and defender was
devised, not one that imparted authority or government, but
a 'personal duty of attending to the actual defence of the land,
as well gainst enemies outward as gainst rebels within': granting
certain power specified in the act and to endure during pleasure.
The duke at that time had accepted the position and subscribed to the Act and the articles regulating the position.
He was called to parliament as duke of Gloucester like any
other lord. 'We know no power or authority that you have,

other than that the Duke of Gloucester should have, the king being in parliament, at years of most discretion.' The lords expressed their astonishment that after this position had been accepted and subscribed to, the duke was now discontented, particularly in view of the fact that the young king would be able 'to occupy his royal power within few years'. They not only exhorted but required him to come to parliament and dispatch business. The lords personally subscribing this outspoken statement were the two archbishops and nine diocesans, including two Welsh holders of sees; four abbots, Westminster, Glastonbury, St. Mary's York, and Hyde; the duke of Norfolk, and the earls of Huntingdon, Stafford, and Thomas Montague of Salisbury; lords Audley, Bourchier, Warre, Scales, Cromwell, Hungerford, Tiptoft, and Poynings. The list is not synonymous with the king's council: of the bishops subscribing London, Ely, Bath, and Winchester were councillors, but Lincoln, Worcester, Rochester, St. Davids, and Bangor were not: the abbots naturally were outside. Among the earls who were councillors Salisbury and Northumberland did not sign; among the lords, Audley, Warre, and Poynings were not members of the council. Of course, to secure the attestation of a reasonably representative group of the elements may be all that was required.

There was another reason why at this juncture Beaufort should retire from the chancellorship: this lay in the part he had played in seconding the efforts of Martin V to secure the abolition of the statutes of Provisors and Premunire. To the Pope, Beaufort was the key man, the chosen instrument of his efforts to remove the obnoxious code. The days of the strong king were over now, and Beaufort might be relied upon, as cardinal and papal legate in England (the legation had been the main difficulty in 1418), to help in the campaign. Martin had been pressing hard. In 1421 he had made the consistorial advocate, Simon de Teramo, collector in England in succession to Walter Medford, dean of Wells, and on 15 May that year the collector addressed the convocation of Canterbury on the Pope's need 'to have provision in the kingdom of England'. In other ways Martin had shown his ignorance of, or perhaps his disregard for, the customs of Canterbury, particularly in varying the requirement that suffragans should take the oath of obedience to the metropolitan and in permitting these suffragans to receive consecration from any catholic bishop. Both Richard

Fleming and Thomas Polton were consecrated abroad. The archbishop was suspected at the curia of upholding the statute of Provisors and for the refusal of Henry V to admit Cardinal Nicholas Albergati, papally provided to the archdeaconry of Lincoln, on the ground that the king could not dispense with a statute over the head of parliament. This refusal was to create for Chichele a second enemy powerful in the diplomatic field. As soon as Henry V was dead Martin took the offensive against the archbishop; he fell foul of him in 1423 over the proclamation of the fifth jubilee of St. Thomas Becket, and the issue of a plenary Indulgence at Canterbury (7 July 1420);[1] and from that year onwards he set himself to create a revisionist party among the English bishops and by directing a steady stream of special representatives to this country whose duty it was, among other things, to report on the attitude of leading personages. The lay councillors appeared to be the root of opposition. In 1424 Richard Fleming of Lincoln having accepted translation to York without seeking permission from the council, was summoned before the lay members of the council, and charged with infringing the statutes. In the end he had to promise formally to renounce the provision and do his best to ensure the transfer of the bishop of Worcester to York and of the treasurer, Stafford, to Worcester: he had also to undertake to further 'the cause of the illustrious prince of the Duke of Gloucester' at the Roman court. At the curia both Chichele and the duke were defamed with the charge of anti-papalism, and though the archbishop protested his innocence, the Pope did not believe him, and at the end of February 1427 suspended him from his metropolitan and legatine powers. The council had the bull impounded immediately and the messenger locked up, but it had in fact reached the archbishop who could not ignore it, and made two further appeals on 6 and 14 April. The Pope was still sceptical and wrote back to the archbishop (6 May 1427) telling him that he must plead with the royal councillors clerical and lay for the abolition of the statute. Despite the volume of testimony on Chichele's behalf which reached Rome, Martin insisted that Chichele must display his

---

[1] Martin wrote of the archbishop and the prior and convent of Christ Church as 'inaudita presumpcione et sacrilega audacia commotos': R. Foreville, *Le Jubilé de S. Thomas Becket du XIIIᵉ au XVᵉ siècle (1220–1470)* (1958), p. 179: she deals with the Pope's reaction to the Indulgence on pp. 61–66.

repentance and his devotion to the Holy See by moving parliament to revoke the offensive enactment. This order Chichele, along with his bishops, had to carry out, by addressing separately the lords as well as the commons in their usual meeting-place, the refectory at Westminster. His appeal was without result. A contemporary reported that despite the good will shown to the Holy See the temporal lords would not permit the revocation of the statute,[1] and Bedford, who in the conquered French provinces had shown himself accommodating to Martin's demands for provisions, now followed the example of the Normans and Angevins in England.

Gloucester might well feel some annoyance at the restrictions placed upon him by the council when he had taken a leading part in the defence of the statutes so carefully preserved by Henry V. Upon him and the archbishop it had fallen to resist the demands of the curia, but unquestionably the resistance sharpened his antagonism with Beaufort. Chichele's legation and metropolitical power was restored on 28 July 1428. It was the archbishop's association with the duke of Gloucester, chief upholder of the *leges Angliae*, that had made Martin suspect the reliability of Chichele. Gloucester had fallen foul of the papal collector in 1424, when Simon of Teramo was threatened with arrest. This may have been the origin of the sinister reports which had reached Martin of the attitude of the protector and the archbishop towards the collector, and Gloucester had to ask the Pope not to believe the charges made. The reports, however, had continued (Chichele had his enemies, especially Thomas Polton) and Cardinal Guiliemo Cesarini confirmed them. Chichele was accused of saying that the curia wanted the statute abolished in order to drain money out of England; and it was Gloucester who sent the lieutenant of Dover Castle to impound the bull of suspension and who threatened with penalties any who carried out an order prejudicial to the *leges regni*. It must have been embarrassing for the archbishop that his chief upholder the protector was the *bête noire* of the newly appointed cardinal: for Beaufort, when he left England after the Leicester parliament, was given the honour denied him in 1418, and later was entrusted with the preaching of the Bohemian Crusade (1428).

---

[1] The episode is only known through a letter of John Kemp to the bishop of Dax. MS. Cotton Cleopatra, C. iv, f. 164.

The victories of Prokop and Žižka leading the Hussite armies had to be halted in the interest as much of the empire as of the Church. Martin appealed to the countries of Europe. On 9 July 1428 his nuncio, Conzo de Zwola, appeared in the convocation of Canterbury asking for a 'notable subsidy' to help finance. The delay in answering the Pope's demand—convocation was prorogued from 21 July to 12 November—led Martin to ask for a whole tenth, a demand characterized by Chichele as *ardua et insolita*: to which Convocation replied by the grant of 8*d.* in the mark, 'on condition that no offence be done to the king or to the laws of the kingdom'. The protector was making himself felt. When Beaufort, as legate *a latere*, was authorized to preach the crusade and distribute the Indulgence in England, the official attitude was not dissimilar to that of 1418: the protector invited the cardinal to his lodgings in the city, where a number of the council were gathered, to hear Richard Caudray, archdeacon of Norwich, read, as proctor for the king, a statement protesting against the entry of any legate of the Holy See into England or English possessions, 'save at the bidding, request, invitation or entreaty of the king of England for the time being'; and declaring that to accept Beaufort as legate would be to derogate from English rights and customs. But if they were not prepared to hear him as legate, they were ready to receive and listen respectfully to him as one of the cardinals of the Holy Roman Church specially sent by our Lord Pope. Beaufort had to accept this, and reply that it was not his intention of doing anything contrary to the laws and liberties of the kingdom. His answer was judged sufficient, and he was permitted to address the council at Westminster next day (12 Nov.). Chichele did not dissolve convocation after the grant of the 8*d.*, but prorogued it until 19 October 1428, probably in order that the subsidy could be explained to the dioceses by the proctors in convocation and that the collection might go hand in hand with arrangements for preaching the crusade, and making the Indulgence known. Directions for the administration of the 'letter of the Cruciat' have survived for the diocese of Canterbury showing the role of specially appointed confessors in distributing the Indulgence to the penitent faithful.[1]

Beaufort was not granted permission to preach the crusade till 18 June 1429. In February he had a licence to treat with the

[1] Bodl. Lib., MS. Tanner 165, ff. 84–90; analysed in *Reg. Chichele*, i. xlviii–xlix.

king of Scots over the crusade and other matters and a warrant
for the payment to him of 500 marks for his expenses was sent
to the chamberlains of the Exchequer. But by the middle of
April the claims of France were entering into competition with
the crusade. In the council on 15 April a letter from Bedford
was read asking for reinforcements for the seige of Orléans to
the tune of 200 lances and 12,000 archers. One hundred lances
and 700 archers under the command of Sir John Radcliffe were
what the council authorized, a smaller number than the 500
lances and 5,000 archers which Beaufort was asking to recruit.
In point of numbers, Beaufort was at first allowed 250 lances
and 2,500 archers 'in all to pass out of this land'. They had to
be recruited in England, for the French garrison must not be
drained away. If Beaufort consented to this and was willing
to do all he could to secure the friendship and loyalty of the
king of Scots, the crusade might, the council conceded, be
proclaimed and the troops enrolled. Those taking part were to
be given full protection and the council consented that sufficient
shipping should be released. But the agreement made (shortly
after 16 June 1429) stipulated that the Pope should waive the
tenth,[1] and after the disaster of Patay a postponement of the
Bohemian crusade was judged necessary. Instead Beaufort on
1 July consented to take his own retinue to Bedford in France
and to induce them 'to serve the king in his realm of France for
the time of half a year' (the period mentioned in the indentures).
The council undertook to make it clear that the diversion of the
crusading forces had nothing to do with the Legate, but was a
matter of English policy: and it was agreed that compensation
for this would be paid to the Pope, and that crusading forces
could again be recruited in England from the beginning of May.

It is clear that the good will and support of Beaufort was essential to the council for the maintenance of the English position
in France after the treaty of Troyes. In the treaty the Anglo-
French sovereign had undertaken to conquer the areas still in
the occupation of the Dauphin. Not only had the 'conquest' to
be established, it had to be extended. The theory, which has
already been noted, was that the conquered territory should
pay for itself. But it was quite uncertain whether this could
necessarily include the cost of offensive operations on a large

[1] P.P.C. iii. 334.

strategical plan, or even resistance to punitive raiding and attrition. Nor could it be forecasted exactly what the conquest territorially was likely to contain at a given future date. Until c. 1435 the frontier—if such a fixed line can be thought of, where often defence had to be in depth—fluctuated, according to the movements and initiative of the English captains operating in the border lands and enemy counter-action. There were Dauphinist *enclaves* in Anglo-French country ready, when opportunity seemed right, to take the offensive, and these expeditions could not be dealt with by local forces. Thus on Henry V's death there were Armagnacs in Le Crotoy on the north bank of the Somme estuary (captured 24 June 1423); in Vermandois, Tierche, and the Laonnois where La Hirè and Poton de Xantrailles were engaged by the earl marshal and Sir Thomas Rempston operating with the Burgundian Sir John Luxembourg; and at Compiègne where on 30 November 1423 the Burgundian garrison was surprised and had to be relieved by Bedford (1 April 1424). In the Paris area the Armagnacs had to be chased from the region between the capital and Chartres, and the example of Meulan, which capitulated on 2 March 1423, was followed by Montlhéry, Marcoussis, and Étampes. Farther south-east, Salisbury's commission as governor of Champagne and Brie included the *baillages* of Melun, Sens, Auxerre, Nivernais, Dunois, and the Maconnois and the area round Soissons. At the southern extremities of Normandy, Mont Saint Michel was holding out for the Dauphin in the south-west, and on the Sarthe below Alençon, a belt of doubtful country separated Tenuie and Montfort from the garrisons higher up. Armagnac infiltrations from the right bank of the Seine had to be guarded against, a task assigned to Lord Scales who was captain-general of the Seine towns and Alençon. Ivry (Eure) was first of all in Dauphinist hands, but its capture, after changing hands before, was the preliminary, because it formed an objective in the French counter-measures during the summer of 1424, to the important victory won by Bedford at Verneuil (17 August 1424). After this Nesle surrendered, La Fère was taken, and in the north Guise surrendered. From 1424 to 1426 the English conquest had reached its fullest extent, but in two years time began the breaches which ended in the dismissal of the English from France.

The English position depended partly on economic factors,

partly upon the military situation and the capacity of the Duke
of Burgundy and his commanders to work together with the
English. It is necessary briefly to survey the resources of the
Dauphin and understand the strong and the weak points of
the French position. These latter considerations should be taken
first. After the treaty of Troyes central and southern France
remained loyal to the Dauphin. The struggle was mainly
located in the north and was for possession of the region between Seine and Loire; after 1423 the Burgundian position ran
more or less along a line which followed the Loire between
Gien and Roanne (the two bridgeheads of La Charité-sur-
Loire and Marcigny were at issue); then ran eastward between
the Maconnais and the Beaujolais, and ended at Bresse, belonging to the House of Savoy. In the south-west there was spas-
modic fighting in Saintongè, the Limousin, Périgord, Rouergue,
and the Agenais: that is, an arc to the east of Bordeaux, an area
already devastated in the campaign of the duke of Orléans.
Little places like St. Macaire and La Réole on the Garonne or
the district of Entre-deux-mers were the scene of fluctuating
fights; the Gascons were opportunists; as M. Boutruche has
observed: 'les villes espèrent toujours dans le secour des rois
qu'ils sont Lancastres ou Valois': and the seigneurs followed the
same pattern. As Froissart shrewdly noticed, the Gascons, even
if they hold to the side for thirty years, do not adhere firmly to
one lord: 'il ne sont point estables'; but on the whole they did
better in war under English than under French leadership.
The Anglo-French war thus flared up from time to time in the
south and was not in any way confined to the borders of Maine-
Anjou. In three groups of provinces the Dauphin was acknowledged: the Loire, protected on the north by the domains of
the houses of Anjou and Orléans, on the south by those of the
Bourbons: Poitou, Touraine, and Berry, the favourite area of
Charles of France as his popular title roi de Bourges proclaimed
(the parlement itself was established at Poitiers, where, on the
death of his father, the Dauphin was immediately recognized
as Charles VII): and a southern group, Languedoc and its
dependencies, while in the south-east Dauphiné was connected
with the French kingdom through the Dauphin's possession of
Lyons, strategically important in its proximity to the Burgundian domains. Touraine and Dauphiné had been in the
hands of Charles VI's sons, and ultimately of the Dauphin

himself; the duke of Berry had ruled Berry, Poitou, and Languedoc. The Dauphin was supported by the House of Anjou: he
had been betrothed to Marie, sister of Louis III of Anjou and
of René, who by a later marriage became duke of Lorraine.
When the Dauphin lost the support of the constable of Armagnac, he received assistance from the widow of Louis II of
Anjou, Yolanda of Aragon, known in France as the queen of
Sicily. In addition to Anjou there was Orléans, and while its
duke, Charles, was a prisoner in England after Agincourt, the
Dauphin's officials administered the territory. The Bourbons
also stood by him: while Duke John, also a prisoner, was away,
the Duchess Marie of Berry sent her troops: they were useful
in resisting Burgundian pressure on the border of Charolais and
Beaujolais. The Auvergne was already in the royal hand and
a declaration confirming this was issued on 29 March 1423.[1]
Financially the Dauphin was better off than it might appear,
for the provinces loyal to him were less impoverished than those
ruled by Bedford, and he was able to gather more taxes than
Bedford. It has been estimated that in normal years, when the
Lancastrians obtained £100,000 or £200,000, the Valois got
£300,000 at least; but the Dauphin's army was not so well
equipped and coherent as the English, a better disciplined
force. The French leaders, men like La Hire, Poton de Xaintrailles, even Dunois himself, were little more than leaders of
irregular forces: and for the bigger campaigns Charles had only
the duke of Albany's Scots, whose leaders were Archibald earl
of Douglas, and John Stuart, earl of Buchan. His efforts were
hampered by his own diffidence, his unsureness of being
legitimate, and by correct, suspicious, and lethargic officials
like Louvet and Tanguy du Châtel; perhaps most of all by
Arthur de Richemont, the constable; and when in 1427 he had
gone, by the dangerous Georges de la Trémoille, an able but
entirely factious minister. These men held on to their posts
despite the attacks made upon them: not till la Trémoille was
removed, in 1433, could France make solid progress.

   At first, under Bedford, military operations consisted mainly
of raids and castle fighting: there was the French seizure of
Meulan, its recapture by the earl of Salisbury: John de la Pole's
raid into Anjou (he was supposed to take his force to besiege
Mont Saint Michel) that ended in defeat by the count of

---

[1] Arch. Nat., x. 11a, 9190: Arresta et iudicata in Curia parliamenti.

Aumâle with a superior army; and the Anglo-Burgundian
action, under Warwick, against Jacques d'Harcourt that
terminated in the fall of Le Crotoy. Bedford did not risk any
major movement, but used Salisbury to clear Champagne by
first besieging Montaiguillon, near Provins, some fifty miles
south-east of Paris. The place offered considerable resistance
and, while here, Salisbury heard that the Dauphin had formed
a new army at Bourges, with a substantial Scots contingent
under Sir John Stewart of Darnley, who was put in command
of the whole force. This was destined for Burgundy, with the
capture of Cravant as a first step: it was a move to re-establish
communication with Dauphinist forces in Picardy and Champagne, while at the same time relieving the pressure on Montaiguillon. It was at once countered by Salisbury who had received
a new English contingent led by the earl marshal and Lord
Willoughby. With the aid of a contingent sent by the dowager
duchess of Burgundy, the two corps made their rendezvous at
Auxerre, and on 29 July 1423 were joined by the English.
Together they marched upon Cravant, made contact with the
Burgundian leaders from within the town, and decided to form
a single army. On 30 July the united force took the offensive
against the investing Dauphinist army in the valley of the Yonne:
Salisbury was now on the western bank of the river and the
other side was lined with the French in considerable numbers.
Reconnaissance showed Salisbury that the French were in a
commanding position about a mile and a half north of the town,
so he decided to outflank them and march his troops round to
the south-west where the bridge gave access to the place. The
French, detecting this, moved from their high position down
to the vicinity of the bridge. To get at the enemy the English
had to cross the river, and as Waurin says, they crossed 'each
as best he could', while Willoughby attacked the bridge leading
over the Yonne into the town. After a tremendous hand-to-hand
fight the French gave way and in moving southwards were
attacked in the rear by the garrison of Cravant who, though
weak with hunger, were none the less able to inflict some
damage. To get away the Dauphinist army had to pass between
the garrison and the English now lining the east bank of the
Yonne, and very few escaped. The French lost between 2,000
and 3,000, the Scots perhaps a thousand men. As a fighting
force the Dauphinists were wiped out. To cross the river (a

hallow one, but with deep pockets) in the face of the enemy
was a dangerous operation; but it would have been more
dangerous still, as one military historian has made clear,[1] to
have attempted to dislodge him from the high ground, and
evidently Salisbury was counting, and counting rightly, on help
from the defenders of Cravant.

Bedford continued, after Cravant, the policy of close co-
operation with the Burgundians. Salisbury, with Burgundian
aid, continued the clearing and subjugation of, strongholds
in the east; but the time was to come when Bedford felt more
sure of offensive operations, beginning with the conquest of
Maine and Anjou. This was the work of the following summer
(1424) and it coincided with the congregation of a large new
opposing army, collected from Scots contingents, Italian
mercenaries, and others: an army of some 15,000 strong,
assembled along the lower Loire, with its advanced headquarters at Le Mans, forty miles north of the river. Ivry was to
be the point where it was to be deployed, for Suffolk's troops
had retaken the town on 5 July, all save the garrison which
agreed to surrender on 14 August, unless help was sent. Help
was indeed forthcoming. The advice of the French leaders, the
dukes of Alençon, and Aumâle and the vicomte of Narbonne,
was to avoid risking a pitched battle, but the Scots and younger
French were determined on a fight. Ultimately it was decided
to compromise and try to capture English towns on the Norman
border without being drawn into an engagement. The Dauphinists made a beginning at Verneuil but Bedford did not immediately follow them. On 14 August he took his forces to
Évreux, where he spent the Feast of the Assumption (15 Aug.)
in his devotions, and he must have felt so strong and confident
of defeating the Franco-Scottish army that he sent away
Villiers de L'Isle Adam with his Burgundian soldiers, given by
the Continuator of the *Brut* as 3,000 men, to go on with their
operations in the north. It was 17 August before this deliberate
leader brought his troops into action along the road leading
from Verneuil to Damville facing the Franco-Scottish army,
drawn up into two divisions, with the baggage well back, in
front of the forest area through which the road ran. It was a
conventional battle on the Agincourt pattern, cavalry on the
French wings, archers on the English, but with a mobile reserve

[1] A. H. Burne, *The Agincourt War* (1956), pp. 188, 193.

of 2,000 archers stationed by Bedford to the west of the road and Bedford took steps to safeguard his own baggage from raid of the type that took place at the battle of Agincourt. None the less the Lombard horsemen assisted by the French succeeded in pillaging the baggage enclosure, but they were met and put to flight by the reserve; Bedford on the right routed, by sheer tough fighting against greater odds, Aumâle's forces, while on the left Salisbury, who had engaged the Scots, was aided by the archers, now freed from attending to the Lombard cavalry, and ultimately by Bedford's forces who had returned from pursuing their opponents to Verneuil and beyond. This return of Bedford to deal with the Scots decided the action, for Salisbury's troops were hard pressed. The result of the battle was disastrous to the Scots who lost the earl of Douglas, with his son and his son-in-law the earl of Buchan, as well as to the French leaders, for Aumâle and the counts of Narbonne, Ventadour, and Tonnerre were killed, while the duke of Alençon and Marshal Lafayette were later prisoners. The French losses were round about 1,500 killed, but very few taken prisoner. Of the 6,000 Scots it has been calculated that only a handful can have survived: Bedford's forces have been estimated at some 10,000 troops, but some had been sent away and the total force at Verneuil must have been between 8,000 and 9,000. The French have been variously estimated, but a figure between 15,000 and 17,000 is most probable.[1]

At this moment an advance on Bourges might have given the best hope of ending the war. But Bedford was intent upon conquering Maine and Anjou, at reducing the territories north of the Loire and at the same time capturing Mont Saint Michel. To these ends the army had to be divided up among its commanders: the campaign in Maine was allotted to Sir John Fastolf and Lord Scales, the Loire operations went to Salisbury and Suffolk, and Sir Nicholas Burdet was given Mont Saint Michel to take. Presently, to counteract the effects of an alliance with the Dauphin, it became necessary to undertake operations against John V, duke of Brittany, under the leadership of Sir Thomas Rempston, who, with a small force of about 600, routed the very much greater numbers besieging him at Saint James de Beuvron on the border of Normandy. Bedford had to go back to England in December 1425 and was there until

[1] Burne, op. cit., p. 213.

March 1427 to deal with the Gloucester–Beaufort disputes; and there was only one Burgundian leader in the field, John of Luxembourg, operating in the Argonne, for the duke of Burgundy had withdrawn his fighting troops into the Low Countries for the war against Jacqueline. From the battle of Verneuil to the siege of Orléans is a period of minor action in which, however, two important new figures emerged as commanders in the field: the count of Dunois, a bastard son of the late duke of Orléans; and Lord John Talbot, brought by Bedford to France in the spring of 1427: in 1428 Talbot relieved the garrison of Le Mans from La Hire's troops who had seized the town, and shortly afterwards captured Laval, till then a well-defended Dauphinist stronghold.

The campaign of Gloucester in the Low Countries had unquestionably weakened Anglo-Burgundian co-operation. When the earl of Salisbury entered Paris with a newly raised army in July 1428, a force far greater than John of Luxembourg's 1,500 men should have been at the disposal of the regent. It may have been a consideration of numbers—he could not muster more than 5,000—that led Bedford to prefer the capture of Anjou and its capital to the plan preferred by Salisbury: the capture of Orléans. Orléans was strongly defended, and was guarded by Dauphinist strongholds such as Janville which was made into a base by the besieging army. The next stage was to isolate the city by water, by taking the Dauphinist towns immediately above and below Orléans: Meung, Beaugency, which proved the more difficult of the two (25 Sept. 1428), and Jargeau twelve miles upstream. Orléans was on the right or north bank of the Loire, which was bridged in the middle of the city on the south side, a strong fort with two towers (the fort of the Tourelles) being constructed at the bridgehead across the river. Salisbury's first task was to reduce the fort, which was successfully accomplished, but while he was reconnoitring the city before his move he was severely wounded in the face, and seven days later at Meung he died. He was succeeded, for a period, by the earl of Suffolk who was of a different calibre. Salisbury had brought miners with him and was determined to finish the siege: but Suffolk withdrew his troops to winter quarters in the neighbouring towns, being merely content to leave a garrison in the captured fort. For a time this was left undisturbed by the French: but in December fresh English commanders arrived,

Lord Talbot and Lord Scales, probably in order to stir Suffolk into action. Then began stronger measures for the investment of the town, a line of forts to stop enemies coming into Orléans on the western side of the town, north of the river, connected up with the Tourelles by an island in the stream. Just north of the Loire, by St. Laurent, was located the English base camp, ready to turn out against the Dauphin or his raiders from Chinon if he approached that way.

In fact the Dauphin did march, but along the south bank of the river. With the army was Joan of Arc, fresh from imparting to the Dauphin the message given her by her Voices, that it was the will of heaven that the English should be booted out of France, and that as a preliminary the Dauphin must be anointed as king at Rheims. She had been to Chinon, she had prevailed upon Charles to equip a new army to relieve Orléans, and the duke of Alençon was put in charge. Clad in full armour, she was allowed to ride with it. In front of the troops, not with the baggage (as in the English forces), marched a body of priests, for each soldier had to make confession and attend mass. With banners flying and mail glinting this inspiring and un-precedented vision brought seriousness and purpose to the most disillusioned of the soldiery. The more practical object of the movement was to pass supplies into the city by barge from Chezy five miles upstream, the landing to be effected at the Porte de Bourgogne on the east side of the city. A demonstration against one of the forts was arranged to coincide with this. Joan of Arc crossed over the river at Chezy (29 Apr.) and on 30 April was able to make her entry into the city: the supporting army did not enter by the Porte de Bourgogne but returned to Blois, but several days later it set out for Orléans again by the north bank, entering the city on the morning of 3 May. The attack on St. Loup, probably intended as a diversion, brought Joan of Arc prominently to the notice of the English rank and file for the first time: nor was Talbot allowed to relieve the fort, for before he could bring his troops to the rescue he was chal-lenged by a covering force sent out of the town by the French.

It has been well observed that the capture of the fort of St. Loup was the turning-point of the siege and in a sense the whole war.[1] The next stage was to secure the other two forts, the Augustins and the Tourelles, held by the English. The Augustins

[1] Burne, op. cit., p. 240.

was taken after a fierce struggle on 6 May 1429, and the English were forced out of the Tourelles the next day. They were badly outnumbered and had made no impression on the walls or upon the morale of the garrison of Orléans. On 8 May, after parading within sight of the enemy and waiting in vain for their challenge to be taken up, they marched away. Suffolk dispersed the army in garrison duties at Jargeau, Meung, and Beaugency. A French army was now approaching under the duke of Orléans with Joan of Arc included, to pick up Dunois's force at Orléans and to wrest the town from the English. There was some hesitation among the leaders whether in fact to attack Jargeau, as it was heard that Sir John Fastolf was coming with a new army, but Joan was emphatic about the need for attack, and by the evening of 12 June, after bombardment and assault, the earl of Suffolk had surrendered. The same week Beaugency fell, and knowing that a French army was advancing towards Meuny, the English had to withdraw to Janville. At the end of the week their retreat had taken them to the neighbourhood of Patay, eighteen miles due north, and, persuaded by Joan, the duke of Alençon decided to pursue them. On 18 June Fastolf made contact with the French advanced guard and agreed with Talbot to take up a position on rising ground two miles south-east of the village of Patay, while Talbot with a picked group of archers should stockade themselves in a position to the south of the place. The French did not give the English archers time to drive their stakes into the ground (the normal order) but with their cavalry set themselves to overwhelm the little force (400). At the same time, with none of the delays customary in a formal battle, they brought a preponderating number of men against Fastolf's army, which by now could not count on Talbot's assistance. The speed and weight of the attack on both the English bodies proved decisive. Talbot and Scales were captured, but Fastolf got away, first to Janville, then to Étampes. Because she gave her opponents no time and no rest, Patay was Joan's battle, though she was only in the van with Arthur de Richemont the constable, while La Hire and Poton de Xaintrailles formed the spearhead for the main body under Alençon and Dunois.

After Patay the French might well have attacked Paris, or have made their way into Normandy. They did neither, for Joan was set upon the coronation of Charles at Rheims. This was not solely due to idealism. On the march there the towns-folk of the leading places opened their gates. Auxerre declared its neutrality (1 July), but Troyes surrendered on 10 July, Châlons on the 14th, Rheims on the 16th. On the 18th Charles VII was crowned at Rheims. It was an act of state carried out in defiance of the treaty of Troyes, and one which raised the problem of the status of the Burgundians under the direction of Bedford, whose regency was now wholly negatived. Directly after the coronation Charles made a demonstration march through Champagne, Brie, Soissonnais, and Valois: then again to the Parisis, to stage an attack on Paris from the west (8 Sept.). In this ill-advised attack Joan of Arc was wounded, in the sector near Porte-Saint-Honoré. She was not allowed to try a further attack and the army was taken back for disbandment south of Loire. Then followed a period of controversy and exhaustion, with the treasury unable to subsidize a new campaign in 1430. Military action had to consist of local attacks on garrisons on the upper Loire, and the main value of the Maid as a tactician (contemporaries emphasize her skill in positioning the artillery) and in animating forces to decisive action at the critical moment was wasted. Those jealous of her authority and prestige would give her no chance, and no main army was collected.

In April 1430 Burgundy, hearing that a new English army which Beaufort had tried to mobilize for the crusade, was coming over, took up arms at Montdidier and advanced to recapture Compiègne, thirty miles to the south-east. On hearing this Joan of Arc left the court at Sully and made her way to Compiègne which she entered on 13 May. On 24 May 1430, while she was leading a sortie in the defence of the town against the Anglo-Burgundian besiegers, Joan was caught outside the city when the portcullises which closed the gates had been lifted. She fell dismounted into the hands of the Bastard of Vendôme, a vassal of Jean of Luxembourg—count de Lagny, commander of the Burgundian contingent besieging Compiègne. Philip duke of Burgundy was 'more delighted than if a King had fallen into his hands'. He had Joan imprisoned first in the castle of Beaulieu in Vermandois, and then in the castle of Beaurevoir which belonged to Jean de Luxembourg himself. It was there that the attempt was made to escape: and there that Pierre Cauchon appeared on the scene, arriving to nego-tiate for the purchase of the prisoner on behalf of the king of

England for 10,000 gold crowns, £80,000 by prevalent standards: the money was to come out of the subsidy voted by the
Norman estates. The offer was accepted, and the Maid passed
into English custody. That Burgundy should have traded her
to the English was an action which this particular ally may have
been glad to perform: for Burgundy had not been altogether
faithful to the alliance made in the treaty of Troyes. Du Fresne
de Beaucourt may have over-emphasized the effect of Gloucester's invasion of Hainault, for the duke was not thereby
piqued out of the English alliance; but a truce between him and
France was concluded (Sept. 1421) and through the efforts of
the duke of Savoy renewed for a further period, from 30
January 1423; and if the negotiations which the French had
begun at Mâcon led to no positive results, hostilities in France
were virtually at a standstill, so far as the duke himself was
concerned. The French had since then secured the adhesion
of the count of Foix (1423) and of Henry V's old supporter,
Arthur de Richemont, brother of the duke of Brittany. Orléans
and Patay had raised French hopes in a *détente* with Burgundy.
The optimism that prevailed over the Duke's attitude may have
been due to the constable, but the duke was Bedford's brother-
in-law and was not likely to fall into the arms of France. At the
coronation of Charles VII he did indeed send an embassy to
Rheims, a clear proof that *rapprochement* was not out of his
thoughts; and towards the end of the year he wrote sharply to
the English council complaining of the non-payment of his
troops at Compiègne. The English king, Philip argued, had
arranged to undertake the payment of the Burgundians at the
siege, but this had not been done, and for lack of £19,500 men
were deserting. He also asked that the troops he sent to Calais
should be paid *incontinent, réalement et de fait*. This is followed
by a series of instructions about statements to be made on the
part of the duke of Burgundy to king and council in England.[1]
In December 1430 the duke sent Henry VI a letter on the subject of his truce with France: he had been more or less forced to
it, he said, and he enumerated the occasions on which he had
asked England for more men and money for the defence of
Picardy and the Somme. For lack of wages he had had to
disband his armies; a French embassy was now approaching
and overtures to him in favour of peace had been made not only

[1] J. Stevenson, *Wars of the English* (Rolls Ser.), II. i. 164–5.

by the estates of Artois, but also by English towns nearby, and by Amiens, Abbeville, Noyon, St. Quentin, and Chauny. The letter was written, in fact, five days before the coronation of Henry VI in Paris. Bedford was determined to make it clear that Henry was the legitimate king of France and to undo the effect of Charles's coronation. The English monarch was transferred to France (April 1430), not to Rheims however, but to Paris, and the actual crowning and sacring took place 'in the Cathedral of a mere bishop'.[1] But Henry, if he was in France for more than a year and a half, had aroused no enthusiasm and Charles, far from being discredited, had gained new prestige from the siege of Orléans and the victory of Patay. It was essential, therefore, in English eyes, that Charles VII's claim that the treaty of Troyes was now obsolete and that the dual monarchy had come to an end with his crowning, should be made to look ridiculous. This was to be achieved by the trial of Joan of Arc, in which she had to be discredited through her witchcraft and sorcery being exposed in the course of her examination by the Holy Office. Such was the purpose of the investigation by the Inquisition: the major error to be detected was that she claimed to have visions, in the course of which St. Michael, St. Catherine, and St. Margaret appeared to her in the flesh, and that their revelations enabled her to know the future. That Charles and his entourage were deluded by magic of this kind was to Cauchon and the political clergy the deduction that had to be drawn in the forthcoming trial at Rouen. Joan must be made to admit that she had been hopelessly deceived, and all her supporters involved in the deception. The English had to account for a great reverse: the siege of Orléans represented to them the culmination of a series of expeditions which had enabled Salisbury, by May 1428, to take possession successfully of the country between Dreux and Chartres, and of the fortresses of Toury, Le Puiset, Janville, Meung, and Beaugency. Now under the enthusiasm of the French rank and file and the co-operation of the credulous and deluded Dauphin the tide had turned, while Charles's unhampered march to Rheims and the historic ceremony there had appeared to confirm all that the Peasant Girl had promised. Charles was now in the true line of the true French monarchs.[2] There was more

[1] E. Perroy, *The Hundred Years War* (Eng. tr. 1951), p. 287.
[2] This was itself of great importance, whether immediate or historical. When

than a great upsurge of morale among the French to be explained: there was military victory over captains successful
from Agincourt to Verneuil. Not simple fraud, therefore, but
magic and 'sorcery' were to be exposed, the 'deception' of the
Voices which Joan heard; and the later evidence produced at
the rehabilitation process was collected to show that these
revelations were of God and not of the devil, while to the
vigilant canonist the trial at Rouen became marked by grave
judicial irregularities.

The most sceptically minded have to admit that the evidence
given at the second or official stage of the rehabilitation process
throws a sinister light on the proceedings that began on 21
February 1431 and appeared to have their ending with a preliminary investigation on 21 May. Joan abjured the heresies of
which she had been pronounced guilty. She was detained in a
secular prison, she had nobody to speak for her. Guillaume
Manchon, in 1431 scribe of the Holy Office, reported that the
judges brought compulsion to bear upon him to alter the words
of the French *procès-verbal* when translating them into Latin. In
a window of the hall, behind a curtain, two men 'wrote down
and repeated everything that incriminated Joan and nothing
that excused her'. Under the guise of a friendly priest the *agent
provocateur* Loiseleur was appointed to secure from her con-
fessions that might prove damaging. Manchon said that after
each session, when a comparison was made of his own text with
what the two concealed figures had written, their account was
different from his own and contained nothing of Joan's defence.
'My Lord of Beauvais was greatly annoyed with me about this;
and where the word *Nota* appears in the reports of the case, that
is where there were differences of opinion.' They were not infrequent. Quite apart from these textual discrepancies and the
rough English method of treating a girl who should have been
in the protection of the Church, mention was made, in the
rehabilitation process, of threats and pressure brought to bear

Joan came to the Dauphin at Chinon she put him in mind of the hero-kings: 'car
sainct Louys et Charlemagne sont à genoux devant luy [God] en faisant prière pour
vous': Cousinet de Montreuil, *Chronique de la Pucelle*, ed. Vallet de Viriville, p. 274.
That she had special powers of telepathy was evident to Charles when she revealed
to him her knowledge of his project to vacate the throne through uncertainty of his
legitimate origin: 'elle dist au roy une chose de grant conséquance, qu'il avoit
faicte, bien secrète: dont il fut fort esbahy, car il n'y avoit personne qui le peust
sçavoir que Dieu et luy': ibid.

by the English upon the officers of the court. In addition to the
atmosphere of hatred surrounding her and the hypocrisy of the
trial, the sheer fatigue and distress of spirit that beset a body
weakened by captivity led to her abjuration: but when she
heard of the penance enjoining prison for life, her country spirit
fired up, and she returned to her wearing of man's clothes, one
of the principal charges against her. Brought up again for
examination, she was found to have relapsed, and as such
handed to the secular arm—her English captors—for burning.
A persistent legend that she escaped the fire and that something
else was burned instead of her has been shown to have no
reliability. She was unquestionably burned, and the English
gained greatly by her death, for, as Bedford wrote to the
council, 'she couraged youre adverse partie and enemies to
assemble them forthwith in grete nombre' and 'used false
enchauntments and sorceries'. What she had done had been
to rekindle the offensive spirit in the French army and to prove
that timely aggressive action is the best way of winning fights,
and that energy, speed, and surprise are the qualities most
necessary for the successful conduct of war. That is why, as
Thomas Basin wrote after her rehabilitation, for all her well-
informed and cautious answers to her examiners and for all her
religious devotion, the English were determined to get rid of her,
for they avowed that they would never fight successfully with
the French or secure victory over them as long as that Maid,
whom they thought a sorceress and a wicked person, continued to live.[1]

We left Beaufort obliged to tolerate the postponement of the
Bohemian Crusade and the diversion of his troops to France.
There is nothing to show how he took the disappointment: but
he could defend himself energetically against the onslaught made
upon him in a meeting of the Great Council on 17 April 1429.
The question raised was whether, now that he was a cardinal,
he ought to be allowed to perform, at the Festival of St. George,
his usual service as prelate of the order of the Garter to which
the see of Winchester entitled him. The council agreed that his
position was ambiguous, and that he should be warned not to
appear at Windsor until it was settled.[2] The council's view was
conveyed to him by his friends Humphrey earl of Stafford, the

---

[1] *Historiarum Caroli VII*, II. xv.   [2] *P.P.C.* iii. 323.

earl of Northumberland, Lords Tiptoft and Cromwell: whereupon he came to Westminster and in the king's presence protested that he had been present at the festival, as bishop of
Winchester, for twenty-four years: he asked for justice or at
least a statement of the reasons to the contrary which he was
prepared to answer. The lords were questioned individually on
the point whether the king should delay his visit to Windsor:
their answer was that it was unwonted that a cardinal should
also hold the bishopric of Winchester, and that they thought it
advisable that for the present Beaufort should abstain from
attending. After this until November 1431 active measures
against Beaufort were suspended, probably because his supporters in the council were able to resist Gloucester's efforts.

In 1431 the attack was resumed. Gloucester authorized the
crown lawyers to make out a case against the cardinal before
a great council, at which fourteen spiritual and eight temporal
lords were present. He appealed to precedent: the acceptance
of the cardinalate on previous occasions had involved the
resignation of an English see. Kilwardby in 1278 and Langham
in 1368 had both resigned Canterbury. The king's sergeant and
attorney accordingly petitioned that the cardinal should be
compelled to resign the see of Winchester and refund the
revenues he had received since 1426. The regent asked the
bishop of Worcester whether it was true that the cardinal had
purchased for himself, his city and diocese, exemption from the
jurisdiction of Canterbury, for Polton had been relating a story
about the part played by the then bishop of Lichfield in securing
such bulls from the Curia. The council had been informed that
one of the bulls presented at the time of the cardinal's investiture
at Calais provided expressly for the retention of all his ecclesiastical preferments in England. In November, after consultation with the judges, writs under the statute of Praemunire were
made out against Beaufort, but it was decided to wait for his
return from France, Marmaduke Lumley contending that
nothing should be done in the bishop's absence. In May 1432
the cardinal appealed to the council in parliament, and offered
to defend himself against anyone accusing him of treason. His
case was discussed by Gloucester and the lords in the presence
of the king. Finally at Henry's command and by the advice and
assent of the duke and the other lords present Beaufort was
officially told that nobody had accused him of treasonable

conduct, and that he was held by the king as a true and faithful subject. This declaration Beaufort asked to be exemplified under the Great Seal, and he undertook not to use it in his defence, if a similar accusation was made later. It is worth noting that the charge of treason had never been formally made. Gloucester, proverbially reckless in his language, may have said that the man who treated the statute of Praemunire in so cavalier a fashion was a traitor, and indeed this was not the first occasion on which Beaufort had got into trouble over it. In the present instance, as in the earlier, the writ against him was not issued.

There was, as on the earlier occasion also, a *quid pro quo* almost certainly arranged before the parliament of 1432 met. Beaufort agreed to restore the jewels which he had received from the king as security for his loans: he agreed to pay £6,000, which he executed on 15 July, 'a special and provisional fine with the Crown' (Mr. Steel calls it), in order to recover plate and jewels seized at Sandwich, at the order of the duke of Gloucester, when he was returning from abroad early in 1432; if it was found that Beaufort's property had been wrongly seized, the £6,000 was to be treated as a loan; he was in fact repaid during the Easter term of 1434. He also undertook to lend a second sum of £6,000 and to put off reclaiming past loans to the amount of 13,000 marks until he could recompense himself from the tenth and fifteenth. The arrangements were gratefully received by parliament and exemplified under the Great Seal. On 18 July 1433 he advanced a further £3,333. 6s. 8d., but on 2 June 1434 he was repaid £12,522, part of which represented the fine he had to pay for the recovery of plate and jewels. The cardinal, in effect, bought himself out of an ugly situation, but in such a way as to ingratiate himself with parliament.

Many years before, in 1338, the Walton ordinances had prescribed an annual declaration of the state of the treasury, but only occasionally, as in 1401 and 1421, had such a reckoning been seriously attempted. There were, however, indications of the way things were going: as it has been pointed out, when there was a change of treasurer, the balance of cash in hand was stated in the issue or receipt roll in sums ranging from £200 to £10,000:[1] and, if the meaning of the entries is rightly

[1] J. L. Kirby, 'The Issues of the Lancastrian Exchequer and Lord Cromwell's estimates of 1433', *Bull. Inst. Hist. Res.* xxiv (1951), 122–3.

understood, it is possible to arrive at an accurate statement of
receipts and expenses from the totals of the receipt and issue
rolls which did on the whole balance one another.[1] Totals are
now available for both sets of rolls for sixty out of the first seventy
terms of the Lancastrian period, and very revealing some of
them are. Thus for the period of the Agincourt campaign
(Easter–Michaelmas 1415), it has been calculated that the
issues came to as much as £142,000, assignments reaching
£52,000 and cash issues at least £90,000: none the less Henry
was receiving a sum not far short of this, and for the whole
reign the difference between receipts and issues is less than
£400. 'This difference represents only 0·26% of the total
receipts so that the reign taken as a whole balances almost
exactly.'[2] Henry VI's reign began that way and it was not till
1429–30 that a difference of more than £10,000 made its
appearance in one term: over the first twelve years of the reign
issues exceeded receipts by an average of £1,600 a year, but
they had been down to much less. When Lord Cromwell
succeeded John Lord Scrope an estimate of the king's revenue
and of his expenses for one year was prepared, along with a list
of outstanding debts. The figures given show that, with the
customs reckoned in on the receipt side, the deficit on the year
(1433) was £21,447: but that the debts, for which no provision
had been made, came to a total of £164,815. The chief items
were the household, £11,101; annuities and fees in arrears,
£19,215; outstanding loans, including 10,000 marks from
Beaufort and £6,028 from the duchy of Lancaster, £19,861;
tallies not yet allowed, £56,815; and, among ancient debts on
the English possessions overseas, Calais accounted for £45,100.
These obligations would have to be met term by term, as far
as it was possible; but one point of importance in Cromwell's
figures lay in showing that the gross revenue *apart* from lay and
clerical subsidies amounted to about £65,000, and the net
revenue, when necessary payments and meeting of debts had
been deducted, about £35,000; of this at least £27,000 was
derived from the customs and wool subsidies. In other words,
all the various sources of the ordinary revenue of the crown,

---

[1] e.g. 'The surviving rolls for the first four years of Henry IV—only five terms
have left rolls in both series—were almost all added up at the time, and the largest
difference between receipts and issues was only £346': Kirby, p. 127.

[2] Ibid., p. 130.

when the fees and annuities from them had been deducted, only reached £8,400. The commons could have had no more telling figure to work upon, when they came to consider how to reduce annuities and augment existing farms. A second point of interest is that it was necessary to maintain the lay and clerical subsidy each year if the normal expenditure, calculated at £57,000–58,000, was to be met. The average yield from this taxation, at a tenth and fifteenth and a full clerical tenth, was £45,000 or rather less. The net margin over expenditure, some £21,000, would scarcely be enough to meet the large 'ancient debts' and the repayment of loans but it enabled the Exchequer to meet at any rate some. The English government could in fact have gone on paying its way, had it not been for the war which could not be made to pay for itself. It was when the discovery was made that the conquest was not self-sufficient, and that the non-Norman territories and special military expeditions, like the fighting round Orléans, were draining the steady though diminishing contributions made by the Norman estates, that the council began to be seriously alarmed, and, in spite of a temporary recovery in the military position, to seek a more permanent modification of English commitments in France.

The success of France in 1429 brought Philip of Burgundy seriously to consider a *rapprochement* with her. In sending to Rheims to salute Charles VII his ambassadors, according to Pius II, *aliquid ad concordiam offerebant*. Does this mean that he was prepared to talk peace? *Aliquid* cannot as yet have amounted to much. He had certain demands which in any settlement with France he regarded as crucial: reparation for the death of John the Fearless coupled with a solemn apology, punishment of the murderers, the founding of chapels, the endowment of masses: but now Charles VII was ready for the cession of Mâcon, Auxerre, Peronne, Montdidier, Roye, and Bar, all of which figured in the final agreement made at Arras. The Somme towns had been part of the dowry of Philip's first wife, Michelle of France, and Henry V had confirmed the duke in possession. Philip began by wanting the grant of the towns to be made in perpetuity, but this in the end was changed to cession, with the possibility of repurchase at any time, and further of return without compensation if peace was made with England. In the autumn of 1429 the French were ready for concessions, if they could only secure the duke, going so far as to promise to remi

Compiègne and Creil into the hands of Philip's lieutenant, John of Luxembourg. With England they were ready to negotiate for a triangular settlement involving France, Burgundy, and England. At a meeting held at St. Denis it was decided that a general peace should be arranged and that conferences should open at Auxerre on 1 April 1430 between the representatives of the parties under the auspices of the duke of Savoy, and with the mediation of cardinals nominated by the Pope. On 17 October 1429 the duke accepted the *journée* at Auxerre, having announced his intention of going there in person as well as his 'dear and much loved brother, the regent in the Kingdom of France', and having promised to secure from Henry VI and the regent adhesion to a general peace. He was, as Beaucourt pointed out, playing a double game, continuing to parley with France while strengthening his bonds with England and preparing for the reopening of hostilities.

Martin V was watching the situation. In 1430 he named Cardinal Nicolò Albergati legate in France, and the commission was repeated by Eugenius IV in 1431. That year he was made peace-maker between the three powers: he held four peace conferences, with the French and Burgundians at Semur in August 1432, with the French, English, and Burgundians at Auxerre in October 1432, between Corbeil and Melun in March 1433, and at Corbeil in July 1433, besides paying personal visits to the princes and leaders involved. He did not get very far. The French insisted on the presence of the dukes of Orléans and Bourbon and of the count of Eu, all prisoners in England, and the English held that a truce was the first necessity which the French would not concede. If he made little progress with Burgundy, it was not for any lack of moves by the duke to ascertain the situation in England, but because he had taken his oath to the treaty of Troyes in 1420 and had again, in 1425, made a personal and defensive alliance with Bedford and Brittany which was 'pour le bien du roy nostre sire et de les royaulmes de France et d'Angleterre'.[1] In July 1433 a Burgundian embassy reached London to discover what opinion there was in favour of a general peace. The duke was anxious that Brittany, Richemont, and Amadeus of Savoy should be brought into the discussions, and Hugh de Lannoy and the treasurer of the Boulenois were commissioned to interview the

[1] Joyce Dickinson, *The Congress of Arras, 1435* (1955), p. 68.

duke of Orléans as well as prominent members of the Englis
council. The envoys found Suffolk favourable, Beaufort re
served; Orléans said he was ready to act as mediator in
general peace, if only he was allowed to come over and spea
with some of his friends in France. Their conversation with hir
greatly displeased the English, they said, who found themselve
confronted in the July parliament with the alternative either t
arrange peace with the Dauphin (the English description c
Charles VII), or to 'raise a very large and powerful army; fo
from what we can perceive, they are well aware that the affair
of France cannot long continue in the state they are in now'
On their departure Suffolk expressed himself optimistic abou
a general peace: Warwick, on the other hand, gave vent to hi
displeasure and the disappointment felt by the English at th
duke's failure to visit Henry VI on his visit to France. 'We aske
him how such a thing could have taken place after the hars
words regularly used about the duke', to which Warwick replie
that it was only people of low rank who made such observation
The ambassadors had ascertained the Dauphin's views fror
Johan de Saveuse who had come straight from Orléan
Saveuse reported that the Dauphin had told him that if Orléai
was delivered, without which nothing could happen, all woul
tend towards peace, 'provided that the English should not hav
the crown', for on this point the French would hear nothing
The ambassadors departed and the English council's reply wa
sent in writing to the duke. The council had already under
taken exhaustive negotiations with France, even to the exter
of taking the prisoners over to Calais, 'hoping that the sai
adversary would send his agents to speak with the said captiv
lords, as it had been desired'. The Dauphin only offered a fou
months' truce, which was inadequate: and it was essential tha
the duke should know what the king was actually doing in th
war, and the letter set forth the English war effort for the duke
information. The letter was not encouraging on the main issue
but it stated a relevant fact: Beaufort had been twice to Cala
to attend prospective peace negotiations with the French, o
the second occasion taking Orléans with him. On neither occa
sion was there any conference and the English council might
well claim that they met with no co-operation. Earlier, in 142(
he had been at St. Denis and had won the confidence of th

[1] Stevenson, *Wars of the English*, ii. i. 229-44.

Burgundians: but he had not been able to attend Albergati's conferences in 1432 and 1433.[1] It was natural, therefore, that he should treat Philip's *démarches* in 1433 with a certain reserve.

The position was peculiarly difficult for the English council, since there were two other authorities besides the three protagonists deeply concerned in securing peace. One was the council of Basel which Eugenius IV had eventually been obliged to recognize. When it began Martin V, after attempting to suppress it, had given it authority to deal with peace, and a commission of peace was quickly established. To this aim, even after the bull of dissolution, it clung tenaciously, and pleaded the need for reconciliation among the states as one of the reasons why it should continue. The Basel Fathers sent envoys to Albergati's conferences, and after the legate's failure to secure pacification, they sent ambassadors to Burgundy, to Charles VII, as well as to Henry VI. The other authority, needless to say, was the Pope, whose mediation was preferred by Duke Philip to that of the council of Basel, though at the preparatory council of Nevers he asked that the council should send two cardinals, Cyprus and St. Peter, to the later assembly. By 1434 both the council and the Pope had committed themselves to recognizing the France of Charles VII as an independent power, and one of the main difficulties which England found in being incorporated in the council was precisely the denial of the settlement of Troyes which that recognition implied. That 'France' should stand for Lancastrian France alone neither the Pope (through his legate) nor the council could admit, and the French members of the English nation at Basel were thus in an anomalous position. The attitude of the council can be seen in the fact that its representative, the cardinal of Cyprus, refused to go without legatine powers, for the French had said that their king had the privilege from the Pope that no legate *a latere* should enter his realm unknown to him and that they hoped that Charles would accept the legate. The mediating powers therefore were clear about the standing of Charles VII; Burgundy had been steady in the direction of Franco-Burgundian peace, but as late as 1434 bad relations between the houses of Burgundy and Bourbon prevented Philip from taking any decisive step. The real change came with a meeting of the French and Burgundians at Nevers in 1435.[2]

[1] Ibid., p. 257.   [2] Dickinson, op. cit., p. 163.

At this important encounter three agreements were made: one between Burgundy and the duke of Bourbon; of the other two, which were the result of talks between Philip and the French ambassadors, one provided for a further meeting at Arras for the negotiation of a general peace, to which Henry VI, the Pope, and the Council of Basel were to be invited to send representatives, and the King of France (*le roy Charles*) was to be represented by his ambassadors, while Bourbon and Richemont were to come, and Philip of Burgundy in person. The other clause foresaw the possibility of Philip's departure from the English alliance. It provided that if the duke did make the change, the king of France would hand over the Somme towns in addition to those which in a previous treaty it had been agreed to cede. If, in the forthcoming conference, a general peace was not worked out the duke would strive for a union with King Charles: but he was to undertake the negotiations as far as was possible saving his honour, and in such manner that the integrity of his intentions should be recognized. Evidently the duke was contemplating a Franco-Burgundian alliance, but he had sworn an oath to the treaty of Troyes, and his obligations to keep this were debated in a number of contemporary memoranda, Anglo-French, pro-Burgundian, or pro-French; attacking or defending the settlement of 1420.[1]

The French acceptance of Arras as the meeting-place for the peace council in accordance with the resolutions at Nevers was signified by the duke to the English council early in May 1435. His ambassadors besides urging the English king to send princes and nobles along with the duke of Orléans and the count of Eu, asked that an army be sent over before the meeting, in order to bring the enemy to a reasonable attitude and, if the conference failed, to be prepared to fight with the Burgundians. The English reply grumbled at having to discuss peace at such short notice (July was the date for the opening of the congress), but consented to send emissaries to be at Arras by 15 July (they had been invited for 1 July 1435). It was in fact a distinguished delegation under the leadership of the archbishop of York John Kemp. The first of the ambassadors to be named was Henry Beaufort who remained at Calais from 25 July till 23 August, when he reached Arras. His stay at Calais with Orléans was intended to clinch matters with the French, if the

[1] Described in Dickinson, op. cit., ch. iii, 'The Burgundian volte-face'.

council at Arras decided upon an Anglo-French peace: if they did not, and matters were going badly, he was to go to Arras. Already what Beaufort's role was at the council has been much debated; what seems most likely is that Beaufort's part was to be mainly connected with Burgundy: he was then 'to salvage the Anglo-Burgundian alliance' and do his best to prevent the inevitable result of a rupture in the negotiations with France.[1] Both his country's and his own position were at stake: if the negotiations failed and Burgundy made a pact with France, part of the onus for the failure at Arras would be laid to his account: far more important was the potential loss of the English conquest. Yet in face of this danger the English delegation when it stated its case before the cardinal, mediator at Arras, was not prepared to make a permanent settlement with the French, but only one of truces until the young Henry VI came of age: its instructions were to offer a marriage between their king and one of the daughters of Charles VII accompanied by a truce of twenty years, the question of final peace being deferred till Henry VI came of age. The mediators had to inform the English that the French would not treat save on a basis of general peace. At this point the English made a second offer along similar lines, adding that the duke of Orléans should be delivered in return for a ransom; this offer was refused, and with the proposed marriage alliance they now offered large territorial concessions; all lands south of the Loire except what the king held in Guienne and all the lands held in France by the French, but with the provision for the exchange of inherited territory on either side and with the exclusion of Normandy, Paris, and the Île de France, which were at the moment being fought for. By the end of the bargaining, the English were willing to accept the bride without any dowry, whether in land or money. The duke of Orléans they were, however, unwilling to release without payment, which they apparently proposed to fix themselves. The French suggested that the mediators should fix the sum, but the English replied that they had no authority to accept the proposal. It is noteworthy that the question of what was to happen to Charles VII, already crowned and anointed, was left open. The words of the bishop of Lisieux perhaps best express the intention of the English. They had come, he said, to make peace by giving a part of the king's

---

[1] Dickinson, op. cit., p. 39.

realm of France to the enemy. They were armed with all sorts of temporary expedients to buy off the adversary of France until the young king came of age and the question of final peace reopened. With such a programme, matched as it was by the French insistence on a final settlement or nothing, together with the surrender of the English claims, it was to be expected that neither the exhortations of the mediators nor of Duke Philip himself could prevail in the cause of a general peace. The French always insisted on two conditions: that Henry VI should renounce the French throne and all lands occupied or claimed and that any lands ceded in return should be held in homage and fealty from Charles VII. *Re infecta*, the Lancastrian embassy left Arras on 6 September.

If this was the attitude taken by the English—and the French were equally obstinate—why was there a conference at all? It is difficult to escape the conclusion that Philip of Burgundy had much to do with the meeting. Having found his English ally unco-operative in recent years, and intending to assume the role of a faithful member of the ruling house of France, he saw that his obligations to the English could not be cast aside unless some attempt had been made to arrive at a general peace. By such a peace he could become the friend and ally of both parties: if negotiations failed, it would be possible to justify peace with France, provision for which had already been made at the meeting of the two parties at Nevers. But the terms of a Franco-Burgundian settlement had already been worked out and the Nevers agreement stated that the duke could proceed to the peacemaking, if and when negotiations for the general peace broke down, *son honneur sauf*: he was not to be charged with breaking his word with the English. His honour and the problem of whether he was breaking his word could now be left to the spiritual authority: and Albergati, legate of Eugenius, could give the assurance. The Franco-Burgundian treaty was finally promulgated on 21 September 1435. A good deal of the preliminary period was taken up by the cardinals' examination of Philip's position in regard to the English alliance: in this they acted, not as mediator, but as representatives of the highest ecclesiastical powers, who had commanded him to make peace with France, having declared that his oaths to the English were no longer binding. They had, as they said, taken the opinion, maturely given of profound and notable clerks and sages in the

aw (e.g. Louis de Garsiis, who wrote a memorandum printed
by Plancher, IV). Charles VII was made to denounce the
murder of John the Fearless, to beg Philip's forgiveness on the
ground of his youth, to promise to punish the perpetrators of
he deed. Charles yielded to the duke the counties of Mâcon
and Auxerre, the *prévôtés* of Peronne, Montdidier, and Roye,
and the Somme towns, and a phrase covering the county of
Ponthieu and all the royal demesne north of the river, except
St. Amand and Tournai. Charles was given the right to buy back
he towns at a very high price of 400,000 crowns but he gave
up the claim to levy taxes in Artois and the lands now ceded.
It was stipulated that the duke of Burgundy should be exempt
rom all obligation of doing homage to the king of France, as
ong as either Charles or Philip should be alive; the duke's
vassals could not be called up for military service by the king;
and Charles renounced his alliance with Sigismund against
Philip and undertook to aid him if he were attacked by the
English.

   The council of Arras is a turning-point in English history
during the fifteenth century. The régime laid down in the treaty
of Troyes could no longer be sustained and there was to follow,
both in the council and out, a prolonged and often angry
struggle over the maintenance of its provisions and the need to
sustain the English hegemony in France now so seriously im-
paired. There were those who with Sir John Fastolf advocated
more intimidating methods of conducting the war, and, as it
will be seen, the French war was regarded from a private as
well as from a public angle. The memorandum which Fastolf
drafted in 1435 about English methods to be employed in the
future was a realistic plea for more ruthless measures.[1] On the
other hand, Beaufort and the party which he had created were
set upon extricating the country as honourably as possible from
the Troyes entanglement, knowing perfectly well that the
military help of Burgundy could no longer be relied upon. The
agreements at Arras did not mean the end of Anglo-Burgundian
relations, but a decisive blow had been struck at the old co-
operation.

   [1] Stevenson, op. cit. II. ii. 575–85.

VII

THE CHURCH

THE Church of England in the fifteenth century was an integral part of the western Church, obeying the common law of the Church as expressed in the papal codes. The volumes of the *Calendar of Papal Letters*, containing innumerable entries relating to England from the Lateran and Vatican registers of the popes, exhibit the practical working of papal law as the common law of the Church in English affairs. Only in a few respects did that law suffer any alteration in the way in which it was applied in England from that in the rest of western Europe. It was a principle of the jurisprudence of the Church that a certain custom which could claim to be *reasonable*, and had been in existence for a number of years, could become law and even abrogate positive written law, and in England local custom had altered the common law of the Church as contained in the *corpus iuris canonici*, but in no very important direction. For instance, by the common law of the Church the rector was responsible for the upkeep of the parish church; but in England local custom had made the rector responsible only for the upkeep of the chancel, while the parishioners had to look after the nave. Again, by the common law of the Church each church in matters liturgical was supposed to follow the example of the metropolitical Church of the province: theoretically in the province of Canterbury the Use of Canterbury should have been followed: in practice throughout the province of Canterbury local customs had made the Use of Sarum the model use for the whole province. Again English custom went far beyond what was laid down in the decretals of Gregory IX about wills. The canon law claimed that bishops had jurisdiction over wills bequeathing property *in pios usus*: but by the thirteenth century, the ecclesiastical courts in England are found exercising a very extensive jurisdiction over wills bequeathing personal estate. The jurisdiction had come to include their interpretation, the settlement of disputed wills, grants of probate and administration, and the conduct of executors and administrators. The secular power in England limited the control of the Church courts over cases of advowson and over benefit of clergy, and there was invariably an inquiry in the secular courts into these cases where clerks were accused of crime; it is also to be noted that sentences of excommunication pronounced by ecclesiastical courts were, as a matter of routine, enforced by secular authority. The large number of significations of excommunications which have survived for the fifteenth century is evidence of the co-operation of the civil power.

A canon of the fourth Lateran council, inserted in the decretals of Gregory IX, ordered provincial synods to be held once each year for the purpose of reading over the decrees of general councils and of enacting constitutions framed to remedy abuses which had been brought to light by the synod. The constitutions passed by the English provincial synods did not aim at creating an exhaustive national system of Church law which was to be applied even when its provisions contradicted those of the papal codes; rather they were, as Professor C. R. Cheney has called them, 'ad hoc remedies to meet abuses'. They thus reiterate the provisions of the papal codes, and amplify them to meet local conditions. The only actually new legislation which they contain is on points not covered by the papal codes.

The best illustration of their scope and character comes from the gloss and commentary of the chief English canonist of the middle ages, William Lyndwood, whose *Liber provincialis*, finished on Whitsun eve 1430, was accepted by the convocations of Canterbury and York. Lyndwood, Chichele's auditor of causes (1414), by 1417 his official principal, took the provincial constitutions and after abbreviating them, arranged them in five books, subdivided into titles and chapters, and added an illuminating commentary[1] which is the chief source of our knowledge of how the *ius commune* of the Church was

---

[1] The Christ Church, Oxford, copy of the 1525 (Paris) edition has a note by Sir William Fleetwood, recorder of the City of London, that Lyndwood was born in Lonsdale (Lancashire) and was related on his mother's side to the Lancashire family of Tunstall. For his father, John Linwood (Lincs.), see *Reg. Chichele*, ii. 183 f.

actually applied in England in the middle ages. Nowhere does Lyndwood ever suppose that the law of the Church of England is independent of the law contained in the papal codes: rather he regards the decretals and their supplements as coming from the highest legislative authority in the Church, in the light of which all local constitutions and customs have necessarily to be interpreted. At every point in his commentary both the decretum of Gratian and the decretals, along with the dicta of commentators and glossators, are copiously quoted, to supply the necessary authority for his statements.

The old controversy between Stubbs and Maitland about the nature of English Church law in the middle ages has therefore been laid to rest. Legally, *Ecclesia Anglicana* was an integral part of the western system, acknowledging the primacy of Rome. The archbishops took the oath of canonical obedience to the successor of St. Peter after receiving from Rome the pallium, the symbol of their office. The words used when the representatives of the Holy See assigned and handed the pallium to a newly elected archbishop were:

We hand to you the pallium taken from the body of blessed Peter, the symbol of the pontifical office, so that you may use [wear] it in your church on the fixed days expressed in the privileges granted it by the apostolic see.

And the archbishop swore to be 'from henceforward faithful and obedient to the blessed Peter and the holy apostolic Roman Church and to my lord the present Pope and his successors that entered that office canonically'. English bishops made a similar profession of obedience to the Holy See. In 1427, when the papal campaign for the revocation of the 1390 statute of Provisors was at its height, Bishop Robert Neville of Salisbury in making his profession was obliged to promise to obey the apostolic decrees, injunctions, reservations, and provisions.

Such, then, is the legal position: but in the actual relations of the English Church with the Roman see there were notable modifications of the theory, modifications caused primarily by the attitude of the state. While nobody doubted the spiritual supremacy of the Pope, or the validity of his legislative powers for the Church at large, the practice then was a working compromise between the claims of the papacy and the claims of the English government.

Until the middle of the fourteenth century the popes had done pretty much what they liked with English benefices: the reservation of bishoprics, dignities in cathedral churches, and of well-endowed livings, was practised as a matter of course, and every bishop with canonries and prebends in cathedral chapters at his disposal was faced with a long waiting list of candidates furnished with papal provisions. The first check to this was the limited anti-papal legislation of the middle of the fourteenth century which aimed at curtailing the petitioning for benefices by Englishmen to Rome. Such legislation could be got round by licence, and it did not exclude the foreign provisor; the only way of excluding whom was by negotiating settlements with the curia. It was only during the course of the Great Schism that the foreign ecclesiastic came to be for the greater part excluded: and the English *Romipeta* or seeker of benefices from Rome was completely suppressed by the second statute of Provisors, January 1390, which put an end to the system of obtaining licences out of the statute. Behind this legislation lay a certain amount of national feeling, but equally in evidence was the determination of the king to secure a good reserve of higher benefices for the officials of his own civil service. On the whole the king was successful in the struggle to keep the foreign provisor out of the English prebends. By the beginning of the fifteenth century there were few in Italian hands. But in the matter of appointment to bishoprics the honours were more even, with the advantage perhaps on the side of the king.

If the Pope found himself hampered over providing bishops to vacant sees—and since 1363 he had reserved to himself the appointment of archbishops and bishops—he could at any rate use his unchallenged power to translate a bishop from one see to another; and when he translated, he was entitled to provide an incumbent to the see just vacated. The popes made increasing use of their power to translate: after the first statute of Provisors, from 1351 to 1400, out of 86 appointments to bishoprics, there were 31 translations, and in consequence of translation, 13 sees were filled by papal provision.[1] Roughly the

---

[1] A number of translations were asked for on purely political grounds by the king's council. Thus in 1388 Alexander Neville was translated to the schismatic see of St. Andrews by Urban VI, and the consequent shuffling of the bishoprics was essentially the work of the government which had the king in control.

same average of translations took place during the fifteenth century.

But bishops were too important a factor in the state to be left to the nomination of the Pope. It was a useful expedient, says Dr. Hamilton Thompson, to throw upon the Pope the responsibility for their appointment, but the nominations were none the less those of the government in power, and during the Great Schism the Roman popes, anxious for English support, were on the whole compliant. The normal practice was for the king, after a discussion in the council, to convey his wishes to the Pope, and unless the council was hesitant or divided, the Pope accepted: if he did, the government offered no opposition to the Pope formally *providing* the royal nominee. In Archbishop Chichele's register practically every new appointment to a see begins with the papal bull of provision. Even for the time when the Holy See was vacant (1415–17) the Pope when elected (Martin V) quashed as uncanonical appointments made during the vacancy and provided the same nominees to their bishoprics. This system set aside two very important parts of procedure: election by the chapter and confirmation by the metropolitan. Election under these circumstances, though it was formally carried out, was a foregone conclusion: what normally happened, when the Pope signified his assent to the regal suggestion, was that the king sent his *congé d'élire* to the cathedral chapter, and at the same time told them whom they were to elect. Thus freedom of election to bishoprics was seriously curtailed, and it was no use the chapter protesting. And there is a further point: during the vacancy of the see, the king had the temporalities in his own hand. He could always refuse to hand them over to a papal provisor, and if he did not agree with the Pope's choice this gave the king a very powerful position and made it very difficult for the Pope to run counter to the royal nominee. A very good example occurred in 1400. In the spring of that year the see of Bath and Wells fell vacant and Boniface IX provided Richard Clifford, dean of York and archdeacon of Canterbury. The provision failed, because the king, Henry IV, refused the temporalities to Clifford: in the end a royal nominee, Henry Bowet, went to Bath and Wells and Clifford obtained the see of Worcester after election by the cathedral chapter. This time it was a canonical election and the king offered no objection.

A clash between king and Pope might and did occur. On two occasions in 1405 (after Archbishop Scrope's murder) it manifested itself over appointment to the see of York. In 1405 the chapter elected their dean Thomas Langley, whom the king accepted: but the Pope, perhaps out of indignation against Henry IV for the death of Scrope, refused his consent and appointed the distinguished clerk Robert Hallum, the archbishop's auditor, a man of the highest calibre, who was to lead the delegation at Pisa and Constance. After some negotiations with the curia Langley was sent to Durham, Hallum translated from York to Salisbury, and the *curialis* Henry Bowet, two years after Scrope's death, was translated from Bath and Wells to York. When Bowet died in 1423 Martin V, a determined man, translated Richard Fleming from Lincoln to York, in spite of the assent given by the king's council to the election by the chapter of Philip Morgan. The council would not have Fleming, and two years later, Bishop Fleming had to be released from York and translated back to Lincoln, while the ambitious John Kemp, bishop of London and chancellor of Normandy, was in the end provided with the vacant archbishopric. We are lucky enough to have a series of Kemp's letters to William Swan, an English proctor in the curia, and can follow the tactics of this ambitious and not too scrupulous character, in adroitly pushing himself forward in the dispute. During the reshuffle which the appointments occasioned there was a great deal of lobbying done by the parties affected, and the Pope had to listen to a good deal of insinuation (in the technical sense of the term) not least by the duke of Bedford, always favourable to Kemp. In the end the Pope translated Kemp.

Thomas Gascoigne, chancellor of the University of Oxford in 1434, 1443, 1444, and 1445, one of the severest critics of the Church of his time, was very fond of castigating provisions: he said a characteristic thing when he observed: 'there are three things today that make a bishop in England: the will of the king, the will of the pope or the court of Rome, and the money paid in large quantities to that court; for thousands of pounds of English money were paid here in England to Lombards for exchange, to the impoverishment of the realm'. The last sentence is an exaggeration, for he is evidently confusing the 'common' or 'little' *servitia* paid by bishops on appointment to Rome, with the 'douceurs' paid to the Roman curia and particularly to the cardinals in the hope of favours to be received. But one need only read the letters of William Swan, English proctor in the Roman curia,[1] to understand that the tariff for the higher apostolic concessions while governed by precedent was not a rigid one and that the chancery and the camera could not easily disregard a client who was affluent and well connected. To refrain, in the face of probable rebuffs, from any attempt to put Italian cardinals into English sees and English prebends; but at the same time to maintain, in appointments to sees, the right to translate, and, when possible, to provide: that on the whole represents the Papal attitude towards the crown during the fifteenth century. While the king every now and then was allowed, and even encouraged, to modify the statute of Provisors, primarily in favour of the universities who desired to petition Rome for benefices for the graduates, the statute and its executive instrument, the great statute of Praemunire, were never relaxed. This, therefore, is a time which sees a steady growth in the influence of the crown over appointments to sees, and a firm determination on the part of parliament not to waver in excluding petitions for benefices to Rome.

We say 'the crown'. Gascoigne was, perhaps, a little misleading when, under Henry VI, he spoke of the 'will of the king'. It was predominantly the will of the lords dominant in the council. There are various instances. In 1446 Henry tried to get his confessor Stanbury recommended for the see of Norwich; in the end it was Lyhert, the earl of Suffolk's chaplain, who was promoted. When in 1448 London fell vacant, both Henry and Nicholas V agreed on the desirability of Thomas Kemp, and Nicholas made the provision, only to receive, shortly afterwards, a letter from Henry suggesting Marmaduke Lumley. Suffolk was Lumley's patron, and the government for the moment was in his hands. When the Yorkists came to power upon the king's illness in 1454, Bourchier and Grey, their adherents, were sent to Canterbury and to Ely, and George Neville, Warwick's brother, was recommended for early promotion; and after the king had recovered, his weakness was evident when in 1457 there was a vacancy at Durham: he recommended John Arundel to Calixtus II, but

[1] A large number are preserved in Bodleian Library, MS. Arch. Seld. B. 23, and in MS. Cotton Cleopatra, C. iv.

the pope promoted Lawrence Booth who was supported by the queen and by many nobles.[1]

The personnel of the episcopate that Henry IV found in the southern province on his return falls largely into four groups: *nobiles*; civil servants and king's clerks who had arrived at their position through service to the government; the academics who had made themselves useful to the crown through their legal studies or in an ambassadorial capacity; and (sometimes overlapping with the latter class) the religious. In the first category the archbishop, Thomas Arundel, was brother of the earl, having recovered the see of Canterbury from Richard II's treasurer and secretary, Roger Walden formerly of London; Henry Beaufort, second son of John of Gaunt and Katherine Swinford, after being dean of Wells had become at an early age bishop of Lincoln; Henry Despenser, since 1370 bishop of Norwich, *nostre trescheur cousin* as Henry IV called him, was the son of Sir Edward le Despenser and grandson of the young Despenser (executed in 1326); and Edmund Stafford, bishop of Exeter since 1395, who had been keeper of the privy seal 1389–96, chancellor 1396–99 and again 1401–3, was the second son of Sir Richard de Stafford, summoned to parliament as Lord Stafford of Clifton, 1371–9. In the northern province there were two *nobiles*, the Archbishop Richard le Scrope of Masham and William Strickland, bishop of Carlisle, one of the Stricklands of Sizergh, the prelate who built the tower at Rose Castle and the tower and belfry at his cathedral and gave Penrith its water-supply. The professional administrators were Ralph Erghum of Bath and Wells who had been John of Gaunt's chancellor; Richard Medford of Salisbury, king's clerk and royal secretary (1385–8), formerly bishop of Chichester; John Fordham of Ely, formerly keeper of the privy seal and a member of the court party; and the veteran William of Wykeham, bishop of Winchester, who had first risen to high office through the keepership of the king's works. The southern province had no lawyer academics to equal, in chancery service or in experience of foreign diplomacy, Walter Skirlaw of Durham, the builder of the chapter house at Howden. Its academics were few: most interesting of them are the canonist John Trefnant of Hereford, an Oxford D.C.L., an auditor of

[1] Some of the examples given by R. J. Knecht, 'The Episcopate and the Wars of the Roses', *Univ. of Birmingham Historical Journal*, vi (1958), 110–11.

the Rota with long experience of Rome; and John Bottisham, master of Peterhouse, of Rochester, who had been Arundel's chaplain. The three religious were John Burghill, Dominican, bishop of Coventry and Lichfield, the Cistercian Tideman of Worcester, formerly abbot of Beaulieu, Richard II's doctor, and Robert Reade, Dominican bishop of Chichester, who had been with Richard II in Ireland, formerly bishop of Waterford and Lismore (1394–6) and Carlisle (1396–7). It was a bench by no means lacking in distinction: in the reigns of Henry V and during the minority of Henry VI it was to become even more noteworthy, as it grew more representative of the class of able graduates who had made their careers in ecclesiastical administration and were to prove valuable public servants. The strengthening of this element, marked in the twenties, may have been partly due to the efforts of Henry Chichele, archbishop of Canterbury 1414–43, who, representing the union of the burgess and the university graduate, made it his business to get graduates appointed to the higher benefices. By 1461 the personnel had changed somewhat: the religious had fallen to one; the *nobiles* had risen to five; the academics in the service of the crown to six, and Edward IV was to augment the number of ex-civil servants. Theologians among the bishops had decreased: there was nobody equal to Stephen Patrington, Henry V's Carmelite confessor, or to Reginald Pecock who was forced into resignation from Chichester in December 1457: but humanism, of which the pioneer among the bishops had been Adam Moleyns of Chichester, done to death by the mob in 1450, was represented by Thomas Bekynton of Bath and Wells, and William Grey of Ely (son of Sir Thomas Grey of Heton), the bibliophile and benefactor of Balliol College library, who was chancellor of Oxford in 1440–1.

In contemporary opinion the English bishop was far from being a benign father in God, who knew all his clergy and went round preaching in their churches. When he was in his diocese and not at court or on the king's business the medieval bishop was known to his clergy either at their institution in the chapel of one of his manors or through his visitations, and on these latter occasions they would normally see his commissioners, and not the bishop himself. The relationship was mainly a legal one, and on the visitation he resembled the judge of the *Dies irae*: he came *cuncta stricte discussurus*. It is perhaps unfortunate, remarks Professor Hamilton Thompson, 'that we see medieval bishops so entirely through the medium of documents and records which are official and impersonal that we have little opportunity of becoming acquainted with individual traits of character'.[1] It is quite true that a bishop's register is the record of his official acts, which in the fifteenth century are cast in common legal form, but it would be most unfortunate if we thought of the fifteenth-century bishop as a *ministerialis*, an administrative official only, well versed in business, or as hard and formal, without personality or the common touch, devoid of idiosyncrasies. Archbishop Arundel cannot have been as hard a prelate as he is depicted. It is customary to think of him as the hammer of the Lollards, the author of the preaching constitution of 1409, a cautious, almost alarmist prelate, who in his anxiety to defend orthodoxy does not hesitate to visit the university of Oxford against the protests of the younger regent masters: the man who pressed Henry V into action against his old comrade-in-arms in Wales, Sir John Oldcastle. Yet this is the prelate who, when Margery Kempe, the East Anglian visionary, visited him at Lambeth to ask for his direction to the bishop of Lincoln to accept her vow of chastity, allowed that strange enthusiast to rebuke him for the licence of his household: as she and her husband came into the hall at Lambeth, in the afternoon

there were many of the archbishop's clerks and other reckless men, both squires and yeoman, who swore many great oaths and spoke many reckless words and this creature [as she always described herself] boldly reprehended them, and said they would be damned unless they left off their swearing and other sins that they used.

These were the words she used to Arundel out in his garden:

My lord, Our lord of all, Almighty God, has not given you your benefice and great worldly wealth to keep His traitors and them that slay Him every day by great oaths swearing. Ye shall answer for them, unless ye correct them, or else put them out of your service.

Then his reply:

Full benignly and meekly he suffered her to speak her intent, and gave her a fair answer, she supposing it would then be better. And so their dalliance continued till the stars appeared in the firmament.[2]

---

[1] *The English Clergy and their organisation in the Later Middle Ages* (1947), p. 41.
[2] *The Book of Margery Kempe, 1436.* A Modern Version by W. Butler-Bowdon (1936), p. 65.

By the latter part of the middle ages the English diocese wa
a territorial unit containing elements that were both diocesan
in the sense of being subject to the bishop's visitation, and
exempt, i.e. bodies over which the bishop had no control o
only a small amount of control. These exempt or quasi-exempt
bodies were mainly collegiate foundations, corporations lik
the royal free chapels of Hastings or St. George's, Windsor
monasteries or friaries subject to visitation by special com
missioners. A diocesan bishop could not visit a Cistercian or
Cluniac house or any place technically exempt from his juris
diction. No bishop of London could visit St. Albans, and even
the primate himself who kept clear of the place on his metro
political visitation of 1425 had to complain that at Barnet, when
he was passing through the liberty, the bells were not rung fo
him: the *reverencialia* were lacking. During the fifteenth centur
such exemptions were regarded with increasing suspicion b
the bishops as a whole. Archbishops like Chichele did not lik
the power granted to the abbots of St. Augustine, Canterbury
to ordain their own monks, when other religious in the dioces
had to get their orders from the archbishop. When Abbot John
Whethamstede went to the council of Pavia–Siena, it wa
mainly with the intention of defeating the machinations o
Bishop Richard Fleming of Lincoln who, he had heard, had
been inveighing against the exempt orders. This dislike wa
increased by the mass of privileges granted to the exempt in
previous centuries. Dr. Walther Holtzmann has noted 120
privileges granted to St. Albans by the middle of the thirteenth
century:[1] and at York St. Mary's Abbey could claim that it
franchise (which included Bootham) was free from all aids and
tallages which had to be paid by the city.

The diocese, divided into archdeaconries which in turn were
constituted from so many christianities or rural deaneries, wa
administered mainly from the episcopal manors by the bishop
who did not spend much time at his cathedral city. The clergy
went to him rather than he to them, but it was unlikely tha
they saw much of him: for the routine work he relied upon
deputies. Two of these were the vicar-general (normally selected
from the cathedral chapter at the beginning of an episcopate
and an assistant bishop, for duties which only a bishop could
perform—particularly ordinations, confirmations, consecration

[1] *Papsturkunden in England* (1930–52), ii. 40.

of chapels and churchyards, reconciliations of consecrated places polluted by effusion of blood, and the making of the chrism on Maundy Thursday. The vicar-general received a commission which specified his duties: he could institute clerks and receive the oath of obedience, issue dispensations for non-residence and letters dimissory for orders, summon and hold diocesan synods; he could examine and approve elections of heads of religious houses in cases where the bishop had such power: he could collect and receive the revenues of vacant benefices, and examine presentations to benefices and so forth. One of the most important episcopal duties was that of seeing that the benefices in the diocese were filled by accredited persons: if the clerks came from another diocese, they must bring letters dimissory: and the same applied to candidates for ordination who came from a diocese outside. The assistant bishops were mostly bishops *in partibus* or Irish bishops who could not live upon their sees. 'When assistance was wanted', Dr. Hamilton Thompson noted, 'there was always a bishop of Philippopolis or Sidon, Annaghdown or Cloyne, ready to accept an offer of temporary work.' Robert, bishop of Ross, or John Chourles, bishop of Dromore, got through a mass of diocesan duties, the latter acting in the sees of Canterbury 1421, London 1419–26, and Rochester 1423.

The third and a more permanent officer than either vicar-general or assistant bishop was the bishop's official who presided over the diocesan consistory exercising the bishop's office in legal matters. His court did not supersede the bishop's own tribunal which, a far more formal body, might be held at one of the bishop's manors or wherever he might chance to be. The great body of cases coming before the official in the fifteenth century was concerned with matrimony, probate and testamentary bequests, debt, tithe (one of the most frequent of all), the purgation of clerks claimed from the secular tribunals, perjury, defamation, and moral offences where the bishop himself promoted the suit. In pleas between individuals[1] the

[1] The clergy themselves were assiduous litigants. 'An analysis of the suits brought by clerics into Consistory Court [of Canterbury[during 1482 gives some indication of the numbers and types of suits brought by the different ranks of ecclesiastics. Heads of religious houses brought eight suits for perjury and one testamentary suit. Rectors and vicars brought thirteen suits for perjury, fourteen tithe suits, one testamentary suit and two other suits for the recovery of "dues". Out of the 636 cases introduced into the Consistory court in 1482, 77 were brought by

'instance' cases were began by *libelli* or written statements of the plaintiff's case, to which the defendant made a formal reply. The other type of business was the *ex officio* case, promoted by the Church authorities themselves. Excellent examples of the latter type are found in a surviving fragment of Bishop Alnwick's court book;[1] this shows the bishop of Lincoln acting in a disciplinary capacity, probably in a good many cases on the information of his archdeacon or the archdeacon's officials or even of the churchwardens: proceedings against absentee rectors; in one case against a rector who did not celebrate mass on ordinary days, who sold the vessels of his church, cut down trees in the rectory orchard, and refused to church a poor woman unless she paid him, or another who let his manse fall into ruin and refused to appear when cited; one or two of them are interesting: e.g. in the Buckinghamshire archdeaconry the vicar of North Marston committed the crime of blasphemy by digging up the head of a dead person from the ground and placing three drops of blood upon it, asserting that it was the head of a saint, to wit 'Master John Shorn':[2] the vicar was also accused of violent assault on Master Richard Farney, official of the archdeacon of Buckingham. He appeared on 24 September 1448 and confessed his misdemeanour. For violence he had to make four pilgrimages to Lincoln, on foot from his vicarage, offering each time a candle of one pound weight in wax. Another man, the rector of Shenley, was promoted to his church simoniacally for he bound himself to Sir Thomas Grey the patron in £20 for his presentation to the church and paid £10 down.

Another case began with an accusation of the simoniacal resignation of a vicarage, the late vicar, it was alleged, having been paid 20 marks by the present incumbent to resign: the accused denied the charge and successfully purged his innocence by the testimony of twelve rectors of neighbouring parishes: *unde dimissus est.* One lively incident reported in a promoted

ecclesiastics, clerics, and churchwardens. The great bulk of the remaining cases were those of middling people who resorted to the courts to recover debts, bring suits for defamation and for recovery of legacies.' B. L. Woodcock, *Medieval Ecclesiastical Courts in the Diocese of Canterbury* (1952), p. 105. In Canterbury the earliest surviving court *acta* date from 1292; ibid., p. 19.

[1] Printed by A. Hamilton Thompson, *The English Clergy and their Organisation in the Later Middle Ages*, pp. 206 f.

[2] The local saint, famous for conjuring the devil into a boot, who died in 1314 and whose body was translated into St. George's Chapel, Windsor, in 1478.

case was when a woman threw a chicken at the rector during divine service. As in all consistory suits, the vicar-general or the bishop pronounced the sentence, after the *officialis* had heard and terminated the suit. In Canterbury diocese the court might sit at various centres while on circuit.[1]

Discipline the bishop exercised through his *oculus*, the archdeacon; but the latter came into contact with his own subjects, clerical and lay, through his official, through whom the visitation of the archdeaconry was often concluded: it was the official who normally increased the procurations which the archdeacon was entitled to collect, and who acted as the moral supervisor of the laity. In the popular mind he was associated with clerical exactions:

> Denes and suddenes, drawe yow togideres,
> Erchdekenes and officiales, and alle yowre regystreres
> Lat sadel hem with silver, owre synne to suffre
> As auoutrie and deuorses, and derne (dark) usurye,
> To bere bischopes aboute, abrode in visytynge.

Langland's lines call to mind the Summoner's statement in the *Canterbury Tales*: 'Purs is the archdeacon's hell', and in a gloss Lyndwood has an apt word for that frame of mind: *bursalitas*, the quality necessary in a good bursar. But it was more general than that, since in the later middle ages the benefice, higher or lower, became the normal reward of the clerks in the royal service and the source of income for secular churchmen of every description. Hence the importance of sequestration as a means of canonical coercion, and of compelling unwilling incumbents to fulfil their obligations; hence, therefore, the growth in importance of the diocesan sequestrator, who became the principal officer in all testamentary matters within the diocese, with the sequestrator-general above him in the archdiocese.[2]

The total number of livings in England must have been round about 9,500. Like real estate, the benefice could be divided into moieties or split into portions. In the institutions carried out by Robert Grosseteste in the archdeaconry of Lincoln it appears that there were no less than twenty-six parishes divided into halves, five into two-thirds, two into quarters and three into smaller portions. The living could also

---

[1] Woodcock, op. cit., p. 33.
[2] See the account of their functions in R. L. Storey, *Diocesan Administration in the Fifteenth Century* (St. Anthony's Hall Publications, no. 16, 1959), pp. 8–16.

be farmed out: the farmer might be the incumbent or a group of persons, including the incumbent, receiving all the dues and paying a fixed sum to the rector for them. The Canons of St. George's, Windsor, for instance, leased their interest in the churches acquired by the college at a fixed rent, leaving to the lessees the collection of the parish revenues. Although leases to farm were restricted by a statute of the college to a term of five years, they were frequently renewed on expiring, and churches remained in the same hands for considerable periods. The atmosphere of such transactions was entirely secular: at St. George's the lay farmer received from the college an annual livery which was generally a 'robe' (outfit of clothing) or its money equivalent.

The incumbent of the great tithe of a parish was called its rector. The rector might be an individual, a dean and chapter, a college, or a monastic house. If he was an individual, normally he had the cure of souls; if the rector was a corporate body, the cure was usually deputed to a vicar, a vicarage having been or- dained within the church. The later middle ages saw an increasing amount of the tithe of benefices passing into the hands of cor- porate bodies through the practice of appropriation. As Canon Watson observed, 'every year down to the dissolution saw further rectories reduced to vicarages'. These transactions were not confined to the religious orders: for when the secular cathedrals substituted prebends for a share in the common fund, the estate with which the prebendary was endowed was commonly a church. In his place the prebendary established a vicar, retain- ing the patronage of the benefice and the larger part of the income for himself. During the half century of Edward III's reign the number of churches for the appropriation of which royal licences were issued has been computed by Miss Wood- Legh as 539: the number for which papal licences were granted was 140: some 40 to 50 occur in both lists, but it is clear that not all would-be appropriators obtained the papal licence. During the period 1378–1402 there were 105 granted by the Pope *motu proprio* and 58 confirmed by the Pope on petition from the bishop (163) and some 80 to 90 granted by the king. There were thus nearly 700 over less than 80 years. It is natural that Richard Ullerston, canon of Salisbury, should in his *Petitiones ecclesiae militantis*, a string of grievances and a call for their remedy written for the English delegation at the council

f Pisa, complain of the 'abnormal' number of appropria-
ions.

There is considerable evidence for the deterioration of
vicarages in the first half of the fifteenth century, particularly
.fter 1420. In 1425 a list was forthcoming from the diocese of
Canterbury of those livings in which residence was due but
vhich did not exceed 12 marks annually. There were 37
vicarages as against 54 rectories: in the diocese of Hereford
here were equal numbers, 30 to 50 reported by Bishop Spofford.
n 1440 a Chichester return revealed in the archdeaconry of
Chichester 25 rectories and 34 vicarages not exceeding 12
narks. There were too many instances, as the Oxford complaints of 1414 made clear, of the body that subsidized the
vicar keeping him on so low a scale of income that he was
scarcely able to support the 'burdens' of the living, by reason
of which the provision of hospitality and the relief of the poor
suffered proportionately. By 1439 certain religious houses were
unable to maintain their vicarages or even less their chap-
aincies. The constitution of December that year provided some
remedy for incumbents pleading for relief: such parsons were
now allowed to plead *in forma pauperis*, and the bishop was to
hear the case gratis and supply the necessary legal aid. The
constitution declared that vicars should be assigned reasonable
portions from the fruits and emoluments of the churches they
served. An entry in the second Chichester *sede vacante* register
preserved in Chichele's own record shows a vicar of Barnham,
which was appropriated to Boxgrove, unable to live on the
stipend of the vicarage, being instituted, at the presentation of
a lay patron, to the chantry in the same church 'out of charitable intent, considering the scarcity of chaplains and the
poverty of the said vicarage'.[1] Some of the manses must have
been extremely uncomfortable. John Lovelych, rector of St.
Alphege, Canterbury, left to his successors in the rectory all
the furnishings, mainly tables and chairs he acquired for the
house, and directed that the bed-boards were to remain in
every room; 'and yet I found none, nor stool nor table of any
sort when I came'.[2]

There is a tendency to depreciate the learning and mental
equipment of the medieval parish priest and to apply to him

[1] For a discussion of this poverty, cf. *Reg. Chichele*, i. cli f.
[2] *Reg. Chichele*, ii. 561-2.

the strictures of the *Gemma ecclesiastica* or the satires of the thirteenth century; or, socially, to think of him as a superior peasant among peasants, divided *longo intervallo* from the holders of prebends and the ranks of the higher clergy. Yet the parish was then the fundamental unit, as real and, in an age of subdivided townships, more unifying than the manor; and the incumbent of its church, who had its cure of souls (or, if he had licence to be absent, his deputy) had a charge which was both spiritual and material. He had to preach the faith along the lines prescribed by Archbishop Pecham and others for his flock's instruction,[1] he had the power of absolution which no bailiff or secular official possessed, and he had to vindicate his claims to receive from his parishioners the tithe, great or little, to which he was entitled. The higher scholarship was not his first need, though the efforts made by the convocation of Canterbury to secure an academically trained priesthood gradually bore fruit in the course of the fifteenth century; but he had to teach his congregation the meaning of reverence and the simple essentials of manners in rude environments where they could learn from nobody else, and to do so he used all the devices that could create the impression of awe, at the promised ultimate retribution, and of hope, through the prospect of intercession and mercy. The fifteenth century was rich in such parochial mechanism, touching and beautiful still;[2] it was, almost as much as the fourteenth, a century of the sermon, the century of Bromyard and of collections giving the most concrete illustrations of virtue and vice, venturing near to disrespect for the institutions of society, even of the Church itself. The medieval countryman easily fell asleep, and his attention had to be held. Hence the priest had to employ colour, illustration, and the

---

[1] In *Ignorantia sacerdotum*, which prescribed explanations of the Creed, the ten commandments, the seven deadly sins, the sacraments, the Lord's Prayer, and the Hail Mary. The greater part of the constitution is 'taken almost verbatim from a manual of priests composed by Pecham's old master, Walter of Bruges, the last part, on the sacrament of penance and most of the citations from the fathers being omitted as unnecessary for the laity': Decima Douie, *Archbishop Pecham* (Oxford, 1952), p. 135. See the section on the manuals for parish priests in W. A. Pantin, *The English Church in the XIVth Century* (1955), ch. ix, especially the amusing recommendations on getting the laity to pay tithe in the treatise *Regimen animarum*, p. 203.

[2] One may refer here especially, among a great wealth of descriptions, to M. R. James, *Suffolk and Norfolk* (1930), for detailed iconography of a series of parish churches.

technique of modernization, to present the saints and local heroes in a 'live' way.[1]

It was most of all in the sacraments that the devotion of the parishioners could be stimulated and the bonds of the spiritual community drawn more tightly. The adoration of the Blessed Sacrament, carried in procession, had increased since the institution of the Feast of Corpus Christi, and the vital importance of the ceremony of the Mass was stressed by all preachers who would echo the words of John Myrc that it was ordained by Christ at the Last Supper as 'a perpetual memory of his passion forto abyde with hys pepul' and for four reasons, 'for manes gret helpyng, for Cristis passione mynnyng, for gret love schowyng, and for gret mede getyng'.[2] It was the 'mynnyng' or memorial of the Passion on which emphasis was laid. The shedding of Christ's blood upon the Cross 'in helpe of al mankynd' is said by Myrc to be repeated in the Mass.[3] In this service the congregation becomes a community of remembrance.

Such was the greatest function of the *parochianus*. On the material side, he had the support of his laity, represented by the *yconomi*, the churchwardens, who are their representatives; their duties developed in the thirteenth century because of the need for keeping and safeguarding the contributions of the faithful, both to the fabric and for alms. The great increase of bequests in wills to churches, sometimes to the *opus* or *opera ecclesiae*, which means a building fund, or for specific decoration, lights or books, involved the incumbent in business administration which he could not manage alone. The custody and disposal of the contents of alms-boxes was the subject of various diocesan statutes in the thirteenth century,[4] and the problem of the usurpation of funds by the parishioners was a serious one for the Church authorities. They (the laity) could urge that gifts should be withheld, unless they were spent in the right way: and the conflict between the clerical and the

---

[1] Cf. especially John Myrc's (14th-century) description (*Festial*, pp. 38 f.) of St. Thomas of Canterbury as the contemporary English gentleman, doing himself well, having a tussle with the king on horseback in Cheapside, then after becoming archbishop, changing into 'hard heyre' (hair shirt) and undergoing other discipline: in G. R. Owst, *Preaching and Pulpit in Medieval England* (1933), p. 134.

[2] *Festial*, p. 169.

[3] Cf. C. W. Dugmore, *The Mass and the English Reformers* (1958), p. 77.

[4] They are dealt with by C. S. Drew, *Early Parochial Organisation in England* (St. Anthony's Hall Publications, no. 7, 1954), pp. 15 f.

lay view of alms and almsgiving necessitated full confidence between the incumbent and the representatives of his congregation.

It was characteristic of Lollardy to attack those elements in the life of the Church which most emphasized its institutional aspect: excommunication, the payment of tithe to the incumbent (rather than to some other good purpose), the forms of penance prescribed in the confessional, prayers to, and adoration of the saints, along with the cult of their relics, and above all the reverence paid to a spiritual authority based on a law which in Lollard eyes was not the law of God. Fundamentally the Lollard protest against these things was of a deep, if mistaken, spiritualism: it was against taking allegory for reality and being seduced by symbols. This was, of course, expressed in more philosophic form by Oxford masters and by the academically minded who thought that the teaching of Wyclif and his friends was at least 'opiniable': but the priests and others brought before convocation after the constitution of 1416 showed also the more popular aspect of Lollardy, particularly in their confusions on the sacrament of the altar: and it should be remembered that these men were only a limited category of persons about whose guilt or innocence convocation needed to be quite clear, nothing like the rank and file dealt with by the diocesans. Thus the banning in 1428 of the Norfolk priests William White, Hugh Pie, and William Waddon are referred to by the St. Albans chronicles and their trials confirmed by local records, while the municipal register of Colchester alludes to the death of another Lollard next year.[1] All the available evidence points to the fact that Lollardy, so far from being suddenly arrested in 1428, as Gardner thought, was very much alive.[2] It was very active in the north during the early sixteenth century, when it had a continuous history through to the Reformation.[3]

The Lollards had all the marks of a true English sect, with a type of puritanism which after its violent and political phase (1413–17) was of the latent and obstinate kind. At the root of their complaints against the Church lay, according to Bishop Pecock who wrote against them in the *Repressor* and the *Book of Faith*, three 'trowings' or opinions on the part of the 'Bible men':

---

[1] *Reg. Chichele*, i. cxxxvii.   [2] Ibid. i. cxxxviii.
[3] A. G. Dickens, *Lollards and Protestants in the Diocese of York* (1959), *passim.*

the first, that no precept of the moral law is to be esteemed a law of God unless it is grounded in scripture: the second, that every humble-minded Christian man or woman, the meeker he or she is, can arrive at the true sense of scripture; and that when the true sense of scripture has been reached, the believer should listen to no argument of clerks to the contrary. It was natural then that Lollardy was highly suspicious of the appeal to emotion and had a great contempt for popular devotion. Thomas Garenter confessed before convocation (1428) that 'for the legendes and lyves of saintes I helde hem nought'.[1] The Lollard priest Robert Hoke refused to adore the Cross in the traditional manner on Good Friday, and had allowed his parishioners to remain seated; and Thomas Bagley brought charges of idolatry against those who went on pilgrimage in different places, 'putting their hope in images and praying to them'.[2] The Church had an elaborate reply, in treatises and sermons, to those who deprecated the journey to Walsingham or Compostella. But it was the 'trowings' which were the obstacle, and reverence for the word which inspired the un-learned apostles and saints who were not 'graduat men in scolis, but þe Holi Goost sodenli enspirid hem, and maden hem plenteous of hevenli loore; and þei þat han traveilid in deedli lettirs mekid hem silf as symple ydiotis as seint Jerom seiȝ'.[3]

One can understand the need for Arundel's preaching con-stitutions (1407–9) and for his rules controlling biblical transla-tions into English. The difficulty about the clergy themselves was not with the parish priest, so much as with the unbeneficed; for during the later middle ages a change was taking place in the character and numbers of the secular clergy. Their numbers are generally much greater than the total of resident rectors and vicars in any diocese. By the middle of the fourteenth century stipendiary chaplains and chantry priests were to be found in many parishes. In Wiltshire a subsidy list of Henry V's reign gives sixty-three chaplains then resident in the arch-deaconry of Salisbury and a similar list of 1449 shows that there were 121 chaplains in the two archdeaconries of Salisbury and Wiltshire. Territorially it has been calculated that there were not far short of 500 parish clergy in Wiltshire, at least, during

[1] *Reg. Chichele*, iii. 206.
[2] Ibid., iii. 106, 222.
[3] *The Lanterne of Liȝt*, ed. L. M. Swinburne (E.E.T.S. 1917), p. 5.

the later middle ages.[1] The subsidies granted in convocation bear out the importance attaching to the stipendiaries. The convocation of October–November 1419 demanded in addition to the half tenth (to be levied along with the tenth due on 2 February 1419) a noble from chaplains of parish chantries of 7 marks annual value and upwards, and from all unbeneficed secular chaplains of similar income. In the long Convocation of 5 July 1428–20 December 1429 there was a grant of 1s. 8d., 13s. 4d., and 20s. according to the scale of the stipend from anniversary priests, parish chaplains, and chantry chaplains. Clerical legislation was also concerned with the question of the stipendiaries and the amount which they could exact for their services. The problem of disciplining the great body of the untitled clergy, especially the anniversary priests, was a difficult one. In 1419 Archbishop Chichele was asked to extend Winchelsey's constitution of 1305 (*presbyteri stipendiarii*) to safeguard the rights of incumbents against stipendiary chaplains celebrating in their churches, by making the permission of the rector or vicar necessary before those officiating received any fees or offerings. This constitution followed immediately upon Chichele's first taxation, to which we have alluded, of chantry and other stipendiary chaplains, and the next step which was taken, we are told, 'at the instance of some of the clerical proctors', aimed at curtailing fees which chaplains demanded. Sudbury's constitution *Effrenata* (26 Nov. 1378) had limited payments made to clerks without cure, celebrating anniversaries, to 7 marks or 3, with an allowance in kind. It is evident that anniversary celebrations were more popular than the steady work of the parochial chaplain wanting (as we should say) a curate for one of his dependent chapels. The secular clergy had a wide range of employment. They could serve as vicars, as domestic chaplains, as anniversary chaplains, or as men brought in to sing a daily mass or to serve a cure in the absence of an incumbent. As the fifteenth century went on fewer men ordained to major orders possessed an income sufficient to support themselves. It has been suggested from an examination of the Hereford registers that between the years 1328–1448 the number of men ordained to the title of their own patrimony shows a steady decrease. By the middle of the fifteenth century very few ordinands of the financially independent sort were forthcoming.

[1] *Vict. County Hist.* Wilts. iii. 22.

At the same time it will not do to underrate the status or possessions of the beneficed clergy. Wills and inventories of the clergy give some indication of the facts about the circumstances of the testators. The inventories provide details of the goods, plate, and furniture of the deceased, when they were discoverable: for the valuations made after death are often incomplete and the 'four decent and discreet men' who do it have to confess the fact. In 1472 John Pyckeryng, chaplain of the diocese of York, died on 10 October, and when the valuers came they found nothing in the hall or chambers except the clothes he wore daily: everything inside, pots and pans, the sheets and cups and all ornaments had been removed by 'the wicked woman' (probably his housekeeper).[1] There were three horses in the stable, 24 quarters of wheat, 20 quarters of oats, and 10 quarters of peas in his barn. He owned six bovates under corn, had six oxen to plough them, five bullocks, six heifers, and four cows and calves: total value £19. 6s. 8d. The bulk of clerical wills have the inventory of the farm and stock, for the rector or vicar drew his income mainly from the land. Convocation cannot continue in London throughout the late summer or early autumn because the harvest has to be got in and the clergy must collect their own produce. The inventories show a wide variety of furnishing, particularly of beds, and, in the case of prebendaries and the higher ranks, of property and personal possessions, especially books and armour. Roger de Kirkby, vicar of Gainford, left household goods and corn to the value of £99. 11s. 3d.,[2] and bequeathed a set of armour, including two basinets, to a friend. Leaving as much as £36. 13s. 4d. in money, Kirkby disposed of various covered cups and beds of diverse upholstery; he owned a *Legenda aurea* and another book called *Gemma ecclesiae*, which may be the *Gemma ecclesiastica* of Gerald of Wales; his other books he left to his nephew William, son of his brother Adam de Kirkby, on the condition that he became a priest. He had four horses in his stable and was evidently a man of substance to judge by the cups, the vestments, and the ornamentally upholstered bedding. The most interesting books left by the ecclesiastical lawyers were those of John de Scardeburgh, rector of Titchmarsh, notary public, whose goods amounted to £116. 11s. 4d.[3] He left to the church

---

[1] *Wills and Inventories*, Surtees Society (1833), p. 96, no. lxvi.
[2] Ibid., p. 56.   [3] *Testamenta Eboracensia* (Surtees Soc.), iii. 1.

of Arundel 'a book called *Summa summarum* [by William of Pagula] and the Clementines with two glosses'. He had a clerk to whom he left 10 marks, his best horse, and other accoutrements, and a servant to whom he bequeathed 5 marks and his bed *cum floribus deliciarum*, his second horse and all his armour and equipment. The largest library seems to have belonged to John Newton, treasurer of York, who made his will in 1414. His standing can be judged from the fact that Thomas Haxey, the well-known king's clerk, and Richard Norton, Justice, were his executors. He describes himself as one who although *deliciis affluens* was yet bound to seek the face of his Lord. The thought of departing from these delights, the embroidered garments, the plate, the barge upon the Ouse, which he left to St. Mary's Abbey, must have cost him a spasm of pain. His books he left to the dean and chapter of York ('in subsidium et relevamen librarie faciende'). They are a representative collection of bibliographical, patristic, and moralist works containing, beside rare treatises like those of Hugh of St. Victor on the Cloister of the Soul, comparative rarities like the *Hieronianum* of Johannes Andreae the Canonist: the books of John Howden, Richard Hermit (Rolle), Canon Walter Hilton, William Rymyngton, and Hugh (of St. Victor) on the 'Institution of Novices' in one volume; while the Sunday sermons of Holcot the Dominican which he possessed were not likely to be found outside the best theological collections. Newton was modern enough to have Petrarch's *De remediis utriusque fortunae*: his legal literature included Henry Bowyk on the decretals, in two great volumes, Cino of Pistoia on the Codex and Bartolus of Sassoferrato on the New Digest. Other service books, chalices, and vestments he left to his own prebendal churches and to other churches of the treasury, i.e. belonging to the dean and chapter of York. In a codicil he gave directions that the notable collection of canon and civil law books should be deposited in a chest to stand in the vestry (*vestibulum*) of the cathedral with the sole reservation that if any nephew of his took orders and wished to specialize in law, the books were to be handed over to him for his lifetime and after his death to go to his son or nephew,[1] if he satisfied the conditions. Otherwise they were to form part of the library of the dean and chapter: but there were more books than these; Roman law texts, and an abundance

---

[1] *Testamenta Eboracensia*, i. 364 f.

of works in history and literature which were destined for Peter-house, Cambridge.

These were comparatively important testators; the legal service of a dean and chapter, or better still of the archbishop, was, if not a nursery for bishops or keepers of the privy seal, an avenue of promotion, or at least a guarantee of the intellectual respectability of the testator. William Petyr, rector of Patrington (E. Riding), a York prebendary, also a canon of St. Davids, left to one beneficiary his 'long jupe of red medle' of the 'livery of the Lord Archbishop of York', showing that there was a distinctive household dress. The livery of the court of Canter-bury seems unknown, but the interests of its leading jurists have left more record: John Estcourt, dean of St. Martin-le-Grand, examiner-general of the court of Canterbury and commissary-general of Archbishop Chichele, who called his master 'my singular and unique lord, and after God, my most worthy creator'[1] was a lawyer with musical interests, who in his will directed his executors to buy an organ (*unum par organorum*) for the choir of Great St. Martin. His chief friends were John Lyndfield and Thomas Brouns, both archbishop's men, the former dean of the Arches and prolocutor in convocation (1438), the latter Chichele's chancellor, later bishop of Norwich. John Lyndfield, B.C.L., left (1440) the archbishop's college of All Souls his 'best' (*meliores*) books of civil and canon law to the value of £20.[2] Brouns's long and valuable will is in Stafford's register at Lambeth. Today, naturally enough, medicals, architects, producers of plays and spectacles are no longer among the clergy. In their wills, doctors like Master John Parker or Nicholas Colnet, Henry V's physician, have left little trace of their activities. To what extent either surgery or physic were paying professions for the clerk it is difficult to say. The medical staff of Edward III has been investigated by Professor Gask and the collection of doctors enumerated here shows the grants to Londoners of messuages and shops and rents of any-thing up to £20; while in 1349 a grant for life to a king's yeo-man shows that the king's surgeon lived in a house 'by the gate of the palace of Westminster'. The indentures made with doctors, e.g. Thomas Moorstead, on service in the fifteenth century mention (1415) a 40 mark fee, and 20 marks to be

---

[1] *Reg. Chichele*, ii. 373.
[2] Ibid. ii. 577.

distributed as the wages of fifteen persons for a year.[1] The indenture made by Henry V with Nicholas Colnet was very similar to that of Moorstead, but he was to be accompanied by three archers and no other physicians. Parker, mentioned above, was a custodian of St. Mary's, York, who appears to have lived in the parish of St. Martin, Coney Street. He was a regular visitor at the great hospital of St. Leonard in York, had lands in Rawdon and Churt, and rode upon his duties armed as it was necessary for a doctor to be.[2] Colnet had various prebends, he maintained three servants and a chaplain. He left to Stephen Payne, dean of Exeter, a silver covered cup and a 'ewer which I had as a gift from the duke of Orléans', possibly for attending upon him. One medical book, the *Lilium Medicinae*, is mentioned among his bequests. The architects are represented by the chaplain Thomas de Malton, possibly a son of the mason, William de Malton, who supervised the completion of the nave of Beverley Minster,[3] whose will enumerates the contents of what appears to be a small builder's yard at Cottingham containing 'wainscots, pumice, tiles, a clock with great spindles and iron wheels'. He left most of this tackle to the Austin Canons of Haltemprice (E. Yorkshire); the gift to the rectory of St. Nicholas, Durham, of a chair 'in the shop under my chamber' shows that he was doing business in Durham also. He was evidently an actual craftsman as distinguished from a merely computing or counting clerk like the well-known Simon de Membury, Wykeham's clerk of the works, who left most of his money to the canons and the various *ministri* of the cathedral at Salisbury,[4] or Master John Druell, clerk of the works at All Souls.

The country clergy, especially in areas of great lordship, are found taking an important part in the affairs of their patrons and masters. There is the famous case where the vicar of Paston[5] came into conflict ('the great fray made at the time of Mass') with his parishioners because he carried out the instructions of Agnes Paston. A rector like William Coting of Titchwell was anxious to vindicate his patron's authority when 'in the grey morning three men of my lord of Norfolk with long spears carried off three good horses from John Poleyn one of your farmers at Titchwell', telling him 'to treat with my lord

[1] Thomas Moorstead: George Gask, *Essays in the History of Medicine* (1950), pp. 77–93, 95. [2] *Test. Ebor.* i. 342.
[3] John Harvey, *English Medieval Architects* (1954), p. 176.
[4] *Reg. Chichele*, ii. 260–1. [5] *Paston Letters*, Library ed., iv. 24.

of Norfolk', if he desired redress.[1] The parish priest while loyal
to his patron could also be a local man of business, or even an
advocate acting for his patron or influential friend in cases at
a manor court and reporting whether the tenants were to be
trusted or no. The parson could help his lord by urging the
tenants to pay their farms (i.e. rents), and act very much as a
bailiff. The vicar of Stalham acted as the agent of the Pastons
in his parish and he would write to Margaret Paston giving her
an account of the numbers of her sheep and lambs on her various
estates. A good many of the parish priests drawn from humble
origins and being intimately associated in the daily life and
pursuits of their parishioners had to share and suffer in the
troubles caused by the great. The *Paston Letters* show that even
in church such a parson was not immune from attack, though
on occasion he might be put outside until the ransacking was
over. When the duke of Suffolk's men attacked Helsdon, the
rector was taken outside until the church had been stripped.[2]
There are many bad cases of assaults upon the clergy. None
perhaps worse than the attack upon William Tyrell, rector of
the church of Winchelsea, who was assaulted while reading
the Gospel at Mass. His opponents who beat and wounded him
took away the Book 'that was before him' and the oblations,
and carried them off.

The lawyer and the constitutional historian will regard the
later middle ages as the time that witnessed the greatest extension of corporate and collegiate life known in this country. If it
was that, it was also the period when laymen and clerk alike
found the greatest opportunity to participate in common
worship and to use their legal and administrative gifts in the
service of the Church, most of all in the mother church of the
diocese. Not only in appearance, but constitutionally, a medieval
cathedral was a great ship with many decks or departments.
Modern practice makes one think only of dean and canons,
organist (very important), choir, and vergers: but the pre-
Reformation cathedral maintained a formidable hierarchy of
secular clerks of various descriptions: each residentiary canon
and a number of the non-residents too had a vicar choral to
represent him in choir, and in time the vicars became a corporate body or college capable of holding common property: such
minor colleges were found in most medieval secular cathedrals.

[1] *Paston Letters*, v. 6.   [2] Ibid., v. 206.

Below them came the cantarists who sang, for their chantry foundations, the anniversaries or masses commemorating individuals who had left gifts and bequests to the cathedral. At Salisbury, for instance, the cantarists were subject to the dean and chapter for discipline, and the Dunham Act-book shows that charges against them on the score of incontinence, drunkenness, brawling in the city, and the like were heard in the chapter house before the dean or president and a special chapter of residentiary canons.[1] Below the cantarists came clerks 'of the second form', who sat in the second row of choir stalls beneath the vicars choral and the cantarists, but above the choristers, and whose duties were mainly connected with the cantarists. Below these were other *ministri inferiores*, down to those who performed the more menial tasks. All these groups were ruled by the chapter with its dignitaries, dean, chancellor, archdeacon, treasurer, as the main departmental heads of the cathedral, if we may so call them: and above them, in a very special, delicately adjusted, and frequently contested relationship which varied from cathedral to cathedral, stood the pastor of the mother church of the diocese, the bishop himself.

But the cathedral chapters were only part of the rich corporative life of the later middle ages; in which the secular colleges, or colleges of secular priests, played a most important part. They, of whatever brand they might appear to be, all arose from the purpose of maintaining intercession for the living and the departed. In all of them masses for the departed were offered daily at altars throughout the church. To the majority of them gifts of property in frankalmoign were made on the understanding that the service done for them should be a service of prayer. Religious houses furnished benefactors with letters of confraternity, admitting them to share vicariously in the works of piety and the prayers of the community. Most of these pious foundations were chantries, either temporary or permanent. A chantry is a service endowed by one or more benefactors at an altar of a church or chapel for the comfort of his soul or the souls of persons whom he wished to commemorate. Some of these services had to be kept up for a period of years only, as we can see from wills, in which a specified sum and no more is left; in other cases the services were perpetual, main-

---

[1] Ff. 262–3, cited by K. Edwards, *The English Secular Cathedrals in the Middle Ages* (1949), p. 298.

tained either by the gilds, the chaplain usually being paid out of the gild's funds, most of which were derived from entrance fees and annual subscriptions of the members, or provided for by one or more grants in mortmain, the evidence for these being the royal licenses to alienate property into the dead hand or amortize it. They might be founded in the lifetime of the donor, with the provision that a daily mass be sung for his good estate until masses for his soul were begun after his death. Buildings like the chantry of Bishop Bubwith at Wells, of Beaufort at Winchester or of Humphrey, duke of Gloucester, at St. Albans, and above all the chapel commemorating Richard Beauchamp in St. Mary's, Warwick, constitute a series 'unique in the history of European art'.[1] At one end we have chantries founded by rich patrons, by gilds, or municipalities: but there were other chantries founded by groups of humble villagers, who contributed according to their means, to common stocks of money or cattle or sheep. The fund was capable of maintaining a yearly obit or anniversary. At Ellesmere in Shropshire the service of Our Lady was maintained by annual subscriptions of 4 pence from each married man and 2 pence from each servant taking 5 shillings wages or above: the principle is expressed by Archbishop Zouche of York:

It is befitting to encourage with affectionate sympathy the sincere devotion of those who desire to give of their worldly goods to the increase of divine worship, the multiplication of the number of them who minister in God's holy church, and the establishment of celebrations of masses which are the more profitable to Christ's faithful people unto salvation, inasmuch as in the same the King of Heaven is placated by mystic gifts and remedies for sin are more easily obtained by asking.[2]

During the fourteenth and fifteenth centuries one of the commonest phenomena was the conversion of parish churches into colleges of chantry chaplains. There were precedents such as the conversion of Cotterstock in Northamptonshire (1337) into a college of a provost and twelve chaplains and of Sibthorpe in Nottinghamshire into one of a master and six chaplain fellows. The cure of souls of the parish was vested in the head of the college and the church was appropriated to the college. But there were, of course, extra-parochial colleges found in

---

[1] Joan Evans, *English Art 1307–1461* (1949), p. 181. The whole section on the architecture of chantries should be read.   [2] Reg. Zouche, f. 49ʳ.

chapels built for the purpose in connexion with the cathedral and the other collegiate establishments such as St. George's, Windsor (1348), St. Stephen's at Westminster, and the New College at Leicester. And there were colleges founded *within* a church, as distinguished from the collegiate church itself, e.g. St. William's College at York for chantry priests. Some of the most interesting foundations are comparatively close to Oxford, the Northamptonshire collegiate foundations of St. Peter's, Irthlingborough, completed in the early fifteenth century; Fotheringhay, which received its final form in 1410; and Higham Ferrers in 1425 which included a grammar school and a bedehouse. Fotheringhay[1] was the foundation of the dukes of York: Edmund Langley, duke of York, was the first to form the idea of a grand collegiate church there, and in the lifetime of his father built a large and magnificent shrine at the east end of the old parish church. He did not live to see his intention fulfilled: but his son Edward of Norwich resolved to carry out his father's wish and founded the college in 1411, the six acres of land between the castle and the rectory house being allotted for the purpose: Edward fell at Agincourt and his body was brought back there. The college consisted of a master, twelve chaplains or fellows, eight clerks, and thirteen choristers and was dedicated to the Blessed Virgin Mary and All Souls: the chief duty of the college was to pray for the good estate and for the souls of the king and queen, the prince of Wales, the duke of York, and all the royal family. The endowment charter of Henry IV granted the college a yearly charge of £67. 6s. 8d. from the manors of Newent (Gloucestershire) and Kingston (Herefordshire) belonging to the alien priory of Newent. In August 1415 it received great additional properties, including the castle, town, and manor of Stamford and the town and soke of Grantham in Lincolnshire. Higham Ferrers was founded in 1422.[2] Three acres, parcel of the duchy of Lancaster, were assigned for the site, and dedicated to the Blessed Virgin Mary, St. Thomas of Canterbury, and St. Edward the Confessor. Divine service was to be celebrated daily for the good estate of the king (Henry V) and Queen Katherine and the archbishop during their lifetime and for their souls after death; and also for the souls of the king's father and mother, and the parents of the archbishop. The dean and chapter of the new collegiate

---

[1] *Vict. County Hist.*, Northants, ii. 170.　　　　[2] Ibid. ii. 177.

church of St. Mary, Leicester, were the rectors of the parish church (appropriated to them) and their consent had to be given to any new appointment.

The fifteenth century had a spiritual life of its own: but, with certain exceptions, it was not the life that flourished within the cloister as the great days of monasticism understood it: the voices may be the voices of religious, but their inspiration is not the Rule nor the classic course of learning: it is rather a spirituality free from, and sometimes on the defensive against, a conventual life which had become too much tied to routine and too much bound up with secular government and institutions. Monasticism had survived the frontal attack of Wyclif and the more subtle (because more friendly) castigation of Langland: but it had become affected by what Professor Knowles has called 'that strange paralysis and hardening of the arteries that affected for a time the intellectual life of north-western Europe and was particularly evident in the England of the fifteenth century':[1] whether this was the result of the Black Death or of the eclipse of the papacy in the Great Schism or the strain of the French wars we are not likely to know: but these forces, as Dr. Knowles has observed, certainly tended to lessen the number and impair the quality of the recruits to the religious life. It is noteworthy that after 1350 the new foundations of the monks and canons and friars of all sorts are less than twenty. The remarkable thing is that numbers and quality did not decline more. It would be quite misleading to say that the monks and other religious never made up the fall in numbers caused by the Black Death.

While the reduction of the total population of this country as a result of the first and greatest onslaught of the plague has been estimated at about one-third, and the reduction in the religious orders appears to be nearer a half, the numbers of all the orders rose steadily after the first shock to c. 1422, the increase being a quarter to a third over the post-Death low-water level. The rise in many cases continued more slowly until 1500, except for the Austin canons who barely held to their 1400 figure. It has been estimated that at the end of the reign of Henry VII there were probably more religious in the country than at any

[1] M. D. Knowles and R. N. Hadcock, *Medieval Religious Houses: England and Wales* (1953), p. 48.

time since 1348, the total, over 12,000, being an increase
of some 50 per cent. over the post-Death total of 8,000. The
total is almost equal to that of the older orders before the coming
of the friars. Of these, the Black Monks or Benedictines had by
far the largest houses throughout the middle ages. If the average
size of the fifty largest Benedictine abbeys and priories was
about fifty in the second half of the twelfth century, it was about
thirty in 1516. Evesham, for example, had 67 in 1086, 38 in
1416,[1] and 33 at the Dissolution. The largest recorded number
for a Benedictine abbey, 150 for Christ Church, Canterbury,
was in 1150; but Gloucester, St. Albans, and Reading all
reached 100 during the course of the twelfth century. In *c.* 1500
Christ Church was still the largest house, with seventy monks:
Bury had 60, St. Albans 57, Gloucester 50, Westminster 46,
Ely 42, Reading 40. These are the more distinguished places,
where the monks tended to live not unlike university dons and
in many cases had their own servants. On the other hand, there
were notable losses even in the larger houses: the priory of
St. Swithin's, Winchester, had in 1387 46 monks, a number
about which William of Wykeham was much disturbed. In
1404 the number had fallen to 42; in 1495 to 39, and on
the eve of the Dissolution it was 43. *Per contra*, at Worcester
the fall was not nearly so considerable; and at Durham the
teaching of the novices, usually six, was continued, in preparation for Oxford, until the end of the century, which shows that
the supply of younger monks for the order was not failing,
whereas at St. Albans, during Abbot Whethamstede's period,
it was noted that there had been no grammar master for some
years, and it was necessary to get one appointed. To generalize
is most difficult: on the whole the principle 'To him that hath
shall be given' applied to the larger Benedictine centres, though
not necessarily to the smaller.

The ship of the Black Monks rode upon an even keel; it was
not so with the Cistercians who had suffered greatly from the
Schism. Urban VI set out to defeat the dependence of the
seventy English abbeys upon the general chapter at Cîteaux
and a provincial chapter was devised before 1381: but the
electing body of this chapter came in for much criticism, and it
is to the existence and activity of this small and not very experienced electing body that a good many of the serious disputes

[1] *Chron. Abbatiae de Evesham* (R.S.), p. 310.

among the English Cistercians have been traced.[1] At the end of the fourteenth century and in the first two decades of the fifteenth there were fierce election disputes which had to be referred to the general chapter, ultimately to be transferred on occasion to the general chapter abroad. At Meaux (1396–9) and Beaulieu the cause of religion was nearly ruined by the disputes of rival abbots-elect: at Beaulieu it was discovered in 1399 that one of the contending parties had kept himself in power there by gifts to lay lords and by bribing the royal foresters of the New Forest, and by selling the timber as well as the goods of the abbey on a large scale. The worst of these offences was the contentious election at Fountains (1410–16) when for six years the issue between the contending parties was in doubt, with the plea and counter plea that one or the other competitor was intruded by the secular arm and that force was being employed. The final *diffinitio* of the chapter general in 1416 was based on the discovery that the original account of the election received by it in 1410 suppressed the true facts of the election and was misleading.[2] Had full and final authority been invested in an English chapter whose findings were universally accepted, the case might have been different: but the Schism had made this impossible, and one of the competitors knew that he could take his case both to John XXIII and then to the council of Constance acting with the jurisdiction of the Roman curia and upset the verdict of the original commission which reported on the case. The Cistercians seem to have been slower to act than the white canons of Prémontré, for in their case the abbot of Welbeck obtained letters from Urban VI giving him power to act as the abbot of Prémontré, powers of confirming elections, of appointing visitors, and confirming elections.

In seriousness and in devotion to the religious life a small order, the Carthusians, was uppermost at the end of the middle ages. There were seven English charterhouses in all. Three had been founded between 1170 and 1370: but four more were now to arise, a testimony to the original spirit of utter austerity and seclusion which the order maintained. The last of these was Henry V's own foundation at Sheen, and it testified to the regard paid to the silent contemplative, now gathered with

[1] Especially by Knowles, *The Religious Orders in England*, ii. 169.
[2] Jacob, 'The Disputed Election at Fountains Abbey, 1410–1416', *Medieval Studies presented to Rose Graham* (1950), p. 84.

others of his kind into a community far removed from the hearty country intercourse of orders like the Austin canons. Miss Thompson has drawn attention to the works of devotion which were found in their libraries: copies of Richard Rolle's writings, the *Cloud of Unknowing*, Walter Hilton's *Ladder of Perfection*, as well as the writings of St. Catherine of Siena and St. Bridget of Sweden.[1] The quiet and the atmosphere of the charterhouses continued to draw people from the city, for it was the London magnate, Sir Walter Mauny, whose intention had been (1349) to establish a college of priests on the lines of the Paris charterhouse. It is, incidentally, very interesting to note the regard paid to the solitary under vows, whether we call him recluse or hermit, in the fifteenth century. There was a reclusorium at Westminster, to which royal or very eminent persons might resort: at Lynn and Norwich there were also recluses of importance; Lynn recalls Margery Kempe's description of the friar-recluse with the Dominicans there, while at Norwich was the black monk Thomas Brackley, a recluse in the Chapel of the Fields. Hinton and Mountgrace were charterhouses which preserved the spirit of the new devotion, where there were new brethren who cultivated the mystical approach to Christ in the cells which they had come, as the author of the *Imitatio* advises, to treat with affection and pride.

Very different from the quietly domiciled religious was the less stabilized friar. He was, by the fifteenth century, a genuine conventual, but his tradition of winning souls wherever he was sent and his astonishing adaptability and knowledge of the world made him essentially a missioner in society. The literary folk and any that thought with Wyclif regarded him as a hard case, to whichever order he might belong. 'A good friar is as rare as the phoenix' (*bonus enim frater rarus est cum fenice*). We hear the bad, the scabrous things about the friars, not the good, and it was because many Franciscans—for they it was who are generally satirized—were clerics of such versatility and intermingled so much in the lives of the bourgeoisie that they laid themselves open to the raillery of the *Prologue* and the *Somnour's Tale*. Yet one has only to examine any large collection of contemporary wills to become aware that bequests to the four, if not the five (to include the Crutched Friar) mendicant orders were the normal disposition of the well-to-do testator,

[1] E. M. Thompson, *The Carthusian Order in England* (1930), pp. 147 f.

and that whatever poets and poetasters might write, the intercession of the orders for the souls of the departed was particularly sought after. Thus John Woodhouse of Kimberley, Norfolk, Chancellor of the duchy of Lancaster from 1413 to 1424 and a member of the royal household under Henry IV and Henry V, when providing for six days' exequies in the prior of Holy Trinity, Norwich, directed that on the first night the Carmelites of Norwich were to officiate, and that for the three following days the services were to be taken by each of the other mendicant orders in the city: not till the fifth day were the secular clergy of the city asked to come in.[1] The Carmelites had always been strong in East Anglia; the convent at Norwich was a distinguished one, providing scholarship with men like John Baconthorpe, the two Bales (Robert and the Bishop), John Torpe (d. 1440),[2] Henry Wichingham,[3] and John Kenyngale.[4] The order itself sent a copious stream of theological students to the universities, and acted as the spearhead of the attack on Wyclif: at the end of the fourteenth century Carmelites began to take the place of the Dominicans as royal confessors, and it was one who thus acted towards Henry V, Thomas Netter of Walden, pupil at Oxford of William Beaufeu the Franciscan,[5] who produced the standard work of apologetic against Lollardy, the *Doctrinale fidei catholicae*, and took part in the events earlier described in this book. Netter who was prior provincial of the Carmelites was early befriended by Stephen Patrington, one of the more distinguished Cambridge Carmelites, who was confessor to Henry V and became bishop of Chichester. His surviving letters[6] are of some interest, for while he is clearly the main advocate with the king against Lollardy, he also reveals himself as a moderate and cautious man, forbidding, for instance, his religious to discuss controversial topics such as the Immaculate Conception or the need for absolute poverty, or the historical traditions of the beginnings of the Carmelite order or of the Austin hermits. He also took his share in the compilation of the

---

[1] *Reg. Chichele*, ii. 437. He was King's Chamberlain of the Exchequer, 1415–31.
[2] Bale, *Scriptorum illustrium maioris Brytannie . . . catalogus* (1559), p. 579.
[3] Ibid., p. 585: A. B. Emden, *A Biographical Register of the University of Oxford*, iii. 2045.   [4] Emden, ii. 1035.
[5] Not William Wodeford. The correction is given in Emden, ii. 1343.
[6] B. Zimmermann, *Monumenta historica Carmelitana*, i (1905), 1448–64; Knowles, op. cit. ii. 146.

very heterogeneous collection of documents, the *Fascicul. zizaniorum*. The task of Catholic defence was falling into the hands of the four orders. Netter himself was present when John Badby was tried at St. Paul's, as well as at the trial of Sir John Oldcastle. Chichele used the orders in the more complicated trials for Lollardy in Convocation. At the examination of Master William Taylor (1423) at which Thomas Netter was present, two friars from each of the four orders, save the Carmelites which had three, acted as assessors to examine articles extracted from the Oxford principal's writings.[1] Yet the orders were not always models of orthodoxy, for Fr. Thomas Winchelsey, one of the assessors at the Taylor trial, was made to answer by convocation to the charge of receiving back, at the London Franciscan convent, a heretical minorite, William Russell, who had maintained publicly that the payment of personal tithes to clerks with cure of souls was not enjoined by the divine law and that they might be applied to works of piety and mercy instead. The Franciscans and the London convent in particular were interested in the issue, for the minorites had to live on alms and could not claim the type of subvention paid to rectors of parish churches. Russell actually got as far as breaking his imprisonment and taking his case to Rome, but there he got no satisfaction from Cardinal Branda, the papal judge and commissary, whose sentence he disobeyed to return to his old haunts. The emphatic condemnation by both universities of such dangerous doctrine was characteristically expressed: Oxford sent a flowery letter to the Convocation of Canterbury, expressing its indignation and sorrow that such a plan could be conceived; Cambridge, avoiding such fustian, produced a more solid condemnation supported by biblical and patristic texts.[2]

As the century moved on, people were used to hearing attacks upon the wealth of the possessioned religious and had come to see that the mendicants, while technically poor, were adding to their convents and building up a strong corporate position which Lollard attacks could not weaken. To Lollardy in the mid-fifteenth century the reply of the English Church was not to produce more and sounder theology, after the manner of the Carmelite Netter, nor to argue the case out along philosophical lines as Reynold Pecock tried to do, but to increase the

---

[1] *Reg. Chichele*, iii. 169–70.   [2] Ibid. iii. 131–3, 134–8.

motional and artistic appeal of the churches, to encourage books
of piety, and generally to fan the flame of faith. For this the
sermon was the readiest method; and the absence of good
sermons was what most of all distressed the chancellor of
Oxford, Dr. Thomas Gascoigne, who in his *Dictionarium theo-
logicum* constantly lamented his own failure to preach and
attacked those who did not consider that preaching was the duty
of prelates.[1] It was for this reason that he found the attendance
of bishops at the court and the formation of a clique of such
attenders a matter of serious complaint: and it was the reason
why at Oxford preaching was insisted on in the statutes for all
who had incepted in arts and for the great importance given
there and at Cambridge to the *ars praedicandi*. It was not the
anecdotal sermon of the 'popular' mendicant preachers which
Gascoigne saw to be necessary, but solid and carefully argued
discourses by way of exposition which the intelligent laity might
hear and understand. For that reason the homiletic work of the
Dominicans was specially regarded with favour, particularly
in the towns, and the vogue of Bromyard's *Summa praedicantium*,
to judge by the place it held in English libraries, testifies to
warm appreciation of the homilist's art.

The mendicants lay outside the scope of diocesan supervision like the larger exempt abbeys, the Carthusians and the
Cistercians, along with the Premonstratensians. The evidence
for the state of the religious houses is mainly based on three
series of episcopal visitations: those of the diocese of Norwich,
1492–1532, edited by Dr. Jessop; Bishop Redman's visitation
of the English Premonstratensian houses, covering the last
quarter of the fifteenth century (Redman was the appointed
official visitor of the order in England); and the visitations of
three bishops of Lincoln, Fleming (1420–1), Gray (1431–6),
and Alnwick (1436–50), edited by Professor Hamilton Thompson. Of these the Lincoln visitations are the most exhaustive as
well as the most illuminating for the light thrown upon the
internal life and economy of the houses with which they deal.
A certain amount of material is available for the exempt
monasteries, whether Benedictine or Cluniac. But before discussing the latter, as well as the alien houses, some observations
should be first interposed.

Cluny, in contrast with Cîteaux, was a monarchical system,

[1] *Loci e libro veritatum*, ed. Thorold Rogers (1881), pp. 30–31, 179 f.

with houses dependent upon the mother-houses of the order in France. When the papal schism reached its penultimate stage with the election of Alexander V in 1409 it was not possible to revert to the earlier relationship. National feeling against French superiors had been accentuated by the French wars and some French Benedictine monasteries had sold their English possessions. The abbots of Cluny aimed at recovering all the rights which they had lost during the wars and the schism. The history of the English houses in the fifteenth century is a record of their efforts to shake off the control of the French mother houses, and of the special privileges which they secured. Thus in 1399 Bermondsey had been created an abbey by Pope Boniface IX at the request of Richard II, and by the same bull the monks obtained the right of electing their abbot after applying to the king as patron for the usual *congé d'élire*. The prior of La Charité thus lost the right to nominate or confirm the head of the monastery. Thetford had secured a papal bull granting freedom of election before 1376 and Boniface confirmed the privilege in 1399. St. Andrew's, Northampton secured freedom of election in a denization charter of 1405, and Montacute Priory by a special charter from Henry V in 1417. Meanwhile a small number of priories, not necessarily under Cluny, had passed permanently into lay hands: but the general view of the Church was that foundations made for prayer and for the souls of benefactors should not be alienated, and such of the priories as were sold passed to ecclesiastical bodies like the two St. Mary Winton colleges or the royal chapel of St. George's, Windsor. When Henry IV came to the throne he restored unsold but confiscated alien lands to their owners and appointments were made to a large number of priories: but the commons were not prepared for the *status ante bellum* to be restored and petitioned for the seizure which came about in 1402, the funds accruing to be diverted to the Exchequer. A rather similar situation came about in 1414, when it was feared that alien priories might be restored again to their owners. An act of 1414 provided for the expulsions of foreign religious, with the retention of their possessions hitherto confiscated in the king's hand. It was this act which finally suppressed the alien priories: it must not be imagined, however, that these were uniformly small houses or cells of foreign houses: many were granges or farms in the possession of aliens. Bec, for nstance, had priories of its own such as Stoke-by-Clare in Suffolk, St. Neots (Huntingdonshire), and Ogbourne; but Ogbourne was the centre of an estate system with an extensive number of manors, organized for agricultural production,[1] and Bec counted some forty manors in the southern half of England. Alien lands thus provided a valuable endowment for the colleges and chantry foundations which were coming into existence during the fifteenth century. The Grandmontine house of Alberbury, for instance, which was confiscated in 1414 was granted as part of their endowments to the warden and fellows of All Souls College in 1441,[2] and the same college received the small priories of St. Clere and Llangenith in Gower during the course of that year. It is scarcely necessary to say that such treatment of land belonging to the Church, which nobody at the time regarded as exceptional, may have served later as a precedent for the greater confiscations of the sixteenth century.

We can now return to the problem of the visitation evidence. Conscientious bishops like Alnwick and Gray carried out their visitations with great thoroughness, examining each member of the house and the matters revealed to the bishop by individuals as well as those which he himself discovered were carefully recorded in preparation for the immediate instructions which the bishop issued and, where need existed, for the written injunctions that formed part of the statutes of the house. The problem in dealing with this evidence lies in its highly confidential character, as well as in the question of what had happened at the house after the bishop's mandate for visitation arrived. When Alnwick came to Thornton in 1440 the succentor revealed the situation there:

He says that, since my lord's mandate was received, a discussion was held in Chapter amongst them all concerning defaults that should be reformed among them before my lord's coming; and when some of them joined in complaining of certain things that ought to be reformed, they were immediately met by the others with such terrible retorts that the abbot said, clasping his hands: 'Woe to me. What shall I do? I am undone.' and, had he not been hindered and kept back by force, he would have gone away from the chapter-house almost like a madman.[3]

[1] Marjorie Morgan, *The English Lands of the Abbey of Bec* (1946).
[2] A.S. College Archives, Alberbury no. 128.
[3] *Visitations of Religious Houses in the Diocese of Lincoln*, ed. A. Hamilton Thompson, iii (1940–7), 376.

It has to be remembered that many of the houses showed
great fluctuations, both morally and economically, so that
generalization is extremely difficult. There were indeed some
houses which had a permanently bad record: in the diocese of
Lincoln, Bardney, Eynsham, and Peterborough were in this
category, and among the Austin canons, Dorchester and
Huntingdon have been described as being in 'chronic trouble'.
The two chief problems lay in the difficulty of getting rid of a
spendthrift or undesirable head, and in the degree to which
religious houses became involved in the secular life of their
areas and in the influence, on the councils of the abbot or prior
of important lay persons. A religious house was an economic
system as well as a retreat from the world, and much of the
evidence given points to the fact that the world was too much
with the monastery, starting with the small accumulation of
private property and ending with the superior and sometimes
the obedientiaries living away from the monastery itself and
with lay persons, often of the undesirable sort, being introduced
into the cloister. The weight of evidence in the Lincoln visitations is not against misdoings in the houses so much as against
the absence of fervour and the inability to keep intact the spirit
of the rule.

Representatives of both secular and religious clergy were
joined together in the provincial council or convocation. Not
all assemblies were recorded in the archbishop's registers, but
the records of a considerable number survive. The provincial
assembly was summoned either on the archbishop's initiative
or on the royal instructions; normally it was the latter and the
archbishop in summoning his diocesans cites the king's writ.
The summons went to the dean of the province, in the case of
Canterbury, the bishop of London or his vicar-general. It went
to all bishops who were the essential element of the provincial
council: 'Others', said Lyndwood, 'will be summoned who
have a necessary part in the business or whose council is essential'.[2] The others who were normally summoned were the deans
and priors of cathedral churches and their chapters, arch-
deacons, abbots, and conventual priors 'and other prelates of

---

[1] Knowles, op. cit., p. 211.
[2] *Provinciale* (1679), iii. 9, p. 154, v. *provinciali Concilio*.

churches exempt and not exempt and clergy of each diocese, convents and chapters each by one proctor'. But the summons might be varied on occasion to include distinguished graduates. In the autumn convocation of 1417 when the question of promoting graduates was first discussed the cathedral chapters were told to send 'one or two canons or monks . . . sufficiently lettered, provident or discreet, one of them, at least, in the case of canons, being a residentiary'. It was Chichele's aim to bring the graduates into convocation particularly when questions of heresy were being discussed.

The normal agenda was that the first day was set aside for the reception of proxies and on the second at a meeting of both houses' the archbishop generally expounded the cause for meeting. Convocation then proceeded to business and if taxation was on the agenda, a delegation from the king's council usually appeared. For the discussion of matters with which they were particularly concerned the bishops and the clergy met separately. In Chichele's time the undercroft of the chapter house in St. Paul's was the place where the clergy usually held their discussions. The clergy did not withdraw to its own 'house' automatically. It was done at the requirement of the archbishop. But the habit of separate discussion was growing through the century and the first fifty years saw the prolocutor of the clergy develop into practically a standing official of convocation. He tended to be, in the southern province, the official of the court of Canterbury, but for the purpose of framing and discussing constitutions the two houses met together after drafting bodies had done their work. It would, of course, be impossible for the whole body to discuss the wording of a constitution for keeping the festival of St. Frideswide (19 Oct. 1434),[1] where the liturgiologists and the canon lawyers had to combine. Indeed the habit of committees was growing throughout the century Such committees were appointed to discuss the arrangements desired for the promotion of university graduates (1417 and 1421–2) and for the discussion of a difficult matter like the attitude of convocation towards the papal dissolution of the council of Basel.

It should be emphasized that both in their constitutions and in the putting forward of *gravamina* to parliament the clergy acted on their own without permission from higher authority.

[1] *Reg. Chichele*, iii. 256.

For *Ecclesia anglicana* the convocations were supreme law-making bodies, however much ecclesiastical business which verged too near civil might be stopped in the courts by the writs of prohibition. In making its constitutions the Church was unhampered by the state.[1]

---

[1] For the financial business of Convocation, see below, Ch. IX, pp. 421-3.

VIII

(a) THE KING AND THE GENTLE FOLK (*GENEROSI*)

BEFORE faction reaches its height and we study the φλεγμαί-νουσα πόλις, the state inflamed, the foundations of lay society in the fifteenth century must be briefly explored. No summary account of them could be adequate, but even the briefest can act as a corrective. In a period of faction and tension the historian is liable to read too much into political events and be impatient with the slower-moving rhythm of the country-side, with the local relationships, both in law and in fact, which constitute so much of ordinary life.

Impatient also, perhaps, with the mentality of the age when it considered problems of government and order: with the conservative nature of thought about the state and the obliga-tions of the subject. One cannot expect works of constitutional theory in 1400. The nearest approach is to see the prince against the background of law, human or divine. His actions are judged by their conformity to English law and custom, to what is considered morally right or, in matters ecclesiastical, to the common law of the western Church. English speculation about government and society in the fifteenth century was less political than moral and dogmatic. The study of man and his duties in the community, his moral nature and his rights was, with a few exceptions, left to the homilist or to the regents in the universities, where a handful of teachers in the faculties of arts and theology considered questions about the moral excel-lence of a citizen mainly as a branch of theology or in relation to the obligations of the classes or grades in society. Richard Ullerston (d. 1423), canon of Salisbury and former chancellor of Oxford, when dedicating (*c.* 1404–8) his treatise *De officio militari* to Prince Henry of Monmouth,[1] was concerned with the spiritual and moral requirements of a knight's office: the virtues which a knight should possess and the vices he should avoid; and as he wrote for a future king, a large proportion of the

---

[1] MS. Trinity College, Cambridge, 359, ff. 16ᵛ–22ʳ; MS. Corpus Christi College, Oxford, 177, ff. 179ᵛ–184ʳ.

work was devoted to expounding the virtues and duties belonging to such a prince. Not unlike Ullerston's exhortations were the precepts given in a work which achieved wide popularity in the fifteenth century: the *Livre des bonnes meurs* by the Austin friar of Paris, Jacques Le Grand (Jacobus Magnus), which is the French version of chapters 6–10 of his own *Sophilogium*,[1] a moral treatise on the Vices and the Virtues and their social implications, with abundant examples from biblical and from Greek and Roman history. This work, written 1405–10, the friar presented in a naïve and engaging form in the *Livre* which was translated into English as 'the Booke of good condicions, otherwise called the Sophiloge of Wysdom' (manuscript in Campbell Library, Beaumont College)[2] and printed, in another translation, as 'The Book of Good Maners', by Caxton,[3] Pynson,[4] and Wynkyn de Worde.[5] In this the moral attributes of a good prince are emphasized: the prince must be able to forgive; for, as Seneca says, there is 'no thynge more necessarye than for to be piteous and enclined to mercy'; princes ought, as Solinus advises, to be 'meure [grave, modest] sage and of ryght good lyfe'; they must avoid covetousness and avarice:

And therfor sayth Saluste that Rome shall but lytell endure, for covetyse wasteth all and lecherye brenneth all. Moreover Orace sayth in one of his dytess [poems] that a prynce evyll mannered causeth the countre for to perysshe.

The moral and controlled prince ought to be 'as a stomake whiche dystrybuteth the mete that it receyueth to all the members and reteyneth no thynge to hym selfe but only the nouryssynge. . . '. The greatest recommendation of the prince is that he is prepared to do justice, his foremost obligation; and the author repeats a story of Helinandus of Froidmont about an old prince who, asked by his council to retire in favour of his son, declined 'that his sone shoulde have it to his prouffyte, but a man that wolde do justyce'. Yet the greatest magistrate must not glory in his power: princes must be 'soft,

---

[1] For MSS. and full discussion, cf. A. Coville, *De Jacobi magni vita et operibus* (Paris, 1889), pp. 50–96.

[2] Identified by Mr. M. F. Bond in 1953; and briefly described by him in *Berkshire Archaeological Journal*, liv (1954–5), 54.

[3] The translation is by the publisher, 1486–7.

[4] Caxton's translation. Dated 30 Sept. 1494. The citations below are from this text.   [5] Undated, probably 1498.

meke and debonnaire', with proper humility before their heavy task:

If prynces consyder well their estate, they shall fynde that theyr seygnoryes conteynen more trouble and thought than plesaunce or deduyt [delight].

They ought to follow the example of Julius Caesar of whom 'we rede in the book of Fyccyons phylosophyke how he was moche humble in spekynge to his knyhtes and servauntes and as redy to serve them as he was to receyue theyr servyce'. He must not 'set by hymseuf' or think that everybody ought to serve him, for much pride 'maketh a prynce lyke a beest and to forgete his condicioun and his byrthe'. To sustain this character he must live chastely and not be 'vanquished' by women; must not fill his days with dice-playing, but with 'honest plays no man ought to reprove'. Princes, therefore, should 'exercise and accustom them in feates of armes'; their knights should not prefer private pleasures to the 'payne of chivalry':

I suppose if a serche sholde be made how many knyghtes that knowe theyr horses wel and theyr horses them, and haue their harneis and abylmentes of warre redy, I trowe ther sholde not manye be founden without lacke of such as they ought to have.

They must keep their oaths to their lords; they must maintain the Church: and they must not only rely on their bodily strength, but 'ought to be wyse and subtyll and byleue good counseyll'.

Neither in these ingenuous musings nor in Ullerston's treatise is there any hard core of instruction in duty or in the administration of justice; in Ullerston's there is plenty of moral exhortation based on Aristotle for the conduct or the life of a knight who is to be *perfecte virtuosus* and virtue includes the nine conditions Aristotle was held to have laid down as essential for the prince displaying 'epikeia' (i.e. *epieikeia*), justice with moderation: virtues which he must apply not merely to himself but to the conduct of his own household. But if the doctrine of *epikeia* came mainly from conciliar writers abroad (Gerson is addicted to the term), nearer home there had been a much greater challenge. It was the challenge of the Renaissance. Richard II's use of the terms 'liberty', 'will', and 'grace' had caught people's imagination and after a long period of conciliar government had made men speculate about the way in which the royal power ought to use them. The term the king's 'estate' seemed to sum up the attributes of kingship within which these assertions of the mind and spirit were exercised. A good example came in 1399 in the articles against Richard II, when it was stated that Richard had said that he understood the *libertas* of his predecessors to mean that he could turn the laws to his own will. Notwithstanding that, the commons later declared that they wished Henry IV to be 'in as great royal liberty as all his noble progenitors were before him'.[1] To this wish Henry IV with medieval wisdom replied that it was not his intention or his will to turn the laws, statutes, or good usages, nor to take advantage of the grant of such a liberty, but only to keep (*garder*) the ancient laws and statutes ordained and used in the time of his noble progenitors and to do right to all men in mercy and truth according to his oath. The king had liberty in order that he might keep the laws and do justice. As it has been observed: 'the king had a discretionary power but his discretion was to be used not for his personal purposes but in the interests of law and justice'.[2] This liberty had to be willed. The king wills that the liberties of the whole Church and the liberties and franchises of lords, cities, and boroughs should be maintained. It was the king's liberty of will that maintained the liberties of others. The king also has grace: grace enables him to accept novelties and innovations so that English custom may remain inviolate and yet new things can be done.[3]

What gives English thought its special character and sometimes its peculiar incoherence is that while people are in a vague sense aware of the problem of harmonizing the customary structure of English law and institutions with the executive needs of monarchy, they try to express their awareness in contemporary terms borrowed often from other subjects and categories. Thus the kingdom is sometimes represented as a piece of property which belongs to the king. The kingship is spoken of as real property: fines made with the king, the amercements inflicted by the justices are the profits of the king's court: so also, in another instance, are taxes levied in the highest court of all, his parliament. At the same time there is extreme

[1] *Rot. Parl.* iii. 434.

[2] S. B. Chrimes, *English Constitutional Ideas in the Fifteenth Century* (1936), p. 9.

[3] Chrimes, loc. cit. The *gratia regis* is inherent in the king's prerogative. His use of it is discussed in the Introduction of Professor G. O. Sayles to his *Select Cases in the Court of King's Bench under Edward III* (Selden Soc.), v. lxxx–xci.

constitutionalism: the king will say that he cannot change a statute without the assent of the estates: he promises not to persecute the Speaker if that voice of his commons says things unpleasant to the royal ear; and in many quarters, not least in the inns of court, there is a strong adherence to the traditional views of nature and the law of nature, particularly as St. Thomas had interpreted it. The harmonizing is not always complete: yet it is looked for, even struggled for.

The survival and importance of the concept of natural law which is natural reason applied where considerations of equity are involved, can be seen in the work of Sir John Fortescue, by no means one of the greatest English thinkers, but one of the more significant English minds of the fifteenth century. If there was much in his writings which seems to run counter to contemporary fact and if some of them (e.g. the *Governance of England*) fail to achieve what they set out to do, it is still impossible to disregard such a contemporary; for he is the man whose contradictions and incoherences result from this attempt to harmonize. A few words about him may not be a digression.[1]

Fortescue was the second son of Sir John Fortescue of Winston in south Devonshire who was one of Henry V's knights at Agincourt and became governor of the fortress of Meaux in La Brie. He was a member of Lincoln's Inn before 1420 and he rose to be three times governor and was official treasurer in 1437. Before that date he had been elected member of parliament for Tavistock (1421, 1423, 1425), Totnes (1426, 1432), Plympton (1429), and Wiltshire (1437). He was made a sergeant-at-law in 1430 and had a remarkable judicial career. He was justice of the peace 35 times in 17 counties or boroughs at different dates, and in the course of 25 years he was to receive no fewer than 70 commissions of *oyer* and *terminer*, of assize, of gaol delivery, or special inquisition. He was made chief justice of the King's Bench on 20 January 1442 and was knighted shortly afterwards, and although he was constant in his judicial functions he became, as was natural with a justice of his ability, drawn into politics. He spoke for the justices when consulted in the trial of the duke of Suffolk in 1450 and in Thorpe's case in 1454. His last appearance in the year-books is in the early part of 1460.

[1] A chronology of his life and biographical details are given in Professor Chrimes's edition of the *De laudibus legum Anglie* (1942), pp. lx f.

In November 1461 he was attainted by parliament and had to go north with the royal party accompanying Henry VI to Edinburgh—a period in which he describes himself as 'the King's chief counsellor', and possibly it was at this time that he composed his treatise *De natura legis Naturae*. He brought Queen Margaret and Prince Edward over to France from Scotland and remained with the prince in the castle of Kœur near St. Mihiel (Bar) for seven years, with occasional visits to Paris and Angers. It was here in exile that he wrote his work *De laudibus legum Angliae*, a notable achievement of faith in English institutions by an exile. Fortescue took a leading part in the negotiations that resulted in the alliance of Queen Margaret and the earl of Warwick, but neither he nor the queen was summoned to England immediately and his advice at this juncture was confined to paper whether in the Memorandum printed by Dr. Plummer, or in his more lengthy treatise, *The Governance of England*. At any rate, Margaret, the prince, and Fortescue arrived at Weymouth on the same day as Warwick was slain and Henry VI was captured at Barnet (14 April 1471). Fortescue himself was taken prisoner at the battle that was to seal the fate of the house of Lancaster at Tewkesbury on 4 May 1471. Fortescue's life was spared but the attainder was not reversed nor were his estates restored to him until he had written in favour of Edward IV's title and had refuted his own arguments against it. From the time of his release (he had been pardoned by October 1471) he seems to have lived at his manor of Ebrington in Gloucestershire where he died between 1477 and 1479.

Fortescue is a significant figure because he shows how a purely secular lawyer could acquire at the inns of court a great deal of the theoretical training which might be expected from a clerk. In the *De laudibus legum Angliae* the chancellor who is addressing the prince, his pupil, shows why the laws of England are not taught in the university.[1] It was a matter of language. Pleadings in the law courts, the chancellor says, are all in French and very many statutes of the realm are written in French. But they are also learned in English and in Latin, the language of many of the statutes themselves. Thus 'since the laws of England are learned in these three languages they could not be conveniently learned or studied in the Universities

[1] C. xlviii: *De laudibus legum Anglie*, ed. S. B. Chrimes, pp. 114 f.

where the Latin language alone is used. But those laws are
taught and learned in a certain public academy (*in quodam
studio pupplico*)' and that academy situated between the site of
the law courts and the City of London is not located in a place
'where the tumult of the crowd could disturb the students'
quiet', but a little isolated in a suburb of the city. Fortescue
gives a most interesting account of the inns of court and of the
great expense (which he fully upholds) involved in the course,
one which poor and common people cannot bear: it costs the
student at least £13. 6s. 8d. a year to live in one of the greater
inns. 'Hence it comes about that there is scarcely a man learned
in the laws to be found in the realm who is not noble or sprung
of noble lineage.' It is an aristocratic society whose members
'do not only give themselves to the study of legal science but at
festivals to the reading of Holy Scripture and of Chronicles'.
Fortescue says that instead of the degrees of Bachelor and
Doctor in Law the inns confer a certain estate not less eminent
or solemn than the degree of doctor which is called a degree of
sergeant-at-law.[1] It is clear that not merely proficiency in the
law but some knowledge of more academic forms of jurisprudence was required from students at the inns, and Fortescue's
own quotations from the canon and the civil law show that he
had acquired much of the technique of the civilian and the
canonist; it satisfied his academic *snobisme*.

The passage in his *De natura legis Naturae* in which he points
out the relation between law natural and law positive (*jus regis*)
make it clear that the legal student of the fifteenth century did
not go to Westminster straight from the grammar master but
began in his inn with the scholastic philosophy of the canon
law. The *Dialogues between a Doctor of Divinity and a Student of the
Laws of England* by Christopher St. Germain published between
1523 and 1530 show, for example, that the law student of the
later middle ages took his background of general notions from
Gerson's *Regulae Morales* (especially for the exposition of equity
or *epikeia* there set forth). The Doctor in St. Germain's dialogue
starts with a summary of the teaching of the eternal law, the
basis of the order in the universe, and then passes to an exposition of law natural. All this is what one might expect. The
common lawyers of the fifteenth century had to be prepared to
defend their position against the encroachments of the chancery,

[1] Cc. xlix, l: ed. cit., pp. 116–20.

to know the basis of their opponents' arguments. It should not be imagined that all the pleaders dealt with in the year-books had this scholastic grounding, but a substantial propor-tion of them would with some further training have been quite prepared to meet the academic clerical lawyer, the bachelor of both laws, on his own ground; and the universities were turning out an increasing number of these. It is natural then that Fortescue in treating of the law of nature must consider what to do if there is any serious discrepancy between natural law and royal law (*jus regis*). Such a discrepancy might very easily exist when the claim to the succession to the crown of Eng-land was put forward by a man who based his possession on a claim of valid descent rather than of reason, established by the facts.

That is the issue in his *De natura legis Naturae*.[1] The question was a practical one. 'A king recognizing no superior has a daughter and a brother; the daughter has a son. The king dies without a son. Does the kingdom descend to the daughter, or to her son, or to the king's brother?' In other words, could the female descendants of Lionel duke of Clarence, possess and, possessing, transmit a valid claim to the throne of England? Were Philippa and Anne Mortimer *coronae capaces*? To the solu-tion of this both theology and philosophy have to be applied, and the law of nature it is which must decide, not the strict law of inheritance.

The law of nature, he says, was the code prevailing until the Mosaic law was granted upon Sinai, a period of 3,644 years, but it remained in operation after the new code had been revealed, and Our Lord Himself confirmed it and enjoined it when He gave the command: 'All things whatsoever ye would that men should do, do ye even so unto them, for this is the law and the prophets.' The canon law expressly declares this to be the law of nature, and Fortescue quotes approvingly the dictum of Aquinas that the law of nature 'is nothing else but the participation of the eternal law in the rational creature'.[2] This law, all the laws of the Old and New Testaments have approved. It is 'natural equity' and under it kingship made its first appearance.

---

[1] Analysed in the writer's *Essays in the Conciliar Epoch* (1953), ch. vi.

[2] The great *Questiones* on natural law are in *Summa theologica*, II. i (prima Secun-dae), xc et seqq. especially xci, articles 1 and 2.

Having, therefore, first described the law of nature in general Fortescue applies it to the present case. He makes the three parties, the late king's daughter, her son, and the king's brother come and plead before *Justitia*. After a number of arguments *Justitia* sums up: in the nature of the universe the woman is subject to the man. In the state of innocence the first man had priority over the woman by reason of the virtues with which he was able to direct and teach her. These virtues are the moral virtues, prudence, bravery, temperance. The superiority of the man over the woman is like that of the soul over the body, the superior part of the reason over the inferior. The judge then gives the verdict in favour of the king's brother. Then comes a conclusion of which Bracton might not have approved. Owing to the government of the kingdom being suspended while such debates are continuing, and lacking a defender, the situation is likely to damage the Church through the disturbance of peace that inevitably accompanies these circumstances. Fortescue, therefore, urges his treatise to go to Rome and submit to the examination of the Pope 'for to him as is mentioned in the previous treatise Moses remits any difficult and arduous judgement that may arise in the courts of men showing that whatever he judges or teaches, according to the law of God all sons of man may teach'.[1] The final resort to Rome is not perhaps what one would have expected of an English justice, but to Fortescue as to a number of the post-glossators law is a multiform system. There is the law of the Church, the Roman law, the appeal to principle whether deep in the eternal mind or apparent to human reason, and there are human positive laws, regulating the practice of the courts. All these alternatives are permissible, though, of course, they are not of the same quality. The law of nature throughout its history has never been capable of being treated as a code to which judges can turn and yet it might be appealed to in the courts and determined in the Chancery where considerations of reason and conscience had frequently to be weighed.

Fortescue's political thought has been termed descriptive rather than analytical. This, if it be so, explains why he is of more interest to the historian pure and simple than to the political philosopher. The *De laudibus* and the *Governance of England* are descriptions of English legal and governmental institutions, the former especially useful for the information it

[1] *Works*, II. lxx. 183.

gives (they will be referred to later) about the council during
the minority of Henry VI or about the inns of court, about the
sheriffs and the executive officials of the country; there are
recommendations for reform, administrative proposals about
the increase of the royal revenue, which must be made to exceed the ordinary charges, by keeping in the royal hands the
greatest possible amount of land: there are proposals for re-
constituting the council by providing a permanent nucleus of
twelve spiritual and twelve temporal men, with additional persons selected by the king and a system of written standing orders
for procedure. Both sets of proposals are made in the interests
of the executive, so as to strengthen the effective power of the
crown in the country. They are not 'constitutional' suggestions.
Interlarded in these books, dragged almost irrelevantly into the
De natura legis Naturae, is the theory for which Fortescue is best
known, the differentiation between the types of *dominium* or
sovereign rule. Fortescue distinguishes between regal dominion
and dominion regal and political (*regale et politicum*). He says
very little about political dominion as such, but a great deal
about the mixed dominion which he calls regal and political.

The essentials of regal domination are that the head rules
according to such laws as he makes himself and the law is in his
own mind. He possesses the realm in hereditary right: the
people cannot legislate without his authority and they are subject to his dignity. He can change the law and impose taxation
without consulting them. Regal domination like this has been
exemplified in the ancient history of Nimrod, Belus, and Ninus;
in part of the history of the Roman empire and in the monarchy
which the Israelites desired. More recently the French kingdom
has given an excellent example of this type. Such a dominion
when under *good* princes was like the kingdom of God. In
political dominion these features were lacking. Here the head
rules according to the laws instituted by the citizens. Under this
régime there could be a plurality of rulers and Fortescue includes under this head Rome under the consuls. The third type
combines the merits of both the regal and the political dominion. Fortescue maintains that in England the two are blended.
In this state the king's power is supreme save in certain spheres
reserved by law and custom, for in England kings do not make
laws or impose subsidies without the consent of the estates (for
Fortescue had sat in the commons for both shire and borough)

and the judges are all bound by their oaths not to give judgement against the laws of the land even if they hear the king's mandate to the contrary. This is political dominion. Now a king reigning *tantum regaliter* would sometimes in practice find it advisable to rule politically, that is, with a rule administered by the council of many, as in the case of the Roman king consulting the senate; likewise the king ruling politically may for some purposes find it desirable to act royally. Fortescue clearly believes in the blending of the two. His definition of political dominion in the *De natura legis Naturae* is that it is *plurium dispensatione regulatum*. In other words, the state is compounded of various parts or communities each regulated by law or custom which the king is bound to respect, though with their approval he may change or vary it.

Both kinds of monarchy, Fortescue thinks, originated under natural law. All the rights of kings (*jura regum*) were ultimately derived not from the prince's authority but from the law of nature. This law not only established the royal dignity but also governed it. Both royal law alone, and royal and political law, are subject to natural law. None the less the two sets of kingly rights originated differently. The regal dominion was established by force, but the political and legal by consent. Of the two, the former was the more ancient. The regal and political came at a later stage when large communities of their own accord decided to unite and form themselves into a body politic establishing one ruler as king. At the time of this incorporation or institution both the king and the people ordained that the kingdom should be ruled by such laws as they would all assent to. In such a union it was necessary to elevate a single person to rule, or any people desiring to erect itself into a kingdom or any other body politic must needs prefer one man into the ruler's place. But the king who was established held his position for the protection of his subjects' laws, bodies, and goods, and his power was authorized by the people for this purpose and for no other. To him, as Fortescue says, this famous *Quod principi placuit, legis habet vigorem* applies, because he has been given power *a populo effluxam*.

It is interesting to speculate whether Fortescue derived this idea of regal and political dominion from contemporary England or from his reading of Aquinas and his continuator Ptolemy of Lucca (the joint authors of the *De regimine principum*) or from

both. In this connexion chapter xiii of the *De laudibus* is particu
larly important. It shows that Fortescue has an earlier sourc
than either St. Thomas or the system, as he knew it, of Lan
castrian England. It lies in the organic theory of the state, th
comparison of the state to the body natural.

The law, indeed, by which a group of men is made into a people
resembles the nerves of the body physical, for, just as the body i
held together by the nerves, so this body mystical is bound togethe
and united into one by the law, which is derived from the wor
ligando, and the members and bones of this body, which signify th
solid basis of truth by which the community is sustained, preserv
their rights through the law, as the body natural does through th
nerves. And just as the head of the body physical is unable to chang
its nerves, or to deny its members proper strength and due nourish
ment of blood, so a king, who is head of the body politic is unable t
change the laws of that body, or to deprive that same people of thei
own substance uninvited or against their wills. You have her
Prince, the form of the institution of the political kingdom.[1]

This is pure John of Salisbury.[2] The differences in the powe
of kings Fortescue derives from the diversity in the setting up c
those dignities which he has mentioned. England blossome
into a dominion regal and political out of Brutus's band c
Trojans 'whom he led out of the territory of Italy and of th
Greeks' and thus Scotland, which at one time was boun
thereto as a duchy, grew into a kingdom political and rega
This does not tell us why the mixed dominion arose, an
Fortescue goes no farther in his quest for origin than to expres
the consensual nature of the act. His early history, needless t
say, is characteristically mythical. For him in the long run it i
partly organic principle and partly the facts of contemporar
society which are responsible for a mixed dominion.

Certainly the facts. The king cannot be isolated from th
other members of his body of state. Described—to chang
the metaphor—by the chancellor, Bishop Russell, in 1483 as th
rocks and the firm ground in a fluctuating sea, the magnat
class and its numerous dependents constituted the governin
element in English society throughout the fifteenth century.
Naturally Russell was referring to the baronage proper, perhap

---

[1] *De laudibus legum Anglie*, C. xiii, p. 30.
[2] *Policraticus*, books v, vi, esp. v. 2: ed. C. C. J. Webb, pp. 282 f.
[3] For his famous sermon, cf. Ch. XIII below, p. 630.

） the actual lords in the council; but the magnates were
social group, with a rare ducal and comital element at the top
nd a great spread of *generosi*, knights, and *armigeri* or esquires
elow. Among these *generosi*, those attached to the king or to
byal or noble households were socially and politically more
mportant than the unattached or unaffiliated element, the
milies living independently upon their ancestral estates in
ne country who often shared the work of the shire on commis-
ons of one sort or another. The author of the *Book of Nurture*,
rritten about 1460 by a former marshal of Duke Humphrey of
iloucester, wrote:

If the king send any messenger to your lord, if he be a knight,
squire, yeoman of the Crown, groom, page or child, receive him
onourably as a baron, knight, squire, yeoman or groom, and so
rth, from the highest degree to the lowest, for a king's groom may
ine with a knight or marshal.
The estate of a knight of blood and wealth is not the same as that
f a single and poor knight.[1]

'he marshal, responsible for the seating, was offering his own
otion of the diplomatic order: yet in fact the families of
nightly rank which often provided members for the shire in the
ommons were a powerful and respected element, capable of
ndependent criticism when drawing up and discussing the
ommon petitions and essential to the work of government.[2]
Many of their members along with the *generosi* around and
elow the magnate nucleus were increasing their position,
dding to their wealth by the gains of war or the profits of
ommerce, building new houses, some not afraid to marry into
urgess families. The parliamentary distinction between lords
nd commons must therefore not obscure the fluidity of this
pper-class element throughout its ranges.

The kingdom of England is curiously compacted of old and
new. The new or 'substitute' feudalism, which now attached a
nan to his lord by indenture and retaining fee, had supplanted
he old tenurial relation: yet land remained the heart of the
ystem and land is the inheritance and reward of those tenants

---

[1] Edith Rickart, *The Babees Book, Medieval Manners for the Young* (1918), p. 73.
'he king's messenger is to be accounted one degree higher than he is.
[2] 'Their existence forbids us to divide that society [parliament] into powerful
arons on the one hand and humble commoners on the other, into leaders among
ne peers and led among the knights': K. B. McFarlane, 'Parliament and "Bastard
eudalism"', *Trans. Roy. Hist. Soc.*, 4th ser., xxvi (1944), 69.

in chief who, owing their liege lord the king *consilium et auxilium*
serve him at the highest deliberative level, that of the grea
council. Though the actual duty of service in the field ha
largely been superseded by money rents and payments of variou
kinds, yet there were still moments as before the battle o
Shrewsbury or in the civil wars when the king can and wil
claim the *servitium debitum* from his tenants in chief, will stil
demand an aid *pour fille marier* as Henry IV did for Philippa
and, going back behind that to Anglo-Saxon times, will pro
claim the ban, as it were, by directing sheriffs to order out th
posse comitatus and by ordaining commissions of array. When a
expedition is planned for Scotland or overseas the obligation
by now extra-legal, is still with the magnate to make with hi
overlord a contract of service, for it is part of the duty of th
lords to maintain the royal estate. Indeed, its maintenance i
axiomatic. In 1477 Thomas Rotherham, preaching in parlia
ment on the text 'The Lord reigns over me and I nothin
lack', showed that the royal majesty was not only right, as if i
were the hand and counsel of God, but was also established fo
the advantage of the kingdom. The magnates are the props o
a monarchy that is both the territorial owner of the land an
the personal wielder of a prerogative which has to be recognize
as high above any subject. When Richard II was made t
renounce the kingdom, he absolved his subjects from thei
oaths of fealty and homage, but also gave up, according to thos
who drafted the parliament roll, the 'royal dignity, majest
and crown' and renounced also 'lordship, power, rule, gover
nance, administration, empire, jurisdiction and the name
honour, regality and highness of king'. This was an attempt t
put into words the high and mysterious position of a king wh
was both a mortal person and the embodiment of undying
regality.

If it was the infrequent occasion of a deposition which con
fronted the lawyers with the problem of saying what was in th
king, of giving expression to his tenurial superiority and hi
moral and legal supremacy, a usurpation brought the subject
of the usurping claimant nearer to the level of their new
master. Even though the duchy of Lancaster was a unit hel
by members of the royal house, it was still a franchise, thougl
the greatest of all the franchises, and in Yorkshire as elsewher
its possessions marched with those of Neville and Percy or thei

dependents. The union of crown and duchy brought valuable new resources of power to the crown, a financial addition, as Mr. Somerville has shown,[1] equal to £14,810 gross, besides no less than thirty castles that served as centres for local administration. To a section, at any rate, of the northern baronage, Henry Bolingbroke's strongest claims to return lay in his determination to be recognized as the rightful owner of the duchy from which he had been unreasonably ousted, and those who accepted the challenge of the crown started from that point of view: he was a successful claimant, more than likely to make good. To the greatest magnate families of the north it was a question during the first weeks of the adventure how far to go in supporting the duke of Lancaster. A clan with great independence and pretensions to vice-regal status in Northumbria, one which bestrode the boundary of the kingdoms to hold Jedburgh and other Scottish lands, might accept the new régime far less easily than a baronial house more recently advanced to power, owing its position to its administrative abilities and its service to John of Gaunt when in command of the eastern and western March, but vulnerable for that very reason, since its representative, John Neville, had suffered impeachment in the Good Parliament (1376) when his own liege lord, Lancaster, was directly attacked. Yet while the adhesion of Ralph Neville to Henry Bolingbroke brought to the Lancastrian standard Cumberland and Westmorland lords like the Cliffords, the Dacres, and the Greystokes, with their dependents, it was the decision of the Percies to sustain Henry IV throughout 1400 and not to let disillusionment get the upper hand that made the effective difference, and allowed the usurper to become established. The great rivals of the Nevilles, the family which had spread from Yorkshire to Alnwick and Warkworth and the Northumbrian littoral, held the key to the position and knew it.

Such calculation was characteristic. At the risk of overcrowding the canvas it may be worth taking some examples, derived mainly from the north, of family policy conducted through personal influence, legal skill, and pressure at the right moment.

More recent arrivals in the baronage than the Percies, the Nevilles were a shrewder and more adaptable family. John Neville of Brancepeth and Raby had shown acute business instinct and exercised careful family diplomacy. By the time of

---

[1] *Duchy of Lancaster*, i. 162.

his death (1388) the Nevilles were well on their way, and b
1425 had won a position of commanding influence. In littl
short of forty years Ralph Neville, the first earl of Westmorland
had succeeded through his enormous family of children i
creating a dynastic network to include many of the nobl
houses of England. Ralph's eldest son, John, died in the lifetim
of his father. He had married Elisabeth, a daughter of Thoma
Holland, earl of Kent, but it was not till 1422 that any advan
tage came of the match: for in that year died Lucy, widow c
the earl of Kent who had been beheaded in the conspiracy c
1400. Her brother-in-law had died in 1408, leaving no mal
heir, and the property descended to the five daughters of Luc
and her heirs, in virtue of which Richard Neville kept a fifth c
the vast estates of the earldom until Ralph, the son of Elisabetl
reached his majority. John's brother, Ralph, married Mary
coheiress of the Baroness Boteler, who died in 1411, and in tha
year the manor of Tirley in Staffordshire and the manors c
Oversley and Merston Boteler in Warwickshire fell to th
Nevilles. Earl Ralph's daughters by his first wife were all mar
ried off to prominent north country landowners: Matilda th
eldest to Peter, Lord Mauley (d. 1414), previously a ward c
Thomas Percy, earl of Worcester; two others to young lords c
whom Ralph had had custody and wardship; Philippa t
Thomas Dacre of Gillisland and Anne to Sir Gilbert Umfra
ville, lord of Kyme. Dacre held an important Cumberlan
lordship, the Umfraville territories were in Northumberland
Lincolnshire, and Yorkshire. The fourth daughter married th
heir of Lord Scrope of Bolton. These were respectably ambitiou
northern matches. But it was the children of Ralph's secon
wife, Bishop Beaufort's sister Joan, that were guided into th
most brilliant alliances of all. Soon after Ralph's marriag
(1396) there began the flow of offices, lands, wardships, an
pensions which only ceased on the death of Joan's half-brothe
Henry IV, in 1413. Many of these grants were made to Ralp
Neville and his wife jointly—they were either for life or in ta
male—so that by 1436 Joan Beaufort was secured of ampl
revenue from past grants of the crown, quite apart from th
estates which the late earl had settled on her. It has bee
pointed out that between November 1396 and October 139
Ralph Neville and his countess had received from the kin
lands and annuities in Westmorland and Northumberlan

worth almost £200 of annual income: and besides confirming
the grants already made, Henry IV shortly before his death
gave the earl and countess of Westmorland all the royal rights
in the lordship of Bainbridge and the forest of Wensleydale.[1] In
the Neville estates themselves, by an elaborate series of fines
and conveyances to trustees, the earl succeeded in depriving
his grandson, Ralph, the heir to the title and second earl, of the
bulk of the lands in favour of Joan (Beaufort), through whom
they were transmitted to the younger branch of the family
represented by Joan's eldest son, Richard Neville, earl of
Salisbury.[2] Ralph was left in possession only of the lordship of
Brancepeth, Co. Durham, some manors in Lincolnshire, the
Neville Inn, Silver Street, in London and some property in
Ripon. To Joan went the original Neville lordships of Middleham and Sheriff Hutton in Yorkshire and Raby in Durham
along with the family estates in Westmorland and Essex.

The profitable marriages Joan's family made were palpably
a recognition of the relationship the Nevilles had acquired with
the royal stock. The nephews of Henry IV and cousins of
Henry V were suitable husbands for the best family in England;
wealthy heiresses provided for the future of two of the younger
sons, William and Edward, who became Lords Fauconberg
and Abergavenny. To a third son, George Neville, the earl of
Westmorland passed on his claim to John Neville's barony of
Latimer.[3] Four of Neville's daughters by Joan Beaufort married
magnates: two of them obtained papal dispensations to marry,
the one Humphrey, earl of Stafford, later duke of Buckingham, the other Richard, Lord Despenser. On Despenser's death
at the age of eighteen, Eleanor Neville married in 1416 Henry
Percy, second earl of Northumberland. On 20 July Ralph
Neville paid the king 3,000 marks for the wardship and marriage
of John Mowbray, the earl marshal; his wedding to Katharine
Neville (later her mother's principal executor) was celebrated
a year later at Raby. She was to survive her husband by more
than fifty years. The earl marshal was one of Neville's sureties
when, in December 1423, his father-in-law bought from the
crown the marriage of Richard, duke of York, again at a cost
of 3,000 marks. He was to have a maintenance allowance of

---

[1] C. D. Ross and T. B. Pugh, 'The English Baronage and the Income Tax of
1436', *Bull. Inst. Hist. Res.* xxvi (1953), 7–8.   [2] Ibid.
[3] So created in 1432. *Complete Peerage*, vii. 479.

200 marks (Richard was brought up in the Neville nursery at Raby).

The grand manœuvre by which Joan's children displaced those of the first marriage produced much trouble later when Richard Neville who had married Alice Montaque, daughter and heiress of Thomas earl of Salisbury, and had been admitted as earl of Salisbury, was opposed by Ralph the second. Ralph could have prevailed against his half-brother by legal methods, but his main threat to Richard's security was through physical violence. Richard wished to avoid the harm which Westmorland might inflict on his bailiff, servants, and tenants and to protect himself against illegal seizure of his estates or of those in the hands of his father's trustees. He brought the matter before the council and on 18 August 1430 both parties were bound over in sums of £2,000 to keep the peace.[1]

For all Richard's intimacy with the Beauforts, despite the renown of his success in France, he could not prevent disorders from continuing on the Border. On 13 May 1431 he undertook the custody of the west March of Scotland and Carlisle for three years at a salary of £3,400 (war), £1,250 (peace), on condition that the government put some pressure on Westmorland to keep the peace; and on 16 May Westmorland was bound over in the sum of £4,000 'that he shall not do or procure hurt or harm to Joan Countess of Westmorland, Richard Neville, earl of Salisbury, or any of their officers, ministers, bailiffs or servants until one month after Michaelmas 1434: till one month after his contract on the West March'. Another crisis arose when in the parliament of December 1435 the king inquired of Richard and William Neville whether they were prepared to serve abroad: they made their acceptance conditional on the consent of their mother whom they professed themselves unwilling to leave exposed to 'sutes, unlawful entries . . . by Ralph now earl of Westmorland, John and Thomas his brother'. Joan Beaufort, summoned before the council,[2] demanded a guarantee of Westmorland's good behaviour during her son's absence: and Westmorland undertook in another bond of £4,000 to keep the peace. As a further guarantee to Salisbury, the government promised on 7 March 1436 that should Joan Beaufort die while

---

[1] *Cal. Close R., 1429–1435,* p 67.

[2] *Select Cases before King's Council,* ed. Leadam and Baldwin (Selden Soc. xxxv), pp. 101–2.

he was overseas, the custody of her estates should be given to Richard Beauchamp, earl of Warwick, John Lord Greystoke, William Lord FitzHugh, Christopher Conyers, and Christopher Boynton, who were to pay nothing of their value to the king but were to transmit their revenues to Salisbury.

After Joan Beaufort's death a final settlement was reached in the family dissensions. On 26 August 1443 Westmorland made a formal undertaking to Cardinal Beaufort, Richard Neville, and William and George his brothers as well as to seventeen supporters and servants of Joan Beaufort's sons, in which he agreed to recognize Richard Neville's claim to succeed to all the inheritance of the first earl of Westmorland in the counties of Yorkshire, Cumberland, Essex and Westmorland, London and York, with the exception of the Neville Inn, London, his yearly £20 and the Ripon holdings. Salisbury abandoned, at a price, all claims to the Neville inheritance in county Durham; but he had to pay a yearly rent of 200 marks from the manors of Langley, East Brandon, Newsome, Halliwell, and elsewhere, and 100 marks annually for Bywell in Northumberland.[1] Similar compensation was made to the other Nevilles of the second family. The settlement proved secure and Ralph took no part in the disputes that broke out subsequently between Salisbury and Northumberland.

The Neville family well illustrate a tendency to be remarked in the fifteenth-century baronage: the absorption of the smaller units by the larger, corresponding perhaps with the economic tendency of the rich to get richer but fewer. Three Yorkshire baronies, Furnival, Fauconberg, and Latimer, came into Neville hands during the first earl's lifetime. The Furnival lordship did not remain with them long: the others, Fauconberg and Latimer, belonged to junior branches of the house of Neville for several generations.[2]

The Furnival lordship in Yorkshire lay in the south-western corner of the county, consisting of the manor and town of Sheffield, the manors of Weeton, Triston, and Aston, and the overlordship of the Wapentake of Stafford. These lands formed a group with the Furnival properties in Derbyshire and

---

[1] *Cal. Close R., 1441–1447*, pp. 150–1.
[2] For some of the following material grateful acknowledgement is made to Dr. C. D. Ross whose dissertation, *The Yorkshire Baronage in the Fifteenth Century*, will, it is hoped, later be published.

Nottinghamshire. The lordship came to the Nevilles in 1383 on the death of William the fifth lord, whose only child and heiress, Joan, married Thomas Neville, second son of John Lord Neville of Raby, in 1370. Neville's first wife, Joan Furnival, died in 1395 and six years later he married Ankaret Talbot, widow of Richard Lord Talbot of Goodrich Castle, Herefordshire, who inherited besides the Talbot dower, the possessions of her father, John Lord Lestraunge of Whitchurch in Shropshire. Already a rich man, he thus secured much valuable territory in the March and western counties, but his life was to be short and the barony passed to the husband of his heir by Joan Furnival, John Talbot, second son of Richard Lord Talbot and Ankaret Lestraunge. The Furnival lordship therefore became part of a marcher barony.

The Nevilles had more success with the Fauconberg inheritance, belonging to a family prominent in Holderness and Cleveland, holding as their chief residence Skelton near the Yorkshire coast. The last lord of the original line, Sir Thomas Fauconberg, had spent most of his life in prison, partly for treason, partly because of his insanity. His son John joined Archbishop Scrope's rebellion and lost his head thereby: he himself died, loyal and ultimately *compos mentis*, in 1407; but his heir, Joan Fauconberg, was reported to be an idiot from birth. The custody of the Fauconberg estates and marriage of the heir were transferred to the charge of Earl Ralph, and remained there until the heir came of age in April 1422. Ralph then married her to his sixth son by the Beaufort marriage, William Neville, and ultimately, on 28 April 1428, they were given livery of Joan's Yorkshire estates. On 3 August 1429 William Neville was summoned to parliament as Lord Fauconberg in right of his wife. If Joan did in fact share her father's malady, the marriage was a scandalous piece of family diplomacy, two lives sacrificed to the interests of finance.

Children might be sacrificed too. The care shown by the upper ranks of society in extending their patrimonies and providing for their children can be seen in large numbers of marriage contracts made by parents on behalf of their children or prospective children. The contract (1464) between Lady Elisabeth Grey (Elisabeth Woodville, later Edward IV's queen), who was the widow of Sir John Grey, and William Lord

Hastings for the marriage of her son Thomas Grey, or in case of his death, of Richard his brother,

with the eldest daughter to be born within the next five or six years to lord Hastings; or failing such a daughter, with one of the daughters to be born within the same period to Ralph Hastings his brother; or failing such a daughter, with one of the daughters of Dame Anne Ferrers his sister

is a fair instance of the way in which material considerations entirely outweighed the happiness or misery of the children united.[1] An essential part of the marriage settlement was the list of the lands to be set aside often with feoffees, for the benefit of the newly married. Such marriages were frequently purchased. In the case cited Lord Hastings was to pay Elisabeth the sum of 500 marks for the marriage, but if Thomas or Richard died before such marriage took place, or if there was no female issue as above, she was to pay him the sum of 250 marks.

Less openly unscrupulous than the acquisition of the Fauconberg heritage by the Nevilles, though not free from traces of sharp practice, was the method by which the Latimer barony was brought into Neville hands. The connexion between the families of Neville and Latimer dated from the early years of Richard II's reign, when William, the fourth and last Lord Latimer of the original line, and John Lord Neville, had been associates in the minority government, with a resulting marriage between William's only daughter and heiress, Elisabeth Latimer, and Lord Neville. The estates lay chiefly in the counties of York, Northampton, and Bedford: but her first husband's family as custodians of her son and heir, John Neville, secured a considerable share in the keeping of the Latimer estates, and Ralph Neville was able to induce John Neville, Lord Latimer to convey all the estates to him, the transfer taking place in 1418. This conveyance was doubtfully legal, because it was put through only at the expense of John Neville's sister of the whole blood, Elisabeth, then wife of Sir Thomas Willoughby, third son of Robert Lord Willoughby. Elisabeth and

---

[1] Hist. MSS. Comm., *Report on the Manuscripts of R. R. Hastings*, i. 301–2. An excellent example is the covenant made (pp. 303–4) between Hastings on the one hand and Sir Oliver Manningham and Eleanor his wife, Lady Hungerford and Molyns, on the other side, for the marriage of Mary, Eleanor's daughter, to Edward son and heir apparent of lord Hastings, 'or in the event of her refusing or his dying, to Richard another son, or, in like case, to George, another son.'

her two sons were the undoubted heirs of John Neville, Lord
Latimer, and the method by which the estates eventually
reached George Neville shows, in the words of a recent writer,
that 'George had powerful backing in relation both to the
Countess and to Willoughby'.

It was an essential feature of the life of the upper ranks of lay
society in later medieval England that the road to success lay
in the service of the crown. The lesser barons realized this. The
knight or gentleman might seek his fame in the service of a
magnate, but few men of baronial rank chose to take the pay of
a member of their own class unless their employer were a man
of the unique standing of John of Gaunt, or another prince of
the blood, or duke or high officer near the king. For the poorer
barons the rewards of royal service, although often earned by
hard and unremitting work, were greater and more secure. A
good example is the career of Henry Lord FitzHugh, retainer of
Henry IV, chamberlain of Henry V, and for a time treasurer of
England. FitzHugh, born 1352, whose family seat was at
Ravensworth in Yorkshire (Richmondshire), commended himself to the first two Lancastrians first and foremost as a knight
with experience of travel and prowess abroad: he had fought
against the Saracens and had built a castle in Rhodes, and as
late as 1408 he left England for east Prussia to fight against the
Letts—'tres grand seignior et tres brillant et tres noble chevalier', who was likely to commend himself to the ex-Prussian
warrior, Henry Bolingbroke. Though FitzHugh had not been
prominent in the public service or on local commissions before
1399—there were a number, but not many—Henry was quick
to attach him by a retainer, for life, of 100 marks yearly
(19 Nov. 1399). He proved his value by his loyalty in the civil
disturbances of the early years of Henry IV and played a
prominent part in the repression of the rebellion of 1405: he
was present at Shipton Moor at the end of May, and helped
Ralph Neville to deceive Scrope's followers by announcing that
the leaders had reached agreement and so persuading them to
disband. He did not get much reward from his services in this
respect, merely a rent of £11 yearly from a Sussex manor which
had formerly belonged to Lord Bardolf. In July 1406 he was
sent to Denmark to treat with King Erik about the dowry of the
king's daughter Philippa, and was evidently much impressed
by what he saw of the Bridgettine rule. The first substantial

reward he received was the custody of the estates of John Lord Darcy of Knaith in 1411, and these he held practically throughout his lifetime, for the Darcy heir Philip died while under age, leaving two infant daughters who did not reach majority till 1431. For the first part of Henry IV's reign he was mainly devoted to local government in Richmondshire: but when Henry V succeeded he found a man of like sympathies, particularly over the establishment of the Bridgettine rule, for in the Sion archives under 1431 was recorded a statement that it was he 'who first caused the Order to be brought into this realm, and gave to this house [Sion] the sum of £20 annually'. In April 1413 he was commissioned as constable of England, and in May appointed chamberlain of England with permission at the king's coronation for himself, his men, and horses to reside in the township of Harrow, whenever he was staying in London, Westminster, or Kennington with the king's household. In November 1414 he was appointed an ambassador to the council of Constance and took with him his son and forty royal men. When Henry was on the point of departing for France he was made an executor of the king's will, with a legacy of 500 marks, and became a feoffee of the estates of the duchy of Lancaster set aside for the payment of bequests. After the Cambridge conspiracy had been discovered and punished, he received all the confiscated Scrope manors in Richmondshire to the annual value of £260 for life (6 Aug. 1415), and then on 10 June 1417, in tail male. More was to come: on 1 May 1416 he was given the custody of the Lovell estates, without payment of farm.[1] These payments may have been to recompense for sums owing to him and his men on the Agincourt campaign, when he had 29 lances and 90 archers. He was in Bedford's Harfleur expedition with 59 men-at-arms and 209 archers. We know that of his lances a great number were from the East Riding of Yorkshire, with a good sprinkling of local notables, names like Redvers, Boynton, Mauleverer, Metham, and Grandorge.

Before the 1417 expedition he was made treasurer of England (he held this post till 1421), but as he was with the king in France the duties in England were carried out by William Kynwolmersh of Derbyshire, a canon of Lincoln and St. Paul's. He was with Henry all through the conquest of Normandy, present at the siege of Meaux, and captain of Falaise, March—

---

[1] C. D. Ross, op. cit., p. 254.

April 1422. He was named executor of the last will of Henry V. He died and was buried, as he desired, before the high altar in Jervaulx Abbey.

FitzHugh was a good and restful companion to a king who lived at high pressure and valued simpler-minded soldier companions. But his acquisition of the Richmondshire inheritance of the Masham Scropes brought many troubles to William, his son and heir. When he died, Henry V had expressed the wish that the forfeited estates of Henry Lord Scrope of Masham should be returned to his rightful heir: but this applied only to such property as the Scropes could prove to have been entailed.[1] When Henry Lord FitzHugh gave his consent to the restitution of the Scrope estates in Richmondshire, as reported in the 1423 parliament, he did not, as yet, suspect that the evidences by which John Lord Scrope secured provisional restoration were actually forged: as this became clear to him, he shifted his ground, and opposed the transfer as strongly as he could. By 1424 the parties were practically at war and had to be bound over to keep the peace; and there is little doubt that Scrope actually sent his own agents to take over FitzHugh property.

Such a clash occurred on the other side of the Scrope family, the Scropes of Bolton. After Richard Scrope, who had followed Henry V faithfully in his wars, had died (1420) the custody of the Scrope castles became occasion for a dispute between Scrope's executor, Marmaduke Lumley (bishop of Carlisle 1440, later treasurer of England), and Sir Richard Neville. Marmaduke and his brother Sir John Lumley were sons of Ralph Lord Lumley who had been a rebel in 1400. Ralph's wife was Eleanor Neville, daughter of John Lord Neville of Raby and sister of the more famous Earl Ralph. Sir Richard Scrope had himself married a Neville of the elder line. It appears that Scrope had conveyed to Lumley and his servant William Mayhew, as feoffees in tail, all his estates in Yorkshire and Durham, apart from East and West Bolton and Askrigg, and that earl Ralph had consented. The king, however, took the Scrope estates into his hands and put keepers into possession of Scrope's Yorkshire estates. In September 1420 the custody of all the Scrope inheritance was given, without payment or farm, to Sir Richard Neville. This was to neglect Lumley's

[1] Ross, op. cit., p. 215.

claim and Neville was prepared to use force, while Lumley had to give a bond under pain of £2,000 to abstain from law-suits or disturbances, and to recognize Neville's right to peace-ful occupation of the Scrope estates.

To these northern examples of legal and extra-legal action in the pursuit of territorial power, disturbing the peace of the country, others could be added; it is enough to note here that the great Neville concentration with all its ramifications was matched in a more peaceful way in the midlands and the south by the massive Beauchamp inheritance which was spread over eighteen counties, with its chief castles in Warwickshire and Worcestershire. There were outlying lordships in the palatinate of Durham, at Barnard Castle and at Pain's Castle in the Welsh March. Richard Beauchamp, who succeeded to the earldom of Warwick in 1403, added to these by his marriage to Elizabeth Berkeley, daughter of Thomas Earl Berkeley, who through her mother was heiress to the barony of Lisle, consist-ing mainly of lands in Wiltshire, Berkshire, Northamptonshire, and the south-west of England. His second marriage brought the earl the estates of Isabel Despenser, countess of Worcester, which composed some fifty manors in England, along with important properties in Wales, including the lordship of Glamorgan. Not long before he died the earl of Warwick succeeded his aunt, Joan Beauchamp lady of Abergavenny, in that lordship in the Welsh Marches along with eight manors in Warwickshire, Worcestershire, and Oxfordshire. Warwick was away in France with Henry V during most of that reign, and the main work of administration, apart from that of the sur-veyor and the receiver-general, fell upon Warwick's auditors and his council, a group composed, like most baronial councils, mainly of lawyers, who had retaining fees of the earl. Warwick had his attorneys in the court of Exchequer, the King's Bench, and the Common Pleas, and also paid six other counsel. How necessary the council was can be seen from the period when the countess of Warwick was trying to establish her claim to the Berkeley inheritance against James Berkeley, the heir male.[1] In course of this Warwick's council held a conference with Berkeley's council and with the three justices who had been appointed to arbitrate. The councils of the magnates, served by

---

[1] C. D. Ross, *The Estates and Finances of Richard Beauchamp, Earl of Warwick* (Dugdale Soc. Occasional Papers, no. 12, 1956), pp. 11–12.

a legal staff domestic as well as resident in London and other cities, were the means by which the lords pursued their invariable aim: to conserve and add to, by every available means, the family patrimony. The lawyers could provide the historical knowledge of title, would know what land was unencumbered and so sound to buy, and the receivers might be able to hazard a guess as to its true value.

A Beauchamp was born with a silver spoon in his mouth: others had to struggle for ennoblement. Recognition came as the result of successful service of the crown in diplomacy, in the royal household, or in local administration. Once they had arrived, very few came to grief by any other means than political miscalculation: as has been remarked: 'if there is a charge against them it is one of harsh proficiency'. The secular lords in the minority council (1422–7) are of particular interest, combining, as they did, hard-headed acquisitiveness in their own affairs with a constant readiness to devote themselves to the king's business. They were, of course, well salaried and the readiness was not wholly altruistic, for their official knowledge of the availability of crown leases, of escheats, and the king's feudal rights stood them in good stead and they were on terms of close acquaintance with the justices of either bench. Ralph Cromwell who held manors in the counties of Nottingham and Lincoln, owner and rebuilder of Tattershall Castle[1] and founder of the college there, treasurer of England 1433–43, and in the end, on retirement, chamberlain of the Receipt, left his executors the duty of making restitution, for conscience's sake, of £5,481. 6s. 8d. which he must have extorted.[2] From the period of his treasurership till his death in 1455 he was steadily adding to his wealth, as a steward of Birkwood and Clipstone parks, steward and keeper of Sherwood Forest, lessee of alien priory lands, profiteering out of advantageous farms, and building up a territorial fortune. Cromwell was executor and feoffee to Lord Fanhope from whom he received the manor and advowson of Ampthill and Millbrook, Bedfordshire, and feoffee to Lady Elizabeth Grey of Codnor as well as to Sir John Fastolf. The family had been prominent in the midlands since the Ralph

---

[1] Hist. MSS. Comm., *Report on the MSS. of Lord De L'Isle and Dudley*, i. 208 f.

[2] *Test. Ebor.*, ii. 197. There are signs, Mr. McFarlane kindly informs me, that there were further restitutions made after that date 'before the administration of the will broke down in hopeless confusion'.

Cromwell who served Edward I. There was a rough side to him: his abuse of the clergy in convocation (for which he was asked to apologize)[1] seems characteristic of his type. A more conventional, and better balanced but no less self-propelling, counsellor was Sir Walter Hungerford, who like his father became steward for the duchy of Lancaster south of the Trent. Hungerford's large estate was built upon the nucleus of three manors in Wiltshire and Gloucester. His father's other lands had been entailed upon the male issue of his second wife who lived on until 1412 and he did not succeed to the whole until that year. By both his marriages he did extremely well: his first marriage to Katherine Peverell, daughter of a Cornish squire, was the occasion for a settlement which provided for estates in Wiltshire or Gloucester worth £40 a year to be settled by Sir Thomas on the pair with the final prospect of entailed estates worth 300 or 400 marks annually. Katherine's mother, a niece of Hugh Courtenay, earl of Devon, died in 1422 and part of her dower estates came to Hungerford that year, lying mostly in Somerset. In 1439 the Cornish and other Devon lands of Peverell and Courtenay came in. The marriage of the grand-daughter of Lord Burnell to Edmund, Sir Walter's third son, occasioned a settlement of thirteen manors in Surrey, Oxfordshire, Worcestershire, Somerset, and Essex, which passed into Sir Walter's hands by 1421 when Lord Burnell died; and during the minority Hungerford was able temporarily to augment his lands by grants and royal wardships, as well as by direct acquisition (some thirty additional manors mainly in Wiltshire and Somerset, along with his London inn in Charing). He bought some of these before he was treasurer of England (1426–32) and many of the rest before the end of his term of office.[2] By 1430 the estates were large enough to carry three stewards; and another was needed to administer the lands brought under his control by his second marriage, to Eleanor, countess of Arundel, the daughter and heiress of Sir John Berkeley of Beverstone (Glos.). In her right Hungerford came to hold thirteen manors in Dorset, six in Wiltshire, five in Gloucestershire, and two in Somerset; estates that brought him after 1440 nearly £700 a year. By this time his grandson Robert had been

---

[1] *Reg. Chichele*, iii. 110.
[2] J. S. Roskell, 'Three Wiltshire Speakers', *Wilts. Arch. and Nat. Hist. Mag.* lvi (1956), 303.

married to Eleanor Moleyns, whose father William had been killed at the siege of Orléans: a marriage which was to bring into the Hungerford family possession some twenty to thirty manors in Buckinghamshire, Oxfordshire, Wiltshire, and Cornwall. The construction of this patrimony was the territorial concomitant of Hungerford's continuous service of the crown: as shire knight for Wiltshire and Speaker in the Leicester parliament of 1414; as chief steward of the duchy of Lancaster in the south, a position which his father had held; as royal ambassador at the council of Constance; as one of the feoffees and executors in the will made by Henry V on 22 July 1415 at Southampton just before leaving for France; as steward of Henry's household abroad and (on Henry's decease) as a member of the council charged with the exercise of the royal authority when parliament or great councils were not sitting. He was first summoned to parliament as Lord Hungerford on 7 January 1426 and served on the council which had to handle the Beaufort–Gloucester *fracas* in 1425–6, and with his co-feoffees Beaufort and Chichele took his part in the slow process of administering Henry V's will until the enfeoffed duchy of Lancaster estates could be resumed by the king. He must have handled, or at least known about, practically every important piece of business that came up in the council until 1444. That year he was excused from being present at the chapter of the Garter, having since his election (1421) attended every chapter (saving those from 1439–43) of which there is a record.[1] He was fortunate in dying before the chaos of the fifties. He was too cautious a public servant to risk his life and fortunes by the gangster methods followed in East Anglia by the two William de la Poles, or in Kent by James Fiennes, Lord Saye and Sele.

Fiennes, a good example of a household figure ennobled, a squire of the body before 1438, chamberlain of the household 1447–9 and treasurer of England 1449–50, was, Viscount Beaumont apart, the richest recipient of grants from the crown between 1440 and his death, his pensions and other rights being estimated worth £302 in 1450. These grants enabled him to support his peerage (1447) and to build up a prominent position in south-east England. He was chief steward of the duchy of Lancaster lordships in Sussex in 1440 and in 1447 succeeded Gloucester as warden of the Cinque Ports. He was the younger

[1] J. S. Roskell, op. cit., p. 333.

son of Sir William Fiennes of Hurstmonceaux, brother of Sir Roger, treasurer of the household 1439–46. His own inheritance was small but he built up a large estate around London in Kent and Sussex, acquiring the manors of Mereworth, Kenarton, and Huntingfield. He and his friends ruled Kent, Surrey, and Sussex in the 1440's. Through a series of associates holding the shrievalty of Kent, especially William Crowmer, who married his daughter Elizabeth, Gervaise Clifton (sheriff 1440–1) and Stephen Slegg (sheriff 1448–9) he was largely responsible for arousing the indignation against the corrupt deals, sharp practice, and perversion of the sheriff's jurisdiction, which culminated in Cade's rebellion. The execution of Fiennes and Crowmer bears witness to the indignation against their harshness and the monopoly they exercised over county politics. Fiennes's lands, given him by royal grant, were involved in the Resumption of 1451, despite his heir's marriage to Margaret, daughter and heiress of William Wykeham of Broughton Castle in Oxfordshire.

In an attempt to evaluate the resources of upper lay society, Professor H. L. Gray, using the taxation returns of 1436, ranked its members thus. At the top, fifty-one lay barons enjoying incomes from land and rents which averaged £768 each, or, with annuities added, £865. Below these 183 greater knights, 'actual or potential', with average income of £208, while below these 750 lesser knights and other men whom the government would readily have designated as knights had incomes of from £40 to £100, with an average of £60. Below these stood some 1,200 taxpayers, either esquires or enjoying roughly, as esquire, an income of £20–35. The returns give, underneath this 'somewhat ill-defined' body of men, some 1,600 men each with an income of £10–19, and some 3,400 others having £5–10. Altogether some 7,000 men in England, non-noble in status, enjoyed incomes from lands, rents, and annuities ranging from £5 to £400.

The taxation of 1436 from which these data were extracted was a graded one on incomes, and had to be paid at the rate of 6d. in the pound from incomes ranging from £5 to £100 and at the same rate for the first £100 of incomes ranging from £101 to £399. On the second group any excess over £100 was to be taxed at 8d. in the pound, and incomes of £400 or more were to pay 2s. in the pound on the total. Thus the larger incomes were taxed at 10 per cent. on the entire range. Professor Gray

gave his opinion that the enrolled account is obviously one of
great importance. 'Since few of the peers and peeresses probably derived annual income from other sources than lands,
rents, annuities or salaries, the figures before us, so far as they
are reliable, record the entire fixed incomes of the persons
accounting.'[1] The assessors, the chancellor, Bishop John Stafford,
and the treasurer Lord Cromwell were to be depended upon
as men of public spirit. As the income of Cromwell himself was
among the largest in the list that was some indication of his
integrity in high office: 'in general, baronial incomes correspond
with the value of estates given in Fifteen Century inquisitions'.[2]
These criteria have been subjected to criticism[3] by comparing a
number of incomes where known with the actual assessments;
the outcome being that the suspicion of evasion brought against
certain wealthier members of the baronage can be confirmed.
'Great persons closely related to the king were able to evade a
thorough assessment of their incomes.'

The figures of those persons in the highest group must, upon
examination, be taken as an understatement: they are Richard
duke of York (given as £3,231); Richard earl of Warwick
(£3,116), Anne countess of Stafford who was Anne of Gloucester, grand-daughter of Edward III, one of the Bohun heiresses
(£1,959); and Humphrey earl of Stafford (£855); Humphrey
duke of Gloucester (£2,243), and William de la Pole, earl of
Suffolk (£1,667): in each case annuities counted for sums
varying from £100 to £233; Gloucester got considerably more,
including £666 from that source. Among these the Countess
Anne seems to have come off lightly, for she was 'the greatest
English heiress of the day': a Bohun on one side, she had two
dowers from the earldom of Stafford valued at £338 per annum,
'when assigned to her in 1393 and 1403'. Her income was
assessed at £1,958, but she had in fact more than this, for in
1431–7 the gross receipts of all her lands in England, except her
lordship of Holderness, were £2,186. 15s. 10¾d., and her net
income after costs of repairs, wages, and fees had been paid was
£1,765. 9s. 6¼d.[4] The profits of the lordship of Holderness seem
to have been round about £737 clear, so that her tax assessment

---

[1] 'Incomes from land in England', *Eng. Hist. Rev.* xlix (1934), 611 f.

[2] Gray, op. cit., p. 612.

[3] By C. D. Ross and D. B. Pugh, 'The English Baronage and the Income Tax
of 1436', *Bull. Inst. Hist. Res.* xvi (1953).

[4] Ross and Pugh, op. cit., pp. 5–6.

'may have underestimated her revenues by four or five hundred pounds'. When the countess's land had passed to her son Humphrey, later duke of Buckingham, the gross rental of his lands in England was £4,400, with a balance in clear value of £3,477. It has been estimated that the tax assessments of the Staffords in 1436 represented only about 80 per cent. of their net income. When it is recollected that Joan Beaufort's income was assessed at £667 in 1436, when her full revenues must have been nearer £1,600 or more, the evidence for official underestimation seems pretty clear; and the critics of Professor Gray have established that the assessment of many of the king's nearest relatives among the baronage provides strong grounds for suspecting evasion and underpayments. It may be asked what exchequer machinery existed for challenging and checking the statements of stewards drawing up the *valor*. One point needs emphasis. Many of the greater magnates had extensive lands and revenues in Wales and the Welsh Marches. Most of all Richard duke of York, inheritor of the vast domains of the house of Mortimer in England, Wales, and Ireland. A *valor* of 1443–4 shows that his cash receipts from the Welsh and marcher part of his possessions reached £3,430, after all charges and reprises had been met. The duke's English income was assessed in 1436 at £3,231, and he was thus worth annually twice that sum. In the March there were Lancastrian magnates confronting him: the FitzAlan earls of Arundel were substantial holders on the upper Dee, in Chirk and Oswestry and in Clun, bounded by the Yorkist (Mortimer) Ceri and Maelienydd; the Talbots of Goodrich held in the middle Wye, and the Beauchamp earls of Warwick in Elfael. The holder of a baronial income next in importance to Richard of York was Richard earl of Warwick, with an English income estimated at £3,116 while he drew large revenues from Wales, since he had acquired the Despenser inheritance in Glamorgan and the Marches, by his second marriage with Isabel, dowager countess of Worcester, in 1423. Dugdale, quoting sources no longer available, made out Richard of Warwick's revenues in England and Wales to have amounted to £5,471 in 1432–3 and to £5,538 in 1434–5.[1] When Richard Beauchamp died in 1439 the Lisle estates went to the three daughters of his first wife; and after the deaths of his son Duke

---

[1] Ross, *The Estates and Finances of Richard Beauchamp, Earl of Warwick* (Dugdale Soc. Occasional Papers, no. 12, 1956), p. 18. The list of the lands is on pp. 20–22.

Henry of Warwick (1446) and Henry's infant heiress daughte
Anne (1449), a few lands were lost to the estate, but the bulk o
the Beauchamp and Despenser territories, including the lordshi
of Abergavenny, were held together and formed the basis for th
great estate of the Kingmaker. Before his creation that sam
year as earl of Warwick, when he succeeded to the Beaucham
lands, brought to him by his wife Anne, Richard Beauchamp'
only daughter, Richard Neville had little more than the castle
and lordships of Middleham and Sheriff Hutton: but now h
was the possessor of an immense estate to which, just as wit
York, Wales had made a substantial contribution. Whateve
may have been the income of wealthy commoners groupe
together on either side in the struggle of Lancaster and Yorl
the combination of York and Warwick must, purely from a:
economic point of view, have proved one of the decisive factoi
against the house of Lancaster.

In the Lancastrian party next to the crown with its duchy c
Lancaster, the earls of Stafford were the most considerabl
landholders,[1] but there were a number of large owners amon
the older families. Berkeley, Roos, Clifford, FitzWalter, Burnel
and Sudeley are examples, and some years after 1436 Moleyn
and FitzWarin were to rank fairly high. But among the Lancas
trians who after the early débâcle kept faithful to the crown, nex
to the Staffords came Percy. The Percy wealth was derive
from Yorkshire, Northumberland, Cumberland, and Scotland
along with manors in Sussex, Lincolnshire, and the Scots estate
which could not be assessed in 1436: in 1436 Northumberlan
was rated for taxation at £1,210, including an annuity grante
to the earl of £120; the figure has been considered an under
assessment, if only because in 1415 John duke of Bedford, wh
had been granted most of the Percy estates after the death c
the first earl of Northumberland, was given a compensatin
annuity of £2,000 when he was required to give them up. I
1417, after the death of his mother, the earl had received fror
Yorkshire manors which were valued at £104 annually, whil
in 1423 his wife, Eleanor Neville, obtained livery of her dowe
interest in the estates of her first husband, Richard Lor
Despenser, which were valued at £500, £394 of it being draw
from lands in Wales and the Marches. Confirmation of th

---

[1] See K. B. McFarlane's map, 'England in the Fifteenth Century', *Camb. Me
Hist.* viii, no. 84.

under-assessment comes from recent specialist study of the Percy lands in Cumberland, Northumberland, Yorkshire,[1] and Sussex. The gross value of the estates is estimated for 1455. Mr. Bean gives as the figures that year the following proportions: from the estates in Northumberland and Cumberland £1,500;[2] in Yorkshire £1,000;[3] in Sussex £175;[4] in Lincolnshire £60; and from single manors in Cambridgeshire, Suffolk and Leicestershire, along with property in London, £90: total, £2,825. This is of course nearly twenty years after the 1436 *valor*, but the difference between this and the assessment is interesting. Perquisites of courts, wood sales, and other casual revenue may have brought up the total to a gross revenue of some £3,100 a year. By 1436, of course, the earl had not recovered two of his Yorkshire properties, Healaugh and Kirk Leavington, which had been forfeited after 1408, and he was not yet in possession of Hunmanby in Yorkshire which he was to obtain from Henry Percy of Athol. The same writer has added the comment that his assessment in the income tax of 1450 as £400 a year is an estimate 'ludicrous in comparison with the reality'.[5] We have already mentioned Eleanor Neville's dower interest in the estates of her first husband, which serves to increase the total figure. Nor was it appreciably lower for the third earl (1455–61) when the Percy and Poynings estates were joined.

The particular point of interest which emerges from the study of the receiver's accounts of the Percy estates, between the date (1416) when the second earl received back the greater proportion of the confiscated properties and 1461, is the number of extraordinary fees (over and above ordinary fees to estate servants and others) mostly payments for life, which were a heavy liability on the Northumberland revenues, particularly between the years 1426 and 1454. An analysis of the charges on

---

[1] J. M. W. Bean, *The Estates of the Percy Family 1416–1537*, (1958), pp. 81–82.

[2] *Cumberland*: the honour of Cockermouth, a third of the barony and manor of Egremont, and a messuage in Carlisle; *Northumberland*, the baronies of Alnwick, Warkworth, and Prudhoe, the manors of Newburn, Rothbury, Langley, Thirston, the Talbot lands in Tyndale, and land in the Cheviots; a messuage in Newcastle upon Tyne.

[3] The manors of Leconfield, Scarborough, Arras, Wressell, Nafferton, Wansford, Waplington, Gembling, and Pocklington in the East Riding; Seamer, Topcliffe, Asenby, Gristhwaite, Kirk Leavington, Throxenby, and Catton in the North Riding; Tadcaster, Healaugh, Spofforth, Leatherley, and Lenton, West Riding; lands in Craven, in Ribblesdale and Langsworth, covering the upper waters of the Ribble (Giggleswick, Long Preston, Settle); and a messuage in the city of York.   [4] Petworth.   [5] Ibid., p. 83.

the Percies' Sussex revenues shows that between 1446 and 1453 on an average £105 was charged to the account yearly on total fees and out of that about £66 was for extraordinary fees. This out of total receipts averaging (for Sussex) £132. The charges on the Northumberland revenues in 1442 show that £130. 18s. 5½d. was paid in ordinary fees, whereas the total of extraordinary amounted to £38. 14s. 2d. In Yorkshire from a total revenue of c. £1,076. 16s. 7½d. annually, ordinary and extraordinary fees together comprised £632. 10s. 2d. Of this figure alms accounted for £23. 17s. 2d., ordinary fees £104. 18s. 8d., and extraordinary fees £503. 14s. 4d., including an annuity of £200 held by the earl's wife and payments of £11. 6s. 8d. and £34 to the earl's two sons. Thus even if payments to the family are excluded, 'extraordinary' fees alone consumed approximately a quarter of the earl's revenues in Yorkshire. These extraordinary fees were for retainers. No indentures of retainer have survived nor is there any explicit difference made between a retainer and an annuitant, save the receiver's note that the man who was paid the extraordinary fee is 'retentus cum domino tam pro pace quam pro guerra ad terminum vite sue'; but this is sufficient to show that these are examples of 'bastard feudalism', the well-nigh universal practice of retaining for peace time and civil service *generosi* or well-born members of the area. Mr. Bean has noted that in the private war between the Percies and the Nevilles that broke out in 1453–4, several of those indicted as supporters of the Percies appear in the Yorkshire *valor* of the Percy estates in 1442–3 and in the Cumberland receiver's account of 1453–4.

Throughout the social structure of the fifteenth century ran the principle of patronage and protection. Just as the university student and the rising clerk sought out those who could maintain or 'exhibit' them by presenting them to benefices, so the *generosi* sought out a lord from whom they received both annuities and protection in return for furthering his interests. The indentured retainer, the recipient of 'good lordship', is on a contract no longer purely military but semi-civil, the promise being to assist the lord in peace and in war for a term of years or more usually for life. The early contracts of this sort were of a mixed kind. They did not all promise homage and fealty, but contained the counterpart in the sign manual or seal of the retainer and the explicit mention of faith or faithful service.

By the fourteenth century the practice of retaining groups of men or fellowships in England was an acknowledged one, and the indenting of men for an annual fee or the making of grants for future services well established. The most celebrated example was the retinue of John of Gaunt: but it was more widespread than that: as Mr. Dunham has observed, the peers' companies of feed men in Richard II's reign 'formed what amounted to a peace-time standing army—from the lord's point of view, to retain men for cash annuities was more advantageous than granting them land for future service';[1] and from the royal point of view, the indenting retainers could serve as the nucleus of a force recruited by contract to serve *pro hac vice*: both systems, the retainers and the contracted army, could come into play. Henry V and Bedford employed the dual system, calling up their own men when wanted, but at the same time recruiting under contract. The retainer might, for the duration of a campaign, be paid such wartime wages 'as the king gives to men of such degree', and a clause inserted giving the lord a right to the third of the ransoms of the indentured man's prisoners and to a third of the thirds acquired from his servants in the case of service overseas or in Scotland.

There have survived a considerable number of indentures made between William Lord Hastings, chamberlain of Edward IV (1461) and king's lieutenant in Calais (1471), who became after Warwick's fall his master's most prominent and influential official. The centre of his territorial power was the northern midlands: he had houses at Kirby, Ashby de la Zouche, and Bagworth in Leicestershire, and at Slingsby in Yorkshire. Between 1461 and 1483 we know the names of ninety men retained by him and the indentures are signed and sealed by sixty-seven of them. An example from those already printed may be given:

(G. Nicholas Agarde, Gentleman. 28 April 1474.)

This indenture made the xxviii day of April the xiv year of the reign of our sovereign lord, King Edward the IV, between William, Lord Hastings, on the one part and Nicholas Agarde, gentleman, on the other part, witnesseth that the said Nicholas of his own desire and motion is belaft and retained for term of his life with the foresaid

[1] W. H. Dunham, jnr., *Lord Hastings' Indentured Retainers, 1461–1483* (Trans. Connecticut Academy of Arts and Sciences, vol. xxxix, 1955), p. 61. In subsequent pages various types of early indentures are discussed by Mr. Dunham.

Lord Hastings afore all other, to ride and go with the same lord and him assist, aid, and his part take against all other persons within the realm of England. The ligeance and faith which he oweth to our said sovereign lord the king and to my lord prince and to their heirs only except. And the said Nicholas at all times shall come to the said Lord Hastings upon reasonable warning, accompanied with as many persons defensibly arrayed as he may goodly make or assemble, at the costs and expenses of the same lord. For the which the same lord promiseth to be good and tender lord to the said Nicholas in all thing reasonable that he hath to do, and him to aid and succor in his right as far as law and conscience requireth. In witness whereof the foresaid parties to these present indentures interchangeably have set their seals and signs manual. Given this day and year abovesaid.

Nicholas Agarde (Seal attached).[1]

Of these ninety, twenty are described as gentlemen, fifty-nine as esquires (*armigeri*), nine as knights, while two, Henry Lord Grey of Codnor and John Blount, Lord Mountjoy, were peers. All bore the names of prominent and substantial county families. Lord Grey of Codnor signed indentures on 30 May 1464 to take Hastings's 'full part and quarrel and be with him against all persons save the king'. As a knight Hastings was bound by the statute of 1390 which restricted retaining to the lords temporal; but as a lord he was allowed to retain and to give livery of company to those of gentle birth in his *ménage*.

Two questions about the indentured retinue have arisen: whether the obligation for perpetual service was strictly fulfilled; and whether the system made for the social stability which has been claimed for it. In the former case the contracts make it clear that although the indentured retainer was not normally permanently resident in the lord's household, his ordinary duties were those of a household and personal attendant:[2] yet Hastings himself was in receipt of other fees from various magnates, and was by no means entirely monopolized by the royal service; and the fact that between April and June 1399 Richard II conferred a number of patents of indenture with the expressed condition that the retainer was 'to stay with the king only', looks like a faltering attempt to hold on to men transferring themselves elsewhere, while there is other evidence to suggest that men sought out the best captain to serve under

---

[1] Dunham, op. cit., p. 126.
[2] N. B. Lewis, 'The Organization of Indentured Retinues', *Trans. Roy. Hist. Soc.*, 4th ser., xxvii (1945), 34–35.

rather than remaining faithfully under local lords.[1] Prestige had a lot to do with it. On the second of these problems Dr. Lewis has indeed termed the indentured retinue 'a steadying influence in a society where old institutional loyalties were breaking down and new ones had not yet fully developed to take their place'.[2] Yet this generalization has to be tested in the fifteenth century by the working of local government, and particularly by the success or failure of the sheriff's administration. Influence in the conduct of shire elections by *comitiva* of the great magnates may have worked for peace (at any rate for absence of incident), but it was more likely to do so when the leading nobles who had retinues available for action agreed to unite rather than act independently. It is not so much the existence of the retinue *as such* which had made for peace, but the co-operation of several potential and possibly competing retinues which kept disorder at bay.

The indentured retinue presents another problem which has not yet been fully solved. To what extent did it enable a lord to intervene in local administration and get his way in the appointment of the personnel of the shire? Here the Hastings statistics are of some relevance. Most of the shrievalties held by Hastings's retainers were in the counties of Derby, Stafford, and Leicester. It has been shown that certainly 19 and possibly 22 of Hastings's adherents served as sheriffs during the 22 years between November 1461 and the spring of 1483. In Edward IV's reign 8 retainers in 12 of the 22 years were sheriffs in Staffordshire; 7 of them in 9 of the 22 years held the sheriffdom in Northamptonshire and Derbyshire; and 5 retainers in 5 years held the post in Warwickshire and Leicestershire.[3] Of these 19, however, 9 signed their contracts with Hastings before they served as sheriffs, and 10 others contracted with him after their first shrievalties: the fact, while it attests the Chamberlain's popularity, does not increase any claim he may have had to secure his own men as sheriffs. The numbers of those commissioned as justices of the peace within these years are larger, 33, with the same local limits as before. This is more important, perhaps, but it is exactly what one would expect of people of this kind: the commission and local appointments are what they themselves were entitled to expect of a magnate powerful at

---

[1] K. B. McFarlane, 'Bastard Feudalism', *Bull. Hist. Inst. Res.*, xx (1943–5), p. 168.
[2] Op. cit., p. 39.   [3] Dunham, op. cit., p. 38.

court. His retainers were particularly drawn upon in 1471 and the years immediately following: but to imagine that politically there was a Hastings *bloc* might be to exaggerate what was largely local influence; and the same conclusion might be drawn from the very limited number of his retainers who sat in the parliaments of Edward IV's reign. In 1478 there were '7, perhaps 10'[1] of the Chamberlain's followers in the commons: but that and 1472 are the only instances where he could be said to have placed his men there. The general average is not more than four, if that.

The annuity under this system is a form of fee promised to the retainer who got his money mostly from the receipts of some particular manor or lordship in the possession of the grantor, upon which the annuitant could distrain in the event of non-payment or undue delay. Thus there came into existence between a lord and those who actually worked on his estate a class of pensioners, somewhat like the mesne tenants of the older feudalism. A number of these might be closely attendant upon the lord, clerks who like William of Worcester (a layman) held places of responsibility, 'lesser gentry, expert in accountancy and management', as Mr. McFarlane has called them.[2] This legal unmilitary nucleus fought its master's causes in the spiritual as well as the lay court. Worcester himself was a 'great landowner's "riding servant"', gaining from his visits to Fastolf's many properties in Essex and East Anglia facts as to cost and finance as well as a good deal of antiquarian experience. The England of the magnates and the more important knights is an England organized not horizontally but in depth, the household groups being microcosms of the several classes living together in a locality or distributed over the lord's estate system. They can be seen, gathered and arranged, in the establishment of a prelate like Wykeham, whose clerks kept a careful record of all who were 'dining in' at their master's table from the distinguished invited guests, through great technicians like Wykeham's builders and architect, to those minor clerics who served his chapel.[3] This is, of course, an ecclesiastical establishment: but in the larger noble households there must have been a similar

---

[1] Dunham, op. cit., p. 34.

[2] 'William Worcester: A Preliminary Survey', *Studies presented to Sir Hilary Jenkinson* (1957), p. 199.

[3] Winchester College Muniments, 'Wykeham's Household Roll', *passim*.

organization. Some notion of it can be derived from the journal of Elizabeth Berkeley, countess of Warwick, for 1421–2, which records the names of guests who sat down to the three principal meals, the consumption of food and provisions, and the purchases by the six departments of the household at Berkeley.[1] This shows that 94 meals might be served on one Sunday (2 March), 10 for breakfast, 46 for dinner, and 38 for supper, the party including her *armigeri* down to two charcoal burners and two pilgrims at the gate. When she travelled (with 57 horses) she might stay *en route* at the houses of her retainers (e.g. Robert Andrew, esquire, a Wiltshire landowner) before reaching her London or Walthamstow headquarters; and she took with her, as she moved, people like John Throckmorton who was of her husband's council, the lawyer John Harnett, also a member of the council, and her auditor, William Poleyne. While the number of persons permanently resident in the countess's household was not large, including six gentlewomen and nine gentlemen, among them the clerk and steward of the household, she entertained large numbers of casual guests and people who came to the household on business, but also many who were in the service of her husband, Earl Richard of Warwick. Several subsidized lawyers who drew *feoda* from the earl, such as William Babington chief justice of the common pleas, John Cottesmore, justice of assize, and the king's sergeant, James Strangeways, were entertained. When the duke of Bedford came in June 1421 to Good Rest Lodge near Warwick, he brought his chancellor, his treasurer, twenty-four esquires, and forty-two other persons.[2]

Among those who gathered round the noble patron were the families intent upon consolidating their possessions and marking out for themselves a position in their county. In a fiercely competitive society law, personal favour, connexion through marriage, gratuitous service, and a dozen other methods were invoked to enable the patrimony to be retained and enlarged; and the groupings that came about were the result of the local challenges and attacks made upon title by the unscrupulous who used their attornies to undermine the evidences upon which the sales and transactions of their opponents were based and who frequently resorted to force while the legal processes

[1] C. D. Ross, 'The Household Accounts of Elizabeth Berkeley', *Trans. Bristol and Glouc. Arch. Soc.* lxx (1957), 85–86.   [2] Ibid., p. 75.

were pending. The owner of property needed skilful and persistent counsel in defending himself, particularly if he had succeeded to an inheritance none too firmly secured in law. This
situation underlay the relationship of John Paston, son of the
justice, to many of the more important figures in East Anglia
depicted for ever in the family correspondence, wherein it becomes clear that the retainers are used as the screen between
the rising *generosus* and the great man who is attacking his title.
John Paston's father had bought the manor of Gresham in
Norfolk and left it to his son and heir; but Lord Moleyns was
persuaded by John Heydon, one of Suffolk's men, that he had a
claim to it, and actually sent in his bailiffs to collect rent before
any decision had been reached about the claim. Paston first
invoked the good lordship of Bishop William Waynflete and
through him got as far as Moleyns's lawyers.[1] The lawyers advised Paston to interview Moleyns personally, but Moleyns
avoided the interview, and in the meantime his retainers at
Gresham were kept on the watch all the summer, fortifying the
house that they had no right to occupy. All Paston could do
was to occupy a house in the town, until on 28 January 1450 an
armed force described as of a thousand strong was sent by
Moleyns to turn the family out by destroying the place and
ejecting Mrs. Paston. John did not enter Gresham manor till
the spring of 1451, but when, to vindicate his position, he
brought an action against Moleyns and his agents for forcible
ejection, his counsel were informed by the sheriff of Norfolk
that Henry VI had instructed him 'to make such a panel (as)
to acquit the Lord Moleyns'.[2] Both sides, therefore, set about
working upon the sheriff who told Paston that his right course
was to get a letter from the king, similar to that obtained by
Moleyns, 'especially as you said a man should get such . . . for
a noble'.[3] In this episode the friends and retainers of the parties
seem in large measure to determine the course of action.
Paston's alertness in defence and knowledge of procedure was
the reason why he was sought out by Sir John Fastolf who,
whether he was actually related to Paston or not, used to speak
of him as 'cousin'. The cousin was invaluable to a man bent on

---

[1] *Paston Letters*, Lit. ed., ii. 90.   [2] Ibid., ii. 235.
[3] Ibid., no. ii. 242. Cf. H. S. Bennett, *The Pastons and their England* (1922), p. 7,
for discussion of the events at Gresham. For the tactics of Charles Nowell's retainers,
cf. *Letters*, ii. 260.

acquiring and building up an estate system largely purchased
from gains in the French war. By 1457 Fastolf had made Paston
one of his feoffees and in the end, two days before he died,
bequeathed to him as 'the best friend and helper and supporter
to the said Sir John' an inheritance, including the great house
at Caister and the messuage in Southwark which was to involve
him in much legislation as well as attacks *vi et armis*.

It was not the cause of York or Lancaster so much as the local
situation and the attitude of local personalities that governed
allegiance to the magnates or prompted, in spite of what
the indentures might promise, the transfer of loyalty on the part
of the retainer. Good lordship did not always follow an obvious
party pattern. The career of Philip Wentworth, sheriff of Norfolk and Suffolk 1447–8, 1459–60, and knight of the shire for
Suffolk in various parliaments of the mid-century, provides
some illustration. Wentworth, a true Suffolk supporter, who
had had a grant of Gloucester's house in Ashingdon, Essex, had
along with his brother-in-law Robert Constable of Holme
(Yorkshire) been granted the wardship and marriage of
Thomas, son and heir of John Fastolf of Cowhall, Suffolk, and
the keeping of the manor of Bradwell for 110 marks in 1448.
This followed upon Wentworth's success in securing a judgement for the king that Sir John Fastolf had illegally entered
Bradwell and seized part of the issues. In 1453 Constable made
over his rights to Wentworth. The next year, however, John
Paston disputed the wardship and may possibly have got possession of Thomas Fastolf; he and his followers nearly came to
blows over Bradwell with Wentworth who was supported by
Gilbert Debenham and John Timperley, a retainer of the duke
of Norfolk: Paston was able to get a favourable grant of Bradwell, for according to Wentworth's successful petition for its
annulment (1459) he paid only £110 when it was worth £200.
Was it perhaps this quarrel with the Pastons which may explain
why Wentworth, when he became sheriff, allied himself with
the duke of Norfolk? He was one of those observed to have
been at the siege of Caister in 1460 when Norfolk eventually
seized the Fastolf–Paston Castle, and in fact he had been associated with Debenham, Norfolk's steward, who was a co-feoffee
with him in 1456.

It is important not to regard the retainer grouping of forces
as a development which superseded the ordinary course of

local administration. It cuts across it, may intervene in it, may sometimes strengthen it, as it may do the reverse. To maintain it, the central core of the knights and the senior armigerous families still stands; having borne the burden of Edward I's reforms in the thirteenth century, in the fifteenth the class remains, whether working in the shire or simply keeping going the routine of economics and justice on their own estates. Tried and proved by successive royal inquiries into their titles and surviving the occasional attacks and undermining efforts of their contemporaries, the *legales milites* have gained rather than lost. Farther on, more will be said of their essential work in county and parliament.

The royal power must, therefore, be set and judged against this background of engagement and allegiance. It is imperilled if it cannot offer more than the greatest of its tenants can offer; it is lost if it cannot meet a combination of those tenants with superior attractions, genuine attractions rather than the romanticism and magic of regality. But it cannot defeat such a combination by force without the law. It must itself mould the constitution while appealing to precedent and while using the established forms in its own way.

(b) THE TRADER AND THE COUNTRYMAN

In 1436 Piero da Monte, the papal envoy to Henry VI, described England as 'a very wealthy region, abounding in gold and silver and many precious things, full of pleasures and delights'.[1] It was only an impression: but it was uttered the same year as the Burgundian attack on Calais, when popular indignation mingled with the patriotic advice of the author of the *Libelle of English Polycye*. The council, to which the *Libelle* was directed, was smarting under the failure of the negotiations at Arras and cannot have enjoyed being implored to strengthen the navy and maintain a blockade of the Channel; but Hungerford and Chichele (if indeed it was sent to him)[2] and the other

[1] Letter 18 in J. Haller, *Piero da Monte, ein gelehrter und päpstlicher Beamter des 15. Jahrhunderts* (Rome, 1941), p. 10.
[2] This question and the relationship between the manuscripts which have come to light since Sir George Warner edited the book (*The Libelle of English Polycye,*

members of the council who received it in the first instance would have recognized, despite its chauvinism and Gloucester-like sentiments, the shrewdness and appropriateness of the picture it portrayed. It was an appeal to return to the 'strong' policy of kings who had fostered sea power and used it to nego-tiate from a position of strength: Edward III (probably Henry IV was really the king in the author's mind) and Henry V who built the *Trinity*, the *Grace Dieu*, the *Holy Ghost*, and other great ships and whose early death brought about the sale of some of the largest:

> For doute it nat but that he wolde have be
> Lorde and master aboute the roundè see
> And kepte it sure, to stoppe oure enmyes hens,
> And wonne us gode and wysely brought it thens.

In that spirit he gave his advice: 'Cheryshe marchandyse, kepe thamyralté, That we bee maysteres of the narrowe see', the advice given to Henry V by the Emperor Sigismund, who told him to keep Dover and Calais 'like his two eyes'. Seeing that

> the wyse lorde baron of Hungerford
> Hathe thee [the book] oversene, and verrily he seithe
> That thow arte trewe,

there is some likelihood that Hungerford, who was attached to the emperor during his visit to England in 1416, retailed this to the author and that it so became the text of a treatise which regards the expansion of trade and commerce as a means to promote the material welfare of the country:

> For yef marchaundes were cherysshede to here spede
> We were not lykelye to fayle in ony nede;
> Yff they bee riche, thane in prosperité
> Schalbe our londé, lordes and comonté.

The interesting part of the treatise is the list of the commodi-ties which the author considered that the stronger policy might bring under control: it is not a matter of English imports and exports, but of regulating what was sold in 'the lytell londe of Flaundres', the 'staple to other londes'. It is there that goods from Spain and Portugal, the Baltic, Scotland, Ireland, and

1926), have been discussed by Dr. F. Taylor in 'Some Manuscripts of the "Libelle of English Polycye" ', *Bull. John Rylands Lib.* xxiv (1940), 376 f. It is most unlikely to have been composed by Adam Moleyns who belonged to the peace party and was an opponent of Gloucester.

Iceland were marketed, and by putting pressure on Burgundian Flanders both that industrial market and other countries could be brought to a better frame of mind. Above all, wool, the chief merchandise of Spain, was necessary to the Flemish textile industry, but this and the fine cloths and linen which the Spanish also brought to Sluys could be seized in the Channel through the proximity of the trade routes to the English coast. In the same way Flemish vessels trading to La Rochelle for wine and to Brittany for salt could be halted, if we set about it, and the English could withhold the mixing of their own wool fibres with the Spanish, which was necessary for the manufacture of Spanish cloth. Even to friends like the Portuguese, with whom a formal treaty had been made on 18 February 1436, free passage by sea into Flanders should not be permitted; still less should it be allowed to Brittany, which brings salt, wine, crest cloth, and canvas into Flanders: the Bretons, particularly those from St. Malo, are the worst of pirates and, more, land raiders against whom severe reprisals have been necessary in the past. To the Genoese the author was slightly more favourable, because in their carracks they brought to England gold, silks, pepper as well as cotton and less costly goods: but the luxury goods of Venice, Florence, or Lombardy should be dispensed with, not least because the merchants who brought them were guilty of sharp practice: they would buy wool on credit both in the Cotswolds and in Calais, sell it for ready cash, and use the money so received to make loans at high interest rates to merchants of England:

> And thus they wolde, if ye will so beleve
> Wypen our nose with our owne sleve.[1]

Wisely, perhaps, the council did not take the advice of its memorialist. Control of the Channel, a requisite indeed for the suppression of piracy (as bad on the English side as on the Flemish or Breton) involved the maintenance of a larger fleet than even Henry V had been able to keep in being; but at best it could be no more than a means to the end the writer had in view, and to have regarded it and the supervision of the alien in England—another means advocated in the *Libelle*—as adequate 'policy' would have been a gross over-simplification. In 1436 Calais and the trade in wool and cloth loomed largest not

---

[1] *Libelle*, ed. Warner, p. 24.

merely because the government wanted the maximum subsidy
but because Calais had just been the object of attack: but there
was the wine trade and the whole problem of the Hanseatic
commercial relations to be taken into account, and though the
council may have thought about areas rather than about
streams of traffic, and have been at the time intent most of all
upon Flanders, in every branch of every trade (except that of
wool for the Hansards who did not deal in it) there were two
lines of commerce, native and denizen, to be considered. Thus
in the export trade in 'broad' cloths, 55 per cent. was in the
hands of denizens, 21 per cent. in those of Hansards, and 24 per
cent. in the hands of other aliens.[1] Furthermore, were English
merchants to be encouraged by discouraging the alien? Was
foreign trade a matter of export only? To control, as the *Libelle*
advocates, not only what came here and its importers, but also
what was sent by other countries to Flanders was a tall order
indeed.

The major change in the character of English trade during
the fifteenth century is the growth in the export of cloth and
miscellaneous merchandise in contrast to the export of wool.
Decline in the latter began in the second half of the fourteenth
century. The average for the years Michaelmas 1392 to
Michaelmas 1395 was 19,359 sacks. From Michaelmas 1410 to
Michaelmas 1415 annual shipments averaged 13,625 sacks,
and by the years 1446–8 it was only 7,654 sacks. Broadcloths,
on the other hand, had reached the annual average of 56,000;[2]
the contrast seems to indicate not only that the expansion of
industry accounted for the decline in wool exports but also that
there had been a temporary halt in the breeding of sheep. By
the middle of the century the best-grade wool was being sold
in Flanders at £13. 14s. 0d. the sack, and middle grade wool at
£9: with custom and subsidy at 40s. the sack to denizens and
53s. 4d. to aliens, and with a profit of not much over £2, the
English merchants were making about £57,600 for the 6,400
sacks they sold, and alien merchants some £15,500 for 1,600
sacks. The broadcloths were fetching more than this: on the
basis of an average value for £2 on each of those exported by
denizens and Hansards, and £2. 10s. on each exported by other
aliens, the annual investment of merchants selling cloth came

[1] E. Power and M. M. Postan, *English Trade in the Fifteenth Century* (1933), p. 13.
[2] Ibid., pp. 10–12.

to roughly £61,800. A second group of merchants was therefore now coming into existence, over and above the thirty-eight staplers who towards the middle of the century constituted some of the chief creditors of the crown: these new exporters were not confined to broadcloths, but imported wine and miscellaneous commodities; nor were all the exporters of wool confined to that line: they took over other goods (including wine, reshipped) to Calais. It thus appears that by the middle of the fifteenth century there were four groups handling British trade, first the Staplers, second the exporters of cloth and other commodities, conveniently termed Merchant Adventurers, third the Hansards, and last the non-Hanseatic aliens. Of these it was the Staplers who, as will be seen, maintained in the end the Calais garrison and its defences; but it was the Merchant Adventurers with whom the future lay; and the word merchant came to mean first and foremost the man who was selling all sorts of commodities abroad, as distinguished from the home trader who retailed the goods purchased from the producer.

This differentiation has been specially marked in the cloth industry in which rapid changes were taking place. As the manufacture of cloth could no longer be confined to the town and flowed into the country districts, a new class of clothier arose who arranged for every stage of cloth manufacture and sold the finished product to the drapers: but the drapers themselves were no longer concerning themselves with its sale abroad and there developed a distinct merchant class specializing in this trade. Professor Carus Wilson in her study of Bristol overseas trade has followed out the fortunes of the Canynges family in this respect. In Richard II's reign John and William (the elder) Canynges both produced and exported the cloth they made. But the younger William Canynges does not appear in a list of over 2,000 people accounting at the ulnage for more than a thousand cloths early in the reign of Henry VI; he was probably in the first instance purely a foreign merchant, procuring the cloth he exported from drapers and clothiers. From being a foreign merchant he ended as a shipowner, and William of Worcester in his account of Bristol notes that he kept 800 men for eight years employed in his ships, and had as many as a hundred workmen, carpenters, and masons on their construction. He controlled about a quarter of the shipping at the port of Bristol, and he made his money by carrying the merchandise of other people who paid freight charges, paid on the safe delivery of the cargo and paid at a high rate, for wine merchants £1 for every tun of wine brought from Lisbon to Ireland with a gratuity of 20 marks to the mariners within six weeks of their arrival.[1] The ship used for this carrying trade was normally termed the cog or carvel, carrying about 200 tuns, though early in the fifteenth century most Bristol vessels were round about 100 tuns capacity. The total tunnage of Canynges's ships has been estimated to amount to c. 3,000; but in the latter part of the century large and valuable cargoes might be carried: the George of which William of Worcester speaks (511 tuns) carried the goods of sixty-three merchants worth altogether more than £1,000: many merchants preferred not to put all their eggs into one basket, so to speak, but to distribute cargo for sale over several vessels.

The gradual articulation of the Merchant Adventurers' organizations takes place in the fifteenth century, though its more obvious phase has been attributed to the sixteenth. Both at Newcastle upon Tyne and at York there were groups of merchants so organized, the latter being especially active in the Low Countries. York merchants who, after the Mercers had, in Dr. Maud Sellers's words, 'captured the government of the City', and had secured a charter of authorization,[2] can be seen laying down a scale of payments for those entering the Adventurers' fellowship in Flanders, Brabant, and Zeeland.[3] In time York had a Merchant Venturers hall, which was lacking in London, but the records of the early Merchant Adventurers discoverable in the acts of court and the wardens' accounts of the Mercers' company compensate for the lack of any early

---

[1] E. M. Carus Wilson, 'The Overseas Trade of Bristol', *Medieval Merchant Venturers* (1954), pp. 86–90. The great family was not confined to Bristol. Thomas Canynges, grocer and alderman 1445–61, eldest son of John Canynges, had a son, William, who returned to Bristol: his one son Thomas engaged in trade and in 1478 was described as 'late of Bristol, knight and merchant': Sylvia Thrupp, *The Merchant Class of Medieval London* (1949), p. 328. The Canynges may have established a London branch in the course of the century.

[2] 1430. *York Merchant Adventurers, 1356–1917* (Surtees Soc. cxxix, 1917), pp. 35–36.

[3] 'Ordinances of the Mistery (1474–5)', ibid., p. 65. 'Also it is enacted by the masteres, constables and all the fellyship that everie brother of the said fellyship occupying as maistre in Flanders and Braband, and Zeland shall pay at his hansynge at Bruges, Andwarpe, Barow and Midilburg iis. at everie place aforesaid and no more. And everie apprentice of the said fellyship shall pay at his hansynge in Bruges, Andwarpe, Barow and Midilburg xvi d. at everie place aforesaid and no more.'

public buildings. In the Mercers' acts of court for 1465 the heading 'Court of Adventurers' first appears and the entr shows the 'Merchant Adventurers' along with other 'diver felyshippes aventurers' making representations, to the mayor on a point of diplomatic negotiations with the Low Countries. By 1489 this adventuring is not confined to the Mercers: 'counte of the felishippes aventurers' included wardens c 'drapers, grocers, skinners and others' as well as of one com pany of the Mercery; and in 1492, in the first account book o the Skinners' company, there is a reference to the 'Marchaunte adventurers of this Crafte'. None the less, just as at York, so i London it was the Mercers who took the lead and the Mercer Adventurers formed the nucleus towards which the othe Adventurers groups were drawn. The new organization of the London groups met at the Mercers' hall; but 'only graduall' did the sense of a new corporate personality emerge',[2] since th groups constituting it were still strongly connected with thei own organizations. Still, the fact remained that all the impor tant governors of the late fifteenth and early sixteenth centur were leading members of the Mercers' company.

The outflow of English cloth which was to overtake the Flemish cloth industry and to penetrate to the south of Franc and the Mediterranean was being directed in quantities tha were both welcome and alarming to the areas served by the German Hansa, and particularly to the organizers of trade i the Baltic and Scandinavia. The depreciatory remarks abou the Italian merchant in the *Libelle* recall the fact that a Southampton the Italian merchant was firmly established making the place outside London the main centre of Genoes shipping in English waters. This was in part the result of civi war which broke out in Flanders in 1379, with disastrous result to Flemish cloth production, and a rise in alien exports of woo took place in the early 'eighties. Between November 1380 anc February 1382 aliens exported 2,416 sacks of wool and ove 3,800 cloths from Southampton, and from February 1382 tc May 1383 they took out 1,473 sacks of wool and over 4,15(cloths.[3] The Italians, clearly, were failing to buy it in Flanders so came to Southampton, and there reappeared in the port the

---

[1] Carus Wilson, *Medieval Merchant Venturers*, p. 152.   [2] Ibid., p. 162.
[3] Alwyn A. Ruddock, *Italian Merchants and Shipping in Southampton, 1270–160(* (Southampton, 1951), p. 49.

Venetians who had been the first of their kindred to sail up the Solent. But the Venetians did not carry what a provincial centre and the country behind really wanted, as the Genoese did, and their galleys found that London was the better market for the expensive luxury goods they brought. The main centre of Italian trade after 1395 remained London, the chief market and distributing centre for Mediterranean goods which mostly were transhipped at Sandwich: London was also the chief Italian colony: but Southampton was to be the principal shipping centre for the Genoese, as it was for the Catalans. Towards the end of Henry IV's reign the Florentines made their appearance there, for the conquest of Pisa in 1406 gave the city direct access to the sea and it was using Porto Pisano; and now the competition of the Florentine was the chief reason for the disappearance of Genoese merchants and shipping from Southampton. The Genoese were helping Charles VI and it was not till after 1420 that their carracks appeared at Southampton again. There were ten or eleven anchored in Southampton Water each year between 1421 and 1458, and along with their appearance a great increase took place in the town's overseas trade in Italian hands. Eventually both Venetians and Florentines reappeared in the wonderful harbour. Until 1434 the Venetians had only frequented London and Sandwich; after that date the Venetians entered on at least four occasions during the following twelve years. By 1459–60 there was what has been called 'an unprecedented gathering of Italian shipping in the port', seven galleys and twelve carracks from Italy discharging their imports for the English market.[1] In the eleven months following Michaelmas 1459 alien goods for export valued at £12,899 paid petty custom, and alien merchants shipped 641 sacks of wool and over 8,360 cloths from the port. While the customs of other chief English ports show some falling off during this period, the statistics of Southampton's total trade in the enrolled accounts do not show the decline noted elsewhere.

The cargoes brought in Italian bottoms from the Mediterranean were spices and drugs of various kinds (including senna and rhubarb), oriental silks, cotton, sweet wines, currants, sugar, the alum of Foglia which came from Asia Minor, velvets and satins, gold and silver articles and precious stones as well as fine armour, especially for the royal family, and a great quantity

[1] Ruddock, op. cit., p. 68.

of ecclesiastical vestments, while for the scholar there were books of parchment, writing paper, and paper in reams (paper royal). The Genoese brought the highly important woad, the blue dye which English dyers used to produce green and violet cloth as well as blues. The Venetians specialized in spices, sweet wines, and luxury goods, making Southampton the staple port in England for all sorts of Mediterranean wines. For the return voyages the Italians brought Cotswold wool, bales of cloth, blocks of tin and lead, hides and calfskins, and the ala-baster carvings made in the northern midlands. The tin was brought from Devon and Cornwall in coasting vessels, but it should be remarked that a great deal of Cornish tin was sent direct to London to supply the London pewterers and the foreign market. In 1424 the weather drove nine ships from Fowey into Portsmouth harbour, whereupon the searchers dis-covered that the 2,254 pieces of tin which they carried were bound for London.

The existence of an organized Italian colony at Southampton with agents of the Florentine and Lucchese firms trading with the place provoked in the end the insular hostility earlier voiced by the poet Gower and the author of the *Libelle*. It was the privileges the Italians enjoyed in the wool trade which caused the trouble; people saw Italian agents riding round the Cots-wold towns and competing with English woolmen for the best crop. George Cely reported from Calais in 1480 that there was but little Cotswold wool at Calais and he understood that the Lombards had bought it up.[1] The indignation against the aliens in London which later took the form of rioting in 1456 and 1457, was for long not shared by the people of Southamp-ton, which profited much in its town revenues from the presence of the galleys and carracks, while Italians were prepared to pay good rents for town property they occupied.[2] It was not difficult to find lodgings ashore for the crews, and brawls ashore be-tween the newcomers and the townsmen, though they occurred, were not serious. The townsmen were prepared for widows or daughters to be married to Italian agents, as well as to confer burgess rights and civic office upon Italian merchants once they were permanently domiciled in the town. It was, however, in 1456 and 1457 that the anti-alien movement in the capital spread south-westwards. In July 1457 a premeditated attack on

---

[1] *Cely Papers*, ed. H. E. Malden, pp. 45, 48.   [2] Ruddock, op. cit., p. 145.

he Italian colony in London took place in which the mayoral
orces came into collision with the servants and apprentices
hat had planned to massacre the Lombard colony in Bread
treet. The alarm caused by the rioting prompted the leaders
f the Italian commercial interests in London to leave the capi-
al and make Winchester and Southampton their headquarters.
n October 1457 the Venetian galleys anchored off Cowes,
nd the visitors planned to find the accommodation they wanted
ot in Southampton, but at Winchester, now suffering from the
eparture of the cloth industry into the countryside, and ready
o receive extra reinforcements. Gregory's Chronicle states that
hey took 'grete old mancyons' in Winchester, caused them to
e repaired by their landlords and then never occupied them.
he reason was that Southampton had become insecure as a
ase. The internecine struggle, on the town council and in the
own itself between the party with business associations with the
Aediterranean and an opposition led by merchants who were
itizens of London as well as Southampton and dominated by
he London grocer, Thomas Payne, worked itself out within an
talian context, Payne having conceived a violent dislike to-
vards Italian methods of business, particularly after the Genoese
eet had seized the ships of Robert Sturmy of Bristol on their
vay back from the Levant (1457). Hostility towards the
Genoese mounted in Southampton, and Payne put himself at
he head of it. On royal instructions the mayor threw all the
Genoese residents in Southampton into prison, and tried to
rrest the Genoese carracks in the harbour; but the existing
égime was not drastic enough for Payne, who at the mayoral
lection of 1460, by an alarming display of force, secured the
lection of a man of his own party; and a royal mandate con-
emning these proceedings and ordering a new election was
otally disregarded. A riot, typical of the state of things at the
nd of the Lancastrian régime, placed the control of the town
n the hands of an unscrupulous group of men, and measures
vere rapidly taken against aliens in the town. The story of the
outhampton riot quickly penetrated to Italy where the greatest
larm was felt for the Florentine and Venetian galleys. In 1461
messenger was sent from Venice with instructions to the cap-
ain to return. The story ended in 1463 when Payne, mayor of
he town, as the result of an appeal by the Venetians in the
hancery court in which reference was made to his 'grete

myght and supporte within the said Towne', was deposed from office by order of Edward IV.[1]

Periodical outbursts of anti-alien feeling influenced the course of English relations with the Hansa, the economic organization of the German merchants trading throughout northern Europe. The goods that England chiefly wanted of Germany were corn, timber, pitch, tar, and ashes, as well as furs and wax. Corn came from the east Baltic (i.e. German east of the Elbe). The English demand was considerable, especi ally during years of scarcity: corn might be sent to Gascony in exchange for wine and sometimes to Iceland in return for fish. Timber in the fifteenth century was primarily a Prussian product: boxes, furniture, and small boats were exported from Danzig. The upward trend of the Hansa had come to an end round about 1370–80. In the second half of the fourteenth cen tury changes were taking place all over Europe that threatened to oust the Hanseatic merchants from their positions of privilege; the Scandinavian countries achieved politically a measure of consolidation and aimed at being economically independent of the Germans. English cloth began to compete in the international markets with Flemish cloth, in the sale of which the Hansa held a monopoly: English and, soon after wards, Dutch vessels filled the Zuider Zee ports, and sailed into the Baltic which had been a closed Hanseatic sea: the Teutonic order was engaged in struggles with its own towns and with the newly established power of Poland–Lithuania, and in the east Novgorod, the north-eastern outpost of Teutonic influence, was ultimately to fall to the Muscovite conquerors. Within Germany itself the great towns of the south, Augsburg and Nuremberg, were dangerous competitors through their western business methods and enterprise. Most serious of all for the future of the organization, the Hanseatic towns them selves had begun to lose their sense of cohesion; the fears of Lübeck in particular were aroused against western competitors in the Baltic trade, as well as against the towns of Prussia, the chief distributor of English cloth in Poland and western Russia. This was the moment when English traders were doing their best to establish themselves in Danzig, provoking a reaction in favour of the local market and regional monopoly. This

[1] The narrative of events is given at length by Miss Ruddock, op. cit., pp. 177–80.

reaction and the protectionist tactics followed by individual members of the Hansa in eastern Germany led here to the famous demand of reciprocity. The English asked that they should be given the same treatment in Prussian and in other Hanseatic centres as the Hanseatics enjoyed in England, and that as long as the Hanseatics refused to grant the English demand, their privileges in England should be countermanded. The merchants of Cologne and Westphalia at the outset, then the merchants in more easterly towns had been allowed to form a corporate body, the Hanse, similar to the Flemish Hansa, in London, soon transformed into the Steelyard, with its right to hold property in the city and to sell retail. By a series of royal charters the Hansa had received exemption from the customs tariffs exacted in the fourteenth century and from subsequent increases, so that by 1400 the Hansa merchants were paying less on cloth exported (12*d*. instead of 1*s*. 2*d*.) than Englishmen and were free from the subsidy of tunnage and poundage.

The latter grant was denied to the Hansa in the parliament of 1381. But while the Steelyard immediately complained, English merchants who had been trying to establish a colony in Danzig were equally vocal in their demands in Prussia, which provoked the diet of Prussian towns to try to restrict the English rights of residence and to oppose any settlement which involved transfer of the family. English piracy at the same time exacerbated Hansa feeling and in March 1405 the diet of the Hansa at Lübeck prohibited the trade in English cloth and the export of Baltic goods to England. But the embargo did not last because it was not sufficiently complete and not everybody obeyed it. The English on their side had reason to guard against the attempt then being made by John the Fearless to bring the Hansa into an anti-English alliance, and Prussia found that she could not do without the English. In the end she concluded, though it was not to the taste of Danzig, a treaty by which the principle of reciprocity was recognized. But the agreement reached in 1408 by which the English were allowed to trade freely, wholesale and retail, in Prussia, and to live there as long as they liked, was not sufficient for the English adventurers who wanted admission to the markets of Livonia and west Russia. The Danzigers on their side were afraid that the English merchants might be erecting another Steelyard and creating a common fortress and centre, to use Danzig for conquering the

neighbouring country as they were alleged to have done in
Bordeaux and Gascony. From 1410 the disputes dragged on
with retaliation from the London side, and the preparation
throughout the country, of an anti-Hanseatic campaign in
parliament, particularly at the accession of Henry V. Between
1428 and 1430 there was a period of *détente*, when both side
made efforts to understand the other's point of view, but it was
the colonists themselves who made the difficulties. It was the
English in Danzig who, though permitted in 1428 to have their
own governor, continued to demand full parity and to protest
against taxation. In June 1434 the diet at Lübeck asked for
their expulsion from Prussia, since on the English side a new
method of valuing goods for customs purposes had threatened
to stop the flow of Hanseatic goods to England. Matters had
reached their most extreme crisis to date, and the Hansa determined on the dispatch of a large delegation to recount Hanseatic
claims and grievances and to make a large claim for compensation. The English were too much occupied with the conference
of Arras to consider it, and when Arras was over, they were in
a very different frame of mind: anxious to restore peace with
the Hansa. On the side of their opponents, the embargo on
English trade was impossible to enforce, for, as previously, not
all members of the Hansa would agree. Then the men of
Cologne would have nothing to do with the embargo and talked
of making separate terms; and the Zuider Zee towns acted
quite independently, while the Bergen factory issued permission
to trade with England. The Hansa ambassadors, therefore, could
not maintain the line which Danzig wanted, and found that
they were obliged to forego financial claim after 1408 (the date
of the treaty) and to include in their proposals for a treaty a
clause defining and expounding the English position in the
Hansa more fully than had been done in the past.

The English wanted more than this, but Cardinal Beaufort
acted as a restraining factor and wisely, since the proposals of
1437, in addition to the reciprocity clause stating the right of
the English to enter Prussia, to stay there and trade unrestric-
tedly, gave the English financial exemptions as exceptional as
those the Hanseatics possessed in England, and the exemption
clause was to extend back 100 years.[1] This treaty or group of

[1] Postan, 'Anglo-Hanseatic Economic Relations', *English Trade in the Fifteenth
Century*, p. 119.

proposals in 1437 was never confirmed by Prussia or recognized by Danzig: it represents the farthest that Hanseatic concessions to England could go. It was a success, but one that was not repeated. Thereafter every encounter with the Hansa ended to the detriment of this country: 'most of the clashes were disastrous to English shipping or trade';[1] and in the end the Hanseatics won a notable triumph at the peace conference of Utrecht (Sept. 1473, confirmed by act of parliament in October).[2] That the English lost their gains, step by step, arose very largely from the anti-alien measures to which the Lancastrian government consented, beginning with the parliament of Reading in 1440, and embodied in the assented petitions of other parliaments (e.g. that of 1442). In January 1442 the commons demanded an ultimatum to the high master of the Prussian Hansa if the terms of the agreement made in 1437 were not carried out. Parliament also launched an act for the maintenance of a fleet of thirty-eight ships for the protection of English shipping, in which the Germans detected a measure to sanction privateering. The Steelyard began to suspect that freedom for reprisals and piracy was what the English merchants wanted; and this was unfortunately confirmed on 23 May 1449 when a fleet of 110 vessels, Flemish, Dutch, and Hanseatic, was captured on its way from the Bay of Bourgneuf by English privateers and the property of the Hansa merchants treated as a prize. But events would not have taken the downward course they did if Prussia had been the sole opponent of England in the Hansa. The fact was that after the affray of 1449 Lübeck was brought into conflict with this country. Although at first it was found possible to isolate her, through the friendly attitude of Hamburg towards the English, and owing to the internal jealousies within the Hansa, in the long run English piracy and reprisals, most of all, perhaps, the seizure, in return for the capture (June 1468) of an English fleet bound for the Baltic, of Hanseatic goods in London as a compensation for English losses, united practically all the Hansa towns from Westphalia to Livonia against this country. The reason why in the end they were to prove successful lay in the assistance, probably on the advice of the duke of Burgundy, given to Edward IV when he was planning to return to England after the Readeption. It was on ships of the Hansa that Edward sailed to England, and for

[1] Postan, op. cit., p. 120.   [2] Rot. Parl. vi. 65–66.

their services he promised to satisfy the Hansa's complaints. This was done in the treaty of Utrecht. The treaty renewed the 'oold frendlyhode' between the 'merchauntes and people of the nation of Almayn, beyng under and of the confederation, ligue and company called the Duchie Hanze'; it wiped out all grievances and complaints for compensation begun during the period 21 November 1408 to 19 September 1473, granted free passage for Englishmen 'unto the londe of Pruce and other place of the Hanze' with no exactions or prizes upon their goods, and confirmed *in toto* the liberties and franchises granted to the Hansa. In February 1474 possession of the London Steelyard and other steelyards at Boston and at Kings Lynn was confirmed to them in perpetuity, and they were granted the sum of £10,000 to be levied from the customs over a number of years. They were also given the custody of Bishopsgate, part of which had previously belonged to the citizens.[1]

It was a victory for the Hansa; but the bickering, the exclusion of one set of merchants or the other, the protective measures against the aliens *en masse*, although parliament rolls provide copious examples of proposals to that effect during the middle of the century, could not be allowed to disrupt the international mercantile system for any length of time. The logic of business was against it. This system existed on a basis of credit and it operated by fixed centres where both payments and credit were obtainable, where new contracts or agreements for the terms of credit could be drawn up, and the value of one currency set against another. From the standpoint of the exchange, rates were obtainable in these centres only, and for one of them to be lost or to pass out of working would administer a severe blow to credit. As the German historian Rörig pointed out, there existed before the end of the fourteenth century a European system of financial centres used by the German merchant community, and of these London was one and Calais another.

For the English merchant Calais was essential, for it was the centre of the stapler community which sold the English wool crop and of the traders who were passing on their cloths and other commodities to the Flemish, Dutch, Spanish, and other

[1] The city had taken it over in 1461. The Hanseatics were claiming to guard the portcullis, which was considered 'too dangerous in war time to commit to the custody of foreigners': *Calendar of Letter Books of the City of London*, Letter Book I, p. 14. For the respective parts of the gate and their holders, cf. *Liber Albus*, i. 485–8, and *Letter Book* C, p. 41.

merchants. It is there, and in the correspondence of firms there like the Celys, that the credit system can best be studied. The woolman or professional dealer like John Linwood or William Midwinter bought the wool on credit from the growers and sold it on credit to the staplers who in turn sold it on credit to the foreign buyers. Not on credit for the whole sum, since in each case a proportion of the whole (often a third) was paid down immediately: the stapler, if he was in London, or his London branch depended on the remittance he received from Calais, otherwise he would have to borrow money in London, to pay the wool dealer. Examples are to hand from the Cely papers to show how difficult it was for the stapler if the money did not arrive. Sometimes the dealer found that he could not buy the wool as cheaply as he had been led to think and was now being hard pressed by the growers who normally had allowed him quite a long credit: when he approached the staplers with the awkward news of the price being changed, there was some con-fusion in the firm.[1] The reason for the confusion was that the timing of the transaction had been disturbed; for when the dealer wrote thus, the Celys were themselves selling wool on credit to Dutch and Flemish merchants before they could remit anything to England, and the grower had evidently shortened the dates within which credit for the successive instalments of the price was given. The principle was that wool could not be bought for cash down; yet it had to be sold off, for old wool was not on a par with new, and if kept lost its commercial value. The trade depended upon the smooth working of sale credits[2] and it was this that the merchant always demanded. Any attempt to speed up or to consolidate the instalment system of payments was doomed to failure. In 1430 in the ordinance of Partition of Wool it was attempted to introduce a rigid system of control over the transactions of individual merchants, accom-panied by an order that payments for wool should be made cash down and all the bullion should be brought forthwith to the mint at Calais. The merchants had no hesitation in petitioning against it, and in 1442 it proved impossible to enforce an order to the English merchants to bring in a third of the price they

[1] Cf. examples from the correspondence of William Midwinter and Richard Cely in E. Power, 'The Wool Trade', *English Trade in the Fifteenth Century*, pp. 62–63.
[2] The view of Professor Postan: 'Credit in Medieval Trade' in E. M. Carus Wilson (ed.), *Essays in Economic History* (1954), p. 68.

received in bullion.[1] Sales on credit continued, whatever the
government might decide: the Celys, a good average firm, 'sold
wool on credit in eleven out of every twelve transactions recorded in their letters and accounts'.[2]

Deferment was not *gratis*. On such sales interest was charged,
but expressed in terms of the exchange. On 20 October 1478
Richard Cely sold to John Delopis and a group of his fellow
merchants thirty-one sarplars of good Cotswold wool for 19
marks. He received the 'third penny' in ready money, at
25s. 4d. Flemish to the pound sterling, and the other two-
thirds payable at 24s. Flemish to the pound sterling on 20 April
and 20 October 1479. The exchange rate at which the portions
of the loan were to be paid was stated. Instalments had this
advantage that they kept the pound steady, for prices at Calais
tended to vary but little.[3] If for the moment there were few
buyers for wool at Calais, long dates could be arranged for repayment: as Richard Cely said to his son 'Spare not for a long
day', for merchants might arrange it for even two or three years
ahead.[4] A proportion only, therefore, was paid to the staplers
and the balance had to be collected at the seasonal fairs of
the Netherlands, at Antwerp, Bruges, Bergen op Zoom, and
elsewhere. If and when the money had been secured, there
remained the problem of getting it home, either by the cumbersome method of transferring cash or, more generally, by bills
of exchange drawn upon the London offices of importing
merchants, frequently the mercers who were importing on a
large scale. The mercers needed Flemish money at the marts and
the staplers needed English money for their purchases in the
Cotswolds: the stapler in Flanders delivered his money to a
mercer and from him 'received a bill of exchange payable at a
future date in London in English money, the interest being expressed in the rate of exchange for different terms, exactly as in
the case of the wool sales'.[5]

The studies of the last quarter-century have shown that the
Staple was a valuable instrument of royal finance, enabling the
crown to obtain large sums of money on credit, in return for
which the staplers had asked for and secured the enforcement

[1] Carus Wilson, op. cit., p. 69.   [2] Ibid., p. 81.
[3] Power, op. cit., p. 65.   [4] *Cely Papers*, p. 5.
[5] Power, op. cit., p. 68. For the early bills in the Low Countries, cf. R. de
Roover, *Money, Banking and Credit in Medieval Bruges* (1948), pp. 50–55.

of a strict monopoly for Calais as the market for the goods they sold. They had also asked for relaxation in the bullion laws which previously had compelled them to receive a large proportion of ready money from their customers instead of relying upon the negotiable instruments which were becoming increasingly common. In return for their loans to the Lancastrian government they secured, in 1449, and again in 1458, the withdrawal of licences to export elsewhere than to Calais; and their help to the exchequer would have continued in its existing form, had it not been for the concern of some of the staplers for the security of the place, the 'saufgard of the said Towne', and the fact that in 1454 the garrison mutinied and seized the staplers' wool. At first, it appears, the soldiers tried to organize a 'restraint', i.e. to limit the amount of wool in the market so as to sell at a high price; encountering opposition from the staplers here, they made the merchants forward the ready money got from the sale of the wool: a sum more than 10,000 marks. It was manifest that the government could not provide for the Calais garrison in the way wanted, that is, not by assignments but by ready cash: it was now confronted with the responsibility of financing it from the wool subsidy and had to make a settlement to that effect with the staplers in 1456. In the end Edward IV (1466) made the staplers responsible both for providing the funds as well as for the whole financial administration of the place. It is easy to hold that after the treaty of Arras Calais should have been given up: to retain it cost a matter of at least £18,000–20,000 a year, perhaps more, but the other mercantile advantages deriving from it were not inconsiderable, and the place played a role of great importance under Yorkist policy. It was, indeed, partly responsible for the success of Warwick in bringing his protégé Edward to the throne.

To be a merchant it was essential to be an adventurer. The Iceland trade was opened up by the fishermen of the east coast ports who in the early part of the century (1412) were attracted to the Vestmann islands, the coasts of which abounded in cod and ling. The fishing doggers or, as we might say, smacks from little places like Cromer and Blakeney and Orwell, though their vessels were small, understood deep-sea lining and were prepared to stock their boats with food and fish the whole summer in the northern seas, despite the prohibition of Bergen and the jealousy of the Hansa. They could fish farther out than the

Icelander who came out to no twelve miles radius as is claimed today. Defying the orders of Henry V's government the fishermen were not slow to turn a fishing into a trading expedition, or to do both, for Icelanders were glad to part with salted produce like stockfish in return for the fisherman's victuals. The English also brought back hake, pollack, and salmon. The English fisherman was less popular than the genuine English trader, the merchant from Lynn which had its recognized body of 'merchants of Iceland', or from Bristol, which played the greater part in the Iceland trade; for if Iceland depended politically upon Norway, geographically the island lies in the north Atlantic far to the north-west. The smaller ships of the fishermen were followed by larger merchant craft, whose routine was to leave the ports in the early spring, between February and April, remain in Iceland throughout the summer while the market was open, and to return between July and September, perhaps going on to Gascony for the following spring.

It might be thought that Gascony, as far as foodstuffs are concerned, was self-sufficing. In point of fact her specialization in the vine led her to look elsewhere for consumptibles. England sent grain, fish, and dairy produce, and as the manufacture of cloth developed, this also found a market in Gascony. A good many imports of food and clothing came to Bordeaux from Bristol to be exchanged, wholly or in part, for wine; and wine was an item of the highest importance to England. During the five years of truce, 1444–9, English imports of wine, most of it from Gascony, reached their peak for the whole fifteenth century, some 12,000 tuns in the period September 1447 to September 1448, and in 1448–9 some 13,000 tuns.[1] In 1449, with the renewal of war, the situation changed: less than 6,000 tuns reached England during 1449–50 and in the following autumn (1450), when the French attacked the valleys of the Dordogne and Garonne, and the Gironde was blocked with their fleet, no more than 6,000 tuns were exported. Upon the fall of Bordeaux (12 June 1451) the situation improved somewhat, and under licence from the French crown as many as twenty-six English ships were using the harbour by January 1452, while English firms continued to load on foreign ships, so that imports of wine during the first year of French rule in Bordeaux reached the

[1] E. M. Carus Wilson, 'The Effects of the Acquisition and of the Loss of Gascony on the English Wine Trade', *Bull. Inst. Hist. Res.* xxi (1946–8), 149.

figure of 7,000 tuns.[1] The final surrender of the place (June 1453) caused some dislocation of the trade, but total English imports of wine for 1454/5 were 9,500 tuns. The direct trade still continued, and in 1454 there were no less than fifty-eight licences for trading with Bordeaux. In 1455 Charles VII withdrew all safe-conducts from the English 'his ancient enemies, but the order produced consternation, and he was persuaded to allow eighty safe-conducts to be granted each year, though by himself or his admiral only: in the end he gave permission to his admiral to grant them on the spot.

The manufacture of the cloths sold by merchants over the Continent brought about a change in the location of industry. The west of England, East Anglia, and the West Riding of Yorkshire became new centres of industrial population when abundant water power made it possible to turn the fulling mills. The Cotswolds, and the Stroud valley and Bradford-on-Avon were the home of the fine broadcloth, and places like Stroud and Chalford grew from nothing into thriving industrial centres.[2] The craftsmen lived along the valleys: at Castle Combe seventy were said to live down by the river, each with servants and apprentices, a colony from whom Sir John Fastolf bought each year the red and white cloth to clothe his men in France.[3] The Wiltshire hundreds of Bradford and Melksham were early areas of settlement. By the time that Leland visited Bradford-on-Avon, 'all the town', he could write, 'standeth by cloth-making',[4] but the industry here is probably earlier than the fifteenth century; at Melksham itself by 1555 there were two fulling mills in the town,[5] and the place was one of the more prosperous of the rising Cotswold towns. Trowbridge was another early centre, where in the early fourteenth century the small township of Lovemede had grown up, to provide dwellings for people employed by clothiers like Thames, Dauntsey, or Long. It was not a borough, but had its own customs and the houses are spoken of as *burgagia*, for in 1502 Walter Dauntsey 'did seised of 22 burgages and of other land held in free burgage';[6] it contained by the later part of the fifteenth century a

[1] Ibid., p. 151.
[2] See the map of the Cotswold area in G. D. Ramsay, *The Wiltshire Woollen Industry during the Seventeenth Century* (1943), frontispiece.
[3] *Camb. Econ. Hist.* ii. 418. Cf. below, p. 378.
[4] *Leland's Itinerary*, ed. Toulmin Smith, i. 135.
[5] *Vict. County Hist., Wilts.* vii. 113.
[6] Ibid., p. 137.

number of prosperous manufacturers amongst whom James Terumber is best known for his chantry in the parish church. Manufacture not of broadcloths but of kerseys extended down through Bridgwater and Taunton into Devonshire. Kerseys were the main produce of Essex and Suffolk, where Colchester, Maldon, Coggeshall, and Sudbury had long been known for their cloths. By the fifteenth century it was the banks of the Stour which had become the centre of concentration. Norwich had developed the manufacture of worsteds, but by the fifteenth century the industry appears to have been in decline and little worsted to have been exported. Perhaps the chief kersey producing region was the West Riding of Yorkshire, where by this time there was an active industry concentrated on the upper parts of the Aire (especially at Calverley) and the Calder, in Leeds and Bradford, Wakefield, and Halifax. The West Riding had outstripped the City of York: farther north-west the development of Kendal had been largely due to the spread of the industry which crept up the valley of the Kent, and farther still along the valleys that provided excellent water and ground not good enough for agriculture, where the cloths could be stretched. Wales produced quantities of frieze and some fine-quality material from the southern marches, especially at Ludlow. From Coventry in Warwickshire came the famous 'blue' cloth, used by the cappers. To produce all these goods both for export and for home consumption a great quantity of material from abroad was required: from Flanders, madder and teasels, from Gascony, Picardy, Brabant, parts of Germany, and Italy woad, alum and saffron; the woad and alum brought to Southampton and distributed over the south-west.

The industry, though organized on a capitalist basis, was one in which there were both large-scale enterprise and the small free craftsman. Many of the workers could be described as smallholders, selling farm produce, engaged part-time in agriculture. The cloth industry was one in which many ranks of people could take part: the landowner who turned himself into a large-scale manufacturer, but was still an agriculturalist; the small clothier who was himself a weaver, probably with two or three looms in his own house; and the fullers, dyers, or shearmen, some of whom had risen to the clothier class, some of whom stayed as artisans but made money in other ways. The cloth industry was only with difficulty fitted into the walls of town or city; it needed streams and organized suburbs. Both factories and domestic work done on the clothier's own premises had a place in it and the nascent country town was better suited for the required buildings and the homes for the workers than the classic and compact borough.

This change in the location of the cloth industry is reflected in the population statistics of the period. The data are scarce, but there are two substantial bodies of evidence, the poll tax of 4 Richard II (1380–1) and the subsidy of 14–15 Henry VIII (1523–4), which enable the distribution of the tax-paying population in an area to be compared and study made of the population fluctuations of the town centres and the centres of rural industry. An especially fruitful examination of the Cotswold area[1] has established certain facts about Cirencester, Lechlade, Fairford, Tetbury, and Painswick in the south Cotswolds, and about Stowe, Chipping Campden, and Winchcombe in the north. The chief point that emerges is the decline of Cirencester. In 1381 its taxed population was one-third of the total taxed population of the eight towns: by 1524 it was only slightly more than a fifth of the other towns, while Campden, Lechlade, and Fairford maintained their position. There was slight decline in Stowe, Painswick, and Tetbury, and a decided expansion in Winchcombe, whose tax-paying population in 1381 was only two-fifths of Cirencester's. By 1524 Winchcombe was nearly a tenth bigger. In the northern Cotswolds there was no appreciable move from the towns to the villages, but in the case of Winchcombe, the rise in population may be due to its increasing success as a market centre at the point where the vale meets the wold. In 1381 there is no indication of any specialized cloth manufacture in Winchcombe, though there was fulling in the adjoining hamlet of Cotes from the early fourteenth century. This must have grown up in the fifteenth or early sixteenth.

Generally speaking there was a de-urbanizing movement in process throughout the Cotswold area. This is not without parallel elsewhere. Coventry is a good example. In 1280 its

[1] By Dr. R. H. Hilton in his (unpublished) paper, 'Some Social and economic evidence in Late Medieval Tax Returns' (1959), kindly communicated to the writer. As regards method, Dr. Hilton makes the point that at different dates different social groups escaped assessment. Of those who should have been taxed in Gloucester in 1381 about a third escaped the tax collector as compared with what happened in 1377.

population must have been 10,000 after the Black Death; in
1377 it was 7,000 and in 1521 we know it to have been 6,600.
Stratford upon Avon similarly dropped, with the decline of the
fourteenth-century cloth industry, which had been sufficient to
claim a street of fullers and a drapers hall. York, which had
nearly 11,000 inhabitants in the late fourteenth century, had
fallen to less than 8,000. The tax yield in the subsidy of 1523–4
was only £379, and Exeter had by now equalled it, and more
in population. Among the larger centres the rise seems to have
been greatest in London, to which Professor J. C. Russell attributes, for the early sixteenth century, 67,744. It is difficult to
ascertain the figure for Norwich for the early sixteenth century
it has been estimated at 12,000, and as it must have lost some
population to the country, the figure may hold for the second
half of the fifteenth. Newcastle upon Tyne was about the same.
Of course taxable capacity does not always correctly indicate
size, for individual rich men may greatly increase the liability:
Richard Marler, grocer of Coventry, paid nearly one-ninth of
Coventry's tax and in Leicester William Wigston the younger,
merchant of the Staple, paid slightly over a quarter of the total
subsidy, while in the Suffolk cloth town of Lavenham, which
paid (£402) more than the four wards of York, Thomas Spring
III was accounted the richest man, apart from the peerage,
outside London, owning when he died some twenty-six manors.
Here at Lavenham the Springs paid 37 per cent. of the total
subsidy in 1524. At Norwich Robert Jannys paid rather more
than Richard Marler at Coventry, one-fourteenth of the whole
subsidy, in 1524.[1]

At a time when the rich entrepreneur was collecting labour
and planting out the artisans near his sheds and work centres,
many small villages and hamlets were becoming depopulated,
and some disappearing altogether. The historian and antiquary
John Rous who left at his death (1489) the *Historia regni Angliae*,
in deploring 'the modern destruction of villages which brings
dearth to the Commonwealth', gave for Warwickshire alone a
list of fifty-eight depopulated places, all but two of which have
been identified.[2] This catalogue, twenty-five years earlier than
the first government inquiry, is headed *Destructores villarum* and

[1] H. G. Hoskins, 'Provincial Towns in the Sixteenth Century', *Trans. Roy. Hist.
Soc.*, 5th ser., vi (1956), 6–7.
[2] Maurice Beresford, *The Lost Villages of England* (1954), pp. 81–82.

s unquestionably genuine and not due to a later completing
hand. Rous regarded the evil as wider than a Warwickshire
problem:

If such destructions as that in Warwickshire took place in other
parts of the country, it would be a national danger. Yet not all my
list is of Warwickshire villages: some, although a few, are in Glouces-
ershire and Worcestershire, but none of them more than a dozen
miles from Warwick.

This depopulation has now been surveyed in its wider aspects,
county by county; the North and East Ridings, Lincolnshire,
and the midlands (especially Leicestershire and Warwickshire)
were those affected most. The evidence points less to the successive visitations of the Death than to the extension of grazing
and consequent wool production, sharply stepped up at the end
of the 1460's and the early 1470's. In 1447–8 the figures for
wool production came out at 24,381 sacks; by 1481–2 there was
an increase to 29,100 sacks, or nearly 20 per cent. There is little
doubt that the turn-over to grass is not a Tudor phenomenon
pure and simple, but perhaps was partly the result of the agricultural depression of the years 1430–60.[1] It was the most plaus-
ible way of meeting that depression. Even small customary
tenants were resorting to it. Their few sheep have grown to
many. On the All Souls College manor of Salford in Bedfordshire, a predominantly arable estate, the court roll for 1472
shows the court fixing the maximum number of sheep per
holding of so many acres.[2] It is interesting to observe that it
was towards the end of the depressive years that the population,
reduced to about 2·1 million in the first half of the fifteenth
century, began to rise again, though the steepest part of the rise
was towards the end of the century and the first half of the
sixteenth. A different type of record confirms conclusions mainly
based on taxation evidence. Recent work on the pre-Reformation chapelries of Lancashire has shown that between 1470 and
1548 the number of chapelries dependent upon parish churches
situated in the south-east part of the county was about forty-
six, thirty-nine being new establishments, and of these twenty-
four appeared in Salford hundred and in Blackburnshire south
of the Ribble. This predominance in the south-east of the
county can doubtless be accounted for in part by the expansion

[1] Cf. below, p. 376.
[2] Archives of All Souls College, Salford, Court Rolls, s.d.

of the textile industries and a growth of population more rapid than in the agricultural regions of the west and north.[1]

The fifteenth century is not a time of stagnation but of mobility in the population of town and country alike. Growth where it occurs is selective and according to area. If textiles had much to do with it, an even greater factor was the psychological unrest and migration of the peasantry. The social and economic revolution that was taking place, besides throwing up the budding entrepreneur from families of well-to-do but otherwise wholly obscure freeholders, was bringing to the fore the prosperous virgater, the enterprising tenant who had gone in for a policy of consolidation and inclosure of the arable, and in general, among the lower ministerial class, the clerks, stewards, and administrators upon whom the work of the estates depended. On many estates it was the bailiffs and the sergeants who themselves became the farmers, rendering both money rents and rents in kind.[2] In some cases the proximity of a city may have helped the process. The little parish of Iffley near Oxford provides an example. From the end of the thirteenth century land there had been changing hands rapidly. The Smiths of Littlemore, and two families who took their name from Sandford, another adjoining village, acquired considerable property there, while only the religious houses seem to have kept their lands unchanged. Out of the buying and selling arose a number of minor landowners, notably Thomas Cowley who in the fifteenth century rose to be coroner; or Thomas Bell husbandman and churchwarden, in 1472, who made part of his money as a miller.[3]

In briefest terms, from about 1390 and during the next century, the seignorial estate was breaking down, and being succeeded by the farms of the successful peasant and of the gentry. Leases have a long history, going back to the thirteenth century; the fourteenth saw them widely adopted. After the Black Death, with the consequent shortage of labour, there was at first a keen struggle to keep the demesne working, to retain the old customary husbandry: then, except for some of the larger religious houses, the attempt was abandoned by the lords, the

---

[1] G. H. Tupling, 'The Pre-Reformation Parishes and Chapelries of Lancashire' *Trans. Lancs. and Chesh. Antiq. Soc.* lxvii (1957).

[2] Cf., among many, the leases granted to the reeve at Crawley, Hampshire given below, p. 373.

[3] *Vict. County Hist. Oxon.* v (Bullingdon hundred), 200.

xed labour services owed by the villeins disappeared and were
eplaced by wage labour. Often the new holdings, where they
ad been created, had no dependent tenants attached to them,
he bondman had gone, and hired labour was often more
conomical and all that could be obtained. So great was the
eaction against all forms of bondage that on the new peasant
oldings resident *famuli* were extremely hard to get and in some
illages no farm servants or labourers appear in the tax lists at
ll. Some of the wealthier cultivators got them, but the full-
ime *famulus*, especially if he was a ploughman or a caster, was
uch competed for. Generally speaking, English manorial
conomy had now entered upon a period of leases replacing
ustomary service; the lord, secular or ecclesiastical, no longer
xploits the demesne, but is a *rentier*, receiving what is collected
or him by his steward or his agents. Between 1350 and 1450
enurial serfdom received its quietus, either by the villein, if he
id not fly, becoming a wage labourer, or by the conversion of
arts of the estate from arable to sheep farming and the con-
equent eviction of the villeins through deliberate raising of
ents and through fines upon entry.

To establish any rules about when, where, and how these
hanges took place is most difficult. Often the information is
ntirely lacking. From firm evidence it is known that there are
o many villeins and so many cottagers on the land; the next
eliable evidence is perhaps more than two centuries ahead: the
ervices have altered. Taking Oxfordshire again, the Abingdon
Abbey manor of Lewknor, held with Postcombe in the Chilterns,
vas returned in Domesday[1] as having 8 serfs, 37 villeins, and
8 bordars; that is 73 persons (with the help of their families)
vholly or partially engaged in agriculture. We see that the
nanor was rated at 17 hides but containing lands for 26
eople, of which 4½ ploughlands were in demesne, 3 being tilled
y 6 serfs, 2 to each plough: the remainder were cultivated by
he ploughing service of 30 villeins and 26 bordars who held
etween them 23 ploughs and therefore had 21½ plough teams
or cultivating their land. At the time of the Hundred Rolls
1279) the number of villeins had increased, but they were
olding smaller tenements and land is more subdivided than
n the twelfth century, and there are numbers of freeholders
vhose total holdings amount to approximately 5½ hides.[2] At

[1] F. 156.   [2] *Rot. Hundr.* ii. 782.

the time of the Dissolution the returns show that the demesn
or home-farm had ceased to be kept in hand and was farme
out for a money rent, labour-services had been commuted fo
money payments and the customary tenants were paying rent
£17. 5s. 2d. from Lewknor, £8. 10s. 7d. from Postcombe.[1] Fror
deeds in possession of All Souls College, the present owner c
the estate, we know that it was during the fifteenth century tha
leases increased, with further subdivision of the lands, but ther
is no information about the date of the first lease of the demesne

Many similar changes happened in the second half of th
fourteenth century and can be traced to the pestilences. A
Ramsey every possible measure was taken to encourage artisan
and wage labourers, previously landless, to take up tenements
a new type of money rent, the *arrentata* which commuted all o
nearly all customary works and services, was brought in. Ram
sey's manor of Houghton had 50 per cent. of the village i
arrentata after a few years.[2] Sometimes a new superior migh
start the lease system going; at Canterbury leases were connecte
with the prefecture of Prior Chillenden (1391) who became th
all-important prior-treasurer.[3] It was not the Death, but th
need to swell the rent-roll so that the nave might be recon
structed and other building projects embarked upon, that le
Prior Chillenden to start leasing the demesne and to do s
within five years, the shortest time possible. At the perio
(1330–50) when in much of manorial England landowners wer
meeting the crisis of the Death by granting leases and commut
ing labour services the Canterbury monks were insisting on th
full performance of praedial duties, and it has been observe
that in 1390 compulsory labour services in the Kentish estate
of Christ Church were far heavier than in 1314.[4] On the othe
hand, in more distant Tavistock, the abbot and convent ha
begun their conversion of bond-land into tenements in 128
(at Downhouse) in return for the annual rent of 12s. payable o
the day of the patron saint (St. Rumon) with a pound of peppe
and one pound of cummin to the *salsarius*, and in 1339 othe

---

[1] Dugdale, *Monasticon*, i. 522.

[2] J. A. Raftis, *The Estates of Ramsey Abbey* (Pontif Inst. Medieval Studies, no.
Toronto, 1957), p. 251.

[3] R. A. L. Smith, *Canterbury Cathedral Priory* (1945), p. 191.

[4] Ibid., p. 127. It will be remembered, as Dr. Smith pointed out, that Chri
Church maintained a considerable staff of *famuli* who could be put in where ther
were labour deficiencies.

rable and meadow was offered for demise.[1] At Crowland it was not till 1391 that the flight of villeins and real failure to get substitutes led to the demise, so that by 1430 what were in all respects most conservative districts of all, the abbey's demesnes of Cottenham and Oakington in Cambridgeshire, were leased entirely to villeins.[2] At the bishop of Winchester's manor at Crawley in the Hampshire Downs, the lease of the whole manor was made to the reeve on 29 September 1407 for a twelve-year period; reeves had been having the responsibility for cultivation for some time, from about 1370 onwards, and the lease very largely involved the grain farming, a side which in view of the scarcity of tenants and their unwillingness to give services of any kind had become very difficult.[3] In their case the leasing of the home farm had been reached by gradual stages in which it came to be realized by the accounting office that in an increasingly commercial age a farmer with a good business head gave better value in his own line than a lord whose interests lay elsewhere.

The incidence of leasing is therefore extremely variable; but leases had set in, and with them the emergence of an upper class of the peasantry which had been growing in strength before the opportunity of the domainal lease came its way. From evidence in the records of Leicester Abbey a number of large peasant tenements are seen emerging from a homogeneous class of 20–30 acres of arable: and there was competition to get them, which appears from the number of rents *ad placitum*, rents at the lord's will or pleasure, rather than the customary villein tenure. This type of rent was unprotected by custom, but created a tenure where the terms depended on the market, 'on the balance between the demand for land and the needs of the lord for rent or for the land itself'.[4] On the Leicester Abbey estates all tenements which were not held by free tenure were held at will, and the fact points to a growing instability: there is subdivision and a quick circulation of the land, and one man's

---

[1] H. P. R. Finberg, *Tavistock Abbey* (1951), p. 249.

[2] F. R. Page, *The Estates of Crowland Abbey* (1934), p. 154. The Camb. Rolls begin to show tenements empty for 1391: cf. those printed on pp. 412 f. and the instance of insubordination on p. 435.

[3] N. S. B. and Ethel Gras, *The Economic and Social History of an English Village* (*Crawley, Hampshire*), *909–1428* (1930), pp. 81, 293.

[4] R. H. Hilton, *The Economic Development of some Leicestershire Estates in the Fourteenth and Fifteenth Centuries* (1947), p. 95.

holding (from the same abbatial lord) may comprise parts of
the holdings of four or five people;[1] and some of the land held
ad placitum is new, assarted land, not part of the old virgates.

This interesting market for land finds illustration in various
Leicester Abbey estates, particularly at Thurmaston, where in
1341 there were twenty-four tenants holding in villeinage, nineteen of them from the thirteen virgates forming part of the
foundation grant of Robert le Bossu. In 1477 there were only
thirteen tenants-at-will, with larger holdings than in the fourteenth century: two tenants each with two dwelling-houses and
3 virgates, two with $2\frac{1}{2}$ virgates each, three with 2 virgates
each, and three with $1\frac{1}{2}$ each. The rest had smaller tenements.
It was the same with the freeholdings. In 1341, 27 tenants held
$7\frac{1}{2}$ virgates, one bovate and $38\frac{1}{2}$ acres, 1 rood of arable; in 1477
only ten freeholders remained, some with quite large tenements:
one held the equivalent of 3 virgates, two held $\frac{3}{4}$ of a virgate
each, with appurtenances. What had happened is clear. The
abbey, the owner of the land and title, found that its receipts
were declining and appreciated that its right policy was to cease
demesne farming and to offer its estates on lease to a class of
men 'able to cultivate an arable holding of 60–80 acres'.[3] The
yeoman had arisen out of the break-up of the customary tenements and the increased market in land. An interesting point is
that near Leicester itself there had been no takers among the
upper classes: only those actually resident on the estates or
reasonably near them would have been able to bring the im-
plements and, as we should say, the machinery to work them.
The topographical knowledge and the farming experience were
there to hand: and if it was not a canon of the house directing
the bailiff and the virgaters, then it must be a peasant anxious
to get on.

The Leicester Abbey estates are not lands where there was a
proportion of Danelaw socmen; a free peasantry alongside of
the customary virgaters (though they had free tenants) was not
their characteristic. In the eastern midlands Wigston Magna
was, on the whole, a village of peasant proprietors, not the
village of a dominant lord. The larger free tenants in it soon
sold out to the peasant proprietors; the remnants of the *generosi*
removed early in the fifteenth century, and with them or soon

after the upper *bourgeoisie* migrated to the town, to Leicester. The population left was mainly a peasant one, with a few survivals representative of the larger freeholder: about 110–20 householders, i.e. about 330–60 or rather more, constituted the community, which had grown from the 86 of 1086. The village paid £8 at the collection of the tenth and fifteenth, reduced in 1433 to £7. 8s. 9d. and there was a further reduction in 1446. There were three absentee lords, the place ran its own economic affairs and in the presence of the lords or more usually of their representatives, arranged for the management of the fields. Here, in a communally governed township, one could witness consolidation of tenements by the free tenants of the manor; but the cultivators had always done a lot of active buying and selling of land;[1] and now in the period of agricultural depression during the fifteenth century they hung on to what they had got. They were not big enough people to go away and start elsewhere; it was what Dr. Hoskins has called 'a solid core of middling peasant freeholds' that lasted right through the depression.

The later court rolls of Crowland and the records of the duke of Norfolk's manor of Forncett (Norfolk) have much evidence for the flight of the customary tenants. Others went to live off the manor and paid chevage. On the Crowland estates 'genuine' flights (rather than living off the manor and working within) began from about 1350, but from 1380 to 1400 there were sixteen, and from 1400 to 1415, thirty-eight. One hundred and three in all left between 1350 and 1415; in 1425 twenty-two were missing from Cottenham alone, and from 1425 to 1496 twenty-five more.[2] It looks as if the peak period for departure was the last years of Richard II and the reign of Henry IV and V; it was the time when there was much competition to buy land and create consolidated holdings, less for normal production than for sheep farming. At Forncett sheep had appeared on the demesne by the third quarter of the fourteenth century, and in 1394 three tenants paid fines for having folds for 100 sheep, while the one extant court roll for that year records the initiation of inquiries into tenants who had fines for having folds of that amount. By 1404 a considerable number of tenants had inclosed their lands in the open fields, and in 1401 one of

---

[1] W. G. Hoskins, *The Midland Peasant* (1957), p. 115.
[2] Page, op. cit., p. 149.

the inclosing tenants paid for a licence to have a fold for 100 sheep.[1] But the supply of available land was limited and the would-be sheep-farmer must go elsewhere, if he could afford the price asked and was not sent back. The extension of sheep farming can certainly be connected with the depression in agriculture which set in during the last years of the fourteenth and lasted till the middle of the fifteenth century: the depression which meant the fall of rents and prices has been traced for the eastern midlands, especially for the Leicestershire villages of Newton Harcourt, Groby, Beaumanor and Quorndon, Loughborough, Arnesby, and Whittick. In most of these places the value of the arable fell; assized rents had gone down steeply. An inquisition of 1427 reveals that at Whittick farm houses were in decay and tenants lacking: the Beaumont inquisitions of 1413 and 1427 tell the story of physical ruin and want of tenants.[2] In Cambridgeshire and Huntingdonshire conditions were similar. If there had been a recovery in the 1370's and the 1380's it was wiped out by the statement of debt occurring on the Ramsey manorial rolls. As Dr. Raftis has said of the situation to 1420: 'the long-run trend in payments to the abbey treasury and the increase in debt show that in all manors, whether the demesne was formed immediately or not, there was a gradual worsening of conditions from the last decade of the fourteenth century'. As far as evidence is available, most of the farmed manors were devalued after 1420.[3] The decline of rents and farms in the fifteenth century, to which Professor Postan drew attention some years ago,[4] finds confirmation in the tables compiled for the Percy estates in Sussex (Petworth) and Cumberland (Cockermouth, Wigton), and elsewhere.[5] These show that the first half of the fifteenth century was a period of declining revenues on the Sussex estates, though the decline might vary from manor to manor; and that though rents of assize might rise, this was more than offset by a decline in the farms of the demesne lords. In Cumberland it was mainly the mills that caused the drop in the total figure. In neither county is the fall

---

[1] F. G. Davenport, *The Economic Development of a Norfolk Manor, 1086–1565* (1906), p. 80. For sheep on the St. Albans manors, very limited in amount, cf. the wills of villeins, printed by Miss A. E. Levett, *Studies in Manorial History* (1938), appendix.

[2] Hoskins, op. cit., pp. 83–86.

[3] *The Estates of Ramsey Abbey* (1957), pp. 292–3.

[4] *Econ. Hist. Review*, ix (1939), 161.

[5] By Dr. J. M. W. Bean, *Estates of the Percy Family* (1958), pp. 17 f.

great: but it is steady and symptomatic of what was happening. In Northumberland, at Alnwick, the decline is more marked: between 1434–5 and 1449–50 the demesne lands and tenancies at will dropped from £17. 15s. 2d. to £10. 12s. 3d., but this was 'part of a process going back at least to the beginning of the fifteenth century'. Naturally in Northumberland revenues were likely to be affected by Border warfare, which happened on the manors of Alnham and Fawdon in 1471–2, and in 1449–50 some had to be spent on the repair of buildings burnt by the Scots: but these inflictions were not part of the general picture of decline, and the only 'official' times of warfare with the Scots were from 23 September 1448 to 11 August 1449, 12 July to 8 September 1453, and from 24 June 1455 to 6 July 1457.[1] The general conclusion has been reached for the Percy estates that the average measure of decline must have been between a third and a half during the first half of the fifteenth century.

A journey to the south-west shows an important abbey able to keep at bay the depression affecting central and south-eastern England. Tavistock could do this because of a balanced economy in which pastoral sales—sales of wool, livestock, butter and eggs—could be set alongside of the sales of corn, the one correcting the adverse inclination, where it existed, of the other. There were also the proceeds of the stannary, the rents for the fishery owned by the house, and a perfectly steady series of rents from the burgesses for their burgages; and there were the seignorial profits (the Abbey court, &c.) From among the sixty-nine sales accounts for this period, in thirty-five corn sales are predominant. In the first twenty-seven there are only four accounts in which pastoral sales are on top. In the second period 1427–54, pastoral sales have the advantage, 'swollen by the high rents paid for the demesne grassland'. Then for a few years corn is leading, till in 1463 it falls back, not to recover for a quarter of a century.[2] The financial result of demesne husbandry goes up and down, but at Tavistock there are more favourable balances than adverse; this may be due to the high level of agriculture, seen in the intensive manuring and the interlocking of arable and pastoral husbandry. It would be true to say that on an estate like Tavistock there were more aspects

---

[1] Bean, op. cit., pp. 31–32.
[2] H. P. R. Finberg, *Tavistock Abbey*, p. 158. Cf. especially the table (xxvi) on pp. 244–5.

and sources of revenue, hence a greater variety of occupation than on the great East Anglian estates. The assets are more widely spread.

Devonshire is in many ways exceptional: in the centre and east of England the customary tenants received the full blast of the depression, and farmers of the demesne got heavily into debt. At Ramsey between 1460 and 1470 the only thing to do was to wipe the debts off the account rolls, probably by a general condonation; and to grant a series of long leases, in the hope that later on good years would make up for bad. 'The manor seems to have kept with wonderful conservation what we may call its external shape.' That was Maitland's verdict on its development from the middle of the thirteenth century down to the end of the middle ages: the tenemental framework of acres that were free or unfree, the legal framework of unfree and freemen remained: but behind it was a movement away from customary tenure and unfree status. Yet provided unfree tenure was a matter of rents and licences only, people took a long time in objecting to it. The unfree might themselves engage in the new textile operations. Plentiful evidence is forthcoming in the case of Castle Combe, Sir John Fastolf's lordship, described in the Extent of the Manor, compiled under the direction of William of Worcester in 1454,[1] as a mixture of tradition and novelty:

There are in that lordship two towns, and one of them is called Overcombe where are the husbandmen (*yconomi*) occupied in cultivating and working the land situated on the high ground; and the remainder called Nethercombe, where live the men who are used to make cloth, the weavers, fullers, dyers and other craftsmen, and all tenants and men living within the two towns have privileges and franchises specified below.

Here are the free and copyhold tenants cultivating their strips above and in the new hamlet down in the valley the weavers, tuckers, and other textile folk making money for the clothiers.[2] Not all the customary tenants were actually farming. William

[1] The description of the boundaries is clearly Worcester's. The extent is printed in G. P. Scrope, *A History of the Manor and Ancient Barony of Castle Combe in Wiltshire* (1852), pp. 203–21.

[2] For the new industrialists at Combe, especially William Heynes, cf. E. M. Carus Wilson, 'Evidences of Industrial Growth on some Fifteenth-Century Manors', *Econ. Hist. Rev.*, 2nd ser. xii (1959), 197–205.

Heyne or Heynes, *nativus domini*, at his death (1436) left chattels valued at 3,000 marks or £2,000 sterling. He was a wealthy clothier, big enough to begin, though a villein, an action in the Hundred of Chippenham;[1] and though Fastolf's court objected to this, it allowed him to sue 'outside this court'. Heyne had been obliged to fine with his lord for permission to marry his daughters outside Castle Combe, but the obligations of unfree status were worth the burdens. Though a local jury whittled down the valuation of his property to 300 marks,[1] when Fastolf and his council granted possession of his chattels and houses to the widow, a fine of £100 was the sum levied, as well as all the houses and tenements held at the will of the lord. The fines which had to be paid by the second husband for marrying Heyne's widow and entering upon her tenements were on a high scale, indicating the council's view of the size of the Heyne estate; and Heyne was by no means unique in the means he had accumulated at Castle Combe.

In fact, if there is money to be made, it does not matter very much whether the tenements leased are bond or free. But there was a more substantial tradition of free tenures, not in the west, but in central England, than is generally imagined. Their existence did not necessarily contribute to the building up and consolidation of individual tenements but added to the complexities of a closely subdivided estate as can be seen from the strip maps, when made at the end of the sixteenth century. If blocks from the waste or the woodland have been purchased, in the open fields of the township the strips, somewhat thicker perhaps than they were before, continue to lie scattered. By the time of the hundred rolls inquiry (1279) the population of many villages was already extremely variegated, subdivision of the lands had gone a long way, and in parts of central England the proportion of free rents to servile rents was high. In Warwickshire in the Arden manors of Tanworth, Haseley, Beansale, Cleverdon, and Sutton Coldfield, free rents predominated over servile in ratios varying from 2 : 1 to 4 : 1. In two fifteenth-century rentals, Tanworth and Erdington, on the former, out of 69 tenants, 53 were freeholders: a rental of Erdington (1463) describes 75 tenements, 28 of which are freehold, and only one

---

[1] Scrope, op. cit., p. 239.
[2] The sum was not admitted by the tenants called upon to verify the injunction: ibid., p. 223.

is stated to be customary.[1] Now since free tenants had, as a general rule, the right to alienate their land, many subtenancies in free land tended to be created. These 'complexities arising from subtenancy', as they have been termed,[2] had to be surmounted before genuine consolidation of tenements could take place. The existence of a market in land may help, but does not of itself indicate the beginnings of large-scale severalty.

The weavers and technicians in the valley were a quota of an expanding industry, resettled and permanent. Close in importance to them came the mobile forces of builders and craftsmen of all sorts from the masons and carpenters down to the quarry diggers and labourers, whose business was to work and travel as their contracts took them or as they were impressed by the king. It has been estimated that if the population of London in 1377 was about 35,000, when deductions have been made for women and children, perhaps 10,000 to 12,000 were adult male workmen. 'In its busiest period, the building of one North Wales castle employed a number equal to 13 or 14 per cent. of the workmen employed in the trade and commerce of the capital.'[3] The direction of the industry lay with those who had the right to purvey and the cash to spend on erection and restoration, i.e. predominantly with the monarchy and the Church, with the magnate intervening to crenellate a castle or, later, to construct great country houses in stone or brick. While a certain amount of the labour used in quarrying and in the transport of materials might be local, the higher branches were normally groups of stone carvers who travelled from place to place and were known to the architects and designers who could recommend their employment to patrons. They both come and do not come into the ordinary category of wage-earners. In long jobs the leading mason might be hired by the year at 2s. a week plus food and be paid an extra consideration of £5. 4s. (or 2s. a week) for the year. Moreover, jobs might last longer than the year, even for life (e.g. William Waddeswyk, glazier at York from 1422), and there might be special positions created in order to retain good men on the spot: a 'wardenship'

---

[1] R. H. Hilton, *The Social Structure of Rural Warwickshire* (Dugdale Soc. Occ. Papers, 1950), p. 18.   [2] By Hilton, op. cit., p. 19.
[3] D. Knoop and G. P. Jones, *The Medieval Mason* (1949), p. 3; 35,000 is, perhaps, rather a low estimate. The figure may be nearer 40,000.

or purveyorship, held at 6*d.* a day. The master mason working on the building of William Lord Hastings's castle at Kirby Muxloe got 4*s.* a week plus six payments of 10*s.* during the year. A 'master' mason specially brought in to advise or to supervise may be paid more, or there may be promotion from the existing staff. Wages were nominally regulated by the two statutes of Labourers 1350 and 1360, according to which the master mason received 4*d.* a day and other masons 3*d.* (1351) or 3*d.* or 2*d.* a day 'as they becometh'. In 23 Henry VI, c. 12 (1444) the 'freemason' was to receive 5½*d.* a day from Easter to 29 September, and in the winter months 4½*d.* a day. A 'rough mason' shaping the stones in the yard before they were positioned got 4½*d.* a day in the summer and 4*d.* a day in the winter. In 1495 freemasons got 6*d.* and 5*d.* respectively and the master mason in charge of work, and having under him six masons, 7*d.* a day. The statutes tried to enforce what had been the ruling rates outside London immediately before the Black Death: but evidence from three centres, Ely (1359), Rochester (1364), and York (1371), shows that their local rates were well above the wages prescribed in the statute. The main source for the masons' doings in the early fifteenth century, London Bridge accounts, shows that the bridge authorities did not conform to the official regulation. Masons working on the bridge got 3*s.* 9*d.* a week, in excess of 6*d.* a day in the statutes; the bridge masons were not reduced in wages during the winter; and all the regular bridge masons appear to have been paid for feast days and holidays when they did not work. In 1425 a royal mandate about the enforcement of the statute of Labourers, attempted a new arrangement: the masons were paid 7*d.* per day for 5⅓ days per week: but within a year the bridge scheme of payments had been readopted, though with 8*d.* a day replacing the weekly wage of 3*s.* 9*d.* This is a fair example of the non-enforcement of the wage clauses in the statute. Better perhaps is the case of Master Edward Canon, master stone-cutter working on the stalls of St. Stephen's chapel, Westminster, in 1352, the year after the first statute, who got 1*s.* 6*d.* a day.

How adequate were these wages? It would be impossible to answer this question upon food statistics alone, for rents, tithes and a variety of household goods would have to be taken into account. None the less the relevant parts of a table constructed by Professors Knoop and Jones and based on the price tables of

G. F. Steffen (1901)[1] may help. The daily real wages are compiled from statistics at Oxford and Cambridge, and the accounts of London Bridge. The prices and wages are represented, in ten year periods, as percentages of the levels in 1501-10:

	Food prices	Daily real wages
1391–1400	84	119
1401–10	84	119
1411–20	89	112
1421–30	85	108
1431–40	94	106
1441–50	86	116
1451–60	91	110
1461–70	88	114
1471–80	86	116
1481–90	94	105

The prices given in the tables of Steffen[2] were largely based upon the seven-volume work of Thorold Rogers against which a great deal of criticism has been directed. For the period of the fifteenth century till 1582 Rogers changed his method of tabulation (vols. iii and iv of *A History of Agriculture and Prices in England from 1256–1793*, 1882), but this did not eliminate some of the drawbacks enumerated against his calculations by Lord Beveridge in his study of prices on the manors of the bishopric of Winchester.[3] Lord Beveridge with his helpers found evidence in the Winchester pipe rolls for 1318 and 1354 that the sizes of the bushels used on the diocesan estates differed in many places from those used by the crown when it made purchases in those areas, and upon that basis they reduced or increased the prices for grain according to whether a nine- or an eight-gallon basket was being used. Dr. D. L. Farmer has effectively disposed of this criticism of Thorold Rogers and shown that there was little difference between the price levels in the two parts of Hampshire supposed to have been using Hampshire measures; but with far more evidence of prices available, he has given a new list of prices for the staple grains in the period 1208–1325; yet for the rest of the medieval period there is as yet no fully revised list, since the figures given by Dr. N. S. B. Gras in his earlier book have not won acceptance.[4] Given these difficulties, it may

[1] *The Medieval Mason* (1949), appendix i, Statistics of Masons' Wages and Prices, p. 238.

[2] *Studien zur Geschichte der Englischen Lohnarbeiter* (1901), i. ii.

[3] *Economic History*, no. 5 (1930), pp. 19–44.

[4] *The Evolution of the English Corn Market* (1926). See the remarks of D. L. Farmer,

still be useful to follow the long-term method of Steffen, who calculated in ten-year periods, even though the data on which he worked was neither complete nor fully understood in its local connotation. It is hardly necessary to add the warning that the figures given are averages, for there was not a single market and no common price for grain.

I. FOOD PRICES[1]

Ten years' average prices for grain, cheese, &c., in different parts of England

	Wheat qr.		*Rye qr.*		*Peas qr.*		*Oats qr.*		*Barley qr.*		*Cheese wey*		*Butter gallon = 8 lb.*	
	s.	*d.*	*s.*	*d.*	*s.*	*d.*	*s.*	*d.*	*s.*	*d.*	*s.*	*d.*	*s.*	*d.*
1391–1400 . .	5	3	3	4¾	3	5	..		4	5⅞	10	2		8
1401–10 . .	5	8¼	4	2¾	3	3¼	8	0½	4	3½	10	6½		8
1411–20 . .	5	6¾	3	3¾	3	3¾	8	6	4	5	10	8	1	0
1421–30 . .	5	4¾	4	1½	3	2¼	7	7¾	4	7¾	10	2½		8
1431–40 . .	6	11	5	1	3	8	8	5¼	4	5½	..		..	
1441–50 . .	5	3¾	3	0	2	8¼	6	1½	3	4¼	..			11½
1451–60 . .	5	6½	3	10¾	2	10	6	2	3	10	..			11½
1461–70 . .	5	4¼	3	8¾	2	11	6	4½	3	7½	6	11		7
1471–80 . .	5	4¼	3	6¾	3	5¼	6	7½	3	4¼	6	6		9½
1481–90 . .	6	3½	5	4¾	4	2¼	6	9½	4	1½	..			11½
Average for period 1351–1540 .	6	0⅜	4	6	3	9½	7	9⅜	4	3⅞	10	6⅞		9⅝

During the period on only two occasions has the price of wheat per quarter exceeded the 6*s.* line. The figure for 1431–40 is accounted for by the bad period 1437–9. The year 1438, owing to the long continued rain in the summer and the failure of the harvest, was the only year that seriously approached the famine time of 1315–16. In 1438–9 wheat reached 20*s.* a quarter in some districts, and rye was fairly proportionate in price. The 6*s.* 3½*d.* in 1481–90 was partly due to the wet season 1481–2, when the quarter of wheat reached 12*s.*–12*s.* 4*d.* at various places in the Eastern counties. These exceptions apart, both the price figures and the wage figures are extremely steady. The mason's daily scale, despite the statutes, averages out at 6*d.*, the carpenter's

'Some Grain Price Movements in Thirteenth Century England', *Econ. Hist. Rev.*, 2nd ser., x (1957).

[1] Based on the table of G. F. Steffen, op. cit. I. ii. 254. From the statistics of Thorold Rogers, *A History of Agriculture and Prices in England*, vol. iv.

II. WAGES[1]

Ten-year average figures from different parts of England. Figures unless stated, are in pence

	Time-work (per day)					*Piece-work*	
	Carvers and joiners	*Carpenters*	*Masons*	*Mason's mate* (operarius)	*Agricultural labourer*	*Threshing and winnowing a qr. of wheat*	*Reaping, binding, and stacking an acre of wheat*
1391–1400 . .	6¼	4⅝	5⅝	..	..	3¼	7⅜
1401–10 . .	7	5½	6	3¾	3⅝	3¾	7
1411–20 . .	6¼	5¼	6	4	3½	3¾	7¼
1421–30 . .	7½	5½	5½	4¼	3½	3¾	8
1431–40 . .	7½	6	6	3¾	4	4½	1*s.* 0½*d.*
1441–50 . .	7¾	5¾	6¼	4¼	4⅛	4⅝	11½
1451–60 . .	6¾	6	6¼	4¼	4¼	4¼	10½
1461–70 . .	6¾	6	6¼	4	4¼	3¾	10
1471–80 . .	6	5¾	6¼	4¼	4	2¾	..
1481–90 . .	6½	6	5¾	4¼	3⅞	3	..
Average for period 1351–1540 . .	6⅝	5½	6	4¼	4	4	9¼

[1] Based on Steffen, op. cit. ii. 250.

at 5½*d.*, and the 'Kerver', sometimes called the joiner, i.e. a sculptor in wood or stone, got just under 7*d.* The daily wage of a skilled labourer was about 6*d.* and of an unskilled about 4*d.*, but there were gifts and inducements of various kinds; and in the building trade, just as the architects might receive robes, so the artisans themselves would receive articles of clothing, gloves, aprons, &c. The authorities of King's Hall in 1431 provided robes for the master mason at Christmas, a striped gown for the chief carpenter, and hoods for two layers, as well as gloves for the plumber and nine 'zones' or belts for the workmen.[1]

In more human terms, there was a sufficiency, but not a large margin. Contentment or discontent depended upon a number of factors that made up the local situation: most of all, in the case of the small cottager, upon the sense of justice in the lord's court or the moderation of the bailiff, its executive officer, and his ability to work with or against the community.

(c) THE TOWNS

The main problems of English borough history lie in the period *c.* 1190–1350. It is to these years that the classic riddles of the relation between the municipality and the merchant gild, of the beginnings of the mayoralty and of the nature of burgage tenure (though the latter has far earlier origins) mainly apply. So too the question of when the English boroughs were achieving corporate existence before juridical recognition was given to the fact. With such complicated and absorbing topics the historian of the fifteenth century is not immediately concerned. But he has to take into account two important tendencies in English burghal life which have their roots deep in the past, of which the first is the reassertion, after a sharp reaction at the end of the fourteenth century, of oligarchical control. The growth of oligarchies in the towns dates back, as the late Professor Tait showed, to the thirteenth century, and survives all democratic attempts to secure the popular election of mayors and borough officials through the representation of the less substantial citizens upon a 'common council' or some other local body. The second tendency, the movement towards borough incorporation, along with the erection of the larger boroughs into counties, reaches its climax in the period between

---

[1] L. F. Salzman, *Building in England down to 1540* (1952), p. 80.

the royal charter making Bristol a county in 1373, and the group of incorporations beginning with Hull from 1440 onwards. The historian has also to recognize the growing assimilation of the borough and the county communities, a breaking down of the barriers between the burgess and the country gentleman, the rise of the landowning burghers, and, towards the end of the century, the appearance of the knight who is also the mayor of his town. The armigerous family is finding no difficulty in marriage alliances with the upper bourgeoisie, a course often expedient from the financial point of view. The same man will represent in parliament first a county, then a borough. This greater social integration, which as yet should not be unduly emphasized, springs more from the pursuit of wealth and the increase of business knowledge and ability than from considerations that might have appealed to the contemporary preacher. It is assisted by the growth of the lawyer element, bridging the gap between town and country, and by the mercantile interests and pursuits of the landowning classes, who have come not only to regard land as a form of investment, but also to realize the possibilities of trade. The period is marked by the expansion of the cities and boroughs which are exporting cloth or engaged in trade with the continent and the Mediterranean. It is *par excellence* the period of the London, Bristol, and East Anglian merchant. We shall have occasion to study their organizations, their local and wider influences, the houses they built and the prestige they acquired for their towns; nor must the literary and educational influences of the borough and its schools be left out of account. The English grammar school owes much to the local merchant.

There should be no need to specify here the steps by which the 'administrative islands', as Professor Meyer[1] termed them, were brought into the royal scheme of administration and how borough officials were in effect made 'crown agents'. A broad assumption was growing that the borough officials were the king's officers, and the creation, particularly during the fourteenth century, of special local administrators in the form of sheriffs and escheators emphasizes the point. The functioning of the municipality within the royal scheme, and the need, just as in the county communities, for an administrative class,

[1] In *The English Government at Work, 1327–1336*, ed. W. H. Dunham, jr., iii (1950), 106.

roughly represented in borough documents by the term jurats *jurati*) or as at Winchester and elsewhere 'the twenty-four', almost automatically involved the more well-to-do citizen in public duties. Already this class can be seen coming into existence during the thirteenth century. It tends to consist of the wealthier merchants of the town, members of the merchant gild. At Lincoln, as Dr. Hill has emphasized, the same people were the leading spirits of both gild and city. It has been pointed out that the alderman began his career as head of the gild of merchants, and that as the French conception of the *communes* grew he assumed the new French name of mayor. At Southampton the alderman is described as the head of the town and the gild. At Leicester the alderman of the gild merchants about 1226 is called the alderman of Leicester and he continued as chief officer in the town until his title was changed to that of mayor. It is this alderman class which, owing to royal employment, took control of the local assembly, and through its widespread acquisition of urban tenements became the local oligarchy of which there are many examples: the most famous illustrations being the division at Oxford between the 'lesser commune' and the *maiores burgenses*, the 'old legal men' of the city; and the divisions of the city at Lincoln into the great, the middling (*secondarii*, elsewhere *mediocres*), and the lesser. There were similar classifications in York and Bristol. These divisions, it has been shown, were not class divisions, but arose from property qualifications when assessments and collection of tallage had to be carried out. The disorders at Bristol between the oligarchy and the community from 1312 to 1316 are an excellent example of such a division getting mixed up with the general political situation. The institution of the common councils as a make-weight to the dominance of aldermanic control gave the popular party only a temporary success. As a general rule the oligarchies succeeded in narrowing the basis by restricting the representation upon common councils. In London after the period 1376–85, when in the election of the mayor and sheriffs the misteries were being substituted for wards, the controlling influence of the aldermen was restored and actually increased by the power, virtually given to them along with the mayor, to pack the election meetings of the council. In 1395 the aldermen were made irremovable except for reasonable cause. There was, however, a legacy from the wreck of 1376: a permanent common council not too large and not too small, which was elected by the citizens in their wards and which the mayor and aldermen were bound to consult at least four times a year. Movement for common councils on an elective basis was not entirely in vain, though at election meetings there was careful regulation of the personnel by the oligarchies.

The closing years of the fourteenth century were marked by quarrels between the richer citizens and the rest of the city, known in most places as the 'commonalty' (*communitas*), touching the election of the mayor and bailiffs or the mayor and sheriffs of the town, or about the rights and privileges of the upper citizens and the commonalty. A number of these disputes found their settlement in the reigns of Henry IV and V, and among borough archives the documents recording arbitrations and awards (some being found unsatisfactory and replaced by others) testify to the efforts that were being made to find a *via media* between the demands of the 'great men' and the citizens as a whole. Bishop's Lynn and Norwich provide excellent examples. At Lynn the gild of the Holy Trinity was the chief force in the corporate life of the town during the thirteenth century. The constitution of the gild did not make for free or democratic development: it was essentially an aristocratic body, the head of the gild bearing the title of alderman, and being, by the merchants' charter of Henry III, appointed deputy mayor. The alderman chose the first four of the committee of twelve burgesses whose duty it was to elect the mayor and other officers for the ensuing year. The town was graded into three classes, the *potentiores*, the *mediocres*, and the *inferiores*, with the gild of the Holy Trinity consisting mainly of the former class. The *potentiores* elected whom they would to serve as members of the 'twenty-four', and at a later period they succeeded in choosing the common councillors, who in consequence were not the semi-popular body of London and elsewhere. It is no surprise to hear that Archbishop Arundel, as chancellor, had to be called in in 1413 to allay the discords and controversies between certain of the *potentiores* of the town and the commonalty of the place who alleged 'certain oppressions and extortions done by the wealthier citizens against the *mediocres* and *inferiores*'. Arundel submitted the dispute to the verdict of the three elements in the town, each group of which undertook to stand by the award. The grievances were largely against a former mayor, Thomas Waterden, now character-istically a member of the committee of eighteen, for claiming and receiving various expenses to the cost of the town: one of the clauses was that in dealing with the finances of the town the mayor should be assisted by a council of three from each divi-sion, and that the *inferiores* who were not allowed burgess rights should have the privileges earlier granted to them in a com-position between the bishop and the mayor and commonalty. Whether the award was put into force and for how long we do not know. It reflects a state of tension in the town which may have resulted in a particular ordinance for the election of the mayor, jurats, and other officers which was strongly opposed by the *potentiores*. The situation was such that in 1416 the govern-ment intervened. Henry V seems to have interested himself personally in the disputes and brought the parties together to agree upon the annulling of the constitution and the drafting of new orders for elections in Lynn. The rules now substituted did not, as in the past, give the initial nomination of the electing body to the aldermen of the gild of the Holy Trinity but to the burgesses themselves assembled in their hall. These were to single out two of the jurats or at least two persons of jurat estate, and the two were to select two other members of the jurat body to be voted on by the remainder of their colleagues for the office of mayor. Each jurat was to be consulted privately and asked to put the two candidates in order of merit. If they did not think that the two persons chosen were sufficiently competent, the burgesses were to meet again and select two candidates from among themselves: but the rider was added that candidates must be of free condition and have at least 100 shillingsworth of rent; and that no 'victualler' selling by retail was henceforth to be made a jurat, still less 'by implica-tion' mayor.[1] It will be seen that while the first choice of the electors no longer pertained to the aldermen, it was only in the case of the jurats rejecting the candidates indicated to them by the two nominators that the reference back to the citizen body was to be made.

In Norwich there was a long struggle between the common-alty and the oligarchical jurats. On 12 February 1380 a petition was granted by charter placing the jurats very much in the

[1] Hist. MSS. Comm., *11th Report*, King's Lynn, pt. iii, pp. 195 f.

position of the aldermen of London. It was requested that the
four bailiffs and twenty-four citizens chosen each year by the
commonalty of the town might have power to make ordinance,
and take remedial measures for good government 'as might
seem good to them' and to correct and mend them when
necessary. This was an echo of the London charter of 1341.
This was clearly a move of the jurat body, not of the citizens as
a whole. Trouble was to ensue. After the charter of Henry IV
(1404) substituting a mayor and two sheriffs in place of the four
bailiffs, great disputes arose as to the method of electing the
new officials. The mayor, sheriffs, and the twenty-four jurats
claimed the right for themselves and invoked the charter of
1380. The commonalty affirmed that the grant had been procured privily without their knowledge and consent. Now the
charter of 1404 threatened to be the first step in the development by which the citizens of Norwich passed from the condition of a self-governing community into that of a community
under the control of a practically permanent magistracy. The
matter of securing representation of the commonalty on the
electing and legislative bodies of the town was therefore essential
In 1414 the parties described as 'the men of estate' and the
'commons' agreed to submit their differences to the arbitration
of Sir Thomas Erpingham, and the 'commons' formulated their
grievances in a petition called the 'Complaints on the part of
the major part of the citizens and commonalty of Norwich
against those who are called the more venerable citizens of
the said city'. They protested against the powers given to the
twenty-four in Richard's charter, and against the action of the
prudes hommes in securing the election of the mayor they wanted.
They claimed that these senior citizens were supported by an
assembly of certain people in Norwich called 'La Bachelery . .
who are sworn and allied by their oath to the said *prudes hommes*
to stand by them in all their quarrels'. The answers of the
twenty-four were mainly an appeal to the principle of order.
The complainants were alleging, they said, that every person
of the smallest reputation in the city should have as much
authority and power in elections and other municipal matters
as the 'more sufficient persons in the said city'; and they made
the counter-request that the word *communitas* in the title of

---

[1] *Cal. Chart. R.* v. 264. The petition is document no. 38 in W. Hudson and J. C.
Tingey, *Records of the City of Norwich*, i (1906).

Norwich should be removed from the charter. A compromise was finally arrived at on St. Valentine's Day 1415. This regulated the election of the mayor and of the twenty-four. The mayor was to be chosen in an elaborate piece of procedure. It does not appear that this came fully into force. The number of the common council was shortly changed from eighty to sixty and by 1417 the 'twenty-four' had become perpetual councillors like the twenty-four aldermen of London. The upshot was that while in the election of the mayor sixty representatives of the commonalty played their part, the 'twenty-four' remained a permanent aldermanic body described in the documents as *De consilio maioris*. The mention of the bachelors gild is interesting; its members not only held a strong position socially, but some of them were merchants of sufficient influence to attract trade to their own houses. It may have arisen as the result of Norwich being granted county organization: a large list of jurors for various purposes would have to be made by the sheriffs from a class corresponding to the knightly class in the counties. Norwich, therefore, consists of a governing oligarchy, a body who are *cives* in the fullest sense and a *communitas* represented by the sixty in the common council.

It was normal in the fifteenth century to select five characteristics as indications of a properly incorporated town: perpetual succession, the power of suing and being sued as a whole and by the name of the society, power to hold lands, a common seal, and authority to issue by-laws.[1] As Maitland said, the greater boroughs of Edward I's reign 'have already in substance attained to all, or almost all, those characteristics'. In the later middle ages it was a question of expressing these, or some of these characteristics, in a single document which gave recognized legal status to the community of the town. Such legal charters clarified the structure of the civic bodies and, sometimes, the methods of election. Incorporation charters are, with the various charters of *inspeximus*, the most characteristic burghal documents of the fifteenth century. In many cases incorporation is marked by the erection of the borough into a county. This sunders the borough from the county organization, forbids the entry of county officials into the town, and gives extended powers of jurisdiction to the town's officers. The

---

[1] M. Weinbaum, *The Incorporation of Boroughs* (1937) and *British Borough Charters, 1307–1660*, ed. Weinbaum (1937), pp. xxiii–xxviii.

important charter of Bristol (1373) is the classic prototype of
the new charter of incorporation plus county status. Before its
issue the citizens of Bristol had to attend county courts at
Gloucester and Ilchester. To avoid the difficult journeys it was
decreed that the town should be separated from Gloucester and
Somerset, and be a county by itself: its mayor was to be the
king's escheator. There was to be a sheriff annually elected by
the burgesses and the commonalty, three names being certified
into chancery where the selection was to be made. The sheriff
of Bristol was to hold his county court in the town and the
mayor and sheriff were given power to inquire into all transgres-
sions and disturbances of the peace and were allowed to arrest
the felons and hold them until the justices of jail delivery, of
whom the mayor was one, arrived. The new county court was
to be a court of record and given power to levy fines for licences
to agree and to receive recognizances of charters and other
documents. It could deal with all pleas of lands, tenements,
covenants, and leases within the city. Its record was to be the
roll of the Gild Hall. The precedent of Bristol was followed soon
after by York. The York charter of 1396 says expressly that the
city now 'leaves the *corpus* of the county'. Neither here nor in
the charters granted to Newcastle upon Tyne (1400) and
Carlisle, in 1401, is there any mention of the five points; but
the charter by which Norwich was incorporated in 1404 under
the name of the 'Citizens and Commonalty' of Norwich has the
legal requirement, inasmuch as extensive judicial powers were
granted to the new society, including the cognizance by the
city authorities of all pleas, felonies excepted. In the Lincoln
charter of 1409 county status was awarded to the town, the
mayor was to be escheator, and the mayor, sheriffs, and four
citizens, justices of the peace. After this there is a gap in the
incorporation charters till 1439, when, with the charter of
Plymouth, a new series begins with the five points fully enumerated. The assented petition of Plymouth asks:

let your royal highness ordain and decree that the town, tithing
and parcels aforesaid shall henceforth be a *liber burgus* incorporated
of a mayor and a perpetual commonalty, and let it henceforth be
called the borough of Plymouth: and let the mayor and commonalty
be one perfect body in fact and name and for all time be named the
Community of the borough of Plymouth, and let there be in it persons fit and legally capable of acquiring for themselves, their heirs

and successors in fee and perpetuity or for the term for life or of years or in any other estate, whatever lands, tenements, rents, reversions, possessions and hereditaments from whosoever people, and let them have a common seal and by the name of the mayor and commonalty of Plymouth plead and be impleaded in any of your courts or the courts of your heirs and successors or of any others, and before any judge and in any actions.[1]

Hull (1440), more accurately Kingston-on-Hull, had already by the charters of 1331 and 1334 attained judicial privileges and the withdrawal of the royal warden along with the free election of city officials. The charter of incorporation making it a county has the best-known formulation of the five points. It is noteworthy that Hull was governed by a small and exclusive body. In the charter granted in 1440 Hull had thirteen aldermen, one of whom was the mayor. Each alderman was chosen by the whole body of burgesses, but he was there for his lifetime, unless he was removed at his own request or from some notable cause. If the charter of 1331 vested the power of electing the mayor in the whole community, by 1440 there is the restriction that the mayor shall be one of the select class.

At Southampton there are two charters, one of incorporation (1445), the other making the town a county (1447), and giving Portsmouth similar status. Just as in 1445 Southampton and Portsmouth were to be freed from obeying the ordinances of the constable, marshal, or admiral of England, so in 1447 the town of Southampton and the port of Portsmouth are to be one entire county and have one sheriff; and the fact is noted that in the past the mayor as well as merchants of these places had been arrested and imprisoned by the sheriffs of Hampshire. At Nottingham, on the other hand, the charter of 1448 does not include the separation of the town from the county, but there is a careful statement of the respective spheres of the borough and the county. A curious little charter is that of Woodstock, 1453, which appears to be the first charter discoverable for the borough. In this the townspeople made the incorporation charter a means of securing a variety of liberties which many places had secured years before. Many of these had been enjoyed as local customs, 'free customs' the townspeople call them. The men of Woodstock were to have their gild merchant and similar liberties to those of Windsor. Windsor was a

[1] Weinbaum, *Incorporation of Boroughs*, p. 46.

precedent, because it was not dissimilar in size and adjoined royal property where the kings were frequently in residence.

Whatever degree of administrative convenience may have been achieved, in achieving legal personality the officials and bodies within the town had their rights and their status defined. The process is one of hardening rather than of flexibility. Incorporation has thus been defined as a formal act determining the relation between and collaboration among one or more high town officials on the one hand, and one or more groups of delegates on the other; and the charters effecting it have been termed 'tools of an irresistible tendency towards exclusiveness'. To a good many places this description will indeed apply. It is, however, important to realize that London, though by 1400 it had emerged with a firmly established mercantile oligarchy and had an oligarchical administration, escaped, in Professor Tait's words, 'the worst features of that closing of the borough corporations which was far advanced by the end of the Middle Ages, an escape which it owed in no small measure to the crises through which it passed in the last quarter of the fourteenth century'.[1] Thus the clause of the statute of 1341 which empowered the mayor and aldermen to provide a remedy for custom which proved defective, but only with the assent of the commonalty, never became obsolete. The common council that emerged from the disputes of 1376, when freed of its gild organization and based upon ward representation, was a check upon city bureaucracy that enabled the government of the city of London to escape the more drastic measures applied to cities and boroughs in the Municipal Corporations Act.

It has been observed that the unique feature of medieval urban administration lay in the jurisdiction that city authorities claimed over trade and industry. The primary aim was to ensure an adequate food supply at reasonable prices through the supervision of the market. Secondly the authorities aimed at enforcing certain standards of manufacture in protection of the consumers' interest; at preventing monopoly among merchants and collective bargaining among hired workers; and at controlling brokerage rates. To effect the first of these the government of the city of London used the direct authority derived from the crown over all retailers of victuals, and, with the aldermen, assumed by custom the right of veto over all private craft

[1] Introduction to Ruth Bird, *The Turbulent London of Richard II* (1949), p. xxiii.

legislation. The control of the crafts was not a negation of their authority, but was intended, as Miss Thrupp has put it, 'to secure certain advantages that could not be obtained in any other way. For the most part, the relationships between crafts and the mayor and aldermen were quite harmonious, the crafts fitting conveniently into place as organs of administration, not only in economic policy, but in police work, in defence, in community pageantry, in taxation and ultimately in the matter of elections.'[1] At the same time the mayor and aldermen were the only authority which could decide the disputes between kindred crafts, and the letter books of the city have not a few instances of the ruling given by the mayor and aldermen on disputed points. Thus the cutlers and bladesmiths in 1408 settled an altercation over trademarks used by the respective companies and the price to be charged for knives and blades.[2] Similarly in 1420 the brewers and coopers agreed upon the marking of vessels and all coopers residing within the franchise of the city were to present to the court within fourteen days 'their marks, made of iron, to be there recorded'.[3] In 1421 the mercers and haberdashers contested the right of the linen-weavers 'which was only an inferior mistery', to admit a merchant stranger as a member of their craft. It was adjudged that the merchants should be removed from the freedom of the city and that the masters of the linenweavers should forfeit their freedom and make fines to the city chamberlain for knowing the facts of the case when they presented the merchant stranger for the freedom of the city.[4] While this jurisdiction in cases of borderline or overlapping disputes was resorted to, it is well to remember that the more important crafts did not, like the lesser ones, come before the mayor and aldermen with the petition that they should be constituted as authorized misteries by a grant of a full set of ordinances.[5] From the reign of Edward I they appear before the court of aldermen as recognized bodies of traders, whose right to a certain amount of self-government is taken for granted. Furthermore, before the close of the century many of the greater crafts had come to hold charters from the king, conferring upon them special powers to regulate

---

[1] *The Merchant Class of Medieval London* (1948), p. 93.
[2] *Letter Book I*, ed. R. R. Sharpe (1909), p. 67.
[3] Ibid., p. 237.   [4] Ibid., pp. 257–8.
[5] G. Unwin, *The Guilds and Companies of London* (1908), p. 78.

their several trades, not only in London, but throughout England. Such charters had been granted to the goldsmiths, the skinners, the tailors, and the girdlers in 1327, and to the drapers, the vintners, and the fishmongers in 1363–4. Because of these royal grants the greater companies, in Unwin's words, 'exercised a kind of *imperium in imperio* within the city'. While paying every deference to the mayor and aldermen they were powerful bodies which, when disputes blew up, armed their retainers and occasionally created such disturbance that their members had to be imprisoned.

It was to the greater crafts that the privilege of incorporation was first granted. These are mostly the bodies which had been or were to be recognized as livery companies. Originally the wearing of distinctive dress by the freemen of the city or a particular gild was a matter of domestic concern. Livery was restricted to the elders of each gild. All the members of the Grocers' company were wearing a livery in 1345, but when it was confined to the older and more prominent members, rather less than half were permitted to wear it (e.g. in 1430). Attendance at common hall, the elective assembly of the City of London, was limited, in 1475, to freemen wearing liveries, together with the common council. Thus the assumption of a livery became of great civic importance, as an indication not only of wealth but of power.

It is notable that the body incorporated tends to be not the craft itself so much as the fraternity which is its core. The London Tailors' charter of 1408 constituted them 'a sound perpetual and corporate Fraternity, which is to have a Common Seal, could plead and be impleaded and hold lands'. At York the gild and the confraternity of the tailors existed side by side. The York confraternity (1415) was composed of a master, wardens, brethren, and sisters; the gild, which led a separate existence, was composed of four searchers and a numerous body of tailors, scissors or shearmen, and tailor-drapers. In the royal licence of 10 February 1453 permission was given to fifteen tailors of York to found a gild, of a master and four wardens 'of the said Mistery and other persons, brethren and sisters, in honour of St. John the Baptist in York'. The gild was to be incorporate, capable of pleading and being impleaded, was to have its common seal under the figure of St. John the Baptist, and was to be capable of acquiring lands in free alms to the value of 100s. yearly for the maintainance of a chaplain, while the poor brothers and sisters of the gild were to pray for the good estate of King Henry VI and Queen Margaret, their souls after death, and the king's progenitors.[1]

Such incorporations, particularly in the case of the livery companies, remained on the whole an exceptional privilege; it was the same among the wealthy fraternities, for nearly half a century, until Henry VI began to grant charters on a larger scale. Then at last the charters granted to the four victualling crafts, the Grocers (1428), the Fishmongers (1433), the Vintners (1436), and the Brewers, together with the five manufacturing crafts, the Drapers (1438), the Cordwainers (1429), the Leather-sellers (1444), the Haberdashers (1447), and the Armourers (1442), made incorporation the established rule among the greater London 'misteries'. Yet, as Unwin showed, this incorporation of the 'misteries' by royal charter created a new situation that called for vigorous action by the municipal authorities, as was shown by a statute of 1437, which, on the ground that the new corporations were making 'many unlawful and unreasonable ordinances as well in the price of wares and other things for their own singular profit', required all incorporated fraternities and companies to bring their charters to be registered by the chief governors of the cities, boroughs, and towns. This registration of comparatively recent charters led to disputes about their validity. Thus in London the Drapers' charter of 1438 aroused the jealousy of the Tailors (incorporated in 1408) and led them to secure, in 1439, another charter giving them exclusive rights of search over the cloth trade. It is perhaps the desire to maintain its control over crafts that led in the later incorporation documents to the usual corporate rights conceded being conferred upon the fraternity rather than upon the mistery itself. At the same time many gilds had among their purposes plays, almsgiving, or the maintenance of services and lights, and, under this aspect, cannot be distinguished from fraternities: but it was the gilds, not the fraternities, who maintained the pageants. Thus at Coventry the Shearsmen and Taylors took the biblical story from the Annunciation to the Slaughter of the Innocents; and at a later stage the Smiths enacted Christ before

[1] *York Memorandum Book*, ed. M. Sellers (Surtees Soc.), i. 94–101; see the discussion in B. Johnson, *The Acts and Ordinances of the Company of Merchant Tailors of York* (1949), pp. 20 f.

the High Priest to the Crucifixion, while the Cappers had the Descent into Hell as far as the Journey to Emmaus. The Assumption group, a subject greatly venerated, was allotted to the Mercers, partly because they were the most important craft, but not least because they purported to have been a fraternity in honour of the Assumption, and the arms the Coventry Mercers bore were the same as those of the London Mercers' company; gules, a figure of the Virgin Mary with her hair dishevelled crowned, rising out and within an orb of clouds, all proper; motto *Honor Deo*.[1] At Coventry there would seem to have been no Old Testament plays: but at York and Chester and in the Towneley cycle there were several Old Testament plays, behind which may have lain an original Yorkshire cycle.

At Coventry, just as at Southampton, it was the leet which formed the centre of municipal activity, not the assembly, as at Northampton, nor the meeting of the gild merchant as at Worcester. The gild tended to form such a centre in the mediated towns, where the burgesses did not control the borough courts: the orders of the Coventry leet affected every department of a citizen's life down to his leisure moments, for he was ordered to abstain from daily and weekly games of quoits and bowls so that he should not neglect his business.[2] A fixed price was set upon the common necessities of life, and goods brought into the city by victuallers from without were inspected for quality and price, while every precaution was taken against the regrators,[3] i.e. people who bought up and resold at a higher price goods sent to the market. Much of the debates and the decisions in the Coventry leet concern the common lands. No doubt powerful private people encroached on the commons, and the temptation to convert areas of land bearing 'common' rights into several holdings for public purpose seems to have been found irresistible by the rulers of the city'.[4] It was the leet that decided the levy of murage and the imposition of rates for public works, the preparations that had to be made for fortifications and for the collection and arming of a force of 100 soldiers sent to fight on the side of Lancaster. It was the leet that authorized loans to the crown and gave Henry IV a loan

---

[1] *The Coventry Corpus Christi Plays*, p. xvi.
[2] *The Coventry Leet Book*, ed. M. Dormer Harris (E.E.T.S., 1903–13), pp. 656 661.
[3] Ibid., pp. 25, 197, 623, 780, 798.
[4] Ibid., p. xliii.

of 300 marks in 1400, while for the siege of Harfleur it loaned 200 marks to Henry V, and it allowed both Bedford and Gloucester to borrow substantial sums, to say nothing of Henry Beauchamp's 100 marks in 1444 and a similar sum from the earl of Warwick in 1471. On the other hand York, which had attained county status in 1396 and had sheriffs now rather than bailiffs, is essentially an example of aldermanic government, with a small council of twelve, who were generally wealthy merchants, helped by councils of twenty-four and sometimes by the forty-eight who represented the various crafts. On certain important occasions there is a mention of the *communitas*, at that date as many citizens as could be got into the Gildhall, but the other councils were largely composed of functionaries, serving or past. Most of the twelve were ex-mayors, and the twenty-four counted amongst themselves a good number of ex-bailiffs and other officers. Their activities can be traced in the memorandum book of the city. At Winchester the authority was centred in the twenty-four, not a legislative or an administrative body, but an advisory one, the 'peers' of the mayor called to counsel like the 'fellows' or fellowship at Exeter. The mayor takes their advice and reports to them on important city business, though the action taken is not theirs, but his.[1] They are an order rather than a council, an estate in the civic constitution: but they are the people that count, helping the magistrates of the city, the mayor and bailiffs, to maintain the law and custom of the place.

Assertion of municipal control over trade and industry is well illustrated at Norwich. Here, after Edward III's death, the citizens lost no time in petitioning parliament that strangers to their franchise might be prohibited from buying and selling by retail within the city. They were ordered to abide by the statute of Gloucester recently enacted, which permitted wholesale and retail trade alike, as previously, in small wares, such as spiceries, coverchiefs, and the like, but allowed citizens and burgesses only to retail wines, linen, cloth, and so forth in their own cities and boroughs. The next stage was to control trade; with this aim in view a body of sixteen citizens was formed to secure the necessary funds to buy up the market stalls. To the sixteen was given warrant to collect offerings from citizens and strangers. In 1378 an assignment of £128. 4s. 8d. apportioned for collection

[1] J. S. Furley, *The City Government of Winchester* (1923), p. 68.

among the four great wards was laid upon the city and three-quarters of the total sum was raised during the current year. By these methods three messuages, eighteen shops, forty-two stalls, and 54s. in rent were acquired. The body of sixteen next ordered that all flesh and fish should be sold at the common stalls: a tariff of tolls was drawn up; and orders were given that all ships and boats were to be laden and unladen at the common staithes and nowhere else. The sixteen through a committee of accounts appear to have revolutionized the city accounting system. A similar control was exercised in Norwich over the craft gilds. By a composition of 1415 the gilds were permitted to choose their own masters and present them to the mayor who administered an oath, while no mayor was given authority to assign masters to those crafts who failed to nominate them among themselves. The master's duties were to search for faulty work as before, and, after informing the mayor, he along with others of similar occupation were to assess the fines, half of which went to the sheriffs and half to the masters, for the benefit of the craft. All crafts that had the right of search in London were to have it in Norwich, and in the same form excepting the privileges of the chartered companies. All the present and future citizens were to be enrolled under the craft to which they belonged, as were also those who should henceforth be enfranchised. Anyone who desired to buy his freedom not having been apprenticed in the city, could not do so unless the masters of his craft notified that they were willing to receive him.

Much of the social and religious life of the towns was centred in the fraternities or gilds for religious and social purposes. Two of the more famous examples were at Coventry and York. At Coventry the Trinity gild maintained priests to pray for the welfare of the living and the salvation of the souls of the departed. It drew its members from nearly every quarter of England and included men and women of every rank save the lower. It had political grandees like John of Gaunt, Thomas of Woodstock, Richard Beauchamp, earl of Warwick, and Henry Percy, earl of Northumberland: all gildsmen were strong Lancastrians till 1461, when the depredations of Margaret of Anjou's soldiers proved too much for the citizens. 'Landowners, merchants, craftsmen, all who from far and near resorted for business reasons to Coventry sought to further their business affairs by establishing friendly relations with those with whom they had to deal.'[1] Founded in 1364, the gild absorbed earlier fraternities, St. Mary's (the earliest, 1340), St. John the Baptist's, and St. Katharine's (1364–9). During the fifty years which had passed since the foundation of St. Mary's gild, the town had become one of the chief industrial trading and financial centres of England. As one of the justices of the peace and a keeper of the common treasure chest, the master of the Trinity gild was, saving the mayor, the chief figure in the city, and his connexion with the mayoralty was close: for two years after he had served the town in this capacity a mayor became automatically master of the Trinity fraternity, and the gild paid part of the service of the recorder.[2] In the manuscript register of the Trinity gild the oaths of the city and the gild officials are juxtaposed, and it is clear that, in Dr. Templeman's words, 'only an important member of the ruling group in the city could aspire to the master's office, and even then the choice was strictly limited'.[3] In 1474 the mayor and the master are described as *superiores et gubernatores civitatis*, and in 1484 the master was to take precedence over the recorder and immediately after the mayor, while he regularly appeared at the head of the list of leet jurors.[4] He was the chief executive officer of the gild and was responsible for the proper administration of its revenues and its property. A rental of the property of the Trinity gild for the year 1485–6 made by William Schore, master of the gild, shows that some £120. 16s. 8d. was paid to the receiver-general for the town houses alone, apart from the sums received for the agrarian holdings, the closes and pastures specified in the rental of 1534;[5] but between 1485 and 1529 the gild acquired fresh property in the city, and there was also a considerable quantity of goods, silver of all sorts, cloths and napery in the possession of the gild. The lists of members show that as at King's Lynn the gild drew upon the more substantial citizens, and citizens of London who were merchants in a big

---

[1] *Register of the Guild of Holy Trinity, St. Mary and St. Katharine of Coventry*, i, ed. M. Dormer Harris (Dugdale Soc. xiii, 1936), p. xiii. The gild was an extensive landowner, holding many messuages let to tenants. The total of its rents reached, in 1485–6, £318. 12s. 6d.: Levi Fox, 'Administration of Guild Property in Coventry in the Fifteenth Century', *Eng. Hist. Rev.* lv (1940), 636–7.

[2] *Register*, i, ed. Harris, p. xviii.

[3] Ibid. ii (ed. G. Templeman), 23.

[4] Ibid. ii. 24.

[5] Ibid. ii. 36–37.

way are found among its numbers.[1] At Lynn the alderman
of the gild, at the choosing of the mayor, nominated four
persons, and the four eight others, who selected the mayor from
the twenty-four jurats of the town.[2]

In the north of England the best known of fraternities was
the York gild of Corpus Christi formed in 1408 but incorporated
on 6 November 1459. It was established under the rule of a
master and six keepers who were to be chosen from the parochial
clergy of the city annually on the octave of the feast of Corpus
Christi and had power to admit men and women members.
The statutes were approved by the archbishop (Rotherham)
in 1477; and the next year the master and wardens of the
hospital of St. Thomas of Canterbury without Micklegate Bar,
along with the then brethren and sisters of the foundation,
transferred their house and possessions to the new foundation
of the Corpus Christi gild, and thereafter the two institutions
were under a single government. The gild was specially dedicated 'to the praise and honour of the most sacred body of Our
Lord Jesus Christ', and its members were 'bound to keep a
solempne procession, the sacrament being in a shrine borne in
the same through the city yearly the Friday after Corpus
Christi day, and the day after to have a solempne mass and
dirige'.[3] The dating was in fact different when the procession
was separated in 1426 from the plays performed by the crafts:
the ordinance of that year assigned the plays to the vigil, and
the procession to the feast itself. The procession assembled
at the gates of the Priory of Holy Trinity, Micklegate, with the
parochial clergy of the city in their surplices walking first, and
the master of the gild, in silken cope, followed, supported on
either side by one of the clergy who had previously held the
same office and attended by the six keepers of the gild. The
ecclesiastical part of the procession escorted the jewelled shrine
of silver-gilt bearing the Host, and the proper services for the
day were chanted as the procession moved. Next came the
mayor, aldermen, and members of the corporation in ceremonial robes, attended by the city officers and bearers of

---

[1] Richard Whittington; John Pultney (four times mayor of London who built
the Church of the Whitefriars at Coventry). John Raby, twice mayor of Coventry
was also mayor of the Calais Staple. *Register*, i. ed. Harris, p. xxi.

[2] Hist. MSS. Comm. *11th Report*, King's Lynn, p. 195.

[3] Cited by Robert Davies, *Extracts from the Municipal Records of the City of York*
(1843), appendix, p. 245, from Bodleian Lib., Dodsworth MSS., vol. cxxxix.

lighted torches, followed by the officers and members of the
crafts with their respective banners and torches. From the priory
the procession made its way to the Minster where a sermon was
preached in the chapter house. Thence the procession went to
the hospital of St. Leonard, where the Host was deposited.

The Corpus Christi gild had its own play, the Crede or Credo
play bequeathed by William Revetour, chantry priest of the
chapel of St. William on Ouse Bridge, for performance every
tenth year, for the feast was marked by the performance, by
the various crafts, of the famous York plays staged on the
movable pageants or tiered platforms, which were wheeled
round the city to stop, at fixed intervals, before certain houses
or churches. From the act-books of the city of York it appears
that the decorations for such occasions were kept in certain of
the parish churches. When Richard III visited the city the civic
authorities made a note to send for Sir Henry Hudson, rector
of All Saints, North Street, and for the three parish clerks of
St. Cross, All Saints Pavement, and St. Michael le Belfry 'to
have their advysez for a new syght to be made at the kyng's
cumyng to Mykylgate Bar, Ouse Bridge and Stanegate (Stone-
gate)'.[1] The 'syght', as given before Henry VII, probably
followed the lines of the earlier spectacle, when Eboruc, the
mythical founder of York, Solomon, and the Blessed Virgin
address the king at various points in his journey through the
city. The vicar who produced the scenes and rehearsed the
actors received from the chamberlain the total sum of 66s. 8d.
Each of the pageants covered a number of subjects. The patron
of the chapel was Nicholas Blackburn, the mayor, whose will
two years later the cantarist drew up.[2] The municipal chaplain
was then helping his master to put his effects into order. Already
Blackburn had founded a chantry in St. Anne's, Fossgate; and
his wife Alice, before she followed him to the grave, left to the
chantry a set of green vestments and two cloths painted with
the angelic salutation. One of the witnesses to the bequest made
by Blackburn to Revetour for his good labour and business
efforts on the former's behalf was the wealthy merchant William
Ormeshed, Alice's brother. It was a closely interrelated governing order, pious, supporting the local parish churches which
were the heart of the citizen's religious life, largely because the

---

[1] *York Civic Records*, ed. Angelo Raine, i. 77.
[2] *Testamenta Eboracensia*, ii. 17–21.

chantries founded there kept alive, by constant periodical intercession, the family name and tradition. All members of the
Blackburn circle whose wills are extant made liberal bequests
to their parish churches, though Nicholas himself was buried
in the Minster. The chantry priest, it had been observed of
York, was the real link between the municipality and the
Church. That the civic officials of the fifteenth century regarded
the chantry priests and chaplains as specially in their charge
emerges from an entry in the memorandum book, recording a
civic adjudication on a claim made to the city rectors and
vicars for mortuaries, in the form of the deceased chaplain's
second best gown and hood. Twelve of the leading citizens
supported the mayor in resisting this claim, the mayor declaring
that 'all the chantries of this city have been and are founded by
the citizens and notabilities of this city: therefore both the priests
of this city and its suburbs, having chantries, are the special
orators of the citizens, their patrons and masters'.[1] The rectors
and vicars had to agree to let the chaplains *stare in pace*.

These religious and eleemosynary societies were not always
confined to the upper ranks of the citizens. The less powerful
crafts formed themselves into gilds and confederacies for the
protection of their own interests, not without protest from the
existing confraternities. At Coventry strong objections were
raised to the gild of the Nativity which was formed (1384) to
commemorate founders and the souls of the departed. A commission which investigated its activities described it as composed of 'labourers and artificers of the middling sort' (*laborarios
et artifices mediocres*) and others, 'to resist the mayor and not for
the welfare of souls'. This gild was suppressed until 1449 when
a payment of 40 marks induced the authorities to grant the
necessary licence. The barbers followed, these being accused
of assembly in unlawful conventicles and 'refusing to shave on
feast days', then the confederacy of the dyers, as well as the
yeomen gilds of St. Anne and St. George. The fraternity of
St. Anne consisted, according to complaints made in November
1407, of the servants of tailors and other artificers. The gild of
St. George was also a group of textile workers who held meetings
in St. George's Chapel (St. George was the patron saint of the
shearmen), which became the property of the revived Nativity

---

[1] *York Memorandum Book*, ed. Sellers, ii. 19: the chantry priests 'sunt speciales
oratores civium'.

gild. One body of journeymen were more fortunate in the early stages. The journeymen weavers were allowed to form a fraternity in virtue of each man's contributing 4*d.* to the fund administered by their masters.[1]

At Coventry there were fewer crafts supporting pageants than at York: not more than ten, but these were mostly reinforced by subsidiary or minor crafts, e.g. the mercers had at least five components, besides the mercers themselves, the linen-drapers, haberdashers and vendors of silk wares, grocers and salters, and the cap-makers of all descriptions. There were ten Coventry pageants, which appear to have been acted, one in each of the ten different wards of the city.[2]

---

[1] *Coventry Leet Book*, ed. Dormer Harris, i. 91–96.
[2] Hardin Craig, *The Coventry Corpus Christi Plays*, (i) The Shearmen and Taylors' Pageant, and (ii) The Weavers' Pageant (E.E.T.S. Extra Ser. 87, 1957), p. xiii.

IX

GOVERNMENT

So far our picture has been of a society in process of change, adapting itself, with the aid of precedent, to economic fact and political necessity. In the fourteenth century two royal depositions, a royal minority which brought government by council to the fore and a popular revolt on the largest scale, had been sufficient tests for a constitution in the making; but in the fifteenth there was to be heavier probation: the poverty of the new dynasty, the absences of a soldier king abroad, a minority of unparalleled length and, this ended, the discovery that the sovereign was totally unable to give firm direction on political issues; the failure of the Anglo-French monarchy of Troyes, the *dénouement* of Arras and the diplomatic isolation of England, the strife of parties—all these imposed upon government burdens it had never yet borne. The exceptional resilience of the country in the early Tudor years witnessed, nevertheless, to its having survived the almost complete breakdown of the central period, proving that the association, in government, of the middle with the aristocratic elements in the community was working effectively.

Constitutionally, after Henry IV had grasped the throne, there was no experiment. Everyone, save the avowed supporters of Richard II, was anxious to go on as before. The novelty perhaps lay in the acceleration of the process by which on the one hand the commons were gaining the initiative in parliament and on the other the secular lords, or a group of them, were developing a faculty for government and administration. Much stress has been laid on the 'premature' nature of the commons' development. This is to argue little understanding of the fourteenth century. The crises of 1404 and 1406, as they have just been described, were resolved by establishing controls not unpredictable in 1376 or 1386; the minority council of 1422 went back to Richard II's first year. The acceleration of the commons' advance and the participation of the lords in the continuous work of the council, though the two were not to prove wholly compatible, were the result partly of serious administrative purpose and partly of clever tactics at a critical moment. Perhaps the most promising new characteristic of English government was an administrative one: the general interest taken in the problems of finance, particularly in the question how to anticipate as well as to augment revenue; for anticipation was of the very essence of a system that depended on credit, the credit of the Lancastrian exchequer. This may have been a major problem of parliament under the Lancastrian kings.

The main functions of parliament in the fifteenth century were the granting of taxation and the consideration of petitions. It was the highest court in the land, but that does not mean that it was an ordinary court of law. The receivers of petitions would be quick to dispatch to the appropriate bench or tribunal any request for legal remedy that belonged there: but for matters where the law touched people's estate, or where treason and subsequent attainder might be involved, or large political issues raised, action could be commenced either by official bill or common petition and a process controlled by the council initiated. The hearing and recommendations to be made upon petitions were, of course, within the function of a court.

The fifteenth-century parliament consisted of the lords spiritual and temporal and of the knights representing the shires and burgesses representing the boroughs. The term knights and burgesses must be figurative. Many of the knights were esquires (*armigeri*) and among the burgesses there were gentry, and in time, even knights drawn from outside the borough; the external elements, as will be seen, increasing after the middle of the century. Parliament, when together, met in the Painted Chamber of the Palace of Westminster. When apart, the lords met in the White Chamber or the Marculf Room; and the commons, who in the fourteenth century had alternated between the Painted Chamber and the Chapter House, after 1397 more often than not assembled in the refectory of Westminster Abbey.[1] The attendances of the lords spiritual and temporal varied greatly. So far as the lords spiritual were concerned, though convocation often overlapped with parliament, the attendance of the abbots and priors was very poor: they did not come to convocation either, and Archbishop Chichele's

---

[1] See the discussion in J. G. Edwards, *The Commons in Medieval English Parliaments* (Creighton Lecture, 1957), note A, pp. 25 f.

attempts to mobilize them through threat of fine had only temporary success. The bishops were better in their attendance: it was the lords, reputedly the heart and core of parliament, who tended to default, despite the minatory language used on occasion in their individual writs of summons. The lords' attendances in the last parliament of Richard II and the first of Henry IV were certainly good, for it was to the interest of all peers to be present: of ninety-seven summoned, there were sixty-three attending Henry IV's first parliament.[1] At the great council of 9 February 1400 the bishops showed up well, but the lay magnates could count no more than five earls and fifteen others, and 'on the crucial day of supplies' no more than thirty-three lords had been present. In the important parliament of 1406, when the exemplification of the statute entailing the crowns of England and France upon Henry IV and his heirs male was made, there were 19 abbots who sent proxies, and of the secular lords, the duke of York, 5 out of the 7 earls and 18 out of the 32 barons affixed their seals: the total presence was 41 peers, out of 84 summoned, just under half.[2] The conclusion for Henry IV's reign is that on an average two-thirds of the secular prelates, a handful of the religious prelates, and perhaps seldom more than half of the temporal lords attended.[3] It was better than this at the great council which met in April 1415 on the eve of Henry V's departure to France, but while all 4 dukes came and 9 out of 11 earls, no more than 14 other lords turned up. In November 1414 forty-three lay magnates had been summoned.

While there were special or significant occasions when the muster was particularly good (e.g. at Leicester on 18 Feb. 1426) the number of magnates attending sessions of importance was only a fraction of what it might have been. This is a significant point in view of the tendency to regard the commons as mouthpieces or advocates of magnate policy. They certainly showed themselves anxious to uphold the status of the noble houses, and were prepared to sponsor the petitions of those suing for justice or rehabilitation; and it is true that elections of the shire knights could be, and were at times, influenced by local magnate influence. But the old dislike of attendance at parliament,

---

[1] J. S. Roskell, 'The Problem of the Attendance of the Lords in Medieval Parliaments', *Bull. Inst. Hist. Res.* xxix (1956), 178.

[2] Ibid., p. 179. [3] Ibid., p. 180.

if indeed it ever existed, has passed away: election, extended
now beyond the *milites gladio cincti*, to the general run of county
gentry, lawyers, business men, and administrators, if not sought,
was not avoided, and the commons gave the keenest attention
to maintaining and supplying the new dynasty, and later to the
problem of the royal household. Their progress throughout the
fifteenth century was continuous from the parliaments preceding
the famous one at Shrewsbury (1398): it can be represented in
a twofold light. They constituted themselves an indispensable
element in the process of legislation: and on various occasions
they took the initiative with the lords where a course of action
had to be decided upon: when, so far from being dependants
of the upper house, they were at times the initiators of policy.

Under the Lancastrian kings practically all legislation arose
out of petitions. These might be private requests or requests
bearing upon matters of wider policy or interest. Originally
petitions were addressed to the king or the king and his council.
Towards the close of the fourteenth century a number were
addressed to the commons along with the king and the lords;
but the practice of including the commons or of addressing the
commons with a view to their advocating the petition to the
king and lords was growing at the end of the period. Of the 59
common petitions enrolled for the reign of Henry IV, 9
were so addressed, and under Henry V 29 were addressed to
the commons alone, while under Henry VI 60 of the 150 printed
were addressed to the commons only. It is the same with private
petitions: under Richard II no private petition of those enrolled
was addressed to the commons: but under Henry IV, out of
57 enrolled, 6 were addressed to the commons; under Henry V,
out of 51 enrolled, 26 mentioned the commons alone, and under
Henry VI 60 out of the 198 enrolled were addressed thus.[1] It
became important to get the commons to advocate or include
among their own petitions those of private individuals or
groups. At the same time they were, in return for the grants
they made, putting forward collective requests of their own,
called in legal French the *commune peticion* about which it is
important to avoid ambiguity.

The word common is most difficult to interpret, but it will be
safest to infer that its primary meaning is 'general' or 'public'.

[1] A. R. Myers, 'Parliamentary Petitions in the Fifteenth Century', *Eng. Hist.
Rev.* lii (1937), 400.

'The essential feature of a common petition should be not that it was a petition of the commons, but that it was concerned with a common or public interest.'[1] Such petitions tend to have a definite location on the parliament roll, below the caption or heading which announces that common petitions 'follow'. This is not always the case, since they also stand, at times, in front of the caption. Some of them were brought forward and discussed, before actual framing, by the knights and burgesses: others originated elsewhere, and were sponsored by the commons; and others in turn claimed to be the work of 'the commons', but certainly were not, being the product of groups of people who in medieval parlance were entitled to call themselves a *communa* or collectivity. But the common petition, however it originated, was some request that touched the public interest, and the great majority of them were documents advocated and preferred by the commons. It has been held that from the reign of Edward II to 1423, common petitions were handed in on one single document,[2] evidently to the clerk of the parliaments (for common petitions did not go through the 'receivers' and the 'triers'). Now it is true that, as in 1406, one petition may 'include several articles': but that the common petition before 1423 was exclusively a portmanteau cannot be proved. That it is unlikely can be seen from the number of extant common petitions which we know to have been successful, but for which there is no evidence on the rolls that they were presented by the commons, and this is true for the fourteenth as well as the fifteenth century. The petitions enrolled on the parliament roll before the caption, may well have been presented individually. The fact is that the evidence for large, comprehensive petitions presented on one occasion is weak. At the beginning of a session of a parliament bills or petitions were coming in: some, the private ones, were sent to the receivers and triers: but the common petitions, whether originating with private individuals or the result of deliberation among the knights, would take time to discuss before they went to the clerk of the parliaments to be presented to the council, and there was no need to present them *en masse*. The subjects and topics were

---

[1] A. R. Myers, 'Parliamentary Petitions in the Fifteenth Century', *Eng. Hist. Rev.* lii (1937), 601.

[2] H. L. Gray, *The Influence of the Commons on Early Legislation* (1932), p. 229. Cf. Myers's careful examination and rejection of this theory, op. cit., pp. 607-8.

best taken by stages. On the other hand, the initiative could equally well come from the government instead of from the commons, in the shape of 'official bills' (to use Professor Gray's nomenclature) put forward in the lords and representing the result, sometimes, of discussions in the council, and it is worth noting that with the accession of Edward IV the government recovered much of its initiative in legislation which it kept until the latter days of Elizabeth I.[1]

The assented petition and the answer given to it became the statute: the form was a matter of editing by the clerks of the chancery and in some cases by the justices of both benches. In 1423 the council advised that the clerk of parliament should show its acts, the approved petitions, to the justices of both benches so that the acts which were to be statutes might be seen by them and 'reduced to clear language' (*redigantur in mundum*) before being proclaimed. After this it was to be enrolled: the fair copy was to be lodged with the clerk of the council and by him sent for enrolment in the chancery.[2] How far this practice persisted we do not know: but the fact of editing being mentioned in the early part of the century may help to dispose of Stubbs's hypothesis that at the end of Henry VI's reign occurred a change from procedure by petition to procedure by bill, the bill which 'had within itself the form of the act'.[3] It has been shown that petition and bill were fundamentally the same thing, and one may go farther to surmise that the bill so described is the petition prepared for proclamation and action. It is now in a form which the justices can understand.

In framing their petitions the commons came to rely on the fourteenth-century precedent of consulting the lords. Dealing with the period 1373–84 Professor J. G. Edwards has shown that the working of parliament involved not two sets of deliberation, but three; of either body, lords and commons, by itself, and of a joint group consisting of a delegation of lords and commons acting together, to which he applies the word

[1] Cf. the remarks of Sir John Fortescue, *The Governance of England*, ch. xiv, on the desirability of the Council's control over legislation. On public bills originating in the lords, cf. H. L. Gray, op. cit., pp. 59 f. We follow him in his basic contention of government recovery after 1461.

[2] *P.P.C.* iii. 22.

[3] It occurs in the act for the attainder of Henry VI and certain Lancastrian lords, 1461: *Rot. Parl.*, v. 476, and in the act of resumption in the parliament of 1449–50. Actually, before 1483, it is a *Cedula* which has the form of the act, as H. L. Gray, op. cit, p. 179, pointed out.

'intercommune'.[1] In 1399 the commons deliberated with the lords, with results showing later in common petitions; in 1402 they asked to have 'advice and communication' with some of the lords on matters to be treated. Henry IV granted the request, though indicating that it was unusual and a matter for special favour, not of right; but the four bishops, four earls, and four lords named were in all probability their own suggested nominees.[2] In 1404 the commons requested that some of them might be allowed to confer with the lords, and this was granted. On the final day of the 1406 parliament consultation between the lords and the commons resulted in the archbishop putting forward a petition about the succession to the crown; and in 1407 the Speaker requested the intercommuning of lords and commons on matters of business 'touching the common good and profit of all the realm', and this time in so doing advanced the names of three lords spiritual and four temporal.[3] The commons, therefore, are not standing in any subordinate position to the lords; if their petitions cannot take statutory form without the consent of the upper house, no taxation can be imposed without the assent of the commons, and it is they who draw up the subsidy bills in the form of indentures. 'The granting of a subsidy', Professor Gray wrote, 'was a transaction between king and commons in which apparently each party retained one half of the twice written contract. In its own phraseology it was a grant made to the king with the assent of the lords.'[4] Provisos and amendments are inserted in the indenture itself, just as they are on the *Concessio subsidii* made by the convocations. Grants of tunnage and poundage and of the wool subsidy are therefore legislative acts of the commons, backed by the lords: and no such act is legal without this agreement: the lords cannot make a grant on their own, just as in convocation the prelates could not do so without the consent of the clergy.

The commons have their mouthpiece, their *organum vocis*:

[1] *The Commons in Medieval English Parliaments* (1958), pp. 5 f. 'This intercommuning is the procedural fact that has been largely responsible for shaping the more recent view that the dominant hand in the working of medieval parliaments was the hand, not of the commons, but of the lords.' Professor Edwards has argued that the 'intercommuning' signified exactly the opposite, the initiative coming from the commons. Cf. his note B on 'individual' reference to intercommuning, p. 28.

[2] *Rot. Parl.* iii. 486.

[3] Instances noted in Myers, op. cit., p. 594.

[4] Gray, op. cit., pp. 40–41.

the Speaker, who was not the head of a deputation, but who could speak continuously for the duration of the parliament, emerges in Richard II's reign. It was in April 1384 that the commons were told for the first time to elect him, though less officially, but no less effectively, he goes back to Edward III's reign. Regularly now the order was given for the commons to elect and present their speaker on the second day of parliament, though from 1413 to 1427 they presented him on the third day or even later; in 1426 they took ten days to decide.[1] They took a knight or esquire of standing who had either been closely connected with the king through the household or in some administrative office or was of proved efficiency and ability in presenting a case for consideration by expert lawyers and officials. He was not imposed by higher authority, though authority could bring pressure to bear and get him changed, as when in 1399 John Doreward displaced the Lollard, Sir John Cheyne of Beckford;[2] on the other hand, the commons could reject their own Speaker, if he exceeded his powers as their agent,[3] and replace him by the man who led their opposition to the original choice. Above all parliamentary experience or, if the knight was young—as in the case of John Tiptoft—a parliamentary tradition in the family was what they looked for; seeking out men like Thomas Chaucer who in 1421 was Speaker for the fifth time when he was representing Oxford in the ninth parliament he had attended; or Roger Flore of Oakham, steward of the duchy of Lancaster north of Trent since 1416, who when acting as Speaker in 1422 was sitting for the twelfth time for Rutland. (The legend that knights of the shire were reluctant attenders will not survive a study of these old hands.) The Speaker's protestation in which he excused himself if he said anything offensive to the king or—in certain parliaments—to the lords, and the occasional expression by the commons of their concern lest what was said in their debates might be magnified or distorted, show that so far from freedom of speech being curtailed, there was a good deal of unfettered expression of opinion. Not least was this so in the parliament of January 1410 when the king, in allowing the Speaker's protestation, voiced the hopeful conviction that the commons, because all

---

[1] J. S. Roskell, 'The Medieval Speaker for the Commons in Parliament', *Bull. Inst. Hist. Res.* xxiii (1950), pp. 40–41.
[2] *Rot. Parl.* iii. 424.
[3] Ibid. iv. 4.

estates had met to further the common weal and profit of the realm, 'would wish to attempt or speak nothing that would not be honourable, in order to nourish love and concord between all parties'.[1] There may indeed have been plain speaking sometimes: but there were occasions when none was heard, and it is permissible to wonder what the commons thought about the measures taken by the lords, purely on their own responsibility, in 1422: whether they agreed with the arrangements for the council during the minority, and whether, if they did not, their silence did not imply that a golden constitutional opportunity had been lost. For after 1422 the bumptiousness of the commons was only occasionally expressed: in the altercation with the lords over the grant of tunnage and poundage in 1425; with the council in 1439–40 over mercantile policy and especially the supervision of alien traders, and again with Henry VI and 'his young counsellors' when these attempt to defend Suffolk in 1449–50. The days of Savage and Tiptoft were over.

To secure the right members the Lancastrian parliaments passed a series of measures to determine the personnel of the electors in the interest of electoral freedom and to eliminate corruption or accidents in the conduct of elections and the making of returns. In 1406 a statute guarded against 'affection' on the part of the sheriff with its effect on the choice of the members, providing that the time and place for the assembly of the next parliament should be proclaimed at the shire court following the delivery of the writ of summons, and that elections were to be held 'en plein countee', with the assistance of all those present, 'si bien sueters duement summonez pour cell cause, come autres'. The indenture accompanying the returned writ was to be drawn up 'under the seals of all those who elect them and to be attached to the said writ of parliament'. Those indentures, which did not strictly follow the 1406 statute in being made with all the suitors present in county court when the election was made, stated that the election of the knights was carried out in accordance with the writ of summons and certified the election as taking place 'libere et indifferenter et ex unanimi assensu', giving the knights full and sufficient power to bind the community of the shire to what was ordained in parliament.

[1] *Rot. Parl.* iii. 623.

In many instances it was the sheriff who determined who should seal and attest. In any case, Professor Roskell thinks, those who did so were 'on the score of their local importance . . . the more influential magnates or notables of the shire'.[1] Granted that the notabilities attested, why was it necessary to decree, in the franchise statute of 1429, that the electors should be men who were resident in the shire and worth 40s. a year clear from free tenements in it? There seems no doubt that in peaceful and well-administered shires there would be a group of local notabilities ready at the sheriff's word to attest: but it is also clear that in others there were, at the full and open court, a number of extremely dubious claimants to be the electors envisaged even in the 1406 statute. There were, in fact, too many for the court. In a number of English counties, the 1429 petition said, elections had been made 'par trop graunde et excessive nombre des gentz demurrantz deinz mesmes les countees, dount le greindre partre estoit par gentz sinoun de petit avoir ou de null value, dount chescun pretende d'avoir vois equivalent, quant au tieulx elections fair, ove le pluis vaillantz chivalers ou esquiers demurrantz deinz mesme les countees'. It was partly the danger of noise and disturbance at county sessions which prompted the 40s. freeholder measure:[2] it was more the dislike of the *vois equivalent* and the feeling that gentry should be elected by gentry and by the 'common suitors', the *sectatores communes*, or their representatives, magnates, or persons nearly on the magnate level. It was a more select group which the framers of the statute wanted; and insistence on the residence qualifications would assist to that end. The Act of 1429 prescribed a penalty of a year's imprisonment, without admission to bail, for an offending sheriff. That there was good cause for the passing of an electoral act of some kind can be seen from three disputed elections in Cumberland, Buckinghamshire, and Huntingdonshire. In Buckinghamshire the sheriff returned (31 Aug. 1429) two names attested by eighty-three suitors, although upon inquiry it was found by sworn inquest taken before the justices

---

[1] *The Commons in the Parliament of 1422* (1954), p. 9.

[2] In the Yorkshire election of 1442 the attestors were about 450: C. 219/15/2. Professor Roskell (op. cit., p. 12) draws attention to the Huntingdon election of 1450, when 124 freeholders of the shire complained that although they, with another 300 electors, made their nominations in full county court, 70 freehold commoners appeared at the prompting of gentry from outside, and made another. It will, of course, be remembered that 1450 was a climax year for local disturbance.

of assize that the return was made on the sheriff's sole authority
and that 129 suitors of the shire court had in fact elected two
quite different people. This was due not to an aristocratic
reaction, but to the disturbances that had been going on be
tween the earl of Huntingdon, John Holand, and the duke of
Norfolk. The sheriff, Sir Thomas Waweton, was connected with
Holand.[1] The causes were probably political.

Was the statute of 1429 a reaction against too miscellaneous
a commons? It was probably one against too diluted a body of
county representatives; borough members were perhaps in a
different category. In 1445 it was enacted by statute that
knights of the shire should be notable knights or such notable
esquires or gentlemen by birth as could support the knight'
estate, and not men of yeomen standing. This exclusiveness can
be seen much earlier in the preliminaries of the 'unlearned
parliament of 1404, when Henry IV tried to exclude lawyer
from the parliament altogether, although the immediate pur
pose of the prohibition may have been to prevent private
petitions of the lawyers' clients being manœuvred into the
petitions of the commons. It was, however, not at all easy to
keep the solicitor or attorney out of the shire representation
nor indeed was it desirable: and there were, of course, shire
knights who were themselves lawyers or learned in the law: in
1422 men like John Wodehouse or John Throckmorton
members for Suffolk and Worcestershire, the one chancellor of
the duchy of Lancaster and chancellor to the queen, the other a
chamberlain of the exchequer, coming of a family long con
nected with the Beauchamps of Warwick. Many of the knights
of this parliament had served in the administration of one of
the great lords, having perhaps fought under them in Nor
mandy, or were now key men on their estates or their deputies
in office. In the 1422 parliament Richard Beauchamp, earl of
Warwick, had the largest group of followers, including five
lawyers: John Throckmorton, John Vampage appointed king'
attorney-general in 1429, Robert Stanshaw of Gloucestershire
and Robert Andrew of Wiltshire, both retained as his council
and John Barton, junior, of Buckinghamshire, who had served
as steward to the abbey of St. Alban. Sir William Montfort
knight of the shire for Warwickshire, was steward of War
wick's household and head of his council. Warwick had other

[1] Roskell, op. cit., p. 18.

connexions in the house: Thomas Stanley who had served in his retinue at Calais (1414); and, in all probability, Nicholas Rody, burgess for Warwick, who was appointed one of the earl's executors. Such connexions with leading members of the upper house, with Edmund Mortimer, earl of March, or with Henry and Thomas Beaufort, were inevitable inasmuch as their senior lawyers and administrators were men of standing in their counties. Nor were the ties binding many of the shire knights to the more important peers of parliament only of a professional kind: there were many ties of family relationship.[1] In 1422 Lord Berkeley's father-in-law, Sir Humphrey Stafford, a kinsman of the young earl of Stafford, represented Dorset, while the son of one of the Suffolk knights, Sir John Howard, had married the earl marshal's sister. Thomas Chaucer himself was cousin to Beaufort; and in the north Sir William Eure, whose estates were at Witton-le-Wear and Old Malton and who represented Yorkshire, was son-in-law to Henry Lord FitzHugh of Ravensworth, who has been studied above.[2] As the century moved on an increase is found in the county knights connected by service with the greatest of all lordships, the crown. In the parliament of 1453–4, of the English counties eighteen had a member of the royal household as one of their representatives and two had both. The only counties that did not send a *curialis* of some pattern or other were Bedfordshire, Devon, Shropshire, Somerset, and Westmorland. The two who sent both were Hertfordshire (John Say[3] and Bartholomew Halley[4]) and Northamptonshire (William Catesby,[5] squire of the body, and Thomas Tresham of Sywell,[6] later controller of the household). In the greater boroughs there was also a plentiful supply of king's men: in Kent, there were such in both Canterbury and Rochester and in the boroughs of the counties near London, especially Surrey,[7] they were well represented.

If in 1422 the 188 burgesses returned were mostly resident in the boroughs that sent them, a good deal of non-residence had

---

[1] J. S. Roskell, 'The Social Composition of the Commons in a Fifteenth Century Parliament', *Bull. Inst. Hist. Res.* xxiv (1951), 167.   [2] p. 326.

[3] Squire of the body, with annuity of 50 marks, 1448; J. C. Wedgwood, *History of Parliament, 1439–1509*, Biographies (1936), p. 745.

[4] Usher of the chamber; Wedgwood, p. 409.

[5] Squire of the household; Wedgwood, p. 164.

[6] Cf. J. S. Roskell, 'Sir Thomas Tresham, Knight', *Northamptonshire Past and Present*, ii (1959).

[7] Bletchingley, Gatton, Reigate.

set in by 1453–4. The trading and mercantile interests were well to the fore at both dates: in 1422 members of the Calais staple were prominent, naturally, in the representation of the City of London, but another five Calais staplers were returned from Hull, York, Lincoln, and Nottingham, towns exporting mainly through Hull and Boston. The interests of native shipowners were typified by the two London aldermen, who imported and exported in their own vessels, as did John Bourton, the Bristol merchant, trading in the wine he fetched from Gascony;[1] and by John Tamworth, mayor of Winchelsea, a baron of the Cinque ports, who earlier in the year had been ferrying reinforcements and livestock across the Channel for Henry V's armies.[2] Interesting, in the 1422 parliament, are the connexions of the burgesses with government and administration, two being justices of the peace and fifteen more serving, later on, upon royal commissions in their own counties, some as escheators, while at the beginning of Henry's reign four were coroners in their shires. 'Almost without exception these men holding such crown appointments and commissions were members of the armigerous class or at least men whom a Chancery clerk would not have scrupled to describe as "gentilmen".'[3] By 1454, in addition to the wealthy merchant and the lesser men who had filled responsible posts in their native towns, men like Simon Kent, mercer, and Thomas Clerk, draper, who represented Reading in 1449,[4] new non-burgess types have entered.

Plentiful examples are provided by the parliament which met in January that year. This had, among the burgesses, a large sprinkling of ex-sheriffs, a fair number of ex-escheators and numerous members of the royal household, from yeomen of the crown (Canterbury and Rochester) to yeomen of the buttery (Shoreham, Sussex, borough), a sergeant of the bakery (Steyning, Sussex, borough), and a marshal of the hall (Wells, Downton, borough). Four members of the Exchequer staff are found returned for boroughs. There are not more than nineteen nominees of the magnates filling borough seats: for one (Grimsby), Lord Beaumont put forward the name of Ralph

---

[1] J. S. Roskell, *Bull. Inst. Hist. Res.* xxiv (1951), 157.   [2] Ibid., loc. cit.
[3] Roskell, *The Commons in the Parliament of 1422*, pp. 57–58.
[4] This 'second group' is discussed by M. McKisack, *The Representation of English Boroughs in the Middle Ages* (1932), pp. 104–5.

Chaundler to the mayor and burgesses as a man of the locality in more considerate fashion than the earl of Westmorland, who in 1460 'advised and heartily required' the burgesses to elect two of his council.[1] The borough groups where 'foreigners' are chiefly to be found are those of Dorset, Wiltshire, Somerset, Surrey, and Sussex. In the Wiltshire boroughs there were five royal servants, five 'gentilmen' (including, at Malmesbury, the county coroner, and the victualler of the army, Richard Joynour, grocer of London), an ex-sheriff (Robert Tynely of Ludgershall), and the youthful son of the master of Bishop Waynflete's household: in Surrey, Yatton had a nominee of the duke of Norfolk, John Framlingham of Debenham, and the constable of Bristol and king's servant, John Daundesey of Trowbridge, Wilts.; Reigate had another servant of Norfolk, John Tymperle of Hintelsham, Suffolk, a former escheator,[2] and a member of the Exchequer staff, John Yerman; from Sussex, East Grinstead has two royal household staff, Richard Strykland of Haversham, Bucks., master of the king's harriers, and John Alfrey, yeoman of the crown. The Cornish boroughs provided useful accommodation for officials and the retainers of the great. Bodmin had George Gargrave, marshal of the Marshalsea, Helston a servant of Exeter's, and a member of his council, John Archer, who was beheaded by the Yorkists after Northampton in July 1460; Liskeard had another servant of Exeter, John Watkins, who came from Stoke Hammond in Buckinghamshire. The list[3] when analysed shows that the parliamentary boroughs were catering for a wide range of persons who could not have got in for the counties as well as genuine county types—younger sons of distinguished persons, and so forth. There were eleven *armigeri* in this 1454 parliament and numerous *rentiers* who are termed 'gentilman'.

In the royal eyes and to the mind of the council the convocations of Canterbury and York were part of the fiscal machinery of the kingdom. The two convocations were, of course, the legislative and deliberative organs of the English Church, and came before the notice of the state for the grants they made and the presentation of *gravamina* only:[4] but the tendency of the

[1] *History of Parliament, 1434–1500*, register, p. cxix.
[2] Feoffee for Lord Scales and the duke of Buckingham.
[3] Cf. Professor McKisack's fuller analysis of the 'burgesses' in 1478: op. cit. pp. 106–10.   [4] Cf. above, Ch. VIII, pp. 303–4.

royal officials was to anticipate, in their calculations, a grant of so much to the crown, and to send to the chapter-house at St. Paul's, where the convocation of Canterbury normally met representative lords to urge this figure upon the clergy. This exposition of the royal needs took place at an early stage in the convocation, and might be repeated if the clergy proved unusually stubborn. Such demands were debated by the prelates and the clergy separately, the archbishop having instructed the lower house (meeting thereupon in the undercroft of the chapter-house, the prelates staying behind) to consider the matter and let him know their decision, which was usually reported by the prolocutor (*prelocutor*), one of his own clerks. There, in their *domus solita*, the difficult discussions took place. The grants if made were reported to the king as made by the whole assembly, the *prelati et clerus Cantuariensis provincie*, and details of conditions and exemptions were forwarded in a certificate from the archbishop to the king in chancery. The certificate then went from the chancery into the Exchequer, where writs for the appointment of collectors were issued to the archbishop for the diocese of Canterbury and to each bishop or his vicar-general for the individual dioceses. The collectors for the province were appointed in the convocations, but the sub-collectors for the diocese in the diocesan synods. At this point the Exchequer took over, dealing directly with the diocese rather than the primate, and asking individual diocesans for information on any point of difficulty that arose about exemptions, &c.

While the secular church and the non-exempt religious houses had to pay the tenth or the half-tenth, as demanded, according to the Pope Nicholas assessment, the exempt religious did not pay, and the stipendiaries were often untouched. This may perhaps be the reason why so few of the abbots appeared in convocation. But after 1422, under the pressure of war, measures were taken to collect from those who had avoided payment of the tax, and in the middle of the century the device, known in the fourteenth-century dioceses as the 'charitable subsidy', a 'voluntary' gift of a moderate amount, was reintroduced. It had been tried under Winchelsea (1301) and Islep (1349), but its use both by Bourchier and Morton was more frequent. It touched stipendiary chaplains of all sorts, save vicars choral, if they really sang, and clerks studying at

Oxford and Cambridge; it collected 'from all and sundry regular and secular chaplains, exempt and non-exempt' at the rate of 6s. 8d. on £5. 10s.[1] When collected the archbishop, as an act of grace, handed the money to the Exchequer. This subsidy was mainly from chaplains and pensioners, but the religious in that category did not get off. The king had been dissatisfied with the yield of the clerical tenth, and wanted to touch the stipendiaries as well. It did not affect the exempt monasteries as such.

In their taxation policy the convocations began from the position that certain classes of the poorer clergy were to be exempt, first all those who had been overcome by natural disaster (flooding, storms, &c.), then all those in a continuous state of poverty (e.g. poor nuns and hospitallers): by 1425 the standards of poverty for a benefice to be exempt was 'twelve marks a year and no more'. In 1429 exemption was extended to those indicted for felony, but certified by the diocesan to be of good character. The certificates of the bishops were to be accepted without cavil on all the exemptions claimed. To take a single archdeaconry, Chester (Coventry and Lichfield), the extension of the qualification for exemption in the first thirty years of the fifteenth century had only a slight effect on the yield till 1450. After that there came a definite increase, which in the later half of Edward IV's reign becomes marked. Exemption on ground of impoverishment amounted in 1453 to 6 per cent. of the total sum due for the archdeaconry: in 1463 and 1468 it was 12 per cent.; in 1474, 29 per cent., in 1475, 34 per cent. By 1478 it had advanced to 45 per cent., and had come to include nearly all the religious houses situated or with property in the area. In other words, the archdeaconry, assessed at £172, was, through its exemptions, by 1478 down to £95: £77 had been the figure claimed.[2] Three out of four other archdeaconries of the diocese tell the same story. On a total assessment of £461 the exemptions claimed for impoverishment rose from £54 in 1461 to £157 in 1478. Besides exemption, there were also refusals to pay. In 1473 refusals to pay amounted to 15 per cent. of the assessment and involved seventeen of the

[1] *Registrum Thomae Bourgchier*, ed. F. R. H. du Boulay (C. & Y. S.), p. 113. Cf. du Boulay's article 'Charitable subsidies granted to the Archbishop of Canterbury, 1300–1489', *Bull. Inst. Hist. Res.* xxiii, (1950), 147 f.

[2] E. 359, Enrolled Accounts, Subsidies, no. 35.

seventy-five taxpayers in the area. Of course 1468–9 were year
of internal strife; in June 1468 the earl of Pembroke landed a
Harlech and reduced Denbigh, and during the first part o
1469 there was continual trouble in Yorkshire and Lancashire
it was from the latter that Robin of Redesdale marched soutl
to join Warwick and helped him win Edgecot (26 July 1469)
Curiously enough, the collectors of the tenth met with mor
resistance in Cheshire than in Lancashire, but there wa
trouble in Lancashire also, and no less than one-third of th
taxpayers in the archdeaconry refused to pay the 1468/9 tentl
both in this disturbed period which saw the Readeption as wel
as some time after Edward IV had returned to the throne
Nearly all the refusals to pay the 1472/3 grant were backed by
physical attacks on the collectors.[1] In March 1475 the convo
cation of Canterbury made a generous grant of 1½ tenths, th
first being payable in May 1475, six months after the first hal
of the previous grant was due, and six months before the las
half of that grant was due (Nov. 1475). The remarkable fact i
that in the archdeaconry of Chester, where there had been s
much resistance to payment, there was scarcely any resistanc
to the levy of the 1475 grant, and the clergy of Lancashire an
Cheshire did more than was expected of them. The grant wa
for the renewal of war upon France.

Secular practice in the collection of the tenth and fifteentl
on movables may be compared with ecclesiastical. Taking th
figures for the county of Surrey, one finds that between 1334
and 1422 the amount collected shows little variation. In 1334
the amount was £587. 18s. 7½d. By 1402, owing to allowance
and readjustment, it had become £581. 2s. 6d. In 1422 th
collection was £540. 13s. 10d. Though in 1429 £566. 6s. 5d
was paid, in 1432 the rate for the county was reduced to th
1422 level, and in 1440 the rate dropped for the county (ex
cluding the borough of Southwark) to about £506. In 1446 i
was reduced to £473. 0s. 9d. In 1436 the tax was grantec
subject to the deduction of £4,000 granted for the whol
country, and in 1446 the relief was extended to £6,000 for th
single fifteenth and tenth.[2] It was found impossible to retair
the tax at the old rate, and the government preferred facing th

[1] E. 159/251, Recorda, Trin. Term, m. 12.
[2] *Surrey Taxation Returns, Fifteenths and Tenths, Part B*, ed. H. C. Johnson (Surre
Record Soc. xxxiii, 1932), pp. lvi–lvii.

acts to granting exemptions. After 1453 grants of fifteenths and
tenths became rarer; when the tax was imposed again (1463)
an attempt was made to get it back by an additional assessment
on the whole country) of £6,000, according to a rate on inhabitants with landed property or rents to the yearly value of
20s. or of goods and chattels to the value of 10 marks. This
attempt to restore the 1334 level failed and the £6,000 was
remitted. It may be wondered whether the tax bore any real
relation to the wealth of the country at any time during the
fifteenth century: the assessments were antiquated: in 1334 the
method of assessment chosen was not a final assessment of goods,
but a conference and agreement with the local people on the
amount the district was to pay. With that action, undoubtedly
just at the time, 'the taxes upon movables lost their elastic
character and their history is that of a standardised levy, the
amount of which was fixed in advance for every township,
hundred, borough and county throughout the kingdom'.[1]
When one thinks of the growth of the borough of London it is
curious to find Southwark, taxed at £17. 2s. 11¾d. in 1336,
paying the tenth at £17. 3s. in 1489.

It may be of some interest to contrast the structure and proceedings of another parliament with the elaborate organization
just described. The Irish parliament at Dublin, which under
Edward I can be described as a solemn and special session of a
court held before justiciar and council,[2] throughout the greater
part of the fourteenth century placed all its emphasis on the
two bodies of the council and the magnates, and gave little
indication of the presence of the commons before 1370. The
commons were not invariably summoned: the writs of summons
have survived from the years 1375, 1378, 1380, 1382, and 1394.
There were 26 constituencies in all, 14 counties and 12 towns at
the maximum, but it is unlikely that 52 commons ever assembled at any time. By the 1370's the lower clergy had their
representation in parliament, probably for the granting of
subsidies, certainly for a very limited context. The operative
body was the council in parliament, and it was only very

---

[1] *Surrey Taxation Returns, Fifteenths and Tenths, Part A,* ed. J. F. Willard (ibid., no.
xviii, 1923), pp. v, vi.
[2] H. G. Richardson and G. O. Sayles, *The Irish Parliament in the Middle Ages*
(1952), p. 69.

gradually that the commons came to share in the big general
matters dealt with, taxation, the presentation of grievances,
legislation.[1]

To trace this process before the first Irish parliament rolls
appear is very difficult because of the absence of records, due
in part to the extreme informality of taxation procedure. Under
Henry IV, when a severe reduction was made in the lieutenant's
stipend (Sir John Stanley in 1413 had 3,000 marks a year with
1,000 added for the first year), the lieutenant contracted to
maintain a military force of an agreed strength in consideration
of an annual payment from the English Exchequer. If the payment proved inadequate, the lieutenant had to look for assistance to the lords and commons in parliament or great council
or to the inhabitants of a particular shire to make up the balance.
The Irish moneys so granted him were granted *personally*, and
no account was rendered at the Dublin exchequer. Thus there
were in 1401 and 1404 special grants by local communities in
which magnates, nobles, clergy, and commons are mentioned
as taking part. The subsidies, which had to be reinforced by a
further grant to enable 800 foot to be maintained, were paid to
receivers appointed by the lieutenant and he was to receive the
money as 'soldier and governor of the wars' and not as justiciar.[2]
From a record point of view, therefore, the commons seem right
out of the picture, though they were not far off; but when we
reach a period where there is more evidence, membership of
the commons house seems to have been little valued and the
difficulty of getting the right sort of representative pronounced,
since an attempt in 1476 to do for Ireland what the 1429 enactment did for England and require a property qualification
broke down after two years, on the ground that the dangers and
difficulties of travel made it useless. The special characteristic,
however, of the Irish parliament in the fifteenth century is, to
quote the two scholars who have studied it most extensively,
'the concentration there of administrative and judicial business
introduced by means of private bills'.[3] In England the chancellor's equitable and remedial functions diverted a good many
petitions which would otherwise have claimed consideration
by the council, with consequent overloading of business. The
reason may lie in the decay of local justice and order. When

---

[1] H. G. Richardson and G. O. Sayles, *The Irish Parliament in the Middle Ages*
(1952), p. 87.   [2] Ibid., p. 156.   [3] Ibid., p. 174.

Richard of York was in Kildare in 1454 he was told that the 'true liege people' of those parts did not dare to appear in the court 'for dread to be slain, taken or spoiled of their goods'. The fear was significant: it was marked by the great raids of the Butlers upon the Geraldines of Kildare and the counter-move of the lords and gentry of Kildare to expel the invaders.

There was, therefore, some reason for approaching a higher court and if the number of peers attending were seldom more than twelve, the commons in the fifteenth century were more numerous. In 1420 and 1421 there were forty-two, twenty-four knights and eighteen burgesses; but no representatives came from Ulster or Connaught, nor from Galway town. As the century went on, only the counties of Dublin, Kildare, Louth, and Meath, along with their boroughs, were represented with any regularity. In 1399 the council at Dublin had complained to the king that the counties of Meath, Ulster, Wexford, Tipperary, and Cork, the recipients of palatine liberties, yielded no revenues to the crown, which also got nothing from Carlow, Kilkenny, Waterford, Kerry, Limerick, Connaught, and Roscommon. This may have been an exaggeration, but Meath and Leinster was all that was now left of the true 'English land'[1] and despite a term of soldier-lieutenants, the lordship of Ireland was never recovered. The native chiefs gained possession again of half the island; the Anglo-Irish lords consolidated territory around them and subjected Gaelic chiefs and Anglo-Irish tenants into admission of their sovereignty. The viceroys made every effort to retain and reinforce the gentry in the towns and the common people in the Pale, but no law for its defence nor absentee Acts could check the migration from the countryside into the towns and into England of the agricultural workers and of priests and of English freeholders whose places the lords preferred to fill with Irish tenantry. The Gaelic revival had set in, and so far from opposing it, the Anglo-Irish fostered it, largely because they found the prerogatives of Irish kingship more lucrative and suited to native tradition than their feudal ones.[2] The whole process was of the utmost danger to the future, because to add to feudal rights the prerogatives of Gaelic chiefs was to create a type more irresponsible than the greater English magnates of the forties and fifties. As Curtis has said: 'Before long "March

---

[1] E. Curtis and R. B. McDowell, *Irish Historical Documents, 1172–1922* (1943), pp. 68–69.   [2] Curtis, *A History of Medieval Ireland* (1938), p. 284.

lords" had their hired kerns or standing gallow-glasses; their heads became "captains of nations"; and the quartering and enforced payment of these troops at the expense of the tenantry, English and Irish, became universal, except in the small areas where the government could check such practices.'[1]

English administration in the fifteenth century was made up of the council, the three secretaries, the Exchequer, and the courts. The mainspring was still the king and a few professionals, members of his household, with the signet, writing letters direct or sending warrants that might be transmitted through the privy seal to the chancery. Under the Lancastrians the signet was frequently used to 'motivate' the privy seal which then issued its warrant to the Great Seal: but it could be used for direct orders, and this was to be specially the case under the Yorkist régime, where the power of the secretaries was greatly increased. The direct system and the warrant system coexisted: however much the seals were departmentalized, the king and his own little group of advisers were there to short-circuit the offices, if there were reasons for doing so. More and more the small continual council acting in closest conjunction with the king had come to be the governing and originating authority in the country, and between 1402 and 1407 this was fully appreciated by those who tried to afforce the council by adding names acceptable to the commons as well as to the king.

The keeper of the privy seal was more often than not an attender of the council, regularly present at its smaller routine meetings, and the clerk of the council was normally a member of his staff. The importance of the privy seal needs no emphasis. It had grown to be the main secretariat in the fourteenth century: every year a great mass of requests in the form of written petitions were made to the king and council for grants of land, money, letters of pardon or letters of remedy. Most of these were considered by the king himself, and, if they were viewed favourably, a writ under the privy seal was issued. Many of these documents were warrants for action to be taken under the Great Seal, classified as chancery warrants; and in the same way the privy seal sent its warrants to the Exchequer. In these Exchequer warrants under the privy seal the increasing part

---

[1] E. Curtis and R. B. McDowell, *Irish Historical Documents 1172–1922* (1943), p. 285.

played by the council in the early fifteenth century is evident. In the year 1404–5, for example, 3·2 per cent. of the chancery warrants are known to have been considered by the council, but 36·6 per cent. of the privy seal warrants to the treasurer and chamberlains and 46·9 per cent. of those to the treasurer and barons are known to have been considered by the council, and by it alone, without reference to the king.[1] The council's share in exchequer business was high throughout the period. Quite apart from warrants, the privy seal had its own original jurisdiction, so to speak, in authenticating diplomatic documents like letters to foreign princes, in dispatching the summonses to parliament, issuing pardons, licences, safe conducts, and so forth; nor could the king dispense with it when he was campaigning or when he was *in remotis*. In the 1405 expedition to Wales, Henry took with him the golden Great Seal and the signet: between 24 April 1405 when he set out and 31 May there were at least sixty-six signet letters sent to the keeper of the privy seal, for action of one sort or another.[2] Henry V had a duplicate privy seal in use in France from 1417. Most of the important royal letters addressed to the Exchequer for the payment of captains and commanders were made under the privy seal, at first by the system of writs current, by which periodical disbursement was made to those serving in the field, the writ being rather like a standing order; but the system had its dangers, and when applied to household expenses involved giving most of the initiative in making payments and assignments to the Exchequer; after 1406 it is plain that the council, through the warrants issued under the privy seal, was controlling assignments in detail. This careful scrutiny and control of the warrants was part of the prince's policy when he came to dominate the council for a short period. It need not be said that a king anxious to get all he could for the household and a prince who put defence and the garrisons first were not likely to see eye to eye.

The striking point is the very active part taken both by Henry IV and Henry V in the financial affairs of the kingdom. When in 1406 the king did what the commons had previously asked for and promised that grants which diminished the revenue should only be made with the advice of the council, the

---

[1] Figures given by Dr. A. L. Brown, 'The Privy Seal n the Early Fifteenth Century' (Dissertation, Oxford, 1954), p. 38, by kind permission consulted here.
[2] Ibid., p. 53.

initiative appears to have come from the king. When the lords chosen to be of the council asked that the 'bill' giving effect to this should be enrolled, the reason they gave was that 'ceste bille fuist la volunte du Roy et de sa mocion propre'.[1] The king had evidently raised the matter in the council before parliament. At the times when on account of health Henry IV has been suspected of retiring or withdrawing from considerations of this kind, the warrants show that his activity was with one exception continuous. And as for his successor, Henry V exercised his personal authority, though absent, through the microcosm of the English administration which he took to France. Perhaps 'microcosm' is the wrong word for an organization—signet, privy seal, Great Seal—which sent large quantities of writs every week across the Channel. After 1422 a substitute had to be found for this active royal solicitude, and for a single royal will a plurality of magnate wills, even when united, was no substitute.

Government has been described as the art of sending the requests of the governed to the right quarters. If parliament canalized the *clamores regni*, enabling some to be discussed and settled at high level and others to be remedied in the courts, it was the council, of which parliament was a highly developed aspect, which had to dispose of the greatest questions of all, relating to finance, supply, public order, and the external relations of the country. Not all its business could be determined by the small body of high officers which met constantly to do much of the day-to-day business. The sessions of this group were unminuted: they were attended by the chancellor, treasurer, keeper of the privy seal along with the clerk of the council as a nucleus, and judges or barons of the exchequer might be warned to attend. It is from the larger body chosen, as Fortescue says, 'off grete princes and off the gretteste lordes off ye lande both spirituelles and temporelles and also off other men that were in grete auctorite and offices' that limited memoranda survive and, with the warrants tested in the council, provide the main source of information for its activity.

Though at times members of the commons were added to it, the council was never a representative body like the knights and burgesses. To the king it was too much a personal matter to be that. Professor Baldwin was surprised that Fortescue, in his

---

[1] *Rot. Parl.* iii. 573. The king's expression of his will is on p. 572.

account, should not have advocated a measure of parliamentary control.[1] That judge was more concerned with the king getting a body of important public servants as counsellors, instead of being 'counseled by men of his chambre, of his householde, nor other which can not counsele hym'. But for Henry IV they must be men he knew very well. That was why in the earlier part of his reign Henry relied, as we have seen, mainly on the professional administrators, John Scarle (chancellor, formerly master of the rolls), John Norbury (treasurer, previously a duchy administrator), Bishop Thomas Langley (keeper of the privy seal), Sir Thomas Erpingham (the king's chamberlain), and on experienced persons like John Doreward of Essex and John Cheyne of Gloucestershire: Doreward had been on Richard II's council, and was made Speaker of the commons in Henry's first parliament. Another valuable addition who came in before the end of 1402 was Sir Arnold Savage of Bobbing (Kent), one of the chief members of the prince's council in Wales. The addition, on 1 November 1400, of three citizens of London—Richard Whittington, John Shadworth, and William Brampton—indicated the king's need to get the maximum help from the city. In the reconstruction which took place in 1404, when Lords Berkeley, Willoughby, Furnival, and Lovel were brought in, the important commoners added were Piers Courtenay, Hugh Waterton, John Curson of Derbyshire, while Savage, Norbury, and Cheyne retained their places. The commons, while anxious that the views of the lower house should be heard in the council, were not imposing strangers on Henry, and if a new council was nominated in public and given a measure of responsibility for the forming of policy, the knightly element was well known to Henry and trusted by him. In the Long Parliament of 1406 Waterton, Cheyne, and Savage were retained, but the new council was more aristocratic, having Prince Thomas as steward of England, four bishops beside Archbishop Arundel, and four barons apart from Lord Furnival the treasurer. To keep in old friends like Waterton was a tactful move on the part of the commons probably intended to counterbalance some of the irritating criticisms of the king's ministers in the lower house. As for Savage, his sententious remarks as Speaker could not hide the fact that he was at the same time a

[1] *The King's Council*, p. 207: 'Strange to say, Fortescue does not advocate in his scheme any degree of parliamentary control.'

most active administrator when in the service of the crown. All these commoner importations made, in fact, very little difference to the administrative machinery of the council under the influence of the civil servants.

Strongly magnate was the complexion of the prince of Wales's council in January 1410. In the reconstruction called for by parliament, Beaufort, Langley, and Bubwith among the bishops, the earls of Arundel and Westmorland and Lord Burnell came in, and vacancies were before long filled by the earl of Warwick and by the bishop of St. David's (Chichele). Although in 1411 this council was dismissed with thanks and (to some) rewards, it had produced the model for the small aristocratic body with a strong professional nucleus which it was Henry V's purpose to retain.

When Henry began the serious conquest of France, he put the administration of England into the hands of a lieutenant and council. The lieutenant was made the military defender of the realm, and was granted certain powers: he could summon and hold parliaments and councils, consult with the lords and commons, make ordinances by their assent and put them into execution; grant licences for all elections of capitular bodies; and receive the fealty, but not the homage, of feudal tenants in chief and grant them livery. He was empowered to act in these and in all other things concerning his governance by the assent of the king's council 'and not otherwise'.[1] These powers were in effect not very extensive. The lieutenant could not exercise the authority of the king in parliament. Petitions might be addressed to him, but he could not grant them at his discretion. He might summon parliament, but the writs issued on the king's orders. On 8 October 1420 the king ordered Gloucester to call a parliament for 2 December.[2] He had none of the prerogatives or powers of patronage belonging to the crown; and Henry was determined to exercise complete control over episcopal appointments. He maintained direct contact with the Roman curia, and received Martin V's bulls in France. The king made presentation to all benefices he had in his gift; and in the case of secular appointments, temporary grants (of the custody of lands and marriages) were made on his warrant. The royal prerogative to grant pardon and dispensations was

---

[1] *Foedera*, IV. iii. 9; *Cal. Pat. R., 1416–1422*, pp. 112–13, 234–373.
[2] Chancery Warrants, 1543/19.

exercised by him alone. The extent of his exercise of crown patronage can be seen on the rolls of his chancery in Normandy,[1] full of English appointments in addition to Norman business. The lieutenant's warrants for chancery letters were confined to the subjects within his commission, such as licences to elect bishops, notification of the royal assent to episcopal elections: but when he was asked for redress of injuries, payments of arrears of pensions, or letters of safe conduct, he submitted the petitions to the council for its assent. Neither Bedford nor Gloucester ever attempted to evade the restriction that the lieutenant could act only with the assent of the council. He was naturally the president, but he did not always sit: the effectives were the chancellor, Bishop Langley, the deputy-treasurer, William Kynwolmersh, the keeper of the privy seal, if in England, and a few prelates and secular peers: between 1417 and 1421 during a period of $3\frac{1}{2}$ years, Archbishop Chichele is known to have attended five times, the bishop of Winchester and Sir John Pelham twice, and the duke of Exeter, the bishop of Bath and Wells, and the earl of Westmorland once. The attendance was very small: on one occasion it was only Langley and Kynwolmersh.[2] More people turned up when Henry returned in 1421, after Beaufort had been restored to favour. At the end of the reign there were Chichele, Morgan of Worcester, Henry Beaufort, Bishop Bubwith, and the keeper of the privy seal attending the last recorded sessions.

The officials were certainly overworked, but owing to the great ability of Langley, the chancellor, the council was immensely efficient: Langley was, in fact, of much greater importance than Bedford or Gloucester: he understood the king completely, and realized that Henry was determined to direct the operations of the home government as much as the course of the war in Normandy. A constant stream of letters and warrants came from the king's headquarters: his warrants for the Great Seal show that he seldom interfered in the executive work of the home government. The council constantly appears in the chancery rolls as ordering action of various kinds: but it is very doubtful whether it acted on its own initiative. The king retained a very tight control over its activities. Projects would be put up to him by the council and Henry gave his fiat to some

[1] Printed, *Deputy Keeper's Report*, pp. xli, xlii.
[2] *P.P.C.* ii. 245–6.

and not to others.[1] Administratively, there were now two privy
seals. When in 1418 Philip Morgan was appointed chancellor
of the duchy of Normandy, it was found necessary to employ
the privy seal and its keeper there. When the king was at home
there was only one in use.

The amount of business transacted by the council was very
great: financially there was the raising of taxation and the
administration of loans made to the crown: from a military
point of view, it controlled the whole of the quartermaster side,
both reinforcements and stores for France, as well as the defences of the country and the territories overseas; it had to
engage workmen and labourers of all sorts for the king in
Normandy: not least it had to see to the impressment of thirty-
four tailors.[2] It looked after the commissariat and the naval
stores: it organized a fleet each spring to keep the Channel open
and preserve the lines of communications: it provided the staffs
for the royal captains in Ireland, Calais, and Guienne: it saw
to the defence and improvement of the fortresses on the northern
Border. Henry also committed to it a good deal of diplomatic
negotiation both with Flanders and the Genoese, though he was
always to be consulted on the line taken. It has been well said
that when the king charged the council to take action in a
certain matter, he usually left it to his ministers' discretion to
plan the means and put them into execution. He could not
provide for every detail. In addition to its administrative work,
Henry V's council was active as a judicial body. There are
numerous instances of undertakings made in chancery for
persons to appear before it on a stated day or upon summons:
for one of its main duties was the preservation of order; not
merely by land, but on sea, piracy being one of the subjects
of the council's jurisdiction. The council appointed a number of
commissions to inquire into the reported seizure of foreign ships,
to cause restitution to be made and sometimes to have the
offenders brought before it.[3] Alternatively, it took action
against foreign pirates: it ordered Breton and Dutch ships to be
seized so that English merchants might be compensated. One
compelling reason for its jurisdiction being exercised in land
cases was the fact that in 1417, before departing to France,

---

[1] Cf. *P.P.C.* ii. 363–7, suggested arrangements for the administration of Calais;
for north Wales, ibid. ii. 318–19.   [2] *Cal. Pat. R., 1416–1422*, p. 387.
[3] Ibid., pp. 135, 146, 202–3, 208, 209, 267, 329, 384, 390–1.

Henry V had an ordinance made suspending the taking of all assizes. This was to protect his soldiers, absent in France, from disseisin. It is worth noting that of the 400 surviving petitions addressed to the chancellor, half concerned cases of alleged disseisin.

On the death of the king it was essential to have the administrative personnel continued into the first council of Henry VI's minority. Langley went on as chancellor, Kynwolmersh as treasurer (for a brief space, and on his death John Stafford, keeper of the privy seal, replaced him). More of the higher magnates were now put in, the duke of Exeter, the earls of March, Warwick, Northumberland, Westmorland and the earl marshal, along with Lord FitzHugh, the chamberlain; and, with great significance, for the future, an able group of knights, all but one soon summoned as peers, Ralph Cromwell, Walter Hungerford, John Tiptoft, and Walter Beauchamp. These, along with the spiritual peers, the bishops of London, Winchester, Norwich, and Worcester, determined to claim, as the condition of accepting responsibility, the appointment to all offices and benefices not specially excepted and the disposal of all farms, wardships, and marriages, and to require the presence of six or four of the *domini de consilio* at least, without the permanent officers[1] as a quorum for the council's meetings, while a further demand was that the lords of the council should have exclusive rights to information from the Exchequer about the state of the finances. The 'lords of the council' were henceforth, till the minority ended, to exercise the royal prerogative on behalf of the infant king. It was not for the duke of Gloucester to do this, save with the council's assent. This move was a quiet usurpation of the royal authority almost on a par with that of Henry Bolingbroke; at the back of it may have been an understanding between Bishop Henry Beaufort, Bishop John Wakering of Norwich, with his long chancery experience, and the knights: but the evidence is insufficient. The council of 1422 represents a successful conspiracy, on the lines of 1377 and (as we said) away from Henry V's last wishes, on the part of an ambitious group who wanted to keep Gloucester from exercising a vice-regal power and probably were banking on Bedford being kept in France, as actually happened. In the council minutes the whole of the counsellors are called *domini de consilio*.

---

[1] 'Withoute officers of þe said conseil': *P.P.C.* iii. 18.

It is important to emphasize that this phrase includes the arch
bishops and the bishops; and there is nothing to suggest tha
the 'lords of the council' were in any way active against the
great officers, chancellor, treasurer, or keeper of the privy seal.
Yet after Langley and Wakering had gone, the most constar
attenders were the original knights, two of whom, Hungerfor
and Cromwell, became successively treasurer, later to b
joined by Scrope, Bourchier, and from the household, Stourto
and Tiptoft. The council itself, for all its nomination in publi
did the co-opting when it needed to be strengthened. Whe
Thomas Chaucer and William Alington came in (1423) the
were said to be *esluz et nomez* to be councillors assisting in th
government of the realm; the nomination was done 'per advy
et assent de tres toutz les seigneurs espirituelx et temporel
avauntdiz'.[2] This means the lords in parliament; but in th
council minutes they are said to have been 'per dictos dominc
[de consilio] ad consilium Regis predictum electi . . . et iurati
which is more accurate. The council of *domini de consilio* is sel
electing. It was the *domini de consilio* who voted Glouceste
3,000 marks on 21 October 1426 as a douceur for the indignitie
to which he had been (and was to be) subjected; it was th
domini de consilio who under threat of Praemunire forced the un
happy Richard Fleming to abjure his provision to York an
to go back to Lincoln, admitting

Quod de benevolencia dominorum procederet ut Episcopus ipse i
sua priori ecclesia Lincolniensi per declaratoria Papae stabilitetu
vel de ea sibi nova provisio fieret secundum beneplacitum sedi
apostolice.

In other words, it was the *domini de consilio* who dictated t
Martin V. Were the bishops present at that meeting? We d
not know: but the 'lords of the council' when they interviewe
Bedford and Gloucester included Canterbury, York, Ely, Bat
and Wells, and Norwich among the spiritual peers. Yet i

---

[1] *P.P.C.* iii. 154, 166, 193, 213. Professor B. Wilkinson thinks that the settlemen
with Gloucester in 1427 reversed the settlement of Feb. 1424 and strengthened th
exercise of the royal authority by the lords of the Council. 'The idea that the lord
of the Council assisted either the great officers or the government disappeared
This was not only a defeat for Gloucester; it was also a set back for the grea
officers.' *Report of the Anglo-American Conference of Historians, July 1957, Bull. Inst. His.
Res.* xxxi (1958), p. 20. But after 1427 some of the great officers were, themselves
called *domini de consilio*, the chancellor and treasurer especially.

[2] *Rot. Parl.* iv. 201: 3. *P.P.C.* iii. 155 (*domini et nobiles*).

omini de consilio, as we suggest, meant everybody of lord's estate
n the council, the nucleus came to be the group Stafford,
Suffolk (by 1437), Hungerford, Tiptoft, and Cromwell. It was
heir labours that had produced a comparative degree of
tability while the minority lasted. The question was whether
he council set-up, standing orders for which had been revised
n 1433, was sufficient as a guide for the royal majority, and
whether the lords of the council would permit the young king
o step into the position which Bedford had tried to persuade
hem to concede him.[1] Henry VI whose mind disliked exacti-
ude about the limits of authority, as he disliked most consti-
utional questions, had in 1434 stopped Bedford and Gloucester
rom discussing their respective powers, and was not prepared
o make a revision now. He was satisfied merely to reappoint,
o make the obvious proviso that they were not to settle the
weightiest matters without his advice and to have the articles
ppointed for the council in 1406 read in that body. It was a
magnate council, and while its members were genuinely
ssiduous and were well salaried for their pains the king could
do nothing to check their desire for private enrichment which
aused Fortescue many qualms. The period 1437-44 is when
nnuities were granted with reprehensible profusion, while the
rown's alienation of important estates, like Chirklands to
Cardinal Beaufort and lands valued at £400 a year including
he earldom of Kendal to John duke of Somerset, provoked no
isapproval in the council. Yet it was a stronger and more
nited régime than its successor, till the time when the ascend-
ncy of Suffolk at court began the process by which the house-
old and the party of the queen concentrated the executive
unction in their hands, and through the direct exploitation of
he sheriffs and the control of local government officers estab-
shed a hegemony some features of which the Yorkists, interest-
gly enough, were prepared to utilize. Henry VI very rarely
ttempted to rule, and the interests of the household group
ominating the royal authority and influencing the distribution
f rewards created in the council first of all the opposition to
uffolk, and after military defeat and a financial crisis prepared
he members to work for his overthrow.

The protectorates of Richard of York never lasted long
nough for the council greatly to change its complexion; but

[1] *Rot. Parl.* iv. 423-4.

under Edward IV a different type of body, chosen with the king's practical eclecticism, came into existence. The number of councillors was greatly expanded. For the period between 1461 and 1485 no less than 124 men called councillors have been traced; and while these were sworn, there was never definite nominated membership. 'Even the most important councillors were frequently away from the king's side for long periods.'[1] Lawyers were in the majority; well over half being canonists and civilians; but there was also a substantial contingent of magnates, for Edward needed all the support he could find and the local influence of magnates was essential for him.[2] The king, as we shall observe, made use of any well qualified man who could serve him; his choice might give rise to the complaints of Warwick, Clarence, and George Neville in 1469 that he was following the example of Edward II, Richard II, and Henry VI in estranging the great lords of their blood from their secret council. Edward could not afford to be prejudiced against 'great lords', but they had, in his eyes, no special advantage when it came to the brainwork on which he relied.[3] This in the main concerned military preparations and finance. The protection of Calais was one of the council's chief concerns, involving transactions with the Staple, and a discussion of the Act of Retainer; and there must have been extensive investigations into the working of the customs and of the system of granting, managing, and supervising the crown lands.

The study of the Exchequer during the later middle ages has been of late focused on the borrowing by the crown and its credit operations. Were Madox, the eighteenth-century historian of the Exchequer, to rise again, he would find that it is not the upper exchequer with its pipe and memoranda rolls so much as the lower which has been systematically explored in a prolonged attempt to understand the nature of its records

[1] J. R. Lander, 'Council, Administration and Councillors, 1461–1485', *Bull. Inst. Hist. Res.* xxxii (1959), 161. See his list.
[2] 'The system of maintenance was inherent in Yorkist and early Tudor government and Edward seems quite deliberately to have built up the power of some of his followers in certain districts.' Lander, op. cit., p. 153.
[3] J. R. Lander, 'The Yorkist Council and Administration, 1461 to 1485', *Eng. Hist. Rev.* lxxiii (1958), 29 f., argues convincingly, we think, against Baldwin's view that Edward's use of officials left the activities of the council 'much reduced'.

particular of the Receipt rolls, the record of the incoming of
sh, tallies and the loans made to the crown, which were
tered in the office of the treasurer and chamberlains.

The story of this exploration is long and complicated, and
e barest outline only is possible. The resources of which the
ancastrian monarchy disposed were at no time sufficient to
ver its commitments; the tenth and fifteenth, the customs and
e farms of the counties and of the towns had to act as local
urces of repayment to its creditors, who often had a protracted
riod of waiting to be repaid sums which they in turn had
obably been obliged to borrow from others in the interim.
his network of credit went for long unperceived or at least
nstudied, and the efforts of financial historians were directed
wards ascertaining the sum total of receipts and out payments
om the receipt and issue rolls, the entries taken at their face
lue. An article of Principal A. B. Steel in the *English His-
rical Review* of April 1932, 'Receipt Roll totals under Henry IV
nd Henry V', by breaking down the nominal totals term by
rm into the categories of cash receipts, assignments, and the
arious forms of book entries which were not really revenue at
l, gave the decisive blow to the older method, used by Dr.
Vylie, Sir James Ramsay, and other historians, of simply
lding up the totals in the receipt and issue rolls, term by term,
order to secure a grand total of receipts and expenditure year
y year. Instead, regarding indebtedness as a permanent and
cessary feature of medieval finance, the historian's purpose
as rather been to examine the scale of that indebtedness, to ask
hat steps the crown was taking to keep it within control and
hat the Exchequer was paying lenders for the sums advanced to
, and to see how people could be induced to make these advances.
Vhat has emerged, as embodied in Mr. Steel's larger work,
he Receipt of the Exchequer (1954), has been, after an exposure
this method, a study of the extent to which individuals figuring
the rolls, now grouped into classes according to their status
nd occupations, subsidized the government through loans
uring the Lancastrian and Yorkist periods, and of the credit
hich the government, in its successive phases, enjoyed.

Most of those lending money to the crown received, in re-
ayment, not cash but assignments. These are, simply speaking,
nticipatory drafts on revenue in the hands of sheriffs, customers,
nd other accountants. The system might take a number of

forms: whatever they might be, an assorted bundle of evidenc
would invariably be brought to Westminster so as to explai
why the collectors could not bring as much cash as was expecte
of them; and as soon as this evidence had been sifted an
allowed, they would receive a tally or tallies, quite distinct fro
the simpler form of tally which they got when they paid in cash
but none the less a kind of tally for receipt of revenue which ha
indeed been collected but had already been spent.

Now from marginal annotations on the receipt rolls it ha
been possible to discover how many entries represent cash pai
in and how many credit or book-keeping transactions. Talli
of assignment often failed to be met.[1] Again and again in a
periods entries are found recording the receipt of a certain sur
from some accountant, followed by the marginal note *pro* some
body else, the sure sign of an assignment to the latter. After
wards the entry has been struck through and an interlineatio
made which records the receipt of a so-called 'loan' from th
individual mentioned in the margin. The loan is, of course,
metaphorical or fictitious one: the king's creditor had bee
marked as paid (by the *pro* entry), but in reality had failed t
cash his tally. To save trouble with the totals, therefore, th
original entry was cancelled, and the amount in question re
corded over again as a 'receipt' in the form of a loan from th
creditor, which, in a sense, it was, as the king still owed him th
money. This is usually followed by an attempt to pay off all o
part of the 'loan' with fresh tallies of assignment, so that th
same amount of money does duty as revenue twice over; perhap
oftener, as the process is repeated. Hence any student of th
receipt rolls in this period will come to associate confusio
cancellation, and bad finance generally with the practice o
assignment, and, on the other hand, will find clarity, order, an
simplicity accompanying the record of cash payments. It seem
then that a high percentage of assignment must naturally be
feature of any period during which there is a strain on th
revenue produced by abnormally large expenditure or by a
equally abnormal reduction in the revenue itself; not havin
the cash to meet its obligations, the Exchequer will anticipat
revenue, and in a phase of falling income confusion will resul
In point of fact, as Mr. Steel cautions, things did not alway
work out thus. So far from a period of peace being a period o

---

[1] Cf. Ch. III, pp. 74 f. above.

ash payments, Dr. Willard has shown that in 1327-8, a year
f peace, it was assignment that prevailed, whereas in 1332-3,
year of war, cash payment was more common. Cash payment
redominates during Henry V's reign, in spite of the French
vars, though there are some notable relapses into assignment,
.g. in the Easter terms of 1415 and 1421. The test seems rather
o be the strength of the government and its ability to collect
evenue. Weak governments were driven to assignment when
ubjected to any strain, and the commonest types of strain were
lomestic strife or foreign war. Assignment, not necessarily
ernicious when revenue is collected and debts paid, easily
ecame so.

It is very interesting to watch the beginnings of the Lancas-
rian dynasty in its relations with its creditors. Mr. Steel has
ermed it 'a pauper government ruling with the consent of its
vealthier subjects'. The real change in the financial position
f the crown after 1399 lies, he thinks, in the comparative weak-
ess of its collecting power and the rapid narrowing of the gap
etween its financial resources and those of its greater subjects.
Repeated disappointment, whether his or theirs, can hardly
ave improved Henry's relations with his creditors, and may
ven be held to have played its part in the growing discontent
vith his rule which marks the early years of his reign. In the
ast ten and a half years of Richard's reign 'fictitious loans' were
asily at the lowest figure they reached perhaps for half a
entury, viz. £37,000, of which, moreover, £26,000 were owed
o his own household and local officials, and only £11,000 to
ersons outside the administration. This must be contrasted
vith the £95,000 to the household and £39,000 to outsiders in
he thirteen and a half years of Henry IV.

But (one may interject) if the present facts are as stated and
here is so much dishonouring of loans, how is it that people will
till go on lending? Do they demand higher security (more
late, valuables, &c.) or rewards of a different kind?

This raises the problem of interest. Nobody now supposes that
he canon law effectively excluded usury from commercial
ransactions, and it is almost certainly untrue that in the four-
eenth and fifteenth centuries, when concealed usury was an
veryday affair, 'English kings were powerful enough to refuse
a *quid pro quo* on that special class of loans made to the crown'.[1]

[1] Steel in *Eng. Hist. Rev.* li (1936), 45.

The consideration evidently varied. It might sometimes be cash
or assignments; there are entries in the issue rolls marked *dono
regis*, and their recipients were often merchants, especially alien
merchants, who had lent money, apparently free of charge, to
the crown. Other lenders on a large scale might receive their
reward in the form of grants or favours, get licences to export
wool duty-free, might amass keeperships of royal manors, or
even, as in the case of Beaufort, establish a lien on the customs
revenue of a great port over a number of years. The remarkable
thing was the amount of fluid capital that was about. The
wealth of the speculator in lands and rents contrasts with the
limited resources of the crown. In so far then as the lenders in
question were either great capitalists like Sir Robert Knolles,
John Hende, Richard Whittington, or Bishop Beaufort, or
favoured officials such as Henry Somer, the Lancastrian chancellor of the exchequer, they secured their ample *quid pro quo*
in a number of ways, among which lending at a heavy discount
was perhaps the most common. Beaufort in particular is said
to have doubled his working capital by his great loans to
Henry V and his successor. A careful study of the recognizances
made in the chancery does, in fact, indicate the conditions on
which money was lent. The close rolls of the fifteenth century
have a good many such acknowledgements of indebtedness
which state the total sum in which 'the borrower is bound to his
creditor with condition that a lesser sum shall be paid upon or
by the given date'. A Warwickshire knight recognizes a bond
on £30 to two Oxfordshire merchants. The conditions are that
he shall pay 10 marks on three successive Easter days. This
pound-mark equation implies that what was actually lent was
30 marks, and that if the creditors are not satisfied by the
specified date, interest of $33\frac{1}{3}$ per cent. per annum will be
exacted on the unpaid portion or portions. A date-line is fixed,
and nobody could call the transaction usurious.[1]

The most interesting result of the new method of study is
achieved in the years 1413–32 by a comparison of the nineteen
receipt rolls of Henry V's reign with a similar number for
Henry VI. The comparison makes clear that Henry V's reign
represents a peak period of borrowing by the crown, and that
there is some decline in this respect, though not perhaps as much

[1] K. B. McFarlane, 'Loans to the Lancastrian Kings: The Problem of Inducement', *Cambridge Historical Journal*, ix (1927), 51 f.

as we should expect, in the ten years after his death. It is also clear that, in comparison with Henry IV's reign, there was a marked drop, under Henry V, in the amount of fictitious loans or bad tallies, a fact which probably reflects the increased efficiency of the government revenue collectors; but this index figure, a sort of inverted barometer for the fifteenth-century exchequer, as Mr. Steel calls it, rises ominously again in the early years of Henry VI. The conclusion is that, in comparison with 1413–22, the years 1422–32 saw a 17 per cent. fall in the amount of money borrowed by the crown, together with a 75 per cent. rise in exchequer inability to meet its obligations. A second point of great interest is the increase in fictitious loans from the magnate class during the minority of Henry VI. In both periods, Henry V's reign and the minority of Henry VI, the main brunt of the fictitious loans is borne by magnates filling local offices. Already under Henry V, Henry Percy, earl of Northumberland, was owed £5,737 arrears of salary as warden of the east March on account of bad tallies; Lord Richard Grey another £1,007 in the same capacity, and the duke of Exeter £1,054 as keeper of the west March: but turning to the minority, in the period 1422–32, we find that the Percy earl of Northumberland alone received £19,836 worth of bad tallies for his salaried wardenship of the east March, an almost exact equivalent to the entire total of bad tallies cut for all the magnates during the whole of Henry V's reign.

The gross nominal revenue for Henry VI's first decade works out at a yearly average of £96,700 on a summary basis, or just under £95,000 on a rather closer calculation, and his real revenue is computed by Mr. Steel at something between £75,100 and £75,700 annually. In his second ten years, when he was still under age most of the time, Henry's average *nominal* revenue rose appreciably, viz. to £115,000 or so, though his real revenue lagged behind at £75,000, practically unchanged. In the third phase, when the Lancastrian party was being formed and Suffolk and Queen Margaret of Anjou were in power, the average gross revenue fell sharply to 'a new low level' of only £85,000 while real revenue declined in sympathy to only £54,000, since the percentage, though not of course the gross total, of book-keeping remained almost the same in both periods.[1] These calculations are on the supposition that 1432–42

[1] Steel, op. cit., pp. 240–1.

was a period of such military disaster that it shook the council, and in time even the commons, into abandoning the 'cheap and niggardly finance' which had marked the 1420's together with the attempt to make the French conquests pay the whole cost of their own administration. But it was already too late to recover France: by the 1440's it was clear that the French possessions must be written off completely and, in the time of Suffolk and the foreign queen, confidence in the administration broke down. Grants of lands and tenements, made for the purpose of party-building, ate away the hereditary revenues.

Only the customs remained buoyant, and became in fact the main financial stand-by of the dynasty, but precisely for that reason they were deluged with assignments and exemptions, grants and licences, which heavily reduced their yield. In these conditions, the serious, though not yet catastrophic, fall in revenue, not to mention the increased recourse to borrowing and to anticipation, are easily accounted for.[1]

Much light has been thrown by this notable study of exchequer mechanism for loan and repayment upon the sources of supply. Perhaps at present it is the individuals and the classes that put up the money rather than the period totals that are impressive; Beaufort the equivalent of £200,000 (over many years); Lord Cromwell £4,170 on one occasion (1433); Chichele £14,218 in eleven years,[2] while all the other bishops did not produce more than another £5,000 or so; the Calais Staple £28,393 out of £31,006 in repaid loans in 1432–42, and £18,673 out of £201,203 in 1442–53; the household £3,188. 19s. 10d. in repaid loans 1422–32, and £9,186. 19s. 8d. in 1442–53, when its members were helping to govern the country. One thing, however, requires emphasis. Borrowing was the essence of finance in the fifteenth century as much as in the twentieth. It would be wholly surprising, now that the great Italian finance companies had had their warning about England and were no longer prepared to stake their money on the old scale upon its sovereigns, if English borrowing had not to be spread over the categories of people likely to be able to assist. The point to be noticed is the credit the English kings were accorded and enjoyed from a wide range of their subjects. This

---

[1] Steel, op. cit., pp. 240–1.

[2] It will be remembered that Chichele paid out, 1438–43, £4,302 for the building of his college and for its lands. Jacob *Vict. County Hist. Oxon*, iii. 175.

was the more remarkable because in general the delay and default of the government in paying its debts, especially those owed for services, was considerable, and reached a formidable sum by the later years of Henry VI, which Edward IV did his utmost to pay off.

We have already expressed agreement with the criticism made of the concept of the 'fictitious' loans and the 'bad' tally.[1] It was inherent in the exchequer system that there should be an uncommon amount of competition ('labouring' would have been the contemporary expression) to get repaid, and what we have still to discover is any calculated scheme of priority in meeting the repayment demands, in whatever way they were expressed. Nobody knew who would be successful and only the experienced knew the right approach: with certain sources of revenue the chances were good; with others decidedly worse. It was not conscious deception that lay behind the 'bad' tally, nor even official negligence in considering what might be likely to pay or not; it was just that the revenue on which the assignment was held might already be several times pledged. Thus creditors would to their utmost to secure priority, sometimes by obtaining a special writ from the king to the treasurers and chamberlains. It would be an error to emphasize the fate of the unlucky at the expense of the many who got repaid as soon as they took their tallies to a local accountant, instead of being told that they might have a fraction of the sum or should try again, or had in the end to go back to the Exchequer. Both lucky and unlucky knew what they were in for:[2] but it could hardly be called businesslike.

The problem that haunted the treasurer was the gap between the crown's revenue and its obligations. In repaying the loans how was the priority to be awarded, when the revenue was so

[1] See above, pp. 89–90. There is the further consideration that 'over the whole period the nominal totals under this head are inflated by repetition; that is to say a man may be disappointed, for example, three times over in a sum of say, £100, which is owing to him; on, for example, three successive occasions he may receive a "bad" tally for the same sum. *Hence what is really only £100 will appear as £300 under the head of fictitious loans*' (italics our own): Steel, op. cit., p. 114.

[2] 'Most of those who appear in the exchequer rolls as its creditors were not seeking payment of an isolated debt: they dealt with it continuously on a variety of accounts and were well acquainted with its practice. They or their attorneys were familiar with the technique of assignments, they measured the hazards of the system and their own chances within it as narrowly as any exchequer official': G. L. Harriss, 'Preference at the Medieval Exchequer', *Bull. Inst. Hist. Res.* xxx (1957), 39.

limited? There could be no more expressive account of the
situation than Lord Cromwell's statement to parliament in
1433 that

Daily many warantis come to me of paiementz . . . of much more
than all youre revenuz wold come to, thowe they wer not assigned
afore . . . the which warrantes yf I shuld paye hem, youre Household, chambre and warderope and youre werkes, shuld be un-
servid and unpaide and yf I paye hem not, I renne in grete indignation of my lordes and grete sclandre, noyse and maugre of all
youre peple.

He asked parliament 'to tell him who shuld be preferred in
payement, and who shull not, and who shuld be paied and who
shull not'.[1] Along with this problem came the further and
ultimately more political question: how was the treasurer to
assure a fixed and permanent income for the royal household,
one which should be assured of absolute priority from certain
sources of revenue?

The greatest client of the Exchequer, the body that incurred
expenses which in the end the Exchequer had to meet, was the
royal household, through its purveying and spending departments, the wardrobe and the chamber. The latter, the *Camera
regis*, might be described as the department of the privy purse,
the office where the king's own personal expenses were recorded
and paid through the counting-house. The household, the
domus regia, was the social and material organization of the
court, which maintained the state expected of the king: this
involved a personnel larger than that of most magnates with
their indentured retainers, entailed payments for their board,
lodging, and liveries, and all the expenses inherent in the private
entertainment of ambassadors, guests, and visitors who frequented the court for any purpose whatsoever. The numbers
and organization of the household are considered later in connexion with the household ordinance of 1478: here one may
only note that by 1432 the arrears were growing, for in that
year fifteen accountants of the household were having to ask in
a parliamentary petition to be pardoned arrears of accounts
going back to the beginning of Henry's reign, and by 1433 the
debts of the household reached approximately £11,000:[2] its
expenses were reckoned at about £13,000; by 1449 they were

---

[1] *Rot. Parl.* iv. 439: cited by Harriss, op. cit.
[2] *Rot. Parl.* iv. 436.

put at £24,000 against a *basic* royal revenue, from farms and lands, of not more than £5,000.[1]

'The wardrobe accumulated debts by its purchases and services and received advances from the Exchequer in exchange. The real history of wardrobe finance is the constant incurring of obligation and its discharge by the Exchequer in recurrent payments or promises through the wardrobe.'[2] There were two complicating factors: Henry as he got older, became increasingly concerned with financing the foundations of Eton and Cambridge, more so than with the cost of his household and his 'ordinary charges', the royal estate.[3] At the same time as he urged the Exchequer to help, he was not wholly dependent on it: he could finance the household from private resources, especially from the duchy of Lancaster, and he might also secure the withdrawal of certain revenues from the Exchequer for payment direct.[4] At the worst he could refer the wardrobe's creditors to the Exchequer and issue writs of *Liberate* when there was little hope of their getting anything: it was wiser to do this than to do nothing at all and risk a series of parliamentary petitions from angry creditors. On the whole, when things were bad, the creditors were right in seeing that control of the Exchequer through parliament was the best way of getting something done.

Of all sources of revenue the customs were by far the most lucrative: they were also the most suitable for assignment, and the tendency was to over-assign. This meant that the wardrobe would be entering into competition with other creditors for the satisfaction of its prests, and for the wardrobe to rely exclusively on such a source would invite serious delays. Other creditors might well have been preferred. The success of the wardrobe depended on the degree of preference it enjoyed, and this might depend on the political situation at the moment. Such problems as these were well known to the commons in parliament. Their determination in 1440 to provide the wardrobe with a steady £10,000 a year for five years led to a resolution to the council naming the sources of income from which the money was

[1] But Ramsay (*Lancaster and York*, ii. 122-4) held that the last figure was too low.
[2] G. L. Harriss, 'The Finances of the Royal Household from 1437 to 1460' (Oxford D.Phil. thesis), p. 12, to whom the writer expresses grateful thanks for the above passage and other comment and criticism.
[3] Harriss, ibid., p. 13.
[4] Harriss, ibid., p. 14.

preferentially to be drawn;[1] the duchy of Lancaster still in the king's hand, 5,000 marks a year; the enfeoffed part of the duchy,[2] 3,000 marks; the duchy of Cornwall, 3,000 marks, and the Exchequer itself, 4,000 marks.[3] This was the sum specified for Henry V's household in 1413, and on the whole it was reasonably well met from the sources named. But it was not enough. Under Sir Roger Fiennes's treasurership expenses rose; in the first extant account for 1441–2 they were £12,500, and in the 1443–4 account, £12,700. The problem of over-assignment was not yet cured and was to underlie the formidable financial crisis of 1449–50. There is, therefore, a technical, financial explanation of Lancastrian failure in the mid-fifteenth century: it is not a complete explanation, but one that must be seriously taken into account.

The late fifteenth-century Exchequer was not like the modern treasury. It was entirely governed by routine: there was no elasticity of any kind. Accounting in it was very cumbersome; the officials of the upper exchequer were terrified of admitting any claim for allowance without the fullest authority: they tried to safeguard themselves behind a mass of paper. They tried to deal with the mechanism of accounts only: they had nothing to do with questions of fact and of practice. If an accountant claimed that a letter or list had not been delivered to him, the clerks of the Exchequer did not decide his claim: he would have to explain on oath in the chancery, and the decision was certified under seal to the Exchequer. Thus it kept everyone in order, but with methods as formal as pleading in the common bench: this prevented any possible error through quick decisions, but delayed cases depending on reference which had to be made outside the department. In many respects caution was indicated: the Exchequer had to receive many directions from the outside, principally in the form of writs under the great and the privy seal. Each year it received about 850 writs under those instruments, directed to the treasurer and barons, both general and particular, affecting individual accountants.

Caution could be carried a long way. The annalist of Meaux relates the story of his abbey's attempt, made for the first time in 1396–7 and continued in Henry IV's reign, to secure an

---

[1] Exch. T.R. Council and Privy Seal, E. 28/63. Dr. G. L. Harriss kindly supplied this reference.   [2] Set aside to meet the provisions of Henry V's will.
[3] Harriss, op. cit., p. 74.

allowance of £10. 2s. 10½d. in their share of a tenth granted by the clergy of the northern province in 1396, because of the inundation of their lands by the Humber. The claim was put forward by the convocation of York on the strength of the archbishop's certificate, and the abbot, to augment his case, tried, without success, to get the Benedictine abbots of St. Mary's York and Selby to make similar claims. When the archbishop died the new one (Richard Scrope), in certifying the grant to the Exchequer, omitted, when the claim for Meaux was being made, the essential words 'possessions both of spiritual and of temporal things'. For this the abbey was to suffer. In the collection the Exchequer officials refused for the time being to allow any abatement for spiritualities destroyed; and there was to have been an inquiry on this claim, but it was interrupted by political events. For the next two years nothing was heard, but in 1399 the Exchequer returned to the charge and claimed the unpaid portion of tenth: the sheriff was told to distrain the abbey, but was bought off temporarily by the payment of 20s., and the abbot thought it time to sue for a writ of inquiry into the damages by inundation. The archbishop was told by the Exchequer to make inquest, and this inquest returned an answer both to the main (temporalities), and the new subsidiary question (the spiritualities), but the barons found that the claim was too large because the wastage of spiritualities had been added, and suspecting fraud, deferred allowance of the £10. 2s. 10½d. to Easter 1401, when the abbot's attorney exhibited the king's writ commanding the court to allow the amount claimed in the petition. But, king's writ or no, the court still wanted further time and adjourned the case to the Trinity term. Meanwhile some diligent person in the Exchequer had found that no mention had been made in the Exchequer rolls of the whereabouts or nature of the temporalities of Meaux, and the barons accordingly decided that an inquiry ought to be held in the Michaelmas term (1401) at Beverley. The jury at the first meeting found that they had not got the facts, so adjourned till a later occasion, when they (or someone from the monastery to help them) drew up a complete list of the temporalities destroyed by floods and the temporalities remaining unwasted. When it had appeared that the sum claimed in allowance was 21¾d. less than the taxable value of the wasted land, the barons eventually allowed the claim, 'salva semper actione regis, si alias etc.' The monastery had a sense of humour and secured an exemplification of the documents from the Exchequer.[1] But the barons were, from their point of view, right. To slip in the *consumptio spiritualium*, assessed at a high figure, was the sort of device which it was the business of good auditors to prevent.

The official who had as much as anyone to do with the Exchequer was the sheriff. Frequently it is said that the great age of the sheriff did not extend beyond the year 1300, when he had most of the work of the shire on his shoulders; and that in the fifteenth century he was just a debt-collector and a server of writs. Now it is true that his main routine work in this period is still chiefly connected with collecting the farm of the shire and the summonses of the pipe and green wax, and with receiving and executing the precepts in, and returning, the king's writs. But he had two highly important duties: it was he who summoned the *posse comitatus*, and this in the period of civil war was by no means a negligible duty; and he was the returning officer *par excellence* in the shire, the assembler of juries and the officer who put to them the questions which they had to answer and was responsible for putting these in the right way. When all was going against him in Norfolk upon the fall of his patron, Suffolk, John Heydon boasted: 'rather thanne he shuld fayle of a shiref this yeer comyng for his entent he wole spende £1000': he did not covet the sheriffdom for himself.[2] With the sheriff friendly to him a magnate could hope to command a maximum of control in his shire: he could expect to overcome an individual private enemy. This was recognized, for a council ordinance had been found needful in 1426 to reaffirm the provision of the statute of Lincoln that no bailiff or steward of a lord should be sheriff unless he were unemployed. But with the crown in Henry VI's reign paying the attention it did to getting sheriffs well disposed to its interests, it is hardly likely that a magnate would lose the chance of putting in his own sheriff, if he could.

When the fall of Suffolk appeared to have cleared the ground for the duke of Norfolk in East Anglia, the duke tried to seduce William Calthorpe, a squire of the body, from his de la Pole

---

[1] *Chronicon monasterii de Melsa*, ed. E. A. Bond (Rolls Ser.), iii. 246–55, 275–95, 296–314.   [2] *Paston Letters*, ii. 181. Heydon had been sheriff in 1432–3.

affinities. Hoping that the duke of York would have the nomination of the sheriff at the end of 1450, Norfolk, it was rumoured, was trying to secure Calthorpe either as knight of the shire or as sheriff 'to the fortheryng of othir folks'. Justice Yelverton hoped for a good sheriff 'that neyther for good favore nor fere wol returne for the Kyng, ne betwix partie and partie none othir men but such as ar good and trewe, and in no wyse will be forsworne'.[1] The type which the justice feared and probably had in mind was Thomas Daniel whose heart was set, when sheriff 1446–7, on defrauding the Wodehouse family of their Rydon estate. Daniel appears to have acquired Rydon fraudulently, and had the duke of Norfolk's support in his usurpation. The house had been built by John Wodehouse, chancellor of the duchy of Lancaster, a friend and executor of Henry V, at a cost of £2,000. In 1455 his son and heir Henry told the commons that Rydon along with his father's other manors had been conveyed in trust to Daniel, for the use of Daniel's sister Elizabeth and Henry, should they marry, as they had contracted to do. The marriage did not come off, as Elizabeth preferred somebody else, but Daniel with a large force temporarily occupied the house. In 1454, as Worcester relates in the *Itinerary*, Henry Woodhouse pulled Rydon down to stop Daniel settling there. As sheriff Daniel was notoriously partial, using his influence widely for Suffolk against Norfolk. He usurped Brayston from Osbert Mountford and pretended to be Sir John Fastolf's heir.[2] Norfolk's sheriffs were like Daniel in avarice, but Norfolk and Suffolk certainly had enterprising ones. Thomas Sharnburn was such, a man who, the duke of Norfolk said, 'ymagynyng and purposyng to make knyghts of the shire after his own interests', made a return to the common bench accusing the duke's men of creating such a disturbance at the Ipswich shire court that he had to close the county court before the election could be got under way.[3] Another method beside closing the

[1] Ibid. ii. 190. On Heydon's misdemenours cf. Winifred Hayward, 'Economic Effects of the Wars of the Roses in East Anglia', *Eng. Hist. Rev.* xli (1926), 174.
[2] Early Chancery Proceedings, C. 1/19/115. Mr. R. M. Jeffs kindly supplied this and the following reference.
[3] Council and privy seal, E. 28/84. Cf. *P.P.C.* vi. 183–4, petition of the duke that those of his tenants who had been returned by Sharnburn might appear by attorney in the common pleas. The list of tenants, including Sir William Asheton, Sir Geoffrey Radclyf, Thomas Daniel, and the duke's brother-in-law John Howard; Thomas Calburne who had been sheriff in 1435–6; sixteen esquires, eleven yeomen, one groom, &c.

county court was to substitute another name of an electe(
knight to the chancery, though this device appears to have bee)
more affected in the boroughs.

During the fifteenth century the sheriffs found the conserva
tism of the Exchequer extremely burdensome. The baron
looked at all sheriffs alike, as revenue officers who were likel
to evade where they possibly could. They considered the sheri(
to be in debt for every farm placed for his county on the pip
roll. Many of the farms were now obsolete, bearing all sorts o
deductions and most of them were over-assigned to meet th
king's increased household expenditure. Often the sheriff coul(
not meet the annuities he was supposed to pay. In 1445 th
sheriff of Kent complained that he had paid in annuities an(
proffers £15 more than he had collected.[1] Thomas Stonor'
petition for allowances as sheriff (1466) is an admirable exampl(
of the 'course of the exchequer' in operation, when the sherif
asks for exoneration of summonses and payments of variou
kinds and the barons make their marginal award on each case
some going back a considerable time, and including the sum
monses not collected by his predecessor in office. It is remark
able that the barons should have gone on summoning certai)
Oxford colleges for taxation in respect of their estates, whe)
exemption had been already granted; not only did they try t(
collect this, they also demanded from the sheriff arrears of :
clerical tenth which the ecclesiastical authorities had not suc
ceeded in gathering.[2] All the mass of explanation about hi
inability to meet the farms and the summonses, the sheriff (o)
more likely, his head clerk) sitting in his office at the castl
would have to provide *ad unguem*, missing no point in his justi
fication. It was the sheer burden of this work that made Joh)
Harrington, sheriff of Lincoln, in 1445 successfully demand a
the condition of holding office the power to declare his accoun
on oath, rather than submit to the 'course' of the Exchequer
He was lucky, for declaration was a very exceptional privileg(
till the middle of the next century;[3] and it may have been th(
sheer burden of office work and the fact that the sheriff made s(

[1] L. T. R. Mem., E. 159/222, 'brevia directa baronibus'.
[2] *Stonor Letters and Papers*, ed. C. L. Kingsford, i. 89–92.
[3] Declaration was a large concession: it did not merely mean that dead items i)
the farm should be discharged by the sheriff's oath, but that the farms of the shir
should be abolished along with other heads of account. Naturally the sherif(

little out of his job that accounts for the large number of sheriffs from the royal household who held office from roughly 1445. To hold office in this way may have been enjoined upon them as part of their duty to the king; and there were plenty of servants in the household after 1440: in 1441 there were 150 esquires of the body; in 1443-4, 225; in 1446-7, 354; in 1447-8, 260; in 1449-50, 310: these in addition to the hereditary element in Henry VI's household, represented by men like Thomas Tyrell and his brother, Edmund Hungerford, Thomas Tresham, Edward Hull. By this household control of the county administration the Lancastrian government in its last phases were constituting themselves a royal party in the fullest sense of the word.

In any judgement on the sheriffs, it would be one-sided to concentrate on a handful of not too scrupulous individuals. The work of the shire, secretarial and financial, was mainly done by the staff of the sheriff's office. The Bedfordshire sheriff's roll of writs and returns for 1333 makes the organization clear.[1] There were two head clerks, the retainer of writs and the receiver of monies, who ranked first. They were the responsible men in the office dealing with the correspondence and the writs that came in while the sheriff was round and about his bailiwick on the king's business. There were 2,000 writs on the Bedfordshire roll, about the same number as on a contemporary patent roll. From the office, writs went out to the bailiffs of the hundreds and their replies or returns came in, often very late, sometimes not at all, because of various delays or obstacles encountered. Frequently a man who had to be detained could not be found, and in the case when the message had to go to lords of liberties who had return of writs, the formulas had to be carefully observed. The chief clerk, the receiver, had his accounts audited before the audit at Westminster: he had had to collect both the farm and the two types of summons, the summons of the pipe (for smaller debts) and the summons of

wanted it, as petitions introduced in the parliaments of 1461-2, 1463-5, 1467-8 make clear. It was conceded a few times before Henry VII came: after 1487 the sheriffs were made to go through the old course, and it was not till 1549 that it was abolished. This information was kindly supplied by Mr. R. M. Jeffs.
[1] M. H. Mills, 'The Medieval Shire House', *Studies presented to Sir Hilary Jenkinson* (1957), pp. 254-69: Dr. G. H. Fowler, *Rolls from the Office of the Sheriff of Beds. and Bucks*. (Bedf. Record. Soc., Quarto Ser., vol. iii, 1929) has analysed the Bedfordshire Roll in detail.

the green wax (for the fines and amercements of the central courts and of the eyre or assizes). As detailed evidence had to be furnished at Westminster about the tallies, receipts, and final payment, not only of the present sheriff's time but also for the times of his predecessors, the fullest records had to be kept in the office. In the final audit before the journey to Westminster the accounts of the bailiffs of hundreds were produced first, followed by the account of the receiver, and if this procedure was not followed in the county, the barons of the Exchequer wanted to know why. A Warwick and Leicester account of two receivers of William Mountfort, the sheriff in 1441–2, taken before the sheriff's auditor shows the receivers charging themselves with the farms of the hundreds separately, and claiming various expenses over and above the £62. 13s. 4d. which they had paid to the king, as their exchequer tallies proved.

Upon the work of the sheriff's office the efficiency of the county organization depended. A frequent visitor to this office must have been the clerk to the justices of the peace. He and they were not of the county court, but held their sessions there. Their powers had grown from the commissions issued in the first half of Edward III's reign, the landmarks being early in 1350, when commissions of the peace were issued with authority to enforce the ordinance of Labourers and with the right to determine felonies, the act of 1360 when the keepers (as they were) were transformed into justices and the commissions of 1362 when they were again given jurisdiction over all labour laws. They came to replace the justices of trailbaston and the commissions of oyer and terminer, both unpopular forms of justice, except on extraordinary occasions like the Peasants' Revolt and the Lollard Rising of 1414, when special commissions, led by magnates in each shire-group, were appointed with full powers to hear and determine. In the early fifteenth century they were a peacetime expedient. 'Whenever in England', Dr. Bertha Putnam has said, 'an orderly government seems in danger, even the commons, instead of turning to the justices of the peace, petition as in 1410 for a commission of oyer and terminer, in this instance to suppress disorder in the north.'[1] So after the Cade rebellion (1450) a large number of com-

[1] *Proceedings before the Justices of the Peace, Edward III to Richard III* (Ames Foundation, 1938), p. 1.

missions of oyer and terminer were issued to magnates and lawyers, with results to be found still in the ancient indictments in the Public Record Office. But in 'normal' disorders, riots, and forcible entries, it was the justices of the peace to whom people looked for justice. In the civil war their relations with the justices of jail delivery are not always clear; in some counties the justices of the peace delivered the jails, in some cases sent the indictments to the justices of gaol delivery.[1] But the commons showed their confidence in 1461 when in the statute it was laid down that all indictments and presentments normally taken at the sheriff's turn with consequent arrest and imprisonment of offenders should be taken before the justices of the peace in the shires. The penalty for failure to do this was £40. The justices were to have power to make process upon all such indictments and presentments as the law required and 'in lyke fourme, as though the seid Enditementz and Presentementez hadde be take bifore the seid Justices of the peas in the seid Shire or Shires, and also arraiyn and delyvere all such persone or persones so endited'.[2] This was evidently a blow at the Lancastrian household sheriffs rather than 'the outstanding concession to the commons' which Professor Gray imagined.[3] But the commons could not secure for the justices the right to assign a coroner to take approvements, and it was not till 1483 that justices of the peace were empowered to admit to bail prisoners arrested by the sheriffs on suspicion of felony. There were still forces favourable to the sheriff, who believed that the man who took the turns knew more about the patria than the justices themselves. The Worcestershire justices' manual printed by Miss Putnam, a case-book dating from c. 1422,[4] shows the wide range of actions in which their jurisdiction was involved, not least those based on the statute of Lollards,[5] the statute of Northampton, and on the statute of Labourers, the latter accounting for sixteen out of the seventy-eight documents which the manual contains. In many instances the compiler of the manual uses the actual case that came into court, and some of the more interesting are those involving accusations against

---

[1] Putnam, op. cit., p. lv.

[2] *Rot. Parl.*, v. 494.

[3] *The Influence of the Commons*, p. 127.

[4] *Early Treaties on the Practice of the Justices of the Peace in the Fifteenth and Sixteenth Centuries* (Oxford Studies in Social and Legal History, vii, 1924), ch. III.

[5] Passed at the Leicester Parliament, 2 Hen. V, St. 1, c. 7.

members of an important county family, the Burdets of Abbots
Lench; the father was Sir Thomas Burdet of Arrow, Warwickshire, sheriff of Warwick and Leicester, 1 December 1415–
29 November 1416, whose son Nicholas of Abbots Lench
became great butler of Normandy and was killed in France in
1440. Various indictments were brought against Nicholas in
June and July 1413 for attacking officials and for murdering
two men. These indictments for trespass and felony were summoned into the King's Bench by *certiorari* on 12 September
1413, but it took nearly two years to bring the indicted persons
into court, and it was not till Easter 1415 that Nicholas Burdet
brought into court his charter of pardon, one of many hundreds
granted by the king in accordance with the decision of the
parliament that met on 19 November 1414, including trespasses
and murders committed before 8 December 1414. The other
people mentioned in the indictment eventually, after a series of
summonses, escaped through pardons by Michaelmas 1417.
But in the meantime the Worcester justices had identified a
number of the unknown who had been at the murder, and sent
them before the justices of jail delivery either in March 1416
or the spring of 1418. Of six indicted before two of the justices
five were acquitted and the last produced a pardon as Burdet
had done. Nicholas's father, Sir Thomas, along with his son
were indicted on 8 January 1418 as accessories to three separate
attacks on the property and servants of the abbot of Evesham
committed sometime in 1417 'by the servants of Nicholas
Burdet and others': the abbot thought that a special commission
of oyer and terminer would be more effective in the case of the
second of the attacks and secured Chief Justice Hankford to
begin the inquiries. This resulted in the surrender of five of the
indicted persons, including the two Burdets, and the outlawry
of the rest. Then came a *certiorari* from the King's Bench summoning before it all five indictments made in the quarter
sessions. The Burdets finally appeared in the Hilary term of
1420, two years after the attacks, and were released on bail
because they were about to join the staff of John of Bedford
abroad. After their return they were sent to prison and finally
tried by the nisi prius justices in 1422 and were acquitted.[1] The
case of the Burdets shows the relation of the Worcestershire
justices to the King's Bench: the bench constantly kept the

[1] The account of Miss Putnam, op. cit., pp. 71–72, has been followed here.

felony and disorder cases in the counties under review. It did not move about much now, as in the fourteenth century, but succeeded in getting before it, somehow or other, the prisoners whom before the middle of Edward III's reign it would have discovered in the counties. 'In any normal year of Henry VI or of Edward IV nine-tenths, as a guess, of the Rex Roll is filled with cases from the sessions of the peace.'[1] The *coram rege* tribunal removed the cases by *mandamus* or *certiorari* or writ of error, and dealt with them during term. The evidence of the *coram rege* rolls points to the large number of pleas that were being so handled and indicates that under the Lancastrians and Yorkists the local justices were being very hard worked.[2] It also shows what a great deal of disorder pervaded the country not merely (as one might expect) in a *tempus turbationis*, but at times normally regarded as peaceful. When a justice of the peace, escheator, and knight of the shire for Warwick could be set upon and murderously attacked by his enemies as he was returning from parliament;[3] or when in St. Dunstan in the East on Easter Sunday (1417) Lord Lestrange and his followers could make a lethal attack on Sir William Trussell and kill one of the parishioners who was trying to stop the tumult, it became obvious that the veneer of peace and order was very thin.

While felony and trespasses of all kinds were matters for the criminal side of the common law, and occur in considerable quantities on the rex roll of the King's Bench, there were cases in which the plaintiff was either not satisfied with the remedy provided or was unable to obtain it. Plaintiffs who brought action for the recovery of goods and chattels had to be prepared to accept damages in lieu of them. Here the equitable courts could order restitution. Again, particular circumstances might be against the petitioner, either his own poverty or the power of his opponent. Many criminal offenders were too powerful to be dealt with in the common law courts. The solution was resort to the king in chancery, where proceedings were begun by petition and the parties summoned by writs of *quibusdam de causis* or *sub poena*. The parties and witnesses were subjected to

---

[1] Putnam, *Proceedings before the Justices* (1938), p. lxiv.

[2] The fifteenth-century commission is printed for 1413 (14 Hen. IV) in *Proceedings*, pp. 88–91.

[3] James Belers: *Cal. Pat. R., 1413–16*, 114 for commission to William Roos of Hamelak and his colleagues to arrest and bring before the Council William Perwyche and his adherents for the attack.

examination, and there was no 'trial' in the strict sense of the word: or the case might be sent where there was. Whether the chancellor owed his equitable powers to the council is a difficult historical point. From the beginning the council was broadly a court of equity in that its action was a dispensation of the royal prerogative: the council received cases on petition, showed mercy and leniency in the application of the law, admitted suitors legally disabled, and required specific performance in the restitution of goods and chattels.

Did the council then delegate its powers to the chancellor? It may be recalled that the chancellor had also a common law jurisdiction and could hear cases on either side, the equitable (the 'English') and the common law (the 'Latin') side.[1] There is no evidence for delegation. The *placita in cancellaria* and the Early Chancery Proceedings (to reverse the order) both arise from his original function as royal administrator and secretary, the second nearest official to the king, from whose household he was long in departing: the man who, as confidential adviser, knew and could help to direct the royal mind and held high rank in the council; and without more ado, one may go back to the saying of the Master in the *Dialogus de Scaccario*: 'Cancellarius in ordine illo [on the President's left] primus est et sicut in curia sic ad scaccarium magnus est adeo ut sine ipsius consensu vel consilio nil magnum fiat vel fieri debeat.'[2] *Sicut in curia* are the important words. When the great justiciar ceased the chancellor remained. He was the man who could dispense the royal prerogative. By the reign of Richard II, even in the second half of Edward III's, the chancellor was summoning parties before him *sub poena*, and the chancery was recognized as a place where the king's grace, mercy, and even (may we say?) inventiveness were displayed. In 1389 there were protests in the commons against writs *quibusdam de causis* or any such writ 'devant le Chancellor ou le Conseill le Roy'.[3] But the jurisdiction was too valuable to be stopped by the disgruntled, and by the middle of the fifteenth century it was hearing a great number of civil as well as criminal suits of various descriptions,

---

[1] On origins, cf. A. D. Hargreaves, 'Equity and the Latin Side of Chancery', *Law Quarterly Review*, lxviii (1952).

[2] Ed. Charles Johnson, pp. 18–19.

[3] *Rot. Parl.* iii. 267. In 1393 there were also complaints that parties were being summoned by *sub poena* to answer untrue suggestions 'devant le dit conseill ou en la Chancellerie'.

appeal to the chancellor being often interposed in a common law suit where plaintiffs or witnesses were threatened. Thus in 1422, when Sir Robert Poynings brought an assize of novel disseisin against Robert Knyvet, William Scot, counsel for Poynings, was threatened in life and limb by Knyvet, and complained to the chancellor that he went in fear of his life, the more so, he alleged, because the defendant had already procured certain persons to lie in wait to kill John Kenton, Poynings's farmer. Scot asked that Knyvet should be summoned into chancery and there find security of the peace.[1] Fear of injury to the body was the cause of a number of such summonses. Richard Ferier complained that he could not go outside his house or attend to the cultivation of his land because of the attacks of John Hundiby *et plusours gentz* and asked for them to be summoned.[2] So did Archbishop Chichele when his park at Otford was raided, his game killed, and the throat of his parkkeeper cut so that the man just escaped with his life.[3]

The Essex and Kent cases between 1426 and 1460 have been analysed.[4] Between 1426 and 1432 fifty-seven petitions reached the chancellor. Of these, thirty-nine, nearly 70 per cent., related to uses. From 1443 to 1456 just over 400 petitions[5] came in: 67 per cent. were cases of uses; from 1456 to 1460 there were 114 sent to the chancellor; 90 per cent. concerned uses. Contract also claimed a considerable number: half of them concerned private transactions relating to land, i.e. sales and leases; but uses appear to predominate and there is a great mass of litigation under *Cestui-que-use* against feoffees. The usual type is re-enfeoffment. A enfeoffs X, Y, Z on going off to the Holy Land so that they re-enfeoff him on his return: they fail to do so, and the case is brought.[6] A man who is a tenant in fee-simple wishes to hold in fee-tail; he enfeoffs a number of people who then are supposed to re-enfeoff him, but something goes wrong, and they do not. As is well known, feoffments to uses were often made in order to provide for the younger sons or the daughters of the trustor, while trustors are frequently found directing their feoffees to create an entailed estate: they are to enfeoff B and the heirs of his body, with remainder to C. Finally, in the

---

[1] C. 1/6/276.   [2] C. 1/4/172.   [3] C. 1/4/177.
[4] By Miss Margaret Avery who has kindly permitted these statistics to be quoted here from her thesis (Univ. of London) 'Proceedings in the Court of Chancery up to *c.* 1460' (1958).
[5] C. 1, Bundles 13–25.   [6] C. 1/9/186.

creation of life estates and fees-tail, feoffees are found making determined attempts to prevent alienation and to keep the land within the family. It was the chancellor's business to see that the wishes of the feoffor to uses were respected, and that the feoffees fulfilled the charges laid upon them. He had to be satisfied that a use had in fact been raised. The number of uses petitions struck Samuel Burroughs who in his *History of Chancery* (1726) observed:

> The court grew in esteem and more Business by the invective Broils that soon after followed between the Houses of York and Lancaster. The Partisans of each knew their estate would certainly fall a morsel to the prevailing House; the unfortunate were sure to be called Rebels and Traytors, so many put their land secretly into Use, to secure their possessions against the event of that doubtful combat.

There would appear to be some truth in the statement. Estates held to uses were made liable to forfeiture for treason in 1388, but there is reason to think that the statute was not always strictly observed.[1] Only detailed investigation of the early chancery proceedings would show to what extent the chancellor succeeded in protecting lands so placed to use.

The weakness of common law procedure clearly shows in the petitions coming to the chancellor. 'Hyt is open known', said one litigant, 'that hyt were het [i.e. hat, called] folly to your seyde suppliant to sue the common law.'[2] Petitions often complain of violence committed by persons of standing who would use their influence in the county for preventing the normal machinery for justice taking effect. There are a number of Westmorland petitions from the early fifteenth century which show that jurors were intimidated if they made presentation of defects on estates for which the bailiffs (who were now threatening them) were responsible,[3] or that groups of men upon whom the chancery *sub poena* had been served pursued the plaintiff to London with intent to slay him.[4] The petitions make clear the lawless and insubordinate attitude of certain families, who did not scruple to collect soldiers, 'as if they were

---

[1] T. F. T. Plucknett, *Concise History of the Common Law*, 5th ed., p. 578.
[2] C. 1/15/37.
[3] C. 1/6/158, cited by R. L. Storey, 'Disorders in Lancastrian Westmorland: some early Chancery Proceedings,' *Cumb. and Westm. Antiquarian and Arch. Soc. Transactions*, New Ser. liii (1954), p. 71.
[4] C. 1/6/282, cited by Storey, ibid., p. 73.

making a foray into Scotland'; but their opponents, who complained, were certainly no better. One of the families presented along with their opponent were described as firing beacons, both night and day, when they wanted to collect their forces for attack.[1] Most significant of all were the petitions of Robert Crakenthorp of Newbiggin, a tenant of the Cliffords, which the justices of the peace, the earl of Westmorland and Sir Thomas Parr, were asked to investigate. Crakenthorp reported that there had been many grave breaches of the peace caused by large unlawful assemblies of armed men. These were inquired into by local justices at Appleby, and at the inquiry Sir Henry Threlkeld and William Thornburgh of Meaburn so threatened the jurors that they dared not speak the truth about the disturbances; and the plaintiff was also threatened with ambush by a group of men instigated by Sir John Lancaster and his wife and relatives, who were obviously incriminated. Plaintiff got wind of the ambush in time, but his enemies continued to threaten his life. On 11 March 1439 a strong commission was appointed to look into the allegations. Crakenthorp was himself a justice of the peace, but could not hold any of the sessions in the county, and the case is one of flagrant disregard for the courts. It is noteworthy that Sir Henry Threlkeld who threatened the jury at Appleby was knight of the shire for the county of Westmorland in 1433, when the commons had petitioned that lords should take an oath not to maintain robbers and other breakers of the peace.[2] Threlkeld was not the only hypocrite. There was also Sir Thomas Parr, commissioned to investigate the attempted assault on Crakenthorp who complained of Henry Belyngham for coming to his home at Burnside, with a great multitude of people, and threatening to burn it down. Parr was under-sheriff of the county (sheriff, the petition called him) and 'the coroners of the same shire bene his meynyall men'. Without hope of getting redress through common law channels, Belyngham had appealed to the chancellor.

The interesting point is that the offenders included men who had sat in parliament for Westmorland and had held commissions of the peace. So powerful was their local standing that it would have been useless to sue them in the county. Westmorland, therefore, is not unlike the Norfolk of John Paston's time: like armies muster, like fellowships turn out, the protagonists

[1] C. 1/7/256, Storey, ibid., p. 75.   [2] Storey, ibid., pp. 75–76.

are the magnates and the gentlemen of the county. The chancellor could at any rate have the circumstances of the petition reported on, and bind the parties over or take the matter to the council which, if the case reached that degree of seriousness, might issue orders. There are numerous complaints brought by petitioners living in the large franchises and liberties of Essex and Kent. One petitioner alleged that he had no remedy at common law, because the cause of action arose within a franchise, 'la ou le brief notre seigneur le Roy ne court miye'. This is remarkable after the statutes of Westminster I and II;[1] but in view of other complaints it is not improbable. William Tanner complained that William Lambert refused to pay him a quit rent upon lands lying within the liberty of the abbey of Battle. He was unable to distrain upon the lands 'par cause de graund maigntenaunce quil ad et auxi par enchesse des les grande libertes et privileges al mesme Abbe grauntes deins mesme la franchise'. Large boroughs like Canterbury and Colchester were especial offenders. A bad case from Canterbury was one in which William Rose, bailiff in 1431, 1439, and 1440, was delated to the chancellor by a certain John Aldburgh. Rose owed the prioress of St. Sepulchre's a rent but, wishing to avoid payment, persuaded her to bring an action for debt against Aldburgh, promising to maintain her and paying all the expenses of the suit. The prioress agreed and went on suing, so Aldburgh brought the action.[2] There is no record how this case of embracery ended. A number of complaints were brought against local officials, for example for violent treatment during plaintiff's arrest: one would expect, where fatality occurred that the coroner would have pronounced against the bailiffs,[3] but evidently this did not happen.

One major difficulty that faced suitors who might otherwise have gone to the common law courts was the time taken over mesne process both in the common pleas and in the King's Bench. Mesne which proved 'the longest and most exhausting part of an action in a fifteenth-century court of law', as Miss Hastings has said,[4] was concerned with securing the appearance

---

[1] T. F. T. Plucknett, *The Legislation of Edward I* (1949), pp. 31–33.

[2] C. 1/9/105.

[3] e.g. in C. 1/13/58 where the men of Stephen Amyot, Constable of the Hundred of Rolvendon, 'smote off the leg' of John Mongeham who subsequently died.

[4] *The Court of Common Pleas* (New York, 1947), p. 169.

of the defendant in court, either through process by distraint or through process of arrest and, when necessary, outlawry. Process by distraint might continue until the goods of the defendant were exhausted; arrest and, after continued exigent, outlawry might lead to a process of reversal which took various forms, and meanwhile the plaintiff was waiting. Entries of mesne process take up the greater part of space in the rolls of the common pleas.[1] In the King's Bench mesne process seems to have been shorter, but a good number of the criminal suits on the rex roll are cases where defendants have already been produced before the justices of the peace or justices of some other commission. It was not so much the delays in the law itself—the number of essoins allowed, the licences to imparl (talking the matter over till a later day), and the writ of *supersedeas* which emanated either from the chancery or issued under the privy seal—the writ by which Lord Moleyns successfully countered John Paston's attempt to have his men punished for attacking Paston's wife at Gresham[2]—as the attempt to pervert or corrupt it in its course which constituted the greatest evil of the fifteenth century. It is not the direct bribery of jurors so much as pressure, the influence upon them of some great lord whose favour the twelve men of the patria would not be willing to lose. 'Steward, the chief constable', having been put on an assize between John Paston and another man, consulted Edmund Paston what to do, because, as he said, the suit was maintained by Sir Thomas Tuddenham, a powerful figure in the county. Edmund replied: 'I counselled him to swear the truth of the issue that he shall be swore to, and then he needs never to dread him of no attaint.' Steward then asked Edmund what he thought 'of the rule of my master Daniell and my Lord of Suffolk, and asked which I thought should rule in this shire: and I said both as I thought, and he that surviveth to hold by the virtue of the survivor, and he to thank his friends and to acquit his enemies.'[3] Security depended on giving 'right verdicts', the verdict in the interest of the stronger.[4] To give the true verdict against might could be dangerous; to give a false verdict would be to risk prosecution by the writ of attaint, a severe and formidable

---

[1] Thus in the roll for Michaelmas 2 Edward IV, about 3,650 out of 4,000 are such entries. This does not imply that plaintiffs were generally unsuccessful. Hastings, op. cit., p. 183.   [2] *Paston Letters*, ii. 248.

[1] Ibid., ii. 79–80 (June 1447).   [4] Hastings, op. cit., p. 222.

process which involved prison, seizure of goods and destruction of houses. It was not easy to sue the twelve jurors by such procedure, and pliancy was better. Best of all was to get the right jury. Sir John Fastolf both rewarded the sheriff for a grand jury panel favourable to himself and also planned to get the two defendants who had lost the verdict in the original action into the household of the duke of Norfolk, so as the better to influence the jury of attaint.[1]

Pressure could take all sorts of forms and juries were not always involved. One instance out of many is the melancholy story of the manors of Chicklade and Hindon in 1452. Richard Page of Warminster, a retainer of the earl of Wiltshire, had set his heart on possessing these two manors lying on the downs to the north of Shaftesbury, and they had been made over, under covenant, to Thomas Tropenell by a debtor, Richard Hurdell. Hurdell had a life interest only, as they were the property of a certain John Lyngever of Kingston Deverell. Tropenell was himself a rich *familiaris* of Robert, Lord Hungerford, and at his request it was Hungerford who with justices and other local personages held an inquiry into the petition for recovery made to the Chancery by Tropenell. Page's friends called Tropenell a 'perillous covetous man', and he was evidently doing well for himself, since he is described as 'the squyer which had the lyvereys of King Harry the VIth and of King Edward the IIIIth'.[2] He was a substantial enough landowner to have a cartulary of his own and to believe that he could trace his pedigree to the forgotten past, certainly from 'before the Conquest'.[3]

Richard Page first got at the debtor, Hurdell, and persuaded him to accept the award of a shady lawyer, William King, that he (Page) would acquit the debt to Tropenell in return for which the manor should be made over to Page for the sum of £10. At first Hurdell refused and Page resorted to threats.

The seid Richard Page seyng unto me upon the same awarde and rewle so made, when I refused it, and wold not abide hit: 'I shold abide it mawgre my tethe and alles else shold nat I dwelle in no shire in England; to spende thereon the utmost of his goodes and undo me he wold, and sette me fast in prison; no man in England had better lordshippe to help hym then he had.

---

[1] *Paston Letters*, iii. 10–11 (1456); noted by Hastings, op. cit., p. 224.
[2] *Tropenell Cartulary*, ed. J. C. Davies (Wilts. Arch. and Nat. Hist. Ser. 1908) ii. 163.　　　　　　　　　　　　　[3] Ibid., i. 272, ii. 162.

Page and King also told Hurdell's wife that Tropenall was 'fast in prison at London' and 'never like to come out'. Hurdell in fear agreed. Before the consent could be translated into a charter, Hurdell, thinking better of the matter, made over the two manors to Tropenell (23 Oct. 1452): but Page and King had got at the original owner, John Lyngever, and at a meeting arranged under cover of getting Lyngever a wife, when drinks were going round, bullied him into demising all his right in the manors, as he imagined, for the term of a single life, his own, at a rent of 10s. a year to Richard Page. Lyngever, who could not read, stated without ambiguity the terms of the lease to which he said he would agree, as he and other witnesses deposed at the inquiry. Unfortunately he did not inspect the deed itself, already written and only waiting his seal, where his intended words 'for life' were fraudulently rendered 'in fee'. When he found this out he sold (28 Sept. 1453) the whole property to John Tropenell,[1] though the unpalatable fact emerged that Page and King had already handed the manors over to feoffees. Tropenell eventually secured judgement at an assize of novel disseisin, but did not get possession till five years later, when the Yorkists were in power.

[1] Ibid. ii. 43.

X

RICHARD OF YORK

RICHARD DUKE OF YORK was heir to all the claims of the House of Mortimer. His father, the earl of Cambridge, was beheaded by Henry V as the result of the Southampton plot, for trying to put his brother-in-law upon the throne. Richard himself was married into the Neville family. His wife, Cecily, was the youngest daughter of Ralph Neville, the first earl of Westmorland by his second wife Joan Beaufort, daughter of John of Gaunt and Katharine Swinford. It was a powerful and prolific clan. The earl's first marriage had produced two sons and seven daughters, married into noble northern families, including Dacre of Gilsland and Scrope of Bolton: the second marriage produced fourteen children, nine sons, five daughters. Cecily's eldest brother Richard married Alice Montagu, daughter of Thomas earl of Salisbury, to become earl of Salisbury in his wife's right. William, Cecily's sixth brother, married the daughter and heiress of Sir Thomas Fauconberg, to become Lord Fauconberg; the ninth brother Edward married the daughter and heiress of Richard Beauchamp, earl of Worcester, and became Lord Abergavenny; a fifth brother, Robert, became bishop of Durham. Cecily's sister Katharine married John Mowbray, duke of Norfolk, and their son John II was to be an ally of Edward IV: Katharine had four husbands, the fourth being Sir John Woodville, brother of Edward IV's queen. Eleanor married Henry Percy II, earl of Northumberland, and another sister Anne married Humphrey Stafford, duke of Buckingham: not all these supported the Yorkist cause: the duke of Buckingham, the earl of Northumberland, and Lord Dacre of Gilsland were confirmed Lancastrians. Perhaps the greatest of Cecily's relatives, her nephew Richard, son of the earl of Salisbury, who married Anne Beauchamp and through her became earl of Warwick and ruler of the Beauchamp estates, ended his Yorkist career by seeking the favour of

Margaret of Anjou and bringing the storm-tossed Henry VI once more to the throne.

Despite his father's attainder, Richard of York could claim the entailed lands of the earldom of Cambridge. In 1425 his maternal uncle Edmund Mortimer died childless and his immense possessions and estates, many in the Welsh Marches, were due to come to Richard: with these went the earldom of Ulster, which like that of March had descended to the house of Mortimer, an accumulation of wealth, which, as Professor Tout once observed, 'made it possible for the House of York to dethrone the House of Lancaster'. Knighted in 1426, made constable of England in 1430, serving in the retinue of Henry VI in France during 1431, Richard did not receive livery of his estates until 1432 when he petitioned parliament for them: he was allowed to enter into possession on finding security that he would pay in five years the sum of £1,646. 0s. 6d. A valor in 1443-4 shows that the duke of York's cash receipts from the Mortimer inheritance amounted to £3,430 after all reprises and charges had been met. In 1436 he was assessed for taxation at £3,230 of which sum £761 came from income from annuities inherited from his grandfather, Edward III's son, Edmund Langley, first duke of York. His total annual income from England and Wales must have been between £6,500 and £7,000.

Wealth was here and Neville territorial influence when needed, for the bulk of the Neville estates had been transmitted through the Countess Joan to the younger branch of the family in the person of Joan's eldest son, Richard Neville, earl of Salisbury: it was, none the less, great place rather than great power. Direct voice in the minority council was not had by young Richard of York who was sent abroad and, on the whole, kept abroad: he was made into a military rather than a political figure. He was first appointed to the lieutenancy in France in February 1436, a few months after the duke of Bedford died, and shortly after the treaty of Arras. He was then twenty-four years of age: an able soldier, but without much experience of government. That he returned to England the next year (1437) has been attributed to the struggle in the council, also to the fact that 'he soon grew weary of his task', and 'had apparently failed in France'.[1] There is no evidence for the second of these statements. He fought effectively in association with Talbot to

---

[1] Cf. Cora Scofield, *The Life and Reign of Edward IV* (1923), i. 7.

drive French forces from upper Normandy. The reasons for his
return were probably different and certainly more complex:
the shortness of his time of service stipulated in his indentures
needs explanation. At the beginning of April 1437 the council
noted that those indentures were *quasi expirate*; and the duke
was asked to stay on in Normandy, 'knowing for certain that if
the duke returns to England when the king's ordinance for
those parts had not been made, this would seriously prejudice
the king and his domains and subjects therein'.[1] It seems likely
that the financial terms of his appointment had proved unacceptable and that York did not ask for a prolongation of an
office which was costing him too much;[2] in 1436 he was not
allowed the proceeds of the Norman taxation, though he were
granted them later. Besides, all monies which reached Rouen
from England, apart from York's own personal allowance, were
paid to the chancellor of Normandy. When Richard left for
Normandy he received advanced payments of two quarters'
wages for his army of 2,700 men, the remaining six months to
be paid, as usual, from Norman sources, though Normandy
was desperately hard pressed at the time; and there was always
the competition of Calais, which might be serious.

But there may well have been another reason why York gave
up so quickly his first tenure. Throughout the summer of 1437
the council was discussing arrangements for a great embassy to
be accompanied by the duke of Orléans to discuss with France
terms of a general peace. It may have been made clear to York,
even as early as 1436, that the lieutenancy in Normandy was
not a long commission, but a short-term appointment pending
a general settlement with France. Moreover, he must have
known that he was to be succeeded by a distinguished soldier,
the earl of Warwick, when negotiations with France had broken
down in September 1437. When Warwick died he was succeeded
first by a governing commission which fulfilled its purpose
adequately enough, but it was found unsatisfactory to leave
Normandy for long without even a nominal lieutenant governor.
It is possible that the appointment of Gloucester himself was
under discussion, for a reference to York's second tenure in

---

[1] *P.P.C.* v. 7.
[2] In 1437 debts to him totalled £1,500, a large part of which was soon repaid
with the £2,000 owing to him for the defence of Calais. In the warrant of 1439
£18,000 was shown to be owing.

1440 describes his power 'as my lord of Gloucester had or shoulde have had now late'. But Gloucester did not take the offer, and a temporary compromise was arranged in the form of John earl of Somerset, until Gloucester was able to go. The wording may have been a way of quietening Gloucester; but it is noteworthy that Somerset, drawing a salary of 600 *l.t.* a month, for some while tenaciously continued to bear the title of lieutenant-general for war after York had been reappointed (2 July 1440). By the time, however, that York actually arrived in Normandy (1441) Somerset, relieved of his commission, had departed. It was Somerset's appointment as lieutenant and captain-general in Aquitaine and in the France not under York's control, made (April 1443) during York's second period as lieutenant, that turned the duke against Beaufort and his friends in the council. By that time negotiations with France, conducted by the great embassy, which met the antagonists at Calais, had hopelessly broken down. Under the most elaborate arrangements the duke of Orléans had been brought over, the aid of Isabel of Burgundy sought, and elaborate instructions had been given in the council to the English ambassadors who were still to uphold the English claim to the French throne. It had all come to nothing. However much territory the English negotiators were prepared to concede, the French were adamant on the point that any land held in France by the English must be held of the French king. The affront to York of Somerset's second mission was obvious and bare-faced, because there was now no alternative to going on with the French war and protecting Normandy and the coast. To launch the unsuccessful Somerset expedition when York was already in command was an act of great imprudence. Financially, too, York upon his second tour had a difficult time.

For the first years of his second appointment York remained in England, and payments made to him were for the troops he was assembling, advanced payments of wages being essential before an expedition could be staffed. Even so, because he stayed in England and did not cross personally with his men, he was only allowed payment of less than half the troops (200 lances and 600 archers) in his employment. In the second year York's allowance of £20,000 was paid remarkably promptly, through the diversion of assignments intended for the house-hold. Yet, in fact, Somerset received more than York. On

10 July 1443 exchequer issues record £25,000 paid to Somerset, while from the central exchequer no more payments went to the duke until 21 February 1444, when a total of £10,300 was recorded in his favour. The restriction can be accounted for. In 1443 Guienne caused the diversion of considerable sums of money intended for Normandy, and the council, who had certain feelings of remorse, were often at pains to justify their attitude. They were naturally reluctant to send over money which might be received by non-Englishmen. Earlier, a council minute of 9 November 1437 suggested that Warwick must be asked to say at once if he had received money sent over with Sir John Popham; to send over £24,000, 'and there were noon Englishmen to receive it, it were but in vayn'. Clearly the Exchequer thought that York was quite well off owing to the grants of the Norman estates. The figure at which the Norman subsidy was put was 340,000 *l.t.* but this was guesswork, for in March only 30,000 *l.t.* had been granted, while in September the unusual scheme of an individual sales tax of 2*s.* per *livre* had been granted. York, therefore, had £20,000 on his second tour in Normandy, the wages of his men, but only a fraction of the subsidy granted by the Norman estates. He must have been aware that Normandy was not popular with the council. In 1443 it took the council a month to decide whether to send relief to Normandy or to Guienne or both. Cromwell had to rule that it could not be both and that a choice was inevitable. It may indeed have been Somerset's *amour-propre* that led the expedition in directions where he would have supreme command: but it was foolishness to give way to him. At the risk of repetition it may be well to review some of these events in greater detail, since the conduct of the English council at this point had much to do with York's subsequent career. It was the failure of the 1439 embassy, after all the hopes raised, that convinced the Cardinal Beaufort's following in the council that greater concessions must be made and a peace with France sealed by diplomatic marriage.

The first step must, in the view of the majority of the council, be the ransoming and release of the duke of Orléans who would serve as an advocate for peace in the French camp. This took place in 1440, greatly to the displeasure of Gloucester who put into writing the reasons for his opposition to it. The prisoner's ransom was set at 120,000 gold nobles or 24,000 *écus*. The terms were that 40,000 nobles or 80,000 *écus* should be paid down forthwith by Orléans, who named certain of the French nobility as his securities; upon which he was to be set at liberty (*elargiri*), and within half a year he was to find the balance when his final *liberatio* was to be sanctioned, or faithfully return to the captivity which he had endured for twenty-four years. His liberation, Henry VI stated in the agreement, was to be 'the means of the pacification of the kingdom of France and England' and in that year he was to do his utmost to end the long contention 'super iure et titulo ad coronam et regnum Francie'.[1] Should disputes arise over the non-observance of any part of the agreement, Orléans agreed to accept the award of the apostolic *camera*, which should have complete jurisdiction, and no appeal or exception owing to privileges (e.g. the taking of the Cross) was to be allowed. The introduction of the *camera* suggests that papal merchants may have undertaken to advance the 40,000 nobles on the duke's behalf. The version of this on the French roll had certain additions to the original convention. If his efforts resulted in final peace within the year prescribed, the king promised to pay all his expenses for that time, except those owing for the period while he was still in captivity. If the peace was not concluded, then immediately after the breakdown of negotiations the duke undertook to return to England as the king's prisoner once again.[2] The French king on 16 August 1440 ratified the arrangement. The duke's final release was therefore made conditional not only on the payment of the ransom, but upon his successful prosecution of negotiations for peace, about which Charles VII, in his ratification, was silent. The extensive series of documents ratifying the arrangements, the commission for the custody of the duke in Lancastrian France, the safe-conducts, the oaths to implement them, show how much importance the English council attached to the release of their prisoner who was to co-operate with an English embassy, led by the bishop of Rochester, and Lord Fanhope, already in the Marches of Calais. Gloucester's objection to the arrangements was largely based on the fear that as Charles VII was 'be comune report and fame' in a state of weak health mentally, the duke would be made regent, and that he might very well reconcile Charles and his son, at that moment at loggerheads: the duchy of Normandy which had borne so

---

[1] *Foedera*, v. ii. 82. [2] Ibid., p. 84.

much expense would consider itself abandoned by Henry. The duke regards himself as the liege man of the king of France and whatever promises he may have made, still thinks himself bound by this feudal relation. Moreover, Orléans has alliances, both with the count of Armagnac and with the duke of Burgundy (made at Calais) which are not likely to favour this country, which lacks allies to help it to retain Henry's conquests, and stands too much isolated. Finally, as Normandy has to bear the brunt of the action likely to follow upon this release, would not it be as well to ask for the opinion of the Normans in the matter? In a final sentence Duke Humphrey returned to the last will of Henry V who there ordered '. . . the manere and the fourme hoough he shuld be delyvered, as it sheweth playnly in the said will'. The council which in 1422 had set aside the provision for Gloucester made in Henry V's will was not likely to return to that document at the duke's request: nor was Orléans successful in the negotiations he had undertaken. Pontoise fell in September 1441, and Orléans turned to more indirect methods to bring pressure to bear on Charles VII. Together with Burgundy and Alençon he thought to win over John count of Armagnac by a marriage alliance. In May 1442 the count offered Henry one of his three daughters as a bride. Early in June Thomas Bekynton, Henry's English secretary, and Sir Robert Roos were commissioned to visit Armagnac, arrange the preliminaries of a treaty, and bring back portraits of the three daughters for Henry to make his choice.

Bekynton reached Bordeaux on 16 July 1442, but could not establish contact with the count because of the presence of Charles VII's powerful army which had successfully attacked Tartas and St. Sever at the end of the previous month. Together with Roos, Bekynton reported to Henry on the dangerous condition of Gascony and also wrote to the treasurer, Cromwell, a letter which was taken to England by a representative of the municipality of Bordeaux accompanied by the archbishop, deputed to explain to the council the plight of the duchy. The letters to Henry set forth all too plainly the tactics of Charles VII and the Dauphin. They had come in person to make a great effort to win Gascony, first by assaulting Dax and Bayonne and afterwards Bordeaux itself: and Gascon morale had been at its lowest on hearing a report that assistance had been expressly denied to the Gascons who had petitioned

Henry VI for it.[1] It had been reassured by the encouragements
of the ambassadors, but the main object of their visit, to see the
count of Armagnac, proved impracticable because the French
king could not be approached. On 22 October Sir Edward Hull,
an opponent of the duke of York, arrived at Bordeaux from
England bearing letters to Roos which informed him that the
earl of Somerset was about to leave England with a large army,
with a special letter to this effect, direct to the townsfolk. With
him he brought 'an artist to take the likenesses',[2] the German
Hans. Only one portrait was finished, but there is no record
that it came to hand. After long delays, due less to the cold
affecting the artist (as the count of Armagnac alleged), than to
Armagnac's realization of the hostility of the French court to
the proposed marriage alliance and to the proximity of the
French army, the ambassadors returned: they had become impressed with the overwhelming and immediate need to defend
Gascony and expressed themselves to the count of Armagnac's
chancellor as unable to wait for the portraits.[3] Somerset, in
point of fact, was not to see Guienne. He went, at his own
request, to France to carry out operations which were pro-
fessedly York's business. The decision had to be broken to
York by garter king of arms. Somerset was to be 'the shelde
[shield] to his said cousin of York . . . he shall be betwix him
and the adversarie'. York was to be informed that it was 'not
the intent of his said cousin of Somerset to doo any thing that
might prejudice in any wise the power that his said cousin of
York hath of the Kyng in this cuntrees of Fraunce and of
Normandie.'[4] In point of fact he was now the military commander *par excellence*. Meanwhile York was instructed to fortify
and defend Rouen. He had been asking for the £20,000 due to
him under the terms of service agreed upon: the final insult
was Henry's request that as so much had been expended on the
equipping of Somerset's force he 'wol take patiens and forbere
him for a tyme'. Had the council concentrated on saving
Gascony there and then and not permitted Charles and the

---

[1] *A Journal by one of the suite of Thomas Beckington*, ed. N. Harris Nicolas (1828),
p. 15.
[2] Ibid., p. 60 (un overir avec lui pour faire les figures).
[3] Ibid., p. 81. 'But as we plainly see and are confirmed in this by your letters,
that it is necessary in the first place to provide as quickly and effectively as possible
for the general security, we are now preparing to go back to our own country.'
[4] *P.P.C.* v. 260-1.

Dauphin to make their invasion, York might have saved the situation in Normandy. But the council was too late, and when it sent its reinforcements to Normandy, they were placed under an imprudent and amateurish commander, Somerset.

Somerset's failure in his campaign of 1443 and his death in 1444 brought to the forefront, as a peacemaker, the man who had for some time been the mainstay of the Lancastrian lords. Suffolk has been presented as a 'man of lofty sentiment and principle', tragically misunderstood by his generation: 'one of the finest types of the old chivalry that was passing away, and also through his intellectual sympathies a fore-runner of the new order'. It is possible to sympathize with his desire for peace, but no attempt to idealize him will survive an examination of his territorial ambitions or his treatment of Normandy in the council. The most that could be said is that he was rather a better man than his unprincipled son. William de la Pole's grandfather, Michael (de la Pole), the friend of Richard II and sufferer from the assault of the Appellants, had added to the original lands of the family in Holderness, Lincolnshire, and Nottinghamshire important estates and rents through his marriage with Katherine, daughter and heiress of Sir John Wingfield of Wingfield, Suffolk. He was holding the manor of Lowestoft and the hundred of Lothingland when in August 1385 he was made earl of Suffolk. He had already been given (7 August 1382) the manors of Benhall, Suffolk, and Dedham in Essex which the last Oxford earl had held. On 20 August 1385 he was granted, besides the usual third penny (£20) from Suffolk, the reversion of lands belonging to Isabel countess of Suffolk when she died, along with £500 annually till that event took place, and in 1389 his son, on doing homage, had livery of eight whole manors and some rents in Norfolk and Suffolk.[1] The second earl, who died on the Harfleur campaign, was thus a substantial landowner in East Anglia, though not so preponderant as the duke of Norfolk or the earl of March, the former representing the Bigod interest, with land centring around Bungay and Framlingham, the latter the Gloucester interest around Clare. When Norfolk was banished and March died in Ireland, Michael de la Pole became the most important man in Suffolk; forgetting his father's friendship with Richard II, he threw in his lot with the usurping Bolingbroke. 'In consideration

[1] *Cal. Close R. 1389–1392*, p. 41.

of his services at the king's advent', he was restored to the earldom of Suffolk and had the lands of the Ufford earls. Round him gathered the families of Lancastrian leaning—Sir Edward Hastings, Sir William Clopton of Kentwell Hall, Sir William de Elmham, Sir John Heveningham, Sir William Argentein, and others. When the young earl of Nottingham, Norfolk's heir, was put to death for conspiracy against Henry IV, the Pole influence was greatly increased. But the death both of Michael at Harfleur and of his son and heir at Agincourt, left the Pole estates to the absentee earl, William de la Pole, serving in lower Normandy and the Cotentin: for seventeen years William was abroad and in his absence the Norfolk and March influence increased.

Great-grandson, therefore, of the Hull merchant, William had early cast in his lot with the Beauforts when he married the widow of the earl of Salisbury, with whose help he had fought in France. The Countess Alice de la Pole was daughter of Thomas Chaucer, the king's butler, formerly Speaker of the commons, member for Oxfordshire over a long period of years: the son of Geoffrey, the poet. On the tomb of Alice in the church of Ewelme, Oxon., home of the Chaucers, are the wheels of Alice Chaucer's mother, Philippa Roet, and Philippa was sister of Catherine Swynford, the mother of Cardinal Beaufort and his brothers. In July 1432 Suffolk was given the custody of the duke of Orléans, and by then, or at any rate by the next year, his desire for a peaceful settlement with France had become clear. He gave expression to it in 1433 (the year he was made steward of the household), when Hugh de Lannoy came over to agitate on behalf of Philip of Burgundy, saying that the king of England was inclining to use the services of the duke of Orléans in promoting peace. When Suffolk took leave of Lannoy he told the Burgundian to inform the duke of Burgundy that he had greater hopes of a general peace than ever before. In 1434, in preparation for the council of Arras, Suffolk, who was to be one of the English delegation there, was employed as an intermediary in negotiations with the French lords in England, and he went to Arras next year. The failure, from the English point of view, of the Arras negotiations brought Humphrey of Gloucester once again to the lead in the council, and an attempt to return to the policy of active warfare. Suffolk had been in Normandy with York, and at the defence of Calais in

1436, but when he came home he no longer had charge of the
duke of Orléans; nor was he employed in the negotiations with
France in 1439. The failure of these negotiations at Oye made
it clear to Suffolk that nothing was to be gained by the stubborn
maintenance of the English claim to the French throne and that
England had to go to the limit of concession. With the liberation
of Orléans in 1440 there followed a train of negotiations which
took English ambassadors first to Brittany where Lord Fanhope,
and probably his retainer John Wenlock, now of the royal
household, tried to persuade the duke into an alliance with
England or, along with the duke of Alençon and other princes
discontented with Charles VII's government, to press their
sovereign to leave off his campaigns in Poitou and Gascony;
and in the late autumn to France where York and a strong
Norman delegation, with the earl of Shrewsbury, were instructed to treat for peace. In the autumn of 1443 Suffolk was
supporting the suggestion of the marriage of Henry to a French
princess, though he was against the king marrying one of
Armagnac's daughters. In the late summer of 1443 John
Wenlock was sent over to conduct preliminary negotiations.
Early in 1444 it was proposed that Suffolk should lead an embassy to France, but he excused himself on the ground of his
friendship with Dunois whose prisoner he had been after the
battle of Jargeau in 1429 and with Charles of Orléans as whose
custodian he had acted. He was, however, pressed by the
council (1 Feb. 1444) to go, and gave way, at the same time
guarding himself by the request that if negotiations did not end
satisfactorily, he should not have to bear the responsibility. On
11 February 1444 he went with Adam Moleyns, keeper of the
privy seal and dean of Salisbury, Richard Andrew, first warden
of All Souls (1438), later dean of York, Sir Robert Roos, Sir
Thomas Hoo and two esquires of the Chamber, Sir John Say,
and John Wenlock (later to aid the Yorkists), to negotiate
a peace with Charles VII, with the duke of Orléans assisting as
mediator. The embassy reached Harfleur on 15 March and
joined Charles of Orléans (who despite the absence of peace had
not returned to England) at Blois, and on 16 April arrived at
Tours where the French king and his party of ambassadors had
been waiting for them for a fortnight. On 17 April, in the company of Réné of Anjou, Charles of Anjou, and the duke of
Calabria, they presented themselves to Charles at Montils-les-

Tours. There the serious negotiations began: the princess for whom Suffolk had persuaded the English council to opt as Henry's bride was Réné's daughter Margaret, and the plan was being discussed in the autumn of 1443; Suffolk now saw her (4 May 1444) for the first time and was much attracted by her. On the actual terms a year later he stated that he informed the French of his instructions which were to claim, irrespective of the question of the French crown, Guienne, Normandy, and other territories, and it is thought that the question of Maine was raised at this meeting. The matter did not get very far. The French offers, he said, he did not consider serious enough for consideration. C. L. Kingsford was probably right in concluding that probably both parties avoided tacitly the more difficult issues, and, when they realized that agreement on a general peace was out of the question, 'fell back on the simple alternative of the marriage accompanied by a truce of two years'.[1] He might, however, have added that the English council was already determined to surrender the claim to the French crown, if suitable territories could be awarded to England: the claim and the territories were in point of fact interdependent, and in the end Suffolk was forced into being the agent by whom both were lost.

Réné of Anjou, king of Sicily, had for some time been considering a suitable marriage for Margaret. He had thought of the count of Charolais and of a son of the count of St. Pol. With the count of Nevers, also related to the duke of Burgundy, a provisional marriage contract had been signed in February 1443, but this was not to the taste of Charles VII, however much Philip of Burgundy may have liked it. The duke now viewed with suspicion the proposed marriage of Henry VI with Margaret and feared that Charles VII was plotting to give the English, in exchange for Normandy, a free hand in Holland and Zealand. The French, however, won: on 22 May Suffolk's embassy arranged a truce between Henry and the kings of France, Sicily, and Castile and a treaty followed arranging the details of Margaret's marriage to Henry. Réné had little to give by way of a dowry. He was determined not to surrender land in Anjou or Maine: the proffering of the islands of Majorca and Minorca over which he had merely a claim through his mother was a poor substitute for substantial territories or sums in specie;

---

[1] *Prejudice and Promise in Fifteenth-Century England*, p. 186.

but the English embassy were saved from getting back empty
handed and Margaret's expensive father could at least resor
to the clergy of Anjou, which granted a tenth and a half and
to his estates for an *aide* of 33,000 livres. The formal betrotha
took place on 24 May, and the truce began on the 28th. Suffol
reached London, to the tune of great rejoicing, on 27 June and
was made a marquess: in his absence, as a further mark o
favour, he was granted the wardship of Margaret Beaufort, the
duke of Somerset's infant daughter, who was later to be the
mother of Henry VII.

There was to be considerable delay before Margaret could
be brought to England, and Suffolk did not start his new mis
sion to fetch her until early in November. In the meantime
Henry had sent his envoys to express to Charles VII his satis
faction at the result of the Tours meeting and his desire to
develop the truce into a permanent peace. Charles replied in
a friendly way, promising to let Margaret go whenever the
English party could receive her. There is no warrant for the
story that he detained Margaret and declared that she could
not be released to Suffolk without ransom, whereupon the
latter was forced, in compliance with the demand, to buy her
out with the promise to concede Maine and Anjou: Gascoigne's
malicious interpretation of the delay experienced by Suffolk
will not bear examination. Soon after the meeting at Tours just
described both Charles VII and Réné of Anjou were involved
in war against the city of Metz. Réné owed the place large sums
of money and the citizens, taking matters into their own hands,
had pillaged the baggage train of Isabel of Anjou while on a
pilgrimage to St. Antoine, Pont-à-Mousson. For this Réné went
to war and persuaded Charles to assist. During the late autumn
and winter of 1444 there were 30,000 besieging Metz and it was
not till the beginning of March 1445 that their resistance ended
with a promise to return the baggage, to forgive the debt owed
by Réné, and to pay Charles VII 200,000 *écus d'or*. All this
meant that Charles and Réné could not arrive till the early part
of March 1445—though they had been waited for by Suffolk at
Nancy since the beginning of January and by Margaret since
early February. When they did finally arrive the actual marriage ceremony could be carried out. Suffolk stood proxy for
his king. It is sufficiently plain that no actual promise or agreement to surrender Maine, as he was to be charged in 1450 with

making, was ever entered into: none the less he and the English council which he represented had been put in a weak position by accepting Margaret while leaving the major question unsettled. Hoping optimistically to end the war, Henry had incurred liabilities that passed their imaginations.

Still, reconciliation was in the air. In parliament on 2 June 1445 Suffolk reported that a French embassy would shortly arrive to discuss the permanent peace that would replace the truce due to expire on 1 April 1446. He added that while he was in Normandy he had not discussed the treaty in any shape or form. His mission won general approval and there is no evidence to suggest that in 1445, at any rate, Gloucester was critical: as for the duke of York, his concurrence can be inferred from the fact that he had asked to negotiate for a French princess as a bride for his son.[1] On her arrival in England Margaret, as the result of the crossing, lay ill for several days in Southampton. The wedding could not be celebrated till 23 April, in the Benedictine abbey of Titchfield. She entered London from Eltham on 18 May and on Sunday, 30 May, was crowned at Westminster. The festivities were lavish: their scale and the contrast of the provision which parliament made for the maintenance of her estate with the actual resources of the crown are noteworthy. In 1433 the treasurer, Lord Cromwell, had put the net income deriving from the crown lands as no more than £8,399. 19s. 2d.; and it has been estimated that at this period the average amount of cash received by the Exchequer each year was not more than £9,907. 11s. 7d. None the less £5,129. 2s. 5d. was the figure provided for the expenses of bringing over the queen from France. Fifty-six ships were chartered to convey her, her household, and her escort which was to include five barons and baronesses, thirteen knights and forty-seven esquires, eighty-two yeoman, twenty sumptermen, and others, and expenses on the journey exceeded receipts by £500. In 1446 parliament fixed her dowry as £3,000 from the duchy of Lancaster (estates £2,000, cash annuity £1,000) and £3,666. 13s. 4d., the Southampton customs providing £1,000, the duchy of Cornwall £1,008. 15s. 5d., and the Exchequer £1,657. 17s. 11d.[2] This was the same as Queen Joan had

---

[1] Kingsford, *Prejudice and Promise*, p. 159.
[2] A. R. Myers, 'The Household of Queen Margaret of Anjou', *Bull. John Rylands Lib.*, xl (1957–8), 80.

received on her marriage to Henry IV and as Queen Catherine
had been assigned by the treaty of Troyes. A dowry of 10,000
marks seems not unsatisfactory: and indeed Margaret's income
for 31–32 Henry VI might appear to have exceeded this, since
the total receipts reached £7,563. 12s. 1d. Of this, however,
£2,805. 19s. 10½d. was arrears from former years, while many
items were not received until after Michaelmas 32 Henry VI.
The bulk of the arrears were in fact from the customs of Southampton.[1] The Lancaster revenues were firm: they came from
the honours of Tutbury, Leicester, and Kenilworth, from land
in the 'home counties' and the south of England: and to ensure
efficiency the receiver-general of the Queen's revenue, William
Cotton, was also receiver-general of the duchy, while the
auditors of the queen's household were also duchy officials. On
the other hand, the Exchequer source was far from satisfactory:
it has been pointed out that although it should have provided
the queen's household with £6,631. 11s. 8d. over four years
(28–32 Henry VI), during one single year, 1452–3, it provided
£1,037. 5s. 1d., mostly by tallies and assignments. The earldom,
shire, and lordship of Pembroke, granted to her in 1447, should
according to an inquisition of 20 May, 29 Henry VI, have produced a net income of £400. 2s. 8d. The queen lost it in the
Resumption of 1450 when it was granted to Jasper Tudor, earl of
Pembroke, and by 1452–3 at any rate, no revenues granted in
compensation for this had yet been received. Margaret, therefore, had to utilize every possible means to realize the little she
had been granted, for she was generous in her spending and
kept a large establishment. She rewarded her councillors and
officers liberally and did her utmost for them. The Bothe
(Booth) brothers, William and Lawrence, who had been her
chancellors, both reached the archbishopric of York, the former
in 1452, the latter in 1476, while at her intercession the clerical
members of her household were rewarded with prebends or
deaneries.

The French embassy arranged to follow Margaret arrived in
July 1445. A fortnight of meetings ended in nothing better than
an extension of the truce. The ambassadors came with the expectation that after the marriage England would undertake to
surrender Maine. It is possible that Henry VI himself went so

[1] A. R. Myers, 'The Household of Queen Margaret of Anjou', *Bull. John
Rylands Lib.*, xl (1957–8), 81–82.

far as to promise this. The instructions given by Réné of Anjou to his two envoys, Guillaume Cousinot and Jean Havart, on their return to England in October 1445, make it clear that the surrender had been discussed in July, and the two ambassadors brought letters from Charles VII and Réné to Henry, Margaret, and Suffolk urging this step as the best avenue to a permanent peace. On 17 December 1445 Queen Margaret wrote to Charles VII that she would do all she could to make Henry consent to the surrender. What methods she adopted are not known: but on 22 December Henry gave Charles VII a definite promise to give up the city and fortress of Le Mans and everything held by the English in Maine to Réné and Charles of Anjou before the end of April 1446. The French envoys, he said, had assured him that the French king considered this the best way of making peace, and he also desired to show favour to Queen Margaret who had asked him several times to surrender the country. On the basis of this promise the Anglo-French truce was extended till 1 April 1447. In writing thus, Henry did not wait for the decision of the council, and thereby placed Suffolk in a most difficult position. Suffolk preferred to negotiate from a position of strength, and the atmosphere in the intercourse between the two courts was totally different from that prevailing in the negotiations between the ambassadors. Throughout 1446 negotiations between the courts of France, Anjou, and Westminster continued without result, the suggestion being for a personal meeting between Henry and Charles VII, but Charles was beginning to think that despite Henry's promise, no result would be achieved, and that a renewal of the war was desirable. He would only consent to a meeting with Henry, before November 1447, if Henry fulfilled his promise to surrender Maine. In the winter renewed pressure was brought to bear upon Henry VI, and no progress was made save to secure a nine months' extension of the truce from 1 April 1447 to 1 January 1448; this permitted another French embassy to come over, and by 27 July, 1 May 1448 had been fixed as the date of Henry's visit to France, while Henry agreed to surrender Le Mans and Maine before 1 November 1447 provided that reasonable compensation was paid to the English commander and garrison in Maine. On 28 July Henry commissioned Matthew Gough and Fulk Eyton to receive Le Mans and Maine from the marquess of Dorset and hand them over to Charles VII.

Commissioners were appointed to arrange for the transference to the French: but then there happened a contretemps which displayed how strongly people felt about Maine. Dorset's lieutenant, Osbern Mundeford, declined, without special permission from his master Dorset, to hand over, and Dorset though commanded in plain and severe language by Henry VI, declined to do so. Meanwhile French forces were gathering round Le Mans which by February 1448 was practically in a state of siege. Only when the garrison said that it could hold out no longer was the promise to surrender carried out. Adam Moleyns and Sir Robert Roos arrived at Harfleur on 14 February to arrange the final handing over, and on 16 March Le Mans was surrendered to Charles VII, with agreements negotiated for the take-over of the other fortresses. Thereupon the Anglo-French truce was extended 15 March 1448 to 1 April 1450.

The arrival and establishment in a commanding position of the young queen altered the situation by reintroducing the court as the highest embodiment of English society. As an influence in politics it had been for long virtually in abeyance: only a few would remember the days of Queen Anne of Bohemia and Queen Isabel. Henry IV had been in poor health the latter part of his reign and his sons were not exactly harmonious: Henry V had been mostly absent on his campaigns and his brief married life was spent mainly abroad: he had yielded to his dark superstitious vein when he struck at his stepmother, Queen Joan, on the charge of practising magic against him. His was too intent, too dogmatic a nature to encourage joyous formality or to be amused by the intrigues of Sheen or Eltham. Even granted his love of aristocratic chivalry, he was too formidable a young man to ler others relax. Margaret energized, while slightly scarifying, the sticky and perplexed court of Henry VI and created her own community, most of all in the royal household. She had distinguished names among her personal attendants: Lady Scales, whose husband had fought well in the French wars and was to oppose Jack Cade's rebellion and to be killed at London in the Lancastrian cause; Lady Margaret Roos, the daughter of Lord Thomas de Roos, who was to marry Lord Botreaux (1458) and Lord Burgh (1464); Lady Isabel Dacre, the daughter of Thomas Lord Dacre, and Isabel Lady Grey, probably the wife of Sir Ralph Grey, one of her attendants; and among her ladies (*damicellis*) the wives of Sir

Robert Whittingham, usher of the king's chamber, who after Towton went into exile with Margaret in Scotland and France and died fighting for her at Tewkesbury; of Gilbert Parr who had been yeoman of the crown to Henry V and was an usher of the king's chamber; and of John Merston who had been treasurer of the king's chamber and keeper of the king's jewels since before 1445; besides the Angevin and other French ladies whom the queen brought with her. Her esquires included a Bourchier, a Roos, a Chichele (son of Robert the grocer and alderman), and a Stafford. Her steward was to be John Viscount Beaumont, constable of England, killed at Northampton fighting on the Lancastrian side (1460), her chancellor Laurence Booth the future archbishop of York, and her attorney-general the Northamptonshire lawyer Robert Tanfield. The best accountants of the duchy of Lancaster looked after her finances;[1] only her chamberlain, Sir John Wenlock of Someries, who had acted as usher of her chamber, was to turn his coat and prove for a time a distinguished servant of Yorkist interest (1455); yet fifteen years later Lord Wenlock, K.G., as he had become, went over to Warwick and, after accompanying his queen on her journey back to Weymouth, was killed at Tewkesbury in 1471.[2]

Margaret was to give her whole support to the duke of Suffolk who had coached her to the best of his ability and told her the little she knew about England; and Suffolk who could see far but never could resist the charm of great place and the lure of self-aggrandizement, both succumbed to, and used to the full, the confidence placed in him by the new régime. In the council he generally got his own way. He is described by Chastellain as like a second king 'menant François et Anglois à deux mains en coupple': but he was not above reckless suspicions and making charges against his opponents and—though this cannot be proved—it is more than likely that he poisoned the mind of Henry, never friendly to Gloucester, against his uncle, and suggested that he was plotting the king's overthrow. The train of events which he put on foot found its tragic ending in the arrest of Gloucester on 18 February 1447, and his death. Some reflections on the miserable story may be in place here.

---

[1] Myers, op. cit., pp. 47–54.
[2] See the biography, 'John Lord Wenlock of Someries', by J. S. Roskell, *Publ. Bedford Hist. Record Soc.* xxxviii (1958).

It does not matter very much how Gloucester died, and it is unlikely that fresh evidence will reveal the guilty. The chief point is that by the end of 1446 Gloucester had ceased to attend the council. Later chroniclers report formal accusations against him, but these are uncertain. We only know that he hid under a cloud since the autumn of 1445. In such cases it is the first step that counts. This had already been taken in the sorcery scare of the summer of 1441. Gloucester's position was seriously weakened by the trial of his wife, Eleanor Cobham, for being implicated in a case where two clerks were indicted on a charge of using magical arts against the life of the king. Before the ecclesiastical court Eleanor had to abjure her heresies and witchcraft, to undergo public penance, and be committed to custody for life. There is no evidence that the duke had anything to do with his wife's practices, which reflected a fashionable current interest in the occult and more suspect arts: but it has been noticed, with some relevance, that when in 1425 Gloucester had almost come to blows with Beaufort, one of the charges against him was that he had removed from custody a certain 'Frere Randolff' who had been imprisoned for treason. Randolph, a literary follower of Gloucester, was the friar who had acted in the same way as the clerks now charged, in the scandal implicating Queen Joan in 1419, and it would scarcely be forgotten that he had had the patronage of the duke.[1] Books on the borderland of science, astrology, and medicine were eagerly devoured by people of Gloucester's temperament and imagination, and if the duke himself had no responsibility for his wife's interest in Roger Bolingbroke, the Oxford clerk now accused, to bring the duchess to trial was a sure way of damaging his reputation. This was the reply of those supporting Beaufort when Gloucester attacked him for the liberation of the duke of Orléans in 1440. Gloucester had indeed concurred in the Angevin marriage. He had even delivered in parliament a speech thanking Suffolk for negotiating it: but this did not imply that he had forsaken his old advocacy of the war and of the maintenance of the English possessions in France. There is the testimony of Polydore Vergil to his speech in parliament urging that it was necessary to break the truce, which was, he argued, no more than a device to gain time and allow the forces of Charles VII to recoup themselves. Political realism

[1] K. H. Vickers, *Humphrey, Duke of Gloucester* (1907), p. 276.

had never been Gloucester's strong point: yet a French chronicler who could estimate the situation in 1446 shrewdly, even if retrospectively, said that later events supported Gloucester's determination to continue the war.

Before 1446 it is unlikely that Gloucester knew about the proposed surrender of Maine. It was important then for the success of the council's plan that he should be out of the way when Henry VI's support for it became known. There had to be no anti-French publicity: and the king had to be kept from listening sympathetically to his uncle: his mind had to be 'conditioned' so as to believe the worst about Gloucester. The sorcery trial was thus a not-too-distant preliminary to the charge of treason which Suffolk, along with Dorset, Grey, and the dean of Salisbury, Adam Moleyns, were to bring against Gloucester. By the late summer of 1445 the conditioning was done. When the French embassy appeared before the king on 15 July Henry openly showed his contempt for Gloucester, and Suffolk declared that what the duke said did not now matter, since the king had no longer any regard for him. Such animus, against a man who, despite his grave faults, had for years borne a heavy burden of responsibility for English policy in the council he so assiduously attended, implied further action. It was decided to summon him to answer accusations in a parliament at some place outside the sphere of his power, first Cambridge, but ultimately Bury St. Edmunds. A rumour was put about by Suffolk that a rising led by Gloucester might break out at any day and Bury was heavily guarded. None the less Gloucester obeyed the summons and unsuspectingly arrived in the town on the morning of 18 February, shortly afterwards to be put under arrest at his lodgings by a deputation of lords including the duke of Buckingham and the marquis of Dorset, Sir Ralph Butler (Lord Sudeley), and the high constable, Viscount Beaumont. The shock of the arrest brought on what appears to have been (on the medical evidence) a stroke, and after lying three days in a coma, the duke died (23 Feb. 1447). There is no reliable evidence that he was physically maltreated in any way: still less that he was murdered. His servants had been kept under arrest, and he knew what that implied. There was no hope of escape for him from a heavily guarded place like Bury, among the retainers of a hostile council, with nobody to rescue him. He had none of the bland effrontery that was to serve Edward IV on a not dissimilar occasion. He was an anachronism, the victim of his own florid and impetuous nature, standing for Henry V's ideals in an atmosphere of political hatred and aesthetic ridicule. In these hours nobody thought of the other Humphrey, the patron of learning, the employer of the simple scribe and the copyist, the lover of culture and the arts, the instigator of the new humanistic lectures at Oxford; only the monks of St. Albans remembered the man who had helped to enrich their library and was the literary ally of their abbot who now brought the duke's body from the Grey Friars at Babwell to the Saint's chapel in his abbey of St. Albans, where behind the high altar and under the splendid canopy the vault for his funeral had already been prepared in his lifetime.

It is seldom possible to see into the personal aspect of such events: the sorrows, the frustration, the human tragedy. The injustice of life had long weighed upon Charles of Orléans; but he, the poet of *amour courtois*, had at any rate found in England two ladies to comfort him for the absence of Bonne d'Armagnac his first wife whom he had married after Isabel of France, Richard II's widow, had died in childbirth (1409). While he was in the charge of Sir John Cornwall (later Lord Fanhope), living mainly at Ampthill in Bedfordshire, he formed a passion for Lady Arundel (Maud Lovell), the earl's second wife. The countess, who went to and fro between England and Normandy to join Bedford's court at Rouen, was almost certainly in England with her husband from November 1433 to May 1434. Arundel, now duke of Touraine, died in June 1435 and Maud Arundel survived him by only eleven months. The cryptograms in the verse Charles addressed to the duke of Bourbon make the identification clear, and the death of the countess 'at the manor of Non Chaloir' evoked some of his most melancholy verse. From this mood he was duly restored by the appearance of a new lady whose resemblance to 'Lady Beally' (Maud Arundel) was at first the chief attraction. This was Anne Moleyns, *née* Whalesborough, a connexion of Suffolk's by marriage, whose anagram is contained in the English poems of Charles (MS. Harleian 682). In the poem entitled 'Love's Renewal' in which he looks forward to a jubilee or celebration of his freedom (he had now passed from Suffolk's keeping at Ewelme and Wingfield into the care of Lord Cobham) he says that all his

occupation was to pray for his lady's soul and to write roundels
or ballades when other unhappy wooers asked him. He then
represents himself as falling asleep, and seeing a vision of Venus
reproaching him for his unnaturally dull life and bidding him
find another lady. And when he demurs, Venus insists and
produces a chariot bearing Dame Fortune and with her a lady
who astounds him by her likeness to the Countess.

> Allas quod y but lyvith my lady yet?
> Nys she not she that y se yondir sitt.
> I am so smyten with her goodlihede
> That next my lady but y love hir best
> I am not lijk to sett myn hert at rest.

But Anne who might, as he reproaches her, have been his 'lady
and maistres for ever mor' proved wilful and difficult: and soon
after he had met her he was taken from Cobham's charge and
banished to Stourton House in Wiltshire, where he could not
see her again. Late in 1440 he was released to claim his third
wife, Marie of Clèves.[1]

   The hard fate of Eleanor Cobham, Gloucester's wife, has
been traced in the poem 'Compleint against fortune',[2] in which
the 'playntiff', in prison, appeals against Fortune who answers
that sin is the cause and that adversity in this world may bring
salvation in the next.[3] This, which may have been written by
Sir Richard Roos, shows in the anagrams which it contains,
names prominent in the trial of the duchess, and may have been
written in 1441, during the actual course of the duchess's
trial, for Chichele and Kemp, who conducted the trial, appear,
along with Sir John Steward, Eleanor's first keeper, and Nicholas Wymbish, her cousin.[4] In prison Eleanor laments that her
friends have deserted her:

> Thei wold me onys not yeve a draught of drynke
> Ne say ffrend. Wilt thow aught with me
> The soth is said. Such frendship some doth synke
> That from his frend fleeth in adversite
> And will not [bide] / but in prosperite
> Such fayned frendis lord there be full many
> ffy on her flateryng / that are not worth a peny.

[1] Ethel Seaton, *Studies in Villon, Vaillant and Charles D'Orléans* (1957), ch. iii,
'Charles d'Orléans and two English Ladies'.   [2] Harleian MS. 7335.
[3] Printed by Ben Hammond in *Anglia*, xxxiii (1909), pp. i–vi.
[4] The identifications are by Dr. Ethel Seaton (MS.) to whose remarkable studies
of fifteenth-century anagrammatic poetry this section is indebted.

> I have no ffrende that will me now visite
> In prison here to comfort me of care
> Of sorow ynow I have of ioy but lite
>
> Fare wele my blys, and all my welfare
> To lette my sorowe / my wittes be all bare.
> Here is no man can tell my hevynesse
> Save oonly. Ekko that can bere mee witnesse.

Roos went on writing anagrammatic poems for Eleanor Cobham after Duke Humphrey's death. In January 1450 Henry Gray, Lord Powys, the husband of the duke's natural daughter, Antigone, died and his widow married Jean d'Amancier, master of horse to Charles VII. That meant that Eleanor had to say farewell to Antigone, and in a famous lyric she complains of death in life, heaviness and sorrow, comfort and remedy:

> This ys no lyf, alas, that y do lede;
>   it is but deth as yn lyves lyckenesse,
> Endeles sorow assured owte of drede,
>   Past all despeyre & owte of all gladenesse.
> Thus well y wote y am Remedylesse,
>   for me nothyng may comforte nor amende
> Tyl deith come forthe and make of me an ende.[1]

Sir Richard Roos, a king's knight for twenty years, whose family was so closely identified with the queen's struggle, was in Edward IV's reign (probably he was captured at Towton in 1461) imprisoned at Windsor Castle and from prison wrote, in 1468–9, verses to John Vere, thirteenth earl of Oxford (who later was to defend St. Michael's Mount and to suffer long incarceration in the castle of Hamme) containing a stirring appeal to Lancastrians to rise and join Warwick's conspiracy: a poem full of double acrostic anagrams which Vere would evidently be able to decode, giving the names of influential or useful Lancastrians.[2]

To return to Suffolk. Is it then possible to concur in the view that Suffolk must be 'held innocent of any direct guilt for Gloucester's death'?' He had prepared the ground for the

---

[1] *Secular Lyrics of the XIVth and XVth Centuries*, ed. R. H. Robbins (1952), no. 165.
[2] 'The Prisoner to Vere'. Printed by Todd in his *Illustrations . . . of Gower and Chaucer*, 1810; and by E. E. Piper (from Todd's text) in *Philological Quarterly*, v. (1926), 331–5.   [3] Kingsford, op. cit., p. 164.

removal of his chief opponent, he had seen to it that the new queen should hear no criticism of his policy in the council. He was now establishing a personal ascendancy of a highly dangerous kind. Between 1445 and 1450 he had become chamberlain of England, captain of Calais, warden of the Cinque Ports, constable of Dover Castle, chief steward of the duchy of Lancaster north of the Trent, chief justice of Chester, Flint, and north Wales, besides being steward and surveyor of mines for the whole country. In 1448 he reached his climax and was made duke. He had curtained the queen from any criticism either of himself or her. Sir John Fastolf, governor of Anjou and Maine, captain of Le Mans under Bedford, returned to England in 1440. He, as the author of the memorandum on the position in France after the treaty of Arras, had no reason to favour the surrender of Maine: but as a Suffolk neighbour of Suffolk, he had much to say about Suffolk and his council in East Anglia; in 1455 he drew up a bill of complaints against the crown (*Billa de debitis Regis*): he complained that he had been:

vexed and troubled seth he came last into this lande by the myght and power of the Duke of Suffolk and by the labour of his counseill and servaunts in divers wyses, as in grete oppressions, grevous and outrageous amercienants and manye grete horrible extorcions, as it may appere more pleynly by a rolle of articles thereuppon made, the damage of which extenden to the somme of V m marc. Item the seyd Fastolf hath be gretely damaged and hurt by the myght and power of the seyd Duc of Suffolk and his counseill, in disseising and taking awey a maner of the seyd Fastolf, called Dedham, in the counte of Essex, to the value of C marks of yerly rent which was halden from the seyd Fastolf by the terme of iii yere day and more, to his grete hurt, with CC marks in costs exspended in recouvere of the same, the some in all V c marks.[1]

Fastolf professed himself frequently 'damaged' by the duke's officers of the hundred of Lothingland, both by undue amercements and the distraint of cattle at Cotton and by the officers of Cossey.[2] A number of these grievances were, naturally enough, 'land agents' points' which Fastolf would be quick enough to seize upon; and often he barked up the wrong tree; but in the Suffolk ménage the knight was confronted with a business-like council, quick to note any weakness in the title-deeds of any places to which it was thought they had any claim.

When the Suffolk esquire John Lyston received 700 marks damages for disseisin against Sir Robert Wingfield, and Sir Robert eventually got it back from the treasurer of England by having Lyston outlawed on another charge in Nottinghamshire and securing the confiscation of his goods, 'here is great hevyng and shovyng be me lord of Suffolk and all his counsell for to aspye hough this mater kam aboute'.[1] The 'heaving and shoving' was characteristic of a time when justice was being perverted and competition for lands and rents was made the fiercer by researches of the lawyers and the tactics adopted by the councils (estate and finance committees) of the more notable land-owners. It was this type of 'oppression' involving, lower down the scale, the employment of ruffians and toughs that raised the indignation of a great many of the gentry, and in Kent was to result, among other factors, in the rebellion of Cade. The townsman and the well-to-do peasant were being given a lesson in the power and effectiveness of force. They could see quarrels like those of the Courtenay and Bonville families in Devon or of Archbishop Kemp and Sir William Plumpton in the north, or (a little earlier) the defiance of the bishop of Durham by his senior tenants, men like Sir William Eure, who refused to accept his palatine jurisdiction. In all cases the king's law meant nothing, and prestige depended on the size and efficiency of a private army. This state of things, to which reference will again shortly be made, is the background to the struggle of interests between York and Suffolk. York returned home from Normandy in 1445, complaining that he had not been paid the whole £20,000 due to him for his last year and £18,000 for his fourth year. All through his governorship he had been kept down to the minimum allowed him, and had the greatest difficulty in obtaining payment of that. Yet he probably wanted a renewal which he did not succeed in getting. The English council had appointed (1445) Sir Thomas Hoo to succeed the chancellor of Normandy, and Hoo, one of Suffolk's men, was clearly unfriendly to York. Again, a Somerset was moved into York's place. John Somerset's brother Edmund, marquess of Dorset, was appointed to succeed York in Normandy. He arrived (1448) during the truce, promised that he was to enjoy the £20,000 allowance only if war broke out. War was not officially reopened until the beginning of August 1449,

---

[1] *Paston Letters*, ii. 47.

when the Exchequer made payments to captains embarking from England, but no payment of the £20,000 to the king's lieutenant can be traced and the reinforcements leaving this country could expect little in the way of subsidies from England.[1] English subsidies could make all the difference to the ability of the Norman treasurers to make ends meet, but the state of the Exchequer made them impossible now, and the advance wages of newly indentured troops was the demand which it was mainly forced to meet. In these conditions of parsimony, the queen's penury and the complaints and representations from Normandy met with little response from the English council. There was no sympathy with York or with the group of English and Norman soldiers and ecclesiastics constituting his advisory council.

During the truce negotiations conducted by Suffolk there was little sign of opposition between the two parties, and Suffolk even assisted York to find a French princess for Edward earl of March: but the underlying division was made manifest by the accusations levelled at York by Adam Moleyns, bishop of Chichester, after his return from France, against which he had to defend himself in parliament. This he did successfully with the help of Norman financial officers who came over specially for the purpose, retorting that Moleyns had bribed soldiers of the Norman garrison to complain that he had defrauded them of their pay. If Moleyns was able to rebut the charge, the council still found it awkward to have the legitimate heir to the throne and the greatest landowner in the country as an opponent. To get him away York was created the king's lieutenant in Ireland (9 Dec. 1447), an appointment which he did not take up for two years. By this time Charles VII had sent his armies into the field (June 1449) and had declared war (July 1449) despite the fact that the English commanders had obeyed Henry VI's command to evacuate the garrisons in Maine. But this evacuation was rendered politically fruitless owing to the seizure by François de Surienne of St. James de Beuvron and other forces placed along the Breton border and by the sack of the town of Fougères. This provocative action had been followed by the French capture of Pont de l'Arche, Gerberoy, and Conches.

[1] In July 1446 York was assigned sums amounting to £28,000 to cover what was described as a 'loan' to the king, he having agreed to 'remit' the remaining £12,666: E. 404/62/224; E. 403/763.

The situation immediately after the capture of Fougères when the lords were discussing in parliament the worsening situation and how to meet the needs of France and Gascony is depicted in the report of a debate which has come down to us in a seventeenth-century transcript.[1] The parliament in which the discussion may have taken place opened at Westminster on 12 February 1449. On 30 May 1449 it was prorogued for the Whitsunday festival until 16 June, when it was ordered to assemble at Winchester. It seems likely that the report is the précis of a debate made specially for the information of the commons who needed to hear the views of the lords on the best means of supplying men and arms to France. Somerset had reminded parliament during February, through the abbot of Gloucester, that the truce was drawing to an end and that provision must be made to avoid 'the shamefull losse [of Normandy] the which God ever defende'. In this debate the first speaker, Lord Stourton, instead of discussing the imposing of taxes or the tightening up of the machinery of collection, spoke for the appointment of commissioners of oyer and terminer to establish better order before anything could be done. They were to inquire 'of murders and Ryottes agaynst the peace'; 'also of liveries and that every sheriff should certify to the commissioners the names, knights, and esquires and all other men of might within his shire that they may know whom they may empanel, such as be sufficient'. Lords Sudley and Cromwell, one a strong governmental supporter, the other an ally of York, agreed in thinking that the first task was to get agreement among the lords, for the raising and empanelling of groups or bodies of men might be used for fighting in England rather than abroad: it was important to secure pacification at home first. The bishops of Norwich and Coventry and Lichfield (Chester) concurred in the need for securing justice, but thought that only half the shire archers should be sent abroad with the available grants. The bishop of Chichester was the only one who made a strictly business reply to the question, urging contributions from

[1] A. R. Myers, 'A Parliamentary Debate of the Mid-fifteenth Century' in *Bull. John Rylands Lib.* xxii (1938), 388 f. One may agree with Professor J. S. Roskell ('The problem of the attendance of the Lords in Medieval Parliaments', *Bull. Inst. Hist. Res.* xxix (1956), 188 n.) in thinking it to be a discussion in the council, held during the period of the parliament, for 'ten of the fourteen lords taking part in the debate had been present in a single meeting of the Council only 5 days before parliament was to be opened at Winchester'.

royal grantees and annuitants. The treasurer (Lumley) thought
that the views expressed in the discussion should be referred to
the commons who might be impressed with the urgent nature
of these requirements and make a grant. The noteworthy point
about this discussion is the priority given to the problems of
order. They met to decide whether to ask for subsidy: they
decided to do so, but not without the burning issue of local
order being raised by certain lords.

If this was in 1449, it was only next year that the same difficulty raised its head in Norfolk and Suffolk. The council decided
to take Stourton's advice and to send the justice Yelverton into
Norfolk, at the same time to take strong measures against Sir
Thomas Tuddenham and John Heydon, supporters of Suffolk,
who had, like Lord Moleyns, been tyrannizing the county and
displaying contempt for the impartial processes of law. On the
commission of oyer and terminer was, unluckily, a judge favourable to Tuddenham and Heydon, and though Yelverton at the
sitting of the court rebuked his colleague, it was no good.
Justice Prisot refused to let the court sit at Norwich, which was
too unfavourable to the two magnates, so it was adjourned to
Walsingham, where their supporters were stronger. At Walsingham, Heydon and Tuddenham had collected a formidable
body of supporters and 400 horsemen rode to the court attending on them. The judge would allow no advocates to speak for
the complainants. The state of things prevailing in 1452 when
the duke of Norfolk had to go down to inquire into 'the great
riots, extortions and horrible wrongs and hurts' shows how
inadequate was the protection afforded to the law-abiding: and
men were terrified by the threats of what could be done to
them after authority had been invoked.[1]

The lords in the debate reported heard François de Surienne's
account of his attack on Fougères written in a letter to Suffolk.
'The whiche was thought right notabley wrytten.' If they
approved this action, they were soon to be disillusioned. At the
end of October 1449 Rouen fell to Charles VII, and in the
early part of 1450 the defeat of Formigny sealed the fate of
Normandy. The news was received with anger and alarm.
Lumley resigned the treasurership in September and Moleyns
found it necessary to give up the privy seal in December.

---

[1] See the instances collected by H. S. Bennett, *The Pastons and their England*,
pp. 18 f.

Parliament assembled on 6 November, but it was not till after an incident had taken place at Westminster on the 28th, that charges were brought against Suffolk: this first time for plotting, with William Tailboys, the death of Lord Cromwell. Suffolk and Tailboys both denied the accusation brought by Cromwell, but in the recess Adam Moleyns was murdered by sailors at Portsmouth after having confessed to the misdeeds of Suffolk, and on 22 January, at the reassembly of parliament, Suffolk found it necessary to make a defence, recalling his own services and the services of his family both at home and in the French war. He referred to 'odious and horrible langage that renneth thorough your lande'. In so doing he admitted that he was the object of slander and misconception, and this fact was used three days later by the commons in a petition that he should, on that account, be placed in custody. The lords consulted with the people and declined to commit, on the ground that there were no specific charges. This gave the commons the chance for which they were waiting to present a formal petition of indictment (7 Feb.) in eight articles, the chief of which was that in July 1447 Suffolk had conspired with the French embassy for an invasion of England (on 28 Jan. they had affirmed that he had fortified Wallingford Castle, as a 'place of refuge and of sucour' for the invader), and the deposition of Henry VI in favour of his own (Suffolk's) son John who was to be affianced to Margaret Beaufort, 'presumyng and pretendyng her to be next enheritable to the Corone of this youre Reame'.[1] The commons alleged that he had taken money to advise the release of Orléans and had got him 'to excite and moeve' Charles, 'callyng hym self Kyng of Fraunce' to reopen the war, with the result that the earl of Shrewsbury and Lord Fauconberg had been taken prisoner; that he had promised the delivery of Maine and Anjou to Charles 'without the assent, avyse or knowyng of other youre ambassiatours' which would be the chief means whereby the duchy of Normandy would be lost; that he had given to Dunois and other ambassadors in July 1447 information about the decisions of the English council and had disclosed to the enemy the nature of the English defences; that for money he had prevented English armies going to Normandy and Guienne, and that he had failed to comprise old friends of this country like the king of Aragon or the duke of

[1] *Rot. Parl.* v. 177.

Brittany in the truces. Nearly a month elapsed before Suffolk was called to answer the charges. The king had decided that the case should be put in respite for a period. In the meantime the commons had thought up other accusations of a more domestic and administrative kind, which they presented on 9 March—malversation while in office, embezzlement of money, misappropriation of taxes granted, and so forth. Two of them are of special interest: one complaining of the action of Suffolk in prevailing upon the sheriff of Lincolnshire not to serve writs of *exigas* against William Tailboys sued out by 'dyvers wymmen' for the deaths of their husbands, and then persuading the king to grant a pardon to the sheriff for taking no action, though he was liable to 'great amercements for the said embezzling'. The other, where a sheriff was again involved, was the charge that Suffolk had controlled the appointment of the sheriffs for many years, some for 'lucre of good' (money payments made to him), some 'to be appliable to his entent and commaundement, to fulfylle his desires and writynges for such as hym liked'. Those who would not be 'of his affinity' in their counties were set aside, and business that he favoured was 'furthered and spedde'

many of your true Lieges by his myght, and helpe of his adherentes disherited, empoverished and distroied, and therby he hath purchased many grete possessions by mayntenaunce, and doon grete outragious Extorsions and Murdres; Mansleers, Riottours and comon openly noysed mysdoers, seyng his grete rule and myght in every part of this your Reame, have drawen to hym and for grete good to hym yeven, have been mayntened and supported in suppressyng of justice, and to open lettyng of execution of your lawes, to the full hevy discomfort of the true subgettes of this youre Reame.[1]

Suffolk, as he had done in the first instance, denied both sets of charges: on the treasonable action in the first set of articles the king held him 'neither declared nor charged', i.e. was not prepared to accept them as a true bill of indictment. On the second, 'touchyng mesprisions which be not crymynall', the king without reference to the lords or the judges banished Suffolk from the country for five years (from 1 May); he must not go to Lancastrian France or any other of his lordships. To preserve their rights to judge Suffolk as peers, the lords, none of whom concurred in the sentence, asked that it should be enrolled

[1] *Rot. Parl.* v. 181.

on the parliament roll. Henry had undoubtedly saved Suffolk's life by an action of his prerogative. For, given the temper of the commons the duke would almost certainly have been found guilty on the first set of articles, had there been a formal trial. How much he had promised in France in 1447 we are unlikely to know. The charges about his son and the allegations about the fortification of Wallingford Castle seem hardly likely; on the other hand, the non-criminal charges may have a firmer foundation, though the most damning of them, that of tampering with elections to the shrievalty, did not appear to contemporaries to have the significance we might attach to it today. But his association with Tailboys has a sinister sound. William Tailboys of Kyme, a powerful gangster who sat for Lincolnshire, was sent to the Tower at the request of the commons and had to pay £3,000 for his attack on Lord Cromwell. He had a feud with Lords Willoughby of Eresby, Cromwell, and Welles, an echo of which is in the letter he wrote to his other protector, Lord Beaumont, professing himself ready to serve Beaumont's interest. On 24 August 1451 he and nineteen others of the Kyme faction were outlawed for the murder of John Saunders some years previously. That did not affect his activities. In October 1455 and in January 1458 he joined Queen Margaret and was knighted for his conduct at St. Albans (17 Feb. 1461). Edward IV's government attainted him and in the end, after Hexham, he was caught hiding in Redesdale with 3,000 marks of Lancastrian money in his possession. He was beheaded at Newcastle on 20 July 1464.

Suffolk spent six weeks at Wingfield before leaving for France. The epistle he wrote to his son John (who was to be an even greater menace to peaceful possession and good government in East Anglia than his father) has been described as a 'noble and touching letter of farewell'. It counselled devotion to God and loyalty to the king, virtues not very prevalent in high places round about 1450; a pious and conventional piece of advice which may be compared and contrasted with Sir Philip Sydney's letter to his son a hundred or more years on in a humaner age. On 30 April Suffolk set sail southward for France, but when in the Straits of Dover his ships were intercepted by the *Nicholas of the Tower* and other vessels which were expecting him. The next day he was put aboard a rowing boat and beheaded, 'the body being thrown on to the beach at

Dover', where it lay until the king had it taken up and buried at Wingfield. By whose machinations Suffolk met his end is uncertain. Bishop Adam Moleyns was treated as a 'traitor' likewise, but in this case there is a possibility that Suffolk was caught by a west country pirate determined to exact a ransom which the duke would not pay: upon his refusal, and as Suffolk was now universally detested, he could safely be disposed of. He was a valuable prize, worth waiting for off the coast. Suffolk was the shrewd organizer of a faction which destroyed the reputation of the council for equitable government: he became the symbol of influence and excessive territorial power. But he was capable of devotion and loyalty, and in his poem describing 'how ye lover is sette to serve ye floure', he narrates his capitulation to the young queen:

> Myn hert ys set, and all myn hole entent,
> To serve this flour in my most humble wyse
> As faythfully as can be thought or ment,
> Wythout feynyng or slouthe in my servyse;
> For wytt the wele, yt ys a paradyse
> To se this floure when yt begyn to sprede,
> Wyth colours fressh ennewyd, white and rede.[1]

Suffolk's death was the signal for further violence. On 29 June 1450 Bishop Ayscough of Salisbury, well known to be a friend of Suffolk, was dragged from the chancel at Edington, where he was saying mass, and murdered on a nearby hill. Ayscough had been bishop some twelve years. He had been a canon of Lincoln before his consecration to Salisbury, and had served as one of the chaplains in the royal household. He had married Henry VI and Margaret at Titchfield on 21 April 1445 and had served as one of the bishops who examined Eleanor Cobham for heresy. Gascoigne said of him: 'he was killed then because he was the confessor of Henry VI and did not remedy the defects around the king, nor depart from the king because these were not remedied' and later, 'when the community of England in different places rose against the ecclesiastics', Gascoigne held that the contempt and hatred the prelates were in arose 'because they do not provide examples of good life nor do they preach to the people, but collect money and do not visit in their churches nor display hospitality'.

[1] *Secular Lyrics of the XIVth and XVth Centuries*, ed. R. H. Robbins, no. 188.

Ayscough, he implies, was a court, not a diocesan bishop. He was an absentee and a member of a disliked administration.[1] There was more in it than that. The bishops of Salisbury dominated their cathedral and city, which by the agreement of 1306 in the term of Simon of Ghent had been forced to recognize his claim to the lordship of the soil and the complete jurisdiction of his court. The struggle between the citizens of Salisbury and their bishop over the position he claimed flared up several times in the middle ages, and was to break out with particular violence under Ayscough's successor, Richard Beauchamp. It was evidently boiling up now, and Bishop Ayscough was unpopular in the city: his persecutors are alleged to have been led by a butcher of Salisbury. Ayscough and his dean, Gilbert Kymer, along with others, blamed popular preachers: 'if preachers had not been, people would not have risen against Churchmen.' It is worth recalling that the Lollard preacher, Richard Wyche, was vicar of the Winchester College living of Harmondsworth where serious opposition of the tenants against their ecclesiastical landlords occurred from time to time.[2] It can hardly have been a coincidence that it was at Edington in 1428 that a lay revolt of parishioners took place against the offerings demanded by the clergy at occasional services. In June that year Bishop Neville had before him in the chapel of Ramsbury six parishioners who, on the Sunday before Whitsun, had assembled at the cross at Tinhead and there pledged themselves not to offer more than a penny at weddings, churchings, and burials. The 'laudable custom of making offerings', as it was later called, had been forbidden in a constitution of Bishop Richard Poore: but in most parishes such offerings had become a regular practice, and now had the authority of the Church lawyers behind them.

Too much should not be read into these local cases of indiscipline, for events were maturing on a larger scale. On the day Ayscough died the rebels of Kent were marching to Blackheath, their rendezvous. The revolt associated with Jack Cade differed greatly from the rising of 1381 except for the East Anglian section of that movement; for it had respectable upper middle-class support and was aimed less at landowners as such than at

---

[1] *Loci e Libro veritatum*, pp. 42–43.

[2] It is called 'rebellio tenencium . . . pro operibus custumabilibus' in 1461: Winchester College Account Roll, 1461–2.

officials found to be oppressive, particularly when they were members of the royal household and magnates who abused their power: most of all against the sheriff of Kent, William Crowmer, who had married the daughter of Sir James Fiennes, the hated Lord Saye and Sele who was treasurer the year the revolt broke out. Crowmer was sheriff in 1444–5 and again in 1449. Both father-in-law and son-in-law had to be put in ward to protect them against the royal army when it turned mutinous: they were pulled out by the rebels, and the heads of both murdered men were displayed on poles on London Bridge. If Crowmer's widow lost husband and father together, she had the satisfaction of marrying Sir Alexander Iden, who caught Cade in his hiding and killed him. These grisly events and the bloodshed in London itself might scarcely have happened had the government acted in a more determined manner and at a crucial moment had been upheld by its own troops.

With Saye and Crowmer were joined, in the propaganda the rebels uttered against Henry VI's advisers, Thomas Daniel and John Trevelyan. Daniel, a Cheshire man from Frodsham, a knight of the shire for Cornwall (1445–6) and Bucks. (1447 and 1449), was a member of the royal household, surveyor of the king's forests in Cheshire (1444), and chamberlain of Chester (1445). He had various grants as *armiger regis* in Westmorland, particularly at Troutbeck.[1] Politically ambidexterous, ready to receive money from both sides, in 1447 he was opposing the duke of Suffolk at a time when he was sheriff of Norfolk and Suffolk, but by 1449 he was regarded as an adherent of the duke, and was a special object of enmity to Cade's followers. In October 1451 it was proposed to indict him for treason and felony, but by November he had been pardoned. A Lancastrian at heart, he survived the 1455 crisis and continued to hold Castle Rising (to which he was appointed, 1448), while his brother-in-law John Howard, later duke of Norfolk, was always ready to put in a word for him at an awkward moment. Attainted in 1461 he got his lands back in 1472 and ended his days in Ireland. Trevelyan the Cornishman from Restormel (the 'Cornish Chough' of Cade's satire), who sat in parliament first for Huntingdon (1442 and 1447) and then for Cornwall (1453 and 1454), was equally a member of the household. A yeoman of the crown and (1442) steward of the duchy of Cornwall in

[1] *History of Parliament, 1439–1509*, Biographies (1936), p. 254.

Cornwall, keeper of Trematon Castle, he was denounced in parliament (Dec. 1450) and in April 1451 ordered to be indicted, but by March 1452 had reached security and was regranted the office of armourer of the Tower (1453, the first grant being in October 1446). A staunch Lancastrian Cornish under-sheriff (1459–60), he held several administrative commissions in his county, and on 10 June 1460, when the earls landed at Sandwich, Trevelyan was sent to Cornwall to imprison all who adhered to the duke of York. When Edward IV was established he was attainted, but received a pardon (June 1462); was ordered to be arrested (May 1463) but was pardoned again (14 July 1468); and raised a third pardon from the Yorkists after the period of the Readeption. Daniel was slippery; Trevelyan more constant, but evidently regarded by the Yorkists as useful in spite of his sympathies. The rebels also included in their list of 'traitors' Sir John Fastolf as John Payn, writing in 1465 to John Paston, recalled. In the revolt, Fastolf sent Payn to Blackheath, to ascertain the 'articles' for which the 'comens of Kent' had marched to London; and the messenger was announced by a herald at all quarters of the field as a spy sent by the 'grettyst traytor that was in Yngelond or in Fraunce, ... oone Syr John Fastolf, knyght, the whech mynysshed all the garrisons of Normaundy and Manns and Mayn, the whech was the cause of the lesyng of all the Kyngs tytyll and ryght of an herytaunce that he had by yonde see'. Fastolf, as 'the captain' (Cade) added, had bought a home in Southwark and filled it with soldiers back from Normandy and with habiliments of war, 'to destroy the comens of Kent whan that they come to Southewerk'. Payn was made to fight on the rebels' side, but not before he had brought Fastolf the articles and had advised him 'to put a wey all his abyllyments of were and the olde sawdiors'.[1] The charge of minishing the garrisons is scarcely one which Fastolf would have recognized. The revolt must have epitomized the grievances—administrative, social, financial, and economic —which were on the lips of a great many ordinary people. It may have been difficult in sober fact to connect the parlous position abroad with the breakdown of order and government

---

[1] *Paston Letters*, ii. 153–4. Payn lost many clothes and valuables and was eventually arrested on the in ormation of the bishop of Rochester at the queen's command and put in the Marshalsea. He was released at the intercession of his wife and a cousin.

at home: but it was easy to hold up to obloquy certain prominent personalities who seemed responsible for both, and to contrast them with their predecessors. A poem directed against
William Booth, Queen Margaret's chancellor:

God keep our King—ay and guide him by grace,
Save him from Suffolk and from his foes all;
The Pole is so parlous men for to pass,
That few can escape it of the bank riall
But set under sugar he showeth them gall;
Witness of Humphrey, [Gloucester] Henry [Beaufort] and John
  [Duke of Bedford]
Which of late were alive and now they be gone[1]

and when no remedy save force was forthcoming, and that
force had failed, it was natural to fall back upon the *deus ex
machina* who had been watching events from the Dublin Pale.

The recall of the duke of York had been mentioned in Cade's
propaganda and Cade had himself used the name Mortimer. It
was unwise (though very natural) that he should return,
landing at Beaumaris in Anglesey during August and marching
at the head of 4,000 troops to London. The threat provoked the
government to recall Somerset from France and make him
constable of England. York's coming in a Mortimer context
made it appear that the throne was being challenged. In the
recall was the Lancastrian reply to York's claim, for Somerset,
nearest of kin to Henry VI, claimed through his grandfather
John of Gaunt, *fourth* son of Edward III, while York's claim was
on his father's side from Edmund, duke of York, the fifth son of
Edward III, if through his mother he was descended from
Philippa, daughter of Lionel duke of Clarence, the third son
of Edward III. But the duke did not put it forward now; he
reserved it for the emergency of 1460 when the *coup d'état* of
June placed the earl of Warwick in charge of the king's person
and the Yorkists in charge of the administrative offices. He
came now as a reformer, though the majority of the baronage
did not believe it and regarded him as a usurper. The queen
had no doubt why he came and threw her influence on to the
side of Somerset. When York was granted an interview by
Henry in September he assured the king of his loyalty but
pressed upon him certain reforms which the king declared his
intention of submitting to a committee. Parliament had been

[1] C. L. Kingsford, *Contemporary History in Contemporary Poetry* (1913), p. 34.

summoned and there was some incentive for preparing at any rate the draft of a report which might be conceded by the council. Nothing emerged from the king's suggestion, and parliament, which met on 6 November 1450, was mainly concerned with putting into effect the Resumption Act passed in the 1449–50 assembly and with providing for a fixed and regular income for the household. The commons in this measure showed themselves favourable to York's cause by the election of Sir William Oldhall, the Norfolk landowner, as Speaker.

In 1450 a Speaker favourable to the duke might go in peril of his life, and Oldhall who had been on the duke's council in Normandy and was his chamberlain, had more powerful connexions than had the unhappy William Tresham who only two months before the parliament of 1450 met had been brutally murdered by a gang of desperadoes at Thorpland Close in Milton when on his way from his Northamptonshire manor of Sywell to join the duke in obedience to a summons from him. In his widow's petition for redress[1] it was stated not only that the assassins had worked out Tresham's movements with exactitude, knowing exactly where her husband would be at a given moment, but that the gang had terrorized the coroner's jury and charged them on pain of their lives to give a verdict of suicide. Nobody had dared to arrest the malefactors or issue any writ against them, and it was now requested that the guilty parties be tried in Northamptonshire and that the sheriff should empanel a jury, ensure their presence in court, and return the writs addressed to him under payment of £200 for each default. As the chief organizer of the murder Isabel Tresham indicated Simon Norwich 'late of Bryngherst in the shire of Rutland, Squyer'. Norwich, cousin and heir of a wealthy Northamptonshire clerk, Richard Holt, succeeded to his various properties in 1452, so despite the royal assent to the petition, no action can have followed. From another source, William of Worcester, it is clear that the murder was organized by Lord Grey of Ruthin. It is therefore significant that the actual murderers bore Welsh names. Such a petition would not have been put forward to commons unfavourable to the duke; and the commons themselves 'exhibited' a petition asking for the removal from the royal presence of a considerable list of persons they named, including the duke of Somerset; Alice

[1] *Rot. Parl.* v. 211–13.

duchess of Suffolk, William Booth, bishop of Chester, Sir John Sutton, Lord Dudley, Thomas Daniel, John Trevelyan (both noticed above), the abbot of St. Peter's, Gloucester, and others, including Thomas Kent, clerk of the council, Thomas Hoo, Lord Hastings, and Sir Thomas Stanley. These lords, royal knights, were not only to be elongated from the court, but to forfeit their lands and tenements. The king's reply was non-committal: to profess that he knew no cause for such treatment, but to agree, subject to excepting the lords from the list as well as a few unspecified persons who normally were in attendance upon the king's person. The remainder should 'absente theym frome his high presence and from his Court for the space of an hoole yeer', during which time they could be sued for any misconduct they might have committed, though if war broke out the king could require their services.

The commons had reacted strongly to the financial position during the years immediately before the Cade revolt. The problem of raising an adequate supply of earmarked funds for the expenses of the household was no new one, but further measures of appropriation for the household, and on the issues of wardship, marriages, and vacant temporalities, were taken in the parliament of 12 February 1449. The normal grant was cut down to a half tenth and fifteenth less half the allowance for impoverished towns, which stood at £6,000; and the persistent agitation of the commons for an act of resumption led to a dissolution on 16 July 1449. The next parliament was the one that carried out the impeachment of Suffolk. In this assembly a new kind of household appropriation was drafted at the petition of the commons, detailing individual items to be derived from specified farms and fee-farms throughout England and Wales, from the ulnage, the customs and subsidies at the ports, and from other sources, totalling £11,002. 6s. 1d. a year, to go entirely to the current expenses of the king's household.[1] This proposal was followed by an extensive petition for resumption, which held out hope of some relief from the direct taxation, recently calculated at a complete tenth and fifteenth, every two years since 1429. Such a measure, if put into effect, would help to remedy the very real grievances about purveyance. That the resumption had been eagerly canvassed can be seen from

[1] B. P. Wolffe, 'Acts of Resumption in the Lancastrian Parliaments', *Eng. Hist. Rev.* lxxiii (1958) pp. 596–7.

the complaints made, while parliament was yet sitting, that the royal ministers were preventing the resumption being drafted while they purported to carry out the demands of parliament.[1] Rattled by the charges against Suffolk, the council, Cromwell, Say, Beauchamp, Sudeley and others, were forced to advise a limited amount of concession to the resumption demand. The petition for a resumption of all grants made since the reign began (1 Sept. 1422) along with fifteen modifying clauses was assented to by the king. Henry reserved the right to add any exemptions he thought necessary. In effect 186 provisos of exemption were added to the roll. This, it has been claimed, was not an excessive number, given the fact of the number of royal grants recorded since the beginning of the reign. None the less what the persons enjoying the royal favour gave up was 'only a fraction of what they retained'. The household men gave up only what they had agreed among themselves and with the king to surrender, and Cromwell, Say, Sudeley, and other chief officials, were given exemption in the widest possible terms.[2] Yet even if the act had not done what the commons hoped, it had put the officials on the alert, especially when it induced them to surrender their life grants and instead to have them converted into leases of ten, twelve, or twenty-five years. Against such half-hearted policy by the government York had some reason to protest, and his criticisms emboldened the advocates of resumption to submit again the petition accepted at Leicester in the spring of 1450, but with a very careful revision of its wording. To the new act the 186 provisos of exemption did not apply: there were forty-three, framed on general rather than personal lines. As a general result of the act, a considerable measure of control over the endowed revenue of the crown took place; at the same time the Reading Parliament of 1453, one especially generous to the king, endowed the royal family with the best of the resumed estates, and in that year Queen Margaret received permanent endowment of other lands in part satisfaction of her dower.[3] The persistence of the commons in this matter of resumption indicates their concern for a more adequate revenue from the crown lands.

After 1450 the political struggle was between York and Somerset representing the Beaufort party. In his two protecto-

[1] Wolffe, op. cit., p. 598.   [2] Ibid., pp. 600–1.
[3] Ibid., pp. 608–10.

rates, the first during the king's illness, March 1454–February 1455, the second, Nov. 1455–February 1456, York tried to establish himself as a reformer of the government, but the king's recovery brought his enemies to power again. His difficulties lay in the council and in the upper house. This had been clear as early as the end of 1450. By the activities of the commons that year the lords remained on the whole unshaken. Somerset, it is true, was arrested on 1 December 1450, but soon afterwards he was made chamberlain of the household: and how little the council was impressed by commons' petitions on the duke's behalf can be seen from the appointment of William Booth to York and the committal (11 June 1451) to the Tower of the member for Bristol, Thomas Young of Shirehampton, who had presented the commons' petition that York should be recognized as heir to the throne. From the lords as a whole the duke got little support. To them a Yorkist succession implied the predominance of Neville, Mowbray, Vere, and their dependants, the consolidation of important power-groups in central and southern England. Locally, in the Paston country, it spelled the ascendancy of Sir John Howard whose estates were concentrated round Sudbury, Clare, and Stoke by Nayland and of the landowners on the borders of Suffolk and Essex whose attachments were to the Howards and the Mowbrays; and the corresponding abasement of the Lords Scales of Nayland, Beaumont, and Moleyns and the notorious Sir Thomas Tuddenham, along with the professional desperadoes who helped them—Heydon, Daniell, and Tailboys. In every instance a change in the succession raised the problem of the local balance of power, and to think of the dynastic struggle as fought out simply between the supporters of Somerset and the queen on the one hand, and an opposition with the traditions of Mortimer, Clare, Salisbury, and the great baronial consolidations of the fourteenth century on the other, is to neglect its organic nature. Just as the barons' wars of the period 1258–1267 were far more than a contest between crown and opposition and involved questions of shire government and the land law, so behind the clash of parties in the middle of the fifteenth century lay problems of local order and economic advantage.

For York, watching the situation from Ludlow, the attitude of the court was now clear. The question was only when he should act. In January 1452, accompanied by the earl of

Devonshire and Lord Cobham, he advanced on London from the north-west, while the king moved as far north as Coventry to meet him: but the duke 'tooke an other way'. On reaching the London neighbourhood, but denied access to the city, he crossed the Thames at Kingston Bridge to take up a position at Dartford in Kent. The king, who could go straight through the city, met him at Blackheath, and might well have brought him to battle: but the intervention of the bishops of Ely and Winchester and of the earls of Salisbury and Warwick stopped this trial of arms and brought Henry and the duke into contact on the understanding that Somerset should be placed in ward for the matters on which York charged him: whereupon York sent his army away. Somerset, however, was very far from being relegated to the Tower. Henry made no effort to remove him from attendance, and York, when he entered the royal tent, found himself treated like a prisoner and made to ride before the king, 'lyke as he shuld have been putt in holde'.[1] The matters of dispute between himself and Somerset, assessed monetarily at £20,000, were referred to an arbitration committee of bishops and magnates, and as these did not concern 'principally the estate of the king and realm', they (or some of them) must have been financial claims left unsettled from York's lieutenancy in Normandy. York had to agree to swear allegiance to Henry publicly at St. Paul's; and his movements would have been farther curtailed, had it not been announced that his son, the earl of March, the future Edward IV, was coming with 11,000 men. York had been tricked and only escaped by good fortune and the devotion of his son. In company with many others he took advantage of the general pardon issued on 7 April 1452, and Henry, always hoping for reconciliation, visited Ludlow in the summer (12 Aug.) during the course of a progress through the land.

Such peaceful intentions were not echoed by Henry's court. York was not summoned to the council till 1453. The year saw a worsening of the position at home and abroad. Abroad the council was too late in its attempts to save Gascony. On 30 June 1451 the French had entered Bordeaux, but the Gascons did not regard themselves as 'liberated'. Six years later Charles VII, writing to the king of Scotland, called it common knowledge that Gascony 'has been English for 300 years and that the

---

[1] *Great Chronicle of London*, p. 186.

people of the region are at heart completely inclined towards the English party'. That was how they felt in 1451, and in March 1452 they sent some of the leading citizens of Bordeaux to London to beg for an army to deliver them. Henry complied, though with a force of not more than 3000 under the command of John Talbot, earl of Shrewsbury. When Talbot landed on 17 October 1452 Bordeaux expelled the French garrison and opened its gates, while other towns in the west of Gascony did the same. In the spring of 1453 Charles VII opened the last campaign of the Hundred Years War in overwhelming force. Three armies made simultaneously for Bordeaux, one from the south-east, one from the east, and one from the north-east, with the king and the reserve in the rear. By the middle of July the French army in the centre had reached Castillon, a defended town thirty miles eastwards of Bordeaux. Talbot was for waiting till the French armies advanced closer, when he could fall on the nearest of them, but the natives of Castillon and the municipality of Bordeaux pressed him to relieve the town and the earl yielded against his better judgement. The French commander, who had with him a notable force of siege and field guns, and an army of some 7,000 to 10,000 men-at-arms and archers, was Jean Bureau, who had earlier been in English service. Bureau, instead of making lines of circumvallation, had constructed to the east of the town a large fortified camp for his army, 700 yards long and about 200 yards wide, its long side parallel to and abutting upon the river Lidoire. The layout of this camp was designed to give the artillery a maximum of oblique and enfilade fire.[1] Talbot marched out of Bordeaux on 16 July to Libourne, where there was a short halt, and then, by night, to surprise the French outpost in the Priory of St. Lorent, on the east side of the forest flanking the Bordeaux road and just outside Castillon. The defenders were evicted and soon Talbot received a report that the French were in full retreat from their position in the fortified camp, and decided to follow quickly and make an attack on the camp from the south. Unfortunately the report was a misleading one, due to the Gascons seeing a large number of horses that had been turned out of the camp; when Talbot arrived the camp proved to be held and, what is more, fully manned with guns. None the less Talbot decided on a frontal attack by dismounted forces,

[1] A. H. Burne, *The Agincourt War* (1956), pp. 338–9.

although the French guns were likely to do—and did—considerable havoc: and matters were going quite uncertainly until a force of Bretons, stationed in the woods north of the camp made their appearance and enabled the main body of the French to press the English back on to the Dordogne. Some reached a ford, the Pas de Rozan, but here Talbot himself and his son Lord de Lisle were killed, and with the death of their commander the English force disintegrated.

One tragedy of Castillon is the scant recognition which the efforts of John Talbot received from his English contemporaries the French were more generous in their praise. The numbers of which he disposed were insufficient, for even when reinforced by his side with a force of roughly 2,500, it was most unlikely that without a large Gascon contingent he could have held the duchy against the three armies of Charles VII. We do not hear that this Gascon contingent was forthcoming. Furthermore, he was sent out with inadequate artillery: a country which had depended so largely on its archers had not yet fully realized the importance of artillery fire when it could be brought to bear at close range. It was a cannon-ball that struck the white palfrey on which the picturesque earl used to ride, throwing its master. Worse than these things was the failure to appreciate and support those elements in Gascony still loyal to the English connexion, particularly the municipality of Bordeaux itself, if only for the sake of the valuable trade running between Bordeaux and Bristol, Southampton, and London. Even if, in the wine trade, the native vintner had for some years in English cities superseded the wine merchant from the Bordelais,[1] the English merchant colony was by no means negligible in Bordeaux, and the social connexion between the countries were close; nor was the appointment, in parliament, of triers of Gascon petitions a mere formality.

The survivors of the expeditionary force had to find their way back to fight in the internecine struggles of England. No money was forthcoming for the Gascons long faithful to England, as indeed nothing was sent to help the poverty of loyalists in Maine. When the inhabitants of that country represented to Henry VI that the lands and offices they had received from the English crown for their good services had been torn from them

---

[1] Cf. M. K. James, 'The Medieval Wine Dealer', *The Entrepreneur* (Econ. Hist. Soc. 1957), p. 6.

and that so great a number of people, loyal subjects, had been abandoned, *qui est grand pitié*, without any compensation at all, the note written by William of Worcester on the document tersely ran: 'Note that this petition was not carried out nor granted, by occasion of which many soldiers were brought to poverty and some fell sick and died of grief, some were imprisoned for robbery and condemned to death as felons, and some are still rebels dwelling in the parts of France.'[1] No compensating clause had been inserted in the truce, for which only Suffolk could have been to blame; for if he had suggested it, he would undoubtedly have said so later in his defence.

Before Castillon had been fought, parliament, summoned to Reading (6 Mar. 1453) had shown its dissent from the proceedings of 1451 and its determination to ward off military measures such as the duke of York's march to London the previous year. The commons petitioned that all measures enacted under the pressure of the Cade rebellion should be declared void; and that York's chamberlain, Sir William Oldhall of Hunsdon, should be attainted for his support of Cade. This was a vindictive measure against the Speaker of the last parliament, and indeed Oldhall had had an agitating time in London during the past year. He had twice been accused of theft, notably of Somerset's goods at the Blackfriars, and had been obliged to take sanctuary at St. Martin-le-grand (31 Nov. 1451); whence he was dragged out by certain lords of Somerset's party and carried to Westminster, only to be returned to St. Martin's under the protest of the dean. He was charged first with treason and on this outlawed; later attainted, his goods and properties being divided among his opponents, Walter Burgh (who had brought the first charge of theft), Somerset who was awarded Hunsdon, and the earl of Pembroke, who took Oldhall's Norfolk estates. Not till November 1455, when York was protector, could he obtain a writ of error annulling the outlawry. The attitude of the commons in the 1453 parliament is therefore quite clear. Besides the grant of fifteenth and a tenth, and tonnage and poundage, 'for terme of youre lyfe naturell', the prolocutor (Thomas Thorp) announced the ominous provision of 20,000 archers, to serve the king 'for the space of a half year'. The king dispensed with 7,000 out of the number specified, while the 13,000 were to remain 'as a hoole hoste or a

[1] Stevenson, op. cit., II. ii. 598–603.

hoole companie'. Even this concession left a large number to
be assessed upon the counties and boroughs, from the 476 o
Wiltshire to the thirty of the town of Nottingham.[1] By July the
king had rehabilitated most of the household officers, whose
privileges or annuities had been recently forfeit.[2] Under the
atmosphere of tension Henry now fell gravely ill and in Augus
became insane. The queen and the officials tried to conceal thi
fact as long as they could, for fear of a regency under York, bu
in October matters came to a head when a son, called after the
saint, was born to Henry and Margaret upon St. Edward'
Day. This necessitated the summons of a great council (24 Oct.)
to which Somerset and his friends purposely did not invit
York, but it proved impossible to dispense with him, and he wa
instructed to attend 'to set rest and union between the lords o
the land'. The phrase, it was added, referred to difference
between York and other lords: but it could have borne anothe
explanation. In one area above others pacification was imme
diately necessary. In July the council had written to the earl
of Northumberland and Westmorland directing them to se
that the peace was kept, for the old feud between Percy and
Neville had broken out between Northumberland's sons, Lord
Egremont and Sir Richard Percy, supported by Exeter, agains
Richard Neville, earl of Salisbury. On this occasion the feud
aggravated by the political climate, flared on till Northumber
land himself was killed at St. Albans.

In London the atmosphere of 1454 had been dramatically
rendered by a correspondent of the duke of Norfolk. Cardina
Kemp was arming his household; the earl of Wiltshire, Lord
Beaumont, Poynings, Clifford, Egremont, and Bonville were
collecting an army to march on London; Thomas Tresham
William Joseph, Thomas Daniel, and John Trevelyan had pu
in a bill to the lords for the safeguarding of the king and the
prince; and the duke of Buckingham had ordered 2,000 'bende
with knottes' for his fellowship, while Somerset's billeting
officer had been booking all the accommodation he could in
Thames Street and in the neighbourhood of the Tower. Somer
set was building up a formidable military power: he had spie
'goyng in every lordes hous of this land', some as friars, some
as sailors captured at sea, and Norfolk should beware of 'busshe
ments' (ambushes). It was at this point that the queen emerged

---

[1] *Rot. Parl.* v. 232.   [2] Ibid. v. 237.

ιs the leader of Somerset's faction. She had grasped the funda-
mentally weak position of York with the lords and in January
1454 demanded to have the government of the realm in her
hands, along with the appointment of the chief officials, as well
ιs the sheriffs and bishops. She had lost for the time being the
support of the Speaker, Thomas Thorp, who had been committed to the Fleet and fined £1,000 for trespass in an action
which York brought against him, a sentence against which he
was not allowed to plead privilege of parliament. On 27 March
1454 the spiritual and temporal lords nominated York protector
and defender, after a vain attempt had been made, by a personal visit, to ascertain whether the king was still *non compos
mentis*. York was careful to protest, in his own interest, that he
had not nominated himself, and asked for the assistance of the
lords in a co-operative task ('I shall employ my persone with
you'). He further sought definition of his power,[1] remembering
perhaps the council's action in interviewing the dukes of
Gloucester and Bedford, and was told that he was to be 'chief
of the Kynges Counsaill' a name devised for him 'different
from other counsaillors, nought the name of tutour, lieutenant,
governor, nor of Regent' (a clear reference to the council's
declining duke Humphrey's request for the *tutela* of Henry VI).[2]
He also raised the matter of the allowance, and received the
answer that precedents should be looked at, but that there
should be an agreement on the point. An act thereupon constituting him, on the grounds of the king's health, protector and
defender was drafted and embodied as a patent; and a further
debate simultaneously put the prince into a similar position
when he had reached years of discretion. The council thus
shelved the succession question and established a temporary
presidency of the council while Henry's mind was disordered
and until Prince Edward could take on the work. York then
nominated his brother-in-law, Richard earl of Salisbury, as
chancellor; Somerset, after the opinion of the peoples had been
taken, was left in prison: and York took care to control both the
Channel by making himself captain of Calais (28 July) in place
of Somerset, and of the western approaches, by securing a

---

[1] 'That I mowe knowe how ferre the said power and auctorite, and also the
fredome and libertie shall extende, duryng the tyme that it shall plaise our said
Soveraine Lord that I shall have hit': *Rot. Parl.* v. 242.
[2] See above, p. 216.

confirmation of his own earlier appointment as governor of Ireland. The north and the south-west were firmly dealt with: the latter through the detention, as a hostage for likely Lancastrian activity, of the duke of Exeter, arrested on a visit he unwisely paid to London, while York himself visited the north to control the activities of Northumberland and Egremont. Exeter had been organizing support there: in January 1454 he was reported as having been at Tuxford 'beside Doncaster', to meet Lord Egremont and they 'been sworne together'.[1] But York's power was not to last. Early in 1455 Henry returned to his senses and reasserted the remains of his own personal will. Archbishop Bourchier was given the chancellorship, the earl of Wiltshire was made treasurer, and Somerset and Exeter were released, and there began the period of the queen's domination when the issue was joined between administration by the household and a legitimist opposition run by a limited number of magnates and friends of York. Yet it is no use drawing boundaries too sharply. The loyalties of the country were determined less by principle than by pre-existing interests and groupings, each assisted by the 'fellowships' of tenants and supporters, an extension into peacetime of the military indenture system which was found to appeal to the lances and archers now returning from France.

Watching the balance of forces in Wales and the March, the queen made every effort to secure the help of the influential. The position in south-east Wales was roughly this: Richard earl of Warwick had secured possession (1449) of Glamorgan and Morgannwg. The families of Herbert and Roger Vaughan were dominant in Raglan and its neighbourhood. Monmouth had been annexed to the duchy of Lancaster by Henry IV. Abergavenny was held by Edward Neville son of Earl Ralph Neville of Westmorland. The duke of Buckingham, Humphrey Stafford, was lord of Brecknock and Newport and one of the great supporters of Lancaster. In the north lay the Mortimer estates of the duke of York, running from Builth to Denbigh, including beside the two fortresses, Clifford, Ewyas Lacy, Maeliennydd, Radnor, and Denbigh, with Ludlow as the centre, and sometimes Montgomery. These estates stretching practically unbroken from Cardiff to Chester would be a serious danger if united under York. It was important for the

[1] *Paston Letters*, ii. 296.

crown to retain the allegiance of the Nevilles and of Sir William
Herbert, and much of the manœuvring of the fifties was the
securing of Herbert by one side or the other. Technically he
was York's steward of Usk, but at the critical moment after
Jasper Tudor had secured west Wales and made it the basis of
his operations, Margaret made every effort to secure him, as he
balanced delicately between the two sides. From the middle of
1457, after he had been pardoned for various border offences,
he and his brothers were acting on the queen's side. Margaret
was counting upon the aid of Jasper Tudor, the duke of Buckingham, and of the Herberts in Gwent. But in the south-east of
Wales Herbert had to go carefully since he was liable to be
enveloped by Yorkist supporters. For a time he seems to have
done so without sacrificing the friendship of York and Warwick
and it was his diplomacy that in the end emboldened the queen
to take the field with the Cheshire levies in the spring of 1459
in order to prevent the forces of Salisbury effecting a junction
with those of York, and with Warwick, after he had arrived
from the continent.

The reversal of York's plans after Henry's recovery sent
him to the north to join the two Nevilles, Salisbury and
Warwick, and to muster forces. They were reinforced by Lord
Clinton and Sir Robert Ogle. Thence the three nobles marched
with their forces down into Hertfordshire from where they
issued a letter to the king protesting their loyalty and asking
that the charges made by their enemies should not be believed:
a manifesto of 20 May declared that York had assembled his
followers because it was not safe for him to go unarmed to the
council which had been summoned at Leicester: both documents were withheld from Henry with serious results, so that at
St. Albans on 22 May 1455, Henry and Margaret marching
with considerable force on their way to the council at Leicester
found an enemy force waiting for them outside the town. The
conflict was deferred three hours, while York tried to get his
complaints against Somerset heard by the king; but as in 1452
he failed, this time through the opposition of Buckingham who
was hoping to refer the case to the council at Leicester, while
Henry refused to surrender certain leaders designated by York
as traitors. The ensuing engagement lasted less than an hour and
was decided by York's larger numbers and by a flank attack
from Warwick. Somerset, Northumberland, and Clifford

perished and the earl of Stafford, Buckingham's son, sub
sequently died of wounds, while Henry was wounded in th
neck by an arrow. After the engagement York and the Neville
knelt before the king and asked his favour. He and the quee
travelled back together with York who now assumed Somerset'
title of constable of England, while Warwick became captai
of Calais and York's brother-in-law, Viscount Bourchier, wa
made treasurer. The duke of Buckingham and the earl of Wilt
shire made their peace with the Yorkists, and one Lancastria
who had fought at St. Albans, Sir John Wenlock, became
whole-hearted supporter of York, and was chosen Speaker i
the parliament of 1455.

The securing of Calais for Warwick was not complete unti
a settlement had been arrived at with the staplers company
To gain for the Yorkists a bastion of such importance was
vital move in the struggle of York with Lancaster. The Calai
garrison has been termed 'the largest single force in the King'
pay'.[1] For long the place had held out for Somerset wh
attempted to make its payment a government priority; an
when York in his struggle with Beaufort had resolved to seve
the connexion which his rival had established with the garriso
and secure his own authority in Calais, he was forced into
series of complicated negotiations[2] with the garrison, badly i
arrears for pay, which in desperation seized the staplers' woo
for reimbursement. The company itself, none too confident i
the stability of the Yorkist régime, in the end, however, under
took to find the garrison's arrears and the wages of a new com
mander (for a limited period) on the security of the customs an
upon the satisfaction by the king's council of other sums owin
to the company. Warwick's command in Calais, so valuable t
the Yorkist lords, was retained throughout the pressure of 145
when the attacks of Henry duke of Somerset threatened it. Bu
some of the garrison commanders proved still loyal, as the battl
of Ludford was to prove, to the Lancastrians. It was the stapler
who held the key to the situation and sustained the Yorkis
lords.

In his first protectorship York had been grappling wit
finance, and in particular with ensuring a reasonable incom

[1] G. L. Harriss, 'The Struggle for Calais, an aspect of the rivalry betwee
Lancaster and York', *Eng. Hist. Rev.* lxxv (1960), 30.
[2] Recounted by Harriss, op. cit., pp. 40–45.

to the household without undue raiding of Exchequer funds. He had reversed the usual order and was set upon restraining the wardrobe's receipt at the Exchequer before curtailing its expenditure. First the wardrobe's preference on the customs assignments had to be reduced in favour of Calais and the keeping of the high seas. In point of fact wardrobe preference at the Exchequer was now very largely destroyed. After St. Albans a new resumption act could, in York's eyes, lead to a new household settlement, and £10,000 per annum was the figure suggested for the latter. By the beginning of 1456, therefore, parliament with the encouragement of the protector had embarked on a programme of financial resumption and allocation no less widespread and even more radical than that of 1450–1. But with the king's emergence into activity and the restoration of personal government (25 Feb.) the main provisions of the act of January–February 1456[1] were nullified. A fairly lengthy list of exemptions safeguarded the duchy of Lancaster estates and numerous grants to household servants.

Roughly from 1456 the government of England was conducted not from London but from the provinces. At the beginning of September that year the court settled at Coventry, there to remain for the following year. This was a signal for the restoration of the crown's absolute authority. At the end of September Lawrence Booth became keeper of the privy seal; on 5 October the earl of Shrewsbury succeeded Viscount Bourchier as treasurer, and six days later Archbishop Bourchier ceded the chancellorship to William Waynflete. The fact of a midland headquarters and the political absence of the court from London made a cleft in the administrative system by emphasizing the personal authority of the crown over the old domestic offices, now the offices of state, and over the wardrobe. In the remaining three and a half years the crown was to abandon the attempt to govern the country, and had devoted the political and administrative resources at its command to the task of strengthening its material power and the protection of the dynasty. Between Michaelmas 1457 and Easter 1458, when the court had returned to London, large amercements were imposed upon the sheriffs for non-return of writs, for escapes from jail, and so forth: e.g. £100 from Berkshire, £100 from Wiltshire, 40 marks from Devonshire, £40 from Yorkshire. By

---

[1] *Rot. Parl.* v. 300–1.

October 1458 the extreme curialist party were in power. The earl of Wiltshire, James Butler, was lord treasurer, Thomas Tuddenham was treasurer of the household, and then began a systematic exploitation of the shrievalty by the household. At least sixteen of the sheriffs named received household wages. The wardrobe was securing its income from these sources, sources amenable now to the personal influence of the crown, and this fact may be detected in the assignments on farmed lands made to the wardrobe. For the household thus to draw directly upon the sheriffs without first going through to the Exchequer takes one back to the bad old days of Henry III, when he was building Westminster Abbey from the monies that accountants ought to have sent into the national treasury. Over such a system there could be no sort of control by the estates. Of course the shires and boroughs might be glad not to be asked for taxation, but it meant that during the last four years before Yorkist rule there was a personal government organized by the queen and based upon her retention in the royal service of public officers in which York, reconciled in outward appearances to the queen, predominated in the council.

The reconciliation did not prevent brawling and local fighting at the palace of Westminster in one episode of which (11 Oct. 1458) Warwick had to escape for his life. The years 1456–8, a period of hollow and unrealistic trial, saw both sides intriguing out of England. Margaret in particular was bargaining with the Scots. If their historian Lesley is to be believed, in return for a promise of help against the duke of York and the earl of Warwick, English commissioners pledged to James II the counties of Northumberland, Cumberland, and Durham along with 'other' sheriffdoms which the king of Scotland had earlier held or had been withheld from him eleven years past. The pledge, if given, was never fulfilled. The queen put herself in the wrong by allowing, if not encouraging, Piers de Brézé, grand seneschal of Anjou, Poitou, and Normandy to land on the coast of Kent and pillage Sandwich. He and his men were driven out by Sir Thomas Kyriell, but the disgrace of the raid was not forgotten. Yet Margaret was prepared to use Brézé as a negotiator for a treaty with France, a *bonne paix* which Brézé's agent, Doulcereau, was commissioned to discuss with Richard Beauchamp, bishop of Salisbury. For this raid Margaret had to find a scapegoat, and Exeter, who had been admiral for ten years, was singled out to be the victim; but the immediate impotence of the defences had shown Warwick at Calais that he had only to judge the moment right and that it was from that town that the decisive expedition to England could be made.

It was the beginning of Warwick's opportunities. From Calais, as keeper of the town and custodian of the sea, he had made himself master of the Channel by the destruction of a Spanish fleet. His attacks on the Easterlings and on Italians were favourably viewed by anti-alien elements in England, and his aggressive tactics against French and Burgundians alike made him popular when he paid his periodic visits to Kent. The duke of Burgundy could not tame him, but could not ignore him, and a second understanding with the duke was arrived at by Warwick in the early summer of 1458 which, as Chastellain observes, led to *hautes merveilleuses fins*.[1] At Calais the earl through his follower Sir John Wenlock was working, often simultaneously, for marriage alliances with French and Burgundian princesses: the former offer made on behalf of the queen, the latter on behalf of Henry VI and the duke of York, quite without authority, and so awkward did this diplomacy become that Queen Margaret resolved to remove Warwick from Calais. In the summer of 1459 York and Salisbury sent word to Warwick that the queen and her lords had determined to crush the Yorkists and that it was time for him to return. He obeyed. In September he was marching from London towards Warwickshire, while the earl of Salisbury was coming from Yorkshire to join the duke at Ludlow. On the Lancastrian side the king was assembling an army in the midlands while the queen was at Eccleshall, south-east of Market Drayton. A royal army had been raised in Cheshire and Shropshire by Lord Audley. As soon as Margaret heard that the earl of Salisbury was marching to join York she ordered Lord Audley to intercept him. This he did at Blore Heath on 23 September 1459, the queen's forces staying at Eccleshall. The Lancastrians though considerably outnumbering their opponents were repulsed, partly owing to the defection of 500 of them to the enemy.[2] This action was the preliminary to the arrival of Warwick with

[1] Chronique, in *Œuvres de George Chastellain*, ed. Kervyn de Lettenhove, iii (1864), 428.
[2] The latest account of Blore Heath is in A. H. Burne, *More Battlefields of England* (1952), pp. 140–9.

600 men under Andrew Trollope and John Blount to the appointed rendezvous with York and Salisbury at Ludlow. The rout of the Yorkists at Ludford Bridge on 12 October 1459 has been attributed to the desertion to the royal army of the troops of the Calais garrison, but it is more likely that it was the weakness of York's own following, his general lack of support that was responsible. Herbert did not help him at the time of need. The diplomacy of Margaret and Jasper Tudor had done its work even if Sir William Devereux and Lord Powys had in the end supported his side. Ludlow Castle, the family home, was robbed and pillaged, and the Yorkists had to make their escape, York himself to Ireland, March and the two Nevilles to the Devonshire coast and then to Calais, Warwick to Guernsey and so back to his Calais stronghold. Meanwhile York, his son Edward, earl of March, Salisbury, and Warwick were attainted in the parliament summoned at short notice to Coventry (20 Nov. 1459). Attainted also were Clinton, Wenlock, John and Edward Bourchier, William Stanley, Lord Stanley's brother, Sir William Oldhall, Sir Thomas Harrington, Sir John Conyers, Sir Thomas Parre, and Sir James Pickering; and while the Yorkist lords were at Calais, a vigorous attempt was made to uproot Yorkist supporters in England; the lords were asked to take an oath of loyalty to the prince of Wales as well as to Henry himself and to promise to protect and support Henry's wife and son. The oath was taken by the two archbishops, sixteen bishops, including George Neville, bishop of Exeter, the dukes of Exeter, Norfolk, and Buckingham, all the kinsmen of the duke of York, five earls and twenty-two barons: and the offices and estates of the attainted were distributed among the king's friends.

The attainder did not affect York's position in Ireland, even though the earl of Wiltshire (also earl of Ormond) had been nominated lieutenant in his place. The Irish parliament showed itself ready and eager to protect him, and one of its statutes enacted that anyone seeking to procure his death or incite rebellion was guilty of high treason. When the earl of Wiltshire sent over an agent with writs for York's arrest, the emissary found himself attainted and after being tried before the lieutenant himself was hung, drawn, and quartered. Meanwhile the duke of Somerset had been appointed captain of Calais and was doing all he could to put the Yorkist earls out. But he could get no farther than clashes and daily skirmishes with the Calais garrison. It was all very well for the Coventry parliament to forbid merchants to carry wool, woolfels, and other merchandise to Calais, for English wool merchants would hardly wish to be obliged to carry their wool directly to the Flemish markets until some new arrangement for the Staple could be made. Furthermore, Duke Philip showed some interest in the Yorkist earls in Calais and concluded a truce of three months with them: the English government had not renewed the commercial treaty between England and Burgundy, dating back to 1439, due to expire on 1 November. Its thoughts were upon expelling the earls from the Channel ports, and by the end of 1459 they had fitted out an expedition under Lord Rivers and Sir Gervase Clifton. They took some time to collect the fleet at Sandwich and on 15 January Warwick sent a force under John Dynham to raid and capture Sandwich. This was extraordinarily successful: Lord Rivers, his wife the dowager duchess of Bedford, and his son Sir Anthony Woodville were seized while in their beds and carried off to Calais, and the ships in harbour, saving the large *Grace Dieu*, sailed thither under the direction of their captains. The chiefs of the expedition were soundly rated by the Calais lords. The government thought that their capture was the sign for invasion by the Yorkist lords and made a great effort to raise a force to prevent it taking place. A fleet had been engaged under Sir Baldwin Fulford, but before it could be fitted out the news came that Warwick had left Calais for Ireland. This prompted the government to bring back the duke of Exeter as admiral and steps were taken to secure the help of a Venetian flotilla then in the Thames: but the masters of the ships, hearing of what was being planned, made haste to depart, whereupon the council gave the order for the incarceration of all Venetian merchants living in London. This unfortunate step showed the state of nerves in which ministers were living; despite Warwick's departure Somerset, for all the reinforcements sent him, was unable to force an entry into Calais; *per contra*, Sandwich was again raided by Dynham, Wenlock, and Fauconberg as a revenge. Warwick had by now returned, and the fleet fitted out by Exeter and Fulford had failed to catch and destroy him.

The failure led to a fresh persecution of Yorkist supporters in England, and the government renewed its local inquiries for traitors. The commissions of inquiry and punishment of treason, insurrection, rebellion, &c., indicate a good deal of local disorder over and above the manifestation of Yorkist sympathies: but confiscation of property and the hanging of inhabitants as at Newbury in Berkshire under Lords Wiltshire and Scales, in other words judicial terrorism, proved in effect valuable material for York whose supporters circulated frequent propaganda, the most effective being the manifesto of the early summer of 1460 drafted by York and Warwick while in Ireland, and pointing to the oppression and misgovernment, both by churchmen and seculars, suffered on all sides, and to the dangers of the control exercised by Shrewsbury, Wiltshire, and Beaumont. Interestingly enough, it was claimed in the Yorkist manifesto that the hated ministers had now begun to try a new imposition never hitherto seen, i.e. conscription, after the French manner, for the king's guard. It has been pointed out that if the measures recently adopted for the safety of the king-dom did not warrant the conclusion about the French method of conscription, in the commissions of array sent into almost every county in December 1457, as well as in those issued almost immediately after the Coventry parliament, there had appeared a clause empowering the commissioners to demand that every village, township, and hamlet according to its population and wealth, and as soon as commanded, should provide the king with a certain number of able-bodied men and archers at its own expense for the defence of the country against the Yorkists.[1] The charges were not the generalities which Stubbs thought them. But was it true, as the manifesto stated, that Henry had been persuaded to send letters to the native Irish encouraging them 'to enter into the conquest of the said land'? This seems more difficult to believe. Yet by and large the charges brought in the manifesto against the royal ministers have been considered by critical opinion to be well founded.

The government, then, expected invasion, and it came. On 26 June 1460 Edward earl of March, Warwick, Salisbury, Fauconberg, and Sir John Wenlock landed at Sandwich. With them was Francesco Coppini, bishop of Terni, the legate of Pius II for collecting the subsidy against the Turks, whom the Pope was sending to England charged with the duty of com-

[1] Cora Scofield, *The Life and Reign of Edward IV* (1923), i. 68.

manding the country to send representatives to the projected
diet of Mantua, where the European powers were to be asked
to join in a crusade against the Turks. Coppini had formed
another subsidiary project which answered to one part of his
commission; besides imploring aid against the Turks he had, as
it was optimistically stated, to 'quieten the people' (*placen-
dumque gentem*). His desire was for the Pope to strengthen his
authority still further by making him a cardinal: this done, the
new cardinal was to throw all his weight on the side of the
Yorkist lords, who having been raised to power through his aid,
would show their gratitude by sending an expedition against
Normandy and Gascony, both now firmly in the hands of the
French king. This would be entirely to the taste of Duke Philip
of Burgundy and Louis the dauphin, Charles VII's son,
who after quarrelling violently with his father had sought
Philip's court. The original conceivers of the plan were Coppini
himself and Francesco Sforza who was trying to force Charles
VII to withdraw his support from John of Calabria, the Angevin
candidate to the throne of Naples. John of Calabria, the brother
of Margaret of Anjou, was no friend of the Yorkists, but they
were attracted to the legate's project mainly because they hoped
that it would prepare the ground for an alliance with Philip
of Burgundy. The attitude of London to the Yorkist earls was
uncertain. On the day after the earls landed the common
council agreed that the mayor and aldermen must be supported
in opposing the rebels and a deputation was sent to inform them
of the order. But Warwick overcame their doubts and a deputation was sent to welcome the earls, while Lords Hungerford,
Scales, and Sir Edmund Hampden shut themselves up in the
Tower, along with Lord de Vescy, Lord Lovel, Lord de la
Warr, the earl of Kendal, and the duchess of Exeter. On arrival
(2 July 1460) the earls removed, for burial, the Yorkist heads
putrefying on London Bridge, and the next day addressed convocation, dwelling on the misgovernment of the kingdom and
the determination to assert their innocence before the king, if
necessary to die for their cause. It was a militant body whom
Coppini had accompanied to London, and he had to admit to
Pius II that in spite of the leadership of Holy Church and his
own presence as 'an angel of peace and a mediator', the Yorkists having been brought back 'as it were on my shoulders or
rather on those of the Church and your Holiness', the intention

of the earls was anything but pacific. Leaving Salisbury, Cobham, and Sir John Wenlock behind to besiege the Tower, March and Warwick accompanied by Archbishop Bourchier and the bishops of London, Exeter, Lincoln, and Salisbury set out to find the king at Northampton. The bishops had to endure some rough speaking for their evident hypocrisy from the duke of Buckingham, who made it clear that there could be no peace with Warwick. In the battle which followed (10 July 1460) the king's army found its entrenched position flooded by heavy rain and the guns on which it relied were useless in the mud and water. The fight lasted only half an hour, in which March bore his father's banner, but in that time the duke of Buckingham, the earl of Shrewsbury, Viscount Beaumont, and Lord Egremont met their deaths, and the royal army suffered heavy casualties. March, Warwick, and Fauconberg had to find the king (the queen had taken refuge in Denbigh) and as at St. Albans in 1455 assure him of their loyalty and of their desire to promote the good of the country. Henry was escorted to London and the capture of the Tower, stubbornly defended against heavy bombardment, shortly followed. Scales and Hungerford were granted their freedom, but Scales, in an attempt to reach sanctuary at Westminster, was recognized and murdered. Of the others, Hungerford and Lovel, Sir Edmund Hampden and Sir Gervase Clifton succeeded in joining Margaret of Anjou, while the earl of Kendal and Lord de la Warr went over to the Yorkist side.

The victory of Northampton determined the duke of York to leave Ireland and make his claim to the throne. He landed at Chester and marched through Ludlow and Hereford. Reaching Abingdon, he sent for trumpeters and gave them banners with the whole arms of England undiversified. The parliament summoned by the earls met on 7 October and on the 10th the Duke arrived with about 300 armed men. Westminster Hall he entered with the sword carried before him, but when he presented himself to the lords and laid his hand for a moment on the empty throne, there was no acclamation, but silence, and the tense and difficult scene was finally interrupted by the archbishop of Canterbury who asked him if he wished to go and see the king. The duke's famous reply, 'I know of no one in the realm who would not more fitly come to me than I to him', and his general demeanour in the palace made it perfectly clear to the lords what the duke had wanted: it was equally clear that nobody thought of that moment as a suitable occasion for a change of dynasty, and the remarkable thing is that the duke so misjudged the temper of the lords who had treated him, when he was protector, very much as they had treated the duke of Gloucester. When after a few days the duke actually sat down upon the royal throne and addressing the lords claimed that the crown was his by inheritance, he got no encouragement. On 16 October he sent the lords a genealogical statement of his claim, making perfectly clear that he was claiming on the ground of indefeasible hereditary right alone.

The question now was whether the succession settled through the enactment of a statute (7 Henry IV, c. 2) was to be defeated by such a claim. The lords heard the statement and on 17 October consulted the king who asked them to state objections to it. They then turned to the judges who declined the responsibility of advising, since they were the king's justices and had to determine such matters as came before them in law, when two parties appeared before them in the courts: it was not their business to advise, since it was a matter between the king and the duke of York as the contending parties, and it was not customary to have to resort to counsel in such matters. They also contended that the matter was so high that it was above the law and beyond their learning: it was one for the lords of the royal blood and the lords in general. The sergeants at law and the king's attorney equally refused to advise, and the lords had to fall back upon themselves. Here, they said, they were confronted by a great difficulty, the oaths of allegiance taken to Henry and the promise to protect the queen and accept Prince Edward as heir, made at Coventry scarcely a year ago. They reminded York that he had taken an oath of allegiance to Henry VI, and of the fact that Henry IV had claimed the throne as heir of Henry III, not by conquest—whereas he had claimed both by inheritance and conquest.[1] And they suggested that York might call to remembrance 'the grete and notable Acts of Parlements made in dyvers Parlements of dyvers of the Kyng's Progenitours, the which Acts be sufficient and resonable to be leyde ageyn the title of the seid Duc of York: the which Acts been of moch more auctorite than eny cronycle, and also of auctorite to defete eny manere title made to eny persone'. The

---

[1] See above, p. 13.

acts, they therefore thought, could rebut the evidence of any history of a title or descent: but the lords must have regarded them as doing more than just that; they were in fact final authority; 'final in the sense of conferring statutory recognition on Henry's title'.[1] York's reply was that the oaths of allegiance were invalid in view of God's law and commandments, because the nature and purpose of an oath was to confirm truth, and the truth was that the peers and the lords ought to help him in truth and justice, notwithstanding any oaths of fealty taken. If Henry had had a really good case for succession to the throne, he would not have had resort to parliament to produce a statute which 'taketh noo place, neyther is of any force or effect ayenst hym that is right enheriter of the said Corones'.[2] In the end, not at the moment, the lords found themselves bound to decide that York's claim could not be defeated: but, as Professor Chrimes has said, in arriving at it, 'the *theory* of parliamentary right to determine the succession . . . to the throne was subordinated to the *theory* of the right of God's law of inheritance to determine it'. This was the theoretical line taken at Edward's accession: he had taken upon him the reign and governance of the realm into which he was righteously and naturally born;[3] for Henry of Derby, the commons' petition alleged, was a usurper; and by God's law, man's law, and the law of nature the right title was and had been since his father's death, in Edward.[4]

The actual settlement arrived at after these debates was a compromise. Henry was to retain the crown for life, and York was assured of his own succession and of his heirs thereafter. To this Henry agreed (28 Oct. 1460), whereupon the attainders of the Coventry parliament were reversed and York received, during the king's lifetime, the assignment of the principality of Wales with lands to the value of 10,000 marks: he was to take one half; 3,600 marks were to go to Edward earl of March, and 1,000 marks to his second son, Edmund earl of Rutland. On 8 November York was proclaimed heir-apparent and protector.

The protector met his end by underestimating—it was characteristic—the strength of his opponents. His visit to the north, undertaken (9 Dec.) to control and punish the Lancastrian earls who were maltreating his tenants in Yorkshire, was

---

[1] S. B. Chrimes, *English Constitutional Ideas in the XVth century* (1936), pp. 29-30.
[2] Ibid.   [3] Ibid., p. 31.   [4] Ibid.

hazardous enough, since near Worksop he was attacked by a body of Somerset's men with great loss, and when he reached his castle of Sandal he might have known that a very much larger force than his own was mustering under the duke of Somerset and the earl of Northumberland at Pontefract. These leaders decided to cut his supply lines and besiege him in Sandal. By the end of the month his position was serious and Edward of March had to come to the rescue. Although advised not to risk a battle, the duke none the less decided to march out and confront the enemy. He fell in the brief engagement known as the battle of Wakefield (30 Dec. 1460). His head, crowned with a paper cap, was stuck on the walls of York, along with that of Salisbury, who had been taken alive and was 'headed' after the engagement. As in 1450 and 1458-9, the Lancastrians showed themselves adepts at such publicity.

The death of Richard of York left the queen and her party face to face with Warwick and the earl of March. After Wakefield the legate tried to negotiate and bring the parties together: but Margaret was justifiably suspicious of Coppini. She went into Scotland where she found two factions at strife round James III, one headed by the queen mother, Mary of Guelders, who was strongly inclined to obey her uncle the duke of Burgundy: the other headed by the bishop of St. Andrews, James Kennedy, who was anxious to follow Charles VII. At a personal meeting at Lincluden Abbey Margaret was able to impress Mary of Guelders and arrange a marriage between the prince of Wales and Princess Mary, sister of James III. Margaret offered to surrender Berwick to Scotland as the price of this arrangement. At York on 20 January 1461 before a large assembly of notables, including the dukes of Exeter and Somerset, the earls of Northumberland, Westmorland, and Devonshire, and Lords Neville, FitzHugh, and Roos, the arrangement was confirmed and the agreement notified to Charles VII, who thereupon opened the harbours of Normandy to the supporters of Margaret. Having played this trump card and believing that Charles VII would effectively help her, Margaret made her famous march to London to catch Warwick and treat him as the Yorkists had treated some of the Lancastrians in the Tower. The action which then followed determined the future of both parties. First, Edward of March with the forces raised from the Mortimer lands in Wales overtook the earls of Pembroke and

Wiltshire who had landed there to support Margaret with Frenchmen and Bretons and Irishmen. He beat them at Mortimer's Cross (3 Feb. 1461), and chased them as far as Hereford. Wiltshire fled, Pembroke escaped, but his father Owen Tudor and other friends of his were caught and beheaded in the marketplace at Hereford. This was the Owen Tudor who had married Katherine of Valois, Henry V's queen. He died, as Gregory said, 'weening and trusting alway that he should not be beheaded till he saw the axe and the block'. The second dramatic episode was Margaret's capture of the king through Warwick's inability to keep her at arm's length in the country. The earl had been supine in London when he should have been collecting men and supplies to stop the queen with her formidable army from passing through the midlands. He let her get as far as the outskirts of St. Albans, where he had an elaborate piece of field engineering constructed on the assumption that her army would attack along the roads leading from Luton. In fact, on approaching Luton (16 Feb. 1461), she had swung west to Dunstable and made her approach along Watling Street from the north-west, entering the town not along what is now the Verulam Road but by the eastern end of St. Peter's Street. Warwick's flank had thus been turned and he had to make his left wing his centre and bring up forces from his centre and right flank for its support. Warwick's troops and their commanders were thrown into confusion by this change, but might have held on to the Lancastrians had not the Kentishmen, under Lovelace, deserted to Queen Margaret. By this time it was getting dark and Warwick, seeing that things were hopeless, was able to extricate his men and take them to join Edward of March, not to London, but to the Cotswolds. Then either at Burford or Chipping Norton was formed the plan that Edward should replace the king whom Margaret had just recovered. (Guarded by Lord Bonville and Sir Thomas Kyriell, Henry is reputed to have laughed and sung while the battle was in progress.)

Margaret had rescued her king, but after the rout of the Yorkist forces a characteristic thing happened. Entertained at the abbey of St. Albans the Queen's soldiers ransacked both the town and convent. The pillage on the march and now the typical conduct of her 'Northern men' had their effect. She was hoping that London would receive her; but the Londoners were extremely suspicious and sent a deputation of ladies, the dowager duchess of Buckingham and the dowager duchess of Bedford to her to say that the gates would be opened if there was no pillaging; she waited at St. Albans till arrangements were made; but the citizens of London refused, over the heads of the mayor and aldermen, to have her in. William of Worcester says that if Margaret had marched to London immediately after her victory at St. Albans she could have done what she pleased with the city.[1] But it was to Warwick and March London opened its gates on 27 February and with their return to London Margaret took herself to York with the prisoners she had captured at St. Albans, who included Lords Montagu and Berners, and Charleton.

Now Henry was in Margaret's hands again the earls had to act. They must either give up the struggle or depose Henry and set up another king. Constitutionally, this was an important moment. Parliament was not in session and what was done had to be an appeal to the acclamation of the Londoners: the *populus*, whose assent, according to custom, was necessary. The populace in the first instance was the soldiers. On 1 March in St. John's Fields they shouted for King Edward: then on 4 March the citizens, being summoned to St. Paul's, acclaimed the earl of March as King. At the chancellor's invitation he and his party proceeded to Westminster Hall, and Edward took the oath there in the chancery. After that, according to the *Ordo* or coronation directions of 1308, he was arrayed in royal robes and a cap of estate, and was installed in his seat as king; then he walked to the Abbey where the abbot and monks placed in his hands King Edward's sceptre. He offered at the high altar and at the confessor's tomb and then, returning to the choir, took his seat on the throne and expounded his hereditary title. The people, appealed to for the fourth time, shouted that he was their lawful king and all the lords present knelt and did homage. Finally the *Te Deum* was sung, and after more offerings Edward left and went back to the city by boat. This was not the coronation, but a recognition of the earl and his title made by the soldiers and citizens of his own capital. It was enough to go upon, enough to justify the appointment of Edward's first ministry, in which George Neville was chancellor, Lord Bourchier treasurer, and the earl of

---

[1] *Annales* in Stevenson, *Wars of the English in France*, ii. ii. 776.

Warwick great chamberlain, constable of Dover Castle and the Cinque Ports, captain of Calais, Guynes, and Hammes, controller of the entrances to England, and the indispensable brain behind the great adventure. Significantly, when Edward marched north to find and defeat Margaret's forces, he had with him the Seigneur de la Barde who bore the banner of the Dauphin Louis and led a band of men sent by Philip of Burgundy as a testimony to his friendship.

Between 13 and 29 March 1461 Edward was moving up to find the Lancastrian army. There was no time to be lost. Uniting his forces with those of Warwick (who had left London on 7 Mar.) and Fauconberg, but not waiting for Norfolk with the East Anglian contingent, he discovered it near Tadcaster where the road from Ferry Bridge to York dips into a little valley. The Lancastrians had stationed themselves on a plateau just beyond it at Towton, bounded to the right by the Cock brook, then in flood, and on the left by the high road to Tadcaster. Towton was a decisive action of the most desperate kind fought in snowstorms in the which the sheer numbers of the Lancastrians (their force was more than 22,000, far greater than the Yorkist) seemed to be determining the day until Norfolk arrived to fall upon the left flank of the Lancastrians and reinforced the weary Yorkists. In this late reverse the Lancastrians were routed and some of their best leaders killed: the earl of Northumberland, Lord Dacre of Gillesland, Lord Neville, Lords Wells and Willoughby, and Andrew Trollope. The dukes of Exeter and Somerset, with Lord Roos and Sir John Fortescue, escaped, but the earl of Wiltshire was captured eventually at Cockermouth and beheaded as soon as Edward reached Newcastle. Queen Margaret, the prince, and Henry VI fled north, accompanied by Exeter and Somerset.

The weakness in the Yorkist position lay in the fact that beyond Newcastle Edward could not go. If he could have closed the doors of Scotland against Henry and Margaret, they would have fallen into his hands. But the queen had got permission from the bishop of St. Andrews to enter Scotland, Linlithgow Palace was put in readiness for her, and thereafter the bishop procured for Henry and Margaret a more permanent abode in the dominican convent at Edinburgh; James III refused to evict them since Margaret had already laid plans for the marriage of the prince of Wales and James's little sister, and now he was being offered Berwick. On 25 April 1461 Berwick was surrendered to the Scots in Henry VI's name and soon Mary of Guelders had the prince of Wales in her household and was making loans of money to Margaret. The loss of Berwick sealed off Scotland for the time being, provided a notable base for Scoto-Lancastrian border fighting, and prepared the way for the diplomatic activities of the France of Louis XI.

In Wales the parties were balanced, with the Yorkists progressively in the ascendant until the end of the sixties. From the outset of the struggle between York and Lancaster, Wales was deeply involved. As we saw above, supporting the Yorkists were powerful families, such as the Nevilles of Abergavenny, and the Warwicks of Elfael and Glamorgan, but on the Lancastrian side were the important families of Talbot and Beaufort. Humphrey Stafford, duke of Buckingham and lord of Brecknock, was now dead; but Welsh help was secured for the Lancastrian king by his half-brother Edmund Tudor, and, on Edmund's death, by Jasper Tudor who was made earl of Pembroke, thus retaining that strategic region for the Lancastrian party and keeping open the connexion with France, Ireland, and Scotland. While the task of reducing the north of England was entrusted to the earl of Warwick, William Herbert of Raglan, now made Lord Herbert, had the duty of subduing Wales. Pembroke which was attacked by land and sea surrendered along with Tenby, and Jasper Tudor had to fly to north Wales and thence to Ireland. Only Harlech held out to serve as a link between Ireland and Scotland. But it is not impossible that jealousy of Herbert was largely responsible for the later defection of the earl of Warwick. When in 1468 Warwick intrigued with the prominent Lancastrian to restore Henry VI to the throne, Jasper Tudor returned to north Wales; and if Jasper's nephew Henry Tudor fell into the hands of Herbert, now made earl of Pembroke, Herbert was himself defeated by Warwick at the battle of Banbury 1469. The history after 1469 bears out the vital importance of Wales, and especially Pembrokeshire, as the connecting-point with France and Brittany.

XI

EDWARD IV (1)

THE coronation of the earl of March could not take place until Sunday, 28 June 1461. Edward was at York for Easter receiving the submission of Yorkshire towns, and issuing commissions of the peace and for the arrest of his opponents. Before he went the mayor of King's Lynn and various of the Norfolk gentlemen were ordered to seize and bring before the king in chancery Sir Thomas Tuddenham and Robert Halyday, 'rebels and adherents of Henry VI', and to seize their goods.[1] To stamp out resistance by the Lancastrians was a long labour in which both Edward and Warwick were to be occupied during the next three and a half years. The battle of Towton did not solve the problem of the north. It gave the assurance that Edward's government would be unmolested; but the English Lancastrians had still to be cleared out of Northumberland. This meant that any Percy castles that gave trouble had to be besieged and any raids by the lords of the Scottish Border met and defeated. The task of covering the line of the Tyne was undertaken by Warwick, while his brother John Neville, who for his services at Towton had been made Lord Montagu, took over the forces fending off Scottish attacks on the western Marches.

The western Marches felt the first impact. In June 1461 the Scots with the English refugees made a move upon Carlisle, which Exeter and Lord Grey de Rougemont had promised to hand over to the Scots, just as they had done Berwick. Carlisle shut its gates and Montagu relieved the siege which was forming—the suburbs had already been destroyed. At the same time Warwick defeated another raiding party led by Lord Roos and Sir John Fortescue and guided by Thomas and Humphrey Neville of Brancepeth. This was an attempt upon Durham, but it was driven back on 28 June. The main fighting, however, centred upon the attempt of Margaret and her friends and French allies to use the Northumbrian castles of Bamburgh, Dunstanburgh, and Alnwick as the basis of her attacks upon the

---

[1] *Cal. Pat. R., 1461–1467*, p. 28.

Yorkists, as the places from which the recovery, with French help, of England could be achieved. Of these Bamburgh was to be the most fought over, partly because it was to her the nearest, to Warwick the most remote. Dunstanburgh standing on its splendid black rocky cliffs was the largest in circumference, Alnwick the most powerful and at the same time the most civilized. Bamburgh consisted of the castle and the parish, forming the shire of Bamburgh, one of the ancient divisions of Northumbria, the castle, held by the Bretwalda of Bamburgh, was a natural fortress.

The castle was surrendered to Edward IV some time after the battle of Towton and was entrusted by him to the keeping of Sir William Tunstall, a member of a well-known Lonsdale family. In the autumn of 1462 a successful plot enabled Sir Richard Tunstall, a firm champion of Lancaster, to seize the castle from his brother and prepare it for Margaret, who was about to make a descent on England in the company of Pierre de Brézé and other French knights. Writing to his father from Holt Castle in Denbighshire on 1 November 1462, the younger John Paston remarks: 'Syr Wylliam Tunstale is tak with the garyson of Bamborowth and is lyke to be hedyd, and by the menys of Sir Rychard Tunstale, is owne brodyr'.[1] On 25 October 1462 Margaret had landed near Bamburgh expecting that there would be a general rising in her favour, but the country folk finding that she had brought so few French auxiliaries with her remained passive. Margaret laid siege to Alnwick which had to yield for lack of foodstuffs. Dunstanburgh also admitted an English garrison. The approach of Warwick with a large army for the siege of Berwick caused Margaret who was in Bamburgh with Brézé to put to sea in the hope that the arrival of a French fleet would save her. She got off in a 'carvyle' but owing to a storm had to anchor off Holy Island. Some of the French ships went ashore near Bamburgh. Brézé got away and Margaret reached Berwick in a fishing boat on 3 November. On 10 December Warwick began the siege of the three castles from his headquarters at Warkworth. Inside Bamburgh were the duke of Somerset, Lord Roos, Sir Ralph Percy, the earl of Pembroke: the besieging forces were led by John Tiptoft, earl of Worcester, and the earl of Arundel, while there were also there Lords Montagu, Strange, Say, Gray of

[1] *Paston Letters*, iv. 59.

Wilton, Lumley, and Ogle. On Christmas Eve the castle surrendered conditionally: life and limb were to be spared, the
leaders were to be restored to their estates on swearing allegiance
to Edward, and Sir Ralph Percy was to have the custody of the
castles of Dunstanburgh and Bamburgh. None the less by Lent
1463 Percy had let the French into the latter. Sir Ralph Grey,
out of indignation about not receiving the governorship of
Alnwick, by trickery secured the castle and handed it over to
the Lancastrians. Two months later Henry VI came to Bamburgh from Scotland with Margaret and Brézé. After an unsuccessful attempt on Norham (on the Tweed) Margaret had
to fall back on Bamburgh, with her husband and son: Henry
was left in the castle and on 3 July Margaret and her son set
sail for Flanders accompanied by the duke of Exeter and Sir
John Fortescue, along with Brézé and his Frenchmen in four
balingers. The Scots were not altogether sorry to see them go.
Gregory has a story of an episode 'at the departing of Sir Persy
[*sic*] de Brasyle and his fellowship', of a valiant French bands-
man who wished to meet Warwick. He took his stand on some
high ground by himself with his tabor and fife, 'taboryng and
pyping as merely [merrily] as any man myght' and would not
give ground till Warwick came up to him. The earl took him
into his service, in which he continued 'fulle good' for years.[1]

Warwick made no headway in the north and, in spite of
Edward IV's preparations, Henry VI in the old Northumbrian
capital of Bamburgh continued for the next nine months to
reign over that little shire and Alnwick. Such was his principality from the autumn of 1463 till the end of May 1464. In the
winter of 1463-4 a new Lancastrian conspiracy began, with
branches extending from Wales to Yorkshire. The outbreak
started at Christmas 1463 with the unexpected rebellion of the
duke of Somerset, who made for the garrison at Alnwick: his
coming into the north, when he arrived almost alone, was a
signal for a new Lancastrian outbreak. Simultaneously Earl
Jasper Tudor of Pembroke tried to stir up Wales. From Alnwick
a band set out which seized the castle of Skipton in Craven, not
far from Warwick's estates in the North Riding: and Norham
on the Border fell to the Lancastrians. There was a rising in
south Lancashire and Cheshire. Thrice Warwick had already
subdued—or thought he had subdued—the north. He had no

[1] *The Historical Collections of a London Citizen*, ed. Gairdner (C.S. 1876), pp. 220-1.

difficulty in dealing with the rising in Cheshire, but this was perhaps the time to make peace with Scotland and prevent the reception there of Edward IV's enemies. The Scots appeared willing and Montagu was sent north to escort the Scots commissioners to York. He had to fight his way past Somerset and the Lancastrian survivors of the campaigns of 1461–2–3, Lord Roos and Hungerford and the two turncoats Sir Ralph Grey and Sir Ralph Percy. At Hedgeley Moor, Montagu dispersed the Lancastrian army, was able to march to Scotland and bring the commissioners to York, where a fifteen years' peace was concluded, the Scots promising to give no further shelter to the Lancastrians and the English to disarm the earls of Ross and Douglas whom they had armed against the Scotch regency. The last stand made by the Lancastrians was at Hexham on 15 May 1464: but their army broke when the Yorkists came in sight and those that stayed were either killed or captured on the hill a mile outside the town. Montagu beheaded Somerset and Sir Edmund FitzHugh; on the next day but one he had Lord Roos, Lord Hungerford, and three others put to death at Newcastle: on the morrow he moved south to Warwick's great castle at Middleham and there had Sir Philip Wentworth and six squires executed.[1] For these deeds of blood this much can be said, that Somerset and several others of the victims were men who had claimed and abused Edward's pardon, and that Roos and several men had been spared at the surrender of Bamburgh in 1462. Yet these judicial executions made any reconciliation of the parties more difficult than ever. For his services in dealing with the rebels Montagu was created earl of Northumberland by Edward, who handed over to him, together with the Percy title, the greater part of the Percy estates. Of these Alnwick was not yet actually in Yorkist hands, but on 23 June the earl of Warwick appeared before it and summoned it to surrender: the garrison did so, on promise of their lives. Dunstanburgh and Norham followed Alnwick: only Bamburgh held out, where Sir Ralph Grey had taken refuge: with him was Sir Humphrey Neville who had fought Montagu at Hedgeley Moor. Both of these were excepted from the offer of free pardons by Warwick. The custodians when summoned refused to surrender Bamburgh, and Warwick had with his

---

[1] The list of those executed at Newcastle, Middleham, and York is given by Gregory, *Collections*, pp. 224–6.

ordnance to shoot a breach in the walls: 'so all the King's guns that were charged began to shoot upon the said castle.' A breach was made and the place carried by assault. Grey was brought to the king at Doncaster when he was tried before John Tiptoft the earl of Worcester and sentenced to be beheaded. The fall of Bamburgh meant that there was now little danger of a Lancastrian rising in the north.

In the meantime Margaret was seeking French aid. Wholly determined to meet Louis XI, she had already formed good hopes of a Lancastrian–French alliance. In July 1461 she had asked Charles VII for a loan of 20,000 crowns and the help of a French army to fight for her in Wales: but the letters were never delivered, for Charles died on 22 July; and, it seemed, little could be hoped for from the Dauphin who had been friendly to the house of York. Yet between the Dauphin, as he was then, and Louis XI, as he was now, there was a substantial difference: a strong Yorkist England was no part of Louis's plans; it was best to keep the country divided: and although he was already holding some of the Lancastrian leaders who had escaped from England, he was very agreeable to the ambassadors sent by Queen Margaret. For her that was enough to go upon. She had landed in Brittany on 16 April 1462, and the duke, Francis II, received her warmly. In May she went to see her father at Angers and to meet her energetic helper Pierre de Brézé. In June the earl of Pembroke and Sir John Fortescue followed her to France. Pembroke joined Margaret in time to be present at the meeting with Louis XI which took place in Touraine. At Chinon on 23 June 1462 the queen offered Louis Calais in return for a loan of 20,000 francs; promising that if Henry ever recovered it, either the earl of Pembroke or the earl of Kendal should be made captain, and that whichever of them was given the office, should deliver the town and the castle to the king of France within a year from the present or else repay the 20,000 francs. Louis in exchange promised that if Calais came into his possession thus, he would pay Henry VI 40,000 crowns. On this basis a treaty between Louis and Henry VI was signed (28 June). A hundred years' truce between Henry and Louis was to begin at once, the subjects of either king being able to visit each other's kingdoms freely, though while the troubles lasted any Englishman coming to France had to show a certificate from Henry and Margaret proving that he was their subject, and until Henry and Margaret were re-established in England, no subjects of theirs were to go to Gascony for trade or for any other purpose without a licence from the king of France. Each king promised not to enter into any alliance with rebellious subjects of the other.

The attitude of Louis XI to these negotiations was characteristic. By his league with John II of Aragon and Gaston de Foix, Louis had brought himself into awkward relations with Castile, which Edward IV did all he could to exploit, even to the extent of sending two members of the council to Spain to treat with its ruler, Henry the Impotent. The ambassadors when they left London were charged with the task of renewing the alliance that had formerly existed, and Louis saw himself liable to have to contend with an alliance between Edward and Henry of Castile. He was doing his utmost to prevent John of Aragon from making an alliance with England, and having succeeded in this, he could do something for Margaret: he could help her projected invasion as a means to keep Edward occupied and so have a better chance of capturing Calais. The difficulty about this plan was the attitude of Philip of Burgundy. Louis tried to get the father's permission to use the count of Charolais for an attack on Calais; but this was refused, and then he thought of using for this purpose Margaret and the forces she was raising at Rouen. The garrison were in rather a worse state of underpayment than usual, but the hopes of Margaret and Louis were dashed when the merchants of the Staple again consented to lend Edward the £41,000 he required to pay the wages. Meanwhile Edward had fitted out a fleet of seventy ships, manned by at least 12,000 men, to raid the French coast from Le Conquet in Brittany down to Bordeaux, and Louis was occupied with counter-measures. Neither he nor Francis II could be of much immediate use to Margaret who, short of money, accepted a loan of 1,000 crowns from Brézé himself. With this limited support to subsidize an expedition of 2,000 men, Margaret and Brézé sailed for the Northumbrian coast to garrison and man the Northumbrian castles, but Edward's riposte sent them to sea again, this time with their fleet dispersed by a storm which destroyed much of their money and the military stores they had brought, while 400 of their troops had to shelter on Holy Island and surrender to the Yorkists. This danger overcome, Edward determined to prevent France becoming a refuge for malcontents set upon destroying his government and decided to feel his way towards a treaty or at least a truce. At that moment (early in 1463) Aragon was threatening to leave Louis, and the French king found the moment right for negotiations with England, for he had other aims; to bring Francis of Brittany to heel and to take advantage of the clause in the treaty of Arras allowing the king of France to repurchase the Somme towns. A surprisingly appropriate offer on the part of Philip of Burgundy to mediate between them provided the occasion, and it was agreed that English and French negotiators should meet the Burgundians at St. Omer on 24 June 1463. Any binding agreement between the three powers was exactly what Margaret did not want. She was determined to state her case to Duke Philip who was equally determined not to have her at the St. Omer conference for fear she might wreck it. Philip complied with her wishes and gave her, non-committally, 1,000 crowns. But nothing she could do could prevent agreement being reached at the conference to conclude a truce between England and France, in which the territories of the dukes of Burgundy and Brittany were comprised. When the convention was made public one clause seemed to give a final blow to Lancastrian hopes.

That the king of France shall neither give nor suffer his subjects to give, any help or favour to Henry, late calling himself King of England, Margaret his wife nor her son, nor to any other enemies of the king of England; and similarly the king of England shall not give, nor suffer his subjects to give, any help or favour to the enemies of Louis of France.[1]

Before the St. Omer diet had broken up the commercial treaty between England and Burgundy was continued to All Saints' Day, 1464: Philip was anxious that England should take part in a crusade against the Turks and send some of their best archers.

During the conference Louis was staying at Hesdin, and there the matter of Edward IV's marriage received discussion. At Warwick's suggestion Edward through his envoys had asked for the daughter of Louis XI. The French king replied that she was too young but offered one of his wife's sisters, Bona, daughter of the count of Savoy. Burgundy, alarmed at the possible conse-

---

[1] *Foedera*, v. ii. 117 (from the Close roll).

quences of such a marriage, offered the hand of one of his
nieces, and in March 1464 the ambassadors of the king of
Castile, Henry the Impotent, urged Edward to marry his sister
Isabella of Castile. Edward, aware of his own eligibility, played
the card of his bachelordom as long as he could: for some
time he concealed both from Warwick (who had been much
attracted by the idea of Isabella) and from his ministers the
fact that he was already married, for on 30 April 1464, when he
was staying at the guest house of the abbey of St. Albans, he
had ridden to Stony Stratford where he stopped the night, and
then on 1 May had gone over to Grafton Regis where he
married Elizabeth Woodville, the eldest daughter of Lord
Rivers and the dowager duchess of Bedford, and widow of
Lord Ferrers of Groby who had been killed at St. Albans while
fighting for Margaret of Anjou against the earl of Warwick.
For three months Edward kept the matter secret while Warwick
was planning to get Bona of Savoy. The French king was
equally anxious to cultivate Warwick. Louis hoped to get him
to a meeting at Hesdin on 24 June 1464; but Warwick would
not come: he got as far as Calais, but wrote to Louis that he
was prevented from going farther by certain matters affecting
the welfare of England. Louis was extremely disappointed.
He and Philip met the English ambassadors accredited to the
conference but found that they could do no more than prolong
the truce: they asked for a long postponement: 'the siege of
Bamburgh was on', and so forth. The ambassadors were shown
the queen's sisters, particularly Bona, beautifully dressed for
the occasion, and Lord Wenlock was offered a large reward if
he would help to bring about the marriage between Edward
and Bona.

Edward had stopped Warwick at Calais: he instructed the
earl, after returning to London, to cross again and interview
Philip of Burgundy, and the mission, Miss Scofield thought,
'had some connection with the alliance the Duke of Brittany
(Francis II) and the Count of Charolais (future Charles the
Bold) contracted against Louis, which ended in the War of the
League of the Public Weal'.[1] Francis and Charles began to deal
diplomatically with Edward, and Louis got wind of it from the
Scots, who had heard about it, when they had been negotiating
with the English at York. The bishop of Glasgow and Sir

[1] *The Life and Reign of Edward IV* (1923), i. 348.

William Monypenny went over to France to report to Louis about the state of affairs in England and Scotland. Monypenny said that there had been much useless haggling, but in the end Francis had promised 3,000 archers to be placed under the command of Lord Montagu. Louis tried to seize the ambassadors of Francis II on their way back from England and failed. The French king did his utmost to find out what was going on between Edward and Francis but could ascertain nothing certain: meanwhile the postponed date of the meeting with Warwick, 1 October, came, and no Warwick. On 4 October Louis heard the story of Edward's marriage and what was described as a break with Warwick; and he let the Milanese ambassador know confidentially that if it turned out to be true that a rupture had occurred between Edward and Warwick, he would take Warwick's part, and that he could count on the aid of the two brethren of the duke of Somerset. By 10 October Louis knew what had happened. Edward had already revealed it at a council held at Reading on 14 September 1464. The announcement, as Lord Wenlock wrote to Lannoy (9 Oct.), caused 'great displeasure to many great lords, and especially to the larger part of all his council': but for Warwick the only course was to make the best of it. On Michaelmas Day Elizabeth Woodville was escorted into the chapel of Reading Abbey by the duke of Clarence and the earl of Warwick and honoured as queen: and Edward tried to appease Warwick by securing the translation of George Neville to the archbishopric of York. Warwick, however, got a foretaste of what was coming when he heard of the betrothal of one of the queen's sisters to Lord Maltravers, son and heir of the earl of Arundel. The earl, we know, wrote a number of letters on Edward's marriage which have disappeared, but in the one written to Louis he stated, according to the French king himself, that he and Edward were on bad terms, and he hoped to send in a few days one of his secretaries with news that would be pleasing to the king of France. From this Louis concluded that Warwick desired to make himself king: he told the Milanese ambassador that he thought the earl would succeed, and that, as he considered him one of his best friends, he was disposed to help him.

In taking up the policy of an Anglo-French alliance Warwick was following in the footsteps of Beaufort and Suffolk; but with this difference, that the pact he aimed at was to exclude another

state—Burgundy. On 27 October 1464 a plan for the continuance of mercantile intercourse between England and Burgundy
was agreed, even though shortly before this Philip had prohibited the import of English cloth and yarn into his lands and
territories, an unfriendly act and one much resented, but
undertaken probably at the request of the Flemish towns who
had told the duke that the import of English cloth was destructive of their own cloth industry. Unluckily this restriction was
imposed just when Warwick was becoming entangled by Louis.
Warwick listened too closely to the dislike many persons expressed for Philip and brought himself to think that he could
lead England into an alliance with France at the cost, if need
be, of her friendship with Burgundy. He misjudged the amount
of opposition that Edward would offer to his French policy and
underestimated the determination of his affable protégé to
remain on good terms with Burgundy.

The period before the Woodville marriage, while fighting was
going on in the north and the new government was occupied
in suppressing Lancastrian centres of rebellion, gave neither
Edward nor Warwick the leisure to think much about their
mutual relationships. Warwick was content to be the mayor of
the Palace with an authority more or less supreme in military
matters and defence and a general supervision of the north:
Edward, also engaged in curbing Lancastrian resistance, had
the more general problem of pacification and order at his doors,
as well as the inveterate question of finance. In any event the
king who flung himself passionately into life brooded but little:
he was an opportunist, though some principles of policy were
to develop and to be maintained by him with great tenacity.
Warwick, far more difficult to assess, had the pride and some
of the reserve of the Nevilles, their love of great state and
magnificence, and, peculiar to himself, the tendency to build
up and realize in action an image, a projection of what he
thought to be his own fundamental nature. This imaginative
portrait seems to have grown upon him and to have haunted
him increasingly in his later days.

Before considering the development and consequences of
Warwick's breach with his former protégé, it is worth while
to note the caution and consideration displayed by Edward in
the first few years of his government. He had reached the throne
on a full tide of reaction against the Lancastrian usurpation to

which the general disorder affecting England, the commons thought, might be traced. In giving sanction to Edward's succession the commons, petitioning in the parliament of November 1461 for the acts of Coventry parliament to be considered void, laid down that the 'Coroune, Roial Estate, Dignitee and Lordship . . . of right apperteynd to the seid noble Prynce Richard, Duc of York' who was 'verry true and rightful heir to the throne'.[1] Henry VI, by his attempt in February 1461 to despoil the then earl of March from the city and earldom of Chester and by his refusal to recognize Edward's hereditary right, had gone round upon his admission that Richard of York was heir to the throne: for abstaining to press his claim, Richard of York had been promised castles, lands, and rents to the tune of 10,000 marks. Yet for all that Somerset had killed the duke at Wakefield. Edward's title rested thus upon the admission of his Lancastrian predecessor whose conduct and acts had rendered him guilty of perjury, just as his claim to rule rested upon usurpation. In this attempted return to constitutional rectitudes, reassertion of the moral and legal authority of parliament was the necessary aim of Edward's first assembly. At his beginning the personnel of the lords presented many changes. His kinsman and friend John Mowbray, duke of Norfolk, had died (6 Nov.); there were new earls of Essex and Kent; the earl of Oxford had asked for a licence to absent himself from the last parliament of Henry's reign and did not appear, and Warwick, Arundel, and Westmorland were the other survivors summoned. New to the band was John Tiptoft, earl of Worcester, just home from the Mediterranean, who was made a member of the king's council on 1 November 1461 and later constable of the Tower, then (7 Feb. 1462) constable of England, and shortly afterwards a knight of the garter. The Speaker of the first parliament was the Yorkshire knight Sir James Strangways, connected with the Nevilles, who gave Edward some good advice on rewarding the friends who had helped him to establish himself and on the need for keeping better order in the country than during the previous reign. Of the lords present in that first parliament there are lists of day-to-day attendance for a part of the first session, which show an extraordinarily full presence of the peers in the period covered by the surviving fragment of a Lords' Journal: ninety-nine

[1] *Rot. Parl.* v. 465.

spiritual and thirty-eight temporal lords. Listed, but not in attendance, were nine spiritual and eleven temporal. Roughly four out of every five peers were present. Only three of the bishops failed to come, Thomas Bekyngton, now discharged permanently, and the bishops of St. Davids and St. Asaph.[1] As many as twenty-one abbots put in an appearance. These may, of course, have been alarmed about the possible resumption of lands, particularly alien priory lands, given them or once in the possession of the crown. The exempt religious were already in bad odour for their evasion of taxation, and were aware of it. The attendance at daily meetings was also considerable: the smallest number of peers present on any one of the recorded occasions was forty-seven and the largest sixty-seven, a remarkable number.[2] It was an important parliament, for besides the recognition of Edward's hereditary right to the throne (as was noted) the declaration that the Lancastrian kings were usurpers made it necessary to establish the validity of certain acts of the last three kings and to ratify accordingly judicial acts of the previous reigns not done by the authority of any parliament, as well as patents creating titles, franchises, and other grants made to municipalities, gilds and crafts, presentments to benefices, assignments of dower, &c.[3] In the second place, a general resumption act had to be carried through, attenuated to a certain extent by the exemptions which these validations made necessary, but none the less formidable in scope and effect. It was also necessary to attaint the chief supporters of Henry VI, and there was no lack of reprisals for the measures taken in the Coventry parliament of 1459: besides Henry, Margaret, and Edward her son, the duchy of Lancaster (declared forfeit) and royal adherents, like the dukes of Somerset and Exeter, the earls of Devonshire, Northumberland, Pembroke, and Wiltshire, Viscount Beaumont, Lord Roos, Clifford, Hungerford, Welles, Neville, Dacre of Gillesland and Humphrey his brother, Sir John Fortescue, Sir Andrew Trollope, Sir William Tailboys, all came under the measure. This was done in the form of a statute, not by petition. There was the sentence pronounced on the earl of Cambridge in Henry's V's reign to be reversed, as well as the attainder of

---

[1] *The Fane Fragment of the 1461 Lords' Journal*, ed. W. H. Dunham, jnr. (1935), pp. 93 f.

[2] J. S. Roskell, 'The Problem of the Attendance of the Lords in Medieval Parliaments', *Bull. Inst. Hist. Res.* xxix (1956), 196. [3] *S.R.* I Ed. IV, c. I.

John Montagu, earl of Shrewsbury, and Thomas Lord Despenser in 2 Henry IV.

Parliament was for long occupied in two special causes: in the first place there was the claim of the merchants of the Staple at Calais, for ratification of previous acts made to issue to them repayment of past loans to the crown amounting to £41,000. This was put 'in respite' pending further investigation, and they were, in fact, paid in the following year. The chronicler Fabyan states that two staplers had lent Edward and Warwick £18,000 when they were at Calais waiting to cross to England, and that as the council held that the loan was made by the treasurer the earl of Wiltshire, without the king's knowledge, therefore, because Wiltshire's goods had been forfeited for treason, the sum remained confiscated to the crown.[1] In point of fact the £18,000 had been originally a sum claimed by Wiltshire's agent, Richard Heron, from the staplers on the ground that they had prevented the sale of wools which he had exported to Calais, and when he could not for the time being recover it from the merchants he began processes against them, in the court of the duke of Burgundy, and then afterwards both in the parliament of Paris and at the papal curia no less than on two occasions. At the time it was thought that Heron had received permission to sue abroad, but in reality it was not so, and the king's council was able to show that Heron should have prosecuted his case in the king's courts and not outside the realm. His action is not uncharacteristic of an unscrupulous agent trying to make out that the money he claimed had been loaned by the staplers for Edward IV's expedition and that he had received official permission to sue for it abroad.

The other case was the dispute between Bishop Waynflete of Winchester and his tenants in the manor of East Meon. These were claiming release from the works and customs demanded of them by the bishop by reason of their tenures, and from other customary rents, on the ground that they were freeholders and not copyholders, all tenures within the lordship being, as they asserted, 'charter and free land' and not copyhold lands. In 1461 special commissioners had been sent into Hampshire to hear and decide the issue,[2] but no solution had been reached,

---

[1] *The New Chronicles of England and France*, ed. H. Ellis (1811), pp. 652–3.
[2] *Cal. Pat R., 1461–1467*, p. 38, when it was alleged that the tenants were 'throwing off their allegiance'.

and it was now judged that the case was one for a special legal committee to examine the complaints brought to parliament by the tenants themselves at the suggestion the king himself made when they approached him at Winchester. The committee duly reported to the lords who heard the arguments of both sides at length and upheld the bishop's pleading on the ground of title-deeds, court rolls, and the pipe-rolls of fifteen successive holders of the see. It was adjudged that the tenants must pay the rents and perform the services required by the bishop. This award[1] did not, however, deter them from again complaining (May 1462) to the king about imprisonments which they alleged that Waynflete had carried out. The king sent them home with instructions that at Whitsuntide two or three men from each hamlet in the lordship should appear while the bishop was also to send fully empowered representatives. Both sides put in an appearance, but the tenants, before waiting to be heard, left the town of Leicester where the case was to be held, and the matter was left to come before the council in the Star Chamber (3 July 1462); here judgement was given againt the tenants, and it was decided that the sheriff of Hampshire should be instructed to help Waynflete in maintaining his rights.[2]

The Fane fragment of the Lords' Journal shows the lords sitting from day to day to consider and amend when need be, petitions in parliament. One of them which passed on to the statute book (1 Ed. IV, c. 2) laid down that all indictments and presentments in the sheriff's tourn should be delivered to the justices of the peace at their ensuing session, and not heard and determined by the sheriffs themselves. The criminal jurisdiction of the sheriff was by this measure abolished. The sheriff thenceforward was to be an administrative guardian of the shire, not a judicial officer, and while it was his business to secure the persons and set out the evidence which had to be laid before the local justices, he could not do more. The preamble to the assented petition speaks of the 'infinite Indictments and Presentments' leading to copious arrests, and, in the trials, to the compliancy of 'jurors having no conscience' who obeyed the sheriff and his officers, as well as to the scale of the fines and amendments levied. It was now for the justices, not the sheriffs,

---

[1] *Rot. Parl.* vi. 475.
[2] *Select Cases before the King's Council*, ed. J. S. Leadam and J. F. Baldwin (Selden Soc. 1918), pp. 114–15.

to decide whether the process of trial in the case of presented persons was to be carried through, and to do the arraigning, delivery, and fining themselves; and penalties were determined for sheriffs who arrested and then refused to deliver the indictments to the justices. The lords, when they had the petition before them the first time, made special provisos for those who had view of frank-pledge and were the lords of private jurisdictions.

In his first parliament Edward IV took the opportunity to thank the commons for the support which they had given him. Addressing the Speaker, he voiced his recognition of the 'true hearts and tender considerations that ye [the Commons] have had to any right and title that I and my ancestors have had unto the crown of the nation', and for the way in which they had remembered to correct (by the act legitimizing his heir) the 'horrible murder and cruel death of his father and of his brother the Earl of Rutland and his cousin of Salisbury'; he promised to be 'as good and gracious sovereign lord as ever was any of my noble progenitors to their subjects and liegemen'. It was appropriate that after this forthright speech of thanks the chancellor should announce an ordinance against maintenance and the granting of liveries which called upon the king's subjects to make every effort to capture thieves and murderers and cautioned those who had received pardons of the consequences of reiterating their offences. No grant was asked for in parliament, but it must have been plain to Edward that a great many people expected to be rewarded for their assistance to him, while the question remained whether the resumptions and the confiscation of the duchy of Lancaster would bring in sufficient for this purpose. The first actual grant was made for defence only in the parliament of 1463, which because of Lancastrian and other interruptions was prorogued from 17 June until 4 November (while the king was in the north), then prorogued to York (20 February 1464), then again to 5 May (York) and later to 26 November (the same). In this Edward was granted an aid of £37,000; £31,000 of which (in two instalments) was to be raised 'in manner and form of payment of the last fifteenth and tenth of shires, cities boroughs and places'. All persons receiving below 10s. yearly from lands and rents or having goods and chattels not to the value of 5 marks were excepted. The remaining £6,000, the sum deducted from the localities' last grant on account of the impoverishment of certain localities, was to be levied from persons having land, &c., to the value of 20s. or goods and chattels to the value of 10 marks: the sum to be assessed 'by such commissioners as shall thereto be severally assigned by your highness'. This last £6,000 Edward remitted (4 Nov.) and declared that the £31,000 should be levied 'oonly by the name of a XVᵉ' which meant that it was not to be assessed in the form of a tenth in cities and boroughs. The convocations for 1461–3 were more forthcoming. The Canterbury provincial council, meeting on 6 May and continued from day to day until 15 July 1461, granted a tenth, payable in moieties in March and November 1462; a half tenth was granted in the convocation 21 July–2 August 1462, in which strong measures were taken against the formidable list of absentees by regaining earlier payment of one of the previous moieties;[1] and a full tenth in the convocation meeting 6–23 July 1463. York granted two moieties in the meeting begun on 30 April 1460 and continued, with interruptions till 23 March 1462, and in the assembly of 1 September 1462. The third Canterbury contribution must have been increased by a 'charitable subsidy' on a graded scale from the stipendiary clergy of the province payable to the archbishop and the bishop of Exeter,[2] George Neville. We know that Edward IV was dissatisfied with the traditional clerical tenth, and in 1461 expressed his views on the subject to Bishop Bekyngton;[3] hence in all probability the re-emergence for the first time since 1377 of the 'caritative' subsidy to buttress up the normal clerical grant. For it has now been proved that the archbishop normally sent the subsidy of the stipendiaries to the Exchequer. It is noteworthy that, at this stage, the clergy were more generous to Edward IV than the laity; they did it, as the wording of the grant in Edward's first convocation shows, 'considering the abundant favour and grace which the king (as they were confidently hoping) will show to churchmen and moreover the urgent needs and the many various perils that threaten the realm from enemies . . .'.[4] The 'favour and grace' were most

[1] The lists, strikingly large, are in *Cal. Fine R., 1461–1471*, pp. 84 f.
[2] *Reg. Thome Bourgchier*, ed. du Boulay, i. 112–15. These subsidies granted 'for the praise of God and the reformation of the Church' are discussed by F. R. H. du Boulay, 'Charitable subsidies granted to the Archbishop of Canterbury', *Bull. Inst. Hist. Res.* xxiii (1950).
[3] Ibid., p. 158 n.   [4] *Cal. Fine R., 1461–1471*, p. 29.

necessary in order to provide against the darker consequences of royal resumptions.

It would have been interesting to read the comments of the lords on the petitions presented in the 1463 parliament. The largest and most important of these were economic: to ensure a proper standard in the cloths produced in this country by laying down regulations for the length, breadth, and quality of the broadcloth and providing an adequate staff of ulnagers accounting regularly at the Exchequer: to ensure that a 'suffisant plenteth' (plenty) of wool remained in the country, and that all wool exported should go to Calais, saving only 'the growyng of the counties of Northumberland, Cumberland and Westmorland' and the 'growyng of the Bishoprick of Durham, betweene the waters of Tyne and Teese, and of the [said] shires of Allerton and Richmond'—the Neville country; to restrict the importation of corn and silken goods brought in by the Lombards; to curtail extravagance in garments and apparel; no grade and rank to exceed his or her allowance. The fact that costly fabrics have a longer life did not appeal to the sumptuary legislators. The present petition is typical of the complaints periodically made in the later medieval parliaments to check the 'inordynaunt arayes' of men and women: its purpose was perhaps less concerned with morality and the setting of a bad example of extravagance than with the desire to curtail the sales of imported stuffs, goods brought by Lombard silk merchants, the damasks, satin, and velvet with which Italians travelled round the country; and, even on a humbler scale, London 'artificers' petitioned for a restraint upon 'Merchauntes Straungers' that brought in saddler's wares, leather goods, and ironmongery, and a host of household utensils which the medieval wife must have been only too glad to buy.[1] Edward, a great sinner in the matter of costly clothes, furs, and jewels,[2] exempted the Teutonic Hansa and made room for wares imported from Ireland and Wales; he also exempted the dean and chapter of St. Martin the Great, the royal free chapel, strongly protected with immunities which in 1432 and again in 1440 had been successfully upheld against the mayor and citizens of London.[3] While appreciating to the full the friendly attitude of the

---

[1] *Rot. Parl.* v. 506–7.
[2] See the warrants cited by Scofield, op. cit., i. 283 n.
[3] *Letter Book K*, pp. 151–61.

commons and particularly of the city which had helped him
on his return, Edward had to be on his guard against the extreme
protectionism that continually found its voice in parliament,
and in the city itself took either peaceful or unpeaceful forms of
action against Genoese and Venetians especially.[1] Only three
years subsequently there were demonstrations against the
merchant strangers which induced the city authorities to prose-
cute rowdier offenders in the Crafts.[2]

The genial and affable king has been the subject of no contemporary portrait by fifteenth-century English writers, saving
only the second continuator of the Croyland Chronicle. It is to
Sir Thomas More and Polydore Vergil, who must have known
people that either saw or knew Edward, that recourse must be
had for an estimate, and these give a view scarcely possible to
contemporaries. More, the contrast of Edward with Richard III
always in his mind, calls him 'princely to behold', a man

of hearte couragious, politique in counsaile, in adversitie nothynge
abashed, in peace juste and mercifull, in warre sharpe and fyerce, in
the fielde bolde and hardye and natheless no farther than wysedome
woulde adventurouse. Whose warres whoso will consyder, hee shall
no lesse commende hys wysedome where he voyded than hys manne-
hode where he vanquished. He was of visage louelye, of body mygh-
tie, strong and cleane made . . .,

and dwells upon his popularity due to little acts of consideration
which impress people more than large benefits.[3] Vergil says that
he was very tall and good looking, large in build but well pro-
portioned; with a quick wit, high spirit, and retentive memory,
diligent in his affairs 'earnest and horryble to the enemy,
bowntyfull to his frinds and aquayntance'; prone to sexual
indulgence, he made friendships not always befitting his dignity. In later life he began to 'slyde by lyttle and lyttle into
avarice', by contrast with his old liberality: still, after party
disorder had been suppressed, he left his realm in a most
wealthy condition. Upon those who belonged to the genuine
nobility he was always ready to bestow position and office,
especially membership of his council, while lesser men in his

[1] Cf. the report to a panel of justices on the claims of the city (1434) to take
'scawage', a customary tax on foreign imports which arose out of action by the
sheriffs against the Genoese. Ibid., p. 175.   [2] Ibid., pp. 385 f.
[3] *The Historie of Kyng Rycharde the Thirde*, ed. J. R. Lumby (1883), pp. 2–3. The
example of such an act was his invitation to the mayor and aldermen of London to
Windsor 'for none other eraunde but too have them hunte and be mery with hym'.

favour were adorned 'with welth, not with dygnytie'.[1] He was very popular and long mourned after his death. Vergil does not fail to reprove him for breaking his oath to the citizens of York on his return to England before Barnet, or for the secrecy he adopted after marrying Elizabeth Woodville; but thinks of him as liberal and generous, perhaps too much so, as Vergil says: 'he used towardes every man of highe and low degree more than mete famylyarytie which trade of life he never changed'. In personal relationships he had little sense of class; there was nothing stuffy or conventional about Edward; but with people in whom he got interested he was sometimes led to believe that his confidence and affection would be returned, when it was not so. His intimacy with the duke of Somerset after he had returned from the north was a disillusioning experience: there was nothing to be done with Somerset. Vergil's sketch is a more sober and accurate delineation than that of Philippe de Commines, whose desire to exalt Louis XI led him to belittle other contemporaries. With him Edward does not come out well. Commines emphasizes Edward's self-indulgence and thinks that his constant debaucheries brought down upon him the political disorders that afflicted him from 1467 onwards. He admits Edward's brilliance and charm, thinking of him when he was at his height as the *beau prince*, a Renaissance figure, and that is indeed the aspect that struck contemporaries: a splendid-looking, able man with a great faculty for determined action and a notable way of extricating himself from danger; a first-rate soldier who enjoyed the mêlée, yet with more than a tendency to intellectual *embonpoint* and the mental laziness often found in big carnal men. On the other hand, both Dominic Mancini who wrote the narrative of Richard III's reign (referred to hereafter) and the second Croyland continuator[2] are clear that Edward, in spite of his relaxations, was a shrewd and intent man of business, and the latter especially emphasizes his wealth, his attention to financial detail, and the position he held at the end of his reign when he was held in awe by his subjects and 'by glory and tranquillity . . . had made himself illustrious'. This is a different story from the gloomy account of Edward given by John Warkworth, master of Peterhouse, in the

[1] 'Rowmes of honour'. *Three Books of Polydore Vergil: English History*, ed. Sir H. Ellis (Camden Soc. 1844), p. 172.

[2] Cited by J. R. Lander, 'Edward IV: the Modern Legend: and a Revision', *History*, xli (1956), 43.

chronicle written some time after 1473, when he observed that by 1469 Yorkist government was so discredited that there was little to choose between it and the Lancastrian régime preceding. There was, from the point of view of the central administration, a great deal to be said for Edward's government,[1] and in the sphere of justice and police there is no doubt of the part he personally took in suppressing disorder, especially in 1461, when he realized that an effective shrievalty was the key to the problem of Norfolk under the influence of Tuddenham and Daniel, and brought himself to release Sir Thomas Montgomery from duties in the royal household for that particular purpose: and in 1464 he went himself on a judicial tour with the justices Markham and Danby from Coventry to Worcester, Tewkesbury, and Gloucester (4–10 Feb.), and eastwards to Cambridge to punish 'risers against the peace'. But in a sense, the whole campaign of 1462–4 displays the energy of the king against the sources of riot and treason.

Edward's dealings with Coventry, besides testifying to his close personal relationships with the place, illustrate his judicial activities in a city firmly devoted to the Yorkist cause. From 1460 onwards Coventry became closely identified with the fortunes of Warwick and Edward. Both parties drew upon it for troops. In the mayoralty of William Kemp (1459) the Lancastrians had commissioned the mayor and sheriffs to assigne and taxe what noumber of abull men myght be had out of the seid Cite at the costes of the same cite to attende uppon oure soverayn lordes person' against the Yorkists attainted in the parliament held there, and the mayor decided, because the commission came so late, to consult Duke Humphrey of Buckingham in the matter. The mayor evidently preferred to pay £500 in lieu of sending the troops, and the next record in the mayor's register is a severe complaint, from the king, of disaffection in the town, 'unfittyng langyeage against oure estate' and other evidences of disloyalty which the mayor has to inquire into and punish.[2] Coventry was compelled to obey the requisition for troops and 40 *abiles homines* well arrayed were chosen to go at the city's cost to support Margaret's cause. But the city gave conclusive evidence of its true attitude when it collected by wards £100 for Edward's expedition to London after the

---

[1] Cf. below, p. 601.
[2] *The Coventry Leet Book*, ed. M. Dormer Harris (E.E.T.S. 1907–13), p. 309.

second battle of St. Albans, and Edward on the day after his
accession wrote to thank Coventry for the 'feliship as ye sent
unto us to do us service' and promising to send help if any rebel
attempted to get control of the place. To the new sovereign
when he arrived after the Towton campaign[1] the citizens
presented £100 and a cup and gave Warwick £40 for fourteen
men in his pursuit of Henry and Margaret to the north, when
even the little hospital of Bablake contributed its pennies.[2]

On 7 July the city received a strong warning from Edward
against breaches of the peace, wearing of livery without warrant
and taking the laws into private hands, which suggests that
property of Lancastrian sympathizers outside the city had been
seized without authority. Nor was Edward less scrupulous in
enforcing his own rights. In 1464 the city officials had arrested
in Cheylesmore Park, a royal franchise, a man who had taken
refuge there 'according to thauncienne custume and liberte
thereof'. Edward demanded that the man be restored to the
franchise, and the city council in reply decided to send the
recorder and one of the sheriffs to lay before the king at Northampton a statement of the city's liberties, supporting their claim
by Ranulf Blundeville's charter, by Henry III's confirmation
granting the citizens the right to amercements, and by Edward
III's prohibition (1375) to the royal officials of Cheylesmore
forbidding them to meddle with the liberties. To this Edward
professing his affection for Coventry, replied that he would be
indifferent between the parties and asked a group of lords
Warwick, Worcester, Hastings, Dudley, Rivers, and Wenlock
along with Danby the judge, to hear the recorder's case. This
was the opening statement, for Edward professed his intention
of coming to Coventry to hear it, and did so along with the two
chief justices, Markham (C.J.K.B.) and Danby (C.J.C.B.)
sitting in the chapter-house of the priory. The case did not get
very far as it was found necessary to search the records of the
duchy of Lancaster which contained matter on the liberties of
Cheylesmore, so in London at Easter 1464 Edward heard the
recorder again and personally asked his steward of Cheylesmore
whether he had found anything in the records of the duchy
who replied that he had not. Whereupon the king, after discussion with the judges, laid down that Coventry should enjoy

---

[1] 'the which was truly done etc.': Dormer Harris, op. cit., p. 316.
[2] Ibid., p. 318.

its liberties and franchises as before, and if the Cheylesmore franchise could prove its immunity from the city, the officers of the city should be warned and have time to answer. This indeterminate ending which, judging from the mayoral records, seemed to the mayor's writer to award the case to the citizens of Coventry, shows the king's determination to do justice, but also reveals his deep personal interest in customs and liberties of the city, carried to the point of hearing the case himself on three separate occasions. This is not the only example of such interest.[1] The personal part taken by the king in the judicial suppression of disorder can also be witnessed in 1475, when the demobilization after the French campaign produced such a crop of disorder and unrest, especially in Hampshire, Wiltshire, Wales, the Marches, and Yorkshire, that Edward himself took his justices to some of the disturbed areas.

He had come to the throne intending, as he put it to his first parliament, to be 'as good and gracious sovereign lord as ever was any of my noble progenitors to their subjects and liegemen'. Yet whatever his good intentions, however sturdy, for example, his effort to exclude corruption from elections by insisting upon the electors being properly qualified and by eliminating the show of force that so often accompanied them,[2] contemporaries none the less noted that his attitude changed in the later part of his reign, especially when he dismissed Chief Justice Markham for being, as he thought, too lenient, and, in the course of eliminating Clarence, had John Stacey and Thomas Burdet tried and executed on charges of magic. Urged against him has also been the use of the constable's court to try cases of high treason, and the encouragement he gave to John Tiptoft, earl of Worcester, in putting down rebellion through this tribunal has been viewed as a piece of unscrupulous absolutism. It must be said, however, that the country was just shaking itself free, by drastic methods, from civil war; that positive cases of royal injustice in this reign are exceedingly few, and that the intrigues of Clarence were an almost intolerable strain. Furthermore, the standards of justice were remote from modern standards: judges

[1] Cf. the 'matter of William Huet', where a citizen who had been tried for and convicted of creating trouble for his neighbours, was none the less set at liberty and the suit extinguished because the defendant had interested the earl of Warwick in his case. Ibid., pp. 328–32.

[2] Especially over John Paston's election to parliament in 1461, *Paston Letters*, iii. 302–3, 313–14.

were regularly in receipt of retaining fees as well as presents from powerful clients, and pardons could be bought by the most suspected persons, if the offer to the crown was good enough, or if it was to the crown's advantage to close the case. Above all, the inheritance of dynastic opposition, through which Edward had fought his way to the kingdom, led many to expect from him the same methods as Lancastrian leaders like the dukes of Suffolk and Buckingham employed. It was on the whole more important for the peace of the country that the crown should be powerful and unchallenged than that it should be above criticism in its administration of justice.

The opposition of Warwick to Edward IV and the ultimate breach which led to the 'readeption' of Henry VI in 1470 arose not so much from the Woodville marriage in itself as from the thwarted determination of the earl to steer the king's policy, through marriage, towards alliance with Louis XI rather than with Burgundy. Warwick had been fascinated by the address, the unexpected charm, and the ingratiating manner of the French king. Louis who called him 'cousin' set out to attach the earl, both by flattery and more substantial promises. Above all things Edward must be kept from any alliance with the count of Charolais. Warwick must have known that the projected queen, Bona of Savoy, would be unacceptable to a country which had never fully accepted Margaret. Yet for all that he had persisted with his plan. There was now, he found, no marriage to advance the proposed French alliance, but instead the displeasing additional prospect of an alliance between England and Brittany, news of which came to Louis from William Monypenny who got wind of it in Scotland. By 10 October 1464 Louis XI knew about the Woodville marriage and about Edward's negotiations with Francis II. He had also gathered why Warwick had been unable to keep the engagement to meet him in Picardy during June that year. Yet he continued to show the friendliest disposition towards Warwick[1] and did not altogether drop negotiations for an Anglo-French treaty. The Breton alliance was dangerous to him because he had the conspiracy of nobles leading to the war of the Public Weal upon

---

[1] See the extract from the Milanese foreign archives in J. Calmette and G. Perinelle, *Louis XI et l'Angleterre (1461–1483)*, pp. 71–72. The truce, due to expire in 1465, was continued in 1466.

his shoulders. When he had extricated himself from this entanglement, though nearly with disaster at the interview of Péronne
(at which the revolt of the Liégeois against their duke was
clearly seen to have taken place at the French king's instigation), and had succeeded in breaking up the league at a heavy
price, involving the surrender to Charolais of the Somme towns,
he had the satisfaction of receiving from Warwick (Jan. 1466)
an undoubtedly treasonable message, purporting to come from
Edward IV: to the effect that he (Louis) could now push on
with his conquest of Normandy (which he had just seized from
his brother), since at that uncertain time England would
attempt no offensive or aggression against France. At the end
of 1465 Louis XI's relations with Edward had deteriorated, and
Warwick had no conceivable justification for making any such
statement: the message shows that he was posing to Louis as
the director of English policy. Determined to fight Anglo-
Burgundian friendship, in the course of 1466 he was confronted
by the Burgundian proposal that Charolais should marry
Edward's sister, Margaret of York, and that his heiress, Mary,
should be given to Edward's brother, George duke of Clarence.
Warwick had already marked out the impressionable George
for his own daughter Isabel, and the former match he considered disastrous. On 15 April 1466 Warwick met Charolais
at Boulogne and showed his hostility to these proposals quite
unreservedly. Shortly afterwards at Calais he signed an agreement with France providing for a truce until 1468 with a further
conference for a more lasting peace to be held in October.
During the truce Louis promised to give no aid to the Lancastrians, and in return Edward was to give none to the count
of Charolais or Francis of Brittany. Louis was also prepared to
pay Edward 40,000 gold crowns a year for as long as the final
agreement lasted and to provide a match for Margaret of York
with a prince of his own choosing, Louis to arrange the marriage
and provide the dowry. For the moment Edward was prepared
to ratify this as well as to consider Louis' proposals for the conference in October: but only five weeks afterwards he sent
safe-conducts to the ambassadors of Francis of Brittany and
Louis' brother Charles, not exactly in the spirit of the ratification. Westminster then became the 'scene of a high diplomatic
duel between the French and the Burgundians'. The possibility
that Philip's son would bring himself to support the house of

York seemed so unlikely to Sir John Paston that he agreed to pay 6 marks for a horse he had purchased if the count of Charolais married Margaret of York within two years, otherwise half that price, and Warwick himself thought that he could drive the French alliance through. But the marriage eventuated and he had misread Edward's mind. Edward had grasped the fact that the French alliance had, in Professor Kendall's words, 'become Richard Neville's touch-stone of supremacy in the realm'. And if Burgundy was disliked (especially for the embargo on cloth in 1464), France was actually detested, and the loss of the French provinces not forgiven or forgotten. Edward knew this, but played a patient game, hoping to get from Louis such offers as would convince Charolais that he must make better. He said he would meet Louis and wrote him a letter in his own hand promising to send the earl over the Channel to Hesdin. On 6 May 1467 Warwick was commissioned to go on his behalf. Louis had his own plan for counteracting the Burgundian alliance: it was to join Warwick with the woman with whom he had been at most bitter enmity, Margaret of Anjou (her adherents had killed his father, brother, uncle, and a cousin). Warwick might be induced to restore Henry VI. A letter of the Milanese ambassador at the French court to the duke of Milan, 19 May 1467, shows that it was difficult to conceal such a manœuvre: 'there is a fresh report that M. Charolais has again opened secret negotiations to take K. Edward's sister to wife, confirming once more the old league with the English. If this takes place, they have talked of treating with the earl of Warwick to restore King Henry in England, and the ambassador of the old Queen of England is already here'.[1]

Events of 1467 widened the breach between the earl and the king. Edward began to suspect the loyalty of George Neville, archbishop of York and chancellor. He discovered that the archbishop was 'working' both to be made a cardinal and to procure a papal dispensation for the marriage of George of Clarence to Warwick's daughter Isabel. At the inaugural session of parliament of Wednesday, 3 June 1467, the chancellor was not present: he excused himself on the ground of illness, but it is more probable that it was the arrival of the Bastard of Burgundy, who had come to joust with Anthony, Lord Scales, Queen Elizabeth's brother and the splendid welcome given to

---

[1] *Cal. S.P. Milan*, i, no. 150.

the suspected Burgundians, which had upset him. On 8 June 1467 he was dismissed from office and the seal was given in a few days to Robert Stillington, bishop of Bath and Wells. News of the death of Duke Philip caused the Bastard and his company to depart, but the French embassy which followed them, despite their notable reception and a stay of six weeks, including a visit to the king at Windsor, was unable to report any further than the vague promise of the king to send an English embassy to France. It was clear that Edward had taken sides and that the earl considered that the policy was not unconnected with the aggression of a single family. The personal family success of the Woodvilles was extremely distasteful to him. Four of the queen's sisters were betrothed to the chief young magnates of the kingdom; the queen's father had become treasurer of England and was created Earl Rivers: the queen had bribed the duchess of Exeter with £4,000 to transfer the Exeter heiress from Warwick's nephew, George, son of John Neville, and pledge her to Sir Thomas Grey, the elder son of her first marriage; Lord Grey of Ruthin, the queen's cousin by marriage, was given the earldom of Kent; and the queen had received custody of the most valuable royal ward, the duke of Buckingham; her brother Sir John Woodville had married the dowager duchess of Norfolk who was old enough to be his grandmother. The list of such advancements was mounting.

Throughout 1468 relations between Warwick and the king were steadily deteriorating and Edward's policy was becoming more hostile to France. In that year he made formal alliances with the dukes of Burgundy and Brittany, both already in league with the French king's rebellious brother the duke of Berri. These alliances were each accompanied by a commercial treaty of considerable importance. The Burgundian treaty was to last for thirty years: besides a guarantee of free passage for the merchants 'of the duchy, county and country of Brabant, Flanders, the town and lordship of Malines and other countries of our said cousin the Duke' and all merchants 'of England, Ireland and Calais', the treaty made reciprocal arrangements for Flemish merchants in English dominions 'in ports and harbours where customers and other officers are ordained to attend to and receive notice of the coming and going out of ships and merchandise, and not in others'. English merchants could enter fortified towns of the other party, 'without asking permission, save the first time only', provided that the gates were watched, and, if there was nobody on duty at them, could go to their hostels and there remain till word had been sent to the civic officials. Arrangements were also made for pilgrims and for clerks of all kinds 'going to the Court of Rome or to the General Council' to pass through each other's territory, stopping not more than one night in fortified towns. The treaty provided for mutual fishing facilities ('anywhere upon the sea') and for the establishment of hostels for the natives of either side.[1] The Brittany treaty[2] closely resembled the Burgundian: merchants were similarly to have free intercourse, escaping the 'customs, tolls and duties at present and formerly due and accustomed'.[3] They were allowed to arm their ships in self-defence, but were not to carry arms ashore, save to their hostels, and excepting any arms and war material which they were selling. It was stipulated that certain towns such as Calais, Winchester, Southampton, Dartmouth, and Plymouth need not have hostels for Breton merchants if the town authorities did not consider it desirable; and the privileges allowed to pilgrims and *Romipetae* were accorded also to those going to universities. Such a policy was completely at variance with the mercantile nationalism of Warwick, already exhibited in his Calais days, when he had attacked a fleet of the Easterlings and had plundered Italian merchants. Now in 1468, when the Danish king seized four English vessels as they were in the Sound on their way to Danzig, Warwick gave support to the claim that the instigators of the seizure were the Hanseatic League. Trade with the Hansa involved a large cloth export from England to Germany, while in return the former took Baltic products, like timber, pitch, tar, potash, furs, bow-staves, wax. Warwick asked the council for severe retaliation. To this Edward under Neville pressure gave way, and on 29 July the Steelyard was closed and its inhabitants sent to prison; merchants of the Hansa were arrested, and a compensation payment of £20,000 was demanded from the Germans. They refused to pay and, except for the men of Cologne (who were prepared to break with the League), were returned to prison. The remaining Hansa towns were determined not to give way and gathered support from the king of Poland, the duke of Burgundy, and even the emperor

---

[1] *Cal. S.P. Milan*, i, no. 150.
[2] *Foedera*, v. ii. 149–52.   [3] Ibid., pp. 159–62.

and the Pope. The council was divided on the issue, the keeper of the privy seal, Thomas Rotherham, and the king's secretary, William Hatclyf, urging the case of the Hansards. The Hansa merchants left London and a sharp and bitter war broke out at sea. Warwick, as captain of Calais, the advocate of strong measures, believed in a policy of retaliation; but although he got support from a good section of the London traders, it was not a generally popular undertaking to damage the German trade; yet Warwick was prepared to risk attack by the Hansa flotillas if only because they would endanger any successful expedition against France sent by Edward's government.

By 1469 Warwick, with the prospect of Holland and Zealand actually offered him by Louis as his principality, was preparing to displace Edward. The commons had granted £62,000 in the summer of 1468 for an invasion of France, but so far there was no sign of a warlike expedition. Edward was his usual genial self and grants had been made to help the Nevilles, the earl and the archbishop; the plan of the insurgents was to raise the country, particularly the north, by their lieutenants—e.g. Sir John Conyers who went by the name of Robin of Redesdale,[1] and by an anonymous Robin of Holderness in Yorkshire—and to disseminate the rumour that Edward was a bastard and that George of Clarence was the legitimate heir of the duke of York, a story bruited about at the time when Edward married Elizabeth Woodville. The basis of Warwick's operations was Sandwich in Kent. Thither on 7 June 1469 George of Clarence made his way, and between then and the 12th Archbishop George Neville arrived at Canterbury, then stole on to Sandwich with Bishop Thomas Kemp of London and the prior of Christ Church, Canterbury. They must have had rather a shock when two days afterwards Edward's mother, Cicely duchess of York, arrived as a guest of Christ Church on her way to Sandwich to see her son George. It is pretty certain that she had got wind of the conspiracy and was trying to stop her son Clarence from getting involved. If so, she had little success. Early in July Warwick crossed to Calais and then on the 11th the archbishop of York married Isabel Neville to George duke

---

[1] The chronicler Warkworth identifies Robin with Sir John's brother, Sir William Conyers of Marske (*Chronicle*, pp. 6, 44–45), and Gairdner followed him. Sir John is more likely (cf. *D.N.B.* xlviii. 443), who with his son John was at Edgecote on 28 July 1469. See below, p. 556.

of Clarence. After that Warwick got ready to repeat 1460: this time to land in England, in order to present to Edward a petition asking the king to remove the evil counsellors (the Woodville family), cease taxing his subjects, and take the advice of the true lords of his blood—Warwick and Clarence. Warwick had no difficulty in returning, and by 20 July was marching to London at the head of a large force. There was nothing to stop him reaching the capital, and once there he shrewdly gave no sign that he was taking the initiative against the king.

Edward was too far away and too late to stop the invasion. After wandering about in East Anglia, he had gone to Nottingham expecting to be screened, at Banbury, by Herbert earl of Pembroke and the earl of Devon. But Pembroke was caught before he could draw up his force in a good defensive position: at Edgecot he was set upon by Sir John Conyers, and though he had with him his brother Richard Herbert who fought with great courage, the arrival of Warwick's advance troops settled the matter, and he was taken to Northampton, Warwick's headquarters, where both Herberts were beheaded the next day.

After this it was possible to secure the person of the king. Earl Rivers with his two sons had left him, to seek safety: when Archbishop Neville, fully armed, took Edward at Olney in Buckinghamshire, only Lord Hastings and Richard of Gloucester were found with the king. Edward allowed himself to be conducted towards the victorious Warwick and Clarence. He put the best face on his capture and signed everything that Warwick put before him. There could be, for the moment, no help. Earl Rivers and Sir John Woodville, captured not far from Bristol, were executed on 12 August outside Coventry. The treasurership of England, vacant by Rivers's death, was given to Sir John Langstrother: Stillington was allowed to retain the chancery. By great seal parliament was summoned to York on 22 September. An historian of these years has pointed to the action which that body might well take on the model of 1322 and 1399, and indeed after the Yorkists had taken Henry at Northampton in 1460: the deposition of the king.[1] If this was Warwick's intention, if Clarence was marked out to succeed Edward, it was certainly concealed; and the example of Duke Richard of York after St. Albans could hardly be forgotten. It was highly uncertain whether, on this occasion, the lords and

[1] Paul Kendall, *Warwick the Kingmaker* (1957), p. 248.

commons would consent. Meanwhile Edward was transferred, first to Warwick, then Middleham; but while the king was in that impressive Neville fortress, Warwick was to discover by the beginning of September that the country was too disturbed to hold the parliament at York (the writ countermanding it referred to 'great troubles in divers parts of this our land not yet appeased'); with the king under tutelage, Warwick found that he could not control the country and disorder broke out in many areas: for example, the duke of Norfolk found it convenient to beseige Caister Castle until John Paston surrendered, and at Brancepeth in Co. Durham Humphrey Neville started a Lancastrian rising. From Middleham Warwick allowed his prisoner, very much on parole, to go to Pontefract. In return for the promise of more liberty, he had agreed to support the campaign Warwick was proposing to make against Humphrey Neville. But at Pontefract Edward was able to collect his friends and lieges. Here he was joined by the chief lords of his court, secretly summoned: the duke of Buckingham, the earls of Essex and Arundel, Lord Dynham, Lord Howard, Lord Mountjoy: his two most intimate allies, Lord Hastings and Richard of Gloucester, appeared, and John Neville, earl of Northumberland, placed himself at the king's disposal. With these adherents, Edward decided to return to London. The archbishop of York, joined at Moor Park by the earl of Oxford, proposed to follow the king and be there when he entered London, but Edward stopped them. Their presence would have been of doubtful benefit, although, once in London, Edward referred in warm terms of favour to Warwick and Clarence.

The earl and Clarence held aloof in the north. It was remarkable that they should have let the situation slide: but Warwick had not yet brought himself to take the plunge. When summoned to attend a great council at Westminster, he asked for guarantees of safety and did not agree to come to London until December. When he and Clarence made their appearance they were cordially welcomed, and there were evident signs of a reconciliation. The betrothal of Edward's eldest daughter Elizabeth to George son of the Neville earl of Northumberland might have encouraged hopes of peace, but in reality John Neville was loyal to Edward, and Edward had been recruiting all the support possible; the dukes of Norfolk and Suffolk, the earls of Kent, Arundel, Essex, Worcester, Lord Hastings, Howard, and

Mountjoy, besides others. Warwick's best hope was to encourage local rebellion against the government, under cover of which he could implement his design to ally England with France and restore the house of Lancaster. Local discontent in Lincolnshire where Lord Welles had attacked Sir Thomas Burgh, the master of the horse, and was now fearing royal reprisals, was stimulated into a small rebellion. On Sunday, 4 March, Sir Robert Welles, son of Lord Welles, published in all Lincolnshire churches a summons to arms from Warwick and Clarence: by 10 March Lord Scrope of Bolton, Sir John Conyers, and Lord Fitzwalter had engineered a rising in Yorkshire. It was not until Sir Robert Welles had been captured that Edward knew what Warwick and Clarence were about. They were then summoned to appear immediately to answer grave charges. The 'great rebels', as a proclamation by the king at York called them, could get no aid, whence they expected it, from Lord Stanley at Manchester, and turned southwards first to Warwick Castle, then to Exeter (c. 10 April), thence with ships collected from Devon and Dorset to the sea. By 16 April Warwick was in Calais. He had had to fight his way out and the entry into Calais harbour was made under fire. Sir John Wenlock would not admit him into the town itself. From the roadsteads outside he skimmed the Channel, collecting Burgundian and Breton merchantmen. There he sailed for the Norman coast and anchored off Honfleur in the mouth of the Seine (1 May 1470).

With him he brought a number of his captured Burgundian prizes, a point of some difficulty for Louis XI, since to favour the new arrival owning such pirated transport would be to break the treaty he had made to Péronne. The admiral (the Bastard of Bourbon) and the archbishop of Narbonne sent by Louis as his spokesmen were charged to tell Warwick that Louis would do all in his power to help the earl recover England either through the agency of Queen Margaret or by any other means desired. For a personal interview it would be better to wait until Margaret had sent word: in any event this could not be in so conspicuous a place as Harfleur in the domains of the count of St. Pol, a cousin of Edward's queen. The French king was evidently excited at the prospect, but made it clear that he was not committed to restoring Margaret and Henry: the decision must be Warwick's responsibility. Warwick in reply

insisted on seeing Louis, for which interview Louis was prepared, provided that the incriminating prizes could be safely
bestowed in some haven where they would not be seen. But
seen they were, and Duke Charles of Burgundy wrote to Louis
that he was preparing to attack Warwick and Clarence where-
ever they could be found by land and sea, while to the parliament of Paris he wrote charging Louis with breaking the treaty
of Peronne. In the end Warwick got his way. With Clarence he
met Louis in the Loire valley, not far from Amboise. There the
plan for the recovery of England was drafted. Warwick would
restore Henry VI to the throne of England aided by a fleet,
soldiers, and money which Louis was to provide. In return
Warwick promised a treaty of peace and alliance against
Burgundy. Margaret's son, Prince Edward, was to marry
Anne Neville and accompany Warwick. Meanwhile the
presence of Warwick and his captured ships was of great
embarrassment to Louis, for the Burgundian fleet had become
active off the mouth of the Seine, and French merchants at
Antwerp and elsewhere in the Burgundian dominions had been
arrested. The Burgundian fleet demanded the surrender of the
English and their goods, and demonstrated off Harfleur and
Honfleur. The damage they did was the subject of an embassy
directed to the duke and received by him in an explosive interview, but his fleet could not stay long at sea, and Warwick was
able to take his vessels to Barfleur and La Hogue in the Cotentin
and the admiral of France his warships to Chef de Caux. While
this was happening Louis was with difficulty persuading Queen
Margaret to allow herself again to be put on the throne of
England, though she would not consent to Prince Edward
marrying Anne Neville. She would not allow him to go with
Warwick: the pair might only cross the Channel when most of
England had been conquered. The actual meeting of Margaret
and Warwick took some arranging. 'The earl of Warwick',
wrote the Milanese ambassador, 'does not want to be here when
that queen first arrives, but wishes to allow his Majesty (Louis
XI) to shape matters a little with her and move her to agree
to an alliance between the prince, her son and a daughter of
Warwick.' In the end with great reverence Warwick went on
his knees and asked her pardon for the injuries and wrongs
done to her in the past. She generously forgave him and
he afterwards did homage and fealty there, swearing to be a

faithful and loyal subject of the king, queen, and prince as his liege lords unto death[1] (24 July 1470).

It was not long before the invading force materialized. It left on 9 September. Edward's precautions during July and August had been curiously inadequate. Commines rightly criticizes him for undervaluing the Franco-Lancastrian preparations. 'He was not so much concerned about the invasion of the earl of Warwick as the duke of Burgundy was, for he knew the movements in England in favour of the said earl of Warwick, and often warned King Edward of them; but he had no fear—it seems to me folly not to fear one's enemy and not wish to believe anything—seeing the resources that he had.'[2] One new enemy Edward had made in John Neville, his old supporter, whom he had created marquis of Montagu in place of the earldom of Northumberland. The earldom Edward had restored to the Percy heir, Henry, who was supposed to be holding the north along with the marquis of Montagu.

Across the Channel the Anglo-French flotilla watched by the Burgundian fleet, its mariners and troops only barely maintained by subsidies wrung by Warwick from the French king, could not sail till a storm had dispersed the blockaders. It could then cross and land Warwick's forces in Dartmouth and Plymouth. At Exeter Warwick issued a markedly Lancastrian proclamation, coming jointly from the earls of Pembroke and Oxford, Clarence, and himself. Edward was in Yorkshire, and as Warwick moved through the country to bring him to battle the earl of Shrewsbury and Lord Stanley joined him, to augment his forces to at least 3,000. At Coventry he heard that Edward had been forsaken by Montagu who in dudgeon at being rewarded with an inadequate marquesate had urged his troops to join Warwick. This was a serious blow. Since Montagu had defaulted very near to the royal camp, it became necessary for the king to evacuate the place quickly. Along with his brother Richard, with Lord Hastings and Lord Rivers, Edward made for East Anglia, reached King's Lynn, and crossed to the Burgundian mainland (2 Oct. 1470). The news of his departure was the signal for an irruption of Warwick's Kentish supporters into London. They had made for the capital as soon as they heard of his landing and now were engaged in robbing Flemish

[1] *Cal. S.P. Milan*, i. 188, 191.
[2] *Mémoires*, ed. B. de Mandrot (Soc. Hist. France, 1901–3), i. 239–40.

nd Dutch merchants on the south bank of the river. On 5 October Warwick entered London accompanied by Clarence, he earl of Shrewsbury, and Lord Stanley. From the Tower ne conducted Henry to St. Paul's, where the king offered, before taking up his quarters in the Bishop of London's palace. A week later he was presented to the view of the citizens in a procession to St. Paul's, with Warwick bearing the king's train. The Readeption placed upon the earl the true responsibility for government. The former chancellor Stillington, and a number of his clerical colleagues were already in sanctuary. George Neville had taken over (by 29 Sept.) the chancery and on 20 October John Langstrother prior of the hospital returned as treasurer, in place of Tiptoft who met his death on 18 October. The prior had first been appointed in August 1469.

On 26 October Sir John Delves superseded Lord Howard as treasurer of household, and Rotherham as keeper of the privy seal (appointed 24 June 1467) made way on 24 October for John Hales, bishop of Coventry and Litchfield, and a supporter of Queen Margaret. Sir Richard Tunstall replaced Lord Hastings as master of the mint, while the great wardrobe went to Sir John Plummer. The legal officers were swiftly reappointed: the justices of the two benches, the barons of the Exchequer, and the sheriffs. Warwick himself was made king's lieutenant of the realm, and resumed his posts of great chamberlain of England and captain of Calais. The admiralship, in the hands of Richard of Gloucester, was taken over by Warwick on 2 January 1471, not long after he had resumed his former offices of great chamberlain and captain of Calais.

As regards membership of the council it was not Warwick's intention to revert to the earlier type of Lancastrian aristocratic body; it was on the Yorkist pattern, with a strong official and episcopal element.[1] The duke of Clarence was restored to membership, but he had little power and did not receive back his lieutenancy of Ireland till February 1471. Montagu (John Neville), whose desertion of Edward IV had made Warwick's triumph possible, did not appear in the council. He was sent to the north, to take up again the wardenship of the east Marches, and so suspect was his old loyalty to Edward that

---

[1] It has been described as 'a Neville régime in a Lancastrian costume'. Kendall, op. cit., p. 284.

when parliament met he had to apologize for his allegiance to the king. The earls of Oxford and Shrewsbury and Lord Stanley were not found on the council, nor were the earls of Devon (Courtenay) nor Jasper Tudor of Pembroke. Tudor and his nephew, the future Henry VII, came to Westminster early in November, but Henry, whose father had been earl of Richmond, could not have the title which had gone to Clarence. Jasper and Henry were awarded the custody of the lands of William Herbert, the Yorkist earl of Pembroke. Of the remaining Lancastrian lords, Edmund Beaufort 'calling himself Duke of Somerset' and Henry Holland 'calling himself Duke of Exeter' were now being paid pensions by the duke of Burgundy. The two most active Yorkists still in the country, the duke of Norfolk and the earl of Essex, were treated with leniency and Essex was made a member of the council. Only one prominent figure was cut down. John Tiptoft, the humanist earl of Worcester, constable of England, a figure in some respects more Italian than English, was handed over to trial under John de Vere, earl of Oxford, whose father and elder brother he had condemned to death in 1462. On 18 October 1470 he was found guilty of treason, and on the way to Tower Hill had to be protected from a crowd who wanted to lynch him: the execution could not take place until the next day.

Here one may pause a moment to consider the life of the man so frequently called an Italianate Englishman. The Tibetot (Tiptoft) family had acquired lands in East Anglia, the Wrothe estates, especially Wimbish in north-west Essex, where a house is still called Tiptoft's; in Hampshire (Nether Wallop and Brockenhurst); and in Middlesex (the manor of Enfield). Sir John Tiptoft, M.P. for Huntingdon (1403–4) and Speaker of the 1406 parliament, was Henry IV's keeper of the wardrobe and treasurer of England in 1408. An old servant of Henry IV when he was earl of Derby, Tiptoft lived to serve for years on the council of regency, from 1422. John Tiptoft, earl of Worcester, his son, who inherited these scattered properties, was sent to Oxford: a *dominus Johannes Typtot* lodged at University College in 1440–2, paying rent amounting to 33s. 4d., more than half as much again as the rent paid by any other lodger and more than double that paid by most. He left Oxford in 1443, the year when his father died. Tiptoft, therefore, was at Oxford when the University was receiving the earlier instalments

Duke Humphrey's books.[1] In 1449 he married Cecily, widow
f Henry Beauchamp, duke of Warwick, who was born Cecily
eville, daughter of Richard Neville, earl of Salisbury and
ster to the Kingmaker. She died in 1450, but Tiptoft's friend-
ip with Warwick ensured him under the Yorkist régime an
mmediate place in public life. He was treasurer in 1452-5
[5 Mar.) and in 1454 keeper of the sea. In 1457 he made a
ilgrimage to the Holy Land, and on his way back stopped in
taly, where he stayed two years for study, in Padua and in
errara under the celebrated teacher Guarino. In Italy he won
reputation as a Latin scholar, and at the congress of Mantua
nade a notable speech on behalf of the king conveying con-
ratulations to Pius II. On his return to England he was made
onstable and treasurer, and on 7 February 1462 was com-
issioned to try all cases of treason 'summarily and plainly
ithout noise and show of judgement' on simple inspection of
ct (i.e. without a jury). Warkworth says of the earl of Oxford
nd Aubrey de Vere, condemned to death by Tiptoft on 20 and
6 February 1462 respectively, that they were 'brought before
ie Erle of Worcestere and juged by lawe padowe that thei
chuld be had to the Toure Hylle and ther was there hedes
myten off'. Tiptoft held his constable's court after Hexham,
nd his reputation as a 'butcher' derives largely from his sen-
ences against the Lancastrian leaders. Englishmen like Sir John
ortescue disliked Roman legal procedure in criminal cases, and
iptoft with his star chamber methods was perhaps unfortunate
a having so many eminent Lancastrians to liquidate.

No parliament roll has survived for the assembly that met on
6 November, opened by the chancellor George Neville, on the
ext 'Return O backsliding children saith the Lord'. The first
ask was to declare Henry VI the king, and to establish the
uccession for his heirs male and, these failing, upon the duke
f Clarence and his. The attainders upon the Lancastrian lords
1461) were reversed: Edward IV was declared an usurper and,
long with his brother Gloucester, attainted: but there were
to large-scale territorial changes. The earl of Warwick was
ccepted as lieutenant and protector for the king, with Clarence
s his associate, Clarence being recognized as Richard duke of
ork's heir; and the marquis of Montagu was pardoned after

[1] In 1438 he had given 129 volumes: in 1441 sixteen more. R. J. Mitchell, *John
Tiptoft* (1938), p. 17.

he had spoken in apology for his long loyalty to Edward IV
alleging that it was only fear that had prompted his loyalty fo
so long. There was an adjournment for Christmas, but parlia
ment met again in January for special business: meanwhil
French ambassadors had arrived. They had come to tel
Warwick of the arrangements made by Louis XI to help him
but also to discuss the assistance against Burgundy which Loui
had been promised, and to conclude with Henry VI a pac
towards this end 'so firmly secured that neither signatory coul
sign a peace or truce with the duke without the consent of th
other, or cease fighting, until every inch of the duke's territorie
had been conquered'. Louis advanced three plans of campaign
each of which involved an English expeditionary force. Th
exact size of the armies to be placed in the field and the exac
day when hostilities were to begin were also inquired into b
Louis. The French king was looking after Warwick well. It wa
a French merchant of Tours whom Louis had persuaded to pu
up the money to secure, from Rome, a dispensation for th
marriage between Warwick's daughter, Anne Neville, and th
prince of Wales. The ambassadors were nobly received an
the reports they sent back to Louis were sufficient to convinc
Queen Margaret that she and her son could safely come t
England. On 17 December the Exchequer was directed to pa
Warwick £2,000 because the king had appointed him to cros
to France 'with an army of ships and men . . . for the bringin
home of our most dear and entirely beloved wife, the Quee
and of our son, the Prince'. Warwick received more than thi
but he did not cross the Channel. One of his problems wa
finance. He was entitled under an act of 1465 to the custom
and the subsidy on wools, and he had the fee farms of the roy
towns and the revenues of the duchy of Lancaster: the latte
judged by the average of the receiver-general's receipts, woul
amount to rather more than £6,000 after all outpayments ha
been made and other obligations met.[1] It seems unlikely tha
Warwick had, in the absence of tenths and fifteenths, an incom
much above £15,000. The City of London lent £1,000 for th
defence of Calais, but Warwick had borrowed another £1,00
in 1469 and the city was now asking for it back.

Louis in his embassy had laid great stress on the need t
synchronize the Anglo-French move against Charles. He wa

[1] See the calculations in Somerville, *Duchy of Lancaster*, i. 237–8.

nxious to get both Warwick and Prince Edward thoroughly
ommitted to war upon Burgundy before he marched. He made
Edward seal the engagement whereby the Englishman promised
o make war on the duke until all the Burgundian dominions
were conquered and to persuade his father to accept the
obligation. Then on 3 December 1470, in a great assembly at
Tours, he denounced the treaty of Peronne as cancelled by the
duke's hostile acts the previous summer and by his alliance with
the Yorkists. Thereupon he immediately sent his forces against
the duchy, moving powerful forces into Picardy. His embassy
did not leave the court till he had advanced well into the
country. England was thus confronted with a *fait accompli*; but
his ambassadors had the difficult task of making England
swallow the alliance against Burgundy, which was the objective
of all the support he had given to Warwick and Queen Margaret. There were individual magnates to be won over: but
most of all the merchants whom he had to attract and impress,
whether by the grant of two free fairs at Caen or by sending
over with the ambassadors traders of Tours with a stock of
merchandise to show that France could supply what England
wanted. Yet Louis could be relied on to keep Warwick in good
frame of mind: he told his ambassadors to suggest that Warwick, for taking part in the campaign against Charles, should
receive the counties and lordships of Holland and Zealand.
This was to implement an earlier suggestion, made as a bait to
the earl. But the larger question remained: could England be
persuaded to swallow the new alliance? The two merchants of
Tours, suspected of underselling the native traders, were by
no means popular. The Burgundian connexion was strongly
established with the London oligarchy who viewed with
suspicion the support given by Warwick to anti-alien movements. At the moment shipping was at a standstill: save for the
men of Cologne, the Hansa merchants had gone, and freight
was lacking to take English goods abroad.

It was a bad moment for pressing the French alliance:
Warwick saw the necessity of getting a document agreed upon
with the French embassy through parliament: but when it came
to the final drafting at the hands of the negotiators (13–16 Feb.
1471) and the result received parliamentary confirmation, it
was by no means the treaty as originally conceived and
promised by the earl. It was not a permanent alliance, but

a truce, to last for ten years, with provision made for intercourse
between the merchants. During this period the kings of England
and France were to give no support to each other's enemies or
rebels: and a convention was to take place within three years
to settle all disputes between the two countries with a view to a
permanent peace. There was no declaration of war, and the
French envoys had to be content with the knowledge that
Warwick was assembling an army. From a letter of the bishop
of Bayeux to Louis, now confirmed by one from Warwick to the
same king (12 Feb.) which has recently come to light,[1] it is
known that the earl actually started hostilities in the area of
Calais, while promising to aid Louis against Burgundy as soon
as he could. To get the troops, Warwick was reduced to the
expedient of commissioners of array. He secured about forty
archers from Coventry, and the Kentish men provided him with
a good-sized fleet for transport; how many others he gathered
it is difficult to say.

Charles of Burgundy had been maintaining, as was noted
above, two inveterate Lancastrians, Henry Holland, duke of
Exeter, and Edmund Beaufort, duke of Somerset. Both were
bitterly hostile to Warwick. The earl had caused the death of
Somerset's father and brother (Henry had been executed)
while Exeter, to whom Warwick had refused in 1460 to yield
the captaincy of Calais, had been attainted in 1461 while serving
as constable of the Tower. His servants had been charged with
treason and put to death, while he himself fled to the Low
Countries. Both these men, when Charles decided to aid
Edward IV, had the courage to plead for the house of Lancaster; and Charles saw that the way of helping the king was
to make them promise to oppose Warwick, if they were given
permission to return to England. Warwick's son-in-law, the
unstable Clarence, was being implored to return to his old
allegiance and was by no means conciliated when Warwick
required him to hand over to Margaret of Anjou certain lands
of hers at present in his possession. Margaret, at Honfleur,
delayed to return. She had heard that Edward was ready to
sail, and could not overcome her misgivings. At last she promised
to cross in the vessels in which the French embassy, then at the

---

[1] A. R. Myers, 'The Outbreak of War between England and Burgundy, in
February 1471', *Bull. Inst. Hist. Rev.* xxxiii (1960), 114–15.

English court, was to return from England; but the delay had the worst effect upon her cause.

Louis was waiting for her at Beauvais: but the earl in a like fascination could not embark his men, and returned to London to find general expectation of Edward's arrival from Flushing. Just before 14 March Yorkist vessels were seen off the Norfolk coast, making northwards for the Humber. Edward was returning. Yet, the prospect of the small invading force of 2,000 getting any distance in England seemed remote. There was John Neville at Pontefract with Warwick's Yorkshire contingent to stop him, while Oxford, Exeter, and Viscount Beaumont were coming up along the Fosse way to Newark. None the less on 18 March York opened its gates to Edward, who (like Henry Bolingbroke among the northern magnates) had been confusing the civic authorities by saying that he had come to claim his dukedom. Then Edward by-passed Pontefract; it was John Neville who let him go by. Even more menacing for Warwick was the attitude of the Lancastrian earls. Shrewsbury took no notice of the summons (Thomas Lord Stanley took the same line) nor could Jasper Tudor be persuaded to move: they were waiting for the arrival of Margaret of Anjou. The duke of Somerset and the earl of Devon repaired to London, sending word that they were awaiting Queen Margaret: on the other hand, for a short while after 25 March it seemed likely that Edward would be caught by a convergence of three Lancastrian forces, Oxford at Newark, Montagu in Edward's rear, and Warwick at Coventry. But the unexpected appearance of Edward's scouts near Newark so alarmed Oxford and Exeter that they fled and Edward continued his march, right under the walls of Coventry whither Warwick had withdrawn his troops on hearing of the débacle at Newark; here for three days Edward issued a formal challenge to combat, while Warwick kept his forces within. No reply came and Edward moved on to occupy the earl's castle of Warwick. Here in his great opponent's stronghold he learned that the troops of Oxford, Exeter, and Montagu had reached Coventry, but that Clarence had played them false and gone over to the Yorkists. One more attempt Edward made to bring Warwick to terms: he again offered to fight the earl at Coventry and moved his troops there for action. But combat was declined and on 5 April Edward started for London. With a two days' start upon Warwick, he entered the

capital at noon on 11 April. Edward was now in possession o
Henry VI. The same day Warwick heard that Louis XI had
signed a truce for three months with the duke of Burgundy. A
he had failed Louis, this was a natural reply on the part of the
French king: but it showed Warwick that no immediate help
could come from that direction; nor had any help come from
Queen Margaret and the prince. He had to go forward now
with Lancastrian help that included neither Queen Margaret
nor Somerset nor Devon nor Jasper Tudor. He must fight it ou
with Edward IV.

On Saturday, 13 April, Warwick moved through to St
Albans, marching for Barnet, and deployed his forces along the
400-foot plateau which drops to the plain of Middlesex, south
of Barnet village. Exeter had command of the left wing upon
the marshy ground, Montagu the centre on either side of the
St. Albans–Barnet road, and Oxford the right behind a hedge
to the west of the road: Warwick had the reserve and a con
siderable number of guns. During the evening Warwick's scout
were driven out of Barnet by Edward's advanced guard, but the
king's main force had not been located. The next morning
Easter Sunday, was foggy and the first stage of the engagemen
was fought in semi-darkness. It was impossible to see that on
Edward's right Richard of Gloucester had outflanked Exeter
and that on his left, Hastings had been outflanked by Oxford
Oxford got too far away from the main battle which was being
fought out by the two centres, both reserves having come into
action, and when he was recalled in the poor light he fell upon
Montagu's division, thinking it to have been the enemy
demoralization and suspicion of treachery quickly spread
through the Lancastrian ranks. This blunder was the signal for
a renewed attack by Edward upon the Lancastrian centre, and
Warwick's reserves were not sufficient to prevent Montagu'
line breaking. The marquis had in fact been killed already
Warwick ultimately overborne by sheer numbers was retreat
ing, when he was caught by a Yorkist band and killed. A
messenger sent by Edward IV from his own household was jus
too late to prevent the deed.

The same day of the battle, weeks too late to save the Lan
castrian cause, Queen Margaret arrived along with Prince
Edward and his wife, at Weymouth. The news of Barnet had
sent the countess of Warwick into sanctuary at Beaulieu Abbey

but Margaret hoping to gain the support in the south-west which the duke of Somerset and the earl of Devon had promised her, went to Exeter and marched north through Bath and Bristol to recruit men for her cause. As King Edward was pursuing them, Margaret thought it best to cross the Severn into Wales, so as to link up with Jasper Tudor. But she was not in time. King Edward caught her force at Tewkesbury on 4 May and inflicted a crushing defeat. Her son Prince Edward was killed. Somerset was captured, along with Sir Humphrey Audley, Sir John Langstrother, Sir Thomas Tresham, Sir Gervaise Clifton, and Sir Hugh Courteney: all were court-martialled and condemned to be executed at Tewkesbury. Besides the prince, the earl of Devonshire, John Beaufort, Somerset's brother, John Lord Wenlock, Sir Robert Whittingham, and Sir Edmund Hampden, were killed in action. The queen herself was discovered hiding in Little Malvern Priory and was taken. Edward's triumph was complete when the Bastard of Fauconberg who had assaulted London with a force of Kentishmen surrendered to Richard of Gloucester. This enabled the king to enter the capital on 21 May 1471. On that Tuesday night Henry VI was put to death in the Tower by Edward's order.

The grandson of Charles VI, born to succeed to a dual monarchy incapable of realization, Henry bore on his shoulders a responsibility which might have broken a man from a stock far less medically suspect than the Valois. In his later years few in high office paid him the regard, hardly any the understanding affection which might have saved his reason. Had he lived in Flanders or the Empire Henry might have been one of the founders of the New Devotion. But ordinary people who did not control the course of events felt for him sincerely,[1] and in quieter groves there were others to remember his benefactions and his delight in the more permanent treasures of learning and the arts.

[1] Most significant is the tribute in the *Great Chronicle* (which represents a London observer's opinion) upon Henry VI's 'readeption': 'And thus was this goostly and vertuous prince Henry the Syxth ... Restored unto his Rygth and Regally Of the which he took noo grete Rejoyse In pride But mekely thankid God and gave alle hys meynd to serve and plese hym, and fforad lytill or noo thing of the pomp or vanytees of this world, wherffor aftyr my myend he mygth saye as Cryst sayd to pylat, Regnum meum non est de hoc mundo, ffor God had endowid hym wᵗ such grace that he chaze wyth mary magdaleyn the lyfe contemplatyve, and Reffucid of martha the actyff, The which he fforsook not ffrom his tendyr age unto the last daye of his lyffe, how be It he hadde many occacyons to the Contrary. Op. cit., p. 212.

In 1469 Warwick had got rid of a number of Woodvilles, including Sir Richard, the head of the family, who had become Earl Rivers, but four of the queen's brothers were living still: Anthony the new Earl Rivers, Lionel the clerk who became chancellor of Oxford and bishop of Salisbury: Edward and Richard. Anthony was the romantic, decorative figure, a literary knight of an age of gothic baroque, unimpressed by the need for reconstruction at home and wise advice to the council. Edward never had much use for him, but before his flight from England he had granted to him the lieutenancy of Calais. In July 1471 it was granted to Lord Hastings: the king never took the trouble to inquire whether Rivers had actually gone on a crusade as he had been proposing to do; in point of fact he had not, and the appointment led to great hostility between the new lieutenant and the Woodvilles, particularly the queen who looked upon Hastings as having an evil influence over Edward. Though joined with Hastings in unswerving support of Edward, Gloucester had had opportunity to observe the character and peculiarities of William Hastings, and years later did not hesitate to strike down the man who knew more about the inner history of the royal household than any: the greatest obstacle to his authority, just because Hastings represented a strain in Edward's psychology which Richard of Gloucester disliked and a loyalty to Edward's wishes that came in conflict with his own ambitions. But a worse enmity than this was very quickly to arise.

XII

EDWARD IV (2)

EDWARD had pardoned his brother Clarence for the part he took in helping the earl of Warwick. Clarence had hoped for the crown in his dangerous manœuvres of 1469–71: he was deeply jealous of Gloucester's favoured position. After he heard that the duke wanted to marry Anne Neville (betrothed to Henry VI's son), who had been captured with Margaret of Anjou after the battle of Tewkesbury, and when, during the summer, all the huge estates of the earl of Warwick in Yorkshire and Cumberland were granted to Gloucester, rather than to himself, the husband of Warwick's elder daughter, he was angered and disappointed.

Louis XI appears to have told Clarence that if he would engage in another conspiracy against his brother's throne, he would send the earl of Oxford, John de Vere (son of the earl arrested and executed by Tiptoft, and the trier in due course of Worcester), who had escaped to France after the battle of Barnet, to make a descent on the English coast, and would, if he could, get the king of Scotland to help. Oxford did not consider Scottish help likely to be forthcoming. On 28 May 1473 he landed at St. Osith's but embarked again on hearing that the earl of Essex was leading a force against him. All the summer Oxford hovered about the coast of England: he never got the money he wanted from Louis, but kept Edward on the alert, and Clarence's behaviour was equally calculated to keep the king anxious. When the king came to London at the beginning of October 1473, to open parliament, he was given the news that Oxford had descended on the coast of Cornwall, and had occupied St. Michael's Mount. He had only eighty men with him, including his three brothers, George, Thomas, and Richard de Vere, and Lord Beaumont who had escaped with him from Barnet. The Cornishmen had welcomed him with 'right good cheer'. His danger to Edward lay more in the encouragement that his defiance gave to the duke of Clarence than in his military strength: Paston wrote to his brother from London that most of the men about the king had sent for their

harness, and it was said for certain that the duke of Clarence
'makyth hym bygge in that he kan, schewyng as he wolde but
dele with the Duke of Glowcester; but the Kyng ententyth, in
eschyewying all inconvenyents, to be as bygge as they bothe,
and to be a styffeler atweyn them'. At first Edward employed
local help, Sir John Arundel, John Fortescue, and the Cornishman Henry Bodrugan, to hold the Mount, and in December
1473 the command was transferred from Bodrugan to Fortescue
who was armed with pardons for all but Oxford, his brothers,
and Beaumont. Oxford's knights gave in and he himself was
forced to submit. He and two of his brothers were pardoned,
1 February 1474, and after the Mount had surrendered, Oxford
was sent to the king and ordered to be confined in Hammes
Castle, where George Neville, archbishop of York, was already
a prisoner. A year after the earl of Oxford and his two brothers
were attainted and all their lands and goods declared forfeit
to the king. George Neville was pardoned on 11 November 1475
and allowed to return to England: but two and a half years of
confinement had broken his health as well as his spirit and he
died on 8 June 1476.

Edward's foreign diplomacy was still directed towards
securing a treaty with Burgundy: but Charles was in fact
largely occupied with designs on the empire, not on the invasion
of France. Ever since Sigismund of Austria's visit to him in
1469, Charles the Bold had been dazzled by the hope that if he
consented to the marriage of his daughter Mary to the Archduke Maximilian (the marriage suggested by Sigismund) the
emperor would promise to bring about his election as king of
the Romans. By 1473 the invasion of France had begun to look
like a minor affair. When Charles went to Trier to meet the
emperor, all that he obtained was the investiture of the duchy
of Guelders and so little did Frederick III relish Charles's
larger requests, that he left hurriedly in the night rather than
promise to procure the duke's election as king of the Romans,
or to grant Charles the erection of his ducal dominions into a
kingdom.

In 1474 Charles prolonged the truce with Louis until May
1475. The invasion of France had to be postponed for a year.
None the less, with the excuse that the grant of 1472, because
of the refusal of certain parts of the country to pay their share
in it, had brought in only £31,410. 14s. 1½d. and that the

fifteenth and tenth granted in the spring of 1473 was still un-
levied and unpaid, Edward was bold enough to ask for another
war grant. The commons, obedient to his wish, gave him till
24 June 1476 to start for France and accorded him another
fifteenth and tenth in place of the one not collected, authorized
him to collect a year's wages for 590 archers (£5,383. 15s.)
from the districts that had refused to pay in 1472, and granted
him the additional sum of £51,147. 4s. 7¾d. to bring the total
amount up to £118,625; which was the cost of the wages of
13,000 archers. Some caution was, however, shown, for half of
the £51,147. 4s. 7d. was to be levied on St. John's Day, 1475,
and the other half at the following Martinmas (11 Nov.), and
when collected the money was not to be given to the king until
he and the ships were ready to go to France.

As soon as the new grant had been announced, parliament
was prorogued until 23 January 1475. In July the treaty agreed
by Edward's negotiators with the duke of Burgundy, drawn
up in six schedules, was published. The first part was a declaration of amity between Edward and Charles with the former
king's promise to equip a force of 10,000 before 1 July 1475 and
contained Charles's undertaking 'to take . . . the king's part in
person and with his army', until Edward had obtained the
right and title to the realm and crown of France: this was
followed by the promise of each side not to negotiate with
Louis XI. The next part specified the duke of Burgundy's share
of the spoils, which included the county of Champagne, the
Nivernais, Rethel, Eu, Guise, and Rouci with the cities of
Tournai and Langres, and 'all the lands and dominions which
Louis of Luxemburg, called Count of St. Pol, at present possesses, provided they were not ancient domain of the duchies of
Normandy and Aquitaine or the Crown of France'; finally came
Charles's consent to the English king being crowned at Reims,
'which is a city of Champagne and belongs to us by virtue of
the aforesaid donation': and if Edward decided to be anointed
and crowned elsewhere, he or his heirs and successors in the
realm of France might 'carry away from the aforesaid City of
Reims the vessel or ampulla appointed for this purpose, though
they are under obligation to restore it to its usual place'.

A term was fixed for the payment of Margaret of York's
dowry, less than half of which (115,000 crowns) had thus far
been paid (the whole amount was to be paid within three years

after the marriage). Edward arranged to send Charles 5,000 crowns every Annunciation Day and every Michaelmas Day, beginning with 1475 until the 85,000 still owing had been discharged. Having got a settlement with Charles, Edward began to make contracts for his French expeditionary force. He also sent Falcon herald to France to make a formal demand for the surrender of Guienne and Normandy, and to say that a refusal meant war. At the same time, however, a dispatch to Milan from Christopher de Bollati, Milanese ambassador at the French court, said something less bellicose. Edward's herald, said Bollati, brought proposals for a marriage between the king's daughter and the Dauphin, 'showing that he is inclined to return again to those designs which were suggested upon other occasions against the Duke of Burgundy and for the ruin of his state'. At the same time continual rumours were current about the large force which Edward was raising; and Bollati thought that this was either a means of putting pressure on France (Edward could justify himself by saying that the marriage negotiations having failed, he was obliged to use force) or else a genuine, but up till now hidden, threat against Burgundy. In the autumn there were still more rumours of Edward's warlike preparations.

Now Bollati may actually have been right. Miss Scofield thought that in the light of later events, the offer to France, was 'not only made, but made in sincerity'.[1] Particularly so, because during the summer Charles was pursuing an *ignis fatuus* in the east. He marched to the support of one of two rival claimants to the archbishopric of Cologne and on 30 July laid siege to the fortified city of Neuss. On the other hand, Edward was making every effort to secure alliances with other enemies of Louis beside Burgundy. Edward sounded Francis II of Brittany to find out if he was prepared to sign another treaty promising to take part in an attack on Louis: and about the same time the abbot of Abingdon and Bartelot de Rivière departed for Italy to invite Ferdinand of Naples, to whom Edward had sent the garter eleven years previously, to become a member of the alliance against France, and to offer the garter to Federico Ubaldi, duke of Urbino. With Scotland Edward was now preoccupied: on 26 October 1474 came the betrothal of Prince James of Scotland, aged two, to Princess Cecily of

[1] *Life and Reign of Edward IV*, ii. 98.

England aged four. They were to be married 'after the form and by the authority of holy kirk' within six months after they had reached marriageable age. The new marriage treaty was, next to his treaty with Charles, the most important advantage which Edward had yet gained over Louis, and the most necessary to the success of an English invasion of France. By it Cecily was to be entitled, upon the accession of her husband to the throne, to the third part of all his property, and her father should give her a dower of 20,000 marks English money. The treaty was ratified 3 November 1474.

Meanwhile money for the expedition was needed. The quest was pursued during the winter of 1474–5. After Christmas Day at Coventry, and before he finished 'plucking of his magpies',[1] Edward had gone as far north as Lincoln. Soon afterwards his ambassadors to Charles the Bold arrived back. It was not a cheering report that they brought. They had not succeeded in obtaining a treaty with the emperor, who had signed one with the king of France instead. Charles, instead of holding up his strength for an attack on France, was thinking only of Neuss. Louis on his side was desperately anxious for an understanding with Burgundy. The force assembled by Edward was assessed by contemporaries as a threefold one: 30,000 for Calais to join the duke of Burgundy; 10,000 for Normandy and 6,000 for Gascony. This is unquestionably an exaggeration: none the less the army was very large. There were 1,100–1,200 men-at-arms, 10,000–11,000 archers; Clarence's retinue alone had 120 *servientes ad arma* (mounted lances) and 1,000 archers: Richard of Gloucester brought even more. That was the royal party alone. The dukes of Norfolk and Suffolk mustered 40 men-at-arms each and 300 archers; the Earl of Northumberland 60 men-at-arms and 350 archers, while a notable amount of artillery had been assembled. Meanwhile Charles made no sign of leaving Neuss: Margaret of Burgundy was solicited and told that Edward would not leave England without the positive assurance that Charles would be at hand, and finding that Margaret could not help him, Edward sent Earl Rivers and Richard Martyn to Neuss to beg him to come. They found

---

[1] Extracting money from his subjects.

[2] For the leaders, with their spears and archers, see the edition of MS. 2 M. 16, College of Arms, ed. E. A. Barnard, *Edward IV's French expedition of 1475, the Leaders and their Badges* (1925). The total force is given here as 11,457.

ambassadors from Francis II and the count of St. Pol's envoy already there, and together they asked Charles to give up the siege on honourable terms. Charles declined. 'God had troubled his sense and his understanding', wrote Commines of the duke's persistent refusal. But Louis determined to take advantage of this. Two days after Rivers and Martyn reached Neuss, the very day that the truce with Charles expired, Louis sent his army across the Somme to overrun Charles's territories.

In default of Charles, Edward had to fall back upon Brittany, and at the beginning of May the Seigneur d'Urfé and Jacques de la Villéon arrived from Brittany to conclude an alliance. Edward went first to Canterbury to meet his forces on Barham Down. Then (20 June) he moved on to Sandwich, where he had his will sealed. All Charles did was to find Edward shipping, 500 vessels: it took Edward more than three weeks to get his army across to Calais, and Commines observed that if Louis had known how to manage his affairs at sea as well as he managed them on land, the English king would not have found himself in France in 1475.[1] Edward crossed on 4 July, on the 6th the Duchess Margaret arrived in Calais, and on 14 July Charles himself—but only with a small bodyguard. He had come to discuss plans. He proposed that Edward should overrun Normandy with the help of the duke of Brittany and the count of St. Pol, and then make his way into Champagne, while he himself, after returning to *collect his troops*, whom on leaving Neuss he had sent into Lorraine to pillage, would enter Champagne from the east and meet the English army at Reims, where Edward could be crowned king of France. Edward kept his temper, and Charles said flattering things about the capacity of the English army to tackle its task single-handed. So it was decided that Edward should march to St. Quentin, which the count of St. Pol was offering to hand over, by way of Doullens and Péronne. By 27 July Louis was at Beauvais with a powerful army and moved on to Compiègne, while Charles and Edward went to Peronne (Charles being admitted to the city, Edward being kept outside). St. Quentin was only approached, not reached, for its guns fired on Edward's troops and it was found that the count of St. Pol had not kept his word to hand over the city. On 12 August the duke departed to rejoin his army, and Edward, in disgust, prepared to open negotiations with Louis:

[1] *Mémoires*, i. 288.

but he did not do so until after consultation with his leaders.

It was a fateful step: the majority assented, but Gloucester and a few others were opposed. The terms suggested were that the king of France should pay Edward 75,000 crowns within fifteen days and 25,000 crowns every Easter and Michaelmas as long as the sovereign lived; Louis was prepared to marry his son, the Dauphin, at his own expense to the first or second daughter of the king of England and endow her with rents of £60,000 annual value and 'after the estimation of France': in other words, Edward was offering to be bought off, and on receipt of the premium to take his troops back to England. Louis was inclined to consider this a reasonable basis for negotiation because, as Commines wrote, the summer was nearly over; because the Duke of Burgundy had failed Edward, and because he thought that Edward 'strongly loved ease and pleasure'.[1] He was not far out. On 18 August Charles came back to Péronne, having got word of the negotiations, and stormy interviews occurred for the two following days. Charles then departed and Louis planned to meet Edward and the English army. This was done at Amiens, when Louis feasted the English army so lavishly that discipline broke down and Edward finally had to eject his own troops from the town. The two sovereigns met at Picquigny, on 29 August 1475, on a specially constructed bridge over the river; the faithful Commines being dressed up as Louis to reduce the danger of his sovereign being murdered. Edward had with him Clarence, the earl of Northumberland, Lord Hastings, and Thomas Rotherham the chancellor. The terms arranged were as follows:

(i) All differences between the kings of England and France, i.e. Edward's claim to the crown of France—should be referred for settlement to four arbitrators, the archbishops of Canterbury and Lyons, the duke of Clarence, and the count of Dunois; who were to hold their first meeting in England before Easter; their second in France before the following Michaelmas. Their award should be regarded as compulsory.

(ii) The king of England on receiving 75,000 crowns from the king of France was to take his army away, leaving Lord Howard and Sir John Cheyne in France.

(iii) There was to be a seven years' truce between England

---

[1] *Mémoires*, i. 303.

and France. No safe-conducts should be necessary for English-men going to France: all charges paid by English merchants in France and by French merchants, that had been established for the last twelve years, were to be abolished;

(iv) A 'Treaty of Amity' was to be concluded between the two countries, forbidding either king to enter into any league or agreement with any ally of the other without his knowledge or consent, and arranging, within a year, for a marriage pact.

(v) A contract for a pension. Every year, as long as both of them lived, Louis was to pay Edward in the City of London at Easter and again at Michaelmas, the sum of 25,000 golden crowns, and as security, Louis undertook to procure and send to Edward either a bond given by the Medici for the payment of the pension or a bull apostolic with leaden seal confirming the promises made.[1]

Around treaties stories will always gather. Two characteristic of Louis are recorded. At Picquigny he invited Edward to Paris and promised that Cardinal Bourbon, archbishop of Lyons, would absolve him from any peccadilloes of which he had been guilty. Later, Louis de Bretaylle, English envoy to Spain, after-wards to Burgundy and France, gave his opinion to Commines that Edward had made a great mistake by the treaty: the dis-grace of this defeat outweighed the honour of all the nine victories which the king had won. Commines repeated this to Louis, who immediately invited Bretaylle to dinner and offered him large inducements to leave Edward's service and enter his own.[2] But Louis had not found it cheap to get rid of Edward: he had to bestow presents on Edward's chief friends and coun-cillors: Rotherham the chancellor had 1,000 crowns a year: Dr. John Morton *custos rotulorum* had 600 crowns, and Lord Howard and Sir Thomas Montgomery 1,200 each. Lord Hastings, who had done more than anyone (as Gloucester would later remember) to bring the agreement about, was assigned 2,000 crowns a year. He was already receiving 1,000 crowns a year annually from the duke of Burgundy. The accounts of Jean Restout, merchant of Rouen, sent to London in 1476, 1477, and 1478 to pay the pensions have survived: but Louis could now pay Edward no more than 55,000 crowns in cash, giving a bond for the remainder.

Edward returned on 28 September; the mayor and aldermen

---

[1] *Foedera*, v. iii. 67–68.   [2] *Mémoires*, i. 321–2.

and the gilds met him at Blackheath. After his return he remitted a part of the last war grant made to him, the three-quarters of a 15th and 10th which was to be paid at Martinmas. At the end of January 1476 Margaret was handed over to France; she was ransomed for 50,000 crowns: the first 10,000 was paid at the time of her handing over. On 7 March 1476 Margaret renounced in Louis's favour as compensation, so he claimed, for what he had spent in trying to assist her to recover the kingdom for her husband and her son, all rights she had inherited from her mother in the duchy of Lorraine, and from her father, in Anjou, Bar, and Provence. At the time the duchy of Lorraine was in the hands of the duke of Burgundy and Réné of Anjou was still living to enjoy his rights in Anjou, Bar, and Provence. Louis granted Margaret a pension of 6,000 livres; after her father died in 1480 that was all she had. The pension from Louis enabled Edward to build up his own private fortune: to extend his commercial ventures; and to embark on the debauchery and sensuality which characterized his later years. Commines actually declares that he 'nule autre chose il n'avoit eu ne pensée que aux dames, et trop plus que de raison, et aux chasses, et à beau traiter sa personne'.[1] 'Nul autre chose' is, as will be seen, a serious historical error.

Clarence had taken part in the French expedition. He had attended upon the duke of Burgundy in the neighbourhood of Calais in July: he had approved the idea of Edward making peace with France, and at Picquigny he stood upon the bridge with his brother Edward: he was one of the four arbitrators to whom by the treaty differences between the kings of England and France were to be referred for settlement. He had suffered keen disappointment when, after the death of his wife, Warwick's daughter, it was decided that he was not to marry Mary of Burgundy (which had been the hope of the Duchess Margaret, who had always thought Clarence her favourite brother). He took to absenting himself from court, and when he did come, refused to eat and drink in the royal house. He seems to have suspected poisoning, and began suing one of his former servants for administering to the late duchess of Clarence 'a venomous drink of ale mixed with poison' which had caused the duchess to sicken and die. The servant, who insisted that she was innocent, was none the less condemned by the local jury, and

---

[1] *Mémoires*, i. 207.

another man, John Thoresby of Warwick, was similarly accused of poisoning the infant son of the duke and duchess. But he himself was becoming involved in a stranger trail of crime: a member of his household, Thomas Burdet of Arrowe, was arrested for necromancy and attempting to contrive the death of the king by magic arts, tried and put to death, along with an Oxford clerk John Stacey, charged with helping him. There is no reason to doubt their assertion of innocence, and their execution was a warning to Clarence. But he could not keep his mouth shut. Clarence tried to appeal to the king's council over the head of the king, to show that Burdet was innocent; but this had no effect, save to annoy Edward, who in the summer of 1477 was confronted in Cambridge and Huntingdon with an impostor who gave himself out to be the earl of Oxford. The impostor was caught by the sheriff, but Edward became aware that Clarence was mixed up in this rising; and he was encouraged in his belief that the duke was plotting by Louis XI who with his cynical delight in making trouble took occasion to explain to Edward through his *maître des comptes*, Olivier de Roux, how dangerous a marriage between Clarence and Mary of Burgundy might have been, repeating some of the things which Clarence had said he would do in England if he acquired the Burgundian dominions. Yielding to this atmosphere of hallucination and suspicion, the king had Clarence arrested and taken to the Tower on the charge of 'committing acts violating the laws of the realm and threatening the security of judges and jurors'. Then, the day after the marriage of Anne Mowbray and the duke of York, Edward brought forward in parliament a bill of attainder against Clarence, charging him with a 'more unnatural and loathly treason than had been found at any time previously during the reign.' The duke had planned to disinherit and destroy him and his children 'by might to be gotten as well outward as inward'. Among the king's charges was one of obtaining and keeping in secret an exemplification, under the great seal of Henry VI, of the agreement made between himself and Margaret of Anjou 'and other', providing that if Henry and his son died without male issue, he and his heir should rule over England: Edward declared that even after all the charges made, he could still forgive his brother, if he made due submission, but the duke had shown himself incorrigible and the country was demanding his punishment.

This royal bill, discussed in the lords, was assented to by the commons and on 7 February 1478 the duke of Buckingham was appointed to pass sentence.[1] Even after his condemnation to death, Clarence was not immediately executed, for Edward would not give the word, and the Speaker, William Alyngton, had to ask the lords that the sentence be carried out. Clarence was put to death in the Tower on 18 February, probably by being drowned in a bath. The story of his death in a 'barell of Malmsey wine' is given by (among others) the London Chronicler, but there is no means of checking its accuracy.[2] His body was buried beside that of his wife in Tewkesbury.

Clarence was a nuisance rather than a great danger, even though son-in-law to Warwick: but his opposition to Edward and Gloucester and his fostering of local rebellion could not be tolerated. He had few friends. He was out of touch with the atmosphere of the court, unacceptable to the dominant household clique, the creatures and followers of Hastings. Death was perhaps too severe a medicine, but in 1478 there were no places of honourable quasi-banishment sufficiently remote to be of use. Clarence was already the king's lieutenant in Ireland, but Ireland was too close for safety.

The greater part of the duke's lands which came into the hands of the crown as a result of the attainder were administered by royal representatives, the accounts being rendered to the Exchequer. The estates were not treated exclusively as escheats, but as being in the king's hands because of the minority of the son and heir of Clarence, Edward Plantagenet. Clarence's Warwickshire estates had come to him after the death of Richard Neville, earl of Warwick, because of his marriage to Isabel the earl's elder daughter; but the son of that marriage, Edward, never in fact succeeded to the inheritance, and though in 1487 the Clarence properties were granted back to Anne, widow of Richard Neville and grandmother of Edward, she immediately conveyed them back to the crown.[3] The estates, forming part of

---

[1] *Rot. Parl.* vi, 195.

[2] This is the story that reached Philippe de Commines (i. 59). Jean Molinet (*Chroniques*, 1476–1506, ed. Buchon, p. 377) says that Clarence was allowed to decide the manner of his death and made this choice. The report of Olivier de la Marche (*Mémoires*, ed. Beaune and d'Arbaumont, iii. 70) that Clarence was drowned 'en ung baine, comme l'on disoit' seems more probable. Cf. Scofield, ii. 209.

[3] *Ministers' Accounts of the Warwickshire Estates of the Duke of Clarence 1479–1480*, ed. R. H. Hilton (Dugdale Soc., 1953), p. ix.

what was known as the king's 'foraign lyvelode' (the others were Wales, the duchies of Cornwall, York, and Norfolk; and the earldoms of Chester, March, and Salisbury) were up to 1484 supervised by foreign, rather than Exchequer, auditors; they were administered as units instead of being absorbed into the general body of crown lands: but the officials in charge of them had, in many cases, long exchequer experience, including the taking over of escheated estates.[1]

The suspicion which Louis XI had done much to foster in Edward IV against his brother was meant more for the Duchess Margaret than Clarence. Margaret had apparently escaped unharmed and Clarence's death had done nothing to prevent Edward allying with Maximilian and Mary. To prevent this materializing, Louis sent over the bishop of Elne, who was widely suspected of being the French king's spy; but although there was genuine sympathy felt for Mary of Burgundy, now being attacked by Louis XI, Edward, despite his interest in peaceful intercourse with the Flemings, was considerably inclined towards the French view. He was tempted by the offer of a pension of 50,000 crowns a year all the time that a lengthy truce, now being proposed by Louis in place of a treaty of peace, was to endure; Louis actually suggested a truce for 101 years, with the promise that as long as it lasted, the 50,000 crowns should be paid with regularity. He was desperately anxious that England should declare war on Mary, and proposed to Edward's three ambassadors to his court, Lord Howard, Sir Richard Tunstall, and Thomas Langton, that when the war was over, Edward should take all the acquired territories lying outside the kingdom of France, while he (Louis) took all lying within the kingdom, saving places like Lille, Douai, St. Omer, and Aire, which were part of the ancient demesne of the crown of France and therefore due to remain in his own hands entirely. The difficulty of this proposal was that England's prospective share in the conquest of Burgundy, which was to be Holland, Zealand, and Brabant, all lay within the empire, and Edward would thereby find himself embroiled with Maximilian; and if this were to happen, his ambassadors urged,

---

[1] *Ministers' Accounts of the Warwickshire Estates of the Duke of Clarence 1479–1480*, ed. R. H. Hilton (Dugdale Soc., 1953), p. xxviii. This does not imply that there were not still under employment local men who had been attached to the Warwick estates through many changes of régime: cf. ibid., p. xxix.

Louis must not only relinquish all right and title in the four Brabant towns of Lille, Douai, St. Omer, and Aire, but must himself help Edward to conquer Brabant, Zealand, and Holland by furnishing him assistance in the shape of 2,000 lances throughout the year, until the conquest was completed, as well as providing the artillery needed during the summer campaigning season, May to October. Louis replied to this by the counter-attraction of a commercial agreement: as soon as Edward had declared war on Burgundy, Louis promised that all foreign cloth save that arriving from England and all wool and tin (save that coming from England) should be excluded from France while the war lasted. The long and difficult negotiations were cut short in July 1479 by the announcement that Louis had concluded a year's truce with Mary and Maximilian and had promised to restore within a month all places which his armies had taken in the countries of Burgundy and Hainault. It has been suggested with some probability that this halt in the king's diplomacy may have been due to the activities in Flanders of Dr. John Coke, sent over by Edward to negotiate a new commercial intercourse between England and Burgundy. Coke was successful in securing the acceptance of a treaty very similar to that of 1467, except that there was no reservation now about the importation of English cloth into Burgundian territories and the export of war material out of Burgundy: in addition a new set of ordinances was made to settle some of the disagreements between the merchants of the Netherlands and the staplers of Calais.

In the tortuous negotiations of 1479–80 between Louis, Maximilian, and Edward the main lines of Edward's diplomacy are reasonably clear. He would make every effort to continue drawing the pension from France by continuing to plan for a joint action with Louis against Burgundy; when it came to the details of that action, he would haggle and bargain, showing his sympathy with the Duchess Margaret who had large financial claims against Louis, and never getting to the point of agreement. He would do just enough to justify the French pay. Meanwhile he would strengthen the commercial alliance of 1467 with Burgundy. He was determined, having already drawn so many crowns from the pension, to get all he could out of Louis XI; and he used proposals made to him by Maximilian for the marriage of his sister to Edward's eldest son, to step up the offers that Louis had been making for the marriage of his son with the Princess Elizabeth, and even asked the French king to endow the pair before the marriage took place, much to the surprise of Louis who explained that according to the custom of France nobody might demand the dowry until the union was consummated. Try as he might, Louis was never able to undermine the influence of the Duchess Margaret with Edward, set as she was upon strengthening by every possible means the English alliance with Burgundy. She appeared to have succeeded. On 1 August 1480 Edward, Mary, and Maximilian confirmed the treaty of perpetual friendship which Edward and Charles the Bold had agreed on 25 July 1474: but characteristically, if he was now leaning away from France, Edward stipulated that Maximilian must pay him the same pension that Louis was now paying him: and Maximilian, hearing that Edward was agreeable to sending him 6,000 archers, concurred. Complementary to this was a pact for the marriage of Princess Anne to Philip, Maximilian's son, the dowry for whom, if the marriage eventuated, was to be paid by Mary and Maximilian. It is all the more remarkable, therefore, that in the late summer of 1480 Maximilian should have entered into negotiations with Louis which ended, on 21 August 1480, in a seven months' truce and an agreement that plenipotentiaries of both sides should meet in October and conclude a lasting peace: at the same time it emerged that the bishop of Elne, Louis's representative in England, had been put on trial before the parliament of Paris for misconducting his English mission. As a matter of fact the plenipotentiaries never met. By the end of the year Edward was too much occupied with Scotland, and there was never much hope that he would invade France in aid of Maximilian, as the alliance directed him to do, nor be able to preserve Burgundy from destruction, as long as the Scots were threatening to drive over the Border. At a council meeting held at Westminster in November 1480 it was decided that Edward should go north in person to help Gloucester who at that moment, after a raid into Scotland in retaliation for the burning of Bamburgh, was busy repairing the walls of Carlisle. A substantial fleet was fitted out both to harry the Scots coast and to guard the English coast against the French.

For Edward the problem of invading Scotland was largely financial. The failure of the 1475 expedition to France had not been lost upon the commons, and to ask them directly for a subsidy was at first thought to be unwise. Edward resorted to loans and, more valuable in this case, presents made *ex bene-volencia*, while the clergy actually granted a tenth for the defence of the kingdom. The 'benevolences', however, did not come up to expectations and Edward called for payment of the three-quarters fifteenth and tenth which he had remitted after his return from France in 1475, Lancashire and Yorkshire being granted exemption. Meanwhile Maximilian was pressing Edward for an active guarantee of help, unless Louis made a firm peace with him before Easter. He cannot now have ex-pected Edward's own personal intervention, but he wanted, as usual, English archers in as large a number as possible. Edward insisted that if an English force was going to invade France, Maximilian must bind not only himself, but his heirs to help him, and that the duke must promise to give a new bond for the payment of his pension as often as he fulfilled the condi-tions of the bond and sent help to the duke. The pension, Maximilian thought, was worth the help which he would derive from his English ally: but he was to discover that English concentration upon Scotland was the first object of Edward's care, and a formidable naval and land force was equipped in May, the fleet under Lord Howard, and the soldiers under captains responsible to Gloucester. Even by the autumn of 1481 Edward had not gone north: he neither supported his brother nor did he go to the aid of Maximilian. It was suggested that he might go over to Calais in September 1481, to see Maxi-milian and concert measures. But the pension was arriving from France and Edward felt glad to receive the attentions of Louis. Gloucester had to do the work of beseiging Berwick, but the main invasion of Scotland was postponed. Perhaps events justified the delay: for during April 1481 James III's brother, the duke of Albany who had been for three years in France, declared his readiness to help Edward: through an emissary sent to France the king had offered to recognize him as king of Scotland if he would help in driving James from the throne. Albany crossed at the end of April and after Edward had con-sulted Gloucester the terms of an agreement were drawn up. The new king of Scotland had to recognize the right of the kings of England to Berwick, which Gloucester was at the moment besieging, and to Liddesdale, Eskdale, Ewesdale, and

Annandale, in fact to the whole of the western March up to the headwaters of Esk and Liddell. Albany was made to promise that, unless he was granted an extension of time, he would within six months after gaining possession of the crown, do homage and fealty to the king of England; and that within a fortnight of his entering Edinburgh he would deliver Berwick to the English king; that he would break off Scotland's alliance with France; and lastly that if he could 'make himself clear from all other women according to the laws of Christian Church', within a year or sooner he would marry Edward's daughter, the Princess Cecily (already promised to King James) at present aged thirteen; and if it was impossible so to clear him, he would arrange no marriage for his son and heir, should he ever have one, except according to the king of England's wishes and 'unto some lady of his blood such as they both can be agreeable unto'.[1]

This arrangement is worth scrutinizing as a good example of a diplomatic act sealed (or which at any rate it was hoped to seal) by a diplomatic marriage. Edward did not go north to Scotland: he was not sufficiently robust now; and he also wished to keep his eye on Calais which he suspected Louis, in spite of his solemn promise not to invade 'a single village' of the territory, to be coveting. On his side Maximilian had already fixed upon Calais as a favourable meeting-place for a conference with Edward and he was anxious that Edward should know that he appreciated Edward's undertaking, given him on two specific occasions, that he should have aid from England if neither a treaty of peace nor a satisfactory truce could be obtained from the king of France. In point of fact Edward did not cross over to Calais nor did he invite Maximilian to meet him elsewhere. And as he sat tight, the French pressure on Maximilian's Flemish possessions was growing. Did Edward not understand that Maximilian was in a precarious position? He evaded his obvious duty, on the strength of the war with Scotland, where Gloucester had collected a formidable army, and meanwhile the instalments of his pension which he was keenly anticipating were paid. This time Gloucester was in a

[1] *Foedera*, v. iii. 120–1. The truce and marriage treaty with Scotland, planned before the invasion of France, had been judged essential to Edward's success with Louis XI. On 30 July 1474 there had been a preliminary agreement and on 8 Oct. a full embassy had been sent to complete the negotiations for the marriage of James and Princess Cecily and the betrothal had taken place on 25 Oct. Cf. *Rotuli Scotiae*, ii. 441 and *Foedera*, XI. 814, 825.

position to strike. He left the siege of Berwick and marched in real Black Prince fashion, burning town after town and looting the countryside, to Edinburgh, which surrendered to him without serious resistance. Edinburgh secured (1 Aug. 1482), Gloucester marched to meet the Scottish forces at Haddington: he was not opposed and the remarkable thing is that he contented himself with telling the Scots lords that they must pay back all the money which had been sent to King James for Cecily's dowry and also promise to surrender Berwick Castle. Gloucester did not demand the abdication of James in favour of Albany, partly perhaps because he had discovered that James's subjects were not in favour of Albany, and also that Albany had already been approached by some of the Scots lords and promised restoration of his estates if he renounced his pretensions to the throne and had assented to the proposal.

Gloucester was in fact content with the originally arranged marriage alliance between King James and Cecily: he did not want to foist Albany upon the Scots, but what he was anxious to secure he actually obtained: the unconditional surrender of Berwick on 24 August; the defenders to be allowed to depart 'bag and baggage', and so an English garrison marched in, and the town and castle which Margaret of Anjou had sold to Scotland became once more part of England. The continuator of the Croyland Chronicle records that Edward was not satisfied with Gloucester's performance in Scotland, even if the recovery of Berwick was of importance, the place being once more incorporated into the East March.[1]

Louis for his part had hoped that the war between England and Scotland would keep Edward from helping Maximilian and he did not believe that James would collapse so quickly. After August it was evident that he (Louis) could no longer rely upon the Scots to prevent Edward interfering in Burgundy. He had never published the truce he had made with Edward renewing the treaty of 1475. This he now did at the end of September, and caused some consternation in Maximilian and Edward alike. Edward resolved to face the music and, relying on his popularity, to summon parliament; but Maximilian he could not save from the deadly embrace of Louis, and soon he was to hear the outcome: on 23 December 1482 Louis and Maximilian signed at Arras the treaty abjuring all ill will and

[1] In W. Fulman, *Scriptores*, i. 563.

stipulating that Maximilian's daughter should marry the dauphin of France as soon as she was of marriageable age and should be placed in the care of Louis, and that the counties of Artois and Burgundy should be regarded as her marriage portion. There was, it is true, the stipulation, made by Maximilian, that these two territories should revert to his son Philip and his heirs if his daughter's heir failed, and to this Louis had consented: but the king of England was not to be included in the treaty of peace, Louis observing that he had already got a treaty with the English and that this 'did not touch them'. This was the result of Edward's refusal to raise a finger to help Maximilian. Rotherham, in the parliament of 20 January 1483 might well denounce Louis for his deceit: but although the commons were given to understand that a grant for the defence of the realm was expected from them, there was no talk of a French expedition: instead it was the rewarding of Gloucester for his successful attack on Edinburgh and the replacement of James III by Albany which was the most notable act of the sessions. Gloucester and his heirs were placed in permanent possession of the wardenship of the West Marches, of the city and castle of Carlisle, and of all the crown properties in the county of Cumberland. They were also allowed to hold in fee simple, with rights similar to those enjoyed by the bishops of Durham, all the lands they might acquire in Liddesdale, Eskdale, Annandale, Clydesdale, and the West Marches of Scotland. The grant has been criticized as 'extravagant and ill-advised':[1] but the history of the Scottish Marches did not discourage the idea of employing a single family, over a long period of years, in their defence and there was reasonable precedent; and it was not a private family the services of which were being utilized. It is far-fetched to infer from the grant that parliament was 'completely under Gloucester's thumb'. To find someone powerful and influential enough to take over the thankless task of commanding the western March, and to select a man of northern sympathies and Neville affinities to the post surely does not argue that Edward's judgement was 'weakened'. It meant that there would be a strong and unified defence force balancing the Percy defence on the other side; the element of doubt in the arrangement was the linking of the March to the warfare now being conducted upon James III: Gloucester'

---

[1] See Scofield, op. cit. ii. 359.

forces had to hold themselves ready to assist Albany to hold the crown of Scotland; for in the treaty with Albany, the duke was required to work daily for the conquest of that crown so that he and his friends among the Scottish nobility might render the king of England 'great and mighty service against those occupying the crown of France'. Before parliament was dissolved, a fifteenth and a tenth 'for the speedy and necessary defence of the realm' was granted, and on 18 February 1483 a tax on aliens was added. From the fifteenth and tenth, at Gloucester's own suggestion, Yorkshire, Cumberland, Northumberland, and Westmorland were exempted, and York and Kingston-upon-Hull also, for the part they had played in the war against Scotland; nor were all aliens included, for the commons asked for the exemptions of the merchants of Spain, Brittany, and the Hansa towns, to which Edward added the Italian merchants who in December 1482 had secured a ten-year renewal of their exemption granted in 1453.

Albany was not to be relied on, least of all as a confederate against France. On 19 March 1483 the duke signed at Dunbar Castle an agreement with James III containing a promise by James to forgive Albany and to receive him once more into favour, while Albany promised to give up his office of lieutenant-general and never to approach within six miles of James. Albany, it is true, promised to obtain a treaty of peace with England and the marriage of Cecily of York to James's son; but the fact remained that the antagonists had become reconciled and that the English agreement with Albany had been frustrated. Whether Edward was able to appreciate this turn of events is uncertain, for towards the end of March he was seized with illness and on 9 April 1483 he was dead. He had barely the time for the most necessary task of all, to secure at least a measure of reconciliation between Hastings and the Woodvilles; but he summoned the former and the marquis of Dorset and spoke urgently to them on the need to sink their differences in the interest of his children. His words appeared to have some effect, for the two magnates gave a promise of amity and reconciliation.

To what extent was Edward IV a reformer in matters of finance and administration? As yet there is a formidable amount of record scholarship to be undertaken before any reply

can be given to this question. Yet some points are becoming
clearer.

One may start with Edward's interest in money as such. The
problem before the mint was always how to draw bullion by
offering a price at which it was possible to compete with foreign
mints. At the king's accession the output in gold was very small:
it has been pointed out that between 1433 and 1460 less than
7,000 lb. of gold were coined, an average of 250 lb. a year, and
that in 1463–4 the output in this material only amounted to
300 lb. Edward, however, began by first increasing the supply
of silver to the mint, and in 1464, under the mastership of Lord
Hastings, the weight of the penny was reduced from 15 to 12
grains, allowing silver to be purchased by the Mint at 33*s*.
instead of 29*s*. the lb.; and gold coins were increased proportionately in value, a noble being rated at 100*d*. instead of 80*d*.;
the proportion between the metals was the same as fixed in
1411, 100:9. This would be likely to bring gold into the mint
and sustain English gold coins then circulating against foreign
imported gold. At the same time Edward made a new indenture
with Hastings substituting the royal or rose noble, to weigh
120 grains at a value of ten shillings: and to replace the
previous gold noble, a new gold coin of 6*s*. 8*d*. at 80 grains
called the angel was struck. The 1464 reform was certainly
successful. In two years 12,000 lb. of gold and 55,000 lb. of
silver had been coined in London, and new mints were opened:
in July 1465 the royal mints at Canterbury and York started
working, and at Bristol, Coventry, and Norwich mints were
established with permission to coin gold as well as silver.
Coventry and Norwich did not last long; but the castle at York
continued over the period of the Readeption until September
1471 and Bristol went on till July 1472. After Edward had been
restored, Hastings resumed the mastership of the mint. He had
stopped the royals before the Readeption: but he did not close
down—or cause to be closed down—the archbishop's mint
which, at York, normally ceased when the royal mint at York
Castle began working: in 1465 the Castle mint coined gold
groats, half-groats, and half-pence, but not pennies. The arch
bishop now 'assumed the sole coinage of pennies at York',[1] and
at Canterbury the metropolitan was allowed to work his three

---

[1] G. C. Brook, *English Coins* (1932), p. 152. See the illustrations of George
Neville's penny in ibid., pl. xxxv.

furnaces along with those of the king, and coin both pence and half-pence, while for the first time personal and ecclesiastical badges, the Bourchier knot and the *pallium*, appear on the archbishop's coins: a graceful gesture towards the archbishop who had always supported Edward IV.

Edward had been described as 'by the spring of 1463 . . . a full-fledged wool merchant'.[1] That year he was exporting, through shipping agents, wool in considerable quantity: 300 sacks, 10 cloves, part of which was bound for Italy, was carried in the galleys of Francesco Bambow and Marco Dalege. In 1464 Bambow and Dalege carried a further consignment of wool to Italy, rather more than 152 sacks, which was for his own personal gain, quite apart from other large shipments which were going out to Calais to be sold for raising money for the garrison. Edward was also an exporter of cloth. On 23 May 1464 his agent Sanderico was ordered to take charge of the shipment of 8,000 cloths, and Sanderico himself shipped 3,000 of them, made up of 2,997 undyed, worth £6,561. 13s. 4d., two half-dyed worth £16 and one of scarlet, worth £12, in five Italian galleys. Besides Sanderico, a trusted agent, in 1465 Edward was employing John Forster and John Defford to ship his cloths abroad, and in November 1466 he commissioned Alan de Monteferrato to convey through the straits of Marrok 6,000 sacks of wool, 20,000 woollen cloths, dyed and undyed, 10,000 blocks of tin, and 10,000 barrels of vessels of pewter or tin. Alan and another man of the same Christian name, Alan Mounton 'alien merchant', were Edward's principal factors for exporting and importing goods, and the imports in June 1470 included bales of woad, alum, wax, writing paper, and white wine. Mounton was transacting his business from London and Sandwich, the former port predominantly. And what Edward did, the nobles and members of his household found no less profitable: George Neville, Henry Bourchier, earl of Essex, who in 1465 obtained a permit to export 1,600 woollen cloths free of custom, and was an importer as well as exporter, and William Hastings who was himself a merchant of the Staple at Calais and made extensive shipments of wool and pelts. But the principal factor for Edward's private trading was the Florentine, Gerard de Caniziani. Caniziani was the factor and attorney of the Medici in England. By November 1462 he was getting

[1] Scofield, op. cit. ii. 404.

small loans from the Italians, the prelude to a good many others made at Edward's request. Caniziani had a house in the City of London for which he paid, as a foreign merchant, the accustomed 40s. tax: he was not only a lender, but a confidential agent of the king who sent him to Scotland when the struggle was on with Queen Margaret, to see what money could do with bishops and noblemen in the north; and when Edward was trying to collect a dowry for his sister Margaret, Caniziani helped by acting as attorney for the Burgundian duke, while it has been suggested that he advanced a substantial amount of it himself. So indispensable a man did not suffer at the Re-adeption, for Caniziani secured a protection along with his Medici colleagues; and when Edward was restored, his hold upon the king was such that in 1476 there had to be a settlement with him, Caniziani receiving £1,000 a year in ready money, £1,000 in assignments on the last clerical tenth, and £1,000 in 'sufficient and ready payment' as total satisfaction.

Between 1462 and 1475 Florentines lent the king £30,472 and Gerard himself found as much as £24,705.[1] In 1466 when he had lent Edward £8,468. 18s. 8d. he was granted in part payment £3,000 out of the tenth granted by the province of Canterbury. Next to him came the other members of the Medici society, lending £5,000; Genoa put up £4,500 and Venice £2,956. If alien merchants had not lent Henry VI anything, they were prepared to invest heavily in his rival, and Edward has been credited with successfully borrowing far more from aliens in the critical first half of his reign than any previous English government had done since the minority and youth of Richard II or the still palmier days of Edward III.[2] Edward was prepared to employ anyone of drive and ability who could help. An example of his encouragement of persons of obscure birth who might be useful to him by their military or financial ability is given by the career of Sir Edward Brampton, the son of a Jewish blacksmith in Lisbon, who turned up in London in 1468, was baptized, and became a member of the *Domus Conversorum*. As one of the king's converted Jews, he became at his baptism a godson of Edward IV. He was first known in England as Edward Brandon; but the Brandons were Lancastrian partisans, and the name was changed to Brampton. In 1469 he joined his godfather's expedition to the north, but at the

[1] Steel, op. cit., p. 352. [2] Ibid.

Readeption of Henry VI nothing more was heard of him till Edward IV again succeeded, when he appeared in the *Domus*. He left it in 1472 to be given command of an armed force in the Channel and in October that year he was granted certain messuages in the City of London, as 'Edward Brampton, born in the realm of Portugal'. In 1473 he was sent to Cornwall with a squadron of four ships against the earl of Oxford and was successful in inducing the Genoese who supported Oxford in St. Michael's Mount to surrender. He had already become a considerable landowner in Northamptonshire by marrying Isabel, widow of William Tresham, who had recently been the wife, or possibly the mistress, of Sir William Peche of Lullingston in Kent. At all events Isabel Brampton seems to have brought with her lands held by the Tresham family, which included a messuage and two tenements near Holborn.[1] In May 1480 he was granted for life certain estates in Northamptonshire, London, and elsewhere, 'late of Isabel Peche', his late wife, and in the king's hands by the forfeiture of Thomas Tresham, knight, attainted of high treason. As early as 1473 he had been especially exempted from import duties on merchandise which foreigners had to pay. He was trading extensively in *malaguetta*, 'grains of paradise', a spice used for flavouring hippocras, and doing well enough to advance in 1481 the treasury £700 to satisfy a group of Spanish merchants. For this he was allowed to compensate himself by getting permission to send wools through the straits of Gibraltar free of export duty. In 1481 during Lord Howard's attack on the Scottish fleet in the Firth of Forth he commanded a big Portugese carvel. On 24 August 1482 he was appointed captain, keeper, and governor of the Island of Guernsey (which meant Alderney, Sark, Herm, and Jethou as well) till 25 January 1485; and when Richard duke of Gloucester made his bid for the throne, the governor of Jersey (which he does not seem to have visited) gave him valuable help and received grants of money (secured on the customs dues) and lands, and is described as a knight of the body, which means that he had found his way into the householdt when he returned to Portugal, Brampton described himself,

[1] 'On the site in what is now Red Lion Square, the Holborn Borough Council has recently built a block of flats which they have aptly called Brampton, by the name of the former owner—though unaware of his amazing and not wholly respectable career': Cecil Roth, 'Sir Edward Brampton, alias Duarte Brandao', *La Société guernesaise* (Guernsey, 1957), p. 163, which describes his extraordinary career.

though wholly without warrant, as knight of the garter. Brampton, his biographer says, 'had left the country of Portugal twenty years before a penniless, despised Jewish fugitive: he returned a Knight and a man of substance with a distinguished record (which he did not scruple to embroider farther) of achievement in England in peace and war and of personal service to the Portuguese rulers.'[1] He lasted, a distinguished pioneer of Anglo-Portuguese friendship, till 1508, pardoned for the part he took in the career of Perkin Warbeck, who had been in his service and had been instructed by him in the ways of the English court. As Warbeck was to state later in a confession: 'Whatever I told you so readily of past syns or treason, I kept all that in mind as a youth when I was in the service . . . of a certain Edward, a Jew, godson of the aforementioned King Edward: for my master was on the most familiar terms with the said King and his sons.'[2]

Mr. Steel has estimated that during the period 1472 and 1485 real revenue seems to fluctuate between £24,000 and £33,000 per annum. While the figures for Henry VI are probably accurate, he admits that the low totals 'take little or no account of important external sources of income created or acquired by Edward IV,' and that in his reign 'we must add liberally for benevolences most of which were obviously omitted from the receipt rolls': for the bulk of the French pension, from 1475; and very probably for the profits upon trading ventures undertaken by the crown, more frequently and more profitably than the receipt rolls allow.[3] Further investigation seems likely to suggest that the mechanism of the receipt rolls may have been by-passed and that by no means all revenue is showing in the records of the lower exchequer. An interesting archival analogy is to be found in the records of the council. The normal sources where the action of the council is recorded executively, council warrants, and council and privy seal warrants, frequently fail to give any information, though we know that the council was sitting and advising on a variety of matters. A recent investigator has observed: 'Whenever the Council's activities are examined over a selected period, no particular class of documents covers or nearly covers its work.'[4] Exchequer records,

---

[1] Roth, op. cit., p. 167.   [2] Roth, op. cit., p. 166.   [3] Steel, p. 354.
[4] J. R. Lander, 'The Yorkist Council and Administration, 1461–1485', *Eng. Hist. Rev.* lxxiii (1958), 42.

particularly the king's remembrancer's memoranda rolls, have their own quota of entries, while for one year examined by Mr. Steel, 1478–9, there are eighteen entries on the issue rolls, showing various payments made on the orders of the council. These orders were frequently communicated under the signet or the sign manual and not under the privy seal; the privy seal has lost its function as 'the direct and authoritative organ of the king's council' (as Baldwin had called it) which it had occupied earlier and was later to assume again.[1] In the same way the important question of household reforms was dealt with under the signet. It need not be concluded from this that the council was less an executive than an advisory body: but that it frequently had to advise can be seen from the fact that nearly 1,500 references to the council have been discovered between 1461 and 1485.

It is reasonable to suspect that a monarchy as personal as Edward's worked, so far as direct action is concerned, through individuals whom the king had retained and had made members of his household. The list of principal household officials printed by Mr. Myers brings to view the number of extremely influential men of Yorkist England who held some appointment there;[2] and it is noteworthy that the unfinished treatise known as the 'Black Book of the Household', defined by its latest editor as a 'draft intended to be turned later into a formal statement of how the household was and ought to be run', is said (§ 9) to have been compiled at the instigation and with the assent of the king's council, three of whom it names. The councillors so designated are the cardinal of Canterbury, George duke of Clarence, and Richard duke of Gloucester; though it is probable that they instructed an able household clerk to compose the work, and certainly nobody without detailed experience of this sort could have drafted the section on the counting-house. The author makes his acknowledgements also to 'the wise and discreet judges and other said admired and well learned men of England in all aprowments'[3] and especially those who had been long time in the organization. He must have written his work after Edward IV's return and before October 1472. It is partly

---

[1] Ibid., p. 45.

[2] A. R. Myers, *The Household of Edward IV* (Manchester, 1959), appendix i, pp. 286–97.

[3] The Black Book, § 9, in Myers, op. cit., p. 86. 'Aprowments' mean financial reviews.

in English, partly in Latin. The author distinguishes between the two sides of the household administration: the *domus magnifientie* or the household upstairs, which has to impress the world by its magnificence: and the *domus providencie*, the household 'downstairs' or the departments concerned with finance: the administrative officers' wages and allowances, the checking of vouchers with the goods bought, how payments are made and under what authority, and so forth. Throughout, references are made to the ordinance of Edward III. Almost unbelievably, the scale of payments for knights and squires is the same as in 1318, but these were basic rates to which various allowances and supplements were added: and to those who won the king's favour, considerable grants were added. It was possible to rise from the lower grades to the highest of all, the treasurership of the household, through the indispensable and important middle position, that of the cofferer. Of this advance John Elrington, treasurer at Michaelmas 1474, is a good example. Elrington was made clerk of the household in the chancery, constable of Windsor Castle in 1474, and treasurer of war for the French campaign of 1475 and the Scottish campaign of 1482. He was knighted in January 1478. Elrington, as treasurer, was concerned with the old problem of securing in advance revenues for the payment of household expenses, so that the accountants could know what to expect and creditors not be obliged to wait too long. In December 1474 he secured, mainly from customs, ulnage, wardships, and marriages, £4,966. 6s. 8d. a year for ten years; and when the duke of Clarence was attainted in 1478, part of the revenues of his estates was used for the household. Elrington had, at any rate, considerable sympathy from among the commons in parliament for such a cause; for they suggested that part or the whole of various penalties judicially inforced should be applied to the expenses of the royal household. In the last parliament of Edward IV the commons, anxious to ensure that payment be made to those from whom royal purveyors had secured commodities, secured the royal assent to earmarking £11,180 a year for five years for expenses. In the Black Book £13,000 a year is the figure the household estimated as necessary. It would be of some interest to know whether Elrington himself had anything to do with the composition of the treatise.

It was the household, and Elrington in particular, that

organized the raising of the army that Edward IV took to France in 1475. There was a special household company, the lances of which were provided by gentlemen of the household. Its function in later medieval warfare demands further investigation, for knights and esquires and yeomen of the body had not lost their military significance.

Elrington lived to see the worst period of royal indebtedness surmounted. 'By 1478', it has been said, 'it was possible to think of clearing off outstanding debts', for the French pension was coming in regularly, there was additional income from the confiscated Clarence estates, the customs had improved with the revival in the export trade, and in 1478 both convocations made grants to the crown.[1] In this year, therefore, there was a great clearance of old indebtedness. None the less during the period 1476–9 the household was still running at a loss (£2,230), and Edward decided to by-pass exchequer methods of auditing and payment which were found to be too slow and cumbersome, and to appoint special auditors from his own household. In 1476 Sir Thomas Vaughan was appointed surveyor and demiser of the revenues of the Norfolk inheritance (John duke of Norfolk deceased). Vaughan (esquire of the body and keeper of the great wardrobe to Henry VI) had been Edward's treasurer of the Chamber, an indispensable household figure who in 1473 was made chamberlain to the young Prince Edward and was a member of the prince's council. He had a house in Stepney and was co-lessee with the prince of Wales of another which he had built within the precinct of Westminster Abbey 'for his dwelling and for the pleasure of the king and his consort Elizabeth and their son'.[2] It was characteristic of Edward's system to employ in his household a man who served as sheriff and on the quorum of Surrey and Sussex, thus linking county and central administrations. In 1478, as it has been pointed out,[3] a special commission consisting in the main of household officials was given the task of examining the accounts of the recently confiscated Clarence estates, a valuable accretion to the crown, not only on account of their revenues, but also because household officials could be appointed to posts within these lands. As the

[1] A. R. Myers, *The Household of Edward IV* (1959), p. 37.
[2] *Cal. Pat. R., 1467–1477*, p. 455. Vaughan's commissioners, several as administrators of lands that had fallen in to the Exchequer, are numerous.
[3] By Myers, op. cit., p. 37. For appointment, *Cal. Pat. R., 1476–1475*, p. 10.

household grew with the increase of Edward's family (by 1478 there were six children), new positions had to be sought to reward the more numerous personnel.

So also it became necessary to curtail expenses, which was the object of the ordinance of 1478. The emphasis of this document was on economy. The number of authorized persons in the household and the liveries which they were allowed had to be reduced, and the source of inspiration appears to have been the ordinance of 1445. But now from 1478 is omitted the concession that all the king's squires and officials who were not on the establishment should have the right to come to the king's court at the five principal feasts of the year, during sessions of parliament or great councils, which must have put a severe strain on the Lancastrian household. The ordinance of 1478 lays down that all knights of the body, cupbearers and knights carvers, squires of the body, chaplains, gentlemen ushers, and squires of the household are to attend when required; and the names of those who had to be in attendance during the coming quarter were set down in a book which the king was to deliver to the counting-house, from which the counting-house could make up a roll of attendances. The economies appear to have been not without effect. It has been calculated that the expenditure of the household in 18–19 and 19–20 Edward IV were £11,292 and £11,193. To meet this, parliament earmarked the sum of £11,180 for the expenses, and whether this sum was actually forthcoming or not, it is the intention and objective of the commons which constitute the interesting point. But in fact to judge from extant household accounts 'the cost of the royal household in these years seems to have been lower than it had ever been in the days of Henry VI or than it was to be in the reign of Henry VII: only it may be noted such a compilation leaves out the expenses of the Great Wardrobe for clothes, linen, furs, and so forth';[1] and Edward was a notable buyer of jewels, precious stuffs, and *objets de vertu*.

The connexion of the household, the knights and esquires of the body especially, with English government in its various branches has to be realized. The plan adopted as an emergency expedient for financial reasons by the Lancastrian government in its last precarious stage between 1450 and 1460 was now,

[1] See the tables of household expenses for 20–31 Henry VI and 8–20 Henry VII in Myers, op. cit.

with modifications, put into practice by Edward IV in both periods of his reign. The royal household both in its regular and in its more occasional personnel maintained a close connexion with the counties and with local justice. Knights and esquires of the body, and yeomen of the crown acted as sheriffs and as justices of the peace, and these services, in addition to the parliamentary duties of a substantial number, brought the household into contact with practical problems of government. Figures to be noted are Avery Cornburgh, yeoman of the crown and chamber 1455–74, squire of the body 1474–85, a Devonshire man who was sheriff of Cornwall, 1464–5, 1468–9, and justice of the peace for Essex (where he had a residence) from 1468 until his death, besides being sheriff of Essex and Hertfordshire 1472–3, 1477–8; Sir Richard Croft of Croft in Herefordshire, described as *serviens Regis*, who was sheriff of Herefordshire 1469–70, and, after the Readeption, from 11 April 1471 to November 1472; Piers Curtis, burgess of Leicester and bailiff (1461–98), a member of the household (1462–72), later to become clerk of the great wardrobe (1472–94), who sat for Appleby 1467–8, 1472–5, and the borough of Leicester 1478, 1483, 1484, 1485–6, 1487, 1489–90, 1491–2, 1495 (what could he not have told?); Sir Giles Daubeny of Barrington and South Petherton, Somerset, squire, then knight, of the body, who was M.P. for Somerset 1478, sheriff of Somerset and Dorset 1474–5, 1480–1, and a justice of the peace for Somerset 1475–83; Sir Gilbert Debenham of Wenham, Suffolk, king's carver 1471–83, knight of the body 1483–5, who sat for Ipswich in 1455–6, was a justice of the peace for Suffolk in 1471–5, 1478–80, 1482–3, in much the same way as Charles Dinham who became squire of the body in 1485, beside acting as sheriff of Devon (1476–7) and on commissions of the peace for the county 1461–3, 1471–87; the remarkable Sir John Fogge of Ashford, Kent, who was king's squire and treasurer of the household 1460–9, sat on Kentish commissions from 1450 until his death, and was sheriff of the county 1453–4, 1472–3, 1479–80; and the other two Kentish king's squires who are often joined with Fogge and helped him to quell Cade's rebellion, Sir John Scott of Smeeth and Braborne, Kent, was sheriff of Kent in 1460, and justice of the peace for the county 1458–70, 1471–5, 1481–5; and Robert Horne who was on all Kent commissions 1449–May 1460, and sheriff in 1451–2. There are a good many others, and material is abundant to show the connexion of Edward's court with the local administration.

By archival study and research into the title deeds of their neighbours and competitors these *curiales* fortified and extended their position. At an earlier period Sir John Fastolf had suffered from the research and inquiries of Sir Edmund Hull.[1] Exemption from the Resumption Act helped, and pardons saved the situation when it was becoming serious. The resilience of many was remarkable. After the turmoils of the period 1447 (when Suffolk had got rid of Gloucester) to 1461, it might have been thought that no more would be heard of Thomas Daniell, attainted after Towton, and deprived of his constabulary of Castle Rising. But he was again justice of the peace for Norfolk in 1469 and, saved in all probability by John Howard, he was granted in 1472 a general pardon and in the next parliament secured a reversal of his attainder. In August 1474 he was granted lands in Ireland and in 1475 the old squire of the body was made yeoman of the crown. The Berkshire family of Norris (Bray, Ockwells, Yattenden) provides some good examples of royal remissions, and shows that Edward IV and Henry VI were ready, at a price, to forget. The father, John Norris was, under the Lancastrian government, usher of the chamber 1429–40 and squire of the body 1441–60, sheriff of Oxfordshire and Berkshire, 1437–8, sheriff of Wiltshire 1440–1 and 1448–9, and of Somerset and Dorset 1445–6, and held the stewardship of Cookham and Bray. As treasurer of the chamber and keeper of jewels to Queen Margaret, he looked after himself well; in May 1448 he was pardoned for any suit the king might have against him. In the events of 1450 he was denounced in parliament, but survived and secured another pardon in 1452. He was sheriff of Oxford and Berks. in 1457–8 and took out pardons in January 1458 and January 1459.[2] After Edward IV's accession he was pardoned once more (1462), to die in 1466. He thus had five pardons during his acquisitive lifetime; but his son was perhaps even more resilient. Knight of the body 1469–83, 1485–1506, and lieutenant of Windsor (1488–1506), as his father may, with some probability, have been, he is first seen

---

[1] Mr. P. S. Lewis has traced the career and the tactics of Hull over the manor of Titchwell, acquired by Fastolf, in 'Sir John Fastolf's Lawsuit over Titchwell'. *The Historical Journal*, vol. i no. 1 (1958), 3–8.

[2] *History of Parliament, 1439–1509*, Biographies, p. 638.

in the Coventry parliament and was knighted by Henry VI just before the battle of Northampton (10 June 1460). Edward received him into favour, and he was made a justice for Berkshire from 1467 (with a gap for the Readeption) till 1483, and from 1494 till he died (1506), and sheriff for Berkshire and Oxfordshire, 1468-9. He was knight of the body from 1469, but in September 1483 he joined the duke of Buckingham's revolt against Richard III and was arrested in Devonshire with the marquis of Dorset and others. He escaped but was attainted in February 1484; but after Bosworth the attainder was cancelled and he was allowed to retain, despite the Act of Resumption (1485), the keeperships and stewardships received from Edward IV and Henry VI to which he soon added others. He was still knight of the body (1502) and like his father was made steward to the chancellor of Oxford University (1505). There is reason to think that these knights were indispensable men in the household, and if family tradition set them on the wrong side, they got themselves rehabilitated during the ensuing reign by their assiduous service and in virtue of their local positions. It was good policy not to alienate them as long as they behaved themselves.

The vicissitudes of individuals and the need for working through men whose past (and even whose present) was not above reproach should not conceal the fact that administratively the policy of the Yorkist kings is one of reform. Their reforms, as Dr. B. P. Wolffe has pointed out, 'appear to have been modelled on the normal methods of contemporary, large-scale, private estate management'.[1] The owners of large estates depended for their income upon a staff of professionals at headquarters: a surveyor, a receiver, and one or more auditors; and just as in diocesan administration, where there are families which specialized in the secretarial and legal work of the see, there were families which specialized in estate management, like the Heton family in the service of the Stafford dukes of Buckingham, or the families of Kidwelly and Sapcote in the royal service after 1461. One of the latter clan was especially prominent. John Sapcote, squire of the body 1472-85, of Elton, Hants, maintained his place in the household until his death in 1501, and was sheriff of Rutland in 1475-6, after he

[1] 'The Management of English Royal Estates under the Yorkist Kings', *Eng. Hist. Rev.* lxxi (1956), 3.

had sat for the county in parliament 1472–5. In 1480 he had married Elizabeth the widow of Lord Fitzwarren and was appointed to farm the Fitzwarren lands in Shropshire and Staffordshire at a figure of £233 a year. Fitzwarren had been a coholder of the Audley barony in Shropshire, Staffordshire, and Devon, and from the time of that appointment onwards Sapcote lived on the Audley-Fitzwarren estates in Devonshire (his house was at Bampton) and was sheriff of Devon in 1477–8 and a justice for the county 1481–14 May 1483, 20 August 1483 until his death. Through the influence of his brother-in-law Lord Dinham, under Gloucester's protectorate, he was made receiver of Cornwall and he supported Richard III throughout; though he suffered in the Resumption of 1485, his loyalty to Richard did not prevent him from being acceptable to Henry Tudor, and he was knighted on 16 June 1487 and given various commissions. Sapcote was a lawyer like his younger brother Thomas who held land in Co. Rutland where he served on the quorum for nearly fifteen years, and like him was employed in the service of the duchy of Cornwall and was on various Cornish commissions. These two Sapcotes did not hold receiverships, the most important administrative posts in the big estates or complexes of estates, as did the Kidwelly family or the Leventhorpes, a group of men prominently connected with the duchy of Lancaster. The Leventhorpes were a Yorkshire family that settled at Sawbridgeworth, Herts. John Leventhorpe I was Henry Bolingbroke's first receiver-general of the duchy, and most important financial officer, whether at Peterborough or in London, who had met him on his return to England at Ravenspur. He it was, Mr. Somerville thinks, who was responsible for drawing up the great Cowcher books of the duchy. He was executor both of Henry IV and Henry V. His son, John Leventhorpe,[1] member for Horsham 1453–4, was king's squire and like his father receiver of the duchy estates set apart for the payment of royal wills. Other sons of John I were William, receiver of Pontefract 1448, and Nicholas, who

---

[1] 'Leventhorpe's almost unique position as executor to both Henry IV and Henry V . . . and his position as one of Henry VI's duchy of Lancaster feoffees were immediately recognized by his co-feoffees when they appointed him (at a fee of £100 a year) to be overseer of the property under their control, and his son, John Leventhorpe the younger, to succeed him as receiver-general of the same estates. Leventhorpe senior continued to hold his office of Keeper of the records of the duchy': J. S. Roskell, *The Commons in the Parliament of 1422*, pp. 117–18.

may be the man described as 'the king's humble servant and true liege', father to the Nicholas receiver-general of the duchy, who is called king's yeoman, receiver of Pontefract (like his uncle) and surveyor of royal castles, lordships, &c., in the four northernmost counties (1472).[1] There were other Leventhorpes serving the royal household and the duchy.

This estate management personnel—receivers who were the financial officers *par excellence*, auditors who could draw up a valor and advise on problems of accounting and estate management[2]—could be seen at its best and most typical in the duchy of Lancaster lands. But until, at any rate, the time of Edward IV, the system was not extended to other estates. Edward had different views: he was prepared to form new complexes of estates and to put them under his own professionals. A good example was that created in 1461 mainly out of the lands of the earldom of March, along with some lands in the duchy of Lancaster, some belonging to the crown and some lands which were in the king's hands by reason of the minority of the heir, Henry duke of Buckingham. These, lying in ten counties of Wales and the Marches, had as their receiver John Milewater, whose accounts were audited at Hereford by John Luthington, the royal auditor for north Wales and Chester. A number of forfeited estates were placed under the control of receivers and special auditors at the beginning of Edward's reign. Among them were the Richmond and Beaufort lands, the Roos lands, and the lands formerly belonging to the earl of Northumberland, and to James Butler, earl of Wiltshire. Then there were the lands of the duchy of York, of the earldom of March in East Anglia, the home counties, Cambridgeshire, and Huntingdonshire. The sequestrated temporalities of the bishop of Durham were placed under the control of the treasurer and the controller of the household and Thomas Colt. These commissioners rendered their accounts not at the Exchequer, but before special auditors acting in the exchequer of the bishopric at Durham.

The issues of these lands thus acquired were not immediately recorded on reaching the Exchequer, nor is there any trace

---

[1] Somerville, *Duchy of Lancaster*, i. 400–1.

[2] A list of receivers and auditors is given in B. P. Wolffe, 'The Crown Estates and the Acts of Resumption' (Oxford D.Phil. thesis), by kind permission consulted here. Cf. his list printed as appendix to art. cit., *Eng. Hist. Rev.* lxxi (1956), 26–27.

of exchequer assignment being made upon them. The receivers were directly responsible to the king and rendered account in the chamber: the estates were not allowed to pass into the Exchequer farming pools. The issues were in fact written down by the local auditors and transmitted to the Exchequer later, to be deposited among the accounts of subordinate ministers; 'Undoubtedly', as Dr. Wolffe has written, 'Edward did let some forfeited lands and some escheated lands out to farm to private persons for lump sums; but even these assignments were not made through the Exchequer and the rentals were paid into his coffers.'[1] What happened is clear: while the Exchequer of Receipt continued its working, the royal coffers in the king's chamber became his main treasury: 'by means of warrants under his signet, his seal of the earldom of March, or by indentures drawn up between the payer and one of the king's officers on his verbal orders, he took money due to him wherever he could obtain it.'[2] This had been happening from the beginning of his reign. The greatest single accession of lands received by Edward IV was the Warwick, Salisbury, and Spencer estates along with many farms, royal lordships, and manors which came into his control in the spring of 1478 after the attainder of Clarence. By the end of the reign these lands were producing at least £3,500 a year net cash income for Edward. At first this great complex was administered by Edward's clerk, Peter Beaupie, from Warwick. Together with the auditor John Hewyk and other auditors Beaupie was given the job of furnishing all relevant accounts for examination to a commission under the chairmanship of Sir Thomas Vaughan, treasurer of the chamber and chamberlain to the prince of Wales. On the commission were Sir John Say (under treasurer of the exchequer), Sir Robert Wingfield, controller of the household, and Henry Boteler, recorder of the favoured town of Coventry and formerly employed by the duke of Clarence. These men reported to the king, and under their supervision the lands were placed in charge of a number of receivers, all directly responsible to the king in his chamber. The Yorkist receivers were men of initiative and trust. A memorandum of 1484 described their duties: 'to ride, survey, receive and remember on every behalf'

---

[1] Wolffe, 'The Crown Estates and the Acts of Resumption'. This has been freely used in the section that follows.

[2] Wolffe, *Eng. Hist. Rev.* lxxi (1957), 11.

that might be most for the king's profit and thereof yearly to make report'. These reports were made either to the king himself or to persons commissioned to hear them, when they delivered in cash the balance of their receipts. After their appearance in the king's chamber, the receivers of Clarence's lands were normally sent to the barons of the Exchequer with various acquittances and instructions, to make a declaration of account for the purpose of record. The barons could not examine them and could demand nothing of them, but their appearance was necessary in order that the Exchequer should have a record of all receivers' accounts so as to check the accounts of subordinate officials with whom the chamber was not concerned.

Edward had, therefore, made the chamber both a treasury and a centre of audit. It is worth noting that Richard III continued the system which Edward had worked out for the administration of the crown lands and the augmentation of their revenues. The confiscations he made caused an increase in the number of receivers and auditors. When Queen Elizabeth Woodville's lands were confiscated, John Fitzherbert, the king's remembrancer, was appointed as receiver of most of her fee farms and annuities, and a number of her receivers were deputed to control groups of manors; quite a considerable group of local lordships in Surrey, Buckinghamshire, Berkshire, and Wiltshire were administered from Windsor, probably through William Herle; a group of royal manors in Kent and Essex were entrusted to Robert Brakenbury, constable of the Tower and treasurer of Richard's household when he was duke of Gloucester. Richard's treasurer of the chamber, Edmund Chadderton, took personal charge of most of Buckingham's forfeited lands as both receiver and surveyor. The new personnel could be drawn from the household as before.

In 1461 new arrangements were made for the administration of lands farmed out from the Exchequer. The treasurer and barons were commanded not to include in the summons of the pipe demands for farms and fee farms worth 40s. a year and above. New regional officers, eight in number, were appointed for eight groups of contiguous counties with sufficient power for themselves or their deputies, to find out, levy, collect, and receive all manner of rents and services due, to distrain for debts and eject insolvent or bad tenants and put in new ones. All sums collected were to be paid to the treasurer of the household towards its expenses. The persons appointed can, for the most part, be identified as personal servants of the king's household with some training in royal administration. These dealt with the lands formerly appearing in the summons of the pipe, not with forfeited lands or the lands of wards. The Exchequer began in 1463 to demand accounts from them. In reply, they were authorized by writs under the privy seal to make declarations of account before the barons and were dispensed from accounting at the Exchequer under the earlier system of charge and discharge. These declarations of account show that six out of eight receivers, covering twenty-six counties acknowledged receipt of about £2,000 a year until Easter term 1463. The Exchequer farming system continued and an attempt was now made to secure its more efficient working. After Easter 1463 the eight receivers did not render account at the Exchequer; the reason may be that Edward IV now began to make many grants from the farmed lands, to his brother George and Richard Neville and later to his queen, and the receivers must have worked on a reduced scale. It has also been pointed out that throughout the Yorkist period, these lands were mainly responsible for the pensions list.

After the restoration of 1471 a new group of receivers or 'approvers' were appointed for the farmed lands, but this time the country was divided into seven regions. Men of considerable experience, like their predecessors, they were authorized to declare their accounts before the barons of the Exchequer: they included Nicholas Leventhorpe referred to above, receiver and surveyor for Yorkshire, Westmorland, Cumberland, and Northumberland who accounted to the chamber: Geoffrey Kidwelly, made receiver and surveyor for Somerset, Dorset, Devon, and Cornwall: and between 1472 and 1476, Maurice Kidwelly, who collected the issues from the manors of the Gurney lordships. Again these receivers did not pay into the Receipt or account before the barons. This territorial and chamber administration by which Edward by-passed the Exchequer deserves a fuller study: it was a notable step forward in the efficiency of the central government.

XIII

RICHARD III

EDWARD IV had made at least two wills and there were
codicils. In 1475 before he embarked for France he put
Queen Elizabeth at the head of his executors; in his later
will, according to reliable testimony, she did not figure there,
and the care of Prince Edward was entrusted to Richard of
Gloucester. It was a natural appointment. Richard, born in
1452, had been loyal to his brother throughout. At a comparatively early age, not more than twelve, he had been made com-
missioner for the western and south-western counties, from
Shropshire to Devon and Cornwall, against the Lancastrians in
Wales; two years previously he had been given the county,
honour, and lordship of Richmond and of Pembroke also; and on
9 September 1464 the king bestowed on him the estates of Lord
Hungerford, the attainted Lancastrian. In that autumn the
king's marriage had confronted him with the choice of following
his brother or of intriguing with his tutor, the earl of Warwick;
in the spring of the next year he had left Middleham Castle, the
great Wensleydale stronghold where he had been brought up,
for his brother's court, where the Woodville influence was becoming predominant. But there is no evidence that he fell out
with the queen or any of her five brothers: he was too young
for that. When Warwick and Clarence began their struggle for
the readeption of Henry, Richard, along with Hastings, held
firm to his master, and when Edward had been captured at
Olney (1 Aug. 1469) the young prince, at liberty, went northwards to raise forces to rescue his brother and, after being summoned to Pontefract, accompanied Edward to London in the
famous entry planned to vindicate his independence. At Barnet
he commanded the right wing of Edward's army, breaking
eventually through Exeter's force in the Lancastrian centre,
and at Tewkesbury he was in the vanguard of the Yorkist army,
confronting Somerset on the Lancastrian right. After which
campaigning he showed at his best in the downfall of the Nevilles
and the disposal of their lands: he stood up for the countess of
Warwick (then in sanctuary at Beaulieu) against the king and

in 1473 pleaded for the release of Archbishop George Neville; when the marquis of Montagu's son lost his dukedom a few years later, Richard obtained the wardship, and brought the boy into his household; later on, he bestowed an annuity on the earl of Oxford's wife, a sister of Warwick, though Oxford was his enemy. In these years he stood as a representative of royal influence in the north. In the settlement of the dispute with Clarence over Warwick's estates, Richard kept Middleham, Sheriff Hutton, and the other lands belonging to Warwick in Yorkshire; and when Clarence was practically cutting his own throat, Richard spoke up for him.[1] Although he had to attend Edward on the 1475 expedition to France, his main ties were in the north; and his relations with the City of York were of far more than normal cordiality. Richard was deeply interested in the city. He was frequently there, staying with the Augustinians in Lendal; with his wife Anne, he was enrolled in the Corpus Christi gild. It was his influence that could prove decisive in securing the royal confirmation of the election of a mayor, when there existed a certain amount of popular feeling against it.[2] The municipal officers cultivated Gloucester assiduously; and it was to York that, as Protector, he was to send one of his most significant writs asking for assistance against his enemies.

During his brother's lifetime, therefore, Gloucester had behaved both loyally and correctly. It is important, if his later actions are to be judged aright, that the death of Clarence, which Shakespeare attributes to his machinations, should not be attributed to him either directly (Sir Thomas More positively states that he was opposed to it)[3] or by those more oblique methods which historians lacking clear evidence use to confirm their suspicions of the duke. In discussing Richard's religious foundations, Dr. James Gairdner made considerable play with the date on which the duke obtained the licences from the king —21 February, 'just three days after the death of Clarence'. 'Richard was not even yet a hardened criminal and however Edward's conduct may have absolved him from personal responsibility for the death of Clarence, the event must have

---

[1] See P. M. Kendall's note on Richard's advocacy of Clarence, *Richard III* (1955), p. 454, n. 8, citing authorities.

[2] See the documents printed in R. Davies, *Extracts from the Municipal Records of the City of York* (1843), pp. 122 f., on the election of [Sir] Richard York (1478) whose memorial window, formerly in St. John Micklegate, is now in the Minster

[3] *The Historie of Kynge Rycharde the Thirde*, p. 6.

weighed upon his mind in some way.'[1] The foundations are the college at Barnard Castle, consisting of a dean, twelve chaplains, ten clerks, and six choristers, who were to perform the services for the good estate of the king and queen, for Richard and Anne while alive and for their souls after their several deaths; and for the souls of his father Richard of York and of his brothers and sisters, and of all faithful persons deceased. This is a familiar formula of a family foundation, which was now repeated, though on a smaller scale, at Middleham, where there were to be a dean and six chaplains, four clerks, and six choristers. One establishment, therefore, was to be in a lordship of which a moiety belonged to Clarence; the other in his own castle town. Gairdner, criticizing an author who had quite pertinently pointed out in Gloucester's favour that the act authorizing one such foundation (name unspecified) was obtained in the parliament beginning on 16 January 1478, and that Clarence was probably alive then, inferred that Gloucester must have had the Barnard Castle project in mind: if this was so and Clarence was still living, such an anticipation of the duke's death made the case 'look rather worse than it did before'.[2] From an administrative point of view it is curious that Gairdner should have imagined that a substantial foundation like this could be put through right up to the stage of the royal patent in rather less than a month: for that is what his argument implies. It was probably fortified by the belief that after the death of Clarence Richard 'secured undivided possession of Barnard Castle of which he had hitherto held only a moiety'.[3] It has been pointed out that no grant of this kind exists for 1478, and that its absence would itself indicate that Richard's full possession of Barnard Castle dates from the division of the countess's property in 1474. If this view can be sustained, the foundation of a family chantry-college within his own lordship seems capable of a simple explanation. Barnard Castle became like the great Yorkist centre of Fotheringhay, residence and college. There is another and larger consideration. Concentration upon the disappearance of the two princes should not be the sole determinant of the historian's view of Richard III. Obviously it is the most difficult and provocative phenomenon of the period: but it has to be fitted into the story, not stand outside it.

---

[1] *History of the Life and Reign of Richard III* (1878), p. 37.
[2] Ibid., pp. 37–38, and appendix, note 1.   [3] Ibid., pp. 36–37.

As Richard of Gloucester is a figure of controversy, it is important not to read into his earlier actions more than they can bear. It has proved particularly tempting to some writers to follow the narrative of Sir Thomas More and the majority of Tudor historians and to allow, in the interest of psychological consistency, a final adverse judgement upon the duke in the affair of the princes to colour the story of the events from April to June 1483. Both Dominic Mancini, writing for his friend Angelo Cato a humanist's narrative of events, and More, when he put together what Cardinal Morton and other senior contemporaries remembered for him, are valuable sources: but starting from the need to tell a clear and definite story (for humanist writing has to do that), neither is prepared for the confusions and the cross-currents of those critical months, and there are times when the silences or suppressions of the Croyland continuator, watching from the council, are more historically revealing than either. Yet there is a great difference between Mancini and the Tudor historians. He is a contemporary, and even if we discount his decided partisanship, he gives, naturally and subconsciously, information of the highest significance. On a longer historical view, the 'occupation' of England or the seizing of the crown may be compared, in its day-to-day development, with an equally famous occupation with which this story began. Who shall say that Henry Bolingbroke came back to England with the sole and fixed purpose, whatever happened, of displacing Richard for good and all? At the outset, the possibilities of an extreme solution must have flickered in the mind of both aspirants. But at what stage did they become the determining factor? Obviously Richard was not unacquainted with history and precedent. He knew about Henry IV's usurpation, he had heard of his father's bid for the throne; he had been brought up in the Warwick household and knew the story of 1470; he had studied his brother and helped him to win crown and kingdom. The stability of modern constitutional practice is liable to obscure the proprietary aspect of fifteenth-century kingship. *Reale est quod petimus regnum*, Fortescue on the law of nature makes one claimant say. The kingdom is a heritable piece of real property, to be awarded by the highest court to the claimant who has vindicated the right to succeed.

Edward IV died on 9 April 1483. The City of York had the report three days earlier, and the Minster, by a not unknown practice, had the dirge and requiem celebrated while the king was still breathing.[1] Richard of Gloucester was then at Middleham; Prince Edward was with Lord Rivers at Ludlow. The prince's proclamation took place on 11 April, the news reached Ludlow on 14 April, and on the 16th Edward informed the mayor of Lynn that he was intending to be in London with all convenient haste to be crowned at Westminster. In point of fact he did not leave Ludlow till about the 24th. Richard of Gloucester had the news first from Hastings, probably not from Buckingham who quickly afterwards from the Welsh Marches sent his servant Persivall to meet Richard and assure him of his loyalty and to arrange a rendezvous with him. The intimation it is well to note, did not come from the queen or the chancellor but from Edward's chamberlain himself, informing Richard that Edward IV had made him protector of his heir and the realm and advising him to secure the person of the king with all reasonable speed. Hastings appears to have followed this up by reporting to Richard the deliberations of the *proceres* that took place almost immediately after the obsequies. Mancini reports that there had been two views in the council about the government of the realm during the minority: one held to Edward's will and urged that the protector should govern: the other opted for a governing council (on the pattern of 1422) with the duke as chief councillor. The second was the view of the Woodvilles who were afraid of a usurpation and of what would become of them at the hands of a man who knew that they had been the cause of Clarence's destruction.[2] Hastings, according to this account, advised Richard to bring a strong force to London, 'seizing before they were alive to the danger' those of the king's followers who were not in agreement with the former of these views. It was at this point that Richard wrote to the queen to express his condolences and to the council, offering his loyalty to Prince Edward and to Edward IV's issue, and asking, in view of Edward IV's will, that he be given the position due to him according to law and to his brother's disposition. There seems little doubt that Richard had the precedent of 1422 in mind,

---

[1] R. Davies, *Extracts from the Municipal Records of the City of York* (1843), p. 142. Bishop Philip Repingdon in his testament, *Reg. Chichele*, ii. 285, asked that 'tali die et hora missa mea funeralis in ecclesia parochiali S. Margarete infra clausam Lincolniensem *me vivente si fieri poterit* pro anima mea . . . celebrari'.

[2] *The Usurpation of Richard the Third* (*De occupatione regni Anglie*), ed. C. A. J. Armstrong, p. 86.

when through the council's thwarting of the will of Henry V, Humphrey of Gloucester was debarred from the protectorate which his brother had devised for him.

On this occasion a much more powerful figure than Duke Humphrey was claiming observance of Edward's dispositions. The majority in the council which had voted for a return to the 1422 precedent could, when it came to a question of force, be overborne by an alliance of the older nobility (Gloucester, Buckingham, Hastings); but only if that alliance would hold together and not weaken or split on essentials. For Richard one essential was that the queen, the marquis of Dorset, and her son Sir Richard Grey should be removed from the direction of affairs, and that Earl Rivers, appointed ten years previously, should have no control over Edward. But danger lay ahead. Dorset, Elizabeth's eldest son by her first marriage, constable of the Tower, both controlled the main armaments depot and was in charge of Edward IV's treasure. Sir Edward Woodville, the queen's brother, was put in command of the fleet which was now manned and victualled for immediate duty. Great stores had been accumulated, for the country stood ready for war against Louis XI, and, if he had lived, Edward would have sent an expeditionary force very quickly. The treasure itself, as Mancini relates, was divided between the queen, the marquis, and Edward Woodville, too rapidly for the protector to lay hands upon it: this cannot be true of the whole contents, as will shortly be seen: but some part was certainly in their hands. The date suggested by the Woodville interest for the coronation was as early as Monday, 4 May, and no limit was at first proposed for the forces with which Earl Rivers was to bring Edward from Ludlow to Westminster. At this Hastings took umbrage and threatened to retire to Calais unless some limitation was agreed upon. The queen gave way and requested her son to limit his escort to 2,000 men. This was a considerable figure when compared with the 300 which Richard, before he was warned by Hastings, was proposing to bring, while Buckingham had been asked to produce a similar number.

The issue was clear. As soon as Edward V had been crowned the protector's authority was due to cease and the government as noted above was to 'devolve upon the Council'. Even before that happened Dorset and his friends declared that the protector was no more than *primus inter pares*, the chief man in the council. The question before Hastings was whether the council that took the decision to expedite the coronation had any right to do so in the absence of the protector. To that Richard himself could give a clear answer. In practice it took the form of an alliance with Buckingham and the interception of the king by the two dukes while *en route* for London: for Dorset had told Rivers to have the king at his capital by 1 May. On 29 April Richard reached Northampton and found that the king had passed through the town and gone on to Stony Stratford. Rivers, however, was there to meet Richard, and later in the day Henry Stafford, the duke of Buckingham, arrived. This was the signal for action. At dawn on 30 April Rivers was arrested and the road to Stony Stratford was guarded to prevent the king hearing of the deed. The dukes then rode on to Stratford to find Edward who was accompanied by his chamberlain Sir Thomas Vaughan and by Sir Richard Grey. Richard thereupon addressed the king, explaining that his own life had been threatened by a conspiracy of ministers, and that he was obliged to arrest Earl Rivers and to remove all sympathizers with the plot on the protector: and though Edward, according to Mancini, made a dignified and spirited protest in favour of the ministers chosen by his father, he could do nothing but acquiesce in his uncle's tutelage and in the steps that were immediately taken: the arrest of Grey (this took place in the king's presence) and Vaughan and the dismissal to their homes of the majority of the royal escort, a force more numerous than the troops brought by the two dukes. With the king at Stony Stratford was his brother the duke of York who was also placed under guard. The whole party returned to Northampton, whence Rivers and Grey were sent under ward to Yorkshire, the former to Sheriff Hutton, the latter to Middleham. Both were ultimately beheaded at Pontefract (25 June 1483). The Croyland continuator says that they were executed under the direction of Richard Ratcliff, who was bringing southward the troops for whom Richard had sent for from the municipality of York; but John Roos suggests that they were accorded some form of trial under Percy of Northumberland.[1] The former seems the more probable story.

The news of the events at Northampton caused consternation in London. It sent the queen into sanctuary at Westminster,

---

[1] *The Usurpation of Richard III*, ed. Armstrong, p. 152, n. 82.

along with the marquis of Dorset and the queen's brother, Lionel, bishop of Salisbury. Rotherham, the chancellor, is reported by Mancini to have found the queen in sanctuary and 'alone, a-low on the rushes all desolate and dismayed' and to have left the Great Seal in her keeping.[1] In point of fact Archbishop Bourchier on 7 May sequestrated the goods, jewels, and seals of Edward IV, since the executors named in his will hesitated to act under the conditions prevailing. The jewels were entrusted to William Daubeny who had been clerk of the jewelhouse, and to Richard Laurence and Rowland Forster, yeomen of the house: the Great Seal, the privy seal, and the signet belonging to Edward IV while he was alive, Bourchier took into his own possession and retained ('ad manus suas recepit et penes se custodivit').[2] The goods and jewels thus under sequestration were made by the archbishop to pay for the king's funeral expenses which amounted to the large sum of £1,496. 17s. 2d.; Bourchier, as such a debt was the first charge on the estate, authorized the executors to raise the money from the sale of Edward IV's property.[3] But before these things had happened the protector, whose case was presented to the council by Hastings, had written to justify his action in arresting the Woodvilles. He also wrote from Northampton to the archbishop asking him to provide for the surety and safeguard of the Tower of London and the 'treasure within the same';[4] while to the mayor and aldermen he wrote saying that the king and he would enter London on 4 May. On 3 May Richard left Northampton for St. Albans, and with Buckingham and the king entered London on 4 May. In his first council meeting Richard was confirmed in his title of protector, to which defender of the realm was added; he was given power 'to order and forbid in every matter like another king'; and, unlike Humphrey of Gloucester, was awarded the *tutela* and oversight of the king's most royal person. In the chancellorship John Russell, bishop of Lincoln, now replaced Rotherham, and the humanist John Gunthorp was appointed to the keepership of the privy seal. The treasurership went to John Wode, previously Speaker

---

[1] More says that conscious of having violated his trust, Rotherham sent for the Great Seal again. *Life of Richard III*, pp. 29–31. This seems equally doubtful.

[2] *Reg. Bourgchier*, ed. du Boulay (C. and Y. Soc.), i. 53.

[3] Ibid., pp. 54–55. The executors were the archbishop of York, the bishops of Lincoln, Chichester, and Ely, Lords Hastings and Stanley, and Sir Thomas Montgomery.   [4] *Ancient Correspondence*, xlv, no. 236.

of the commons and a friend of Richard's. Hastings retained his offices: he was governor of Calais as well as chamberlain, and one of his protégés, William Catesby, was made a member of the council, while Hastings's deputy at Calais, Lord Dynham, was made steward of the duchy of Cornwall.

The greatest concentration of power, though deliberately away from the capital, was in the hands of Buckingham. On 15 May he was given power to array the king's subjects in Shropshire, Hereford, Somerset, and Dorset, and in these western counties was made constable of the royal castles, as these should fall vacant, as well as appointed steward of all the royal demesnes and manors. By the second grant he was made chief justice and chamberlain in both north and south Wales, and given complete authority over the most important Welsh castles and lordships. His powers were practically palatine in the principality, and within a few days he was appointed steward of the castles and manors within Wales belonging to the duchy of Lancaster and to the earldom of March. These were grants of jurisdiction and authority, not of territory: but they had the effect of concentrating in his hands a unique degree of power in Wales and the west country. He was not a soldier or sailor like John Howard, and unlike John Howard he was by nature an adventurer, anxious to play the leading part, not capable of taking an ambassador's role nor the sort of man to settle down with his steward to go over his accounts.

The Woodvilles were not completely out of the way until Sir Edward, in command of the fleet, had been rendered innocuous and his sailors and soldiers encouraged to desert him. To capture Woodville was a pretty desperate task, as he had a large fleet anchored in the Downs. Woodville's men had to be informed of the pardon to be granted to all who deserted an enemy of the protector; and for that purpose the rougher and abler spirits among the sea adventurers had to be mobilized and sent in. Sir Thomas Fulford, son of Sir Baldwin Fulford, a Lancastrian beheaded after Towton, and Sir Edward Brampton, the Portuguese Jew whom Edward employed against the earl of Oxford at St. Michael's Mount, were chosen for the errand, and somehow they proved able to spread the news of the pardon in Sir Edward Woodville's fleet: but their best achievement was to win over the Genoese captains in the two largest carracks in the fleet, who at a party which they gave made all the English guards within them so intoxicated that the sailors were able to take the vessels back to the port of London. With two vessels only Sir Edward Woodville succeeded in making Brittany. Whether, as Mancini says, he was able to convey a portion of Edward's treasure to aid Henry Tudor, seems very doubtful.

By the end of May 1483 there had been no coronation, but the date, originally fixed for Tuesday, 24 June had been moved forward to Sunday, 22 June, and preparations were pushed on. In the middle of May the council considered the question of the protector's position, and the proposal for a continuation of the office until Edward V came of age was recommended for submission to the parliament that was planned to take place on 25 June. Richard took it for granted that the lords and commons would give their consent. It is likely that he talked over with Bishop Russell of Lincoln the theoretical as well as the more immediate practical reasons for deciding that the protectorate must go on. They were embodied in the first draft of Bishop Russell's sermon to parliament, replaced by the version he adopted after Buckingham's rebellion.[1] It is the intervening period which proved crucial in the development of Richard's policy. 'Having got into his power', says Mancini, 'all the blood royal of the land, yet he considered that his prospects were not sufficiently secure without the removal or imprisonment of those who had been the closest friends of his brother, and were expected to be loyal to his brother's offspring.'[2] This is an over-simplification of the moves that were to follow.

All government springs from some more or less self-conscious group of persons: a community, however small, engaged upon the same task, whether the organization is dominated by a single will or a number of wills. The members must be bound together by considerations of utility or self-interest. What the protector had so far accomplished was to remove such a self-conscious group without putting anyone in their place. Offices had been filled, but the new men did not think alike. It was not exactly a vacuum which had been left: there were able men, Russell, Gunthorp, Stillington, among the new council; but there was something indeterminate, a number of administrators who had not taken the measure of one another and (saving

[1] See below, p. 630.　　　　[2] *The Usurpation of Richard III*, p. 109–10.

always John Morton) had been bewildered by the pace of events. Into this body, if a firm and workmanlike council was to be built up, had to be inserted and fitted the co-operating magnates who were of highly dissimilar character: Hastings, the intimate friend of Edward IV, his chamberlain, the governor of Calais, the pillar of the household system, but no friend of the Woodvilles; Henry Stafford, duke of Buckingham, who had married the queen's sister but detested Queen Elizabeth, highly strung, enthusiastic, possibly even magnetic, now made constable (15 May 1483) of the royal castles in the western counties, Shropshire, Hereford, Somerset, Dorset, and Wiltshire, as well as chief justice and chamberlain of north and south Wales; John Howard, the Essex Yorkist, Paston's opponent, devoted to Edward IV and in April 1483 standing with Hastings against the Woodville influence; Thomas, Lord Stanley, potent in Lancashire and Cheshire, who had been the husband of Warwick's sister, a shrewd man and quick to see on which side his bread was likely to be buttered. Outside these inner powers was the Percy earl of Northumberland, warden of the east and middle Marches; and there were the protector's friends, Viscount Lovel and the earl of Lincoln.

The protector, an individualist, lacked the gift of holding these people together. Ready to consult with his friends, he was less happy at co-ordinating the work of the council's committees which met in different places and often in each other's houses. If the full council met in the Star Chamber at Westminster, Richard's own headquarters were in Crosby's Place. The Tower, where Prince Edward was lodged, was the centre for the issue of chancery letters and the meeting place of the small administrative group within the council; and one of the committees of the council consisting of Hastings, Rotherham, Morton, and Stanley met there and was closely in touch with the king. This was probably the most experienced of the committees and it is likely to have been the one whose activities were most closely watched by Buckingham and the protector himself. The former knew the past records of its members as well as his chief; and could connect the tendency he was coming to suspect in Hastings, that of reconciliation with the queen's interest, with the activities of the former mistress of Dorset, Jane Shore, now unluckily taken over by the chamberlain. The protector was not slow to hear of these developments; and he was

influenced by his evident knowledge that Hastings was dissatisfied with his position and the limited scope of his authority. It
seems more doubtful whether the protector had, before 13 June,
heard of the story, told him by Stillington, the bishop of Bath
and Wells, of the illegitimacy of Edward IV's children owing to
Edward's supposed precontract with Lady Eleanor Butler:[1] but
he had certainly become aware of a recrudescence of the queen's
interest, for on 10 June he wrote to the City of York asking it to
send as many fencibles as possible 'to eide and assiste us aynst
the Quiene, hir blode adherentts and affinitie, which have en-
tended and daly doith intend, to murder and utterly distroy us
and our cousyn the duc of Buckyngham and the old royall
blode of this realme. . . .'[2] On 11 June he wrote to Lord
Neville, son of the earl of Westmorland, asking him to come to
London to do him good service. He gave no other outside sign
of alarm, but he had evidently heard that a *coup d'état* was under
discussion, and he knew that, in any event, a party in the council was prepared, after the coronation, to terminate his powers.
The atmosphere was heavily charged with rumour and suspicion, and the protector was not sure what was going on at the
Tower around the king or what messages were reaching the
queen through Jane Shore, whom he later charged with serving
as the agent for Hastings in establishing contact with the Woodvilles. It looked as if a conspiracy of some kind was developing
and that it centred round Hastings himself. One mention of
Buckingham in the letter to the corporation of York suggests
that the duke shared what information he possessed with the
protector. On 12 June two committees of the council were
appointed to meet next day: a coronation committee, under the
chancellor John Russell, and a second group consisting of Hastings, Rotherham, Buckingham, Morton, and Stanley, and other
advisors of the protector, which was to meet in the White
Tower. At the meeting of this committee on 13 June Richard
charged Hastings, Stanley, Morton, and Rotherham of plotting
with the Woodville interest against the protectorate, and
accused the chamberlain of treason. This started a scene.
Hastings was seized by armed men waiting, and while Morton
and Rotherham were guarded in the Tower and Stanley

[1] Cf. below, p. 619.

[2] Signet letter in R. Davies, *Extracts from the Principal Records of the City of York*
(1843), p. 149.

detained in his own quarters, Hastings was led out for immediate execution. To quieten any popular movement an indictment of the dead man was read by a royal herald: Richard had it all ready. Hastings had been detected plotting against the protector and the duke of Buckingham and justice had been done on him for his treason. And as in another famous blood-bath of the present century, charges of immorality were, according to More, made against the chamberlain of Edward IV, who had set his royal master an example of evil living and had the previous night slept with his mistress, Jane Shore, herself one of the conspirators.[1]

The death of Hastings set in motion the train of events by which the protector, urging the illegitimacy of Edward IV's offspring by Elizabeth Woodville, seized the crown. The first step was to extract the duke of York from the sanctuary of Westminster and to send him to be guarded in the Tower. Neither a Becket nor a Winchelsey in face of such a demand, Archbishop Bourchier was persuaded to plead with the queen for his surrender and his words eventually prevailed. Already Clarence's son, Edward earl of Warwick, had been taken into the protector's household to be looked after by his wife: as with the Mortimers earlier in the century, possible claimants were in safe hands—save one, waiting abroad. It was Bishop Stillington who had told Richard that the children of Edward IV and Elizabeth Woodville were bastards because before his marriage Edward was affianced to Lady Eleanor Butler, widow of Sir Thomas Butler and daughter of the earl of Shrewsbury, Talbot himself, by his second marriage. It has been argued that it was because Clarence was aware of this that he had to be put out of the way when in his last frantic phase he started rumours about the king. In that case it was remarkable that Richard, if he had the sympathy for Clarence with which he is credited, never heard the story. At any rate he heard it now, and decided that Edward V's supposed illegitimacy should act as the lever for his claim to the throne: his mouthpiece was to be Bucking-ham, who was to address the lords who had been summoned to London (but specially instructed to leave most of their armed retainers behind), and according to Mancini, he did so, but according to London sources made a speech to the mayor,

---

[1] This is on More's authority (Richard III), but there is confirmation of the allegation in *The Great Chronicle*, p. 233.

aldermen, and citizens of London assembled in the Guildhall. Whether there were two speeches or only one, Mancini's account shows that Richard used some erroneous history to buttress his statement of fact when he urged that Edward IV had, before ever he married Elizabeth Woodville, sent Warwick overseas 'and betrothed the other lady by word of proxy, as they call it'.[1] At the time of Warwick's journeys abroad Edward was already wedded to Elizabeth Woodville.[2] The lords who had made the journey to London with small escorts found themselves in the hands of the protector and Buckingham in much greater strength than they—*in numero terribili et inaudito*, the Croyland continuator observes.

On 22 June the protector with Buckingham and other magnates rode to St. Paul's Cross to hear a political sermon by Friar Ralph Sha, the brother of the mayor. The friar, after praising the duke, repeated the story of the precontract and claimed that by his character as well as by his descent Richard was entitled to be king. In other parts of the city preachers were going farther and declaring that Edward himself was illegitimate: an old and widely diffused scandal which Clarence had once helped to spread, and one that in simpler minds gained credence from the fact that Edward had been born outside England. Thus propaganda prepared the popular mind for the more solemn but doubtfully constitutional proceedings on 25 and 26 June. On 25 June before an assembly of lords and commons that had been summoned originally as a parliament, and continued, though the chancery had begun to send out writs of postponement, as a *de facto* assembly, a document was drawn up petitioning the protector, on the ground that Edward IV's marriage was not a true marriage, to take over the crown and royal dignity 'according to the election of us the three estates of the land'. To this petition lords and commons unanimously gave their consent, and on 26 June before a great concourse at Baynard's Castle, Buckingham read the petition. Richard assented and then rode to Westminster Hall where he usurped the throne by sitting in the royal chair in the King's Bench, having decided that the acts of his reign should begin that day. Then in the presence of the judges of both benches and the serjeants of the law he adjured the lawyers of all kinds to do justice, and there and then was himself dramatically

[1] Mancini, op. cit., p. 118.   [2] Armstrong's note to Mancini, op. cit., p. 155.

reconciled to Sir John Fogge, an old antagonist of the house of York. It was a gesture on a level with the exhibition, on Richard's entry into London (4 May), of wagons bearing what was described as 'Woodville armour'.

The coronation took place on 6 July, by which time large forces from the north had arrived and no counter-coup was possible.[1] Archbishop Bourchier's register entered the king's oath in contemporary English form, the first clause of which ran:

Will ye graunt and kepe to the people of Englond the lawes and custumes to theym of old rightfulle and devoute kingis graunted and the same ratefie and conferme by your oth, and specialli the lawes custumes and libertees graunted to the clergie and people by your noble predecessor and glorious kinge saint Edward? R. [esponsum] Regis   I graunt and promitte.

Being requested to maintain the privileges of canon law 'to alle the churches that be gevin and committed unto us' (the bishops and religious prelates), the king made the following promise:

Animo Libenti (*marg.*)

Wyth glad will and devoute soule I promitte and perfittely graunt that to you and to every of you and to alle the chirches to you committed I shall kepe the privilegis of lawe canon and of holy chirch and due lawe and rightfulnesse.[2]

It was a noteworthy coronation, not only for its splendour, but for the number of peers present and for the allocation of duties. Though John Howard had been made earl marshal, and had been created high steward, he did not supervise the order of the details of the ceremony. This was done by the duke of Buckingham. The latter's wife, a Woodville, was not present. The duke of Norfolk bore the jewelled crown in his hands. The queen had Lord Stanley's wife, the countess of Richmond (Henry Tudor's mother), to carry her train. Stanley himself bore the constable's mace. When, after the anointing and the crowning itself (by Archbishop Bourchier) Richard and his queen were on their seats of estate in St. Edward's shrine, Buckingham and Norfolk stood on either side and the sword of

[1] 'He had decided to employ them as auxiliary police for the coronation, perhaps as much to give them something to do as for any other reason': Kendall, *Richard III*, p. 228. This, however, was 1483, not 1953.
[2] *Reg. Bourgchier*, ed. du Boulay, i. 60–61.

state was borne by the earl of Surrey. The banquet began at four and was of immense length—five and a half hours.

The scenes and demonstrations of early July were surface-deep. The violence and terror of June had not been an incentive to peace and had shown one magnate at any rate, the duke of Buckingham, that revolutions, if made in the right way, could be successful. Richard apparently suspected nothing. Had he known of it, he would scarcely have set out upon the progress which took him first to Reading, where he gave the widow of Hastings a protection against the consequences of her husband's treason, then to Oxford, where Waynflete entertained him at Magdalen College; thence by Woodstock to Gloucester, Worcester, Warwick and, on 2 August, York, where he and the queen accompanied by the prince, wore their crowns in the streets. Richard was unquestionably popular in York. Buckingham had accompanied him as far as Gloucester, and thence he retired to Brecon. At Brecon, so More relates, he held certain conversations with Bishop Morton of Ely, in which Morton encouraged him in his dissatisfaction with the king. The grievances Buckingham felt were probably not due to the delay he experienced in getting the moiety of the Bohun inheritances to complete his possession of the whole earldom; they were more likely to have arisen from a conviction that he had backed the wrong horse. He was, after all, a Lancastrian and his own descent and earlier background played an important role. He was descended from Thomas Woodstock, Edward III's youngest son: his grandfather, the most notable of the line, had fought for Henry VI. His father had died of wounds received at St. Albans in 1455 while fighting against Richard's father. His mother was the daughter of another casualty at St. Albans, no less than Edmund duke of Somerset. After marrying into the queen's family, which, as her ward, he was practically obliged to do, he had taken little part in public affairs save as seneschal of England when he pronounced the death sentence on Clarence. He had joined Richard's side partly out of anti-Woodville sentiment, partly out of ambition to play the leading role to which his resources entitled him. His support made Richard's usurpation possible and he had been created practically a viceroy to the west of England. He was at Brecon when he was made aware of a movement throughout the home counties and the south to rescue, before it was too late, the sons of Edward IV now in the Tower. Before the end of August Richard had got wind of this and had appointed commissioners of oyer and terminer to deal with offenders. But by 11 October he had heard that Buckingham had become implicated and that a more serious phase of rebellion was at hand. After the rumour had spread that King Edward and his brother had met a violent death—linked by the continuator with the events of October[1]— the movement was becoming transformed into an attempt to displace Richard and to send for Henry Tudor. The actual part taken by Buckingham in these events is difficult to trace. It has been argued, with some plausibility, that Buckingham began by aiming at the throne, between which and him stood both Richard and the princes; that the responsibility for their assumed deaths lay at his door rather than at Richard's, or at Henry VII's (as Sir Clements Markham forcibly argued); but later that he came to see that his own accession would gain scanty support and that the only chance of obtaining agreement among the magnates outraged by Richard was the new king's displacement by Henry Tudor. This hypothesis would make Buckingham the doer or at least the organizer of the deed[2] and at the same time make him partly responsible (perhaps with Morton) for the rumour—and the timing of the rumour—of the violent end of the princes, spread so as to augment the fury and indignation of those whom he proposed to lead against Richard III.

The evidence for this hypothesis is not convincing: no chronicler or contemporary makes any such suggestion. Mancini who places the murder of the princes fairly and squarely upon the shoulders of Richard, by whatever intermediary it was done, left England before Richard's coronation on 6 July. From his text it is clear, as Mr. Armstrong has pointed out, that before his departure Edward IV's children were believed by many people in London to be either dead or as good as dead.[3] The Great Chronicle of London says that after the death of Hastings they had been kept in stricter confinement. During the mayoralty of Edmund Sha (on some occasions between 29 Oct. 1482–29 Oct. 1483) they were, according to the same

---

[1] *Historie Croylandensis Continuatio*, in Fulman, *Scriptores*, p. 568; *The Great Chronicle* says 'after Easter' 1484, p. 234.

[2] P. M. Kendall, *Richard III*, appendix i, especially pp. 411 f.

[3] *Usurpation*, p. 153.

authority, seen 'shotyng and playing in the garden by the Tower'; and 'day by day began to be seen more rarely behind the bars and windows' till at length they ceased to appear altogether. Mancini, in a eulogy of Edward V for his scholarly attainments, his dignity and charm, says: 'I have seen many men burst forth into tears and lamentation when mention was made of him after his removal from men's sight.' 'I have seen' (unless Mancini is to be written off as a mere rhetorician) is one of the casual disclosures which make this Italian *relatio* so significant, pointing to the expectation, not of the inns and ale-houses but of informed citizens—that there was no hope for Edward.[1] This forecast was about by the end of June, and even in an excited state of opinion a prediction of this kind was not based on nothing. Edward V made it, we are told, about himself.[2] He at least had been removed from view by the beginning of July, and there is no reason to believe that his brother was not with him. By October the forecast had become a story of fact. Whatever had happened to the boys, their concealment was now a reality. They were not seen again under Richard III's rule.

It is unlikely that the circumstances of their deaths will be known. The famous story related by More to the effect that Sir James Tyrell had confessed to the murder of the princes and that this confession was let out by Henry VII is now discredited.[3] More convincing, perhaps, is the archaeological and medical evidence, derived from an examination in 1933 of the skeletons of two children found originally in 1674 within a wooden chest below the foundations of a stone staircase outside the White Tower.[4] This shows that the elder skeleton was of a child between twelve and thirteen, and that the younger was of a child of about ten. Edward V was born in November 1470, his brother in August 1473, and if the bones are in fact those of the princes, correspondence of age is indeed found. But how old the bones actually were in 1933 it is more difficult to determine. All that can be said is that if the skeletons are those of the princes, it appears that the children may have been killed

---

[1] A correspondent of the Celys, writing between 13 and 26 June 1483, expresses alarm for what might befall Edward V and the duke of York. *Cely Papers*, pp. 132–3.

[2] 'Quod mortem sibi instare putaret': *Usurpation*, p. 112. This was told Mancini by Dr. Argentine (*Argentinus medicus*) who was the last known person to attend him.

[3] See the discussion by P. M. Kendall, *Richard III*, appendix i, pp. 402 f.

[4] Lawrence E. Tanner and William Wright, 'Recent Investigations regarding the Fate of the Princes in the Tower', *Archaeologia*, lxxxiv (1934), 1 f.

in the summer of 1483: and were certainly dead by the end of the year. But can the identifications be satisfactorily established? There is some degree of probability, but no certainty: and one dental authority has put the age of the elder child as under ten.[1]

Evidence for the continued existence of the princes at any rate into 1484 has been brought forward,[2] but it is very far from satisfactory and there is no clear indication that they or even one of them are referred to. Very naturally it was the policy of court circles during the next reign to make out Richard's responsibility for the death of the princes. Both Gigli and Carmeliano made this point in 1486 and in 1499 William Parron, Henry VII's court astrologer, in his *De astrorum vi fatali* was clear that their lives had ended under Richard III.[3] Moreover, when Perkin Warbeck was executed in 1499 his admission that he was not a son of Edward IV was given wide publicity and printed. But Henry VII himself kept silence. The words 'shedding of infants' blood' were indeed put into one of the charges in the Act of Attainder brought against Richard and his adherents in Henry's first parliament 1485-6,[4] but Henry never made direct charges, although he could have obtained statements from contemporaries like Tyrell and Argentine. The very fact of his silence might be thought to tell against him, but in view of the circumstances of 1483 it is far from conclusive. In this atmosphere of doubt one point seems clear: even if the duke of Buckingham as constable of the Tower had either received, or (which is most unlikely) had himself given, the order for the death of the boys, the fact remains that they disappeared from view while Richard III was on the throne, and the king never took effective steps to counteract the rumour, of which he must have been aware, that they had been disposed of.

The defection of Buckingham had to be met quickly. On 15 October the constable was proclaimed a rebel. In the crisis Stanley, although his wife was preparing for her son's invasion, held firm to Richard. On 18 October the insurrection broke out, but the duke of Norfolk was able to prevent a junction

---

[1] Kendall, op. cit., pp. 497-8.
[2] Based on MS. Harleian 433, warrants for livery of clothes, and regulations for the king's household in the north. Discussed and rightly dismissed by Kendall, op. cit., pp. 407-8.
[3] C. A. J. Armstrong, 'Astrology at the Court of Henry VII', *Italian Renaissance Studies*, ed. E. F. Jacob (1960), pp. 448-9.   [4] *Rot. Parl.* vi. 276.

between the rebels of East Anglia and those of Surrey and Kent: the Kent and Surrey thrust against London, led by Sir John Fogge, Sir Richard Hunte, and Sir John and Sir Richard Guildford might have been formidable, but Norfolk obstructed their way at Gravesend. The royal army had been summoned to Leicester, and on 24 October the king moved to Coventry to prevent Buckingham who had marched from Brecon into the southern midlands joining the rebels from the southern and eastern counties. Buckingham made a difficult passage, harassed by guerilla bands and particularly by the earl of Devon, Humphrey Stafford, from Brecon into Herefordshire: by the time he got to Weobley, a manor of Lord Ferrers, his forces, depressed by the small enthusiasm they had found for his cause and by the bad weather, were melting away. Bishop Morton was with him at first: but seeing that Buckingham's cause drew few adherents he escaped, first to Ely and then to Flanders. Morton's defection threw his fellow-conspirator into panic and he took refuge in Shropshire. When the duke's flight came to the notice of the leaders of his force, Sir William Stonor, Sir William Berkeley, Sir Richard Woodville, and others, they abandoned resistance and dispersed. Richard who had been marching into Wiltshire occupied Salisbury, the seat of Bishop Lionel Woodville, without difficulty; and very soon afterwards Buckingham who had been handed over to the sheriff of Shropshire by one of his servants, was brought in. He was tried by his deputy, Sir Ralph Assheton, and sentenced to be executed. He was never accorded an interview with the king, his plea for mercy was rejected, and he was beheaded in the market-place of Salisbury (2 Nov. 1483).

Meanwhile Henry Tudor had made an abortive attempt to land at Poole. The behaviour of the soldiers guarding the coast excited his alarm and he quickly withdrew. The date given by various authorities whether 9, 19, or 29 October is uncertain: of these 19 October, at the very beginning of the revolt, is not impossible, since Richard while he was at Leicester was warned that Henry was on the way, and his informant, Dr. Hutton, would have taken at least three or four days to come from Brittany. Hutton may have known that Henry had already left or at any rate was leaving the Breton coast. On the other hand, Henry received a loan of 10,000 crowns on 31 October while he was at Paimpol on the Channel, which must have been made either before he sailed or after he had returned from the expedition. The evidence suggests either that there may have been two abortive attempts to land on 19 October and again after 31 October; or that Henry was at sea for some time, touching first at Poole in Dorset and then, as the continuator of Croyland relates, at Plymouth. He must have realized without much delay that the attempt was premature: it was treated very seriously by Richard who took up his headquarters at Exeter between 5 and 8 November 1483: but it was not as yet joined by any leading magnates apart from Dorset or by any bishop except Morton and Lionel of Salisbury. Its supporters were mainly country gentry and the upper ranks of the yeomanry.[1] The executions following it were few, and pardons, along with the partial restoration of confiscated estates, were granted to a number of the leaders. Richard took no vengeance on the Woodvilles, like Dorset or Sir Richard. Even the bishop of Ely was offered the king's forgiveness. The countess of Richmond, while she lost her titles, was not attainted; her lands were given to her husband, Lord Stanley. The main rewards went to members of the household.[2] But one result the rebellion certainly had: offensive measures of all kinds against Duke Francis II of Brittany, the foyer of rebellion against Richard III. At Rennes on Christmas Day 1483 Henry Tudor contracted to marry Elizabeth daughter of Edward IV; the Breton fleet made the Channel dangerous for English shipping, particularly wool vessels destined for Calais, and every effort was made to locate it and bring it to battle, though no full-sized engagement appears to have been fought. All Breton goods within the City of London were ordered to be seized.

It was not difficult to exacerbate anti-alien feeling, but Richard did not give way to it for long. It was essential to evict Henry Tudor from Brittany and the Breton coast and to cultivate good relations with the duchy, so as to prevent any recurrence of the loans that were given to Henry at the end of

---

[1] See the Kentish evidence in Agnes E. Conway, 'The Maidstone Sector of Buckingham's Rebellion', *Archaeologia Cantiana*, xxxvii (1925), 106–14: the confiscations and grants to loyal subjects are in *Cal. Pat. R., 1476–1485*, pp. 427 f.

[2] Grants for loyal service: *Cal. Pat. R., 1471–1485*, p. 424, for Sir Thomas Burgh (manors belonging to Sir Giles Daubeney, Sir William Berkeley, and the reversion of the manor of Colston Bassett, Notts., 'late of Margaret countess of Richmond on the death of Thomas Stanley kt., lord Stanley, who holds the same for life').

October, and with France, as far as possible, so that the French
coast should not form a jumping-off ground. Richard sent an
embassy to Francis offering to yield up the yearly revenues of
the earldom of Richmond if he would surrender the Tudor.
The embassy was not received by Francis on account of illness,
but by his treasurer, Pierre Landois, whose chief concern was
getting money and increasing his own influence by doing a
favour to Richard III; but Henry was warned in time by
Bishop Morton in Flanders: the priest Christopher Urswick,
who bore the message, was immediately sent in by Henry to the
court of Charles VIII to procure a safe-conduct for him and his
friends to enter his dominions. Under pretext of visiting the
duke, who was then on the borders of Brittany and France,
Henry's entourage left Vannes and entered the duchy of Anjou,
where after two days the earl himself joined them. Landois sent
a party after Henry to bring him back, but they were an hour
too late: meanwhile Francis II had recovered sufficiently to
show his disagreement with the tactics of Landois; he sent for
Sir Edward Woodville and Edward Poynings and provided
them with money enough to convey the remaining Englishmen
to Henry: thus the whole party was enabled to reach Charles
VIII at Langeais on the Loire, where they were later joined by
the French council. The council, like the king, showed no doubts
about supporting Henry. On 17 November 1484 they sanctioned the payment to him of 3,000 *l.t.* to help him array his
troops. Louis XI had been polite to Richard and had stated
that he desired Richard's friendship: Commines, on the other
hand, says that he regarded Richard III as inhuman and would
not answer his letters: whether Commines is right or not, Louis
had no intention of continuing the pension paid to Edward
ever since the treaty of Picquigny: nor was Charles VIII inclined to be friendly, for Bishop Thomas Langton, sent over in
March 1484, with powers to conclude a truce with the French
king, made no headway; progress with France was unlikely
after the conclusion of a truce between England and Brittany
in June. With the Archduke Maximilian Richard's relations
were more friendly, and the old alliance with Burgundy might
have brought about close co-operation against France, had the
situation not been complicated by the struggle that was going
on between Maximilian and the Flemings, which led to constant infractions of the maritime agreements with Burgundy.

While Richard's success with these external powers was either mediocre or non-existent, he was, within limits, more effective with both Scotland and Ireland. With the former, the defeat of Albany and the loss as an ally of the earl of Douglas convinced Richard that it was futile to maintain an Anglo-Scottish war and that the right move was to conclude peace. A strong Scots delegation was therefore sent to Nottingham (11 Sept.) to conclude with England a three years' truce and following that a treaty of marriage between the duke of Rothesay, James III's son, and Richard's niece, Anne de la Pole, daughter of the duke of Suffolk. The match never came to effect. When Richard was killed it was broken off and Anne entered the Bridgettine monastery of Sion. In Ireland Richard was never looked upon as a tyrant: on the whole the house of York was popular. It had to be so now, not from choice but from necessity: the old problem for an English government, whether to rely on lieutenants specially sent over or upon the more doubtfully efficient services of the Anglo-Irish nobility, was answered by Richard in the spirit of compromise; he relied upon the earl of Kildare, a Fitzgerald, to support his lieutenant the earl of Lincoln, and did his best to conciliate the earl of Desmond, whose father Tiptoft had put to death, declaring that he had always 'had inward compassion of the death of his said father', though Desmond was required to wear English dress. It must be said that in Richard's time Ireland was quiet, and that the frequent rebellions of Henry Tudor's reign show that the house of York had had some hold on the Irish people.

There is evidence from Richard's brief period of government that he was resolved to carry on the methods of Edward IV's administration and that in the sphere of justice and order he was both a reformer and to some extent an innovator. Owing to Buckingham's rebellion the parliament originally intended for St. Leonard's Day (6 Nov.) 1483, which had to be postponed to 23 January 1484, began with a sermon by the chancellor, John Russell, the bishop transferred from Rochester to Lincoln in 1480, whom More describes as 'a wise manne and good, of much experience and one of the best learned men, undoubtedly, that England had in hys time'. This gremial Wykehamist has been described as a trimmer,[1] for though employed on royal diplomatic missions by Edward IV and by Henry VI at the

[1] S. B. Chrimes, *English Constitutional Ideas in the Fifteenth Century* (1936), p. 168.

Readeption, Russell also commended himself to Richard III and Henry VII alike. To the University of Oxford the former archdeacon of Berkshire (1467) remained as chancellor for the period beginning either in, or shortly after, 1483 and lasting till his death in December 1494. Russell's sermon intended for Edward V's first parliament, on the 'trimembred text'—'Audite insule, et attendite populi de longe, Dominus ab utero vocavit me'—is an appeal to the lords, the more stable element in the country, 'to accord and eche amyabilly to herken apon other', for the nobility is the 'insule', the 'Isles and londes enuirounde with water' where surety and firmness is more likely to be found 'than in the see or in eny grete Ryvers'. There is nothing infallible, no security 'amonges gret waters and tempestuous Rivers' (the allusion would have been obvious): the right channel is to hearken to 'the commyn voyce grownded in a resonable presydent', and for the lords and noblemen to realize that such good sense and experience demands concord among themselves in whom is the 'polityk rule of every region'; for they have the right of speaking with the prince, as Moses and Aaron did with God; and when the prince in his own person conducts a judicial visitation of his realm, 'the ministracion of justice is wont to be so terrible and precise in processe that all the pertees and persones adioignaunt quake and tremble for feer'. 'Attendite populi de longe' is meant for the common people 'that stonde ferre of', bidding them attend to the nobles in authority, and does not refer, Russell hastens to add, to the commons in parliament, but to their constituents. He continued this very Wykehamical address by comparing the body politic to the human body in which the belly or womb is the king's court and his council. This womb waxed great just before the death of Edward IV,

consyderynge the inextricable curis, pensifenesses, thowghtes and charges wharewith ys wyse and fercastinge mynd was hugely occupied and encombreed, a fore hys decesse, seeyng the crafty and fraudulente delynge of the outward princes with whome he was allyed, and howe untruely they varied bothe for mariages, paymentes, suretees and other grete and noble appoyntmentes passed fro them by theor othys and selys.[1]

The king who has succeeded in troubled circumstances required the lords and commons 'as agreabilly [to] pourvey for the sure

[1] In Chrimes, op. cit., pp. 169–78.

maynetenaunce of hys hyghe estate as eny of their predecessours
have done. . . .' This draft, liberally illustrated from Roman
history, was rewritten in two versions, for Richard III's parliament, under the text 'in uno corpore multa membra habemus,
omnia autem membra non eundem actum habent'. The second
version written after Buckingham's revolt had the part about
the belly, but pointed to the lack of unity in the body through
the action of one person 'late ryghte aud gret membir of thys
bodye', whose example and whose punishment would not be forgotten. At the end the chancellor compared England to the
woman who lost one of her ten pieces of silver and had to seek
diligently till she found it. The commonwealth (symbolizing perfection) had departed from this standard, and it was the duty of
the country to get a light and search diligently for the piece lost.
Both speeches, the original conceived for Edward V and the
new version, were primarily exhortations to unity and harmony
within the state. The allusion in the first, to the king on a judicial eyre, showed the determination of Edward's son to do
justice in person, for the sight of the royal person actually so
engaged had a profound effect.

The first duty of parliament, after the election of William
Catesby as Speaker, was to confirm the new king's title and
settle the succession on the heirs of his body. While, the Act
stated, it was clear that the king's title to the crown was based
upon God's law and natural law, as well as upon the ancient
customs of the realm; none the less, because most people had
little knowledge of these laws and could not perceive the truth,
it was necessary to declare in parliament that Richard was the
king because he had inherited the crown, had been elected,
consecrated, and crowned. The king's son Prince Edward was
then declared heir apparent, and the king called upon the
nobles, knights, and gentlemen of the household to swear an
oath of allegiance to the prince as their supreme lord, in the
event of his father's death. Two previous acts of attainder concerning the property of the late duchess of Exeter, the king's
sister, were annulled, and a new attainder act passed against
all those guilty of rebellion.[1] These included 'the leaders of the
revolt at Brecon' and, most significant, groups of twenty-eight
Kentish and Surrey men who included Sir John Fogge; fourteen, headed by Sir William Norris and Sir William Stonor

[1] *Rot. Parl.* vi. 244–9.

who started it, in Berkshire; thirty-three, including Sir John
Cheyne, in Wiltshire; and eighteen, comprising Dorset and two
members of the Courtney family, who revolted at Exeter. The
bishops of Ely, Salisbury, and Exeter were forgiven the penalty
of death, as they were clerks, but had to forfeit their temporalities. The countess of Richmond, as we saw, was condemned to
forfeit her lands, but in view of the service done by her husband
was not subjected to attainder. On the other hand, Earl Percy
of Northumberland (whose ancestors were attainted for rebellion against Henry IV) had an act of restitution passed in his
favour, and there were private acts for Lord Lovel and Sir
James Tyrell.

The statutes made by this single parliament must be judged
against the background of disaffection which the quelling of
Buckingham's revolt had never fully laid. The lands of the
rebels were still being seized, and the ports were carefully
watched: no one could pass out of the realm without special
mandate, and Kent was still a danger. When Richard went into
Kent on tour ten days before the opening of the parliament, he
offered large rewards for the seizure of the rebels, while praising
those who had deserted the leaders of the disaffected. At the
same time Richard showed himself anxious to compensate those
who had lost goods and property in the rebellion: in the same
spirit the king in consenting in the parliamentary grant allowed
merchants paying duty on exports to replace, without further
payment, cargoes lost. If, then, the atmosphere was full of
anxiety, the tone of the measures taken was firm and moderate,
and aimed at the suppression of local tyranny and abuse. The
first of these forbade secret feoffments to use by which a pur-
chaser or other person acquiring in good faith lands, rents, or
resources discovered, after having them, that there were un-
revealed obligations. A second aimed at prohibiting the enforced
taxation under the name of free-will offerings known as benevolences; a third permitted bail to be allowed to persons arrested
and imprisoned on charges of felony, and the goods of persons
so incarcerated were not to be seized before conviction. The
most apposite were the statutes directed towards the improvement of local justice. In order to prevent the return on inquests
and sheriffs' turns of jurors likely to be unreliable and subject to
bribes and intimidations, bailiffs and other officials were not
to empanel persons, 'but such as be of good name and fame,

and having londes and tenements of freehold within the same Shire to the yerely value of xx s at the leste' or else copyhold to the yearly value of 26s. 8d. Whether the replacement, on such inquests, of riff-raff collected by the bailiffs by more solid persons would cure the practice of overawing juries by sheer physical force,[1] was a pertinent question, but the act was content with small beginnings. A further statute forbade the use of piepowder courts (the courts held in fairs) for the trial of contract and debt cases, some of which had no connexion with the fair at all. Of some importance was the act ensuring the proper publication of fines made in the bench; which prescribed that the reading and proclamation of fines should be systematically carried out, and then repeated each quarter of the year, with transcripts sent to the justices of assize and to the justices of the peace in the counties to which the conveyances applied. A number of economic measures regulated the dyeing and the measurement of cloths, their preparation for sale, the sealing and marks of origin to be affixed to the bales, and the process of watering and tentering: and secondly, the practices of Italian merchants who bring in goods to the country which they will only sell at 'the tyme the prices therof been greatly enhanced for their most lucre', and who also buy up goods, sell and carry the proceeds overseas instead of at a favourable time buying again from English people, as they should. This naïvely nationalistic statute enacted that Italian merchants should sell the wares they had imported in gross rather than at the higher price usual to retailers and should do so before 1 May 1485; and use the proceeds 'uppon the commoditees and merchaundises of this realme after deduction of reasonable costs and expenses'.[2] In future they were to have eight months in which to sell their goods, and were to be given two months after that in which to remove the unsold goods. No Italian merchant was to sell wool or woollen cloth bought within the realm. The determination to make aliens sell in gross and not as retailers reflects the commons' anxiety about high prices, but also at the other end the fears of the native merchant about alien undercutting. The commons also showed their determination that the statute of 22 Edward IV prohibiting alien importing of silk goods should be maintained, and hit at the 'Lombards' (Venetians) for the excessive price charged for bow-staves by enacting that every

[1] Cf. the northern examples given on pp. 458-9, above.   [2] S.R. ii. 490.

butt of Malmsey and sweet wine imported should be accompanied by ten bow-staves and that selected bow-staves only be put up for sale and then sold only to natives. The statute reflects the decline of the bow (bow-staves used to be 40s.–46s. a hundred) and the difficulty experienced by the bowyers in getting the material for their craft. More serious were the grievances of the finishing and subsidiary crafts about the importation of merchandise already wrought and complete, which the last of these purely economic statutes sought to remedy by prohibiting alien merchants from bringing into the country a large quantity of household consumer goods.

The personnel of Richard's council is not altogether easy to determine, but some of them have been already mentioned: Rotherham of York, Edmund Chadderton, treasurer of the chamber, and three bishops, Worcester (Alcock), St. Asaph (Redman), Bath and Wells (Stillington). Like the great Rotherham, John Alcock and Robert Stillington were both Cambridge academics; Stillington a doctor in both laws, while Alcock, a canonist only, had been his pupil, and was to be the founder of Jesus College. A little below this group came the *custos rotulorum* and prebendary of St. Stephen's, Westminster, Thomas Borowe, and Dr. Thomas Hutton, Richard's envoy to Brittany in 1484. The lords were John Audeley, treasurer of the Exchequer (1484); Lord Stanley, steward of the household; the chamberlain, Francis Viscount Lovell; and John Lord Scrope of Bolton Castle in Wensleydale. The commoners normally present were the king's secretary, John Kendall (also controller of the mint),[1] William Catesby, Speaker in the 1484 parliament, an esquire of the body; and that knight of the body closest, perhaps, to the king, Sir Richard Ratcliffe.[2] Two others whose speciality was law are also found: Morgan Kidwelly, Richard's attorney, and Thomas Lynom, solicitor to Richard. Clerk to the council was William Lacy who received 40 marks annually from the issues of the manor or lordship of Bradwell, Essex, and a summer and winter livery each year.[3] This group was closely in touch with

[1] *Cal. Pat. R., 1446–1485*, p. 367.
[2] Cf. the lines affixed to the door of St. Paul's cathedral on 18 July 1484, at the instigation of William Colyngburne:
> The Cat, the Rat and Lord our dog
> Ruleth all England under a Hog.

Ratcliffe was sheriff of Westmorland for life.
[3] Harleian MS. 433, m. 24ᵛ and (more fully) *Cal. Pat. R., 1476–1485*, p. 430.

the agents whom Richard appointed in the counties as keepers of castles or guardians of the demesne; such men as Sir John Dynham, Sir James Tyrell (Cornwall) and Sir Thomas Tyrell (Essex), Sir William Berkeley, made keeper of the king's castles in the Isle of Wight and custodian of Carisbrooke,[1] Sir Robert Brackenbury (Kent),[2] constable of the Tower, Sir Richard Neil (Leicestershire). It was Richard's policy to use the knights and gentlemen of the body in command of key posts, e.g. Sir Richard Huddleston, knight of the body, as keeper of the castle of Beaumaris and captain of the towns of Beaumaris and Anglesey; or Thomas Tunstall, esquire of the body, as constable of the castle of Conway and captain of the town.[3]

The Signet office docket book[4] provides a good number of Richard's administrative acts. Diplomatic correspondence and administration of the king's lands are predominant. A scholar who has recently studied this book considers the most interesting of the documents preserved in it are two detailed annual assignments of £10,574. 6s. 8d. and £1,344 made to support the king's household and a separate subsidiary establishment at Sandal Castle, Yorkshire. The assignments were apportioned on the revenues of the king's lands, and the names of the receivers, with the amounts due from each, are given.[5] As was the case under Edward IV, the receivers were accounting to the chamber. The lists show that the king's lands were under duty to pay £11,918. 6s. 8d. a year for the two assignments. From his lands, it is argued, Richard III enjoyed an income of at least £25,000 a year; and there were in addition some £10,000 for annuities and pensions which the lands were made to provide, so that Richard III was enjoying a profit of at least £35,000 from them. The book also contains an important memorandum on the levying of the king's revenues from lands, with some particularly pertinent advice on a number of technical points about the system of farming the king's manors and the need to have really efficient stewards and receivers, who had to be active men, and, in the

---

[1] Harleian MS. 433, m. 25; and *Cal. Pat. R., 1476–1485*, p. 461.
[2] Ibid., p. 383, which shows that Brackenbury was granted the forfeited lands (Merdon, Detling, Newington) of Earl Rivers and of John, Robert, and Humphrey Cheyne (Glastonbury).   [3] *Cal. Pat. R., 1476–1485*, p. 369; ibid., p. 368.
[4] B.M. Harleian MS. 433.
[5] B. P. Wolffe, 'The Management of the English Royal Estates under the Yorkist Kings', *Eng. Hist. Rev.* lxxi (1956), 19.

case of the stewards, must be professionals, not local lords, knights, or esquires, persons tempted to extort fines for their own use. There are instructions on auditing the king's lands in Wales, the duchies of Cornwall, York, and Norfolk; the earldoms of Chester, March, Warwick, and Salisbury; and all other lands in the king's hands by forfeiture should be audited not in the Exchequer but by foreign auditors in sufficient number to do the whole work between Michaelmas and Candlemas each year; and between Candlemas and Palm Sunday the auditors were to make declaration of all the accounts of the royal domain, and, the examinations over, they were to deliver the accounts to the barons of the Exchequer. The whole system of surveyors and receivers for the farmed as well as the crown lands in hand had been evolved as the result of Edward IV's reign, and much thought had been spent upon it as an essential part of the revenues of the crown. Modern research is tending to regard the Yorkist period as one in which a determined effort was being made to see each part of the revenue in proportion, and to believe in the existence of a co-ordinated system of chamber finance.[1] It is of some significance to find the king's cofferer under Edward IV, John Kendall, now coming from the personal service of Richard of Gloucester to supervise the latter's affairs when he became king. 'The officer destined to become the chief instrument of Edward's new financial policy was treasurer of the Chamber.' Kendall in fact had been the fiscal officer closest of all others to the king; but in his new appointment by Richard he was termed secretary and keeper of the mint, and a new treasurer, master Edmund Chadderton, a member of Richard's council and his household chaplain, was appointed.

In the course of 1484 Richard, to his passionate grief, lost the young prince of Wales, who died at Middleham round about 9 April. At first Richard chose as his heir apparent Edward, earl of Warwick, the only son of Clarence: but before long he altered the arrangement and nominated in his place John de la Pole, earl of Lincoln. When in the following year (16 Mar. 1485) his wife Anne died, there began to circulate, not necessarily out of malice against Richard and possibly to test the reactions of his supporters, a suggestion that he might marry Elizabeth of York, his niece. Upon his close friends taking fright, he quickly

[1] Dr. Wolffe's phrase: op. cit., p. 22.

and in public disowned the project; the story, however, may have been more than a mere *canard*; though quite apart from the question of consanguinity, it is difficult to see how he could have been justified in marrying a lady who had been declared illegitimate. Lincoln therefore was to remain the heir of his choice, and it was Lincoln whom he made the first president of the organization which has rightly been called his most important and enduring creation, the council of the north.

The background of this organization has been the subject of much discussion, but the main lines are clear. In the absence of a standing force, the only method of safeguarding the Borders was to make local people responsible. This was done by the creation of the wardenship of the Marches. The power of the Percies was used in the eastern, of the Nevilles in the western March: but the danger of this lay in the rivalries and antagonisms of the families whose members were appointed, and in the overwhelming power which either magnate might accumulate when the landowning families of lesser rank, though quite considerable in themselves, attached themselves to Percy or to Neville. The tenants of these important vassals might themselves turn out to fight. To avoid this uneasy balance it was essential either to make one of the wardens so strong that, like the Leviathan, there was no power to compare with him, and this was done when in 1483 Gloucester was, as we saw, given a franchise comprising royal lands and rights in Cumberland and in districts of south-west Scotland, either conquered or to be conquered by the duke, in which unit the wardenship of the west March was incorporated; or, to reverse the Lancastrian practice, diminish the standing of the wardenship and appoint, for shorter periods than the old wardens enjoyed, lieutenants with strictly controlled powers.[1] Whatever the solution adopted, it came to be realized in the fourteenth and increasingly in the fifteenth century that the problem of order in the north was not simply one of defence against the Scots, but of providing an adequate civil administration, at first through the councils of the great magnate-wardens, to which those aggrieved could resort and obtain justice. Accordingly the crown would issue special commissions of the peace to one or more often both of

---

[1] Cf. the indentures between Henry VII and Thomas Lord Dacre in 1486 cited by R. L. Storey, 'The Wardens of the Marches of England towards Scotland', *Eng. Hist. Rev.* lxxii (1957), 608.

the magnates who associated with themselves the knights and lawyers of their household councils, and so quarter sessions began to have the appearance of a session of the Percy or Neville council.[1] The commissions of the peace and the enforcements of statutes were not the only ones issued: there were special commissions of oyer and terminer as well, and the foundation was laid for the sort of jurisdiction, including what we should term chancery business, that belonged to equity rather than the common law. The council of the north did not originate in the wardenship of the Marches, but in the two commissions thus issued and the relevant legal and administrative action.

Richard, while he was duke of Gloucester, exercised a sort of condominium in the north with Henry Percy. They were both great landlords, as Sheriff Hutton and Wressell show. When he came to the throne he left his council at Sheriff Hutton to administer in the name of his son, but in 1484 Lincoln was made lieutenant in the north, and Yorkshire was separated from the other counties. Lincoln with the majority of the Sheriff Hutton council had to keep order in Yorkshire and exercise a general supervision of the king's peace in the north; and the warden-general of the Marches (Henry Percy) had the military duty of defence, the only precaution against his misuse of power being the retention of Lord Dacre as lieutenant in the west March.[2] Lincoln's council was now the king's council: the household he maintained was the king's household in the north, and for it were issued in 1484 the ordinances copied in the Harleian docket book. The council had to set aside all private considerations ('be indifferent and no wise parcell');[3] every quarter it had to meet at York to 'hear examine and order all bills and complaints and other there before them to be showed': it had complete authority over cases where public order was endangered, and if it felt unable to deal with any of these, a reference must at once be made to the king; and no matter involving freehold was to be determined without the assent of the parties. The ninth clause made it plain that the council derived its jurisdiction from the king, by ordering 'that all letters and writings by our said Council to be made for the due executing

[1] F. W. Brooks, *York and the Council of the North* (1954), p. 4.
[2] Noted by R. R. Reid, *The Council of the North* (1921), p. 61.
[3] Printed ibid., appendix v, p. i.

of the premises be made in our name, and the same to be endorsed with the hand of our nephew of Lincoln below with the words *Per consilium regis*'. The council now established consisted of a lieutenant, the earl assisted by councillors who were both lords, and others including some lawyers who were to be of the quorum and without two of whom and the lieutenant, no important matter was to be determined. The instructions drawn up for the council show that its jurisdiction was both criminal and civil, and that the civil was largely equitable, exercised in accordance with the laws of the realm and good conscience, the procedure to be as in the chancery, on bills of complaint, from examination to decree. Its seat, after the Reformation, was the king's manor on the St. Mary's site, York. Probably the council of the north owed little to the experience of Prince Edward's council in Wales, established after Jasper Tudor and Henry of Richmond had been driven out into Brittany. Then the problem had been not only one of maintaining order but of how to deal with the traditional privileges of the lords marcher. With Yorkist ascendancy, Wales, as Mr. Howel Evans observed, had almost become one vast lordship-marcher.[1] Not only had the lands of the duchy of Lancaster fallen to the Yorkist Edward, but Glamorgan had met a similar fate.

From the spring of 1484 Richard was expecting invasion. He had no idea where Richmond would land and found it most prudent to make his headquarters at a half-way house between north and south, one also which would allow him time to prepare for a threat from Wales. Nottingham Castle, fortified and decorated by his brother, was his choice, and a system of mounted scouts posted along the roads at every twenty miles was established to give early information of an invader. This did not prevent Richard staying in London during August, partly for the reinterment of Henry VI in St. George's Chapel, Windsor. He remained at Nottingham throughout the autumn till 9 November, when he was feeling more secure, though disturbed at intervals by false reports of Richmond's movements. Earlier in the year he had collected his available vessels at Scarborough, where the fleet would be out of the range of French marauders; he was now looking to the south coast, as well as to

[1] *Wales and the Wars of the Roses* (1915), p. 197.

Harwich which he heard to be in special danger, and took urgent measures for its defence. Meanwhile, unwilling to summon another parliament and to interfere with the system of defence already arranged,[1] he had resort to loans. Sir James Ramsay has calculated that £18,600 was the sum asked for in the form of blank bonds, to be placed by the king's agents wherever this was possible. Gairdner commits himself to the figure of 'about £20,000'. How much, says Principal Steel, of all the money was in fact raised and how much of it represented simply paper 'expectations', it seems impossible to determine: 'but what is quite clear is that less than one-seventh of the hoped-for total ever made any appearance whatever on the receipt roll, where the total for the whole of book-keeping, including one fictitious loan for £33. 6s. 8d., is only £4,453. 14s. 8d.'[2] The same writer states that only about £10,000 or £11,000 worth of bonds accompanied by letters of 'request', were in fact addressed to named individuals. If this was the case, Richard can hardly have hoped to gain much by the loan: but may not part of the money have been paid elsewhere than to the receipt, e.g. to the chamber, and by it distributed to local commanders?

The situation was alarming, for prominent people were escaping to France and prosecutions for treason had multiplied. The earl of Oxford imprisoned at Hammes near Calais induced the lieutenant, James Blount, to let him out, and Blount, who had fortified the castle, accompanied his former prisoner to the earl of Richmond. Richard seems to have been expecting Henry to land somewhere in the neighbourhood of the Solent, for before the end of May 1485 he had appointed his chamberlain, Lord Lovel, to command a fleet at Southampton; Milford near Christchurch was the place mentioned in a contemporary prophecy as the most likely spot: but Richard did not lose sight of Milford Haven in Pembrokeshire for, as Polydore Vergil says,[3] he had a system of signalling lamps set up 'on the hills

[1] Commissions of array on a large scale had been issued on 8 Dec. 1484, embracing the majority of Yorkist landowners of position in the counties: *Cal. Pat. R., 1476–1485*, pp. 488–92. On 18 Dec. commissioners were ordered to convoke the knights and gentlemen of Surrey, Middlesex, and Hertfordshire, to find out how many effectives each could bring on half a day's warning in case of sudden alarm: Harleian MS. 433, no. 2028.

[2] Steel, *Receipt of the Exchequer*, p. 321.

[3] *Three Books of Polydore Vergil: English History*, ed. Sir H. Ellis (Camden Soc. xxix), pp. 213–14.

adjoining'. In west Wales he had put Richard Williams in charge of the castles of Pembroke, Tenby, Manorbier, Haverfordwest, and Cilgerran, and the preparations at Pembroke were particularly elaborate. He had also relied on William Herbert, earl of Huntingdon and justiciar of south Wales, whom he installed in the castles, including Brecon, formerly in the possession of the duke of Buckingham, while Sir James Tyrell was watching the upper valley of the Towy from his strongholds of Builth and Llandovery. None the less it was Milford Haven which Henry had selected. Meanwhile Richard took up his residence at Nottingham. On 22 June 1485 he alerted his commissioners of array in the counties, having on the day before proclaimed Henry and his collaborators to be a company of outlaws attainted by parliament, led by 'one Henry Tydder' whose paternal grandfather, Owen Tudor, was a bastard, while his mother was descended from John earl of Somerset, the illegitimate son of Catherine Swynford by John of Gaunt. He had no sort of claim to the throne and were he to be successful the lives and property of all would be at his disposal; moreover he had bargained with France to give up all claim to the former English provinces as well as to Calais, Guines, and Hammes and to separate France and England for ever. Other disherisons and outrages were forecast in a document which, in all its vigorous wording, probably made less appeal than the briefer letters from France which had been reaching Henry's potential supporters in England, asking them to state 'what power you will make ready and what captains and leaders you get to conduct', upon receipt of which information he was prepared instantly to cross.

Henry started from the mouth of the Seine on 1 August and arrived at Milford Haven on the 7th. He had received the information he needed from Morgan of Kidwelly, the lawyer, that Rhys ap Thomas (the grandson of Griffith ap Nicholas) and Sir John Savage were devoted to his cause. His informant Morgan was of a Tredegar family solidly loyal to Henry.[1] The invader who had a force of 2,000 men of very doubtful quality, brought with him Jasper Tudor, John Morton, and the earl of Oxford. After landing at Dale on the northern shore of the Haven, he made straight for Haverfordwest and remained in the neighbourhood, meeting with no serious opposition till the

[1] See the account of them in Howel Evans, op. cit., pp. 216–17.

9th, when he was informed that Rhys and Sir Walter Herbert were at Carmarthen, preparing to challenge him. He decided to reconnoitre and to send a body of cavalry to Carmarthen, which he found friendly, and in the event Rhys proved faithful to the pro-Lancastrian attitude of his house. As for Sir John Savage, there could be little doubt. He was a son of Lord Stanley's sister, and it has been observed with justice that the Stanleys were deeply implicated in Henry's enterprise.[1] The story of the hostility of Rhys ap Thomas and of Sir John Savage which reached Henry after landing was probably a false report, deliberately circulated in order that Richard might be lulled into a false security, and made to think that there were powerful forces to delay Henry. If this is so, the report was successful; and the two plotters joined Henry on his way, Rhys two days before he reached Shrewsbury, Sir John Savage between Shrewsbury and Bosworth. Henry now marched through Cardiganshire and on, probably by Aberystwyth, Machynlleth, and Newtown to Shrewsbury. On the way, while he was in Merionethshire, he appears to have been joined by a north Wales contingent and, when about thirty miles from Shrewsbury, by Rhys ap Thomas to whom he promised the lieutenant-ship of Wales in return for his support. Rhys brought him 'a great baulk of soldiers' and the standard of the black raven now accompanied that of the red dragon. It is thought that Sir Walter Herbert joined Henry at the same time as Rhys, and brought with him the levies of south-east Wales, Monmouth, and the neighbourhood. When they reached Shrewsbury, about 15 August, he found the gates closed and the portcullis down; but not for long: the town quickly surrendered, and from Shrewsbury Henry went on to Newport to be joined by Gilbert Talbot and a Shropshire contingent. At Stafford he had a conversation with Sir William Stanley, whose forces were drawn mainly from north Wales 'and the Dee valley'; from Stafford he then moved to Lichfield. It was while Henry was at Shrewsbury that the king heard of his unopposed passage through Wales: Richard thought that with his small forces he would either have been brought to battle and overwhelmed or else captured by Walter Herbert and Rhys ap Thomas. He immediately sent to the duke of Norfolk, the earl of Northumberland, and the earl of Surrey, to join him, and to Sir Robert

[1] Evans, op. cit., p. 220.

Brackenbury, keeper of the Tower, to bring Sir Thomas Bourchier and Sir Walter Hungerford with all the force they could
collect, as well as to every county, with the threat of death and
confiscation to all refusing to aid him. He then moved to
Leicester. Of Lord Stanley he could not now be sure. Before
Henry had landed the steward of the king's household had
obtained leave to visit his home in Lancashire, and Richard
had placed him, his brother Sir William Stanley, and his eldest
son Lord Strange, in charge of defence against rebels, believing
that if Henry landed in Wales the Stanleys would cut him off
before he was over the Marches and into England. The king
now summoned him, but he excused himself on the ground of
illness: the truth, however, was discovered by a confession made
by Lord Strange, who put himself upon the king's mercy, and
assuring Richard that his father would help, wrote to Lord
Stanley imploring him to fulfil the promise which his son had
made. The king kept him as a hostage and it was this fact that
prevented Stanley from joining Henry openly. Thus when
Henry, at great risk to himself and his army from whom he had
temporarily become separated, sought an interview with the
Stanleys at Atherstone, he probably received an assurance of
support, but a knowledge of Richard would make it impossible
for Lord Stanley to effect any junction with Henry's army, and
his force had to be placed in an ambiguous position between the
two armies shortly to conflict. From Leicester Richard advanced
to Market Bosworth, and on the morning of 22 August drew up
his men with John Howard, duke of Norfolk, on the left, Henry
Percy, earl of Northumberland, on the right, and himself in the
centre. Numerically he was superior. With Richard when he
rode out of Leicester on the 21st were also Viscount Lovel,
William Berkeley, earl of Nottingham, Lords Ferrers and
Zouche, Lords Scrope, Dacre, and Greystoke, Sir Richard
Ratcliffe, Sir Robert Brackenbury, and an army certainly
double the size of Henry's 5,000. Henry on leaving Atherstone
encamped (21 Aug.) not far from White Moors, about three
miles from the royal army, with Ambien hill in between. On the
morning of the 22nd the king moved up to occupy the high
ground, and as he did so, he sent a message to Lord Stanley at
Sutton Cheney calling on him to help, and threatening to put
Lord Strange to death in the event of his not complying. Stanley declined to move and Richard in a passion gave orders to

kill Strange, but his execution was quickly countermanded. To Henry, who was also asking Stanley's help, the answer was given that he should draw up his forces and that Lord Stanley would come when the convenient time arrived.

To neither party was the response satisfactory, and Henry had to make his dispositions without the Lancastrian. The earl of Oxford was the commander of his force, Gilbert Talbot was in charge of the right and Sir John Savage the left, while Henry had the centre. The Stanleys at Shenton and Sutton Cheney were still a problem to both sides, and to watch Lord Stanley Northumberland, who could not absolutely be trusted, had asked the king's permission to take his mounted force to a position on the verge overlooking Lord Stanley's position. Norfolk led the vanguard forward along the ridge; and Henry's forces had to fight up hill. The first part of the action saw the heavy engagement of Oxford by Norfolk's men coming over the brow of the hill, in which Oxford's men eventually had to give ground and were pulled back to the standards of their leader; when this disengagement had taken place, Richard sighted Henry Tudor to the west on the rising ground and decided that whatever happened, he must engage Henry before Oxford's men could rally and before Sir William Stanley could enter the battle. It meant riding directly across Sir William's front against a superior body of troops, but the king thought it was worth risking, especially after he heard the news that Norfolk had been killed. He therefore sent a message to Northumberland asking him to come to his aid—and heard the grim reply: that Northumberland felt that he must stay where he was and watch Lord Stanley. That meant that the earl could not be relied upon; none the less Richard took the knights and esquires of his body forward to the north-west down the slope at the northern end of the battle line, to attack Henry Tudor with the reserve. In doing so he had to risk attack by Sir William Stanley and when he was engaged in a desperate effort to reach Henry's bodyguard and Henry himself, Stanley, judging the moment ripe, brought his troops in from the flank against the royal party. This proved the decisive moment and Richard with his bodyguard destroyed quickly fell. Only a few of the household escaped: Ratcliffe and John Kendall were killed. Lovell and Humphrey Stafford got away, while Northumberland remained at Sutton Cheney, to do homage to Henry when sent for. Richard's body was brought naked to Leicester and lay for two days exposed at the Grey Friars near the river. At the dissolution the tomb was destroyed and the body thrown into the Soar.

That there was a sound constructive side to Richard III is undoubted. He was very far from being the distorted villain of tradition. His early years of probation and loyalty to his brother were entirely creditable; a simple, puritanical strain in him kept him away from the complications of the Woodville court, and his serious nature revolted against the frivolities of his brother's entourage. But when the change of government came he could not be content with the large but temporary authority offered him by the protectorship: he saw that even if the protectorship were continued a governing council might veer in the direction of the Woodville queen and that Hastings could not be relied on to keep it straight. The impulsive Buckingham was too close to his ear, and he could not trust the council over which he himself presided. The fatal step was the murder of Hastings: after that the seizure of the throne was inevitable. He had found, under pressure of his own reserved, tense, and uncommunicative nature, the Renaissance way to quick results, and that way, the way of removal, was to determine his control of events after the middle of June 1483. Having begun by strong illegal action, he was forced to continue it. There was no drawing back: people had come to believe that behind the reforms and the apparent good intentions there was nothing but terror, and the kingdom of England had had too much of that medicine. Yet the latest years of violence should not detract from the value of the Yorkist achievement. If there was an experiment in our fifteenth-century history, it was Yorkist rather than Lancastrian. It was one of particular interest for its use of special personnel, from household and estate, in an attempt at quicker and more business-like government. But it was a party experiment and because it was this, based on legitimism and direct rather than traditional forms of administration, it could not command the adherence and full respect that were, after an initial probation, to be awarded to its Tudor successor.

XIV

THE PEACEFUL ARTS

FIFTEENTH-CENTURY England is a country of contrasts. No amount of political upheaval seems to have affected the continuity of English art. It has been maintained that in the reign of Richard II the arts in England reached a brilliant climax and that the fifteenth century was prosaic in comparison; that there was a great deal of superficiality and carelessness in that period, an abundance of stock sets and ready-made figures; that panels of glass were sometimes put in upside down or in the wrong order and that many designs are routine designs. Yet the curious traveller, still happily extant, who aims simply at observing for himself the medieval past in areas such as Norfolk, Suffolk, Gloucester, south Wiltshire, or farther north in Cheshire, finds himself constantly pulled up short and resorting to his notebook or diary to record some splendour of church roof or screen or spatial enlargement, some achievement of proportion which would have been unlikely in the previous century; and travel abroad may show him that works of art were being produced not only for home consumption, but also for eager buyers there, to whom English alabaster or the entrancing *opus Anglicanum* were products to be sought after. For the woodcarver and for the glassmaker, the fifteenth century is a period of the highest importance. It is certainly an age of advance in the industrial arts.

But not in them only. If there is some danger in relating building and sculpture to politics and political history, the connexion of artistic achievement with economic development is certainly clearer. It was necessary to build or to enlarge for new centres of population or for notable additions to the old numbers. The west of England, where manufacture had grown along the southern fringes of the Cotswolds; the kersey and light fabric region of south Wiltshire and Berkshire; East Anglia, the villages on both the Essex and Suffolk banks of the Stour and the new centres on the Stour's tributaries, like Hadleigh, Kersey, Lavenham and those in the West Riding of Yorkshire along the upper reaches of the Aire and the Calder, all give clear architectural testimony to the connexion of the woollen industry and the building craftsmanship. The Stour churches, Dedham, Stoke by Nayland, East Bergholt, Sudbury, Long Melford, Glemsford, Cavendish, Haverhill are splendid examples of English rectilinear, while Lavenham (begun by a noble and finished by a merchant) and Great and Little Waldringfield owe much to the fifteenth-century builder. Travelling west, one reaches the remarkable line of churches from north roughly to south, Chipping Campden, Winchcombe, Northleach, Chedworth, Fairford, Cricklade, where brasses as well as surviving monuments, glass and tapestry, pay their tribute to the capitalist entrepreneurs who extended and in some cases actually rebuilt the villages of an earlier manorial age.

The new extension of cloth manufacture to rural areas and the growth of new towns, particularly in Wiltshire, led to the creation, or at least to the enlargement, of many parish churches and to the strengthening of parish life generally; in this were involved the lives and fortunes of the *yconomi*, the church wardens, the development of parochial libraries, the enrichment of the plate and vestments, the multiplication of church furniture of various descriptions, and liturgically, new aspects of the cult of the saints and of the Blessed Virgin, and new emphasis upon the Passion and Death of our Lord; most evident of all, in the larger towns, this process of enrichment could be witnessed in the domination of the church services by the gilds, and the employment of extra chaplains, along with the beautification of the altars where these gild services took place. The devotional and, it might be said, the liturgical movement of the fifteenth century found its outlet in the expression of the sculptor and the painter. All these features were subordinated, in the churches, to the general scheme of English perpendicular which we know now to have been derived not from the south transept of Gloucester Cathedral, so much as from St. Stephen's Chapel, Westminster, the basic plan of which, in turn, stemmed from churches in the Île-de-France.[1] This is not to deny the importance of the Gloucester example, particularly on account of the great cloisters which, begun by Abbot Thomas Horton in the middle of the fourteenth century, were finished by Abbot Frocester who died in 1412; the largest in England,

[1] M. Hastings, *St. Stephen's Chapel, Westminster* (1951).

and to leave ecclesiastics to pay for the embellishment of the greater building.[1] Naturally, this point of view should not be exaggerated: it is merely a reminder that in a city like York the glass in St. Denys, All Saints, North Street, and St. Michaels, Spurriergate, is of a quality higher than a quantity in the Minster itself. In smaller churches, where considerations of height and distance from the eye do not apply to the same extent as in the greater fanes, more detailed and more delicate work could be carried out.

The fifteenth century shows abundant difference of styles but a certain concentration of themes, apart from the purely local narrative windows devoted to St. William and St. Cuthbert at York. At York the tense questing faces of the saints are unmistakable, best seen in the figure of St. William himself or in the heads of St. Anne or the bishop from the (so-called) Mass of St. Gregory in All Saints, North Street; but at Malvern Priory, where the eastern part of the church is filled with glass dating roughly from 1440 to 1480, the faces are nearer to the types occurring in earlier fifteenth-century illumination, more pensive, perhaps more placid and less dramatic than in the York examples. The parallelisms between continental and York design particularly in representations of the Holy Family or Holy Parents and their children have been pointed out. The Norfolk windows, particularly at East Harling, and the Suffolk glass at Long Melford, have certainly Flemish traits in the painting of the faces; while jewelled borders of robes, whether the effect is gained from pieces of coloured glass leaded in or by outlines on black pigment or yellow stain, are found more frequently in Gloucestershire, Warwickshire, and Worcestershire than elsewhere.[2] In Oxford, at All Souls College, John Glazier's women saints have a gentle and rather ethereal beauty of delineation. While these local differentiations of style have their own interest, the themes are very much what could be expected from the devotional literature of the time: the Joys and Sorrows of the Blessed Virgin, the Seven Sacraments and the Seven Corporal Acts of Mercy, the Passion of Christ with constant emphasis upon the Instruments of the Passion and the Sacred Wounds; Almsgiving; the Tree of Jesse (still), with one remarkable example of the combination of stone

---

[1] *The York School of Glass Painting* (1936), p. 42.
[2] Christopher Woodforde, *English Stained and Painted Glass* (1954), p. 23.

window tracery and glasswork at Dorchester (Oxon.). In All Saints, North Street, York, there is a most unusual representation of the 'Pains and Terrors of the last Fifteen Days of the World' in a window based upon the scenes from Richard Rolle's 'The Prykke of Conscience'. Votive windows paid for by the donor or by a group of donors (as at St. Neot, Cornwall) are evidence of heavenly help expected. Whether designs are good or inferior, the main interest of the window lies in the subject-matter: as Dr. Woodforde has well said: 'A poorly conceived and badly executed window is often of considerable iconographical interest because it illustrates the religious and devotional fashions of the time.'[1]

In the year of Bosworth William Caxton 'enprysed to enprynte a book of the noble hystoryes of . . . Kynge Arthur and of certeyn of his knyghtes, after a copye unto me delyverd, whyche copye Sur Thomas Malorye dyd take oute of certeyn bookes of Frensshe and reduced it into English'. Caxton did so, he says, in order that noble men might see and learn the 'noble actes of chyvalre', the 'gentyl and vertuous dedes' used by certain knights in those days, by which they acquired honour, while the vicious ones were put to shame. It was characteristic of the fifteenth century that the knightly redactor of these tales which he put into his own prose, principally from a 'Frensshe Booke' and from the English alliterative poem the *Morte Arthur*, had done so mostly from prison where he had been thrust for robbery, theft, and raiding on an extensive scale. Whether some of the charges against him were due to local political faction or not, the contrast between Caxton's (and Chaucer's) perfect knight and the assailant of the Blessed Mary of Coombe who was charged with breaking into the abbey and stealing various jewels and ornaments must strike the eye. And it is instructive; for both the printer of 'certain bookes of ensamples and doctryne' and the knight who handed on to the Tudor age the long epic in all its ramifications that formed the matter of Britain, are characteristic of their time.

While it is difficult to identify the 'Frensshe Booke' which may be one of the late Arthurian compilations circulating in France during the fifteenth century, there lay behind the prose cycle and the English poem on which Malory relied the narrative

[1] Op. cit., p. 21.

of Geoffrey of Monmouth, Wace's *Round Table*, the poems of *courtoisie* written by Chrétien de Troyes and of Robert de Boron, and the Grail legend as handled by the religious, particularly the Cistercians. But Malory, as Professor Vinaver, the editor of the Winchester manuscript, has pointed out, is presenting a picture of Arthur as the victorious king 'crowned Emperor by the Pope's hands, with all royalty in the world to weld forever', and brings his *Noble Tale* to an end at this point, dismissing the rest of the story of Mordred's treachery and Arthur's own downfall.[1] If he is nostalgic, it is not for chivalry in itself (Caxton's theme) as for the prince who displays the chivalric virtues. Arthur appears as the 'true embodiment of heroic chivalry', the English counterpart of Charlemagne, the conqueror and possessor by right of the Roman empire: 'not as a mere abstract centre of the fellowship of the Round Table, but as a political and military leader, conscious of his responsibility for the welfare and prestige of his kingdom'. This portrait of Arthur has been interpreted as a tribute to Henry V, and it has been pointed out that Arthur's itinerary through France is altered so as to resemble the route followed by Henry. Whether Malory had a definite figure in his mind or not, he was at least free from the belief, widely proclaimed by the chroniclers, though acutely criticized by William of Newburgh, in the Trojan origin of the British; if he was confident in the existence, at some early period, of an ideal chivalric prince, his concern with the Arthurian legend was that of an artist rather than of an historian. He had in front of him 'a jumble of stories about Arthur', lacking in structure and proportion; and while he could not always disentangle the various threads in the tangled skein, he was a superb story-teller, using a prose that is simple and yet supple enough for his many needs,[2] with a terse and direct dialogue and a smiting word that rings like the blows of the knights who 'hurteled togedyrs as two wylde bullys, russhynge and laysshyng with hir shyldis and swerdys, that sometyme they felle bothe on their nosys'.[3] It is not all fighting and as the stories went on, the drama of conflicting forces was worked out: the motive of the tale is primarily a conflict of two loyalties, both based on the medieval conception of knightly service: the

---

[1] *The Works of Sir Thomas Malory* (1947), I. xxv.
[2] H. S. Bennett, *Chaucer and the Fifteenth Century* (repr. 1954), p. 201.
[3] *Sir Launcelot du Lake*, in *Works*, i. 267.

loyalty of man to man, a greater thing than fealty, because it involves the knight's passionate devotion to companions as well as to his leader: on the other hand, 'the devotion of the knight-lover to his lady, the romantic self-denial imposed by the courtly tradition and inseparable from any form of courtly romance . . . the clash between these conceptions of human love and service is neither an accident nor a caprice of destiny: it is inherent in the very structure of medieval idealism'.

It could not be claimed that either in his language or in his thought Malory is typical of the prose of the fifteenth century; for as yet there was no common or standard English for literary purposes. There were local varieties in plenty, but for a work to gain a wide circulation a great deal of co-operation from readers was necessary. Chaucer in his Troilus and Criseyde had noted the difficulty:

> And for ther is so greet diversitee
> in English and in wryting of our tonge
> So preye I God that noon miswryte thee
> Ne thee mismetre for defaute of tonge.
> And red wherso thou be, or elles songe,
> That thou be understonde, I God beseche.[1]

The problem of the merchants becalmed in the port of London who, as Caxton narrates, went on shore to buy eggs and could not make themselves understood when they pronounced the word as we pronounce it (they had to say *eyren*) is very relevant. Add to this the fact that a professional literary class did not exist: the author had to make or find his living in other ways: as a clerk in the office of the privy seal (Hoccleve) or as a canon (John Waldon, John Capgrave) or as a monk (John Lydgate of Bury St. Edmunds), or usher of the chamber (John Russell, in the service of Humphrey of Gloucester). The greatest figure of all, Geoffrey Chaucer, the merchant's son who began as a page in the service of Elizabeth of Ulster, wife of Lionel duke of Clarence, was first a yeoman in the royal household and clerk of the king's works, then employed on diplomatic and business journeys and as controller of the customs

---

[1] 'Often indeed no word was available which would express Chaucer's exact meaning and he had to coin a word, or more exactly to take one over from a Latin or a French source. Of the four thousand odd words from Romance languages used by Chaucer, more than a thousand have not been found in earlier writers in English': H. S. Bennett, *Chaucer and the Fifteenth Century*, p. 82.

and subsidies in the port of London; and in the last part of his life he had the management of a large estate in Somerset. But whereas with Chaucer the rubs and contacts of practical life sharpened the powers of observation and the knowledge of men that were to emerge in the *Canterbury Tales*, perhaps only with Hoccleve did his life in the capital give interest and substance to his verse. The other imitators and followers of the great man lacked the *vivida vis animi*: and as far as courtly poetry is concerned, the fifteenth century has been called the hey-day of the poetaster who had little feeling for verse and scant intellectual power. At the head of them stand Lydgate and Hoccleve. Lydgate (*c.* 1370–1450) the monk of Bury produced either in his own monastery or in the priory of Hatfield Broadoak in Essex a vast amount of verse, of which the best known was his Troy Book, the history of the Trojan Wars.[1] Like Osbern Bokenham the friar, he turned out a great deal of minor verse at the request of patrons, written with an 'intolerable glibness and an indomitable energy'. Yet where he cannot be too repetitive, in the shorter poems, there is often humour and good sense, even if the didacticism is obvious and unsubtle: the Dietary (Bodleian Library, MS. Rawlinson C. 86) illustrates these qualities:

> For helth of body, couere for colde þyn hede;
> Ete no rawe mete, take good hede þerto,
> Drynke holsom wyne, fede þe on lyghte brede,
> With an apitite rise from þy mete also;
> With women agid, flesshely haue not A-doo;
> Vppon þy slepe, drynke not of þe cuppe;
> Gladde toward bedde and at morwe boþe to;
> And Vse neuer late for to suppe.

> And yf so be þat leches do þe fayle,
> Thanne take good hede to Vse þynges thre-
> Temperat dyet, temperat traveyle;
> Not malincolius for non aduersite,
> Meke in troubill, glad in pouerte,
> Ryche with litell, content with suffisaunce,

---

[1] Printed by Pynson, 1573, E.E.T.S., o.s., xcvii, ciii, cvi, and cxxvi. Other works of Lydgate are *The Falle of Princes* (Pynson, 1494, E.E.T.S. cxxi–cxxiv); *The Assemble of Goddes* (Wynkyn de Worde, 1498, 1500); the *Temple of Glass* (E.E.T.S. lx, Caxton 1476), *The Chorle and the Birde* (Caxton 1476, also Cambridge 1906, facsimile).

> Neuer grucchyng, but mery lyke þy degre;
> Yf physike lakke, make þis þy gouernaunce.[1]

Moderate food, avoidance of all surfeits bring physical health; spiritual health is a matter of 'charite'. His receipt Lydgate thinks,

> bought is at no poticarye,
> Of master Antony nor of master hewe,
> To all indifferent þe rycheste dietarye.

Lydgate as a monk was reasonably secure: Hoccleve as a secular *clericus conjugatus* was a weaker but more sympathetic character, working in the privy seal office all day, copying in silence, unable to break into song:

> This [these] artificers, se I day by day,
> In the hotteste of al hir bysynesse
> Talken and syng, and make game and play,
> And forth hir labour passith with gladnesse.
> But we labour in trauaillous stilnesse;
> We stowpe and stare up-on the shepes skyn,
> And keepe muste our song and wordes in.[2]

He will admit that songs, especially as on the occasion when Henry Summer, chancellor of the Exchequer, invited Hoccleve's dining club to dinner (May Day 1410), followed in the evenings: but in spite of the gloomy picture he gives of the office and of his own variable health and his poverty, he continued to write a great quantity of verse. In 1411–12 he translated the *De regimine principum* of Aegidius Colonna for Henry prince of Wales, and he presented *balades* to the duke of Bedford and the duke of York, who was interested in all the *balades* he had written. His work is more limited than that of Lydgate, but gives a more naïve and more convincing notion of a poet's personality.

But when the more familiar original poetry like the *Flower and the Leaf*, modernized by Dryden, and the earlier (c. 1403) poem *The Cuckoo and the Nightingale* is left—and it is poetry with a charming pastoral appeal—there is a mass of lyrical poetry, 'practical' and occasional verse, the carol, and the ballad to be reckoned with. 'If courtly poetry fell into decadence with the

---

[1] Printed in R. H. Robbins, *Secular Lyrics of the Fourteenth and Fifteenth Centuries*, pp. 73–74.
[2] Cited by T. F. Tout, *Chapters in Medieval Administrative History*, v. 107.

fifteenth century inheritors of the Chaucerian tradition', Sir Edmund Chambers has remarked, 'a more popular lyric held its own, mainly by virtue of the carol.'[1] The carol is the dance-song, a gesture of welcome on great occasions, accompanied by minstrelsy, sometimes on the return of the sovereign from war-fare abroad, more often at the advent of Christmas, a great secular feast as well as a religious one. In the Black Book of the Household, the festivities in the royal chapel are described

The King hath a song before hym in his hall or chambre vppon All-halowen day at the latter graces, by some of thes clerkes and children of chapell in remembraunce of Cristmasse; and so of men and children in Cristmasse thorowoute. But after the song on All-halowen day is don, the Steward and Thesaurer of houshold shall be warned where hit likith the King to kepe his Cristmasse.[2]

The carol reaches its full perfection in the fifteenth century: 'I sing of a Mayden' and 'Adam lay I-bowndyn' are famous, and there were carols for other parts of the Christian year, as well as for secular occasions, as upon the entry of the boar's head, or the combats between the holly and the ivy: the love song is worked into a religious setting, the rollicking chorus fitted to the Christian's thanksgiving, while quieter slumber songs cele-brated the mystery of the nativity. There were large numbers of refrain poems, hilarious as well as religious in character, 'which seem to have inherited alike the name and the metrical form of the danced carols'.[3] Among the dialogues between the Blessed Virgin and Child there are some reminiscent of the carols for Innocents' Day:

> Þis endres nyght A-bout mydnyght
> As I me lay for to sclepe,
> I hard a may syng lullay
> for powaret[4] sor sco[5] wepe.
>   He sayd Ba-Bay:
>   sco sayd lullay,
>   þe virgine fresch as ros in may.
>
> Sare sco soght Bot fand sco nought
> To hap hyre sone Ihu fro cold.
> Iosef sayd belif,[6] 'scuet wyfe,

---

[1] 'The Carol and the Fifteenth-Century Lyric', *English Literature at the Close of the Middle Ages* (1947), p. 67.   [2] Ibid., p. 84.
[3] Robbins, op. cit., p. 85.   [4] Poverty.   [5] She.   [6] Quickly.

Tell me wat ȝe wald,
Hartly I ȝou pray'.
    He sayd ba-bay,
    Scho sayd lullay,
    þe virgine fresch as ros in may.[1]

The believer peoples a wayside chapel with disciples and saints
on a May morning:

And By a chapell as y Came,
Mett y wyhte Ihû to chyrcheward gone
Petur and Pawle, thomas & Ihon,
And hys desyplys Euery-chone.
                Mery hyt ys.

Sente Thomas þe Bellys gane ryng,
And sent Collas þe mas gane syng,
Sente Ihon toke þat swete offeryng,
And By a chapell as y Came.
                Mery hyt ys.

Owre lorde offeryd whate he wollde,
A challes alle off ryche rede gollde;
Owre lady, þe crowne off hyr mowlde,[2]
The sone owte off hyr Bosome schone.
                Mery hyt ys.

Sent Iorge þat ys owre lady knyȝte,
He tende þe tapyrys fayre & Bryte—
To myn yȝe a semley syȝte,
And By a chapell as y Came.
                Mery hyt ys.[3]

In so many of the lyrics the secular and the religious are as one,
as they were in the Franciscan world. And here are both in a
lament for the untimely death of a fair lady:

O myghty lord, wos goodnesse neuer schal fynyse,
Haue mercy on the soule of my dere maistresse!
The fendis power fro that soule chare & chastise!
Deliuere here, gracious lord, fro peyne and distresse!
Endowe here in thi place of plesaunt paradise,
And receyue here, blyssed lord, vpon thi right side,
In thy blysse eternally whyt the to a-byde.

---

[1] Printed Carleton F. Brown, *Religious Lyrics of the Fifteenth Century* (1939), no. 4.
[2] Head.   [3] Ibid., no. 116.

Of lordis lyne & lynage sche was, here sche lyse!
Bounteuus, benigne, enblesshed wyth beaute,
Sage, softe and sobre an gentyll in al wyse,
fflorishyng ant fecunde, wyth femenyn beaute,
Meke, mylde and merciful, of pite sche bar þe prise.
Comely, kynde and curteis, in nobleye of nurture,
Vernant[1] in alle vertu, plesaunt and demure.[2]

The popular songs include nursery rhymes (e.g. 'My Twelve Oxen', the ancestor of 'When I was a boy, a farmer's boy' or 'My gentle Cock'), verses on money (the various rhymes on Sir Penny are characteristic), satires on lecherous clerks, complaints of serving girls seduced at the fair, rollicking drinking songs and invitations to festivity, bawdy verses, verses abusing women and complaining of their tyranny ('All þat I may swynk or swet, My wyfe it wyll boþ drynk & ete'), quantities of verse with *double entendre*, all the fantasies and conceits of a vigorous and yet barely disciplined people. Yet some of it has the true lyrical note of a later age:

Have all my hert & be in peys,
And þink I lowfe yow ferwently;
ffor in good fayth, hit ys no lese,
I wold ȝe wyst as well as I.
ffor now I see, bothe nyȝt and day,
That my lovfe wyll not sese;
Hawe mercy on me as ȝe best may—
Hawe all my hert and be in peyse.[3]

War-ridden England had a considerable reading public. In an increasingly literate age not only the ecclesiastics, but the knight, the lawyer, the merchant, and the trader were building up small collections. The reading of English was general, and most of the merchant class had some training in Latin. In the City of London parents were genuinely anxious for their sons to be initiated into that world of Latin learning over which the Church presided. A baker could order that his son be brought up 'in all lernyng', just as an alderman desired his brought up ' to connyng lernyng and erudition'.[4] Little divided the attitude of the wealthier merchant families from that of the more cultivated gentry. Most of their sons would attend the city grammar schools, and so have lived at home: but some were sent to

---

[1] Flourishing.   [2] Ibid., no. 153.
[3] *Secular Lyrics of the Fourteenth and Fifteenth Centuries*, p. 135.
[4] Sylvia Thrupp, *The Merchant Class of Medieval London* (1948), p. 160.

boarding establishments or lived with a vicar who took in boys for instruction. The city merchant was, however, very utilitarian. The learning his sons got was useful to the business and, as Miss Thrupp has pointed out, 'the fact that, when printing began, the book trade remains largely in the hands of aliens and that as late as 1520 the mercers were classing books among the "tryfylles" of their import trade, does not look well for the London merchant's intellectual curiosity or initiative'.[1] Small private schools and hostels, some of them run by the scriveners, provided the mixed education that was needed. The scrivener, William Kingsmill, gave tuition in commercial French, and about 1415 a boy of twelve is made to declare that in three months at Kingsmill's hostel school he had learned to read and write, to make up accounts, and to speak French.[2] This is utilitarian learning, not the learning of the schools: the city merchant was literate but not literary. And of the London merchants only Sir William Walworth and Sir Robert and Sir William Chichele show any sign of learned interests: Walworth bequeathed his religious books to churches, and a law library, worth the substantial sum of £100, to his brother; and Robert Chichele commissioned Hoccleve to write for him one of his religious ballads. His brother Sir William was, however, a benefactor of the Guildhall Library to which he bequeathed £10 'to be bestowd en bokes notable to be layde in the newe librarye at the Gildehall at London'[3] as a memorial to the mayor, John Hadley.

Of the fifteenth-century wills of personal property bequeathed by London citizen testators about 20 per cent. mention a few books, but these are mainly liturgical and devotional, missals, psalters, and primers. On the other hand, the noble and the knightly classes, who had chapels of their own, were moderately well endowed with books. In the wills proved by Archbishop Chichele service-books and a certain number of devotional books are bequeathed by laymen such as Sir Edward Cheyne, Richard Bankes, Sir Thomas Berkeley, and Sir Gerard Braybroke. Cheyne of Beckford (Glos.) had a French bible in two volumes and a 'sauter glosid of Richard Ermyte' (Richard Rolle), and the same testator had a halling of curtains 'stained

---

[1] Op. cit., p. 161. [2] Ibid., 159.
[3] *Reg. Chichele*, ii. 340. William Chichele bequeathed a bible, a primer, and a psalter.

with the siege of Troy'.[1] Bankes, a baron of the Exchequer, could possess the *Florarium Bartholomei* by the Austin canon John of Mirfield, Sir Thomas Berkeley a glossed psalter and the *Legenda sanctorum* in English, and Sir Gerard Braybroke service-books and works of devotion. But the noble laity generally went in for history (The Trojan Legend, the Brute Chronicle, and various *gesta regum*), books of courtesy, and treatises describing what a person of coat armour should know. The *Book of Hawking, Hunting and the Blazing of Arms*, commonly called the *Boke of St. Albans*, was published by the St. Albans schoolmaster (as Wynkyn de Worde called him) just after Bosworth. He had been printing *apud villam sancti Albani* since 1480; and Wynkyn de Worde thought it worth printing again (with an addition on angling). It is a compilation devoted to the pursuits and interests of a *generosus*, in this case a country gentleman. The longest treatise in the *Boke*, which was alleged to have been put together by Mistress Juliana Bernes or Barnes, is the *Liber Armorum*, derived from the *De officio militari* of Nicholas of Upton, canon of Salisbury, and the English *Book of the Lineage of Coat Armour*, a fifteenth-century compilation. There is no need to dwell upon the importance of heraldry as a subject of polite study and speculation in the fifteenth century. If to the minds of Malory and Caxton (who printed a translation of the *Ordeyne de Chevalerie*) chivalry had a moral value for its inculcation of the free and knightly attributes, heraldry was the formal way of displaying the gentle lineage which, to contemporary minds, disposed a man towards virtue. The origins of coat armour, according to the *Boke of St. Albans*, were to be found in the siege of Troy, where 'in *Gestis Troianorum* it telleth what the first beginning of the Law of Arms was'. This existed before any law in the world save the law of nature: but even before the siege of Troy knighthood existed and an even greater institution: 'Know ye that these two orders were, first wedlock, and then knighthood.' The treatise goes as far as to claim that Christ was a gentleman and bore coat armour of ancestors: the four evangelists had gentle ancestry, sprung as they were from Judas Maccabaeus; but after his death, his kin 'fell to labours and were called no gentlemen'. The four doctors of Holy Church, however, were 'gentlemen of blood and coat armour'.

[1] *Reg. Chichele*, iii. 46, 48.

Such historical and archaeological snobbery must have had a market: but the average higher ecclesiastic of the fifteenth century was more likely to have in his private collection of books the standard works of theology, civil and canon law, and it is noteworthy how few of them and how few English testators in general bequeathed classical books in any number.[1] Most of the bishops left in their wills books on the two laws, and canonistic prevails over theology. In Arundel's library there was, however, a collection of St. Gregory which was to go to Christ Church, Canterbury, but Henry V borrowed it from his executors and appears to have left it to his own foundation at Sheen. It finally reached Canterbury through the good offices of Humphrey duke of Gloucester upon the petition of the prior. Henry had a bad record as a borrower, and he seized books wherever he could. The countess of Westmorland had to petition for the return of a book after his death. He purloined a 'goodly French book' at the siege of Caen and plundered the library in the chapel of the market at Meaux, bringing 109 books in all to England, mainly works on the canon and the civil law. Some of the bishops had quite copious collections. The valuation of Archbishop Arundel's books amounted to £207. 19s. 2d. for his chapel and £352. 8s. 6d. for his study; and Archbishop Kemp's books of theology and canon law were put at £263. 14s. 11d. Bishop John Trefnant of Hereford who died in 1404 had ninety-one items of canon and civil law, including works on the Decretals by Petrus de Sampsona and Henry Bohic Paul de Zizariis on the Clementines, and a *Tractatus super electione* by William de Mandagod. There were thirty-three listed in the will of Thomas Langley, bishop of Durham, mainly a theological collection, bequeathed to friends and colleagues of his when he was chancellor. Thus Robert Rolston, keeper of the great wardrobe (archdeacon of Durham, 1421), got the *Moralia* of St. Gregory, and John Frank, B.Can.L., canon of Salisbury, had the *Historia scholastica* of Petrus Comestor (another copy went to John Stafford, chancellor and later archbishop). A library, therefore, containing humanistic as well as philosophical books such as was collected by Bishop William Grey for presentation to Balliol College was exceedingly rare: only the university library at Oxford—an astonishing collection —can have surpassed it in its dual aspect.

[1] For the collection of John Newton, canon of York (d. 1414), cf. above, p. 286.

The hunger for books is in part accounted for by the growth of literacy. Here it does not do to exaggerate. Large numbers of people did not get beyond the reading and writing stage reached under local schoolmasters. Yet by the middle of the fifteenth century, England possessed a considerable number of grammar schools. The commons in 1447, when petitioning for an additional four in the City of London, spoke of the 'grete nombre of gramer scoles that somtyme were in divers parties of this Realme, beside tho that were in London and howe fewe ben in these days', but, in fact, the fourteenth century had seen the laity take to founding them. A common form of meritorious act was the endowment of a chantry, the priest of which was required not only to sing mass for the benefactor's soul, but also to keep a school whether for grammar or of a more elementary sort. The grammar schools of Wakefield and Leeds began in chantries; and it was not uncommon for gilds employing priests to conduct services for them to ask the priest to do some teaching also. The late A. F. Leach, when investigating the history of thirty-three gilds, found that all maintained song schools and that twenty-eight also maintained grammar schools. The latter can be clearly distinguished from the song and from the reading and writing schools, the 'petite' learning or English reading schools; for they taught their pupils to be 'perfect Latin men', and so prepared them, or some of them, for the life of the clerk. All the establishments, not merely the grammar schools, had to be under ecclesiastical jurisdiction, and very frequently the master was in Holy Orders, a curious exception being the master appointed for the Sevenoaks grammar school (1432) who was to be *in sacris ordinibus minime* (not at all) *constitutus.*

A number of collegiate churches maintained both types of instruction, song as well as reading. At the collegiate church of St. Mary's, Warwick, the grammar master had to teach dialectic, i.e. logic or rudiments of philosophy, as well as grammar, and it is very likely that he used Isidore of Seville's *Etymologies* (which includes treatises). Training in dialectic meant training in formal logic, and the rhetorical exercises in the large schools were more advanced than we should imagine likely among schoolboys. William Fitzstephen's description of a speech day was written in the twelfth century in an account of three 'famous schools privileged and of ancient dignity', those attached to St. Paul's, St. Mary-le-Bow, and St. Martin-le-Grand.

On high days the masters gather their pupils at the churches and there the scholars engage in disputations. Some present an argument. Some dispute a thesis by means of question and answer, or in syllogisms. There are those who play to the gallery, those who seek the truth, those who hope to make an impression by sheer volume of words, and those who rely on verbal artifice. Boys who are studying rhetoric use every art they know to present a case persuasively. Boys from different schools compete in verifying, debating and even arguing such points of grammar as the rules governing the use of different tenses.

What the London schools could do, Winchester and Eton could surpass: the originality of these foundations is not their connexion with a college in one of the universities: it is that they were colleges themselves, not adjuncts to collegiate churches, monasteries, chantries, and hospitals. They were self-governing corporations, and after them colleges like Acaster (founded by Stillington *c*. 1470) and Rotherham (founded by Archbishop Rotherham in 1483) could arise. But Eton College had its own adjunct. The original statutes of Henry VI added to the Wykehamical example of a provost and seventy 'poor indigent scholars' and the priest fellows, chaplains, clerks and choristers, thirteen poor men unmarried, of sound mind and free from incurable disease: in other words, he linked an almshouse with his college of priests and scholars, and this characteristic, as has been well remarked,[1] emphasized the charitable character of the entire undertaking: for Eton was in fact to give free instruction in grammar to all comers, in addition to the seventy scholars maintained there. With the exception of bastards and the unfree, it was open 'to all others whatsoever whensoever and from whatever parts coming to the said college to learn the same science, in the rudiments of grammar, freely'. Such pupils were not permitted to live in college, but they could dine in hall. The sons of *generosi* and friends of the college could, however, live in upon payment for their accommodation and board. This was like Wykeham's provision for *extranei commensales*, 'sons of noble and influential persons, special friends of the said college, to the number of ten to be instructed and informed in grammar within the said college, without charge to the college': in both cases such statutory provision for laymen, the sort of laymen who had not previously frequented the grammar

[1] Vivian Ogilvie, *The English Public School* (1957), p. 30.

schools, invited a new element to participate in the life of the society. But neither this nor the more democratic provision that admitted 'all others' could save Eton from Edward IV's attempt to unite his predecessor's foundation with St. George's, Windsor, or prevent the dean and chapter of St. George's from removing the bells, jewels, and vestments; until in the end the papal bull authorizing the union was reversed and St. George's obliged to hand back the spoils.

As in the case of the schools, the fifteenth century saw a notable development in the growth of colleges in the universities. Consciousness that the Church was not receiving its proper quota of trained intellect, that arms had taken the place of learning, while the 'unarmed clerical militia' was being depauperated and good scholars kept from the opportunity of study: these and similar phrases show that the appeals made by the universities (and they did not fail to make their voices heard),[1] had gone deep. At Cambridge, King's College was founded in 1441 by Henry VI; in 1448 Queens' College by Margaret of Anjou, refounded by Queen Elizabeth Woodville in 1465; St. Catharine's date is 1473; Jesus College came into being in 1496. Earlier than these was the creation of Godshouse by an ordinary parochial rector William Bingham in 1439 with Henry VI as co-founder (1448): a college to be refounded in 1505 with its present name of Christ's. At Oxford, Lincoln College (1429), All Souls College (1438), and Magdalen (1448) made their distinctive contribution to the medieval university. The beginnings of Godshouse are interesting. Bingham was rector first of Carlton Curlieu, Leicestershire, then of St. John Zachary, City of London, when he was one of a group of able city rectors, among whom were William Lichfield, parson of All Hallows the Great; Gilbert Worthington, parson of St. Andrew's, Holborn; and William Millington, later provost of King's. Bingham was impressed, he says, by the great lack of schoolmasters and convinced of the injury done to the realm by the lack of them. He had discovered in the course of his own journeyings between Hampshire and Ripon that in the part of England lying to the east of that line no fewer than seventy grammar schools were without masters. Mr. Leach saw in the college which Bingham had licence to found in 1439, the first secondary-school training college on record. Bingham asked

---

[1] e.g. *Epistolae Academicae*, ed. H. Anstey, i. 106–8.

that a 'licence might be given to fynde perpetually in the forseid mansion y called Goodeshouse xxiiii scholars to commence [incept] in grammar'. In his petition to the king he not only declared that grammar is 'rote and gronde of all the seid other sciences', but in the licence (representing his own words) it was stated that when that faculty (grammar) is weakened, the knowledge and understanding not only of sacred scripture and the Latin necessary for dealing with the laws and other ordinary business of our said realm but also of mutual communication and conversation with strangers and foreigners were entirely lost. The grammar master at Magdalen School, Oxford, in his English prose passages for translation into Latin, expressed Bingham's point of view with some emphasis:

Ther be many nowadays gon to sophistre [logic] the which can scant speke thre wordes in latyn. They wyll repent it gratly hereafter when they cum to parfyght age, for after my mynde sophistre is not to be comparede to gramere, but sum be of so unstable and waveryng mynde that they cannot perseve ther profytt.

But in the *studium generale* grammar had a preliminary role. At Cambridge, under the direction of a unique official, the *magister glomerie*, appointed by the archdeacon of Ely; at Oxford it was lectured upon mainly with Priscian as the textbook in the first year of the arts student's course by the grammar masters.[1] The colleges contained a number of such younger men; they were, however, for the majority, societies of fellows and *scolares* (probationary fellows), regent masters and members of the higher faculties of theology, law, and medicine. In the first statutes granted to King's College, 1441, the 'poor and needy' scholars were given as seventy, and the link with Eton College, likewise the foundation of Henry VI in 1440, was emphasized by requiring scholars of King's to have been on the foundation of Eton for no less than two years. But the new establishment had one feature which its prototype, the sister colleges of St. Mary of Winchester (Winchester College) and New College, Oxford, did not enjoy: on 31 January 1449 the University of Cambridge under its common seal granted that the provost, fellows, and scholars, along with their servants and ministers, should be exempt from the power and jurisdiction of the chancellor, vice-chancellor, proctors, and ministers of the

---

[1] *Munimenta Academica Oxoniensia* (Oxford Hist. Soc.), p. 286.

university, though in all matters of attendance at scholastic acts, lectures, disputations and degrees, and in meals, processions, congregations, convocations, and other formal acts they were to be obedient to the university authorities. Such exemption was not granted to any Oxford foundation and may have formed the reason why the first provost, William Millington, felt himself obliged to withdraw from his office and be formally ejected by the statutory commissioners. There would have been little dispute about the subjects to be studied in the new King's: theology, the arts, philosophy, but with the provision that two 'keen-witted' masters might devote themselves to the study of the civil law and four to canon law: there could be two medicals and two astronomers, the *scientia astrorum* being carefully confined in method to what the provost and the dean would permit.

The civil and the canon law were totally forbidden in the college founded by Robert Woodlark, St. Catharine's (1475). The foundation was intended to aid 'in the exaltation of the Christian faith and the defence and furtherance of holy Church by the sowing and the administration of the word of God'. Each fellow on his admittance had to swear not to 'divert himself' to any degree in the university save philosophy and sacred theology. The founder may have been alarmed at the number of legal degrees being granted and at the use made of clerks so trained both in diocesan administration and by temporal lords for their own territorial purposes. He also must have seen with anxiety the tendency of the religious orders, especially the Dominicans and the Carmelites, to concentrate theological teaching in their own hands at the expense of the secular masters and doctors.

Thirty years before St. Catharine's was launched, Queen Margaret of Anjou had envisaged a similar object for the college of St. Margaret and St. Bernard and had petitioned that her college should be founded 'to conservacion of our feith and augmentaceon of pure [poor] clergie, namely of the imparesse [empress] of alle sciences and faculties theologie', after the manner of the 'two noble and devoute countesses of Pembroke and Clare'. Her college of St. Bernard was refounded as Queens' College on 21 August 1447 by the king, the previous charter being cancelled and a new site, next to the house of the Carmelite friars, chosen. The actual statutes were given to the college by Elizabeth Woodville (once a lady-in-waiting to Margaret of Anjou) at the petition of Andrew Doget, the first president, and the foundation is given in them as a society of a president and twelve fellows, all of whom were to be in priest's orders, of not lower status than questionist, if a student in arts,[1] or a scholar, if in theology. When elected the fellow had to devote his time either to philosophy or theology until he had taken his doctor's degree. But one provision was made for those who did not wish to pursue theology: they could obtain the consent of the president and the majority of the fellows for studying the civil or the canon law; and herein they were to part company with St. Catharine's.

At Oxford it was equally the century of the pious founder, though perhaps less than the fourteenth: Richard Fleming, Henry Chichele, William de Waynflete were great clerks whose intention it was, in the spirit of Wykeham, to provide first and foremost for the estate of the Church, and the first two foundations, Lincoln and All Souls, were intended to be limited societies of secular priests. Fleming's foundation charter for Lincoln (19 Dec. 1429) incorporating three Oxford churches spoke of his little college (*collegiolum*) being brought into existence in order that the errors and heresies of the time that were leading people astray might be opposed by a body of trained academic graduates; and as has been pointed out, significantly among the early manuscripts recorded as having been given to the college by Richard Fleming is a copy of the *Doctrinale* of Thomas Netter of Walden.[2] Its original endowments were the revenues of the two Oxford churches of All Saints and St. Michael in the North Gate, amounting to not more than £15 a year after the salaries of the two chaplains had been paid; but in 1475 Bishop Thomas Rotherham negotiated with the abbey of Eynsham, patron of All Saints and St. Michael, for the appropriation to the college of Long Combe, Oxfordshire, and in 1478 Twyford, Buckinghamshire, was added. Fleming's intention was that the college should consist of a warden or rector and seven fellows; he never got as far as granting statutes, which was left to Thomas Rotherham in 1480: not before the college

---

[1] Cambridge University statute 139 prescribes that nobody should answer the question before the end of his fourth year: statute 135 enjoins that the questionist shall have been *generalis sophista* for about two years. The questionist was a determining bachelor.   [2] *Vict. County Hist. Oxon.* iii. 163.

had been twice threatened with dissolution, once at Edward IV's accession, when George Neville was able to secure for it letters patent under the Great Seal, 9 February 1462, and again on a drafting technicality in 1474. Rotherham's statutes of 11 February 1480 laid down twelve as the number of fellows, the warden making the thirteenth; and with an area qualification: nobody could be elected unless he came from one of the three dioceses of Lincoln, York, or Wells: one fellow was to come from Wells diocese, eight from the vast Lincoln diocese, and four from the diocese of York. Like University College and Queen's College, Lincoln was for graduates of the university who had finished the arts course and were now prepared to study in the theological faculty.

The graduate nature of the society was maintained in Henry Chichele's college of All Souls (1438). The forty fellows whose duty it was to pray for the souls of Henry V, Thomas duke of Clarence, and the English captains who had fallen in the French wars, were in part (twenty-four) to pursue theological studies, but in part (sixteen) the canon as well as the civil law. The substantial number of civilians and canonists (or either) was an innovation, but Chichele was quite clear that Church administration needed trained lawyers; these, however, must be in Holy Orders and no evasion of the rule could be permitted. Those elected must be persons instructed 'adequately in the rudiments of composition (*grammatica*) and competently in plain song'. They had to have the first tonsure and be fit and disposed to become priests. Most of the *scolares* (probationary fellows) elected were already bachelors of arts and on their first election would be between seventeen and twenty-six years of age. The college stood in particularly close relation, as might be inferred, to the archbishop of Canterbury, its visitor. He could not alter or abrogate the statutes; but his letters and injunctions show him to have possessed considerable legislative powers. The statutes given by Chichele in 1443 resemble William of Wykeham's at a good many points: they show, incidentally, that the library was divided into chained and lending sections, and in both the amount of legal books is considerable. 'Taken as a whole', as a recent history of the college has put it, 'the books which Chichele and others (especially members of his *familia*) secured for the college were a good all-round collection, not an assemblage of specialist theology and philosophy, subjects in which the library of Merton abounded.'[1]

Forty is a moderate-sized society, a good average for a fifteenth-century college. Waynflete's Magdalen, established in 1448 to the west of the present Examination Schools, had forty fellows, thirty scholars called demies or half-commoners (*semi-communarii*), four chaplains (priests), eight clerks, and sixteen choristers. The fellows were to be chosen from dioceses where the college had estates. There was a lower age limit of twelve for the demies, who already knew plain song when elected and were taught grammar, logic, and disputation. Waynflete recognized the need for the study of language, placing a grammar school alongside of his college, though the demies did not automatically, until the end of the sixteenth century, become fellows, as those elected from Winchester did in Wykeham's New College. Magdalen was an aristocracy rather than a monarchy, for while the president, who lived apart and only dined in hall occasionally, had extensive powers, he had to act with the thirteen senior fellows and in matters of great importance with the whole body of fellows. The interesting and novel part about Waynflete's great foundation was its difference from the older type of society which had little or nothing to do with undergraduates. The new feature, Dr. Denholm-Young has said, 'was the legalization of commoners or persons up to the number of twenty who were not on the foundation but were allowed to live in college and to pay their way'.[2] They were to be the sons of *nobiles* or persons of standing and were under a system of 'moral tutors', found within the college.

From a territorial point of view these college foundations are of considerable interest. Befittingly their charters and foundation statutes are often examples of calligraphy. The great charter granted to King's College, Cambridge, 16 March 1445–6, which is confirming the founder's earlier gifts and adding various provisions, has notable miniatures showing the Commons kneeling, with the Speaker at their head, saying *prient les communes*; and above are the lords, cardinals, bishops, temporal peers, and judges, who, auxiliaries, not superiors, are made to say *Et nous le prioins auxi*.[3] The estates conveyed by

---

[1] *Vict. Count. Hist.* Oxon. iii. 176.   [2] Ibid., p. 195.
[3] Illustration in J. Saltmarsh, 'The Muniments of King's College', *Proc. Camb. Antiquarian Soc.* xxxiii (1933), plate ii, opp. p. 87.

more than seventy original letters patent under the silver or Bretigny seal were remarkable for their extent and value, and for their wide distribution. They were scattered over a score of counties, from Lancashire and Yorkshire to Sussex, Hampshire, and Devon, with St. Michael's Mount in the extreme south-west. These suffered diminution as the result of attacks in the Yorkist period and a college whose income in 1460 was £1,000 per annum saw it by 1464 reduced to £500, though it was to go up to about £750 in the 1480's. The majority of these estates had belonged to monastic corporations, the alien priories suppressed by the parliament of Leicester in 1414. Nine belonged to the abbey of Bec-Hellouin in Normandy, including Ogbourn Priory in Wiltshire, Lessingham in Norfolk, the manors of Ruislip in Middlesex, Dunton Waylet in Essex, Atherston in Warwickshire, Brixton Deverell in Wiltshire; there was the estate of St. James by Exeter, formerly a Cluniac cell of St. Martin des Champs, which brought with it about ninety medieval charters; and the lands of the priory of Our Lady and St. Antony of Kersey, Suffolk, a small house of Austin canons, but a native foundation, granted to the college by Lord Powis in 1446. Another house of the same order was the priory of Great Bricett, a cell of the abbey of St. Leonard of Limoges, which contributed some 800 charters to the college muniments.

All Souls College, the granting of whose foundation statutes (1443) was practically the archbishop's last act, bears his rare seal of the Trinity of the Martyr surrounded by the *mitrata capita episcoporum* of the province, as around the figure of Becket on St. Mary's Tower. The alien priories granted to the feoffees who conveyed them to the college were the lands of the Grandmontine house of Alberbury in Shropshire, the priories of St. Clere, a cell of St. Martin-des-Près, Paris, and Llangennith in south Wales, which belonged to St. Taurin of Evreux; but the basis of the landed revenue of All Souls was (as it still is) the Middlesex properties of Edgware, Hendon, Kingsbury, Harlesden, and Willesden; and the rich lands in and around Romney Marsh, particularly Lydd and New Romney. Nearer in income to King's College was Archbishop Waynflete's Magdalen whose receipts at the beginning of Henry VII's reign were nearly £700, which rose to £1,128 in 1504 and over £2,000 in 1552.[1]

[1] N. Denholm-Young in *Vict. County Hist.* Oxon, iii. 195.

Colleges did not account for the majority of the Oxford and Cambridge students whose life went on in the halls and inns under the supervision of principals licensed by the university. The colleges were oases of endowment and privilege within the larger society, and their advantages were envied and sought after, for unless a university clerk was reasonably well 'exhibited' (paid for by parents or patrons) he required a benefice, even though he might make something by masses and occasional turns of duty. To stay away from his benefice he needed a licence and a substitute which might cost him as much as 8 to 10 marks a year. And unless a college was prepared to elect, from time to time, promising people from its own estates, there were complaints, and a number of letters preserved in the Oxford formularies of the later middle ages dwell pitifully on the difficulties of would-be entrants, particularly from the north. One prior of Durham made it his business to see that the complaints of northerners were heard, when Merton, having elected a certain number of Durham scholars, declined to elect them as fellows when their probationary period had ended.[1] The *patria* or native country of secular students took some interest in its scholars and anxiety for provision of some kind makes itself evident in much of the correspondence. They are a reminder that outside the colleges, the existence of students for any length of time in medieval Oxford (and the university course was much more than the average three years of today) depended on the readiness of patrons, ecclesiastical or secular well-wishers, to exhibit the young clerks until they had completed their 'forms' and served the necessary time in the faculties.

It has not infrequently been said that the universities in the fifteenth century had, in their philosophy and theology, ceased to deal with intellectual problems of living interest and were existing on the past. This is a superficial view and one not shared by contemporaries, who thought that there was too much uncontrolled speculation. The humanist Coluccio Salutati at the beginning of his *De laboribus Herculis* defends the poetic art not only against the *profanum vulgus* but also against the philosophers of his time. (He was writing at the end of the fourteenth century.) These persons are prepared to fly the heights of logic and philosophy without understanding or

---

[1] *Formularies which bear on the history of Oxford, c. 1204–1420*, ed. H. E. Salter, W. A. Pantin, H. G. Richardson (1942), i. 227–31.

even reading the texts of Aristotle, for they search out among 'the Britons at the end of the world' this or that treatise, as if our Italy was not sufficient for their erudition. These works they pore over without books and the writers of good philosophy to help them, and they learn from them dialectic and physics and whatsoever soaring (*transcendens*) speculation deals with.[1]

The reference may well be to Ockham and his disciples or others influenced by him, but it is more likely to be to Oxford logic in general. Salutati's attitude is natural to a follower of the humanist tradition centred in grammar, rhetoric, and poetry when confronted with scholasticism which claimed the fields of logic and natural philosophy: it is in harmony with the onslaughts of Petrarch and Leonardo Bruni against the logicians of their time; yet with this factual difference, that the introduction of English dialectic in Italy dates from the very end of the fourteenth century and is probably to be connected with the teaching of Peter of Mantua who appears to have died in 1400. 'Actually', it has been remarked,[2] 'the English method of dialectic was quite as novel at the Italian schools of that time as were the humanistic studies advocated by Petrarch and Bruni, and the humanistic attack was as much a matter of departmental rivalry as it was a clash of opposite ideas or philosophies.' Yet Bruni's half-humorous reference, in one of his dialogues, to *Britannica sophismata* puts an important point: the logicians had profoundly disturbed not only the professional theologians (and thus provoked the realist-Augustinian reaction first of Bradwardine and later of John Wyclif), but in Oxford itself the university authorities as a whole, who were anxious for a more balanced presentation of the liberal arts and an improved system of the 'ordinary' lectures, but lacked the wherewithal to endow them. The movement was started by Gilbert Kymer in 1431, and in 1432 the statutes embodied the new plan of lectures. The correspondence of the university (1433) with the duke of Bedford who had announced his intention of creating a fund to provide lectures in the 'seven liberal arts and the three philosophies', and with Duke Humphrey of Gloucester who had made a similar suggestion, was reinforced by a visit of the chancellor to both these royal personages:[3] very

[1] *Colucii Salutatis de laboribus Herculis*, ed. B. L. Ullman, i. 3.
[2] By Paul Kristeller, *Studies in Renaissance Thought and Letters* (1956), p. 577.
[3] *Epistolae Academicae*, ed. H. Anstey (Oxford Hist. Soc. 1898), i. 106–8.

shortly afterwards Humphrey's new foundation was buttressed by the gifts of books and of money (1435); but the opportunities so created and the competition to lecture became the subject of controversy, for the bachelors of arts who had taken their first degree claimed to be called masters when the public disputations were held, whereas the statutes (14 May 1432) made a clear distinction between the grades, allowing the master to be seated and enjoining that the bachelor should respond 'standing at the desk'.[1] Evidently the endowment was for *magistri*, and must have been large enough to be sought after by the younger inceptors: resistance to them on the part of the regent masters provoked the disturbances in which the university appealed to patrons and magnates like the earls of Stafford and Warwick to prevent the *proterva iuvenum delicta*. The claims of the bachelors of arts were adopted by bachelors of the canon and civil law who in their own houses (*infra suum precinctum*) had been allowed by custom to call themselves 'masters' and the younger members of the law faculty were in the van of revolution.

The university survived the disturbances, but the money received for the lectures was not sufficient to keep them going, and recourse was had to Duke Humphrey once again (1437). We have carried on the lectures in the seven sciences and the three philosophies which Humphrey was supporting (they said) but the expense is more than we can bear. If the *milicia* of the kingdom is to flourish, the true sign of it must be *scienciarum renascencia florida*,[2] a renaissance (if it may be so translated) of the sciences: but we have not the supply of books nor the means of getting them. The appeal was successful and in 1438, 120 volumes arrived, valued at over £1,000. Between 1435 and 1444, as Sir Edmund Craster has pointed out, the duke had not only given more than 281 manuscripts, but had contributed freely to a proposal that a library should be built over the Divinity School to house his books. While no detailed consideration of the list[3] is possible here, the range and interest of the gift is worth remark. Among the theology, patristic works are noteworthy: Chrysostom, Ambrose, St. John of Damascus, Athanasius: among the canonists are works by John Fitz-Geoffrey (Johannes Salford) and Johannes Andreae; in the

---

[1] *Statuta Antiqua Universitatis Oxonie*, ed. S. Gibson (1931), p. 247.
[2] *Ep. Acad.* i. 152.
[3] Ibid. i. 232–7.

category of history, Vincent of Beauvais, Eusebius, Trogus Pompeius, 'Dares Phrygius', Hegesippus, and a quantity of Livy; there is the *granarium* of Humphrey's friend, Abbot John of Whethamstede, and among general literature, the strongest section, four works of Boccaccio, five of Petrarch, the letters of Symmachus, Peter Abailard, Nicholas of Clamanges, two works of Dante, the *Commentaria* (possibly the *Convivio*), and 'the book' (the Comedy), and among classics, works of the two Plinys, Aeschines, Terence, Suetonius, Cato Censorius, Varro, Sallust, Nonius Marcellus, and a 'new translation of the whole of the Platonic Polity' (the *Politics* rather than the *Republic*). There was a Greek–Latin glossary which must have pleased John Farley, the registrar. The duke was interested in history, science, and rhetoric, and there are in addition a number of French versions of the Latin classics. After his death a good many of his 'latyn books', promised to Oxford, were allotted by a special commission to King's College, Cambridge. It is mistaken to represent the duke's gift as remote from the teaching in the Oxford syllabus: the books he presented were wanted for the new and more broadly conceived lectures on the *scientiae*. As Mrs. Leys has said,[1] 'he really does seem to have made an imaginative attempt to provide books that would be useful to students as well as those that pleased his own aesthetic sense'.

But the university library was not the only place to receive additions. Among English travellers to Italy was William Grey, bishop of Ely, the pupil of Guarino of Verona who had resided as a sojourner in Balliol College before 1442, when he took with him two of the fellows to Cologne. Grey was the patron of the humanist John Free, sent by him to Italy. Both Grey and his Balliol colleague Richard Bole employed a Dutch scribe, Theoderec Werken of Appenbroeck, who accompanied them to Italy and returned to England (by July 1450), to do further copying for Bole, whence the manuscripts passed to the Balliol College Library (nos. 310, 287, pt. ii, 127). Werken could write both in German and in Italian script. To Balliol after his death in 1478 came Grey's remarkable collection of books—181 manuscripts, and one printed book, which show the extraordinary range of his interests and refute the idea that a humanist has little interest in medieval theology and literature. The new and the old are sometimes combined in a single volume,

[1] R. J. Mitchell, *John Free* (1935), p. 36.

e.g. Cambridge University Library MS. Dd. 13. 2, written by Werken and given by Grey to Balliol, a Cicero corpus deriving from the English renaissance of the twelfth century combined with a group of speeches which had been some of the most distinguished discoveries of the fourteenth century.[1] Standard medieval theologians are found alongside of works of the new learning, for Grey collected both. Aquinas, Bonaventura, Scotus, Walter Burley, Richard of Middleton, Robert Cowton, Richard Fishacre, Thomas Docking, Robert Holcot, and not least Peter Aureol are found alongside of Gasparino of Bergamo, Benevenuto da Imola, Petrarch, Poggio, and other commentators and editors of the Latin classics. With the gifts of Bole and Robert Thwaites, the Balliol library stood for the new broadening of studies associated with Oxford library policy in the middle of the fifteenth century.

In two special directions this impetus is felt. Readers of the library lists of the period will not fail to mark the amount of Scotus either already discoverable in or actually reaching the libraries as a result of the donations of Wykeham, Chichele, William Reed, and Grey, and for this there was a substantial reason. The reaction against Ockham had gone far. Augustinian theology, reacting against the Pelagianism of Ockham and his disciples, had denied that men through their own actions, uninformed by habitual grace, could gain consideration and reward from God. Ockham had made free will a compelling agent in gaining God's grace; to Bradwardine, and to the Augustinian determinists critical of this view, such a 'Pelagian' position exalted human powers to an importance and value of their own and made them independent of the necessity of grace, while making merit dependent upon human actions. The anti-Pelagian attack was continued later in the fourteenth century by FitzRalph and by Wyclif, who largely took over Bradwardine's views on grace and predestination. Wyclif's polemic against Cunningham's tenets on future contingents continued the dispute between the upholders of free will and those who maintained that, because of God's foreknowledge of the future, the scope of the human will was strictly limited

---

[1] R. A. B. Mynors, 'A Fifteenth Century Scribe: T. Werken', *Transactions of the Cambridge Bibliographical Society*, vol. i, pt. ii (1950), pp. 98 f. Giving a list of MSS. in Balliol library signed by T. Werken: 'the script derives its renaissance quality from association with English humanists of the earlier generation'.

and could only move with the limits permitted by that fore-knowledge. The debate on the Divine knowledge of future contingents, the mould in which the controversy was cast, was the great feature of English fifteenth-century philosophy, and the appearance in the Balliol library, during the middle of the fifteenth century, of Peter Aureol on the Sentences is significant: for Aureol had been one of those who had discussed the problem of God's future knowledge, and had asked the question: if God knows all that will come about, how can this knowledge be contingent? Is the future not eternally determined by God's knowledge? To Aureol Divine knowledge appeared very like Divine determinism, the annihilation of freedom and contingency.

What was at stake, therefore, in the Oxford of Gilbert Kymer and Thomas Gascoigne was an old problem raised in a new setting; freedom upheld to the point of chaos (so the Augustinians thought) by the sceptics who followed in Ockham's track and upheld human deserving apart from God's grace, but challenged by those who in the manner of Bradwardine could see nothing but the dominance of the Divine will intervening immediately, not remotely, in human actions. In this tension it was natural that academic Oxford should return to the *doctor subtilis* who had been strongly opposed, in his days, to extreme Augustinianism: but who also criticized the nominalist view of reality and held that if there were nothing outside the mind save singulars, our understanding of reality would be false, since we do our thinking in universal terms. His balanced metaphysics is paralleled by a doctrine of the will which is given superiority over the intellect. For Scotus the intellect is moved of necessity by its natural object, but the will moves itself freely. Voluntary action is essentially self-determining, not pointed to any universal end: it can turn its attention to any object, even to that which it knows to be evil. Scotus rejected the ancient doctrine, going back to the Platonic Socrates, according to which the will has to conform to the knowledge of the good; and what is true of the human will is even more true of the Divine will. God cannot will what is irrational or contradictory: but since He is absolutely free, the operation of His will cannot be submitted to philosophical treatment. 'The works of creation are the acts of a spontaneous will which cannot be traced to necessary grounds immanent in the divine nature. The Universe is completely contingent and cannot be understood by apodeictic reasoning'.[1] Such an attack threw doubt on theology as a demonstrative science and emphasized the gap that lay between human thought and Divine truth. Theology could never be a department of philosophy; the theologian cannot prove that the great beliefs of the faith are true: when applied to the deity, terms such as wisdom and goodness possess little of the significance they have in relation to human experience.

Scotus had defended and rehabilitated the will, but without seeing it tending to good or thinking that free actions are necessarily meritorious. He had held the balance between the determinists and the extreme Pelagians and it was to him that Oxford theologians were prone to return, if indeed his cult had ever faded. The separation of faith and philosophical reality towards which Scotus found himself drawn was, however, to be strongly resisted by one who had taken it upon himself to provide a reasonable explanation of Christian doctrine especially for the Lollards who continued to be in strong reaction against the teaching and practice of the Church. The career of Reynold Pecock, bishop of Chichester, is that of a man convinced that it was possible to offer a *rationale* of religion, and to do so in the vulgar tongue. Pecock, born in Wales, was a fellow of Oriel between 1414 and 1424; he was master of Whittington College and rector of St. Michael Royal, a living belonging to the Mercers company, from July 1431 until his appointment to the bishopric of St. Asaph in 1444. He was made bishop of Chichester in 1450, and tried for heresy in October and November 1457, as the result of which, in the autumn of 1458, he recanted his errors and resigned. In 1459 he was confined, as part of his penance, to the abbey of Thorney near Peterborough, where he died. Unlike his patron, Bishop Walter Lyhert, Marmaduke Lumley, bishop of Carlisle, or Adam Moleyns, the former clerk to the king's council, his predecessor at Chichester, Pecock took no great part in politics, save to protest, in his *Repressor of overmuch blaming the clergy*, against the continuance of the French war. But he showed himself a true Lancastrian bishop in his dislike of personal evangelization, even going so far as to deliver a famous series of sermons arguing that bishops *qua* bishops were not bound to preach. He was a publicist, a

[1] M. H. Carré, *Phases of Thought in England* (1949), p. 153.

literary figure, pure and simple, contending in all his works, Latin and English, with the problem of winning back the Lollards to the orthodox faith. The clergy, he maintained, ought to labour 'for to bi cleer witt drawe men into consente of trewe feith otherwise than by fier and swerd or hangement. . . .' For him 'cleer witt' meant the employment of syllogistic logic, which is so powerful that it cannot be gainsaid. The disciple whom in his *Book of Faith* he is attempting to instruct, is told that

resoun which is a sillogisme wel reulid aftir the craft tauȝt in logik, and havyng ii premysis, openli trewe and to be grauntid, is so stronge and so myȝti in al kindes of maters, that thouȝ al the aungels of hevene wolden seie that his conclusionn were not trewe, ȝitt we schulde leeve the aungels seiying, and we schulden truste more to the proof of thilk sillogisme than to the contrarie seiying of alle the aungels in hevene, for alle Goddis creaturis musten needis obeie to doom of resoun.[1]

It was the method rather than the contents of the books he wrote which was original. Statements of the orthodox faith, like Thomas Netter's *Doctrinale*, were not lacking: new was the exposition in English philosophical language, with use of a vocabulary which he had had to create for himself in the east midland dialect. His answer to the Lollard theology lay in a definition of faith which emphasized the intellectual element. Faith is a species of knowledge (kunnyng) that man acquires, not by his own natural reason, but from another person who may not lie, or from God:

Feiþ takun propirli is a knowyng wherbi we assenten to enyþing as to trouþ, for as mych as we have sure evydencis, or ful notable likli evydencis grettir þan to contrari, þat it is toold and affermyd to us to be trewe bi him of whom we have sure evydencis, or notable likli evydencis grettir þan to þe contrari, þat þerinne he not lyed.[2]

Reason comes in when, in order that we may believe, we are called upon to determine the probability of the evidence, and in that evidence there can be degrees of likelihood, ranging from probability to the certainty attaching to revelation. Faith, therefore, involves a certain amount of discrimination; and here Pecock echoes the statement of Aquinas that faith is *cognitio*

---

[1] *Book of Faith*, ed. J. L. Morison (1909), p. 174.
[2] *Folewer to the Donet*, ed. E. V. Hitchcock, p. 62.

quaedam, but one that is different from the sort of knowledge inherent in science. But Pecock is so convinced of the varying quality of the assurance of certainty that he made a distinction between 'opinional' and 'sciential' faith, which Aquinas would certainly never have done. In scripture too, there is a distinction of purpose, since beside grounding truths of faith, it is also its function 'to release and witness moral truths of law of kinde grounded in moral philosophie; that is to say in doom of reason'. Now to Pecock this 'doom of reason' is not only the understanding of a truth which is the natural precursor to what, in scripture or revelation, we are asked to believe: it suggests new definitions of the faith and a new list of moral virtues: and Pecock did not hesitate to put forward, on the basis of this doom of reason, his own version of the Creed, and a better and more comprehensive collection of virtues than the ten commandments in his *Four Tables*. The *Four Tables* and the *Creed* were almost certainly his undoing, the reason why his views were discussed by the great council and referred to a theological committee; and because of these two works, the rest of his English philosophical works found circulating were involved in a like condemnation. But the man who 'put forward the law of nature above the scriptures and the sacraments', as Gascoigne complained, was not likely to save his more academic exercises from destruction. One of the matters which Gascoigne, chancellor of Oxford, found especially distasteful in Pecock was his apparent 'vilipending' of the Fathers. He set little value upon or actually repudiated the writings of the holy doctors of the Church, St. Jerome, St. Augustine, and the blessed Ambrose; and in the middle and later fifteenth century the cult of the four doctors of the Church showed itself both in art and in the frequent patristic additions to the library. Pecock's book the *Just Apprising of Doctors* has not survived, but throughout his works his views are sufficiently clear; he often reverts to the theme that the writings of the doctors, even of the Fathers, must be judged according to the canons of reason. They must not be regarded as inspired or accorded any special authority except that in matters of faith special heed should be paid to 'wise holi lettered clerks which lyved in tyme of the apostlis'.

Perhaps the most cogent reason why Pecock was frowned upon lay in the considered opinion of many churchmen, not least Gascoigne and Rotherham, that the English Church needed not the syllogism, but ardour and conviction to maintain the traditional faith. 'Reason is under.' Reason was all right in its place, but religion was the sphere of poetry and devotion; and in the fifteenth century there were many anxious to achieve the peace of the contemplative life. A recent editor of the Middle English treatises, the *Cloud of Unknowing* and the *Book of Privy Counselling*, found seventeen different texts of the *Cloud* and ten of the *Book*, the majority in fifteenth-century hands. These treatises are both in the tradition of the Pseudo-Denys, and give instruction 'how to be knit to God in spirit and in one head of love and accordance of will'; and the way is through darkness, through negation, since the discursive reason must fall short of the truth and its activities are, after a certain stage, a hindrance to the work of contemplation. The intuition of faith has first to reduce the mind to a state of darkness, in which the believer must persevere until the cloud of unknowing is pierced by 'a beme of goostly liȝt'. 'The plunge into the darkness of unknowing is therefore only a vivid image of the decision of faith to love and to press towards a God whom the understanding cannot comprehend, and belief in the power of faith impelled such doctors as St. Bernard, St. Bonaventure, Hugh and Richard of St. Victor to exalt affection above reason in the act of contemplation.'[1]

The epitome of devotional self-surrender is to be found in the book, commonly called the autobiography, of Margery Kempe of Lynn. This remarkable and disturbing woman, the daughter of John Burnham, who at one time had been in the Commons as burgess for Lynn, was married to a freeman of the borough, a respectable civic official, but after fifteen or sixteen years began to hanker after the celibate life, and at the end of a long period of tension with her husband, resolved with his co-operation to live in chastity as one devoted to Christ. This determination was reached through periods of mortification accompanied, with increasing frequency, by spasms of continuous weeping which many sceptical people thought to be under her control, but were in fact the spontaneous expression of her compassion for the Sufferings and Death of Christ. The revelations vouchsafed to her of Divine love as well as the story of her more practical contacts with ecclesiastics and laymen are

[1] The present writer in *Proc. British Academy*, xxxvii (1951), 152.

written, almost at her dictation, in the *Book of Margery Kempe*, the reader of which may well notice, in the story of her life and in her visions, certain traits that conform to those in the revelations of St. Brigit of Sweden, whose cult was of considerable importance in devout circles of fifteenth-century England. Brigit, at an early age, received a vision, after hearing a sermon on the Passion, of Christ speaking to her from the Cross which affected her so powerfully that for the remainder of her life she could scarcely think of the Passion without tears. She was married to a noble layman, Ulf, with whom in 1341 she began a pilgrimage to many of the most famous shrines of western Europe, but on the return journey the husband fell ill and vowed that if he recovered he would enter a monastery. This he did, at the Cistercian Abbey of Alvastia, whilst his wife established herself close by under the spiritual direction of the monks. Her visions and prophecies began after Ulf's death in 1344. With Margery there was a harder period of probation and struggle when she was trying to convince Churchmen that she was not a Lollard, that her visions were genuine and that her desire to have the mantle and ring of the ascetic should be satisfied; in the course of which Bishop Repingdon of Lincoln was impressed, but not fully convinced about the constancy of so temperamental a lady, and sent her to Archbishop Arundel and to the notable interview to which reference has been made above. But the significance of Margery lies less in her pilgrimages, her intercessions, and the scandal and sensation that her behaviour in church often caused than in her absolute conviction of the immediate revelation she received and of its character. Jesus Christ promised her a singular grace in heaven.

A, dowtyr, how oftyn-tymes haue I teld þe þat thy synnes arn forȝoue þe & þat we ben onyd to-gedyr wythowtyn ende? Þu art to me a synguler lofe, dowtyr, & þefor I behote þe þu schalt haue a synguler grace in Hevyn, dowtyr, & I be-hest þe ⟨þat I shal⟩ come to þin ende at þi deyng wyth my blyssed Modyr & myn holy awngelys & twelve apostelys, Seynt Kateryne, Seynt Margarete, Seynt Mary Mawdelyn, & many oþer seyntys þat ben in Hevyn, whech ȝevyn gret worshep to me for þe grace þat I ȝeue to þe, God, þi Lord Ihesu. Þow þart drede no grevows peynes in þi deyng, for þu xalt haue thy desyre, þat is to haue mor mynde of my Passyon þan on þin owyn peyne. Þu xalt not dredyn þe Devyl of Helle for he hath no powyr in þe. He dredyth þe mor þan thow dost hym. He is wroth wyth þe, forþ u turmentyst hym mor wyth þi wepyng þan doth al þe fyer in helle; þu wynnyst many sowlys fro hym wyth þi wepyng.[1]

Unlike St. Brigit she received no political messages from God, nor Divine directive to go to court to promote the establishment of a new religious order, for she was in no commanding social position, nor was her book as authoritative as St. Brigit's revelations. But the way she took was prepared for her and possibly even suggested to her by the circulation in this country at the end of the fourteenth century of the *Revelations*, the Merton text of which[2] gives an account of Brigit's pilgrimage to various shrines on the continent.

Margery's principal confessor was the Carmelite friar, Alan of Lynn, who was the compiler of the *tabulae* to the copy of the *Revelations* now belonging to Lincoln College (MS. LXIX). During her pilgrimage to Rome in 1414 Margery Kempe records a conversation with St. Brigit's maid, and she also visited the Saint's house in the city. Throughout the autobiography Margery is comparing herself to the saint. But St. Brigit had an influence on a very different type of man, Gascoigne himself, who was the author of a life of the saint and had made a careful study of her works. The Balliol manuscript of the *Revelations* is annotated in his hand; he was a friend of the confessor general of Syon Monastery, Robert Bell, and worked in the library of the monastery to which, in his will (*Reg. Cancellarii* i. 406), he left his books and papers. In St. Brigit's revelations he found much to support his views on the evil of the time: 'Sancta Birgitta, vidua et sponsa Christi, de regno Suecie, verba sancta et terribilia dixit contra peccatores'.

The cult of the women saints, growing throughout the century, is characteristic of the devotional movement. So far from running down in this period, religion, not merely in literary and artistic forms, but in the fervour of corporate devotion and in popular appeal achieves a place in the ordinary life of the country which it has seldom been accorded by historians of pre-Reformation England.

[1] *The Book of Margery Kempe*, ed. S. B. Meech and Hope Emily Allen (E.E.T.S. 212, 1940), vol. i, p. 50.
[2] Merton MS. CXXV, f. 238. Quedam notabilia de vita et obitu beate Brigide.

BIBLIOGRAPHY

[In the following lists places of publication are not given when they are in the British Isles]

1. RECORD SOURCES

THE standard guides are, for the Public Records, M. S. Giuseppi, *Guide to the Manuscripts preserved in the Public Record Office*, 2 vols., 1923; V. H. Galbraith, *The Public Records*, 1934; see also H. Hall, *Repertory of British Archives*, part i, England, 1920; and his *Formula Book of English Official Historical Documents*, 2 parts, 1908–9; P. H. Winfield, *The Chief Sources of English Legal History*, Cambridge, Mass., 1925. For local and county records see *British Record Association: Hand-List of Record Publications*, ed. R. Somerville, 1951; F. G. Emmison and I. Gray, *County Records*, 1948. The Historical Manuscripts Commission's list of records in private (including local government) hands is the National Register of Archives at Quality House, Chancery Lane. This National Register publishes its own annual *Bulletin*, and has taken over the 'List of Accessions to Repositories', which was included previously in the *Bulletin of the Institute of Historical Research*. The best guide to serial publications, whether of records or in monograph form, is E. L. C. Mullins, *Texts and Calendars: an analytical guide*, Royal Historical Society, Guides and Handbooks no. 7, 1958; for government publications in general, including those of the Historical MSS. Commission, see *Record Publications, Sectional List No. 24* (H.M. Stationery Office), 1960 (list reissued periodically).

(a) Public Records

The system of the English Secretariat is described by Galbraith, op. cit., pp. 27–34: 'the essential unity by which the great seal was at the disposal of other branches of the administration is reflected by the notes of warranty which the clerks added to the copies of the documents which they enrolled on the various chancery rolls and which it became more and more the custom to enter on the engrossments as well'. The various chancery enrolments require, therefore, for their understanding some knowledge of the system of writs or warrants authorizing the issue of letters under the great and privy seals. In the case of the Exchequer, it is necessary to be acquainted with the practice of warranty and accounting.

Only the most summary mention can be made of the principal classes of records.

Chancery documents are classified as enrolments and files:

(i) The list of chancery rolls is *P.R.O. Lists and Indexes*, xxvii, 1908. The rolls are calendared thus: the charter rolls in *Cal. Charter Rolls*, vols. v, vi, 1916, 1927; close rolls in *Cal. Close Rolls*, Henry IV (4 vols. and Index), Henry V (2 vols.), Henry VI (6 vols.), Edward IV–Richard III (3 vols.), 1927–54; the fine rolls in *Cal. Fine Rolls*, vols. xii–xx (1399–1471), 1931–49; French (or treaty), Gascon, and Norman rolls, briefly in *Catalogue des Rolles Gascons, Normans et Francois*, ed. T. Carte, 2 vols., 1753, more fully in *Cal. of French Rolls*, Henry V and Henry VI, in *Deputy Keeper's 44th Report* (1883), app., pp. 545–638, and *48th Rep.* (1887), app., pp. 217–450, and *Cal. of Norman Rolls*, 6–10 Henry V, in *Deputy Keeper's 41st Rep.* (1880), app., pp. 671–810, and *42nd Rep.* (1881), app., pp. 313–472, cf. *Rotuli Normanniae in Turri Londinensi asservati Johanne et Henrico Quinto Angliae regibus*, ed. T. D. Hardy (Record Comm.), 1835; patent rolls in *Cal. Patent Rolls*, Henry IV (4 vols.), Henry V (2 vols.), Henry VI (6 vols.), Edward IV–Richard III (3 vols.), 1897–1911. Parliament and Scotch rolls are printed in *Rotuli Parliamentorum*, iii–vi, 1767, and index (Record Comm.), 1832; and *Rotuli Scotiae . . . 19 Edward I–Henry VIII*, ed. D. Macpherson and others (Record Comm.), 1814–19. Pardon rolls (unpublished) are under patent rolls (supplementary): see Giuseppi, *Guide*, i, p. 37.

(ii) *Files. Chancery files.* For warrants for the great seal, series i, cf. P.R.O. manuscript list (and see E. Déprez, *Études de Diplomatique Anglaise: Le Sceau Privé, Le Sceau Secret, Le Signet*, Paris, 1908). For miscellanea, cf. manuscript list and Giuseppi, i. 57–62. Inquisitions *post mortem* are calendared briefly in *Calendarium Inquisitionum post mortem sive excaetarum*, 4 vols., Record Comm., 1806–28, and inquisitions *ad quod damnum* in *P.R.O. Lists and Indexes*, xxii, 1906.

Chancery acted as parliament's secretariat. For valuable miscellanea, cf. P.R.O. manuscript list 'Parliament and Council'. Parliamentary writs are in W. Prynne, *A Brief Register, Kalendar and Survey of the several kinds of all Parliamentary Writs*, 4 vols.,

1659–64. Much material of interest is contained in *Reports from the Lords' Committees . . . touching the Dignity of a Peer*, 5 vols., 1820–9. A note on an early Lords debate is in *The Fane Fragment of the 1461 Lords' Journal*, ed. W. H. Dunham, jnr., New Haven, 1935.

(iii) *Exchequer*. The two main archival divisions of the upper exchequer are those of the king's remembrancer and the lord treasurer's remembrancer. A rough distinction is that after the Exchequer ordinances of 1323 the king's remembrancer became responsible for the collection of the casual revenues of the crown while the treasurer's remembrancer was more particularly concerned with the fixed revenue (Giuseppi, i. 77). The memoranda rolls (for an introduction cf. *Memoranda Roll 1 John*, Pipe Roll Soc., N.S., xxi, ed. H. G. Richardson, 1943; *Memoranda Roll 14 John*, ed. Chalfant Robinson, ibid. xi, 1933; and J. Conway Davies, 'The Memoranda Rolls of the Exchequer to 1307' in *Studies presented to Sir Hilary Jenkinson*, 1957) record the day-to-day work (*communia*) of the barons of the Exchequer and other important material. The L.T.R. memoranda rolls give the proffers of the sheriffs. There are contemporary repertories: the K.R. series lists the *recorda* and the L.T.R. the accounts by various ministers and collectors of lay and clerical subsidies. The subsidy rolls (K.R.) also record the collection of these taxes and there is a separate series of subsidiary records. For these see *Deputy Keeper's Report*, ii, app. ii, pp. 132–89; iii, app. iii, pp. 3–101; iv, app. ii, pp. 2–29; and the introduction by H. C. Johnson to *Surrey Taxation Returns, fifteenths and tenths*, part B (after 1332), Surrey Record Soc. 1932.

The other main L.T.R. series are the pipe rolls (the finalized accounts of the sheriffs), enrolled accounts (including customs, escheators, wardrobe, and household) and foreign accounts (including army, navy and ordnance, Calais and Guienne, embassies and works). Many documents subsidiary to these accounts are to be found in K.R. accounts various (P.R.O. *Lists and Indexes*, vi, 1900, and xxxv, 1912).

The chief classes of the Exchequer of receipt (Lower Exchequer) are receipt rolls, 1399–1484 (see A. B. Steel, *The Receipt of the Exchequer*, introduction, 1954), and issue rolls, 1399–1479 (P.R.O. manuscript list); excerpts in *Issues of the Exchequer, Henry III–Henry VI*, ed. F. Devon (Record Comm.), 1847). The tellers' Rolls, 1401–85, provide information when the issue rolls are missing. The warrants for issues often give the circumstances of grants. For the treasury see *Ancient Kalendars and Inventories of the Treasury of H.M. Exchequer*, ed. Sir F. Palgrave (Record Comm.), 1836.

Privy Seal Office. Warrants for the privy seal, series i (MS. list), are formal warrants under the signet. For less formal warrants—authorized drafts and petitions granted (and often signed) by the council or king—see 'Council and Privy Seal' (among the records of the treasury of the receipt). Documents removed from this group by Cotton and others and now in the British Museum are printed as *Proceedings and Ordinances of the Privy Council of England*, ed. Sir N. H. Nicolas (Record Comm.), vols. i–vi (to 1460), 1834–7.

Special collections. These contain four categories of special importance: ancient correspondence, cf. P.R.O. *Lists and Indexes*, xv, 1902; ancient petitions, cf. ibid. i, 1892; court rolls, cf. ibid. vi, 1896; and ministers' accounts, cf. ibid. v, 1896, viii, 1897. The last give valuable economic data.

Palatinates. Duchy of Lancaster: ibid. xiv, 1901; cf. J. F. Baldwin, 'The Chancery of the Duchy of Lancaster' in *B.I.H.R.* iv (1927), 129; and R. Somerville, *The Duchy of Lancaster* I, 1953. Chester, Durham, County of Lancaster and Wales: P.R.O. *Lists and Indexes*, xl, 1914. The Durham exchequer records are in the archives of the dean and chapter of Durham.

State Papers. Two series bear on the reign of Edward IV: *Cal. State Papers, Milan*, ed. A. B. Hinds, 1913; and *Cal. State Papers, Venice*, vol. i, ed. R. Brown, 1864.

For *Legal Records and Judicial Proceedings* see Winfield, op. cit., W. S. Holdsworth, *Sources and Literature of English Law*, 1925, and T. F. T. Plucknett, *A History of Legal Literature*, 1958.

Chancery (as court). Latin (or common law) side, cf. Giuseppi, i. 46, and P.R.O. MS. lists. Jurisdiction in equity (a valuable source for social and economic information), cf. P.R.O. *Lists and Indexes*, xii, xvi, xx, 1901–6. (Cf. *Proceedings in Chancery in the Reign of Queen Elizabeth I, with examples of proceedings from Richard II*, ed. J. Caley and J. Bayley (Record Comm.), 1827–32; *Select Cases in Chancery, 1364–1471*, ed. W. P. Baildon, Selden Soc. x, 1896; and C. A. Walmsley, *An Index of Persons named in Early Chancery Proceedings*, Harleian Soc. 78, 79, 1937.)

Common Law Courts. The chief records are (i) King's Bench. Indictments (Ancient): see P.R.O. MS. list, and B. H. Putnam,

'The Ancient Indictments in the Public Record Office', *Eng. Hist. Rev.* xxix. 479, a most important category, still only partly explored. For the plea rolls (Coram Rege) see *Lists and Indexes*, iv, and P.R.O., Agarde's Indexes, no. 43. The controlment rolls give references to the various stages of pleas recorded on several plea rolls. (ii) Common Pleas. For plea rolls (Placita de Banco) see *Lists and Indexes*, iv; for feet of fines, see the Indexes and Calendars published by local record societies. (iii) Records of the Justices Itinerant, gaol delivery rolls, coroners' rolls, eyre rolls, cf. *Lists and Indexes*, iv. (iv) *Justices of the Peace*. Many records are among ancient indictments (see above), cf. B. H. Putnam, ed., *Proceedings before the Justices of the Peace in the fourteenth and fifteenth centuries, Edward III to Richard III* (Ames Foundation), with a commentary by T. F. T. Plucknett, 1935.

Printed cases from various tribunals are to be found in the following publications: *Select Cases before the King's Council, 1245–1482*, I. S. Leadam and J. F. Baldwin (Selden Soc. xxxv), Cambridge, Mass., 1918; *Select Cases concerning the Law Merchant, 1239–1779*, ed. C. Gross, and H. Hall, 3 vols. (ibid. xxiii, xlvi, xlix), 1908–32; *Select Cases from the Coroners' Rolls, 1265–1413*, ed., with English translation, C. Gross (ibid. ix), 1896; *Select Cases in the Exchequer Chamber before all the Justices of England, I, 1377–1461*, ed. M. Hemmant (ibid. li), 1933; *Select Pleas in the Court of Admiralty*, ed. R. G. Marsden, vol. i, pt. 1 (1390–1404) (ibid. vi), 1892; *Some Chancery Proceedings of the fifteenth century*, ed. C. T. Martin in *Archaeologia*, lix (1904), 1–24; *Year Books of Henry VI: 1 Henry VI*, A.D. 1422, ed. C. H. Williams, Selden Soc. l, 1933; (Year Books) *Les Reports del cases en ley, que furent argues en le temps de les Roys Henry le IV et Henry le V*, 1679; *Henry VI*, 2 vols., 1679.

Collections of documents. J. J. Champollion-Figeac, *Lettres de rois, reines et autres personnages des cours de France et d'Angleterre*, 2 vols., Paris, 1839–47; J. Delpit, *Collection générale des documents françaises qui se trouvent en Angleterre*, Paris, 1847; J. Stevenson, *Letters and Papers illustrative of the Wars of the English in France*, Rolls Ser., 2 vols., 1861–4; T. Rymer, *Foedera, conventiones, literae et cuiusque generis acta publica . . .* 3rd ed., The Hague, 1739–45, vols. iii–v; E. C. Lodge and Gladys A. Thornton, *English Constitutional Documents 1307–1485*, 1935; I. D. Thornley, *England under the Yorkists*, 1920.

(b) Ecclesiastical Sources

The main original source for archiepiscopal and diocesan administration is the registers of the archbishops and the bishops. For the province of Canterbury, the registers of Archbishops Arundel and Stafford, unprinted, are in Lambeth Palace Library. For bibliography see R. C. Fowler, *Episcopal Registers of England and Wales* (S.P.C.K. 'Helps for Students of History'), 1918; C. J. Offer, *The Bishop's Register*, 1929; and E. F. Jacob, *The Registers of Canterbury and York: Some points of Comparison*, 1953; I. J. Churchill, *Canterbury Administration*, 2 vols., 1933, analyses the growth of the archbishop's office as reflected in the documents recorded by his clerks and registrars; *The Register of Henry Chichele 1414–1443*, ed. E. F. Jacob (vol. ii with H. C. Johnson), 1938–47, and *Registrum Thome Bourgchier*, ed. F. R. H. du Boulay, 2 vols., 1955–6 (Cant. and York Soc.), cover much of the Lancaster and Yorkist periods. For the province of York: *Documents relating to Diocesan and Provincial Visitations from the Registers of Henry Bowet* (1407–1423) and *John Kempe, Archbishop of York* (1425–52), ed. A. Hamilton Thompson (Surtees Soc. cxxvii. 131–302), 1916.

Printed diocesan registers for the following bishops are: for *Bath and Wells*, Henry Bowet (1401–7), ed. T. S. Holmes (Somerset Rec. Soc. xiii), 1899; Nicholas Bubwith (1407–24), ed. T. S. Holmes (ibid. xxix, xxx), 1914; John Stafford (1425–43), ed. T. S. Holmes, 2 vols. (ibid. xxxi–xxxii), 1915–16; Thomas Bekynton (1443–65), ed. H. C. Maxwell-Lyte and M. C. B. Dawes, 2 vols. (ibid. xlix, l), 1934–6. For *Chichester*, *Medieval Registers of the Bishops of Chichester, 1396–1502* (abstracts), ed. M. E. C. Walcott, Trans. Roy. Soc. Literature, 2nd ser., vol. ix (1870), 215–44; Robert Reede (1397–1415), ed. C. Deedes, 2 parts (Sussex Record Soc. viii, ix), 1908, 1910; Richard Praty (1438–45), ed. C. Deedes (Extracts), 1905. For *Durham*, Thomas Langley (1406–37), ed. R. L. Storey, 3 vols. (Surtees Soc., 164, 166, 169), 1956+. For *Ely*, Abstracts of John de Fordham (1385–1425), Thomas Bourchier (1444–54), William Gray (1454–78), ed. J. H. Crosby in *Ely Diocesan Remembrancer*, 1897–1902, 1902–4, 1904–8; Ely Episcopal Records (Calendar), ed. A. Gibbons, 1891. For *Exeter*, Edmund Stafford (1395–1419), ed. F. C. Hingeston-Randolph, 1856; Edmund Lacy (1420–35), ed. F. C. Hingeston-Randolph and O. J.

Reichel, 2 vols., 1909, 1915 (new ed. by G. R. Dunstan, Cant. and York and Devon and Cornwall Hist. Rec. Socs. in progress). For *Hereford* (Cant. and York and Cantelupe Soc.), John Trefnant (1389–1404), ed. W. W. Capes, 1914–16; Robert Mascall (1404–16), ed. J. H. Parry, 1917; Edmund Lacy (1417–20), Thomas Polton (1420–2), ed. J. H. Parry and W. W. Capes, 1918; Thomas Spofford (1422–48), ed. A. T. Bannister, 1917–19; Richard Beauchamp (1449–50), ed. Bannister, 1917–19; Reginald Boulers (1451–3), ed. Bannister, 1917–19; John Stanbury (1453–74), ed. Parry and Bannister, 1919. For *Lincoln*, *Visitations of Religious Houses in the Diocese of Lincoln* (1420–49), ed. A. Hamilton Thompson, 3 vols. (Linc. Record Soc.), London, 1915–27, covering Richard Flemyng (1420–31), William Gray (1431–6), William Alnwick (1436–49). For *St. David's*, *The Episcopal Registers 1397–1518*, ed. R. F. Isaacson, 2 vols. (Cymmrodorion Soc., Record Ser. vi), 1917. For *Winchester*, William of Wykeham (1366–1404), ed. T. I. Kirby, 2 vols. (Hants Record Soc.), 1896, 1899.

Papal letters (Vatican and Lateran Registers) are to be found in the following: *Calendar of entries in the Papal Registers relating to Great Britain and Ireland, Papal Letters*, vols. v–xiv (Cal. S.P. 1904–61); *Petitions to the Pope*, vol. i (1342–1419) (Cal. S.P. 1896); O. Raynaldus, *Annales Ecclesiastici post Baronium*, Lucca, 1747–56; Johannes Haller, 'England und Rom unter Martin V' in *Quellen und Forschungen aus italienischen Archiven und Bibliotheken*, bd. viii, Heft 2 (Rome, 1906), Beilagen, pp. 289–304.

Collections of Ecclesiastical Documents. The standard works are D. Wilkins, *Concilia magnae Britanniae et Hiberniae*, vol. iii, 1738; and E. Gibson, *Codex juris ecclesiastici anglicani*, 2 vols., 1761. Provincial constitutions (to 1432) are in W. Lyndwood, *Provinciale, seu constitutiones Angliae continens constitutiones archiepiscoporum Cantuarie e Stephano Langtono ad Henricum Chicheleium, cum ad notationibus*, 1679; translation in J. V. Ballard and H. Chalmer Bell, *Lyndewood's Provinciale*, 1929 (the introduction is faulty). For collections of statutes in the secular cathedrals cf. K. Edwards, *The English Secular Cathedrals in the Middle Ages*, 1949, bibliography, pp. 365–6. For English monasticism see the foundation and other charters printed in W. Dugdale, *Monasticon Anglicanum*, 6 vols., re-ed. J. Caley, H. Ellis, and B. Bandinel, 1846, and the notes of recorded registers in Thomas Tanner, *Notitia Monastica*, ed. J. Nasmith, 1787. The best bibliography is in M. D. Knowles, *The Religious Orders in England*, ii. 1955. The chapters of the Benedictines are recorded in *Documents illustrating the Activities of the General and Provincial Chapters of the English Black Monks, 1215–1540*, ed. W. A. Pantin (Roy. Hist. Soc., Camden 3rd ser.), 3 vols. 1936–7; for the Franciscans see L. Wadding, *Annales Minorum*, 2nd ed., 19 vols., Rome, 1731–46; the Carmelites, B. Zimmerman, *Monumenta historica Carmelitana*, Lerins, 1905; the Cluniacs, C. F. Duckett, *Charters and Records of Cluny*, ii, 1888 (cf. R. Graham, 'The English Province of the Order of Cluny in the fifteenth Century', *English Ecclesiastical Studies*, 1929, pp. 62 f.); for the Austin canons, *Chapters of the Augustinian Canons*, ed. H. E. Salter (Oxford Historical Soc. lxxiv), 1920; for the Premonstratensians, the periodical *Analecta Premonstratensia*, Tongerloo, from 1925. The statutes of the Cistercians are in *Statuta Capitulorum generalium Ordinis Cisterciensis*, ed. J. M. Canivez, Louvain, 1933–41. Lollard documents, in defence or attack, are contained in *Fasciculi Zizaniorum*, ed. W. W. Shirley, Rolls Series, 1858. The heresy is rebutted in Thomas Netter of Walden, *Doctrinale de Sacramentis*, 3 vols., Venice, 1571. Monastic cartularies are listed in G. R. C. Davis, *Medieval Cartularies of Great Britain*, 1958. The following cartularies and register books might be mentioned: Bury St. Edmunds (see *Monasticon*, iii. 117–31), T. Arnold, *Memorials of St. Edmund's Abbey*, ii (Rolls Series 1892) and iii (1896); the Register of Abbot Curteys (1429–46) is Brit. Mus. Add. MS. 14848 (vol. i) and Add. MS. 7096 (vol. ii); Christ Church, Canterbury (cf. C. E. Woodruff, *Catalogue of Manuscripts of Christ Church, Canterbury*, 1911), Register of Prior William Molassh, Bodleian Library MS. Tanner 165 (from 1427); St. Augustine's Abbey, Thomas of Elmham, *Historia Abbatiae Sancti Augustini*, ed. C. Hardwick (Rolls Series, 1858), and *William Thorne's Chronicle of St. Augustine's Abbey, Canterbury*, trans. A. H. Davis, 1934; Lancaster Priory, Brit. Mus. MS. Harley 3764, ed. W. O. Roper, *Materials for the History of the Church of Lancaster* (Chetham Soc., N.S., xxvi, xxxi, 1892–4); London, St. Paul's Cathedral (secular chapter), Muniments of St. Paul's Cathedral, W.D. 11 a, gives the lists of deeds drawn up by Thomas Lyseux, dean, in 1447; London, St. Bartholemew's Hospital, Archives of St. Bartholemew's, 'Cok's Cartulary', Henry VI–Edward IV; Malmesbury, Brit. Mus. MS. Lansdowne 417, cf. J. S. Brewer, and C. T. Martin, *Registrum Malmesburiense* (Rolls Ser.

1879–80), 2 vols.; Meaux, E. A. Bond, *Chronica Monasterii de Melsa*, vols. 2, 3 (Rolls Ser. 1867–8); Norwich Cathedral Priory, 'Reg. IV', cf. H. T. Riley, *Hist. MSS. Comm. 1st Rep.* (1870), app., pp. 87–89, and W. Holtzmann, *Papsturkunden in England*, ii (Göttingen, 1935), pp. 30–35; St. Albans, Chatsworth Trustees, Cartulary of St. Albans Abbey (*c.* 1390, Davies no. 832); Brit. Mus. MS. Arundel 34 (lands acquired by abbots Whethamstede and Ramrigge); *Johannis Amundesham Annales Monasterii St. Albani*, ed. H. T. Riley, 2 vols. (Rolls Ser. 1870–1); *Registrum Johannis Whethamstede*, ed. H. T. Riley, 2 vols. (Rolls Ser. 1873); Westminster, Westminster Abbey, Muniment Books 1 ('Liber Niger Quaternus') and 12 (cf. J. Armitage Robinson and M. R. James, *MSS. of Westminster Abbey*, 1909).

The Courts and Jurisdiction. Extracts from Bishop Alnwick's court book (Lincoln Consistory) are printed in A. Hamilton Thompson, *The English Clergy and their Organization in the Later Middle Ages*, 1947, app. iii. Documents illustrating the tuitorial appeal are in B. L. Woodcock, *Medieval Ecclesiastical Courts in the Diocese of Canterbury*, app. vi; for records of the Canterbury Consistory cf. ibid., pp. 139–42. The chancellor's court at Oxford (Reg. Aaa) has its *Acta* printed from 1434–69 by H. E. Salter, *Registrum cancellarii* (Oxford Historical Soc.), 2 vols., 1932.

(c) Town Records: a select list

BIBLIOGRAPHIES: C. Gross, *Bibliography of British Municipal History and Parliamentary Representation* (Harvard Hist. Studies v), New York, 1897; A. L. Humphreys, *Handbook to County Bibliography*, 1917; M. Weinbaum, *The Incorporation of Boroughs*, 1939, and *British Borough Charters*, vol. iii, 1940.

For CONSTITUTIONAL HISTORY: Beverley: *Beverley Town Documents*, ed. A. F. Leach (Selden Soc. xiv), 1900; Bristol: *The Great Red Book of Bristol*, ed. E. W. W. Veale, vol. i, introduction, Bristol Record Soc., 1931; *Bristol Charters, 1378–1400*, ed. H. A. Cronne, Bristol Record Soc., 1946; Cambridge: *Annals of Cambridge*, by C. H. Cooper, vol. i, 1842; *The Charters of the Borough of Cambridge*, ed. F. W. Maitland and M. Bateson, 1901; *The Victoria County History of Cambridgeshire*, vol. 3, 1958; Colchester: *Charters of the Borough of Colchester*, ed. I. H. Jeayes, 1903; *Court Rolls of the Borough of Colchester*, ed. with an introduction, by W. Gurney Benham, 3 vols., 1921–41; Coventry:

Coventry Leet Book; or Mayor's Register containing Records of City Court Leet, ed. M. D. Harris, 4 pts. (Early English Texts Soc., Orig. Ser.), 1907–13; Leicester: *Records of the Borough of Leicester*, ed. M. Bateson, 3 vols., 1899–1905; London: *Calendar of Letter Books . . . of the City of London*. Letter Books K, L, ed. R. R. Sharpe, 1912; *Aldermen of London*, ed. A. B. Beaven, 2 vols., 1908–13; *Memorials of London and London Life in the 13th, 14th and 15th centuries*, H. T. Riley, 1868; *Munimenta Gildhallae, Liber Albus, Liber Custumarum* and *Liber Horn*, ed. H. T. Riley (Rolls Ser., 1859–62); *Calendar of Select Pleas and Memoranda of the City of London 1381–1412*, ed. A. H. Thomas, 1932; *Calendar of the Plea and Memoranda Rolls of the City of London, 1413–37*, ed. A. H. Thomas, 1943; *1437–57*, ed. Philip E. Jones, 1954; Northampton: *Records of the Borough of Northampton*, ed. C. A. Markham and J. C. Cox, 1898; Norwich: *Records of the City of Norwich*, ed. W. Hudson and J. C. Tingey, 2 vols., 1906–10; Nottingham: *Records of the Borough of Nottingham*, ed. W. H. Stevenson, 5 vols., 1882–1900; Reading: *Reading Records*, ed. J. M. Guilding, 4 vols., 1892–6; Rochester: *Archives of Rochester*, in *Archaeologia Cantiana*, vi; Southampton: *The Black Book of Southampton, 1385–1620*, ed. A. B. Wallis-Chapman, 3 vols. (Southampton Record Soc.), 1912–15; Winchester: *Black Book of Winchester*, ed. W. H. B. Bird, 1925; *The City Government of Winchester from the records of the XIVth and XVth centuries*: by J. S. Furley, 1923; *The Ancient Usages of the City of Winchester*, by J. S. Furley, Glossary by E. W. Patchett, 1927; York: *Extracts from Municipal Records of York during the reign of Edward IV, Edward V and Richard III*, ed. R. Davis, 1843; Angelo Raine, *Medieval York*, 1955 (for sources).

2. CHRONICLE AND LITERARY MATERIAL

1. BIBLIOGRAPHIES

The most valuable is in C. L. Kingsford, *English Historical Literature in the Fifteenth Century* (1913). This contains a bibliography of the printed editions of original authorities and a list of manuscripts described or noted in this volume. It has an appendix of Chronicles and Historical Pieces 'hitherto for the most part unprinted'. There are useful bibliographies in C. W. C. Oman, *The Political History of England*, 1399–1485 (1918), and to the chapters on the Lancastrian and Yorkist kings in *Cambridge Medieval History*, viii, ch. xi, xii (1936), by K. B. McFarlane and C. H. Williams, respectively. J. H.

Wylie, *The History of England under Henry IV*, vol. iv, 1411–13 (1898) has, in appendixes A–G, a collection of extracts from documents in the Public Record Office then unpublished, mainly from the duchy of Lancaster, the Wardrobe Accounts (K.R.), and the K.R. Army, Navy, and Ordnance accounts. For the identification of persons the index (vol. iv) is valuable. The *Cambridge Bibliography of English Literature*, ed. F. W. Bateson, vol. i, 113–24, is also useful for the literary sources. For the occupation of France, R. A. Newhall, *The English Conquest of Normandy, 1416–1424* (New Haven, 1924); for Gascony, R. Boutruche, *La Crise d'une société: seigneurs et paysans du Bordelais pendant la Guerre de Cent Ans* (Paris, 1947), pp. xviii–l; for social and economic history, *Cambridge Economic History*, vol. i, Agrarian history, pp. 605–10, 613 (Professor Neilson); vol. ii, ch. iv, pp. 531–6 (Professor Postan), vi, pp. 560–1 (Professor Carus Wilson); and the periodical lists of publications in the *Economic History Review*.

2. CHRONICLE SOURCES

These are arranged by Kingsford in four main groups, the details of which have now been modified by research, and in a group of 'minor' chronicles (the word 'minor' to be treated with caution).

On fifteenth- and sixteenth-century historiography: J. Bale, *Scriptorum illustrium Maioris Brytanniae Catalogus*, Basel, 1559; *Index Britanniae Scriptorum*, ed. R. Lane Poole and M. Bateson, 1902; F. W. D. Brie, *Geschichte und Quellen der mittelenglischen Prosachronik, 'The Brut of England'*, Marburg, 1905; L. Fox, ed. *English Historical Scholarship in the Sixteenth and Seventeenth Centuries*, Dugdale Soc., 1956 (for John Rous); V. H. Galbraith, *The St. Albans Chronicle, 1406–1420*, introduction (pp. i–lxxi) (1937); D. Hay, *Polydore Vergil, Renaissance Man of Letters*, 1952; Esther Hodge, 'The Abbey of St. Albans under John Whethamstede' (Manchester Ph.D. thesis, 1933); T. D. Kendrick, *British Antiquity*, 1950; N. R. Ker, *Medieval Libraries of Great Britain*, 1941; J. Leland, *Commentarii de scriptoribus Britannicis*, ed. A. Hall, 1709; K. B. McFarlane, 'William Worcester, A Preliminary Survey' in *Studies presented to Sir Hilary Jenkinson* (1957); *Dictionary of National Biography*, notices of William Botoner (William of Worcester), John Free (cf. Mitchell, above), John Amundesham, Thomas Walsingham, John of Whethamstede; W. F.

Schirmer, *Der englische Frühhumanismus*, Leipzig, 1931; T. Tanner, *Bibliotheca Britannico-Hibernica*, 1748; E. M. W. Tillyard, *Shakespeare's History Plays*, 3rd ed., 1951; R. Weiss, *Humanism in England during the Fifteenth Century*, 2nd ed., 1957.

(*a*) *The St. Albans Chronicle*. The work of Thomas Walsingham, who wrote the St. Albans Chronicle from 1376–1422, is divided by a break in 1394–6, when he was prior of Wymondham. He first completed the *Chronica maiora* (1272–1392), contained in British Museum Royal MS. 13 E. IX: then, at Wymondham, a short chronicle, 'a re-written abstract of the larger work' (Galbraith), of which surviving manuscripts run from 1327 to 1392, continuing these after his return. About 1420, MS. Bodley 462 (1257–1420) was completed, continuing the full contemporary history, 1392–1420. Walsingham was thus responsible for a long and a short version of the St. Albans Chronicle, to which can be related what are known as the *Historia Anglicana*, the *Chronicon Angliae*, and the *Annales Ricardi II et Henrici IV*. They are all Walsingham's work.

Editions are:

1. *The St. Albans Chronicle 1406–1420*, ed. V. H. Galbraith, 1937. This is MS. Bodley 462, which copies the short chronicle as far as 1392; after this 'it copies a rather fuller St. Albans Chronicle which served as the direct source for practically the whole of the chronicle called Otterbourne'. It pays much more attention to Henry IV's reign than to Henry V's.

2. *Historia Anglicana*, ed. H. T. Riley, 2 vols., Rolls Ser. 1863, printed from Arundel MS. VII (College of Arms), itself copied (though the editor did not know it) from Corpus Christi Cambridge MS. 195. This is the full text from 1272–1392, followed by the 'shortened version' to 1422.

3. *The Annales Ricardi II et Henrici IV* (1392–1406), ed. Riley, iii (Rolls Ser.), a fragment of the full chronicle, valuable for Henry IV's reign.

Thomas Otterbourne, *Chronica regum Angliae*, has a few passages borrowed from the *Liber metricus* of Thomas Elmham, q.v.: otherwise it is entirely extracted from MS. Bodley 462. John Capgrave, *Chronicle of England*, except for one addition, Henry IV's death-bed confession, is taken with large omissions from the St. Albans Chronicle.

Ypodigma Neustriae, compiled between July 1419 and the

death of Henry V, is an epitome of English History from 911–1419, 'Perhaps the best short history of England produced in the Middle Ages' (Galbraith).

Other St. Albans products: *Gesta abbatum*, ed. H. T. Riley (John V and William II), Rolls Ser., 1869; and *Annales monasterii sancti Albani* (Amundesham and another), 2 vols., Rolls Ser., 1870; *Registrum Johannis de Whethamstede*, 2 vols., Rolls Ser., 1872. The first Chronicle in the Annales is probably by Walsingham.

(*b*) *The Chronicles of London*. These are compared and described in C. L. Kingsford, *English Historical Literature*, and by A. H. Thomas and I. D. Thornley in their introduction to *The Great Chronicle of London*, 1938. There are a large number of city chronicles, the chief of which, for the period under review, are the MSS. Julius B. I; Vitellus F. IX; Julius B. II; the Longleat MS.; Harleian 565; St. John's College, Oxford, 57; Harleian 3775; Lambeth 306; Vitellius A. XVI; Egerton 1995; Cleopatra C. IV; The Great Chronicle (Guildhall MS.). Eight of the more important were discussed and printed in C. L. Kingsford, *Chronicles of London*, 1905. Four versions, of the period 1419–46, were preserved as a continuation of the *Brut Chronicle* (ed. F. W. D. Brie, 1908, pp. 440–90); and five London Chronicles are printed in R. Flenley, *Six Town Chronicles*, 1911.

Mr. Kingsford (pp. 80–81) arranged the various versions in recensions which he attributed to the years 1430–2, 1432, 1440, 1446, and 'the Main City Chronicle', 1440–85. He thought that between 1413–30 the Chronicles were in constant process of re-editing and continuation. Of all the ten, he considered the Great Chronicle 'the most ample extant representation of the English Chronicles of London in their earliest form', and 'the fullest and most valuable copy of the London Chronicles we possess'. Thomas and Thornley hold that the Great Chronicle lacks 'the fulness of wealth and civic detail found in Harley 565 or the accuracy of names and dates in Julius B. II', and that Kingsford placed too much emphasis on passages common to the Great Chronicle and the other chronicles and not sufficient on the divergencies. Kingsford's table of recensions they regard as an over-simplification. After 1399 the Chronicles continually diverge from one another, and the Great Chronicle moves from one to the other, generally adopting the best and fullest accounts. The compiler of the section 1413–39 had before him in a finished form the main constituents of the other chronicles and made a great effort to produce a work that should be comprehensive (*Great Chron.*, p. xxxv). To Thomas and Thornley the Great Chronicle surpasses the other manuscripts of the London chronicles through its inclusion of important public documents.

Other London Collections: Gregory's Chronicle in *Collections of a London Citizen*, pp. 57–183, ed. J. Gairdner, Camden Soc., 1876; Short English Chronicle in *The Fifteenth Century Chronicles*, pp. 1–65, ed. J. Gairdner, Camden Soc., 1880; Harley 565, Julius B. I. in Sir N. H. Nicolas, *Chronicle of London, 1089–1483*, 1827; Robert Fabyan, *The New Chronicles of England and France* (The Concordance of Histories), ed. Henry Ellis, 1811.

(*c*) *The Brut* or the *English Chronicle*. The version 1377–1419 or the continuation closely resembles the London Chronicles, but its compiler had other and richer sources of information, and it is now doubted whether the original was a London Chronicle. It contains (1418–19) John Page's poem on the siege of Rouen (printed *Collections of a London Citizen*, ed. J. Gairdner, 1876, and by H. Huscher (Kölner Anglistische Arbeiten 1), Leipzig, 1927). The second continuation, perhaps completed in 1464, ends in 1461. This was adopted by Caxton for his *Chronicles of England* (1480), known as Caxton's Chronicles, the earlier part from 1419–30 being based on a London Chronicle. The section of the Brut ending in 1437 represents the longer original of *The English Chronicle from 1377 to 1461*, ed. J. S. Davies, Camden Soc., 1856: *The Brut or the Chronicle of England*, ed. F. W. D. Brie, parts i–ii, Early English Texts Soc., Orig. Ser., 131, 136, 1906–8.

(*d*) *Biographies of Henry V. Gesta Henrici Quinti* (i), ed. J. A. Giles, 1846, (ii) ed. B. Williams, Eng. Hist. Soc., 1850, (iii) ed. with notes by F. Taylor, Manchester (thesis), 1938. This is the Life attributed, probably without solid foundation, to Thomas Elmham, Cluniac prior of Lenton. Elmham was the author of *Liber metricus de Henrico Quinto*, Rolls Ser., 1858, included in the volume containing *Memorials of Henry V* (*Vita Henrici Quinti, Roberto Redmanno auctore*). The *Gesta* ends in 1416, the *Liber metricus* in 1418.

The official Life is *Vita Henrici Quinti*, by Titus Livius Forojuliensis (Tito Livio da Forli), ed. Thomas Hearne, 1716; the *Vita et gesta Henrici Quinti*, 1727, in MS. Julius E. IV (and in other manuscripts), Thomas Hearne attributed, on slender grounds, to Elmham, but it was written long after Henry V's death, probably after 1446 and before Gloucester died in 1447, by a master of the florid style. From 1419–22 the Pseudo-Elmham, as he is called, is useful. The *First English Life of Henry V*, edited by C. L. Kingsford (1911), is to be dated 1513; its value lies chiefly in possessing stories of the reign told partly on the authority of James Butler, fourth earl of Ormond.

(*e*) *Other Chronicles*. Special Bibliography, Kingsford, *E.H.L.*, chs. vi, vii; Gross, *Sources and Literature of English History*, 1915, p. 48. For news-letters, cf. C. A. J. Armstrong, 'Politics and the Battle of St. Albans 1455', *Bull. Inst. Hist. Res.* xxxiii, No. 87 (1960), 1–5.

(i) For Henry IV and Henry V: the *Eulogium historiarum, continuatio* iii, ed. F. R. Haydon (Rolls Ser.) 1863, is important for ecclesiastical material; *Chronicon Adae de Usk*, ed. E. Maunde Thompson, 1876, gives a Welsh ecclesiastical lawyer's view of events, beginning with Richard II's reign and ending in the summer of 1421; *Incerti scriptoris chronicon Angliae de regnis Henrici IV, Henrici V et Henrici VI*, ed. J. A. Giles, 1848, which begins with Richard II's reign, is for 1403–13 the work of a writer significantly critical of Henry IV, who appears to have had access to the parliament roll for 1404 and 1406; the Henry V part is borrowed from the *Gesta*, but the writer who did the Chronicle of Henry VI, writing in or soon after 1460, has original material between 1438 and 1453; *The Chronicle of John Strecche*, ed. F. Taylor, 1934, is probably the work of a canon of Kenilworth, who adds, from his knowledge of the castle, certain particulars about Henry V's reign; *The Chronicle of John Hardyng*, ed. Ellis, 1812, written by a clerk with special knowledge of the Scottish Border, an adherent of the Percies and the Umfravilles, consists of two recensions, the first using a panegyric on Robert Umfraville as an occasion for exhorting Henry VI to reform his realm: the second, Yorkist in sympathy, is addressed to Edward IV.

(ii) For Henry VI, Kingsford in his *English Historical Literature* prints the *Latin Brut*, 1399–1437, a Chronicle for 1445 to 1455, the *Waltham Annals* (Cotton MS. Titus D. XV, fos. 7–57), and *Collections of a Yorkist Partisan*, 1447–52 (Cotton Roll, ii. 23); J. Le Fèvre, *Chronique*, ed. F. Morand, 2 vols. (Soc. Hist. Fr.), Paris, 1876–81, covers 1408–35; William Worcester, (i)

Itinerarium, ed. J. Nasmith, 1778, (ii) *Annales Rerum Anglicarum* first printed by Hearne with the *Liber Niger Scaccarii* (1728) and by J. Stevenson in *Letters and Papers illustrative of the Wars in France*, Rolls. Ser., vol. ii, pt. ii, 1864; John Warkworth, *Chronicle*, ed. J. O. Halliwell (*Chronicles of the White Rose*, Camden Soc., 1839), is of value for events in the North in 1464 and for the earlier career of the duke of Gloucester; the continuation of the Croyland Chronicle (*Historiae Croylandensis Continuatio*) ed. W. Fulman in *Rerum Anglicarum Scriptores*, 1684 (Eng. trans. H. T. Riley, in Bohn's Library), the best account of the reign of Edward IV; the second *Continuation of the Croyland Chronicle*, written after the death of Edward IV, by a royal councillor and a doctor of Canon Law, who went on a mission to Charles the Bold in 1471, is a work of cautious and critical judgement; *Historia Rerum Angliae* by John Rous of Warwick (Chantry priest of Guy's Cliff) ed. Hearne, 1716 and 1744, has a venomous attack on Richard III, but Rous is better known as the compiler of the two Rolls of the earls of Warwick (cf. C. E. Wright, 'The Rous Roll: the English Version', *British Museum Quarterly*, vol. xx, no. 4 (1956), 77–81) and as the author of a 'Life of Richard Beauchamp, earl of Warwick' (Cotton MS. Julius E. IV). Sir Thomas More's *History of King Richard III* (also in a Latin version which stops at the coronation of Richard III) first published by Rastell, was written to contrast Richard III unfavourably with Edward IV, and much of the book was due to information given by Morton; *The Usurpation of Richard the Third*, by Dominic Mancini (*De Occupatione Regni Angliae per Riccardum Tercium Libellus*), ed. C. A. J. Armstrong, 1936, is an Italian humanist's account, written to his patron, Angelo Cato, of events in London between the death of Edward IV, 9 April 1483 and the seizure of power by Richard at the end of June that year. Mancini left England shortly after 6 July. A work of humanist character, it is an indictment of Richard III, giving a valuable account of opinion in London during the weeks following Richard's entry.

(*f*) *Miscellaneous Narratives and Chronicles.* Account of the first battle of St. Albans (1455), ed. J. Bayley, in *Archaeologia*, xx. 519; J. Blackman, *Collectarium mansuetudinum et bonorum morum Regis Henrici VI*, ed. with English translation by M. R. James, 1919; Thomas of Burton, *Chronica monasterii de Melsa* (continuation 1396–1417), ed. E. A. Bond, Rolls Ser., iii. 237; *Chronicle of*

Dieulacres Abbey, 1381–1403, ed. M. V. Clarke and V. H. Galbraith, in 'The Deposition of Richard II', see below; *Chronicon Abbatiae de Evesham ad annum 1418*, ed. W. P. Macray, Rolls Ser., 1863; *Kirkstall Chronicle, 1355–1400*, ed. M. V. Clarke and N. Denholm-Young in *Bulletin of the John Rylands Library*, xv (1931), 100; 'London Chronicle of 1460', ed. G. Baskerville, *Eng. Hist. Rev.* xxviii. 24; J. Stone, *Chronicle of Christ Church, Canterbury (1415–71)*, ed. W. G. Searle (Camb. Antiq. Soc. xxxix), 1902.

(g) *Tudor Chronicles*. Robert Fabyan, *Newe Chronycles of England and of Fraunce*, 1st ed. (anonymous), 1516; 2nd ed. by Sir H. Ellis, 1811; Polydore Vergil, *Anglica Historia*, Basel, 1555; *Three Books of Polydore Vergil's English History comprising the Reigns of Henry VI, Edward IV and Richard III* from an early translation, ed. Sir H. Ellis, Camden Soc., 1844; Edward Hall, *The Union of the two Noble and Illustrious Families of Lancaster and York*, ed. Ellis, 1809 (for his sources cf. *E.H.L.*, pp. 263–5); John Stowe, *Annales of England*, 1592, 3rd ed., 1605, of importance for the last ten years of Henry VI and for Cade's rebellion (pp. 388–9, 391–2); R. Grafton, *Continuation of Hardyng's Chronicles*, ed. Sir H. Ellis, 1809; Sir T. More, *History of King Richard III*, ed. J. R. Lumby, 1812 (see above, (e) (ii)).

(h) *Correspondence*. *Anglo-Norman Letters and Petitions*, ed. M. D. Legge, 1933; The *Paston Letters*, ed. James Gairdner, Library ed., 6 vols., 1904; the *Stonor Letters*, ed. C. L. Kingsford, Camden Soc., 2 vols., 1919, and *Supplementary Stonor Letters and Papers*, Camden Miscellany, vol. xiii, ed. Kingsford, 1924; the *Plumpton Correspondence*, ed. T. Stapleton, Camden Soc., 1839; *The Cely Papers*, Camden, 3rd ser., ed. H. E. Malden, 1900; *Original Letters*, ed. Sir H. Ellis, 1st, 2nd, and 3rd ser. (mostly from Cotton, Vespasian F. II, and Vespasian F. XIII; the letters of Richard III's reign are mainly from Harleian MS. 433), 1824, 1827, 1846; *Royal and Historical Letters for the Reign of Henry IV (1399–1404)*, ed. F. C. Hingeston, Rolls Ser., 1860; *The Official Correspondence of Thomas Bekynton*, ed. C. Williams, Rolls Ser., 2 vols., 1872; *Letters of Queen Margaret of Anjou and Bishop Beckington and others*, ed. C. Munro, Camden Soc., 1863 (contains no more than 76 of Margaret's own letters); *Letters and Papers of the Reigns of Richard III and Henry VII*, ed. James Gairdner, vol. i, Rolls Ser., 1861; *Litterae Cantuarienses*, ed. J. B. Sheppard, vol. iii, Rolls Ser., 1889; *Christ Church Letters relating to the affairs of the Priory of Christ Church, Canterbury*, ed. J. B. Sheppard (Camden Soc., N.S., vol. xix), 1877.

(*i*) *Treatises*. Sir John Fortescue, *The Works of Sir John Fortescue collected by Thomas Lord Clermont*, 2 vols., 1869; *The Governance of England*, ed. C. Plummer, 1885; Sir Thomas Littleton, *Tenures*, ed. E. Wambaugh, Washington, 1903; [William Worcester], *The Boke of Noblesse*, ed. J. G. Nichols, Roxburghe Club, 1852.

3. SECONDARY AUTHORITIES

ENGLAND AND WALES

(i) General Histories of the Period

W. Denton, *England in the Fifteenth Century*, 1888 (a pessimistic view); V. H. H. Green, *The Later Plantagenets* (useful genealogical tables), 1955; C. L. Kingsford, *Prejudice and Promise in Fifteenth-Century England*, 1925; K. B. McFarlane, 'England: the Lancastrian Kings, 1399–1461', in *Camb. Med. Hist.* viii (1936), 363–416; R. B. Mowat, *The Wars of the Roses*, 1914; A. R. Myers, *England in the Later Middle Ages*, 1953; C. W. C. Oman, *History of England, 1377–1485* (*Political History of England*, ed. Hunt and Poole, iv), 1918; Sir J. H. Ramsay, *Lancaster and York*, 2 vols., 1892; C. H. Williams, 'England: the Yorkist Kings, 1461–1485', *Camb. Med. Hist.*, viii. 418–48; J. H. Wylie, *History of England under Henry the Fourth*, 4 vols., 1884–98; *The Reign of Henry V*, 3 vols. (vol. iii with W. T. Waugh), 1914–29. The most useful companion to English history in the period is *Medieval England*, ed. A. L. Poole, 2 vols., 1958.

(ii) Biographical

J. J. Bagley, *Margaret of Anjou*, n.d.: H. S. Bennett, *Six Medieval Men and Women* [Humphrey of Gloucester, Fastolf, Hoccleve, Margaret Paston, Margery Kempe, Richard Bradwater], 1956; P. Champion, *Louis XI*, 2 vols., Paris, 1927; *Vie de Charles d'Orléans, 1394–1465*, Paris, 1911: R. Chandler, *The Life of William Waynflete, bishop of Winchester*, 1811; A. Duck, *Vita Henrici Chichele*, 1617 (Eng. transl., 1699); J. Gairdner, *The Life and Reign of Richard III*, 1898; E. F. Jacob, *Henry V and the Invasion of France*, 1947; P. M. Kendall, *Richard the Third*, 1956; C. L. Kingsford, *Henry V*, 2nd ed., 1923; J. R. Lander, 'Edward IV, the Modern Legend and a Prevision' in *History*, xli (1956), 38; Sir J. E. Lloyd, *Owen Glendower*, 1931; R. Lodge, *Cardinal Beaufort*, 1875; David MacGibbon, *Elizabeth Woodville (1437–1492)*, 1938; Sir C. R. Markham, *Richard III*, 1906; A. R. Myers, 'The Character of Richard III' in *History Today*, vol. iv (1954), no. 8, p. 511; C. W. C. Oman, *Warwick the Kingmaker*, 1891; L. B. Radford, *Henry Beaufort*, 1908; Cora L. Scofield, *The Life and Reign of Edward the Fourth*, 2 vols., 1923; L. Stratford, *Edward the Fourth*, 1910; G. M. Towle, *The History of Henry V*, New York, 1866; J. E. Tylor, *Henry of Monmouth, or memoirs of the life and character of Henry the Fifth as Prince of Wales and King of England*, 2 vols., 1838; K. H. Vickers, *Humphrey duke of Gloucester*, 1907.

(iii) MILITARY AND DIPLOMATIC: see also 'England, France, and Burgundy', below, p. 717.

(*a*) *The wars*: E. P. Barnard, *Edward IV's French Expedition of 1475*, 1925 (useful heraldically); A. H. Burne, *The Agincourt War*, 1956; Howell T. Evans, *Wales and the Wars of the Roses*, 1915; J. Gairdner, 'The Battle of Bosworth', *Archaeologia*, lv (1897), 159–78; R. A. Newhall, *Muster and Review*, Cambridge, Mass., 1940; Sir N. Harris Nicolas, *The Battle of Agincourt*, 1827 (valuable for contemporary indentures); Benedicta J. H. Rowe, 'A contemporary account of the Hundred Years War', *Eng. Hist. Rev.* xli (1926), 504.

(*b*) *Diplomacy and foreign relations*: J. Calmette and O. Perinelle, *Louis XI et l'Angleterre* (Memoires et documents . . . École des Chartes, XI), Paris, 1930; E. F. Jacob, 'The Collapse of France in 1419', *Bull. John Rylands Lib.*, xxvi (1948), no. 1; L. V. D. Owen, 'England and the Low Countries', *Eng. Hist. Rev.* xxviii (1913), 13; W. Webster, 'An unknown treaty between Edward IV and Louis XI', ibid. xii (1897), 521.

For Calais, of special importance at this period, see G. L. Harriss, 'The Struggle for Calais: An Aspect of the Rivalry between Lancaster and York', *Eng. Hist. Rev.* lxxv (1960), 30; C. L. Kingsford, 'The earl of Warwick at Calais in 1460', ibid. xxxviii (1923), 544; J. L. Kirby, 'Calais sous les Anglais', 1399–1413, *Revue du Nord*, xxxvii (1955); 'The Council of 1407 and the Problem of Calais', *History Today*, v (1955) 44; 'The Financing of Calais under Henry V', *Bull. Inst. Hist. Research*, xxiii (1950), 165.

(iv) ARTICLES AND MONOGRAPHS ON POLITICAL HISTORY

J. M. W. Bean, 'Henry IV and the Percies', *History*, xliv (1959), 212; Agnes Conway, 'The Maidstone Sector of Buckingham's Rebellion', *Archaeologia Cantiana*, xxxvii (1925), 97; W. H. Dunham, jnr., *Lord Hastings' Indentured Retainers, 1461–1483* (Connecticut Academy of Arts and Sciences, New Haven, 1955); J. Gairdner, 'Did Henry VII murder the Princes?', *Eng. Hist. Rev.* vi (1891), 444, 813; J. P. Gilson, 'A Defence of the Proscription of the Yorkists in 1459', ibid. xxvi. 512; C. L. Kingsford, 'A Legend of Sigismund's Visit to England', ibid. xxxvi (1911), 750; 'The Earl of Warwick at Calais in 1460', ibid. xxxviii (1923), 544; K. B. McFarlane, 'Bastard Feudalism', *Bull. Inst. Hist. Res.*, xx (1945), 161; 'The Investment of Sir John Fastolf's Profits of War', *Trans. Roy. Hist. Soc.*, 5th ser., vii. 91; A. R. Myers, 'The Captivity of a Royal Witch', *Bull. John Rylands Lib.*, xxiv (1940), 263; G. G. Perry, 'Bishop Beckington and King Henry VI', *Eng. Hist. Rev.* ix (1894), 261–74; Glyn Roberts, 'The Anglesey Submissions of 1406', *Bull. Board of Celtic Studies*, xv (1954), 39; Cora L. Scofield, 'Henry duke of Somerset and Edward IV', *Eng. Hist. Rev.* xxi (1906), 300; 'Elizabeth Wydevile in the Sanctuary at Westminster', ibid. xxiv (1909), 90; 'The early life of John de Vere, 13th earl of Oxford', ibid. xxix (1914), 228; 'Five Indentures between Edward IV and Warwick the Kingmaker', ibid. xxxvi (1921), 235; 'The capture of Lord Rivers and Sir Anthony Woodvile in 1460', ibid. xxxvii (1922), 253; J. R. Scott, 'Letters relating to Fauconberg's Kentish Rising, 1471', *Archaeologia Cantiana*, ii (1877), 359; L. W. Vernon Harcourt, 'The two Sir John Fastolfs', *Trans. Royal Hist. Soc.*, 3rd ser., iv (1910), 47; W. T. Waugh, 'Sir John Oldcastle', *Eng. Hist. Rev.* xx (1905), 434, 637; W. Webster, 'An unknown Treaty between Edward IV and Louis XI', ibid. xii (1897), 521.

(v) CONSTITUTIONAL AND ADMINISTRATIVE (for parliament, cf. sect. (vii), below).

Constitutional ideas and contemporary practice are discussed in S. B. Chrimes, *English Constitutional Ideas in the Fifteenth Century* (1936); 'Sir John Fortescue's Theory of Dominion', *Trans. Roy. Hist. Soc.* 4th ser., xvii (1934), 117, and his edition of *Sir*

John Fortescue, De Laudibus Legum Anglie, 1942; E. F. Jacob, 'Sir John Fortescue and the Law of Nature', *Essays in the Conciliar Epoch*, 1953; G. Lapsley, 'The Parliamentary Title of Henry IV', part i, *Eng. Hist. Rev.* xlix (1934), 429; part ii, ibid., p. 577; *Crown, Community and Parliament in the Later Middle Ages*, ed. H. M. Cam and G. Barraclough, 1951; T. F. T. Plucknett, 'The Lancastrian Constitution', *Tudor Studies*, ed. R. W. Seton Watson, 1924, pp. 161–81; I. D. Thornley, 'Treason by Words in the fifteenth century', *Eng. Hist. Rev.* xxxii (1917), 556; B. Wilkinson, 'The Deposition of Richard II and the Accession of Henry IV', ibid. liv (1939), 215.

For constitutional and administrative history see J. F. Baldwin, *The King's Council in England during the Middle Ages*, 1913; H. M. Cam, 'The Decline and Fall of English Feudalism', *History*, xxv (1940), 216; S. B. Chrimes, ' "House of Lords" and "House of Commons" in the Fifteenth Century', *Eng. Hist. Rev.* xlix (1934), 494; 'The Pretensions of the Duke of Gloucester in 1422', ibid. xlv (1930), 101; M. V. Clarke and V. H. Galbraith, 'The Deposition of Richard II', *Bull. John Rylands Lib.* xiv (1930), 125; G. R. Elton, *The Tudor Reform of Government*, 1953; Margaret Hastings, *The Court of Common Pleas in Fifteenth Century England*, Ithaca, 1947; J. R. Lander, 'The Yorkist Council and the Administration', *Eng. Hist. Rev.* lxxiii (1958), 27; H. C. Maxwell-Lyte, *Historical Notes on the use of the Great Seal of England*, 1926; Joyce Otway-Ruthven, *The King's Secretary and the Signet Office in the Fifteenth Century*, 1939; T. F. T. Plucknett, *A Concise History of the Common Law*, 5th ed., 1955; Rachel R. Reid, *The King's Council in the North*, 1921; W. Stubbs, *Constitutional History of England*, vol. iii, 5th ed., 1903; B. Wilkinson, 'The Deposition of Richard II and the Accession of Henry IV', *Eng. Hist. Rev.* liv (1930), 215; B. P. Wolffe, 'The Management of English Royal Estates under the Yorkist Kings', ibid. lxxi (1956), 1; 'Acts of Resumption in the Lancastrian Parliaments, 1399–1456', ibid., lxxiii (1958), 583.

(vi) THE HOUSEHOLD AND HOUSEHOLDS

The best bibliography for the royal and seignorial households is in A. R. Myers, *The Household of Edward IV*, 1959, pp. 300–7, especially the list of original sources, pp. 300–2. From five manuscripts Myers prints the 'Black Book of the Exchequer', an inferior text of which was given in *A Collection of Ordinances and*

Regulations for the Government of the Royal Household made in divers reigns from King Edward III to King William and Queen Mary . . ., Soc. of Antiquaries, 1790. The Household Ordnance of 1454 is given in *Proceedings and Ordinances of the Privy Council of England,* vi. 220. For seignorial households see the following volumes in Hist. MSS. Commission: *MSS. of Lord de L'Isle and Dudley,* i, Tattershall Church and College (Cromwell Family Papers, giving, p. 210, Ralph Cromwell's will and showing his receipts and expenses (p. 212)); *MSS. of R. R. Hastings of Ashby de la Zouche,* i. 300 (Ferrers and Hastings); extracts from the household books of the Willoughbys of Wollaton, ed. W. H. Stevenson, in *H.M.C.,* the Middleton MSS. (1911), p. 324; the Household Book of *Dame Alice de Bryene, Sept. 1412–Sept. 1413* (Suffolk Inst. of Arch. and Nat. Hist., Ipswich, 1931); *Illustrations of the Manners and Expenses of Antient Times in England in the 15th and 17th centuries,* printed by John Nichols for Soc. of Antiquaries, 1797; *Accounts and Memoranda by John Howard, 1st Duke of Norfolk, A.D. 1462–71,* ed. T. Hudson Turner; *Manners and Household expenses of England,* pp. lxxxv–xciii (Roxburghe Club, 1841); *Household Books of John, Duke of Norfolk, and Thomas, Earl of Surrey, temp. 1481–90,* ed. J. I. Collier (Roxburghe Club, 1844).

(vii) PARLIAMENT

C. H. Hunter Blair, 'Members of Parliament for Northumberland (1399–1558)', *Archaeologia Aeliana,* 4th ser., xii (1935), 82–132; J. Cave-Brown, 'Knights of the Shire for Kent, 1406–1500', *Archaeologia Cantiana,* xxi (1895), 198; L. C. Latham, 'The Collection of the Wages of the Knights of the Shire in the Fourteenth and Fifteenth Centuries', *Eng. Hist. Rev.* xlviii (1933), 455; M. H. McKisack, 'The Parliamentary Representation of King's Lynn before 1500', ibid. lxii. 583; *The Representation of English Boroughs in the Later Middle Ages,* 1932; A. R. Myers, 'A Parliamentary Debate of the Mid-fifteenth Century', *Bull. John Rylands Lib.,* xxii (1938), 388; 'Parliamentary Petitions in the Fifteenth Century', *Eng. Hist. Rev.* lii (1937), 385, 590; J. E. Neale, 'The Commons' Privilege of Free Speech in Parliament', *Tudor Studies,* ed. R. W. Seton-Watson, pp. 257–86, 1924; A. F. Pollard, 'Receivers of Petitions and Clerks of Parliament', *Eng. Hist. Rev.* lvii (1942), 202; J. S. Roskell, *The Commons in the Parliament of 1422,* 1954; *The Knights of the Shire for the County Palatine of Lancaster 1377–1460*, 1937; 'The Problem of the Attendance of the Lords in Medieval Parliaments', *Bull. Inst. Hist. Research*, xxix (1956), 153; 'The Social Composition of the House of Commons in 1422', ibid. xxiv (1951); 'Three Wiltshire Speakers', *Wiltshire Archaeological and Natural History Magazine*, vol. lvi (Sir Thomas Hungerford (1377), Sir Walter Hungerford (1414), and Sir Walter Beauchamp (1416)); 'Two Medieval Lincolnshire Speakers, 1. Sir John Bussy of Hougham', *Lincolnshire Architectural and Archaeological Society, Reports and Papers*, vol. 7, part 1; 'Sir Arnold Savage of Bobbing, Speaker for the Commons in 1401 and 1404', *Archaeologia Cantiana*, lxx (1956); 'Sir John Cheyne of Beckford', *Transactions of the Bristol and Gloucestershire Archaeological Society*, vol. 75; 'Two Medieval Lincolnshire Speakers, 2. Sir Henry de Retford', *Lincolnshire Architectural and Archaeological Society, Reports and Papers*, vol. 7, part 2 (1958); 'Sir James Strangeways of West Harlsey and Whorlton, Speaker in the Parliament of 1461', *Yorkshire Archaeological Journal*, xxxix [these and other articles on medieval Speakers by Professor Roskell are to be published in a single work]; J. Wedgwood, ed., *History of Parliament*: vol. i, *Biographies of the members of the Commons House, 1439–1509* (1936); vol. ii, *Register of the Ministers and the Members of both Houses, 1439–1509* (1938); H. T. Weyman, 'Shropshire Members of Parliament (1325–1884)' in *Trans. Shropshire Arch. and Nat. Hist. Soc.*, 4th ser., x. 162; xi. 1; C. H. Williams, 'A Norfolk Parliamentary Election, 1461', *Eng. Hist. Rev.* xl (1925), 79.

(vii *a*) Specialist treatment of financial history is to be found in the following: H. Hall, *History of the Custom-Revenue in England*, new ed., 1892; G. L. Harriss, 'Fictitious Loans', *Econ. Hist. Rev.*, 2nd ser., viii (1955), 187; 'Priority at the Medieval Exchequer', *Bull. Inst. Hist. Research*, xxvi (1958), 2; J. L. Kirby, 'The financing of Calais under Henry V', ibid., xxiii (1955), 165; K. B. McFarlane, 'Loans to the Lancastrian Kings: the Problem of Inducement', *Cambridge Hist. Journ.* ix (1947), 51; R. A. Newhall, 'The war finances of Henry V and the Duke of Bedford', *Eng. Hist. Rev.* xxxvi (1921), 172; T. B. Pugh and C. D. Ross, 'Some materials for the study of Baronial Incomes in the Fifteenth Century', *Econ. Hist. Rev.*, 2nd ser., vi (1954), 183; 'The English Baronage and the Income Tax of 1436', *Bull. Inst. Hist. Research*, xxvi (1953), 1; A. B. Steel, *The Receipt of the Exchequer*, 1954; 'Mutua per talliam, 1399–1413', *Bull. Inst. Hist.*

Research, xiii. 73; 'Receipt Rolls Totals under Henry IV and Henry V', *Eng. Hist. Rev.* xlvii (1932), 204; 'English Governmental Finance, 1377–1413', ibid. li (1936), 291, 577; 'The Receipt of the Exchequer', *Camb. Hist. Journal*, vi (1938), 33.

(viii) LOCAL GOVERNMENT AND LOCAL JUSTICE

C. A. Beard, *The Office of Justice of the Peace in its Origin and Development* (Columbia University Studies in History, xx), New York, 1904; C. G. Crump and Charles Johnson, 'The Powers of the Justices of the Peace', *Eng. Hist. Rev.* xxvii (1912), 226; Bertha H. Putnam, *Early Treatises on the practice of the Justices of the Peace in the fifteenth and sixteenth centuries* (Oxford Studies in Soc. and Legal Hist. VII), 1924; *Select Pleadings before the Justices of the Peace in the fourteenth and fifteenth centuries* (Publ. of the Ames Foundation, London, 1933); 'The Ancient Indictments in the Public Record Office', *Eng. Hist. Rev.* xxix (1914), 479; R. L. Storey, 'The Wardens of the Marches of England towards Scotland, 1377–1489', ibid. lxxii (1957), 9; James Tait, 'The Common Council of the Borough', ibid. xlvi (1931), i; W. P. Williams, *The Council in the Marches of Wales*, 1957.

(ix) SOCIAL AND ECONOMIC LIFE

J. M. W. Bean, *The Estates of the Percy Family, 1416–1537*, 1958; H. G. Bennett, *The Pastons and their England*, 1922; *Life on the English Manor: a study of peasant conditions 1150–1400*, 1937; W. H. (Lord) Beveridge, 'The Yield and Price of Corn in the Middle Ages', *Economic History*, i. 153; 'Wages on the Winchester Manors', *Econ. Hist. Review*, vii. 22; E. M. Carus Wilson, 'Evidences of Industrial Growth on some Fifteenth-Century Manors', ibid., 2nd ser., xii, no. 2 (1959), 197–205; Sir John Clapham, *Concise Economic History of Britain from the Earliest Times to 1750*, 1949; F. Davenport, 'The Decay of Villeinage in East Anglia', *Trans. Roy. Hist. Soc.*, N.S., xiv. 213; *The Economic Development of a Norfolk Manor (Forncett) 1086–1565*, 1906; H. P. R. Finberg, *Tavistock Priory*, 1955; N. S. B. Gras, *The Evolution of the English Corn Market from the Twelfth to the Eighteenth Century*, Cambridge, Mass., 1915; (with Ethel Culbert Gras) *The Economic and Social History of an English Village (Crawley, Hampshire), 909–1428* (Harvard Economic Studies, 39), Cambridge, Mass., 1930; H. L. Gray, 'Incomes from land in England in 1436', *Eng. Hist. Rev.* xlix (1934), 607; *English*

Field Systems (Harvard Historical Studies, xxii), Cambridge, Mass., 1915; W. I. Haward, 'Economic aspects of the Wars of the Roses in East Anglia', *Eng. Hist. Rev.* xli (1926), 170; G. A. Holmes, *The Estates of the Higher Nobility in Fourteenth-Century England*, 1957; W. G. Hoskins, *The Midland Peasant*, 1957; *Essays in Leicestershire History*, 1950; R. H. Hilton, *The Economic Development of some Leicestershire Estates in the later Middle Ages*, 1952; D. Knoop and G. P. Jones, *The Medieval Mason*, 1938; J. Krause, 'The Medieval Household: large or small?', *Econ. Hist. Rev.*, 2nd ser., ix (1957), 420; E. Lipson, *An Introduction to the Economic History of England*, vol. i, The Middle Ages, 5th ed., 1929; P. S. Lewis, 'Sir John Fastolf's Lawsuit over Titchwell', *The Historical Journal*, i (1958), 1; F. M. Page, *The Estates of Croyland Abbey*, 1934; T. W. Page, 'The End of Villeinage in England', *American Econ. Assn. Trans.*, 3rd ser., vol. i, no. 2, New York, 1900; M. M. Postan, 'The Fifteenth Century' (Revisions in Economic History), *Econ. Hist. Rev.* ix (1938), 160; 'Some Social Consequences of the Hundred Years War', ibid. xii (1942), 7; T. D. Pugh and C. D. Ross, 'Materials for the Study of Baronial Incomes in fifteenth-century England', ibid. (mentioned above); L. R. Raftis, *The Estates of Ramsey Abbey, a study of economic growth and organization*, Toronto, 1957; J. E. Thorold Rogers, *History of Agriculture and Prices in England*, vols. 1–4, 1866–82; *Six Centuries of Work and Wages*, 2 vols., 1884; 1886; J. C. Russell, *British Medieval Population*, Albuquerque, 1948; J. Saltmarsh, 'Plague and Economic Decline in England in the Later Middle Ages', *Camb. Hist. Journal*, vii. 23; L. F. Salzman, *Building in England down to 1450*, 1952; *English Industries in the Middle Ages*, new ed., 1923; Maud Sellers, 'York in the sixteenth century', *Eng. Hist. Rev.* ix (1894), 295; Sylvia L. Thrupp, *The Merchant Class of Medieval London*, Chicago, 1948; George Unwin, *The Guilds and Companies of London* (reprint), 1938. The connexion between the social groupings and heraldry is strikingly illustrated by A. R. Wagner, *English Genealogy*, 1960.

(x) Trade and the Towns

E. M. Carus Wilson, 'The Effects of the Acquisition and of the Loss of Gascony on the English Wine Trade', *Bull. Inst. Hist. Research*, xxi (1946), 145; 'The Origins and Early Development of the Merchant Adventurers Organisation in London as shown in their Medieval Records', *Econ. Hist. Rev.* iv (1939),

147; *Medieval Merchant Venturers*, 1954; 'The Iceland Trade' in E. E. Power and M. M. Postan, *Studies in English Trade in the Fifteenth Century*, pp. 155–82, 1933; 'The Overseas Trade of Bristol', ibid., pp. 183–246; (ed.) *Essays in Economic History*, Econ. Hist. Soc., 1954; Engel, 'Die Organisation der deutsch-hansischen Kaufleute in England im 14. und 15. Jahrhundert, bis zum Utrechter Frieden von 1474', *Hansische Geschichtsblätter*, xix. 445, xx. 173; R. Flenley, 'London and Foreign Merchants in the Reign of Henry VI', *Eng. Hist. Rev.*, xxv (1910), 644; N. S. B. Gras, *The Early English Customs System* (Harvard Econ. Studies, xviii), Cambridge, Mass., 1918; H. L. Gray, 'English Foreign Trade from 1446 to 1482', in E. E. Power and M. M. Postan, *Studies in English Trade in the Fifteenth Century*, pp. 1–38; Margery K. James, 'The Fluctuations of the Anglo-Gascon Wine Trade during the Fourteenth Century', *Econ. Hist. Rev.*, 2nd ser., iv (1951), 170, 'Les Activités commerciales et les negociants en vin gascons durant la fin du moyen âge', *Annales du Midi*, t. 65 (1953), 35; C. L. Kingsford, 'The beginnings of English maritime enterprise in the fifteenth century', *History*, xiii (1928–9), 97, 193; 'A London Merchant's house and its owners, 1360–1416', *Archaeologia*, lxxiv (1925), 137; W. E. Lingelbach, *The Merchant Adventurers of England*, Philadelphia, 1902; M. Mollat, *Le Commerce maritime normand à la fin du moyen âge*, Paris, 1952; L. V. D. Owen, 'England and the Low Countries, 1405–1413', *Eng. Hist. Rev.* xxviii (1913), 13; M. M. Postan, 'Credit in Medieval trade' in *Essays in Economic History*, ed. Carus Wilson (1954); 'The Economic and Political Relations of England and the Hanse, 1400–1475' in Power and Postan, *Studies in English Trade* (above); Eileen E. Power, 'The English Wool Trade in the Reign of Edward IV', *Camb. Hist. Journal*, ii. 17; *The Wool Trade in English Medieval History*, 1942; and M. M. Postan, *Studies in English Trade in the Fifteenth Century*, 1933; Yves Renouard, 'Le Grand Commerce des Vins de Gascogne au moyen âge', *Revue historique*, ccxxi (1959), 262; 'Les relations de Bordeaux et de Bristol au moyen âge', *Revue historique de Bordeaux et du département de la Gironde*, 1957, p. 107; R. de Roover, 'La Balance Commerciale entre les Pays-Bas et l'Italie au quinzième siècle', *Revue belge de Philologie et d'Histoire*, t. xxxvii, no. 2, 1959 (important for English trade); L. F. Salzman, *English Trade in the Middle Ages*, 1931; G. Schanz, *Englische Handelspolitik gegen Ende des Mittelalters, mit besonderer Berücksichtigung des Zeitalters der beiden ersten Tudors, Heinrich VII und Heinrich VIII.* 2 vols., Leipzig, 1881.

(xi) RELIGION AND THE CHURCH

C. R. Cheney, 'The Legislation of the Medieval English Church', *Eng. Hist. Rev.* l (1935), 193, 385; Irene J. Churchill, *Canterbury Administration*, 2 vols., 1933; Margaret Deanesley, *The Lollard Bible and Other Medieval Biblical Versions*, 1920; *The Significance of the Lollard Bible*, Ethel Wood Lecture, 1951; A. G. Dickens, *Lollards and Protestants in the Diocese of York*, 1959; F. R. H. Du Boulay, 'Charitable Subsidies granted to the Archbishop of Canterbury, 1300–1489', *Bull. Inst. Hist. Research*, xxiii. 147; Kathleen Edwards, *English Secular Cathedrals*, 1949; 'Salisbury Cathedral' and 'Vaux College, Salisbury', in *Vict. County Hist. Wilts.* iii, 1957; R. Foreville, *Le Jubilé de S. Thomas Becket*, Paris, 1957 (has useful bibliography); J. Gairdner, *Lollardy and the Reformation in England*, vol. i, 1908; E. Gibson, *Synodus Anglicana* (1702), ed. Cardwell, 1854; R. Graham, *English Ecclesiastical Studies*, 1929 (for essays on the Cluniacs and Cistercians during the Schism and the Councils); *Essays presented to Miss Rose Graham*, ed. V. Ruffer and A. J. Taylor, 1953; Johannes Haller, *England und Rom unter Martin V* (Quellen und Forschungen aus italienischen Archiven und Bibliotheken, VIII), Rome, 1905; *Piero da Monte, ein Gelehrter und päpstlicher Beamter des XV. Jahrhunderts*, Rome, 1946; F. Harrison, *Life in a Medieval College* [the Bedern, York], 1951; E. F. Jacob, *Essays in the Conciliar Epoch*, 2nd ed., 1953; 'Wilkins's Concilia and the Fifteenth Century', *Trans. Roy. Hist. Soc.*, 4th ser., xv (1932), 91; 'Petitions for benefices from the Universities', ibid., 4th ser., xxviii (1945), 41; 'Chichele and Canterbury', *Essays presented to Frederick Maurice Powicke*, Oxford, 1948; 'Reynold Pecock', *Proc. British Academy* (Raleigh Lect. 1951), xl, 1953; E. W. Kemp, 'The Origins of the Canterbury Convocation', *Journal of Eccl. History*, iii (1953), 132; *An Introduction to the Canon Law in the Church of England*, 1959: M. D. Knowles, *The English Mystics*, 1927; *Medieval Religious Houses: England and Wales* (with R. Neville Hadcock), 1953; *The Religious Orders in England*, vol. 2, 1955; K. B. McFarlane, *John Wycliffe and the beginnings of English non-conformity*, 1952. R.-P. Victor Martin, *Les Origines du gallicanisme*, vol. ii, Paris, 1939; R. L. P. Milburn, *Saints and their images in English Churches*, 2nd ed., 1957; *Miracles*

of King Henry VI, ed. R. A. Knox and Shane Leslie, 1923;
G. R. Owst, *Literature and Pulpit in Medieval England*, 1933;
*Preaching in Medieval England: an Introduction to Sermon Manu-
scripts of the period c. 1350–1450*, 1926; W. A. Pantin, *The English
Church in the Fourteenth Century*, 1958; *Documents illustrating the
activities of the General and Provincial Chapters of the English
Black Monks, 1215–1540*, Roy. Hist. Soc., Camden 3rd ser.,
nos. 45, 47, 54, 1931–7; E. Perroy, *L'Angleterre et la France
pendant le grand Schisme d'Occident*, Paris, 1933; Eileen E. Power,
Medieval English Nunneries c. 1275–1535, 1922; R. H. Snape,
English Monastic finances in the later Middle Ages, 1926; R. A. L.
Smith, *Canterbury Cathedral Priory*, 1948; A. Hamilton Thompson, *The Organization of the English Clergy in the later Middle Ages*,
1949; B. L. Woodcock, *Medieval Ecclesiastical Courts in the Diocese
of Canterbury*, 1952; Noël Valois, *La France et le Grand Schisme
d'Occident*, vol. iv, Paris, 1902; *La Crise religieuse du XVᵉ siècle: le
pape et le concile (1418–50)*, Paris, 1903; A. Zellfelder, *England und
das Basler Konzil* (Eberings Histor. Studien, 113), Berlin, 1913.

LEARNING AND THE ARTS

(xii) THE UNIVERSITIES AND EDUCATION

F. L. Anstey, ed. *Epistolae academicae*, 2 vols. (Oxford Hist.
Soc.), 1894; A. B. Emden, *A Biographical Dictionary of Members of
the University of Oxford from A.D. 1176 to 1500*, 3 vols., 1957–9; S.
Gibson, *Statuta antiqua universitatis oxoniensis*, 1938; 'Oxford Uni-
versity', *Victoria County History of Oxford*, vol. iii, ed. H. E.
Salter and M. D. Lobel, 1954; N. R. Ker, *Oxford College Libraries
in the Sixteenth Century* (Catalogue of the Bodleian Exhibition),
1958; A. F. Leach, *The Schools of Medieval England*, 1915; *English
Educational Charters and documents*, 1911; *A Fifteenth-Century School
Book*, ed. W. Nelson, 1956; C. E. Mallet, *History of the
University of Oxford*, vol. i, 1924; H. C. Maxwell-Lyte, *History of
Eton College*, 1889; J. B. Mullinger, *The University of Cambridge
from the earliest times to the Royal Injunctions of 1535*, 1873; Winifred
Pronger (Mrs. Maxwell), 'Thomas Gascoigne', *Eng. Hist. Rev.*
liii (1938), 606: liv (1939), 20; H. Rashdall, *The Universities of
Europe in the Middle Ages*, new ed. by F. M. Powicke and A. B.
Emden, vol. iii, 1938; H. G. Richardson, 'An Oxford Teacher
of the Fifteenth Century', *Bull. John Rylands Lib.*, xxiii (1939),
436; H. E. Salter, *Medieval Oxford* (Oxford Hist. Soc.), 1936; ed.,

Snappe's Formulary and other Records (Oxford Hist. Soc.), 1934; ed., *Registrum Cancellarii Oxoniensis*, 1434–69, 2 vols. (Oxford Hist. Soc.), 1932; with W. A. Pantin and H. G. Richardson, edd., *Formularies which bear on the History of Oxford* (Oxford Hist. Soc.), 1942; *Victoria County History, Cambridge*, vol. iii, ed. L. P. C. Roach, 1959.

(xiii) HUMANISM AND LEARNED THOUGHT

Mario Borsa, 'Correspondence of Humphrey, duke of Gloucester and Pier Candido Decembrio', *English Historical Review*, xix. 509; M. H. Carré, *Phases of English Thought*, 1942; R. J. Mitchell, *John Tiptoft*, 1948; *John Free*, 1955; E. F. Jacob, 'The Book of St. Albans', *Bull. John Rylands Lib.*, xxviii (1944), 99; J. L. Sandys, *History of Classical Scholarship*, vol. i, 3rd ed., 1921; vol. ii, 1908; E. A. Savage, *Old English Libraries*, 1911; W. F. Schirmer, *Der englische Frühhumanismus*, Leipzig, 1931; B. L. Ullman, 'Manuscripts of Duke Humphrey of Gloucester', *Eng. Hist. Rev.* lii (1937), 670; R. Weiss, *Humanism in England*, 2nd ed., 1957.

(xiv) ART AND ARCHITECTURE

F. Bond, *Gothic Architecture in England*, 1912; *An Introduction to English Church Architecture from the eleventh to the sixteenth century*, 2 vols., 1913; *Wood Carving in English Churches*, 2 vols., 1910; T. Borenius and E. W. Tristram, *English Medieval Painting*, Paris and Florence, 1927; G. G. Coulton, *Art and the Reformation*, 1928; F. H. Crossley, *English Church Monuments*, A.D. 1150–1550, 1933; *English Church Craftsmanship: an introduction to the work of the medieval period*, 1941; Joan Evans, *English Art, 1307–1461* (Oxf. Hist. Eng. Art), 1949; Arthur Gardner, *English Medieval Sculpture*, new ed., 1951; F. Harrison, *The Painted Glass of York Minster*, 1928; Harvey, John H., *English medieval architects*; *a biographical dictionary down to 1550*, 1954; F. E. Howard, *The Medieval Styles of the English Parish Church, a survey of their development, design and features*, 1936; F. E. Hutchinson, *Medieval Glass at All Souls College*, 1949; J. A. Knowles, *Essays in the History of the York School of Glass Painting*, 1936; E. G. Millar, *English Illuminated Manuscripts of the 14th and 15th Century*, Paris and Brussels, 1928; W. F. Oakeshott, *The Sequence of Medieval English Art illustrated chiefly from illuminated English manuscripts 650–1450*, 1950; G. McN. Rushforth, *Medieval Christian Imagery*

as illustrated by the Painted Windows of Great Malvern Priory Church,
1935; Christopher Woodforde, *English Stained and Painted Glass*,
1954.

(xv) LITERATURE

H. S. Bennett, *Chaucer and the Fifteenth Century*, 1947, reprint
1954; *The Author and the Public in the fourteenth and fifteenth centuries*,
English Association Pamphlets, 1928; W. Blades, *Life and Topo-
graphy of William Caxton*, 1861–3; E. K. Chambers, *The Medieval
Stage*, 2 vols., 1903; *English Literature at the Close of the Middle
Ages* (Oxford Hist. Eng. Lit.), 1945; *Sir Thomas Malory*, 1922;
Religious Lyrics of the XVth Century, ed. Carleton Brown, 1939;
Secular Lyrics of the XIVth and XVth Centuries, ed. R. H. Robbins,
1952; E. Vinaver, *The Works of Sir Thomas Malory*, 2 vols., 1947.
See the bibliographies in *Cambridge History of English Literature*,
vol. ii and in *Cambridge Medieval History*, viii. 902–4.

ENGLAND, FRANCE, AND BURGANDY

PRINTED SOURCES

Abrégé d'une histoire chronologique de 1400 à 1467, at the end of
the edition of Jean Juvénal des Ursins, by D. Godefroy, Paris,
1653, pp. 401–50; Hérault du Roi Berry (Gilles de Bouvier),
Le Recouvrement de Normandie, ed. with Eng. trans. in J. Stevenson,
Narratives of the Expulsion of the English from Normandy, 1449–50,
pp. 239–376 (Rolls Ser.); Th. Basin, *Histoire des règnes de Charles
VII et de Louis XI*, ed. J. Quicherat, t. iv, Paris, 1859 (Soc. Hist.
France), or by Ch. Samaran (Les Classiques de l'Histoire de
France, 2 vols.); R. Blondel, *De reductione Normanniae*, ed.
Stevenson, and above, pp. 1–238 (Rolls Ser., 1863); *Journal d'un
Bourgeois de Paris*, ed. A. Tuetey (Soc. Hist. France), Paris,
1881; P. Le Cacheux, *Rouen au temps de Jeanne d'Arc et pendant
l'occupation anglaise (1419–1449)*, documents publiés avec intro-
duction et notes (Soc. Hist. Normandie), Paris, 1931; *Calendars
of the French* (i.e. Treaty) *Rolls*, 44th Annual Report of the
Deputy Keeper of the Public Records, 1883, pp. 543–639; 48th
Annual Report . . . 1887, pp. 217–451; *Calendar of the Norman
Rolls*, Henry V, 41st Annual Report of the Deputy Keeper of
the Public Records, 1880, pp. 671–810; 42nd Annual Report
(1881), pp. 313–472; J.-J. Champollion-Figeac, *Lettres de rois*,

reines, et autres personnages des cours de France et d'Angleterre depuis Louis VII jusqu'à Henri IV tirées des archives de Londres par Brequigny, t. ii, Paris, 1847 (Coll. de docs. inédits); P. Chaplais, 'Documents concernant l'Angleterre et l'Écosse anciennement conservés à la Chambre des Comptes de Lille', *Revue du Nord*, xxxviii. 185; *Chartularium Universitatis Parisiensis*, ed. H. Denifle and E. Chatelain, t. iv, Paris, 1896; G. Chastellain, *Œuvres*, ed. Kervyn de Lettenhove, i–iii, Brussels, 1883–4 (Acad. royale de Belgique); P. Cochon, *Chronique Normande*, ed. Vallet de Viriville, *Chronique de la Pucelle ou chronique de Cousinot*, Paris, 1864; Philip de Commynes, *Mémoires*, ed. J. Calmette et G. Durville, tt. i, ii, Paris, 1924 (*Les Classiques de l'histoire de France au moyen âge*); Mathieu d'Escouchy, *Chronique*, ed. G. du Fresne de Beaucourt, 3 vols., Paris, 1863–4 (Soc. Hist. France); Clement de Fauquembergue, *Journal*, ed. A. Tuetey and H. Lacaille, 3 vols., Paris, 1903–15 (Soc. Hist. France); Pierre de Fenin, *Mémoires*, ed. Dupont, Paris, 1837 (Soc. Hist. France); J. Froissart, *Chroniques*, ed. Kervyn de Lettenhove, 26 vols., Brussels, 1861–77, esp. vols. ii, viii, ix, xv, xvi, xxiii: Eng. trans. by Lord Berners, 6 vols., ed. W. P. Ker (Tudor Transl. Library), 1901–3; Jean Juvénal des Ursins, *Histoire de Charles VI*, ed. Denis Godefroy Paris, 1653; Ghillebert de Lannoy, *Œuvres*, ed. Ch. Potvin, Louvain, 1878 (Collection des grands écrivains du pays); Olivier de La Marche, *Mémoires*, ed. H. Beaune and J. d'Arbaumont, 4 vols., Paris, 1883–8 (Soc. Hist. France); Jean Molinet, *Chronique* (1474–1506), ed. J. A. Buchon, 5 vols (Collection des chroniques nationales françaises); Enguerrand de Monstrelet, *Chroniques*, ed. L. Douët d'Arcq, tt. iii, iv, vi, Paris, 1859–62 (Soc. Hist. France); Eng. trans. by T. Johnes, 1810; *Procès de condamnation et de réhabilitation de Jeanne d'Arc*, ed. J. Quicherat, t. iii, Paris, 1845 (Soc. Hist. France); *Deutsche Reichstagsakten*, Bd. xvii, ed. D. Kerler, Munich, 1878; *Chronique d'un religieux de Saint-Denis*, ed. L. Bellaguet, tt. vi, vii, Paris, 1852–4 (Collection de documents inédits); Jean de Waurin, *Receueil des chroniques et Anchiennes Istories de la Grant Bretaigne, à present nommé Engleterre*, ed. W. Hardy and E. L. C. P. Hardy, vol. v, Rolls Ser., 1891.

Secondary Works

G. du Fresne du Beaucourt, *Histoire de Charles VII*, 6 vols., Paris, 1881–91; L. Bonenfant, *Du meurtre de Montereau au Traité de Troyes*, Paris, 1958 (contains valuable bibliography for 1418–

21); 'Actes concernant les rapports entres les Pays-Bas et la Grande-Bretagne de 1293 à 1468 conservés au Château de Mariemont', *Bulletin de la Commission royale d'histoire*, t. cix. 53; *Philippe le Bon*, 3rd ed., Brussels, 1955; A. Bossuat, 'Étude sur les emprunts royaux au début du XVᵉ siècle. La Politique financière du Connétable Bernard d'Armagnac (1416–1418)', *Revue historique de droit français et étranger*, 4th ser., 1950, pp. 351–71; R. Boutruche, *La Crise d'une société: seigneurs et paysans du Bordelais pendant la guerre de Cent Ans*, Paris, 1947; J. Calmette, *Chute et relèvement de la France sous Charles VI et Charles VII*, Paris, 1945; and E. Déprez, *La France et l'Angleterre en conflit*, Paris, 1937 (*Histoire Générale publiee sous la direction de Glotz, G., Histoire du moyen âge*, t. vii, part i); J. G. Dickinson, *The Congress of Arras*, 1955; M. Lenz, *König Sigismund und Heinrich V von England*, Berlin, 1874; A. Longnon, *Paris pendant la domination anglaise (1420–1436)*, Paris, 1878 (Soc. Hist. Paris); L. Mirot and E. Déprez, *Les Ambassades anglaises pendant le guerre de Cent Ans (1327–1450)*, *Bibl. Ec. Chartes*, lix–lxi, 1891–1900; R. A. Newhall, *The English Conquest of Normandy, 1416–1424*, New Haven, 1929; E. Perroy, *L'Angleterre et le Grand Schisme d'Occident*, Paris, 1948; *La Guerre de Cent Ans*, Paris, 1945, Eng. trans. *The Hundred Years War*; B. A. Pocquet du Haut-Jussé, 'François II, duc de Bretagne, et l'Angleterre', *Mémoires de la Societé d'histoire . . . de Bretagne*, ix, Paris, 1928; 'Dons du roi au grands feudataires, les ducs de Bourgogne Philippe le Hardi et Jean sans Peur', *Revue historique* t. clxxxiii. 297; 'Les dons du roi aux ducs de Bourgogne Philippe le Hardi et Jean sans Peur (1363–1419). Le don des aides', *Annales de Bourgogne*, x. 261; L. Puiseux, 'L'Émigration normande et la colonisation anglaise en Normandie', *Mémoires lus à la Sorbonne, 1865, histoire, philologie et sciences morales*, Paris, 1866, pp. 313–401; *Siège et prise de Caen par les anglais (1417)*, Caen, 1858; *Siège et prise de Rouen par les Anglais (1418–1419)*, Caen, 1867; F. Quiche, 'Les Relations diplomatiques entre le Roi des Romains et la Maison de Bourgogne', *Bulletin de la Commission royale d'histoire*, xc. 193; J. Richard, *Les Ducs de Bourgogne et la formation du duché*, Paris, 1954; Benedicta H. Rowe, 'Discipline in the Norman Garrisons under Bedford', *Eng. Hist. Rev.* xlvi (1931), 194; 'John Duke of Bedford and the Norman Brigands', ibid. xlvii (1932), 583; 'The Estates of Normandy under the Duke of Bedford, 1422–1435', ibid. xlvi (1931), 551; F. Schneider, *Der europäische Friedenskongress von*

Arras (1435) und die Friedenspolitik Papst Eugens IV und des Basler Konzils, Greiz, 1919: Vallet de Viriville, *Histoire de Charles VII*, 3 vols., Paris, 1861.

4. SCOTLAND AND IRELAND

SCOTLAND

Bibliography: Cambridge Medieval History, vii. 915–18; E. W. M. Balfour-Melville, *James I, King of Scots*, 1936, pp. 298–304; A. I. Dunlop, *The Life and Times of James Kennedy, Bishop of St. Andrews*, pp. 437–46. *Records*: *Acts of the Parliament of Scotland*, vols. 1 and 2, ed. Thomas Thomson and C. Innes, 1814–44; *Calendar of Documents relating to Scotland*, iv, ed. J. Bain, 1888; *Calendar of Scottish Supplications to Rome*, 1418–22, 1422–37, ed. (1) E. R. Lindsay and A. I. Cameron (Scot. Hist. Soc.), 1934, (2) A. I. Dunlop (*née* Cameron), 1957; *Copiale prioratus sancti Andree*, ed. J. H. Baxter, 1925; *Exchequer Rolls of Scotland*, v, vi, ed. G. Burnett, 1882–4; *Registrum magni sigilli regum Scotorum*, i (1306–1424), revised ed., 1912; ii (1424–1513), ed. J. B. Paul, 1882. *Chronicles*. Thomas of Auchinleck, *A short Chronicle of the Reign of James the Second, King of Scots*, ed. P. Thomson, 1819; Hector Boece, *Lives of the Bishops of Aberdeen*, ed. James Moir (New Spalding Club), 1894; George Buchanan, *History of Scotland*, tr. Aikman, 1827; John Lesley, *The History of Scotland* (1436–1561), ed. J. Thomson (Bannatyne Club), 1830; Lindsay, Robert, of Pitscottie, *Historie and Chronicles of Scotland*, ed. A. I. G. Mackay, 2 vols., Scottish Text Soc., 1st ser., 42–43, 1898–9; Alexander Myln, *Vitae Dunkeldensis ecclesiae episcoporum*, ed. C. Innes (Bannatyne Club), 1823; *Pluscardensis liber*, ed. F. J. H. Skene, 1877; *Scotichronicon Johannis de Fordun cum supplementis et continuatione Walteri Boweri*, ed. W. Goodall, 2 vols., 1759 (later edition by W. F. Skene, with trans., Edin., 1871–2); Andrew of Wyntoun, *Originale Cronykil of Scotland*, ed. F. J. Amours, vols. v, vi, 1913–14. *Modern works*: P. Hume Brown, *History of Scotland*, i, 1911; and the following articles: 'The Captivity of James I', *Scottish Hist. Rev.* xxi (1923), 45; 'Five Letters of James I', ibid. xx (1922), 28; 'James I at Windsor in 1423', ibid. xxv (1927), 226; 'The Provision and Consecration of Bishop Cameron', ibid. xxiii (1925–6), 191; Annie I. Dunlop, *Life and Times of James Kennedy* (above); R. K. Hannay, 'James I, Bishop Cameron and the Papacy', *Scottish Hist. Rev.*

xv (1917–18), 190; R. L. Mackie, *Short History of Scotland*, 1929–30; R. S. Rait, *The Relations between England and Scotland 500–1707*, 1901.

IRELAND

Bibliography: J. F. Keaney, *The Sources for the Early History of Ireland: an Introduction and Guide*, vols. i, ii (Columbia Records of Civilization, New York, 1929); Constantia Maxwell, *Short Bibliography of Irish History* (Historical Assn. Leaflet, 23), 1921. *Records and secondary works*: *Statutes, Ordinances and Acts of the Parliament of Ireland, King John to Henry V*, ed. H. F. Berry, H.M.S.O., 1907; *Statute Rolls of the Parliament of Ireland, Reign of Henry VI*, ed. H. F. Berry, 1920; *Irish Historical Documents, 1172–1922*, ed. E. Curtis and R. B. McDowell, 1943; *Rotulorum Patentium et Clausarum Hiberniae Calendarium Hen. II–Hen. VII*, ed. E. Tresham, 1828; *History of the Church of Ireland*, ed. W. Alison Philipps, ii, 1934; M. V. Clarke, *Medieval Representation and Consent*, 1936; E. Curtis, *A History of Medieval Ireland from 1086 to 1513*, 2nd ed., 1938; *Richard II in Ireland, 1394–1395*, 1927; A. Gwynn, *The Medieval Province of Armagh, 1470–1545*, 1946; E. B. Fitzmaurice, and A. G. Little, *Materials for the History of the Franciscan Province of Ireland, 1230–1450*, 1920; J. T. Gilbert, *History of the Viceroys of Ireland*, 1805; H. G. Richardson and G. O. Sayles, *The Irish Parliament in the Middle Ages*, 1952; H. Wood, 'The Office of Chief Governor of Ireland (1172–1509)', *Proc. Roy. Irish Acad.* xxxvi (1921–4), C. p. 206.

INDEX

184; to be heir of France, Charles VI living, 185; seals Treaty of Troyes (21 May 1420), 185; orders Scots captured at Melun to be hanged, 187; joins Charles VI at Corbeil, 187; plans to govern Normandy and the 'conquest' as a separate state, 189; keeps military admin. of Normandy in English hands, 189; firm hand of, on higher clerical appointments in Normandy, 192; policy, while in France, towards the home government, 193; loans raised by, 1421, 195; debts of, while prince of Wales, 195; strength of his hold upon country, 195; as founder, 196; his conception of his duty to religious orders, 196–7; directs Benedictines to reform themselves, 196–7; writes to chapter general, 196; returns, after Beaugé, to France, 200; follows Dauphin to the Loire, 200; besieges Meaux, 200; contracts dysentry at Meaux, 200; hands over to Bedford at Corbeil (1422), 201; his dying addresses, 201; displays his will and codicils, 202, 213; latest will of, lost, 213,—invoked by Gloucester, 470,—council regards as invalid without consent of estates, 233; an estimate of, 202; confessor of, *see* Patrington, Stephen; his debts, at death, to Bp. Beaufort, 227; services for, 292; advice to Sigismund, 347; fleet maintained by, 348; reconciles parties in Lynn, 389.

Henry VI, k. of England: birth of (6 Dec. 1421), 201; authority of, exercised (1422) by the magnates, 212; care and instruction of, 213; Gloucester claims the tutelage of, 214; welcomed by the Speaker (1423), 223; letter to, from duke of Burgundy, on truce with France, 249; crowned in Paris, 250; arouses no enthusiasm in France, 250; coming of age of, 261; relations with Papacy over appointments to sees, 268–70; the *domini de consilio* and the king, 433; stops Bedford and Gloucester from discussing their powers, 435; commissions portraits of Armagnac's daughters, 470; proposal (Suffolk supporting) for marriage with French princess (1443), 474; probable (July 1445) proposals for surrender of Maine, 478; promises to surrender Le Mans and English possessions in Maine, 479; orders the surrender of Le Mans and Maine (July 1447), 479; openly shows his contempt for Gloucester

(1445), 483; saves Suffolk's life, 493–4; m. to Margaret by Bp. Ascough, 495; goes on progress through the country (Aug. 1452), 504; becomes insane (Aug. 1453), 508; wounded at first battle of St. Albans, 512; oath of loyalty to be taken to, at Coventry parliament (1459), 516; after Northampton, escorted to London, 520; with Margaret, resides in Dominican convent in Edinburgh, 526; comes to Bamburgh from Scotland, 530; is left by Margaret and Brézé in Bamburgh, 530; treaty of, with Louis XI (28 June, 1462), 531; at Readeption, presented to the Londoners by Warwick, 561; taken prisoner at Barnet (1471), 310; put to death in the Tower, 569.

Henry VII, k. of England, 293, 624; witnesses 'syght' staged by city of York, 403.

Herbert, family of, 510.

— Sir Richard, executed by Warwick, 556.

— Sir Walter, 642.

— William, lord, York's steward of Usk, 511; relations of, with Warwick, 527; made earl of Pembroke, 527; defeated by Warwick (1469), 527; executed by Warwick, 556.

Hereford, 42, 55, 58, 520, 603; people of, 44.

— Joanna (Bohun), countess of, 26, 63.

Herefordshire, 102, 194.

Herle, William, 605.

Heron, Richard, agent of earl of Wiltshire, 540.

— William, steward of the household, 80.

Hervelinghem (Calais), 106.

Hesdin (Pas-de-Calais), 5, 535.

Hève, Cap de la (Seine-Inf.), 158.

Heveningham, Sir John, 473.

Hexham, battle of, 494, 563.

Hexhamshire, franchise of, 134.

Heydon, John, 344, 448, 491, 503.

Heyne, Heynes, William, 379.

Higham Ferrers (Northants), 47; coll. ch. of, 292.

Hill, Sir J. W. F., 387.

Hilton, Sir Robert, 127.

— Sir William, 127, 128.

— Walter, writings of, 296.

Hindon (Wilts.), manor of, 462.

Hinton, priory of (Carth.), 296.

Hoccleve, clerk and poet, 658, 660.

Hoke, Robert, Lollard priest, 283.

Holcot, Robert, 680.

Holderness (Yorks., E.R.), 2, 59.

— Robin of, 555; lordship of, 334.

3 D

PRINTED IN GREAT BRITAIN
AT THE UNIVERSITY PRESS, OXFORD
BY VIVIAN RIDLER
PRINTER TO THE UNIVERSITY

MAP 1

WALES IN THE GLYN DWR REVOLT

(Adapted, with kind permission, from *A Historical Atlas of Wales*,
by William Rees, Cardiff, 1951)

MAP 2

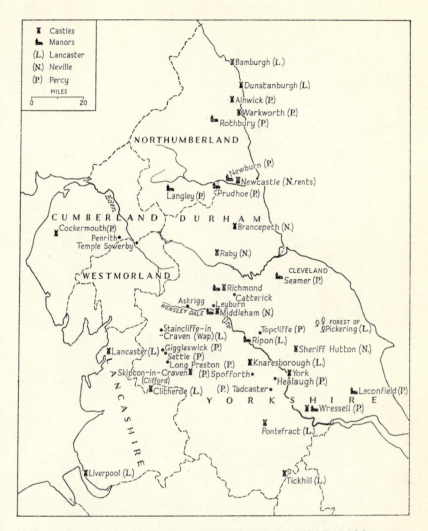

Castles ⬚
Manors ⬚
(L.) Lancaster
(N.) Neville
(P.) Percy

MILES
0 — 20

NORTHUMBERLAND

Bamburgh (L.)
Dunstanburgh (L.)
Alnwick (P.)
Warkworth (P.)
Rothbury (P.)

Newburn (P.)
Newcastle (N. rents)
Langley (P.)
Prudhoe (P.)

CUMBERLAND   DURHAM

Cockermouth (P.)
Penrith
Temple Sowerby
Brancepeth (N.)

WESTMORLAND
Raby (N.)

CLEVELAND
Seamer (P.)

Richmond
Askrigg   Catterick
Leyburn
WENSLEY DALE   Middleham (N.)

Staincliffe-in-
-Craven (Wap)(L.)
Topcliffe (P)
FOREST OF
Pickering (L.)

Lancaster (L.)
Giggleswick (P.)
Settle (P)
Ripon (L.)
Long Preston (P.)
Sheriff Hutton (N.)
Skipton-in-Craven
(Clifford)
(P.) Spofforth
Knaresborough (L.)
York
Healaugh (P.)
Clitheroe (L.)
(P.) Tadcaster
Leconfield (P.)
YORKSHIRE
Wressell (P.)

LANCASHIRE

Pontefract (L.)

Liverpool (L.)

Tickhill (L.)

DUCHY OF LANCASTER, PERCY AND NEVILLE, 1400

MAP 3

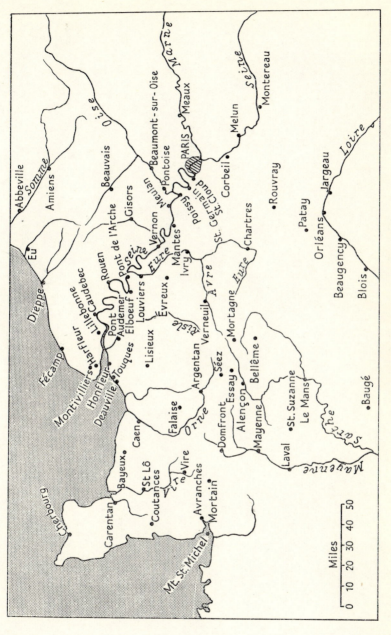

CONQUEST OF NORMANDY

MAP 4

FRANCE 1430

The Anglo-Burgundian territories are grouped thus:

A.   i. The Duchy of Normandy.

    ii. The *Pais de Conquête*: The lands which Henry V had conquered between the Norman frontier and Paris, corresponding to the ancient Vexin, English and Norman.

    iii. The Maine border.

B.   The territories which accepted Henry VI as the result of the Treaty of Troyes: the Île de France, the Chartrain, Champagne, Picardy.

C.   The Burgundian fiefs which Philip of Burgundy held of Henry VI as King of France: Burgundy (Duchy of), Artois, French Flanders, along with County of Burgundy.

D.   Brittany during the time when Duke John recognized Henry's claim.

    The early governorships were:

Lower Normandy, the Earl of Suffolk; Champagne and Brie, the Earl of Salisbury; Alençon, expanded into Maine, 1425, Sir John Fastolf. The Duke of Bedford, was Count of Maine, and as such had headquarters at Le Mans.

Demesne of Charles VII.

Boundary (fluctuating) of Lancastrian France.

(Based, with acknowledgement, on the map of the late Professor James Tait in R. L. Poole, *A Historical Atlas of Modern Europe*, Plate 56)

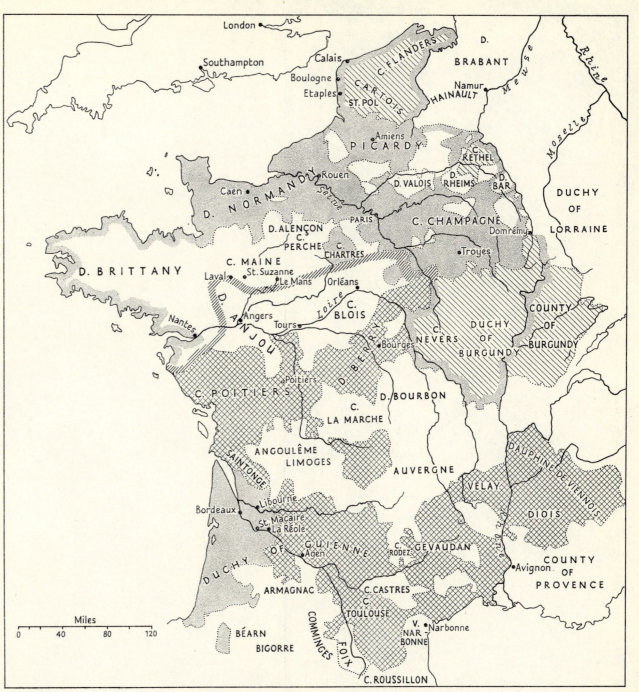

MAP 5

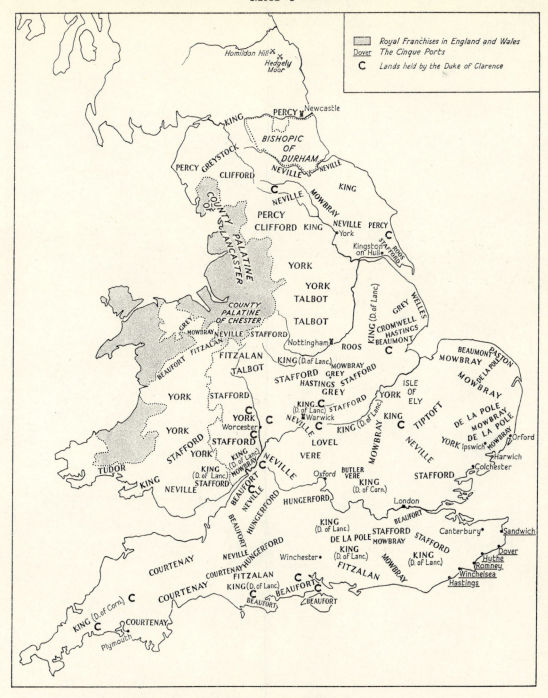

CHIEF NOBLE FAMILIES

(Based, with acknowledgement, on the maps of the late Professor James Tait in Poole, op. cit., Plate 20, and of Mr. K. B. McFarlane, *Cambridge Medieval History*, viii, Map 84)

MAP 6

CASTLES AND BATTLES, 1450–1485
(Based as in Map 4)